CITIES, SAINTS, AND COMMUNITIES
IN EARLY MEDIEVAL EUROPE

STUDIES IN THE EARLY MIDDLE AGES

VOLUME 46

General Editor
Tom Pickles, University of Chester

Editorial Board
Charles West, University of Sheffield
Caroline Goodson, University of Cambridge
Gabor Thomas, University of Reading
Catherine Clarke, University of Southampton
Tom O'Donnell, Fordham University

Previously published volumes in this series
are listed at the back of the book.

Cities, Saints, and Communities in Early Medieval Europe

Essays in Honour of Alan Thacker

Edited by
SCOTT DEGREGORIO AND PAUL KERSHAW

BREPOLS

A catalogue record for this book is available from the British Library

© 2020, Brepols Publishers n.v., Turnhout, Belgium.

D/2020/0095/32
ISBN 978-2-503-56504-0
E-ISBN 978-2-503-56566-8
DOI 10.1484/M.SEM-EB.5.108029

ISSN 1377-8099
E-ISSN 2294-835X

Printed in the EU on acid-free paper.

Contents

List of Illustrations

Frontispiece
Alan Thacker, The Barbican, London, February, 2019. Photograph by Geoffrey West.

Mark A. Handley

Clare Stancliffe

Richard Sharpe

Barbara Yorke

Paul Fouracre

Éamonn Ó Carragáin

Acknowledgements

This collection of original essays is offered to Alan in celebration of his contribution to early medieval studies over more than four decades. While the foundation of that contribution is, of course, his rich, wide-ranging, and ongoing scholarship, his role as mentor, organiser, and collaborator, in the UK and internationally, has also been a significant component of his impact. All of these aspects are, we believe, reflected in the chapters that follow.

Conceived in 2015, this volume has taken rather longer to come to print than originally envisaged and we are grateful for the *patientia* and *constantia* of all our contributors. We regret that several friends and colleagues of Alan's who were initially involved in this project were not able, ultimately, to contribute to the present collection, and we remain grateful for their support and good wishes. Prominent amongst the early supporters of this volume was Jennifer O'Reilly, who died in February 2016. We owe a particular debt to her husband, Terry O'Reilly who, with the support of Máirín MacCarron and Diarmuid Scully, saw her contribution through to publication. The news of the death of Richard Sharpe, another close friend of Alan's and a contributor to this collection, came as the volume went into production. We are sad that neither Jennifer nor Richard will see an enterprise come to fruition to which both gave committed support.

We are very grateful to Guy Carney at Brepols and Tom Pickles, general editor of the 'Studies in the Early Middle Ages' series, for taking on this collection. They gave strong support from the beginning and displayed endless patience towards the end of this volume's path to publication. The frequency with which a Brepols byline occurs in Alan's bibliography — particularly in recent years — is testament to the company's importance to, and investment in, early medieval studies; we are delighted that they are the publishers of this collection. We also wish to thank the anonymous readers for the press, one of whom commented on the initial proposal, the other on the final manuscript, and are particularly grateful for the rigour and learning the latter brought to the task. We owe a further debt of gratitude to Sarah Thomas for her careful and comprehensive copy-editing.

Finally, we must thank Genevra Kornbluth who generously provided the cover image from her extensive archive of digital images (www.kornbluthphoto.com), and Chris Halsted for map design.

Paul Kershaw, Charlottesville
Scott DeGregorio, Ann Arbor

Feast of St Aidan, 2019

Frontispiece: Alan Thacker, The Barbican, London, February, 2019.
Photograph by Geoffrey West.

PAUL KERSHAW

Introduction: Alan T. Thacker, an Appreciation

Alan was born on 6 June 1949 near Lowestoft, East Anglia. The roots of his interest in the past may very well pre-date his eleven-plus exam but they found fertile ground at Lowestoft Grammar School. One figure in particular was responsible for this, the school's History master, Stuart Spalding, known to his pupils as 'Spoof'.

Another Lowestoft pupil for whom Spoof's impact was both pivotal and long-remembered has offered this sketch: 'He was the archetypal after-the-war, been-in-the-war, rode a sit-up-and-beg bike, smoked a pipe, you never knew quite where he was coming from; he would argue one thing one lesson then come in the following lesson and argue the exact opposite.'[1] (On this last point, some might discern a possible early influence upon Alan's own opinions on many matters: always forceful, rarely predictable.) It should also be noted that Spalding belongs to the select roster of school teachers who have been a significant presence in the formation of not one but two scholars of Anglo-Saxon history. The other was James Campbell, Alan's elder by nearly fifteen years and his future tutor; by the time Alan entered the sixth form Campbell was established as a Fellow at Worcester College, Oxford. Spoof's forceful character evidently exerted sufficient gravity to ensure Campbell remained an intermittent visitor to the school. It was in the course of one such visit that Alan was formally introduced to Campbell, though even before then Alan remembers Campbell as 'a presence' by force of reputation, one to be encountered not only in the classroom but also at home: the two were distantly related, and word filtered back through family channels of James' academic ascent. All this meant that, when the question of university selection arose, Alan's sights fell upon Oxford and, specifically, upon Worcester College.

The target was hit. Alan matriculated in October 1967. The eighteenth- and nineteenth-century history of his school days gave way to the study of the medieval past. His first term brought tutorials in Medieval Latin with Michael Winterbottom and 'Prelims': papers on Gibbon, Macaulay, and Bede, whose *Historia ecclesiastica* III

---

1 McInerney, 'Profile: Tim Brighouse', p. 13.

Paul Kershaw • (paulkershaw@virginia.edu) is Associate Professor in the Corcoran Department of History, University of Virginia.

Cities, Saints, and Communities in Early Medieval Europe, ed. by Scott DeGregorio and Paul Kershaw,
SEM 46 (Turnhout: Brepols, 2020), pp. 11–24
BREPOLS PUBLISHERS   DOI 10.1484/M.SEM-EB.5.119620

was a set-book. Here, again, the Campbell effect was in operation. Patrick Wormald, one year ahead of Alan and several hundred yards away at Balliol, would recall James Campbell's accompanying lectures as 'a Damascus Road for many who have gone on to expound the early history of the British Isles and Europe'.[2] For Alan, as for some of Bede's kings, conversion was neither immediate nor absolute. Late medieval England, rather than the late antique West, remained his primary interest. In the late 1960s Stubbs's *Select Charters* was entering the terminal phase of nearly a century as a mainstay on many British medieval history curricula in UK universities, and elsewhere. Like many before him — but few after — Alan tracked English constitutional history (to 1307) through its pages. His third year meant the selection of a Special Subject. Alan chose 'The Reign of King Henry V'. Devised by Bruce McFarlane and taught in the years after his death by Maurice Keen and Gerald Harriss, the class served as something of a forcing house for several generations of late medieval British historians.[3] For Alan it was formative, too, but differently so: the experience confirmed his preference for the study of literary texts — 'or at least with texts which aspired to be literary', in his words — over bureaucratic records, and of intellectual and cultural questions over those of government or administration. Immersion in the fifteenth century catalyzed one further realization: his true interest lay not in the late but in the early Middle Ages.

In 1970 Alan graduated with a First in Modern History. In autumn of the following year he returned to Oxford to begin a D.Phil. The topic he had initially identified, Alcuin's letters, was soon jettisoned in favour of a study of late seventh- and early eighth-century Anglo-Latin saints' lives, in Alan's words, 'the entire corpus of English hagiography from the period before the Viking invasions'. Across six core chapters Alan analysed the Whitby Life of Gregory the Great, the anonymous Lives of Cuthbert and Ceolfrith, Bede's thought on 'hagiography and *historiae*', Stephen of Ripon's Life of Wilfrid, and that of Guthlac by Felix. Alongside detailed analyses of individual texts, Alan explored the networks that linked the insular world with the continent, the forms of intertextuality evident in the lives, and the light these shed upon the multiple textual communities in which they participated and the strategies of sanctity and authority their authors simultaneously drew from and reinforced. In the case of Bede, Alan explored the interplay between his homiletic, exegetical, and historical works. Here, as elsewhere, Alan's work directly anticipated many of the key modes of much current Bedan scholarship, not least the drive towards taking what might be termed a holistic approach to the corpus. Taken in sum, the thesis presented a significantly more sophisticated model of cultural exchange than had prevailed hitherto, one able to accommodate the interplay of influence, imitation and innovation in each of these lives and to interpret these processes in terms of both broader late antique cultural patterns and also the immediate political and institutional circumstances of composition, the unstable, aristocratic world directly beyond the *scriptorium* window.

---

2   Wormald, 'James Cambell as Historian', p. xiv.
3   Brundage and Cosgrove, *The Great Tradition*, p. 76; Macintyre, 'Gerald Harriss', p. xiv.

Michael Wallace-Hadrill was his supervisor. Alan was, then, one of that remarkable wave of Oxford postgraduates for whom Wallace-Hadrill served as supervisor and who, from the later 1970s onwards, would be a powerful, if far from homogeneous, force behind early medieval history's prominence in British universities for decades to come. '[O]n the whole', Ian Wood observed of Wallace-Hadrill's style of supervision, 'those students who demanded most of him got most in return'.[4] By his own account, Alan could not be numbered amongst them; mutual reticence meant that Wallace-Hadrill would remain a relatively remote presence during these years. That said, in 1983 Alan was one of a number of former pupils who contributed to *Ideal and Reality in Frankish and Anglo-Saxon Society*, the Festschrift organised by Patrick Wormald, Donald Bullough, and Roger Collins, themselves all former doctoral students of Wallace-Hadrill. Alan's contribution, 'Bede's Ideal of Reform', would become — and remain — one of his most influential articles, as its repeated invocation in this volume attests. It was the first time Bede or, more accurately, Bede's thought and attitudes to the world about him, became Alan's primary focus in a published piece. It was a new departure in one other way, too. Alan had received his D.Phil. in 1977, but this was the first time key elements of his doctoral research emerged in print. His thesis, 'The Social and Continental Background to Early Anglo-Saxon Hagiography', never became a book, something hard to imagine in today's academic environment but which was far from unusual in the later 1970s, and certainly not in a field such as early medieval history where the tightly-argued article had long been the dominant form.

Alan's contribution to *Ideal and Reality* was not, however, his first publication in Anglo-Saxon studies. It was preceded two years earlier by 'Some Terms for Noblemen in Anglo-Saxon England, *c.* 650–900', a deceptively modest title for an article that offered an authoritative conspectus of the terminology for noblemen and high officials across a wide range of Latin and vernacular sources and which displayed both high sensitivity to regional variation and a tight command of continental comparanda, a study all the more remarkable for having been undertaken before the era of the database and the digitised text. This piece is striking in other ways: first, as a rare instance of Alan focusing solely upon issues of secular political authority and, second, for the fact that the realisation at the article's core — that multiple modes of aristocratic identity could co-exist, some with 'official' titles, others assigned on the basis of individual actions or roles — offered a secular corollary and wider historical context to the image of Bede's vision of the church and its members in 'Bede's Ideal'.

By this time, Alan had left Oxford, first for Durham, where he was the Isabel Fleck Research Fellow for 1974–1975, and then for Chester, where the following year he took up the position of Assistant Editor of the Victoria History of Cheshire. The appointment brought with it a research fellowship at Liverpool University, where Alan also taught. From early on, and throughout his career, Alan has been a frequent and valuable committee member, most recently serving as a council member of the Royal Historical Society. At Chester he was active on the councils of numerous north-western historical organisations, the Chester Historical Association, the

---

4   Wood, 'John Michael Wallace-Hadrill', p. 37.

Chester Archaeological Society, and the Record Society of Lancashire and Cheshire, amongst others. His association with Liverpool University would also be fruitful. Displaying a skill for piloting long-standing collaborative projects to publication that would serve him well in the years ahead, in 1991 Alan steered to successful, if belated, completion an essay collection in honour of Geoffrey Barraclough, who had stepped down from Liverpool's Chair of Medieval History some thirty-five years earlier and who, at the time of publication, had been dead for seven.

The move to Chester was the first stage of a three-decade career with the Victoria History of the Counties of England, one that would see him progress from Assistant to County Editor of VCH Cheshire before returning south in 1994 to the Deputy Editorship of the national VCH project based at the Institute of Historical Research in the University of London's Senate House. Alan's work at the VCH resulted in his participation in a steady stream of collaborative publications. Indeed, one might well imagine a companion volume to this collection, taking English local history as its focus and dedicated to this facet of Alan's career. In Alan's scholarship, of course, any notional distinction between 'early medieval' and 'local' history evaporates; in his many publications on Chester's early history and, more recently, Anglo-Saxon Wearmouth, the two are one and the same. And this same acute sense of the particularity of place informs Alan's approach to the study of places far beyond the VCH's remit. In his recent work on the late antique martyr cults of Rome and northern Italy, Alan has shown a considered sensitivity to the idiolects of early medieval piety, together with a no less intense interest in setting such specifics in productive tension with larger patterns — of the developing practices of piety and cult, of patronage, and political contingency. Or, as Alan himself puts it, far more pithily: '... while all saints are local, some are more intensely local than others'.[5]

The VCH's offices in the Institute of Historical Research meant it shared a home with a substantial community of medievalists for whom the regular Wednesday evening 'Earlier Medieval Seminar' was the focal event. Alan's name soon found its way onto the distinguished roll of seminar conveners and he went on to rapidly become one of a handful of active organisers responsible for co-ordinating each term's programme of speakers, a role he would fulfil for many years. Traffic with the scholarly world beyond Senate House was not one-way, however, and these years also saw a growing number of invitations to serve as a PhD examiner, and to speak. In 1992 Alan gave the Brixworth Lecture, the Deerhurst followed in 1994. He would give the Jarrow Lecture for 2005. And connections were forged internationally; Alan himself began to be a regular international speaker, developing long-standing, affectionate ties with colleagues at University College, Cork and becoming a regular visitor to Kalamazoo from 1997 onwards. These later visits forged a further enduring link, this time to the North American community of established and, at the time, emerging Bedan scholars. (Both connections are, we're glad to say, well-represented in this book.) From its inception in 1992 until 2012 Alan was also a member of the editorial board of the journal *Early Medieval Europe*, which would provide a further outlet

---

5   Thacker, '*Loca Sanctorum*', p. 1.

for his organisational and editorial energies and an additional context for fostering new scholarly connections and, typically for Alan, opportunities for new friendships.

In 2001 Alan was appointed Executive Editor of the VCH and also made a Reader in Medieval History at the University of London, positions he would hold until his retirement in 2009. The latter appointment meant that the mentoring and support Alan had given to many graduate students and several early career colleagues could take on an official character, for he was now able to supervise graduate students formally within the London system, and would go on to direct several doctoral theses.

And concurrently with all this activity he produced a steady stream of articles and chapters. Some developed interests already evident, such as his mordantly-titled exploration of the complex early phases of the cult of King Oswald, 'Membra Disjecta: the Division of the Body and the Diffusion of the Cult' (1995), or his 1998 piece, 'Memorializing Gregory the Great: the Origins and Traditions of a Papal Cult'. Others, however, saw him break new ground, such as the sequence of publications from across the millennium that refocused his interest in the dynastic and material aspects of saints cults from the seventh and eighth centuries to the tenth, to the reign of Edward the Elder and the age of the Benedictine Reform. It scarcely needs repeating that the cultures of cult in Francia, northern Italy, Rome, and, selectively, parts of the wider early medieval Mediterranean, have all been a presence in Alan's scholarship. The early 2000s, however, saw them become subjects of study in their own right, rather than serving as they had hitherto as crucial contexts for making sense of insular phenomena. Alan's contribution to James Campbell's Festschrift, 'Peculiaris Patronus Noster: the Saint as Patron of the State in the Early Middle Ages' and his substantial contributions to the major collection he co-edited with Richard Sharpe, Local Saints and Local Churches in the Early Medieval West, signalled this shift, taking as they did a distinctly European rather than a primarily Anglo-Saxon perspective. Multiple publications have followed that explore the cult of the martyrs in the Latin West from the fourth to the eighth centuries, and especially in Rome itself, publications that hold the promise of constituting, in aggregate, a coherent study in their own right. Membra disjecta, indeed.

If anything, Alan's retirement in 2009 saw a quickening rather than a calming of activity. It also saw a return to Bede, whose works Alan once again engaged with in a series of studies each of which considered his relationship with a text, an authority or a category of thought: Bede and the Ordering of Understanding', 'Bede and Augustine of Hippo' (Alan's Jarrow Lecture of 2005), 'Bede and History', 'Bede and Martyrology'.

Relationships are an organising principle in this volume too, of course, as it exists to honour Alan as friend, colleague, collaborator, and teacher, to celebrate his achievements and to explore subjects of shared interest, often ones that Alan's own work has done much to illuminate. All our contributors have enjoyed long and fruitful friendships with this volume's honorand, and several have been close collaborators. From the outset, all were encouraged to address issues central to Alan's own work, and thus to take the opportunity to enter, on the page, into a dialogue with his thought — the continuation of friendship, it might be said, by other means. Happily, a number of contributors had anticipated our aim and already had an appropriate subject in mind.

Consequently, readers will find several chapters addressing aspects of saints' cults to which Alan has given particular attention: questions of site and setting, the nature of political patronage and the role of local saints in generating and sustaining communal identity. The late antique and early medieval city of Rome is repeatedly revisited by our contributors, explored not only as the seat of papal authority and a centre of apostolic and martyrial cult and the destination for a range of travellers — for some of whom the city would be their final earthly destination — but also as both connector and conduit between the eastern Mediterranean and the western kingdoms of early medieval Europe. As in Alan's own work, Bede is a defining presence in this volume. Here, again, the theme of relationships recurs: the often complex and occasionally fraught ones that existed between Bede and those close to him, relationships conducted as much on the page as in person, reified in rich and allusive terms. The referentiality of this framing is a reminder of another kind of relationship, of course, the one Bede enjoyed with older authorities who provided material for his own thought and exemplars for the development of his distinctive, authoritative voice, one which would in time join with them for new generations of scholars and teachers. It might be said that the shadow side of this earlier scholarship, erudition in the service of error, was heresy. 'Bede, famously, was much exercised by heretics', Alan has written, stressing how here, too, Bede's relationship with the past was an engagement with, and a response to, the problems he perceived in his present.[6] Several of our contributors take up this theme, offering, in concert, a sustained exploration of the place of heresy in Bede's body of thought. Another touchstone is 'Bede's Ideal of Reform', Alan's 1983 exploration of the connections between his exegetical thought and his understanding of contemporary Northumbrian society, its ills, their means of remedy, and the place of the church in the world. And even when Bede himself is not present in a particular chapter, the age of Bede, the seventh and earlier eighth centuries, often is.

Ultimately, these approaches have not only generated thematic coherence — far from a given in celebratory volumes such as this — but also produced a collection that, in sum, amounts to a reflection of its honorand's own thought and interests.

The interplay between saints and kings, patterns of royal patronage, and the political possibilities of cults and their associated centres has long fascinated Alan. In his contribution, Mark Handley takes up these themes as he reassesses the evidence for the Merovingian ruler Childebert I's patronage of the cult of the Spanish protomartyr, Vincent of Zaragoza, and his foundation of a church in the saint's honour, the future Saint-Germain-des-Prés. Childebert's evident devotion to St Vincent led to his burial in the church he had earlier founded, and the beginning of its long-standing use as a royal necropolis. Bringing neglected and marginalised epigraphic evidence into conversation with the relevant, far better studied narrative sources, Handley sets out the evidence for the earliest phases of Vincent's cult not only in Francia but also across much of late antique Iberia, North Africa, and the north-eastern Adriatic. He also offers a provocative reassessment of the fragmentary inscription recovered,

---

6   Thacker, 'Why did Heresy Matter to Bede', p. 47.

along with other pieces of Childebert's highly-decorated sarcophagus, in the early 1970s. In arguing for its contemporaneity with Childebert's interment in 558, Handley assigns the inscription a high historical charge: it is the earliest original description of a Merovingian ruler as *rex francorum*.

In his exploration of the saints cults of late antique and early medieval Ravenna, their changing relationships to local secular and ecclesiastical authority and contributions to collective identity, Tom Brown keeps the focus upon the conjunction of piety and politics. What factors, he asks, drove the support of a particular cult by the city's elites — pre-eminently its bishops — and how was such support expressed and instrumentalised for political advantage? The strategies that emerge, in a paper that moves from the fifth to the tenth century, include elements of assertion, appropriation, and improvisation, all underwritten by a powerful sense of local identity. Brown notes the strikingly sparse evidence for cults in Ravenna with their origins in the eastern Roman world, and the prominence in Ravenna of both Roman saints (Agnes, Laurence), as well as several associated with Milan (Vitalis, Gervasius, Protasius). And, alongside these holy outsiders, Ravenna's own: Apollinaris, the city's protobishop, and his fourth-century successors, Severus and Probus, figures whose cults would play a recurrent role in the assertion and reassertion of Ravenna's urban identity, not least in the tenth century, when the city's late antique imperial past became a resource for asserting its importance in a new, Ottonian imperial present. It was a period that witnessed both the composition of new hagiographies and the reshaping of the city's fabric through the construction of new buildings and the restoration of existing ones.

Catherine Cubitt moves our focus to later seventh-century Rome, the city experienced by visitors such as Benedict Biscop and Wilfrid, and a place at a particular time to which Alan has given special attention, both individually and in close collaboration with another of our contributors, Éamonn Ó Carragáin.[7] For Cubitt, Rome's *loca sanctorum*, its shrines and basilicas, are relegated to the role of backdrop for the volatile and politically freighted world of christological controversy. At the heart of her paper stands the Lateran Synod of 649, convened by Pope Martin I to address the monotheletism subscribed to in the east by patriarchs and the emperor, Constans II, and a position the synod would ultimately condemn as heretical. In particular, Cubitt explores the impact in Francia of Constans' infamous response to the Synod's repudiation: the pope's capture by imperial agents, transportation to Constantinople, trial, and eventual death in exile. In the process she, like Handley, re-evaluates problematic Merovingian evidence, in this case the account of Pope Martin's death in the life of Eligius by Audoin of Rouen, a work putatively composed in the seventh century's third quarter but extant only in a Carolingian redaction, and a source over which doubts about its integrity have long hovered. Cubitt situates the account within the wider discourse of contemporary anti-monothelete polemic, making the case that Audoin did indeed draw, as he claimed, upon the text of an eyewitness account of the imperial attack upon Martin to which he may plausibly

---

7   Ó Carragáin and Thacker, 'Wilfrid in Rome'.

have had access during his visit to Rome in the 670s, a journey contemporaneous with the *Vita Eligii*'s probable period of composition. Implicitly, she demonstrates how a consideration of the monothelete controversy, the breadth of the engagement it engendered and the impact it made, offers a powerful illustration of the continued existence of trans-Mediterranean communication networks in the later seventh century, and Rome's place within them, a nexus as much as a terminus.

The 649 Lateran Synod and its aftermath is also the departure point for Jennifer O'Reilly, in a piece that complements Cubitt's contribution to the present volume and is the first of a sequence of chapters to explore notions of heresy and their uses in Bede's thought. What, O'Reilly asks, did Bede actually know about monotheletism, and where did that knowledge come from? Communication and communicators — that question of relationships again — take centre stage. For O'Reilly, as for Cubitt, this means texts, but it also means people: individuals with whom Bede was in contact who possessed first-hand knowledge of events in Rome, informants capable of connecting Wearmouth and Jarrow to the cultural circuits of Rome and through them to the wider Mediterranean world. What Bede knew of 'real' monotheletism is one question. How Bede thought with it is another. Shifting focus, O'Reilly magisterially explores Bede's treatment of monotheletism and his use of the materials it generated, ranging from his presentation of the Lateran Synod as an event in the *Historia ecclesiastica* to his use of its *acta* as a resource in his exegesis, particularly his commentary on Mark, where the consideration of heresy becomes a means to articulate orthodoxy and propound truth, and thus to sustain the belief of the faithful.

The notion of heresy as heuristic in Bede's thought is also central to Faith Wallis' discussion of Bede's *Commentary on Proverbs*, a direct response both to Alan's larger arguments about reform in Bede's thought and, more specifically, to his passing observation that the treatment of heresy found in this work differed markedly from that found in other works due to the absence of any significant emphasis upon *perfidia*, the faithlessness that Bede emphasised elsewhere in his writings. This was, in Wallis' resonant phrase, 'the toxic heart of heresy'. Why did the treatment of heresy in this work differ so markedly from that present elsewhere? What might have been the purpose of so distinctive a treatment? Wallis offers convincing answers to both these questions. She demonstrates quite how selective Bede was in his treatment of Proverbs, skipping over many verses entirely, and selecting others in order to construct a commentary in which the secular world depicted in the scriptural base text was systematically allegorised in order to propound a set of ideals to be pursued by members of the clerical orders, and especially the church's important learned elite. This elite status brought its own unique perils. The learned were particularly susceptible to intellectual vanity; the thirst for knowledge could be a drive towards heresy. Moreover, these dangers were more than purely personal, for it was from the ranks of the learned that the *rectores* and *doctores* emerged. Thus, they posed a danger to the Christian society as a whole, and were a particularly pernicious internal threat to the Church's mission in the world. Wallis implicitly demonstrates it was clearly a threat Bede felt acutely and to which his Proverbs commentary was a response. Alan's own work has repeatedly shown the centrality to Bede's thought of the notion of the doctor as simultaneously communicator of Christian truth and living exemplar of

Christian values. Here, Wallis demonstrates the need to understand Bede's commentary on Proverbs as a further distinctive expression of that central ideal and, more broadly, to see his exegesis as an engagement with the world around him.

That actual monotheletes were easier to find by the banks of the seventh-century Bosporus than those of the Wear in the eighth century does not mean that the accusation of heresy had lost any of its potency as a charge to be feared. In his paper, Peter Darby, like Faith Wallis, pursues the treatment of heresy in another lesser-studied Bedan text, his letter to Plegwine of 708. Here, however, the tables are turned. Bede himself was the *eruditus* assigned a place in the ranks of the heretical because, it was alleged, in his *De temporibus* he had denied that the Incarnation occurred in the sixth age of the world. As Darby shows, the rapidity and intensity of Bede's response speaks to the seriousness of the charge. That the accusation emanated from Hexham meant that Wilfrid would be a key figure in its resolution — as he may have been in its formulation — and it was in his presence that Bede wished his letter to be read. Rather than the steadily constructed self-presentation Bede projected in some of his other works, his letter to Plegwine was highly reactive, the product of pressure, and a snapshot of its author in the act of rapid and sophisticated scholarly self-defence. Darby's dissection of the letter lays bare Bede's rhetorical strategies, his deployment of layers of pointed and allusive passages of scripture and patristic authority not simply to affirm his orthodoxy, but to assert his position as its defender and advocate, and to evoke — through association by quotation — an antecedent in the role who had himself been wrongly accused of heresy: Augustine.

The accusations against Bede in 708, the rapidity and intensity of his response and the indirect means by which its contents were to reach Wilfrid, passed on by Plegwine to a mutual acquaintance whose identity was disguised, or at least occluded, beneath the cognomen 'David', testify to the fraught relationship between Wearmouth and Jarrow and Hexham, Bede and Wilfrid. Between the two stood the figure of Acca, who seems to have successfully balanced being Bede's friend and supporter whilst simultaneously being Wilfrid's long-standing companion, priest, and eventual successor at Hexham. The tensions within this triangle are the focus of Claire Stancliffe's chapter, a comprehensive reappraisal not only of the evidence for ties of friendship and obligation that bound Acca and Bede but also for the charged and sporadically hostile environment in which they existed. For many earlier commentators a recognition of the putatively formulaic nature of the terms of address deployed by Bede in his prefatory dedication letters to Acca has been the end point of their analysis. It is where Stancliffe begins, in a chapter that sensitively contextualises the echoes and appropriations of Bede's choice of phrase, sifting those Bede employed rather more widely from those directed at Acca alone in order to draw out what was distinctive and the particular about Bede's presentation of this important relationship. She also offers insights into Acca's own perspective, based upon his sole surviving letter, preserved in the preface to Bede's Commentary on Luke.

Stancliffe, like a number of our other contributors, is highly attentive to how Bede's larger message might emerge through resonance and aggregation, much like a chord generated by, but distinct from, the notes from which it was built. For example, she sets the superficially laudatory portrait of Acca in the *Historia ecclesiastica* alongside the pastoral ideal espoused elsewhere by Bede, producing a significantly more complex and ambivalent profile of his patron — a dissonance only perceptible in combination. Stancliffe also offers strong reasons for that ambivalence, reasons grounded in the hostile and hyper-critical attitude towards him that existed within Wilfrid's inner circle, an attitude that evidently survived into Acca's episcopacy and for which the charge of heresy would continue to be a favoured weapon. Stancliffe offers her own take on the accusations of 708, but she also gives close attention to Acca's repeated requests for a commentary on Luke and Bede's sustained resistance to doing so, making a powerful case for it less as a recognition of Bede's learning so much as an exercise in scholarly entrapment, with Bede's self-incrimination as a heretic as its goal.

Wilfrid, second only to Bede himself as a presence in Alan's work, finally takes centre stage in Richard Sharpe's chapter. Sharpe turns his attention to the years of Wilfrid's exile from Northumbria and his close association with the West Saxon king, Ceadwalla. This was a period book-ended by two journeys from England to Rome. The first, in 679, was Wilfrid's, undertaken for the purpose of a personal appeal to the pope against Theodore's subdivision of his Northumbrian diocese the previous year. Ceadwalla was the second traveller, abdicating and taking the road to Rome in late 688 where the following Easter he was baptised by Sergius I, died soon after, and was interred in St Peter's. In Alan's words, Bede's treatment of Wilfrid in the *Historia* is characterised by 'discrete omissions and careful neutrality'. Sharpe's is one of a number of contributions that dive deeply beneath the placid surface of the text and forensically recover detached fragments of evidence. In Sharpe's case they reassemble into a damning portrait of Wilfrid as both complicit in, and the beneficiary of, Ceadwalla's campaigns of conquest and wholesale slaughter. In the process he illuminates Bede's skill in offering a master narrative of conversion whilst simultaneously permitting an image to emerge, by inference, of the messier and more complex reality beneath. Sharpe lays bare the calibration at the core of Bede's historical method, the balance between what could be written and what might be understood. Sharpe's analysis of Bede's treatment of Wilfrid's time with Ceadwalla lead him to identify significant evidence for the *Historia*'s revision at an early stage of circulation, alterations undertaken by Bede, in the hope of either pleasing or placating his friend and patron Acca or perhaps, Sharpe suggests, by Acca himself.

In his own treatment of the subject, Alan argued against any notion that Bede possessed any procrustean attitude towards 'the Irish'. Barbara Yorke builds upon this insight, focusing in particular upon Bede's treatment of Aidan. As with the previous papers, Yorke ventures beneath the surface of the page, in this case exploring the construction of Bede's positive portrayal of Aidan and those linked to him, in particular his highly selective deployment of miracle stories. A considerable number are attached to favoured figures — Aidan and his associates. For others, however, including Wilfrid, Paulinus, and Edwin, miracle narratives are noticeably lacking: less a case of discretion so much as, once again, criticism by omission or, in instances when we know Bede to have had access to accounts associated with a particular individual, suppression. More than two decades separated Aidan's death from Bede's birth; nevertheless Yorke makes a strong case for his significance in Bede's life, as an exemplar — a model bishop — but also as a powerful influence upon figures in the Northumbrian church who had themselves gone on to be influential in Bede's own life.

One of the transformative consequences of the recent explosion of sustained and penetrating scholarship on Bede's exegesis has been the opportunities it has created for a far deeper understanding of the linkages between his works — the intertextuality of his *oeuvre* — as well as their individual distinctiveness, especially when set in the context of the whole. The attempt to explain either phenomenon has, in turn, often resulted in a renewed search for the context that might have generated it. One of the paradoxical consequences of a wave of work that has privileged *opera exegetica* over *opera historica* — placing Bede's theology and commentary, his lifetime devoted to the scrutiny of scripture — front and centre, has been a deepening awareness of the extent to which Bede's exegesis displays a sensitivity to events in the world beyond the cloister. It is the impact of the events of one year, 716, that is the subject of Scott DeGregorio's chapter, a year that saw the death of King Osred of Northumbria, and the departure for Rome of Ceolfrith, abbot of Wearmouth and Jarrow, and one in which Bede was occupied in writing *On First Samuel*, probably his first Old Testament commentary. Taking his initial orientation from Alan's own work, in particular, 1983's 'Ideal of Reform' and 2009's 'Bede, the Britons and the Book of Samuel', DeGregorio argues forcefully for *On First Samuel* as 'a work forged in crisis', written against a backdrop of political instability and under the shadow of an ongoing British threat and one that at points offered commentary, not only on the scriptural passage at hand, but also, discretely and allusively, upon contemporary events. In the process, DeGregorio highlights *On First Samuel*'s distinctive characteristics: its structure (unparalleled elsewhere in Bede's works), the intensity of its allegorising and the obsessive typological mapping of Old Testament phenomena onto those of the New. And, alongside the particular, the intertextual, as DeGregorio explores some of the resonances between the commentary completed in 716 and the Letter to Ecgberht composed some eighteen years later in November 734, offering observations with implications for our understanding of the wider developmental arc of Bede's thought.

Arthur Holder, in his exploration of Bede's understanding of mystical experience and his treatment of the individual faithful granted a 'vision of God in this life', assesses both Bede's debts to, and differences from, earlier theorists. He emphasizes in particular his fluency with the established technical terminology of the visionary and Bede's confidence in making it his own, not least by parsing the mystical as the sensory and gustatory: a synaesthetic foretaste of heaven. His insights, perhaps, offer us a new context in which to understand Cuthbert's account of Bede's final hours, and the striking pairing of his reported distribution of his personal 'treasures' of pepper and incense to his inner circle with the stated hope, quoting Isaiah 33.17, that with death would come the chance to apprehend Christ, to see 'my King in all his beauty'.

In the wake of Alan's own work it has become axiomatic that Bede conceived of a set of roles co-existing alongside the formal orders of church hierarchy, the former instituted, the latter ordained. Holder explores a further taxonomy, one that distinguished between *perfecti*, the select few granted a fleeting vision of God or intimation of heaven; *proficientes*, Christians who were works in progress, pedestrians on the long path to perfection; and *carnales*, beginners who, while still counted amongst the faithful, were yet to travel far, anchored as they were by their sinful flesh. Rather than running in parallel with formal ecclesiastical hierarchy, these categories cut across it: some laity could be counted with the *perfecti*; some clergy could not. For those that were, however, Bede was clear that the mystical was in service to the pastoral, the fleeting theophany should sustain the long-term demands of ministry.

One emerging consequence of the exegetical turn is its potential for reinvigorating our understanding of Bede the historian. In her contribution, Julia Barrow analyses the variety and sophistication of Bede's exploitation of scripture as a resource in the composition of history. While she has much to say on these issues in terms of the *HE* as a whole, her case study focuses in particular upon *Historia ecclesiastica* IV. 23–26, and Bede's treatment of Ecgfrith's defeat and death in battle against the Picts, the Northumbrian double houses of *Streanæshealch* (Whitby) and Coldingham, and those associated with them — Caedmon, Hild, and Æbbe. Barrow is particularly sensitive to the effects of what might be called Bede's micro-quotation of scripture: words or abrupt phrases well below the scale of the substantial 'block' quotation. She demonstrates how, in practice, this often meant the selection of one or perhaps two or three words possessed of distinct associations or the deployment of particular motif-generated fields of allusion, triggering scriptural images and ideas in readers' and listeners' minds, and creating an eductive commentary on his text: 'a Bachian counterpoint' in which the memory of the reader (or listener) became an instrument, providing half the notes. In this, Barrow identifies in the *Historia* the same strategy of argument by allusion that Darby, DeGregorio, Sharpe, Stancliffe, and Wallis identify elsewhere in Bede's works.

In recent years Alan's interests have expanded from the major centres of northern Italy to Aquileia and the Adriatic coast, the location of Paul Fouracre's chapter on the much-discussed *placitum* of Risano of 804. This chapter also shares with Alan's wider work an interest in issues of local identity, its articulation in the face of external challenges, but with the focus falling squarely on the assertion of enduring custom rather than local cult. Istria had long been part of Byzantium's western periphery. In the later eighth century it fell under Frankish rule, still liminal, but now the south-eastern extremity of Charlemagne's power. This reorientation brought new representatives of central authority with new expectations of what might be demanded from those they governed. Worldly, well-connected, an affluent patron of the churches under his control and no stranger to exile, there's more than a touch of Wilfrid, bishop of Hexham, about Fortunatus, patriarch of Grado, the most senior figure to come under Carolingian scrutiny in the Risano inquest. It is Istria's bishops and particularly the local Carolingian appointee, John, and his immediate family, that come in for the most criticism; their treatment of Istrian communities over whom they held sway was exacting, oppressive, and ignored both past practice and established rights.

Many of the previous chapters offer new insights into the complex question of Bede's relationship with earlier authorities, confirming that 'following in the footsteps of the fathers' was a task pursued on many paths to multiple ends. In Jinty Nelson's paper it is Bede himself who becomes the authority, and his footsteps, she argues, that at crucial points showed Hincmar of Reims a way forward as he formulated the arguments of *De divortio*, his critical commentary on the contested divorce of

Lothar II and Theutberga. Through an exploration of Hincmar's explicit citation and silent quotation of a range of his works, Nelson lays bare his considerable familiarity with, and evident high regard for, the scholar he called 'blessed Bede' (*beatus Baeda*). Her analysis also identifies something of a sense of common enterprise in the face of comparable problems and concerns (divorce, possession) and a shared sense of how exegesis generated frameworks not only for interpreting but also acting in — and on — the world. Bede may have aspired to — indeed arrogated for himself — a near patristic weight of authority. The paradox of such an assertion of scholarly authority is that the power to activate or validate does not — cannot — lie with the claimant themselves but only with others, those who choose to recognise the claim. In her analysis of how Hincmar thought with and through Bede, in ways that clearly indicate he saw him amongst the ranks of the *doctores catholici*, Nelson shows this process of retrospective endorsement in action. Bede may have followed in the footsteps of others but, for those who followed after, his own prints had merged with theirs.

Anglo-Saxons continued to take the road to Rome until the end of Anglo-Saxon England itself, and it is the identities, activities, and motivations of visitors in this later period — the age of ecclesiastical reform preceding Gregory VII's pontificate rather than the age of ecclesiastical formation that succeeded Gregory I's — that Francesca Tinti explores. She finds new patterns of practice emerging alongside continuities with the earlier period. Amongst the former, the custom of archbishops of Canterbury (and, later, of York) travelling in person to receive the *pallium* from the pope's hand and the development of penitential pilgrimage; in the latter, the practice of appealing to Rome during moments of crisis or challenge, and of travelling to attend synods. (These were journeys undertaken in their own way in Wilfrid's footsteps.)

Éamonn Ó Carragáin's work has long been characterized by an acute sense of the interplay of the textual, the artefactual and the spatial, interplay in which the liturgy was often the conductive medium. In his, the final chapter, he directs his skills in drawing out dense patterns of meaning he has applied in the past to understanding the Ruthwell Cross and Old St Peter's to a much younger site: the church of San Giovanni Crisostomo in Venice, rebuilt in the years around the turn of the sixteenth century and furnished with art created by multiple hands in various media over several years, most notably three altar pieces. With its dedication to Chrysostom, Church Father and Archbishop of Constantinople, a floor plan indebted to Byzantine forms and a fourteenth-century Madonna *orans* of probably eastern Mediterranean origin, Christian antiquity and the medieval past were both strong presences in San Giovanni Crisostomo. Ó Carragáin, however, brings other aspects of these presences into the light, using the thought of the Carolingian theologian, Paschasius Radbertus, to decode the marble altar piece's initially puzzling depiction of Christ in his thirties crowning a Virgin Mary seemingly only in her teens, and Gregory the Great's mariology to make sense of the treatment of Virgin and Magdalen. By unravelling each artefact's individual knot of meaning, Ó Carragáin is able to trace the threads that bind one piece to another and the ways in which they cohere to form a whole, in the process making clear the compound lessons taught by this early modern *Gesamtkunstwerk*.

Works Cited

Secondary Studies

Brundage, Anthony, and Richard A. Cosgrove, *The Great Tradition: Constitutional History and National Identity in Britain and the United States, 1870–1960* (Stanford: Stanford University Press, 2007)

Macintyre, Angus, 'Gerald Harriss', in *Rulers and Ruled in Late Medieval England: Essays Presented to Gerald Harriss*, ed. by Rowena E. Archer and Simon Walker (London: Hambledon, 1995), pp. ix–xvi

McInerney, Laura, 'Profile: Tim Brighouse', *Academies Week*, 28 November 2014, pp. 13–14

Ó Carragáin, Éamonn, and Alan T. Thacker, 'Wilfrid in Rome', in *Wilfrid: Abbot, Bishop, Saint, Papers from the 1300th Anniversary Conferences*, ed. by Nicholas J. Higham (Stamford: Shaun Tyas, 2013), pp. 212–30

Thacker, Alan T., '*Loca Sanctorum*: the Significance of Place in the Study of the Saints', in *Local Saints and Local Churches in the Early Medieval West*, ed. by Alan T. Thacker and Richard Sharpe (Oxford: Oxford University Press, 2002), pp. 1–43

——, 'Why did Heresy Matter to Bede? Present and Future Contexts', in *Bede and the Future*, ed. by Peter Darby and Faith Wallis, Studies in Early Medieval Britain (Farnham: Ashgate, 2014), pp. 47–66

Wood, Ian N., 'John Michael Wallace-Hadrill, 1916–1985', *Proceedings of the British Academy*, 124. *Biographical Memoirs of Fellows*, III (2004), 332–55

Wormald, Patrick, 'James Campbell as Historian', in *The Medieval State: Essays Presented to James Campbell*, ed. by John R. Maddicott and David M. Palliser (London: Hambledon, 2000), pp. xiii–xxii

A Bibliography of the Publications of Alan T. Thacker, 1979–2019

This list omits editorials, reviews, obituaries, and minor notices.

1979

'[Chester] Castle', in *Chester: 1900 Years of History*, ed. by Annette M. Kennett (Chester: Chester City Council), pp. 13–16

'The Diocese of Chester'; 'The Endowed Schools of Cheshire', in *A History of the County of Chester, Volume II*, ed. by Brian E. Harris (Oxford: Oxford University Press), pp. 36–87; 223–54

1981

Chester Cathedral: Its Music and Musicians (Chester: Mason)

'Some Terms for Noblemen in Anglo-Saxon England, *c.* 650–900', in *Anglo-Saxon Studies in Archaeology and History*, 2, ed. by David Brown, James Campbell, and Sonia Chadwick Hawkes, British Archaeological Reports, British Series, 92 (Oxford: British Archaeological Reports) pp. 201–36

'The Chester Diocesan Records and the Local Historian', *Transactions of the Historic Society of Lancashire and Cheshire*, 130, 149–85

1982

'Chester and Gloucester: Early Ecclesiastical Organization in Two Mercian Burhs', *Northern History*, 18, 199–211

1983

'Bede's Ideal of Reform', in *Ideal and Reality in Frankish and Anglo-Saxon Society: Studies Presented to J. M. Wallace-Hadrill*, ed. by Patrick Wormald, with Donald Bullough and Roger Collins (Oxford: Basil Blackwell), pp. 130–53

1985

'Kings, Saints and Monasteries in Pre-Viking Mercia', *Midland History*, 10 (1985), 1–25

1987

Victoria History of Cheshire: I. Physique, Prehistory, Roman, Anglo-Saxon, and Domesday,
ed. by Brian E. Harris, assisted by Alan Thacker (Oxford: Oxford University Press).
Contributions: 'Anglo-Saxon Cheshire'; 'The Cheshire Domesday'(with Peter
Sawyer); 'Index to Domesday Survey', pp. 237–92; 293–370; 386–91
'The Architectural History of St Werburgh's Abbey', *Annual Report of the Friends of Chester
Cathedral*, 9–17

1988

'Aethelwold and Abingdon', in *Bishop Aethelwold: His Career and Influence*, ed. by Barbara
Yorke (Woodbridge: Boydell and Brewer), pp. 43–64
'Early Medieval Chester: the Historical Background', in *The Rebirth of Towns in the
West, A.D. 700–1050*, ed. by Richard Hodges and Brian Hobley, Council for British
Archaeology Research Report, 68 (London: Council for British Archaeology),
pp. 119–24

1990

with David J. Freke, 'The Inhumation Cemetery at Southworth Hall Farm, Winwick',
Journal of the Chester Archaeological Society, 70, 31–38

1991

The Earldom of Chester and its Charters: A Tribute to Geoffrey Barraclough, ed. by Alan Thacker
[= *Journal of the Chester Archaeological Society*, 71] (Chester: Chester Archaeological
Society). Contribution: 'Introduction: the Earls and their Earldom', pp. 7–22

1992

'Monks, Preaching and Pastoral Care in Early Anglo-Saxon England', in *Pastoral Care before
the Parish*, ed. by John Blair and Richard Sharpe, Studies in the Early History of Britain
(Leicester: Leicester University Press), pp. 137–70
'Cults at Canterbury: Relics and Reform under Dunstan and his Successors', in *St Dunstan:
His Life, Times, and Cult*, ed. by Nigel Ramsay, Margaret Sparks, and Tim Tatton-Brown
(Woodbridge: Boydell and Brewer), pp. 221–45

1994

'Cheshire', in *English County Histories: A Guide*, ed. by Christopher Currie and C. P. Lewis
(Stroud: Sutton), pp. 71–84

1995

'*Membra Disjecta*: the Division of the Body and the Diffusion of the Cult', in *Oswald: Northumbrian King to European Saint*, ed. by Clare Stancliffe and Eric Cambridge (Stamford: Paul Watkins), pp. 97–127

'The Cult of King Harold at Chester', in *The Middle Ages in the North-West*, ed. by Tom Scott and Pat Starkey (Oxford: Leopard's Head Press), pp. 155–76

'The Documentary Evidence', in *Excavations at Chester, the Evolution of the Heart of the City: Investigations at 3–15 Eastgate Street 1990/1*, ed. by Keith J. Matthews, Archaeological Service Excavation and Survey Reports, 8 (Chester: Chester City Council), pp. 33–37

1996

'Saint Making and Relic Collecting by Oswald and his Communities', in *Saint Oswald: Life and Influence*, ed. by Nicholas P. Brooks and Catherine Cubitt, Studies in the Early History of Britain, Makers of England, 2 (Leicester: Leicester University Press), pp. 244–68

'Bede and the Irish', in *Beda Venerabilis: Historian, Monk and Northumbrian*, ed. by Luuk A. J. R. Houwen and Alistair A. MacDonald, Mediaevalia Groningana, 19 (Groningen: Egbert Forsten), pp. 31–60

1997

'Dissolution and Resurrection', *Transactions of the Historic Society of Lancashire and Cheshire*, 145, 21–43

1998

'Memorializing Gregory the Great: the Origins and Transmission of a Papal Cult', *Early Medieval Europe*, 7.1 (1998), 59–84

1999

'Chester'; 'Cuthbert of Lindisfarne'; 'Wilfrid', in *The Blackwell Encyclopaedia of Anglo-Saxon England*, ed. by Michael Lapidge, John Blair, Simon Keynes, and Donald Scragg (Oxford: Blackwell, 1999), pp. 102–03; 131–33; 474–76. Pagination for the second edition, *The Wiley Blackwell Encyclopedia of Anglo-Saxon England* (Chichester: Wiley Blackwell, 2014), pp. 104–06; 134–35; 495–96

The Rows of Chester: The Chester Rows Research Project, Andrew Brown, Peter de Figueiredo, Jane Grenville, Roland Harris, Jane Laughton, Alan Thacker and Rick Turner, English Heritage Archaeological Report, 16 (London: English Heritage)

2000

Medieval Archaeology, Art and Architecture at Chester, ed. by Alan Thacker, The
    British Archaeological Association Conference Transactions, 22 (Leeds: Maney)
    Contribution: 'The Early Medieval City and its Buildings', pp. 16–30
'In Search of Saints: The English Church and the Cult of Roman Apostles and Martyrs
    in the Seventh and Eighth Centuries', in *Early Medieval Rome and the Christian
    West: Essays in Honour of Donald A. Bullough*, ed. by Julia M. H. Smith, The Medieval
    Mediterranean, 28 (Leiden: Brill), pp. 247–77
'In Gregory's Shadow? The Pre-Conquest Cult of St Augustine', in *Saint Augustine and the
    Conversion of England*, ed. by Richard Gameson (Stroud: Sutton), pp. 374–90
'*Peculiaris Patronus Noster*: The Saint as Patron of the State in the Early Middle Ages', in
    The Medieval State: Essays Presented to James Campbell, ed. by John R. Maddicott and
    David M. Palliser (London: Hambledon), pp. 1–24

2001

'Dynastic Monasteries and Family Cults: Edward the Elder's Sainted Kindred', in *Edward
    the Elder, 899–924*, ed. by Nicholas J. Higham and David H. Hill (London: Routledge),
    pp. 248–63

2002

Local Saints and Local Churches in the Early Medieval West, ed. by Alan T. Thacker and
    Richard Sharpe (Oxford: Oxford University Press). Contributions: '*Loca Sanctorum*:
    The Significance of Place in the Study of the Saints'; 'The Making of a Local Saint',
    pp. 1–43; 45–73

2003

Victoria History of Cheshire, V.1: The City of Chester. General History and Topography,
    ed. by Alan Thacker (Woodbridge: Boydell and Brewer). Contributions include:
    'Early Medieval Chester'; 'Later Medieval Chester' (with Jenny Kermode and Jane
    Laughton); 'Topography from *c.* 400 to 1914' (with A. P. Baggs and John Herson),
    pp. 16–33; 34–90; 206–38

2004

'The Cult of the Saints and the Liturgy', in *Saint Paul's: The Cathedral Church of London,
    604–2004*, ed. by Derek Keene, Arthur Burns, and Andrew Saint (Yale: Yale University
    Press), pp. 113–22
'Acca [St Acca] (d. 740), bishop of Hexham'; 'Æbbe [St Æbbe, Ebba] (d. 683?), abbess
    of Coldingham'; 'Ælfflæd [St Ælfflæd, Elfleda] (654–714), abbess of Strensall–
    Whitby'; 'Æthelthryth [St Æthelthryth, Etheldreda, Audrey] (d. 679), queen in

Northumbria, consort of King Ecgfrith, and abbess of Ely'; 'Boisil [St Boisil]
(d. *c.* 661), prior of Melrose'; 'Bosa [St Bosa] (d. 706), bishop of York'; 'Brorda
[Hildegils] (d. 799), magnate'; 'Deusdedit [St Deusdedit, Frithona] (d. 664),
archbishop of Canterbury'; 'Eadberht [Eadbert] (d. 698), bishop of Lindisfarne';
'Eadfrith [Eadfrid] (d. 721?), bishop of Lindisfarne'; 'Eanflæd [St Eanflæd] (b. 626,
d. after 685), queen in Northumbria, consort of King Oswiu'; 'Eata [St Eata]
(d. 685/6), bishop of Hexham'; 'Hild [St Hild, Hilda] (614–80), abbess of Strensall–
Whitby'; 'Stephen of Ripon [Stephanus] (*fl. c.* 670–*c.* 730), biographer'; 'Werburh
[St Werburh, Werburgh, Werburga] (d. 700 × 707), abbess'; 'Wilfrid [St Wilfrid]
(*c.* 634–709/10), bishop of Hexham', in *Oxford Dictionary of National Biography*,
ed. by H. C. G. Matthew and Brian Harrison, 60 vols and index (Oxford: Oxford
University Press)

2005

Victoria History of Cheshire V.2: The City of Chester. Culture, Buildings, Institutions, ed. by
Alan Thacker (Woodbridge: Boydell and Brewer). Contributions: 'Municipal
Buildings', 'Law Courts'; 'River Navigation'; 'Markets and Fairs'; 'Mills and
Fisheries'; 'Churches and Other Religious Bodies' (with C. P. Lewis); 'Major
Buildings'; 'Cathedral Music and Music Festivals'; 'Mayors and Sheriffs'; 'Chester
and Beyond', pp. 15–20; 20–28; 83–90; 94–104; 104–14; 125–84; 185–246; 273–75;
305–21; 322–30
'England in the Seventh Century', in *The New Cambridge Medieval History, I. 500–700*,
ed. by Paul J. Fouracre (Cambridge: Cambridge University Press), pp. 462–95

2006

'Bede and the Ordering of Understanding', in *Innovation and Tradition in the Writings of the
Venerable Bede*, ed. by Scott DeGregorio, Medieval European Studies, 6 (Morgantown:
West Virginia University Press), pp. 37–63

2007

'Martyr Cult within the Walls: Saints and Relics in the Roman *tituli* of the Fourth to
Seventh Centuries', in *Text, Image, Interpretation: Studies in Anglo-Saxon Literature and
Its Insular Context in Honour of Éamonn Ó Carragáin*, ed. by Alistair Minnis and Jane
Roberts, Studies in the Early Middle Ages, 18 (Turnhout: Brepols), pp. 31–70
'Rome of the Martyrs: Saints, Cults and Relics, Fourth to Seventh Century', in *Roma Felix
– Formation and Reflections of Medieval Rome*, ed. by Éamonn Ó Carragáin and Carol
Neuman de Vegvar, Church, Faith and Culture in the Medieval West, 10 (Aldershot:
Ashgate), pp. 13–49
'Bede and Wearmouth'; 'The Buck Prospect' (with Maureen Meikle), in *Sunderland
and its Origins: Monks to Mariners*, ed. by Maureen Meikle and Christine Newman
(Chichester: Phillimore), pp. 24–26; 100–01

2008

Bede and Augustine of Hippo: History and Figure in Sacred Text, Jarrow Lecture, 2005
    (Jarrow: St Paul's Church)
'Gallic or Greek? Archbishops in England from Theodore to Ecgberht', in *Frankland: The
    Franks and the World of Early Medieval Europe. Essays in Honour of Dame Jinty Nelson*,
    ed. by Paul Fouracre and David Ganz (Manchester: Manchester University Press),
    pp. 44–69

2009

'Bede, the Britons and the Book of Samuel', in *Early Medieval Studies in Memory of Patrick
    Wormald*, ed. by Stephen Baxter, Catherine E. Karkov, Janet L. Nelson, and David
    Pelteret, Studies in Early Medieval Britain (Farnham: Ashgate), pp. 129–48

2010

'Bede and History' in *The Cambridge Companion to Bede*, ed. by Scott DeGregorio
    (Cambridge: Cambridge University Press), pp. 170–89
'Priests and Pastoral Care in Early Anglo-Saxon England', in *The Study of Medieval
    Manuscripts of England: Festschrift in Honour of Richard W. Pfaff*, ed. by George
    Hardin Brown and Linda Ehrsam Voigts, Arizona Studies in the Middle Ages and the
    Renaissance, 35 (Turnhout: Brepols), pp. 187–208

2011

'Bede and his Martyrology', in *'Listen, O Isles, Unto Me': Studies in Medieval Word and Image
    in Honour of Jennifer O'Reilly*, ed. by Elizabeth Mullins and Diarmuid Scully (Cork:
    Cork University Press), pp. 126–41; 350–53
'Popes, Patriarchs and Archbishops and the Origins of the Cult of the Martyrs in Northern
    Italy', in *Saints and Sanctity*, ed. by Peter Clarke and Tony Claydon, Studies in Church
    History, 47 (Woodbridge: Boydell), pp. 51–79

2012

'Early Settlement', in *Victoria History of the County of York: East Riding IX. Harthill
    Wapentake, Bainton Beacon Division. Great Driffield and its Townships*, ed. by Graham
    Kent, with David Neave and Susan Neave (Oxford: Oxford University Press), pp. 5–13
'Patrons of Rome: The Cult of Sts Peter and Paul at Court and in the City in the Fourth
    and Fifth Centuries', *Early Medieval Europe*, 20.4 (2012), 380–406

2013

'Popes, Emperors and Clergy at Old St Peter's from the Fourth to the Eighth Century',
    in *Old St Peter's, Rome*, ed. by Rosamond McKitterick, John Osborne, Carole M.

Richardson, and Joanna Story, British School at Rome Studies (Cambridge: Cambridge University Press), pp. 137–56

'Wilfrid, His Cult and His Biographer'; 'Wilfrid in Rome' (with Éamonn Ó Carragáin)', in *Wilfrid: Abbot, Bishop, Saint, Papers from the 1300th Anniversary Conferences*, ed. by Nicholas J. Higham (Stamford: Shaun Tyas), pp. 1–16; 212–30

2014

Victoria History of Shropshire VI.1, Shrewsbury: General History and Topography, ed. by W. A. Champion and Alan Thacker (Woodbridge: Boydell and Brewer). Contributions: 'Introduction'; 'Shrewsbury 700–1200' (with Nigel Baker and Richard Holt); 'Shrewsbury, 1200–1340' (with Dorothy Cromarty, Robert Cromarty, and W. A. Champion), pp. 1–4; 5–30; 31–88

'Rome: the Pilgrims' City in the Seventh Century', in *England and Rome in the Early Middle Age: Pilgrimage, Art and Politics*, ed. by Francesca Tinti, Studies in the Early Middle Ages, 40 (Turnhout: Brepols), pp. 89–140

'Why did Heresy Matter to Bede? Present and Future Contexts', in *Bede and the Future*, ed. by Peter Darby and Faith Wallis, Studies in Early Medieval Britain and Ireland (Farnham: Ashgate), pp. 47–66

'The Origin and Early Development of Rome's Intramural Cults: A Context for the Cult of Sant'Agnese in Agone', in *Le culte de sainte Agnès à place Navone entre Antiquité et Moyen Âge*, ed. by Claire Sotinel, *Mélanges de l'École française de Rome–Moyen Âge*, 126.1, pp. 137–46

2015

'Anglo-Saxon Wearmouth'; 'Churches and Religious Bodies' (with Christine M. Newman), in *The Victoria County History of Durham, V. Sunderland*, ed. by Gillian Cookson (Woodbridge: Boydell), pp. 15–25; 177–218

2016

'Shaping the Saint: Rewriting Tradition in the Early Lives of St Cuthbert', in *The Introduction of Christianity into the Early Medieval Insular World: Converting the Isles*, I, ed. by Roy Flechner and Máire Ní Mhaonaigh, Cultural Encounters in Late Antiquity and the Middle Ages, 19 (Turnhout: Brepols), pp. 399–429

'Bede's Idea of the English: The Toller Lecture. Read at the John Rylands Library, March 2015', *Bulletin of the John Rylands Library*, 92.1, 1–26

2017

'The Saint in His Setting: The Physical Environment of Shrines in Northern Britain Before 850', in *Saints of North-East England, 600–1500*, ed. by Margaret Coombe, Anne E. Mouron, and Christiania Whitehead, Medieval Church Studies, 39 (Turnhout: Brepols, 2017), pp. 41–68

2019

'Pope Sergius' letter to Abbot Ceolfrith: Wearmouth–Jarrow, Rome and the Papacy in the Early Eighth Century', in *All Roads Lead to Rome: The Creation, Context and Transmission of the Codex Amiatinus*, ed. by Jane Hawkes and Meg Boulton, Studia Traditionis Theologiae, 31 (Turnhout: Brepols, 2019), pp. 115–28

'The Church and Warfare. The Religious and Cultural Background to the Hoard', in *The Staffordshire Hoard: An Anglo-Saxon Treasure*, ed. by Chris Fern, Tania M. Dickinson, and Leslie Webster, Reports of the Research Committee of the Society of Antiquaries of London, 80 (London: Society of Antiquaries of London), pp. 293–99

Guthlac: Crowland's Saint, ed. by Jane Roberts and Alan Thacker (Donnington: Shaun Tyas, 2019). Contributions: 'Introduction' (with Jane Roberts); 'Guthlac and his Life: Felix Shapes the Saint', pp. i–xxix; 1–24

MARK A. HANDLEY _____

Gildebertus rex fr[ancorum]: The Least–Famous Epitaph of a Merovingian King and the Cult of a Spanish Martyr in Sixth-Century Paris

In 1973 excavations in the chapel of Saint-Symphorien within the church of St-Germain-des-Prés resulted in the discovery of a highly-decorated sarcophagus. On its lid was an inscription with a cross and three words: + *Gildeb(er)tus rex fr[ancorum]*.[1] No less a figure than Jean Mallon published the *editio princeps* in 1981.[2]

Since then a total of just four scholars have made mention of this inscription. In 1998 Didier Busson included a discussion of the inscription in his volume on Paris within the series *Carte archéologique de la Gaule*, together with a reproduction of the originally-published photograph.[3] In 2003 I cited it as an example of important historical evidence generally ignored by early medieval historians because it is found in an inscription.[4] In 2004 Jean Vezin included a brief discussion of it as an example of Merovingian cursive in his survey of fifty years of work on Merovingian palaeography.[5] Finally, in 2015 Helmut Reimitz mentioned it in a footnote so as to dismiss its evidence.[6] There is little utility in listing scholars who have not made use of or mentioned this inscription, despite its evident relevance to any number of subjects under discussion.

The inscription deserves better. It is an original epitaph of an early medieval king, one found *in situ* during modern excavations of a church that Childebert himself

---

1 The idea for this article was long ago suggested to me by Alan. I remember talking to him about the inscription of Childebert that lay forgotten and how this gave life to Gregory's story of Childebert's foundation of the church of St Vincent (later Saint-Germain-des-Prés). Alan's immediate response was to say that that should be the basis of a short article. It has been a long time in the making, but is offered here in thanks for many conversations about the spread of the cult of martyrs, the reading of many draft articles, and in recognition of the indisputable fact that it would have been a better article if I'd been able to share it with Alan in draft beforehand.
2 Mallon, 'Le graffite Gildebertus rex francorum'.
3 Busson, *Paris. Carte Archéologique de la Gaule*, p. 355.
4 Handley, *Death, Society and Culture*, pp. 2, 46, 145.
5 Vezin, 'Un demi-siècle de recherches' p. 265.
6 Reimitz, *History, Frankish Identity and the Framing of Western Ethnicity*, p. 98.

Mark Handley • (mark3handley@hotmail.co.uk) has published extensively on late antiquity and early medieval history, with a focus upon epigraphic culture.

Cities, Saints, and Communities in Early Medieval Europe, ed. by Scott DeGregorio and Paul Kershaw, SEM 46 (Turnhout: Brepols, 2020), pp. 33–51
BREPOLS PUBLISHERS   DOI 10.1484/M.SEM-EB.5.119621

founded, testifying to his devotion to the cult of St Vincent. It is also the earliest original text that uses the term *rex francorum*.

In the summer of 541 the Merovingian King Childebert led his army from Spain back into Gaul. This had been his second invasion of Spain. The first had taken place in 531 when he had taken his army south to avenge the dishonouring of his Catholic sister Chlotild at the hands of her Arian husband, the Visigothic King Amalaric. Defeated at Narbonne the Arian Amalaric was pursued south to Barcelona where he was killed.[7] In that first invasion Childebert's army marched back north laden with royal treasure. Chlotild, however, fell ill and died during the journey north. Gregory of Tours recorded that 'she was carried to Paris and buried beside her father Clovis'.[8]

Childebert's second invasion may have been just as successful, but the sources differ on this. His army, and that of his brother Chlothar, had crossed the Pyrenees to Pamplona. This westerly route suggests a decision to bypass Visigothic Gaul. The army then marched further south from Pamplona to Saragossa.[9] From there the Frankish army would have had the choice of marching east-south-east along the Ebro valley to Tarragona, or to keep marching south-west to Toledo. By this time Toledo was emerging as the capital of the Visigothic kingdom under King Theudis whose only surviving law, interestingly a *Novella* to the *Breviary of Alaric* and not an early law for the *Lex Visigothorum*, was promulgated at Toledo in 546.[10]

For Gregory of Tours Childebert's invasion of 541 was a resounding success: 'They succeeded in conquering a large part of Spain and returned to Gaul with immense booty'.[11] For Isidore of Seville, on the other hand, the same invasion resulted in a 'fortunate victory' for the Visigoths.[12] According to Isidore, Theudis's appointed field commander, one Theudigisel:

Gothi duce Theudisclo obicibus Spaniae interclusis Francorum exercitum multa cum admiratione victoriae prostraverunt. Dux idem prece atque ingenti pecunia sibi oblata viam fugae hostibus residuis unius diei noctisque spatio praebuit: cetera infelicium turba, cui transitus conlati temporis non occurrit, Gothorum perempta gladio concidit.[13]

> closed off the passes into Spain and laid low the army of the Franks with great amazement at their victory. In response to their entreaties and the offer of a large amount of money, the general provided the remaining enemy troops a path of escape for the period of one day and one night. The wretched crowd of Franks who were unable to pass through within the allotted time were massacred by the swords of the Goths.

---

7 *Chronicle of Saragossa, s.a.* 531.
8 Gregory of Tours, *Decem Libri Historiarum*, III. 10.
9 *Chronicle of Saragossa, s.a.* 541.
10 Zeumer, 'Das Processkostengesetz des Königs Theudis'.
11 Gregory of Tours, *Decem Libri Historiarum*, III. 29.
12 Isidore of Seville, *Historia Gothorum Wandalorum Sueborum*, c. 42.
13 Isidore of Seville, *Historia Gothorum Wandalorum Sueborum*, c. 41.

That the Frankish army was (as ten years previously) laden with sufficient treasure to bribe their way north suggests that the evidence of Gregory and Isidore may not be so very far apart. Other sources give different emphases. Jordanes tells us that Theudis 'assailed the Franks'.[14] The so-called *Chronicle of Saragossa* is another surviving source for the same campaign:

> Hoc anno Francorum reges numero V per Pampelonam Hispanias ingressi Caesaraugustam venerunt, qua obsessa per quadraginta novem dies omnem fere Tarraconensem provinciam depopulatione attriverunt.[15]

>> During this year, five kings of the Franks entered the Spains, through Pamplona and reached Saragossa. They besieged it for forty-nine days, and totally destroyed it, along with the province of Tarraconensis, with their pillaging.

This chronicle gets its name from the concentration of entries relating to Saragossa and surrounding towns in northern Spain. Its latest entry dates from the 550s. It is possible, therefore, that the entry for 541 was written by an eyewitness to the events.

For our purposes, however, this eyewitness account omits a key aspect of the events as told by Gregory:

> Post haec Childeberthus rex in Hispaniam abiit. Qua ingressus cum Chlothachario, Caesaragustanam civitatem cum exercitu vallant atque obsedent. At ille in tanta humilitate ad Deum conversi sunt, ut induti ciliciis, abstinentis a cibis et poculis, cum tonica beati Vincenti martiris muros civitatis psallendo circuirent: mulieres quoque amictae nigris palleis, dissoluta caesariae, superposito cinere, ut eas putares virorum funeribus deservire, plangendo sequebantur. Et ita totam spem locus ille ad Domini misericordiam rettulit ut diceretur ibidem Ninivitarum ieiunium caelebrari, nec aestimaretur aliud posse fieri, nisi eorum praecibus divina misericordia flectiretur. Hii autem qui obsedebant, nescientes quid obsessi agerent, cum viderent sic murum circuire putabant, eos aliquid agere malefitii. Tunc adpraehensum unum de civitate rusticum, ipse interrogant, quid hoc esset quod agerent. Qui ait: 'Tonicam beati Vincenti deportant et cum ipsa, ut eis Dominus misereatur, exorant'. Quod illi timentes, se ab ea civitate removerunt.[16]

>> King Childebert set off for Spain. He and Chlothar arrived there together. They attacked and laid siege to the city of Saragossa. The inhabitants turned in great humility to God: they dressed themselves in hair shirts, abstained from eating and drinking, and marched round the city walls singing psalms and carrying the tunic of Saint Vincent the martyr. Their women folk followed them, weeping and wailing, dressed in black garments, with their hair blowing free and with ashes on their heads so that you might have thought that they were engaged in burying their husbands. The city pinned its hope on the

---

14 Jordanes, *Getica*, c. 58.
15 *Chronicle of Saragossa*, *s.a.* 541.
16 Gregory of Tours, *Decem Libri Historiarum*, III. 29.

mercy of God. It could have been said to fast as Nineveh fasted, and it was quite unimaginable that God in His compassion would not be swayed by the prayers of these people. The besiegers were nonplussed to see them behave in this way: as they watched them march round the walls they imagined that it was some curious kind of black magic. They seized hold of a peasant who lived in Saragossa and asked him what in the world they were doing. 'They are marching behind the tunic of Saint Vincent', he told them, 'and with this as their banner they are imploring god to take pity on them'. This scared the troops and they withdrew from the city.

The usual narrative proposed by modern scholars is to have the siege of Saragossa as the turning point in the campaign, with Childebert retreating after defeat by the combined power of St Vincent and the walls of Saragossa.[17] This ignores the evidence of the *Chronicle of Saragossa* which has the siege ending after forty-nine days with a Frankish victory. There is no way of reconciling these accounts, but in choosing between them we would have every reason to prefer the contemporaneous eyewitness account. Gregory, as we shall see, had every reason to maximise the power of Vincent's relics. Perhaps Childebert's army was ultimately victorious, but had faced sterner resistance at Saragossa than elsewhere.

The doublet to Gregory's account comes later in his Book III. In describing Childebert's death in 558 he states:

Childeberthus igitur rex aegrotare coepit, et cum diutissime apud Parisius lectulo decubasset, obiit et ad basilicam beati Vincenti quam ipse construxerat, est sepultus.[18]

King Childebert fell ill: for a long time he lay bed-ridden in Paris and then he died. He was buried in the church of Saint Vincent, which he himself had built

The general narrative of these events constructed by modern commentators ties Childebert's foundation of St Vincent to his experience at Saragossa, a connection that rests upon an assumption that Childebert brought Vincent's relics back with him from Spain.[19] There are a number of problems with this. Firstly, Gregory himself does not make the connection, although he may have expected the attentive reader to do so. Secondly, Gregory makes no mention of Childebert bringing relics of Vincent back from Spain. The eighth-century *Liber Historiae Francorum*, building upon Gregory's narrative, has Childebert asking the bishop of Saragossa for relics of Vincent after the siege's end, but the bishop tricking the Frankish king and handing over his own tunic rather than that of the martyr.[20] In the context of early eighth-century ecclesiastical politics this anecdote may have been intended as a slight upon the relics of one of Paris's

---

17 There are many such examples and it is unfair to cite just some, but for one example see Kulikowski, *Late Roman Spain*, p. 226.
18 Gregory of Tours, *Decem Libri Historiarum*, IV. 20.
19 I have done this myself. See Handley, *Death, Society and Culture*, p. 145.
20 *Liber Historiae Francorum*, c. 26.

great churches by an author most likely writing in Soissons.[21] More certain, however, is the fact that the author of the *Liber Historiae Francorum* was writing in a milieu where it was thought that Childebert had brought relics of Vincent back from Spain but she (if it was she) was writing nearly two hundred years after Childebert's invasion.

In addressing the probabilities of whether Childebert's relics of Vincent were imported from Spain with the returning army it is appropriate to turn to the evidence for the spread of Vincent's relics and cult into Gaul by Childebert's time. Before we can decide whether Childebert must have, or may have, brought the relics of Vincent back with him from Spain, we need to consider whether it was possible for Childebert to have acquired relics of Vincent from elsewhere within Gaul.

The earliest evidence for the existence of the cult of Vincent in Gaul is the *Calendar* of Polemius Silvius dedicated to Bishop Eucherius of Lyon and written in 448–449.[22] This work blended Roman festivals and Christian holy days into a single calendar. Under 22 January — Vincent's traditional feast day — there is the entry *natalis sancti Vincentii martyris*.[23] Vincent's cult is only one of a handful worthy of inclusion. Only Stephen, Lawrence, and Hippolytus are otherwise mentioned. Unless Polemius Silvius had his own reasons for promoting an otherwise obscure cult into the highest echelon of the saints, it is difficult to avoid the conclusion, at least in this region of southern Gaul and the Rhône Valley, that the cult of Vincent was one of the most prominent of all cults, martyrial or otherwise. For a mid-fifth century writer of a calendar listing the main civic festivals, the feast day of Vincent had to be included.

The next evidence comes from Montady between Béziers and Narbonne in the far south-west of France. The evidence is in the form of a building inscription dated to the seventh consulship of the Emperor Valentinian and that of Avienus (AD 450).[24] It reads:

+ *Othia pr(es)b(yter) anno XXX III +*

Pr(es)b(y)t(eratu)s sui baselic(am) ex vot[o]

suo in hon(orem) s(an)c(to)r(u)[m mart(yrum) Vincenti]

Agnetis et Eula[liae con(s)tr(uxit) et d(e)d(i)c(avit)]

Valentinia[no VII et A[v]ien(o) cons(ulibus)]

> + Othia the priest in the 33rd year +
> of his priesthood built and dedicated this basilica
> in honour of the holy martyrs Vincent, Agnes and
> Eulalia in fulfilment of his vow.
> Seventh consulate of Valentinian and that of Avienus.

---

21 Nelson, 'Gender and Genre in Women Historians' and Gerberding, *The Rise of the Carolingians*, both agree on Soissons, albeit preferring different establishments within the town.

22 This evidence is omitted from Saxer's otherwise useful survey, Saxer, 'Lieux de culte de saint Vincent'.

23 Polemius Silvius, *Laterculus*, p. 257.

24 The best, and most detailed, study of this now worn and damaged inscription is Chalon, 'L'inscription d'une église rurale'.

This inscription has achieved a certain prominence in recent work by Ralph Mathisen as an example of patronage and evergetism by a Gothic Arian priest.[25] The argument is that Othia's name indicates him to be a Goth, and thus an Arian, and that only an Arian priest would have dared to dedicate a church when the Nicene Council of Orange had expressly forbidden the dedication of churches by anyone other than a bishop. These arguments are also not without difficulties. For instance, the Council of Orange had only sat in 441, and had not been attended by bishops from Narbonensis or indeed from Visigothic Gaul.[26] Were the canons of councils from a separate polity really so widely circulated down to the parochial level and so strenuously followed that a priest such as Othia must be understood to have been bound by their tenets? Perhaps not. He was, after all, not the only priest to build and dedicate a church.[27] Lastly, if we are not passed the point where all people with a linguistically-Germanic name are assumed, without the need for argument, to be Goths, and that all Goths were Arians — we should be.

It is noteworthy that the most recent detailed study of this inscription concludes instead that Othia must have been a Nicene priest because of the three martyr cults he was promoting.[28] That argument is, unfortunately, no more compelling. King Leovigild's attempts to wrest relics of Eulalia from Mérida in the sixth century suggests that martyr cults should not be seen in such a denominational manner.[29] Whether Othia was Nicene or Arian may be a puzzle that cannot be solved.

What is not in dispute is the evidence for the cult of Vincent in mid-fifth-century southern Gaul — here coupled with the cults of Eulalia of Mérida and the martyr Agnes from Rome.[30] Although divided by the Pyrenees, the distance from this church to Saragossa or indeed Valentia (the site of Vincent's martyrdom) is not great. The spread of the cult to the far south-west of Gaul may have been more of a process of gradual osmosis, but the combination with Eulalia of Mérida is suggestive of a particular interest in Spanish cults. The combination of these cults with that of Agnes is, moreover, suggestive of a reader of Prudentius. Each of these martyrs was the named subject of three of the 'Crowns' in Prudentius' *Peristephanon*: Crown III was dedicated to Eulalia, Crown V to Vincent, and Crown XIV to Agnes.[31]

The next two pieces of evidence are perhaps best seen together and together attest to a prominent cult for Vincent in early sixth-century Burgundy. The first piece of evidence is a letter from Avitus of Vienne dated to the early sixth century where he

---

25 Mathisen and Sivan, 'Forging a New Identity'; Mathisen, 'Barbarian Bishops and the Churches', p. 682, and Mathisen, 'Barbarian "Arian" Clergy', at p. 159.

26 *Concila Galliae A. 314-A. 506*, ed. by Munier, pp. 87–90 for the different versions of the subscription lists to this council. Bishops attended from *Viennensis*, *Lugdunensis Prima*, *Narbonensis Secunda*, and *Alpes Maritimae*. Also attending was Agrestius of Lugo from Gallaecia. There were no bishops from *Narbonensis Prima*. On Agrestius of Lugo see Mathisen, 'Agrestius of Lugo'.

27 See, for example, *Receuil des inscriptions chrétiennes de la Gaule*, Vol. 15, *Viennoise du Nord*, no. 288.

28 Chalon, 'L'inscription d'une église rurale'.

29 *Vitas Sanctorum Patrum Emeretensium*, ed. by Maya Sánchez, V. 7, VI. 12.

30 In the works cited in footnote 25 Ralph Mathisen states that the inscription records relics of Felix, Agnes and Eulalia. This error of Felix for Vincent is based on a long-since abandoned reading.

31 Prudentius, *The Crowns of Martyrdom*.

pays his annual 'Saint Vincent's day' respects to Prince Sigismund; the other is an epitaph from Vaison in the Rhône Valley recording the relics of Saint Vincent being deployed in a private mausoleum at around the same time.

In his letter to Sigismund, son and eventual successor of King Gundobad, Avitus gently berates Sigismund for not stopping in Vienne when travelling 'from Sapaudia to Provence' and to apologise for the delay in arranging a messenger 'to convey my annual respect to you for the feast of Saint Vincent'.[32]

The inscription raised near Vaison in the Rhône Valley in the early to mid-sixth century is the epitaph of one Pantagatus.[33] It records the building of his mausoleum on his private land, and refers to the relics of Vincent 'together with his companions and peers' looking over the burial. The relevant first lines of the inscription read as follows:

Inlustris titulis meritisque haut dispar avorum
Pantagatus, fragilem vitae cum linquerit usum
malluit hic propriae corpus committere terrae
quam precibus quaesisse solum. Si magna patronis
martyribus quaerenda quies, sanctissimus ecce
cum sociis paribusque suis Vincentius ambit
hos aditos servatque domum dominumque tuetur
a tenebris lumen praebens de lumine vero.

Illustrious in rank and deed, worthy of his ancestors,
Pantagatus, when he departed this fragile existence,
preferred that his remains be interred here on his own land
than to solicit a resting place through his prayers. If one
is to find eternal peace under the protection of the
martyrs, behold! The most-saintly Vincentius, together
with his companions and peers, watches over the approaches to this
place, protecting this house and guarding its lord from the
darkness by casting light from the True Light.[34]

Whether we should envisage a private chapel dedicated with relics of Vincent, or a situation in which Pantagatus was buried with a relic in his own grave is perhaps

32 Avitus, *Ep.* 79; *Avitus of Vienne*, trans. by Shanzer and Wood, pp. 237–38.

33 The exact find spot is unrecorded. Some have interpreted the final line as a dating clause referring to the consulate of Senator in 515. I prefer the interpretation in Martindale and Jones, eds, *Prosopography of the Later Roman Empire*, II, *s.n.* Pantagathus, II, pp. 829–30. Chalon, 'L'inscription d'une église rurale', p. 162 n. 75, agrees with a general sixth–century date for this epitaph.

34 *Inscriptions chrétiennes de la Gaule antérieures au VIIIe siècle*, ed. by Le Blant, no. 492 = *Inscriptiones Latinae Christianae Veteres*, ed. by Diehl, no. 211. The most recent edition is *La collection d'inscriptions gallo–grecques et latines du Musée Calvet*, ed. by Gascou and Guyon, no. 215. Gascou and Guyon prefer the interpretation of the date as 515.

uncertain. Either way we can see the eminence of the cult of Vincent. He was singled out amongst the martyrs and this man with senatorial aspirations (*vir inlustris* being the highest senatorial grade) was an adherent to, and sponsor of, his cult.

Some sixty years after the *Laterculus* of Polemius Silvius these two pieces of evidence suggest that Vincent's cult was no less prominent in the Rhône valley of the early sixth century, than it had been in 449. There is then a gap in the evidence until we reach the late sixth century and the works of Venantius Fortunatus and Gregory of Tours.

Gregory makes room, in his *Glory of the Martyrs* and his *Glory of the Confessors*, for a number of stories about the cult of Vincent in sixth-century Gaul. One such account focuses on a newly-built church at Neuvy-le-Roi, which had no relics as the relics of Andrew and Saturninus which had been held by the church had been taken away. On the same day as the removal a small piece of a relic of Vincent was obtained from a group of 'travelling men' (*errantes homines*).[35] The dating of this episode is uncertain but likely to have been some time in the sixth century. Whether it is evidence for a cult of Vincent in Gaul *before* the dedication of Childebert's foundation in Paris is far from certain.

The same can be said for Gregory's story of one Antoninus, who was buried in the church of St Vincent in Toulouse, but who had committed so many crimes that the holy martyr threw his sarcophagus out of the church, and of Gregory's account of relics of Vincent in the region of Poitiers.[36]

Although not mentioned in Gregory's works, two poems of Venantius Fortunatus indicate that Bishop Leontius II, or Leontius the Younger, of Bordeaux may have been a promoter of Vincent's cult.[37] Leontius was probably related to his eponymous predecessor in office, Leontius I, or Leontius the Elder. Leontius I is recorded as bishop of Bordeaux at the Council of Orléans in 541, and Leontius II was the bishop by the time of the Council of Orléans in 549.[38]

Leontius II was married to Placidina, the great-granddaughter of Sidonius Apollinaris and so also related to the Emperor Avitus. He was also one of Venantius Fortunatus's earliest patrons in Gaul, the recipient in return of a sequence of poems in praise of three of his villas (*Carm*. I. 18–I. 20), verse celebrating several of the churches that he had commissioned (*Carm*. I. 6 and I. 8–I. 13), and panegyric (*Carm*. I. 15 and I. 16). Venantius's final poetic tribute would be Leontius's epitaph (*Carm*. IV. 10).[39] Gregory of Tours, by contrast, says little of Leontius II and what he does say is largely negative; criticising Leontius for describing Bordeaux as an 'apostolic see'.[40]

---

35 Gregory of Tours, *Gloria Martyrum*, c. 30.
36 Gregory of Tours, *Gloria Martyrum*, c. 88; c. 89.
37 Venantius Fortunatus, *Carmina*, ed. by Leo, I. 8, I. 9. See also de Gaiffier, 'Les deux poèmes de Fortunat en l'honneur de saint Vincent'.
38 *Concilia Galliae A. 511-A. 695*, ed. by de Clercq, pp. 142, 161.
39 In general see George, 'Portraits of Two Merovingian Bishops'; Brennan, 'The Image of the Merovingian Bishop' and Roberts, *The Humblest Sparrow*, pp. 16–18, 64–65, 69–77, 79–82, 167. On the epitaph for Leontius also now see Buchberger, 'Romans, Barbarians and Franks' at pp. 298–99.
40 Gregory of Tours, *Decem Libri Historiarum*, IV. 26.

Of Leontius II's career before becoming bishop almost the only detail known from Venantius is that Leontius accompanied an unnamed king to Spain (*Carm.* I. 15, lines 7–10). This king was Childebert. *PLRE* (*Prosopography of the Later Roman Empire*) argues that because Venantius refers to Leontius serving under *one* king in Spain that this must be a reference to the invasion of 531, and not to that of 541 which was jointly led by Childebert and Chothar.[41] This is unconvincing. At any one time a person in Merovingian Gaul was only ever the subject of one king. Whether Leontius took part in the invasion of 531 or of 541, in either case he was there serving Childebert alone.

That Venantius associated Leontius with two churches dedicated to Vincent is perhaps suggestive that Leontius took part in the invasion of 541 and that the events of the siege of Saragossa had an impact upon him, just as perhaps they did upon his king. The significant difficulty with this argument, however, is that several scholars, including Marc Reydellet and Michael Roberts, have argued that the Vincent to whom Leontius's churches were dedicated was Vincent of Agen, and not Vincent of Saragossa.[42]

Vincent of Agen is a saint whose authenticity is widely doubted. He is considered to be a manufactured doublet for Vincent of Saragossa. In some sense, therefore, the creation of the cult of Vincent of Agen is evidence for the spread of the cult of Vincent of Saragossa. By the time of Leontius, however, the cult of Vincent of Agen was long established and if Leontius was promoting the cult of Vincent of Agen that is best not interpreted as indirect evidence for the cult of the Spanish martyr.

In Venantius's poems on the Vincentian churches built by Leontius the method of martyrdom for the saint is specified as beheading.[43] According to Prudentius, Vincent of Saragossa was put through any number of tortures and punishments but having his head chopped off was not one of them.

It follows that although the evidence indicates that Leontius was a senior secular figure associated with Childebert who campaigned with his king in Spain and was probably present at the siege of Saragossa and that when he later became bishop of Bordeaux he took the opportunity to build a church dedicated to a Saint Vincent, the Vincent in question was probably not the martyr of Saragossa.

Let us turn now to Paris, and to the church built by Childebert. Gregory of Tours's evidence gives an indication that this church (despite remaining dedicated to Saint Vincentius) was starting to be seen increasingly as the location for miracles at the tomb of Bishop Germanus of Paris. In his *Gloria Confessorum*, the fact that Germanus's body is working its miracles in the church of St Vincentius is an incidental detail in a story about the holy power of the bishop.[44] As a further illustration of this tendency Venantius's *Life of Germanus* fails once to mention Vincent by name.[45] Venantius's poem *De ecclesia*

---

41   Martindale, ed., *Prosopography of the Later Roman Empire*, III, *s.n.* Leontius, 4, p. 774.
42   Roberts, *The Humblest Sparrow*, p. 69, n. 85, and *Venance Fortunat*, ed. by Reydellet, I, pp. 170–72.
43   Roberts, *Venantius Fortunatus*, trans. by Roberts, I. 8, pp. 26–29.
44   Gregory of Tours, *Gloria Confessorum*, c. 88.
45   Venantius Fortunatus, *Vita Sancti Germani*, ed. by Krusch, pp. 11–27.

Parisiaca (*Carm.* II. 10) has been interpreted as a description of the church of Saint Vincentius, but this is uncertain and it may be describing another church. The poem makes no mention of Vincent. Moreover, this poem refers to the church in question as housing a relic of the true cross. No other source associates the church of Saint Vincent with such a relic. As a result I side with Jean Dérens and Michel Fleury who have preferred to doubt whether this poem is a description of Saint-Germain-de-Prés.[46]

Leaving Gaul there is also significant evidence for the early spread of Vincent's cult and relics to North Africa, where his cult was celebrated in sermons by Augustine and in epigraphic dedications.[47] A fifth- or sixth-century inscription from Salona reading + *Sanctus Vincentius* records the spread of the veneration of this martyr in Dalmatia.[48] By contrast there is little evidence of a cult of Vincent in Italy in the fifth or early sixth century.[49]

In Spain there is significant evidence for the wide spread of the cult by the end of the sixth century. Prudentius's inclusion of Vincent in his *Peristephanon* has already been mentioned, with Vincent appearing in his own Crown, and also in that for the eighteen martyrs of Saragossa.[50] From Toledo, the epitaph of one Arcadius describes himself and his parents as 'Servants of Saint Vincent the Martyr' (*servi sanc(ti) Vincenti marteris*).[51] Bishop Justinian of Valencia's poetic epitaph from the mid-sixth century not only presents the bishop as a devotee of the martyr, but refers to a monastery in Valencia dedicated to Vincent, all the while stressing that Vincent's actual martyrdom took place in Valencia.[52] From Cehegín, just inland from Cartagena, there is a dedication of a church to Vincent by Bishop Acrusminus in either the sixth or seventh century.[53] Further south in Granada at the very end of the sixth century, or very early seventh century, Count Gudiliu [...] dedicated three churches to Stephen, John the Baptist, and Vincent.[54] To the west, near Seville, the town of Carmona has left us one of the most remarkable of all early medieval inscriptions — a partial liturgical calendar for the months from December to June inscribed down the length of two columns. It is likely that two now lost columns completed the year. Unfortunately, the calendar can only be dated broadly to the sixth or seventh century, but it records that Vincent's festival was celebrated on the eleventh day before the calends of February (22 January).[55] From Seville itself

---

46 Dérens and Fleury, 'La construction de la cathédrale de Paris par Childebert Ier'.
47 See Duval, *Loca Sanctorum Africae*, II, pp. 645–48; Castillo Maldonado, 'El culto del mártir Vicente de Zaragoza' and Meyer, *Der Heilige Vinzen von Zaragoza*, pp. 57–72, 225–27.
48 *Salona IV. Inscriptions de Salone chrétienne IVe–VIIe siècles*, ed. by Marin, no. 41.
49 Saxer, 'Le culte de S. Vincent en Italie avant l'an mil'. Meyer, *Der Heilige Vinzenz von Zaragoza*, pp. 200–24.
50 Prudentius, *Peristephanon*, ed. by Cunningham, Crown IV.
51 *Inscripciones cristianas España Romana y Visigoda*, no. 67.
52 *Inscripciones cristianas España Romana y Visigoda*, no. 279, with discussion in Gómez Pallarès, 'Poésie épigraphique en *Hispania*', pp. 143–48. See also the discussion in *Carmina Latina Epigraphica Hispaniae*, no. V6.
53 *Inscripciones cristianas España Romana y Visigoda*, no. 319.
54 *Inscripciones cristianas España Romana y Visigoda*, no. 303, with discussion in Duval, 'Nativola-les-trois-Églises'.
55 *Inscripciones cristianas España Romana y Visigoda*, no. 333.

Isidore's *Chronicle* adds a gloss to Hydatius's account of the sack of a church which is suggestive of a dedication of that church to Vincent by 428.[56] There is, therefore, extensive evidence for the spread of the cult of Vincent throughout at least eastern, southern, and central Spain before the end of the sixth century.

The question needs to be asked, therefore, as to whether Childebert's decision to dedicate his Parisian church to Vincent was, in fact, an indigenous extension of the pre-existing spread of the cult of Vincent into Gaul, or whether it should be seen rather primarily as the result of the events of the siege of Saragossa.

What is clear is that Childebert's dedication did not occur in a vacuum. The cult of Vincent was already spread across large parts of Gaul, even if the evidence from before Childebert's time derives from areas much further south than Paris. Despite this antecedent interest in the cult, the fact that in Paris Childebert came to patronise church building dedicated to Vincent suggests that the events of 541 and the siege of Saragossa did indeed have an impact on the target of his martyrial devotion.

The Excavations at Saint-Symphorien

The excavations of the chapel of Saint-Symphorien within the broader complex of Saint-Germain-des-Prés started in 1970 and continued for several years. It is fair to say that as yet they have not been fully published, although several summaries of progress were published at the time.[57] It was in the north-east corner of the chapel that the sarcophagus with which I began this paper was found during the excavations. It was built into the base of one of the walls. This location confirms that it was *in situ*. The lid was broken, and contains some geometric patterning while the entirety of the visible side is covered in geometric striations. It was on one of the broken pieces of the lid that the inscription was found.

The Inscription

Perhaps the first issue is to discuss the inscription's authenticity. This is because it has recently been doubted by Helmut Reimitz. He has proposed that the inscription was produced perhaps several hundred years after Childebert: 'the scratch is unlikely to be a contemporary inscription'.[58] These doubts must be discarded. Reimitz's first stated reason is that the lettering 'is, however, rather a scratch than an inscription'. This distinction is, for want of a better word, baffling. It is entirely unexplained how the weight of carving is supposed to mean that this inscription cannot be contemporaneous with Childebert. Weight of carving does not equal weight of evidence.

---

56 See the discussion in Handley, *Death, Society and Culture*, p. 144.
57 See Dérens, 'A propos des fouilles de la chapelle Saint-Symphorien de Saint-Germain des-Prés'; Fleury, 'Les fouilles récentes'.
58 Reimitz, *History, Frankish Identity and the Framing of Western Ethnicity*, p. 98.

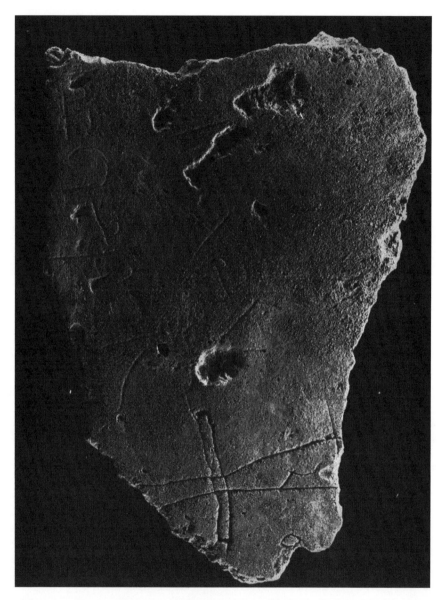

Figure 1. Inscribed fragment of sarcophagus lid recovered in 1973 during excavations in the chapel of Saint-Symphorien, Saint-Germain-des-Prés. Image reproduced courtesy of Cahiers de la Rotonde. Original photograph taken by José Lothe, La Commission du Vieux Paris.

Reimitz's second reason is the 'G for the grapheme Ch in the name Childebertus, which is attested only in a manuscript from the tenth century with a version of the *De virtutibus S. Martini*.[59] At issue here is a concern that the spelling found in this inscription is inconsistent with the known linguistic chronology of the move from Ch– to G–, and thus is an anachronism that makes the notion of its composition in the sixth century an impossibility. A comparable concern about this use of the initial G was raised by Jean Mallon in his 1981 edition of the inscription. Mallon, however, drew attention to the parallel of the name 'Gildobertus' in an original document from seventh-century Tours.[60] Because Reimitz had seemingly not consulted Mallon's edition, he was left unaware of this parallel. In addition to this parallel we might note that another sixth-century Merovingian, Queen Austregild, appears to have always had her name spelled with a G and not Ch. Certainly this is the spelling reflected in the manuscripts of Marius of Avenches and Gregory of Tours, and in the ninth-century manuscript that recorded her epitaph.[61]

People in the early middle ages did not always place linguistic or phonological significance on divergent spellings. The word-initial G– could be used in this, and other, inscriptions, without it being intended to signify a change in pronunciation. The use of G in *Gildeb(er)tus* is not unparalleled. Nor is its use in the sixth century necessarily contradictory to the known chronology of sound changes in Germanic.

Moving on to the title of *Rex Francorum*, it is worth making clear that this full title does not survive. The letters remaining are *rex fr*: due to a break in the lid it is not entirely clear if there were once other letters now lost (i.e. a reading of perhaps *fr[ancorum]*), or if the text finished at *fr* (i.e. a reading of *fr(ancorum)*).

The usage of this term has been studied in wonderful detail in recent years by Andrew Gillett, Hans-Werner Goetz, and Helmut Reimitz. For Goetz, the earliest certain use was in a charter from the reign of Theudebert II in 596;[62] for Gillett the best evidence for the use starts with original charters from the 620s considering that earlier usage in non-original documents was too prone to later editorialising;[63] Reimitz is willing to look beyond charters and sees the earliest usage of *rex Francorum* in the Edict of Guntram of 585.[64] But if we take this inscription as contemporary with the death of Childebert it becomes the earliest original document with this title, predating the Edict of Guntram by nearly three decades.[65] If we accept that the inscription as having been prepared at the request of Childebert himself, or

---

59 Reimitz, *History, Frankish Identity and the Framing of Western Ethnicity*, p. 98.

60 *Documents comptables de Saint-Martin de Tours*, ed. by Gasnault, p. 69.

61 See the discussion of Austregild in Handley, 'Merovingian Epigraphy'.

62 Goetz, '*Gens*, Kings and Kingdoms', p. 323, with bibliography of earlier studies.

63 Gillett, 'Was Ethnicity Politicized in the Earliest Medieval Kingdoms?', especially pp. 94–97, 111–12. A problem with Gillett's study is the lack of interest in evidence of change over time. With kingdoms such as Gibichung Burgundy, the kingdom of Odovacar, and those of the Moors in North Africa this is less of an issue than with the nearly three hundred years of the Merovingians.

64 Reimitz, *History, Frankish Identity and the Framing of Western Ethnicity*, p. 98.

65 This is an important point, as there is evidence that later copyists of royal formulae would on occasion alter *rex* to *rex francorum*. See Gillett, 'Ethnography and *Imperium*', at p. 77.

by those within his circle, it also becomes the earliest use of this term as a form of self-identification.

Significantly, there are, in addition to this inscription, a number of other documents which combine to make a suggestive argument that Childebert consciously adopted this title during his reign. A key piece of evidence is the fact that the very earliest known usage of the term *rex francorum* is found in a text written during Childebert's reign.[66] This is the *Vita Genovefae*, composed in the 520s in (or near) Paris by a writer with close associations to the Merovingian family and specifically to Chlothild, Clovis's widow and patroness of the *Vita Genovefae*. In this *Vita* Childeric, Clovis's father, and Childebert's grandfather, is described as *rex francorum*.[67] The evidence of the *Vita Genovefae* is omitted from the discussions of Goetz, Reimitz, and Gillett. Staying in the reign of Childebert in May 545 Pope Vigilius addressed Childebert as *rex francorum* in a letter to Gallic bishops.[68] This may have been an example of the ethnicization of titles by external actors analysed by Gillett, but in light of the use of the title by the Merovingians themselves, or those close to them, it could equally well be evidence that the adoption of this title had become known to the pope in Rome by the time this letter was written.[69]

Following Childebert's example, a number of other Merovingians were buried at Saint Vincent.[70] Gregory of Tours records that Chilperic I was buried there in 584.[71] His epitaph, now lost, was found in 1643.[72] Chilperic's wife Fredegund was buried in the same church when she died in 597.[73] Two of Chilperic's sons by another woman were also buried at Saint Vincent.[74] Chlothar II, the son of Fredegund and Chilperic, died in October 629. He too was buried in the same church.[75] There is then a gap of nearly fifty years before the next known burial of a member of the Merovingian dynasty, that of Childeric II. That this is also the final known burial of a Merovingian at Saint-Germain is evidence that by this point the practice of royal burials had truly moved away from this church to a new centre: Saint-Denis.

Childeric II was murdered in 675.[76] Fredegar does not record the location of his burial, but an epitaph to *Child(e)r(icus) rex* was found at Saint-Germain-des-Prés in

---

66 Cassiodorus, *Variae* II. 41 and III. 4 each refer to Clovis as *rex francorum*. Gillett, 'Was Ethnicity Politicized in the Earliest Medieval Kingdoms?', p. 106, following Classen, *Kaiserreskript und Königsurkunde*, p. 130, sees this usage as the result of later interpolation. In any event the *Variae* as published post-dates the *Vita Genovefae*.

67 *Les Vies anciennes de sainte Geneviève de Paris: Étude critique*, ed. by Heinzelmann and Poulin, c. 25. See also the discussion of Bitel, *Landscape with Two Saints*.

68 See Jaffé, *Regesta Pontificum Romanorum*, I, no. 918, pp. 119–20. *Epistolae Arelatenses Genuinae*, ed. by Gundlach, no. 40, pp. 59–60.

69 This is one of the key arguments in Gillett, 'Was Ethnicity Politicized in the Earliest Medieval Kingdoms?'.

70 Also see James, 'Royal Burials among the Franks' and Périn, 'Saint-Germain-des-Prés'.

71 Gregory of Tours, *Decem Libri Historiarum*, VI. 46.

72 See the discussion in Handley, 'Merovingian Epigraphy'.

73 *Liber Historiae Francorum*, c. 37.

74 Gregory of Tours, *Decem Libri Historiarum*, VIII. 10.

75 *The Fourth Book of the Chronicle of Fredegar*, ed. by Wallace-Hadrill, IV. 56.

76 *The Fourth Book of the Chronicle of Fredegar*, ed. by Wallace-Hadrill, p. 81.

1656.[77] The death of Childeric I long predated the foundation of Saint-Germain-des-Prés, making it clear that it was the late seventh-century king who was buried there. Childeric II was only belatedly buried sometime after his murder. Those occupying the throne were presumably unwilling to allow his interment at Saint-Denis, the new home for the bodies of the Merovingian dynasty — and so the out-of-fashion Saint Germain was used, not to say permitted, instead.

Conclusion

Childebert's epitaph marked not only his own dedication to the cult of Vincent, but also a new departure for the Frankish ruling house as his epitaph was the first of many in the sixth century to commemorate the Merovingian royal dead. It is fitting, therefore, that this innovative epitaph should also be the earliest original document describing a Merovingian as *rex francorum*. As to whether Childebert's dedication to Vincent grew out of indigenous Gallic interest in the cult, or arose more as a result of the events of the siege of Saragossa, the evidence is inconclusive. Nonetheless, it would be remarkable if the role of Vincent at the siege of Saragossa had *no* impact on Childebert's choice for his church in Paris. Perhaps that choice was made all the more attractive by the pre-existing spread of the cult across large parts of Gaul. If that is correct, it leads to the further possibility that the choice of the cult of Vincent also had a socio-political role in the establishment of the Merovingian capital of Paris.

Works Cited

Primary Sources

Avitus, *Alcimi Ecdici Aviti opera quae supersunt*, ed. by Rudolf Peiper, *Monumenta Germaniae Historica: Auctores antiquissimi*, 15 vols (Hannover: Weidmann, 1887–1919), VI.2 (1883)

Avitus of Vienne: Letters and Selected Prose Works, trans. by Danuta Shanzer and Ian N. Wood, Translated Texts for Historians, 38 (Liverpool: Liverpool University Press, 2002)

Chronicle of Saragossa, in *Victoris Tunnensis ex Consularibus Caesaraugustanis et Iohannis Biclarensis Chronicon*, ed. by Carmen Cardelle de Hartmann, Corpus Christianorum Series Latina, 173A (Turnhout: Brepols, 2001), pp. 1–55

Concilia Galliae A. 314-A. 506, ed. by Charles Munier, Corpus Christianorum Series Latina, 148 (Turnhout: Brepols, 1963)

Concilia Galliae A. 511-A. 695, ed. by Carlo de Clercq, Corpus Christianorum Series Latina, 148A (Turnhout: Brepols, 1963)

Corpus Inscriptionum Latinarum, Vol. XVIII/2, *Carmina Latina Epigraphica Hispaniae*, ed. by Concepción Fernández Martínez, Joan Gómez Pallarès, Javier del Hoyo Calleja (Berlin: De Gruyter, forthcoming)

---

77   See the discussion in Handley, 'Merovingian Epigraphy'.

*Documents comptables de Saint-Martin de Tours à l'époque mérovingienne avec une étude
    paléographique par Jean Vezin*, ed. by Pierre Gasnault, Collection de Documents inédits
    sur l'histoire de France publiés par les soins du Comité des travaux historiques et
    scientifiques (Paris: Bibliothèque nationale, 1975)

Epistolae Arelatensis genuinae, ed. by Wilhelm Gundlach, *Monumenta Germaniae Historica:
    Epistolae*, 8 vols (Berlin: Weidmann, 1891–1928), *Epistolae Merowingici et Karolini Aevi*,
    III (1892), pp. 1–83

The Fourth Book of the Chronicle of Fredegar with its Continuations, ed. and trans. by John
    Michael Wallace-Hadrill (London: Nelson, 1960)

Gregory of Tours, *Decem Libri Historiarum*, ed. by Bruno Krusch and Wilhelm Levison
    Monumenta Germaniae Historica: Scriptores rerum Merovingicarum, 7 vols (Hannover:
    Hahn,1884–1920), I.1 (reprinted 1951)

————, *Gloria Confessorum*, ed. by Bruno Krusch, *Monumenta Germaniae Historica:
    Scriptores rerum Merovingicarum*, 7 vols (Hannover: Hahn, 1884–1920), I.2 (1885)

————, *Gloria Martyrum*, ed. by Bruno Krusch, *Monumenta Germaniae Historica:
    Scriptores rerum Merovingicarum*, 7 vols (Hannover: Hahn, 1884–1920), I.2 (1885)

Inscriptiones Latinae Christianae Veteres, ed. by Ernest Diehl, 4 vols (Berlin: Weidmann,
    1927–1931)

Inscriptions chrétiennes de la Gaule antérieures au VIIIe siècle, ed. by Edmond Le Blant, 2 vols
    (Paris: Imprimerie impériale, 1856/1865)

Inscripciones cristianas España Romana y Visigoda, ed. by Jose Vives, 2nd edition,
    Monumenta Hispaniae Sacra, Vol. 2 (Barcelona: Consejo Superior de Investigaciones
    Cientificas, Instituto Enrique Flórez, 1969)

Isidore of Seville, *Historia Gothorum Wandalorum Sueborum*, ed. by Theodore Mommsen
    Monumenta Germaniae Historica: Auctores antiquissimi, 15 vols (Hannover: Weidmann,
    1887–1919) XI (1894)

Jordanes, *Getica*, ed. by Theodore Mommsen, *Monumenta Germaniae Historica: Auctores
    antiquissimi*, 15 vols (Hannover: Weidmann, 1887–1919), V.1 (1882)

La collection d'inscriptions gallo-grecques et latines du Musée Calvet, ed. by Jacques Gascou
    and Jean Guyon (Paris: Boccard, 2005)

Liber Historiae Francorum, ed. by Bruno Krusch, *Monumenta Germaniae Historica:
    Scriptores rerum Merovingicarum*, 7 vols (Hannover: Hahn, 1884–1920), II (1888)

Polemius Silvius, *Laterculus*, in *Inscriptiones Italiae Antiquissimae*, ed. by Theodore
    Mommsen (Berlin: Reimer, 1893)

Prudentius, *Peristephanon Liber*, in *Prudentius*, ed. and trans. by H. J. Thomson,
    (Cambridge, MA: Harvard University Press, 1953), II, 98–345

Prudentius, *Peristephanon*, in *Aurelii Prudentii Clementis Carmina*, ed. by M. Cunningham,
    Corpus Christianorum Series Latina, 126 (Turnhout: Brepols, 1966)

Recueil des inscriptions chrétiennes de la Gaule antérieures à la Renaissance carolingienne,
    Vol. 15, *Viennoise du Nord*, ed. by Françoise Descombes (Paris: CNRS, 1985)

Salona IV. Inscriptions de Salone chrétienne IVe–VIIe siècles, ed. by Nancy Gauthier, Emilio
    Marin and Françoise Prévot, Collection de l'École française de Rome 194/4, 2 vols
    (Rome: École française de Rome, 2010)

Venantius Fortunatus, *Carmina*, ed. by Frederic Leo, *Monumenta Germaniae Historica:
    Auctores antiquissimi*, 15 vols (Hannover: Weidmann, 1887–1919), IV.1 (1881)

Venantius Fortunatus. Poems, trans. by Michael Roberts, Dumbarton Oaks Medieval
   Library, 46 (Cambridge, MA: Dumbarton Oaks, 2017)
Venantius Fortunatus, *Carmina*, in *Venance Fortunat, Poèmes. Tome I: Livres I–IV*, ed. by
   Marc Reydellet (Paris: Les Belles Lettres, 1994)
Venantius Fortunatus, *Vita Sancti Germani*, ed. by Bruno Krusch, *Monumenta Germaniae
   Historica: Auctores antiquissimi*, 15 vols (Hannover: Weidmann, 1887–1919), IV.2 (1885),
   pp. 11–27
Les Vies anciennes de sainte Geneviève de Paris: études critiques, ed. by Martin Heinzelmann
   and Joseph-Claude Poulin, Bibliothèque de l'École des hautes études. IVᵉ Section:
   Sciences Historiques et Philologiques, 329 (Paris: Honoré Champion, 1986)
Vitas Sanctorum Patrum Emeretensium, ed. by A. Maya Sánchez, Corpus Christianorum
   Series Latina, 116 (Turnhout: Brepols, 1992)

Secondary Studies

Bitel, Lisa, *Landscape with Two Saints: How Genovefa of Paris and Brigit of Kildare built
   Christianity in Barbarian Europe* (Oxford: Oxford University Press, 2009)
Brennan, Brian, 'The Image of the Merovingian Bishop in the Poetry of Venantius
   Fortunatus', *Journal of Medieval History*, 18 (1992), 115–39
Buchberger, Erica, 'Romans, Barbarians and Franks in the Writings of Venantius
   Fortunatus', *Early Medieval Europe*, 24.3 (2016), 293–307
Busson, Didier, *Paris. Carte Archéologique de la Gaule*, 75 (Paris: Académie des inscriptions
   et belles lettres, 1998)
Castillo Maldonado, Pedro, 'El culto del mártir Vicente de Zaragoza en el norte de África',
   Florentia Iliberritana, 7 (1996), 39–52
Chalon, Michel, 'L'inscription d'une église rurale du territoire narbonnais au Vᵉ siècle',
   Pallas, 84 (2010), 145–75
Classen, Peter, *Kaiserreskript und Königsurkunde. Diplomatische Studien zum Problem
   der Kontinuität zwischen Altertum und Mittelalter*, Vyzantina keimena kai meletai, 15
   (Thessaloniki: Kentron Vyzantinōn Ereunōn, 1977)
Dérens, Jean, and Michel Fleury, 'La construction de la cathédrale de Paris par
   Childebert Iᵉʳ, d'après de *De ecclesia Parisiaca* de Fortunat', *Journal des Savants*,
   4 (1977), 247–56
Dérens, Jean, 'A propos des fouilles de la chapelle Saint-Symphorien de Saint-Germain-
   des-Prés. La Basilique de Saint-Vincent puis Saint-Germain-des-Prés, des origines au
   11ᵉ siècle', *Document-Archéologia*, 3 (1973), 11–27
Duval, Yvette, *Loca Sanctorum Africae. Le culte des martyrs en Afrique du IVᵉ au VIIᵉ siècle*,
   2 vols (Rome: Écoles française de Rome, 1982)
——, 'Nativola-les-trois-Églises (éveche d'Acci, 594–607), d'après Vivès, ICERV, 303',
   Mélanges des écoles française de Rome. Antiquité, 103 (1991), 807–20
Fleury, Michel, 'Les fouilles récentes de la chapelle Saint-Symphorien (ou des
   Catéchismes) de l'église Saint-Germain-des-Prés', *Cahiers de la Rotonde*, 4 (1981), 17–32
De Gaiffier, Baudoin, 'Les deux poèmes de Fortunat en l'honneur de saint Vincent (*Lib.
   I, 8, 9*)', in *Études mérovingiennes (Actes des journées de Poitiers, 1ᵉʳ–3 mai 1952* (Paris:
   Picard, 1953), pp. 127–34

George, Judith, 'Portraits of Two Merovingian Bishops in the Poetry of Venantius Fortunatus', *Journal of Medieval History*, 13 (1987), 189–205

Gerberding, Richard, *The Rise of the Carolingians and the Liber Historiae Francorum* (Oxford: Clarendon Press, 1987)

Gillett, Andrew, 'Was Ethnicity Politicized in the Earliest Medieval Kingdoms?', in *On Barbarian Identity: Critical Approaches to Ethnicity in the Early Middle Ages*, ed. by Andrew Gillett, Studies in the Early Middle Ages, 4 (Turnhout: Brepols, 2002), pp. 85–121

——, 'Ethnography and *Imperium* in the Sixth Century: Frankish and Byzantine Rhetoric in the *Epistolae Austrasicae*', in *Basileia: Essays on Imperium and Culture in Honour of E. M. and M. J. Jeffreys*, ed. by Geoffrey Nathan and Lynda Garland, Byzantina Australiensia, 17 (Brisbane: Australian Association for Byzantine Studies, 2011), pp. 67–81

Goetz, Hans-Werner, '*Gens*, Kings and Kingdoms: The Franks', in *Regna and Gentes: The Relationship between Late Antique and Early Medieval Peoples and Kingdoms in the Transformation of the Roman World*, ed. by Hans-Werner Goetz, Jörg Jarnut, and Walter Pohl, Transformation of the Roman World, 13 (Leiden: Brill, 2003), pp. 307–44

Gómez Pallarès, Joan, 'Poésie épigraphique en *Hispania*: propositions et lectures', *Revue des études latines*, 77 (1999), 118–48

Handley, Mark A., *Death, Society and Culture: Inscriptions and Epitaphs in Gaul and Spain, AD 300–750*, British Archaeological Reports, International Series, 1135 (Oxford: Archaeopress, 2003)

——, 'Merovingian Epigraphy, Frankish Epigraphy and the Epigraphy of the Merovingian World', in *The Oxford Handbook of the Merovingian World*, ed. by Isabel Moreira and Bonnie Effros (Oxford: Oxford University Press, 2020), pp. 556-79

Kulikowski, Michael, *Late Roman Spain and its Cities* (Baltimore: Johns Hopkins University Press, 2004)

Jaffé, Philippe, *Regesta Pontificum Romanorum ab condita ecclesia ad annum post Christum natum MCXCVIII* (Leipzig: Lipsiae, Veit, 1885)

James, Edward, 'Royal Burials among the Franks', in *The Age of Sutton Hoo: The Seventh Century in North-Western Europe*, ed. by Martin Carver (Woodbridge: Boydell, 1992), pp. 243–54

Mallon, Jean, 'Le graffite Gildebertus rex francorum découvert à Saint-Germain-des-Prés', *Cahiers de la Rotonde*, 4 (1981), 33–35

Martindale, John R., and Arnold H. M. Jones, eds, *Prosopography of the Later Roman Empire, Vol. 2, AD 395–527* (Cambridge: Cambridge University Press, 1980)

Martindale John R., ed. *Prosopography of the Later Roman Empire, Vol. 3, AD 527–641*, 2 vols (Cambridge: Cambridge University Press, 1992)

Mathisen, Ralph, 'Agrestius of Lugo, Eparchius Avitus and a Curious Fifth-Century Statement of Faith', *Journal of Early Christian Studies*, 2 (1994), 71–102

——, 'Barbarian Bishops and the Churches *in barbaricis gentibus* during Late Antiquity', *Speculum*, 72 (1997), 664–97

——, 'Barbarian "Arian" Clergy, Church Organization, and Church Practices', in *Arianism: Roman Heresy and Barbarian Creed*, ed. by Guido M. Berndt and Roland Steinacher (Farnham: Ashgate, 2014), pp. 145–91

Mathisen, Ralph, and Hagith Sivan, 'Forging a New Identity: The Kingdom of Toulouse and the Frontiers of Visigothic Aquitania (418–507)', in *The Visigoths: Studies in Culture and Society*, ed. by Alberto Ferriero, Medieval Mediterranean, 20 (Leiden: Brill, 1999), pp. 1–62

Meyer, Sofia, *Der Heilige Vinzenz von Zaragoza. Studien zur Präsenz eines Märtyres zwischen Spätantike und Hochmittelalter*, Beiträge zur Hagiographie, 10 (Stuttgart: F. Steiner, 2012)

Nelson, Janet, L., 'Gender and Genre in Women Historians of the Early Middle Ages', in Janet L. Nelson, *The Frankish World* (London: Hambledon, 1996), pp. 183–97

Périn, Patrick, 'Saint-Germain des-Prés: première nécropole des rois de France', *Medievales*, 31 (1996), 29–36

Reimitz, Helmut, *History, Frankish Identity and the Framing of Western Ethnicity, 550–850* (Cambridge: Cambridge University Press, 2015)

Roberts, Michael, *The Humblest Sparrow: The Poetry of Venantius Fortunatus* (Ann Arbor: University of Michigan Press, 2009)

Saxer, Victor, 'Le culte de S. Vincent en Italie avant l'an mil', in *Quaeritur inventus colitur. Miscellanea in onore di Padre Umberto Maria Fasola*, ed. by Philippe Pergola, Studi di antichità cristiana, 40 (Vatican City: Istituto Pontificio di Archeologia Cristiana, 1989), pp. 743–61

——, 'Lieux de culte de saint Vincent en France avant l'an Mil', in Victor Saxer, *Saint Vincent diacre et martyr: Culte et légendes avant l'an mil*, Subsidia Hagiographica, 83 (Brussels: Société des Bollandistes, 2002), pp. 21–44

Vezin, Jean, 'Un demi-siècle de recherches et de découvertes dans le domaine de l'écriture mérovingienne', *Archiv für Diplomatik*, 50 (2004), 247–75

Zeumer, Karl, 'Das Processkostengesetz des Königs Theudis vom 24. November 546', *Neues Archiv*, 23 (1898), 77–103

TOM BROWN

The 'Political' Use of the Cult of Saints in Early Medieval Ravenna

In the late seventh century the anonymous writer of a geographical treatise wrote of his home city:

> Ravenna … quae scilicet non solum nobilitate, sed et autentu regio inter ceteras olim celsior, nunc deo volente dignitate ecclesiastica atque pontificali, martirum in ea coruscantium meritis famosior excelsior excolitur.

> > Ravenna, once the most outstanding of cities, not only because of its fame, but also because of the protection of its rulers now, thanks to the will of God, is venerated as even more outstanding owing to its ecclesiastic and papal dignity, most famous as it is for the merits of the martyrs who shine there.[1]

Such pride in local saints, and martyrs in particular, is central to the identity of cities and other communities in early medieval Italy, and indeed of Europe in general, as the work of Alan Thacker has so effectively demonstrated. His work stands out among the eminent array of historians who have advanced immensely the study of saints' cults and their *vitae* in recent decades, throwing invaluable light both on the nature and institutions of the medieval Church and on medieval mentalities in a broader sense. Not only has he illuminated the role of saints in the Anglo-Saxon Church in general, but he has done much to relate cults to specific areas, demonstrating the complex and dynamic relationship between saints and their centres of veneration, most notably in his masterly paper '*Loca sanctorum*: the significance of place in the study of saints'.[2]

As Alan recognised, local saints, especially martyrs, were a particularly strong and precocious presence in late Roman and early medieval Italy where cities were

---

1 *Ravennatis anonymi cosmographia*, ed. by Schnetz, p. 117, ll. 20–28. The passage survives only in the version preserved by the later geographer Guido da Pisa. The translation is that of Massimiliano David, *Eternal Ravenna: From the Etruscans to the Venetians*, p. 208.

2 Thacker and Sharpe, ed., *Local Saints and Local Churches*.

Tom Brown • (T.S.Brown@ed.ac.uk) is former Reader in Medieval History and current Honorary Research Fellow of the School of History, Classics and Archaeology, University of Edinburgh.

Cities, Saints, and Communities in Early Medieval Europe, ed. by Scott DeGregorio and Paul Kershaw, SEM 46 (Turnhout: Brepols, 2020), pp. 53-69
BREPOLS PUBLISHERS   DOI 10.1484/M.SEM-EB.5.119622

prompt to adopt their own 'patron saint'. The study of this process has been a full and productive area of Italian hagiographical scholarship, as in the work of Alba Maria Orselli and Sofia Boesch Gaetano.[3] More recently, the cult of local saints has been identified as a valuable tool in reconstructing the 'cultural memory' of particular communities, and again Alan's work in this field can be seen as pioneering.[4]

The relevance of saints' cults to the study of local ecclesiastical and urban communities is especially evident in the case of Ravenna, where the plentiful evidence has been well studied by local historians but not become as familiar to early medieval historians as it deserves to be.[5] The city of course is well known as a major centre of the fifth-century Western Roman emperors and their Ostrogothic and Byzantine successors and also for its magnificent churches and their mosaic decoration. Contrary to what is often still believed, Ravenna's importance continued not only in the Byzantine period up to the city's conquest by the Lombards in 751, but also during the ninth and tenth centuries, the time of Carolingian and Ottonian domination.[6]

However, by this later period the dominant force in the area of Ravenna, commonly known as the exarchate, was the Church. The archbishop of Ravenna inherited many of the traditions and administrative systems from the empire and built up a powerful ecclesiastical lordship which stretched from the area of the Po delta around Ferrara in the North to the Apennine mountains of Umbria in the South.[7]

The coherent nature of this large area centred on Ravenna was reflected in its strong attachment to a distinctive set of saints, for the most part either local or 'imported' from centres such as Milan or Rome. Although useful and perceptive studies have appeared on particular cults, the study of saints' cults has not always been prominent in recent studies of Ravenna; for example, not one of the papers in the recent volume on the city edited by Judith Herrin and Jinty Nelson deals with saints.[8] As a cohesive society with a strong sense of identity, Ravenna offers an opportunity for a preliminary study aimed at identifying the most venerated saints, how they were chosen and promoted, and what advantages they brought to local groups. This paper is intended as a preliminary study of the 'political use' of cults, by which I mean their promotion for reasons of power, wealth, and prestige, especially by the archbishop and other elements in the Church for, as we shall see, the main driving force was the powerful bishops, the kind of prelates whom Peter Brown called episcopal 'impresarios'.[9] The state, in contrast, seems to have been less of a player. In

---

3   Orselli, 'Il santo patrono cittadino fra tardo Antico e Alto Medioevo'; Orselli, *L'idea e il culto del santo patrono cittadino*; Boesch Gaetano, *Agiografia altomedievale*.

4   E.g., Pohl and Wood, 'Introduction: Cultural Memory', pp. 1–12.

5   For a useful survey, see Ropa, 'Agiografia e liturgia a Ravenna'.

6   See my 'Culture and Society in Ottonian Ravenna'.

7   Fasoli, 'Il dominio territorio degli arcivescovi di Ravenna'; Fasoli, 'Il patrimonio della chiesa ravennate'.

8   Schoolman, *Rediscovering Sainthood*; Herrin and Nelson, ed., *Ravenna: Its Role in Earlier Medieval Change*.

9   Brown, *The Cult of the Saints*, especially p. 101 and, for an example of such episcopal activity, his 'Relics and Social Status'.

a broader sense the lives, cults and buildings associated with favoured saints throw considerable light on the forging of a distinct communal identity and a strongly felt aspect of 'cultural memory' in Ravenna and its hinterland.[10]

First, we have to be clear about the relatively abundant sources. Perhaps the most instructive and certainly the most attractive are the numerous depictions of saints, usually in mosaic, in Ravenna's splendid churches. As Hippolyte Delehaye famously remarked 'l'hagiographie de Ravenne est écrite sur les murs de ses basiliques'.[11] Perhaps the most impressive example is the remarkable procession of saints in the church of Sant'Apollinare Nuovo, male saints, mostly martyrs, on the south wall and female saints, also martyrs, on the north.[12]

We also have a wealth of other evidence in which saints and their dedications figure prominently, including two remarkable types of source. One is an unparalleled series of documents, first in papyrus and later in parchment, still mostly preserved in the archiepiscopal archive, and constituting the second largest collection of original documents in Italy, after Lucca. Over five hundred survive from the fifth century to the millennium.[13] We also have a number of historical and hagiographic texts, of which the fullest is the *Liber pontificalis ecclesiae Ravennatis* of the deacon Agnellus, who wrote this history of the see in the 840s.[14] In this he concentrates on the power, prestige, and riches of his see and its struggle for independence from Rome, commenting bitterly on the tensions between Ravenna's clergy and some of the bishops, whom he denounces as 'wolves'.[15] However, some favoured bishops are glorified for their saintly lives and for their miracles. Of course many of the early bishops were purely legendary and Agnellus gives a gratifyingly honest account of his methodology in reconstructing their lives:

> Hunc predictum Pontificalem, a tempore beati Apolenaris post eius decessum paene annos .dccc. et amplius, ego Agnellus qui et Andreas, exiguus sanctae meae huius Rauennatis ecclesiae presbiter, rogatus et coactus a fratribus ipsius sedis, composui. Et ubi inueni quid illi certius fecerunt, uestris aspectibus allata sunt, et quod per seniores et longaeuos audiui, uestris oculis non defraudaui; et ubi historiam non inueni, aut qualiter eorum uita fuisset, nec per annosos et uetustos homines, neque per aedificationem, neque per quamlibet auctoritatem, ne interuallum sanctorum pontificum fieret, secundum ordinem quomodo unus post alium hanc sedem optinuerunt, uestris orationibus me Deo adiuuante

---

10   This is a major theme of the valuable book of Verhoeven, *The Early Christian Monuments of Ravenna* esp. pp. 15–18.

11   Delehaye, 'L'hagiographie ancienne de Ravenne', p. 6.

12   See Penni Iacco, *La Basilica di Sant'Apollinare Nuovo di Ravenna*, I, pp. 75–79. For good illustrations see David, *Eternal Ravenna*, pp. 194–97.

13   Cavarra, Gardini, Battista Parente and Vespignani, 'Gli archivi come fonti della storia di Ravenna'.

14   Most recently edited by Deliyannis, *Liber pontificalis ecclesiae Ravennatis* (hereafter *LPR*).

15   E.g. Archbishop Theodore in *LPR*, c. 118, pp. 289–90. The imagery is probably modelled on Matthew 7. 15: 'Attendite a falsis prophetis, qui veniunt ad vos in vestimentis ovium, intrinsecus autem sunt lupi rapaces' (Beware of false prophets, who come to you in the clothing of sheep, but inwardly they are ravening wolves).

illorum uitam composui, et credo non mentitum esse, quia et oratores fuerunt castique et elemosinarii et Deo animas hominum acquisitores. De uero illorum effigie, si forte cogitatio fuerit inter uos quomodo scire potui, sciatis, me pictura docuit quia semper fiebant imagines suis temporibus ad illorum similitudinem.

> I, Agnellus, also known as Andreas, insignificant priest of my holy church here in Ravenna, asked and urged by the brothers of this see, have composed this… pontifical book from the time of blessed Apollinaris and after his death lasting almost eight hundred years and more. And when I found out what they certainly did, these deeds were brought to your attention, and what I heard from elders and old men I have not stolen from your eyes. And when I did not discover any history, or what their life had been like, neither from aged and old men, nor from buildings, nor from any authority, in order that there would be no gap in the holy bishops, in the order in which each obtained this see, one after the other, with God aiding me by your prayers, I have constructed their manner of life; and I believe that I have not lied, since they were encouraging and pure and charitable orators and acquirers of the souls of men for God. Indeed if by chance you should have some question about how I was able to know about their appearance, know that pictures taught me, since in those days they always made images in their likenesses.[16]

In addition to these sources, we have a wide range of other texts, including various hagiographic works, *vitae, passiones, miracula*, and *translationes*, composed between the sixth and tenth centuries, which have only received detailed attention in the last few years.[17] Archaeology has also made enormous strides recently, and provided much rich new data on the churches devoted to particular saints.[18] Here it is worth noting that over seventy late Roman and early medieval churches are recorded in the city alone, and these obviously provide an indication of the main cults venerated in the city.[19]

Before we look at prominent cases of saints and the factors involved in promoting their cults, we need to stress that in many ways the hagiographic landscape of Ravenna is not what one would expect. For a city which struggled for centuries to gain independence from the papacy, Roman saints such as Laurence and Agnes are prominent presences, both in depictions such as those of Sant'Apollinare Nuovo and in church dedications. This can be explained by their great prestige, and also from the strong liturgical influence which Rome exercised over a see which was after all its suffragan, especially before its elevation into an archbishopric in the mid-sixth century, under Maximian.

---

16 Agnellus, *LPR*, c. 32, p. 185, as translated by Deliyannis, *The Book of Pontiffs*, pp. 134–35.

17 By numerous scholars, including Filippo Carla, Giovanni Montanari, Enrico, Morini and Schoolman.

18 E.g., Racagni, *La Basilica Ritrovata* and in general the outstanding work of Cirelli, *Ravenna. Archeologia di una Città*.

19 This figure is based on the survey of ecclesiastical buildings which either survive or are recorded through literary or archaeological evidence, as listed in Deichmann, *Ravenna, Hauptstadt des spätantiken Abendlandes*, II. An important point is that many buildings referred to as *monasteria* were mere oratories usually attached to proper churches.

More surprisingly perhaps are some omissions. There is little evidence of the cult of St Benedict, even although there was a whole book devoted to him in the most influential hagiographical work in early medieval Italy, the *Dialogues* of Gregory the Great, written at a time when two of the pope's close associates were archbishops of Ravenna.[20] Despite their prominence in the mosaic decoration of Sant'Apollinare Nuovo, with the obvious exception of the Virgin Mary there are few dedications to female saints. Those that are attested include: St Agatha of Catania, which may reflect the Ravenna see's close economic links with Sicily, and St Euphemia, whose remarkable tally of four churches or oratories reflects her association with the Chalcedonian orthodoxy which Ravenna sought to uphold.[21]

One of Ravenna's most prominent and learned bishops, St Peter Chrysologus, appears to have only a limited cult even though he was the author of letters and homilies collected in the city and for which he obtained important privileges, including metropolitan status, through his close ties with the imperial court. He is a similar figure to Ambrose, but unlike the Milanese saint, he never became the main 'patron' of his city.[22]

Even more startling is the relative lack of specifically eastern saints. As we have seen, one exception is St Euphemia who was regarded as a champion of orthodoxy since her place of origin was Chalcedon, scene of the great council. There are also cults of Illyrican saints such as Ursicinus and Pollio, which may reflect the associations of early emperors (and soldiers) with the area, and the close economic and cultural ties of Ravenna with the coasts of Istria and Dalmatia.[23] The absence of saints from further east is, however, in sharp contrast to 'Byzantine' cities on the eastern shore of the Adriatic such as Zadar and Rovinj, which were granted relics by the empire in the early ninth century as a way of reinforcing their loyalty.[24] Particularly surprising is the relative lack of Byzantine military saints such as George and Theodore, who

---

20 John III and Marinianus, although the relations between them and the pope were at times fractious. The former is probably the dedicatee of Gregory's *Liber Regulae Pastoralis*: Markus, *Gregory the Great*, p. 21 n. 11 and pp. 143–56.

21 Deichmann, *Ravenna, Hauptstadt des spätantiken Abendlandes*, II. 2, pp. 323–25. Deichmann lists six dedications to Mary (the most prominent being S. Maria Maggiore), but the only other female saints with churches dedicated to them are Agatha, Agnes and Petronilla. I am indebted to Professor John Osborne of Carlton University for discussion on this point who confirmed the high number of female dedications in early medieval Rome.

22 For a brief discussion see Deliyannis, *Ravenna in Late Antiquity*, pp. 84–85; Sottocornola, *L'anno liturgico nei sermoni di Pietro Crisologo*. The important Basilica Petriana in Classe was founded by Peter but was not dedicated to him nor to the apostle Peter, but to Christ, see Deichmann, *Ravenna, Hauptstadt des spätantiken Abendlandes*, II. 2, p. 350. On Ambrose, McLynn, *Ambrose of Milan*. On parallels and links between cults in Milan and Ravenna, see Pilsworth, 'Representations of Sanctity'. There is much useful material on the commemoration of the bishops of Ravenna in Picard, *Le souvenir des évêques*, pp. 109–94.

23 Delehaye, 'L'hagiographie ancienne de Ravenne', p. 8. Venantius Fortunatus, who was educated in Ravenna, mentions the burial of Ursicinus in the city, together with other saints such as Vitalis; *Vita S. Martini*, ed. by Leo, IV, ll. 680–85, p. 369.

24 Examples include the translation of relics of Euphemia to Rovinj, Tryphon to Kotor, and Anastasia to Zadar, see Vedriš, 'Martyrs, Relics, and Bishops'.

possessed prominent cults and churches in other Byzantine cities such as Venice, and even Rome.[25] On the other hand, such saints do appear to have received greater veneration in frontier areas such as Ferrara (a military foundation of the Byzantine period where the cathedral's patron was — and remains — St George).[26]

There are two possible explanations. Ravenna was, contrary to traditional views and its location as seat of the exarch, much more of a late Roman than a Byzantine city and, unlike Rome, its Greek population was small and rapidly assimilated.[27] The other likely reason is that the Church exercised much greater influence than other institutions from early on. One might add that the corollary of this also applied, and there is little evidence of Ravenna saints being venerated in the East, although Apollinaris, Vitalis, and Ursicinus do appear in the *Synaxarion* of Constantinople and in Greek hymnography.[28]

Which saints then were venerated in Ravenna? As elsewhere there was a clear pecking order of holiness, with Christ, the Trinity, and Mary at the top, followed by angels, apostles, martyrs, and then finally confessors. Thus, the original dedication of the present Sant'Apollinare Nuovo was Christ the Redeemer (interestingly an Arian foundation) and S. Maria Maggiore still survives.[29]

One interesting case is the archangel Michael, to whom a lavish church was dedicated by Maximian, who was promoted by Justinian to be the first archbishop of Ravenna. It survives in a deconsecrated state as, of all things, a Max Mara clothing shop, although what purports to be its apse mosaic can be seen in the Bode Museum in Berlin.[30]

Another, even more illuminating, case is that of the apostle St Andrew, widely revered as the brother of St Peter, and for whom Maximian also built a church, which later became an important monastery and whose documents survive in quantity.[31] Andrew was clearly in demand, because the status of a see could be elevated if it had a prestigious apostolic protobishop. This led to competition between Constantinople and Ravenna for the body of St Andrew, because both wanted parity of prestige

---

25   Thus St Theodore *stratelates* of Amasea was patron saint of Venice before St Mark: Demus, *The Church of San Marco in Venice*, pp. 20–21. In Rome S. Teodoro and S. Giorgio in Velabro are Byzantine foundations likely to have been used by the garrison on the nearby Palatine hill. In general on military saints Delehaye, *Les Légendes grécques des saints militaires*.

26   Sgarbanti, *Ferrara. Nascita di una città*, pp. 63–64; Toffarella, *Ferrara. La città rinascimentale e il delta del Po*, p. 34. George and other military saints are common dedications in the *pievi* recorded from the tenth century onwards in the foothills of the Apennines: Gugliotta, 'L'evoluzione della proprietà ecclesiastica ravennate', p. 104. Again, this may reflect the earlier settlement of imperial garrisons.

27   Brown, 'Ebrei e Orientali a Ravenna' pp. 135–49; Sansterre, 'Monaci e monasteri greci a Ravenna'. In Ravenna itself eastern immigrations appear to have associated themselves with local saints from an early stage. For a full discussion Morini, 'Santi orientali a Ravenna'.

28   Efthymiadis, ed., *Ashgate Research Companion to Byzantine Hagiography*, II, p. 394; Follieri, 'Vite e inni greci per i santi di Ravenna'.

29   Penni Iacco, *La Basilica di Sant'Apollinare Nuovo di Ravenna*; Mazzotti, 'La basilica di Santa Maria Maggiore in Ravenna'.

30   Spadoni and Kniffitiz, eds, *San Michele in Africisco e l'età giustinianea a Ravenna*.

31   *Le Carte del Monastero di S. Andrea Maggiore di Ravenna*, ed. by Muzzioli.

with Rome, the burial place of St Peter. Maximian's actions are best described in the words of Agnellus:

> Ecclesiam uero beati Andrea apostoli hic Rauennae cum omni diligentia… decorauit…Tunc ablatum corpus ipsius apostoli Rauennam ducere conabatur.

> Dum hoc praesensisset imperator Constantinopolitanus, iussit beatum Maximianum Constantinopolim uenire et pium apostoli corpus secum deferre. Quo gauisus imperator ait ad eum: 'Non sit tibi grauis, pater, quod primam unus tenet Romam frater, iste uero secundam teneat. Ambae sorores et hi ambi germani. Nolo tibi eum dare, quia et ubi sedes imperialis est, expedit et ibi corpus esse apostoli'.

> At beatissimus Maximianus dixit: 'Fac quomodo iubes; tantum postulo ut in hac nocte cum meis sacerdotibus ad hoc santum corpus psalmodiam peragamus'. Imperator moxque concessit. Tunc tota nocte peruigiles extiterunt, et post expleta omnia arripiens gladium, oratione facta, abscidit barbas apostoli usque mentum. Et ex reliquiis aliorum multorum sanctorum reliquias detulit cum augusti alacritate; dehinc quoque ad propriam reuersus est sedem.

> Et re uera, fratres, quia si corpus beati Andreae, germani Petri principis, hic humasset, nequaquam nos Romani pontifices sic subiugassent.

> He [Archbishop Maximian, 544–556] decorated with all due diligence the church of St Andrew the Apostle here in Ravenna… Then he tried to bring the stolen body of that apostle to Ravenna. When the emperor in Constantinople knew of this he ordered blessed Maximian to come to Constantinople and to bring with him the body of the apostle. The emperor, amused, said to him, 'Don't be displeased, father, that one brother holds the first Rome, this one should hold the second Rome. The cities are sisters, and the apostles are brothers. I do not want to give him to you, since it is fitting that there be the body of an apostle where the imperial seat is'.

> But most blessed Maximian said, 'Let it be done as you command; however I request that I and my priests might pass this night in psalmody over this holy body'. And the emperor agreed at once. Then they spent the whole night in vigils, and after all things were completed, seizing a sword and saying a prayer, he cut off the beard of the apostle up to the chin. And from the remains of many other saints he took relics with the emperor's agreement; and from there he returned to his own see.

> And it is a true thing, brothers, that if he had buried the body of blessed Andrew, brother of Peter the prince, here, the Roman popes would not have subjugated us.[32]

---

32   Agnellus, *LPR*, c. 76, p. 244. The translation is that of Deliyannis, *The Book of Pontiffs*, p. 190, with minor modification.

This failure was a great blow to Ravenna's ambitions to be on a par with the see of Rome. However, the clergy, or more probably, Maximian himself, quickly developed an effective 'Plan B'. It was decided to elevate the mysterious and probably imaginary protobishop of Ravenna himself, Apollinaris, an apostolic associate of Peter. Apollinaris was already venerated — traces have been found of an early church at Classe and in the fifth century St Peter Chrysologus devoted a sermon to his life and virtues.[33] But a later *Passio* survives which I would date to the sixth century, the period of Maximian, which gives him a much fuller life story, as a migrant from Syria and disciple of St Peter who evangelised the Ravenna area in the first century.[34] To house the relics of this great patron, Maximian completed the building of the largest basilica in the Ravenna area, the church we know as Sant'Apollinare in Classe, with its striking apse mosaic which depicts Apollinaris in a prominent Christ-like position surrounded by twelve sheep, signifying his congregation or possibly his own 'posse' of disciples.[35] Dedicated in 549, Sant'Apollinare in Classe thereafter outshone the Ravenna's cathedral, the early fifth-century Basilica Ursiana, and became the main focus of devotional life in Ravenna. The cult played an important role in the temporarily successful attempt of the see of Ravenna to gain independence (*autocephalia*) from the see of Rome in the seventh century, and some scholars have wrongly, in my opinion, attributed the saint's *passio* to Archbishop Maurus (642–671) the promoter of this separation.[36]

The saint's body was so precious that in the ninth century it was transferred from Classe back into the city, supposedly because of the fear of Arab attacks. We have a *translatio* recording the move of the saint's relics to the urban church, then known as San Martino, which was renamed Sant'Apollinare Nuovo. This, however, led to a bitter dispute in the eleventh century, when Sant'Apollinare in Classe was taken over by the monks of Camaldoli, who claimed that the saint's relics had in fact remained in their church. The monks of Sant'Apollinare Nuovo contested this for centuries, despite formal *inventiones* of the relics by the monks of Classe in 1173, 1487, and 1511. The papacy finally recognised the relics as resting in Sant'Apollinare in Classe in the late seventeenth century and the relics were rehoused in their present location within it when the church was restored between 1723 and 1745. The intensity of this dispute reflects the popularity of the saint's cult.[37]

Another early bishop who was promoted as a leading saint at this stage was Saint Severus, who has the merit of having actually existed, being recorded as present at the Council of Serdica in 344. A *vita* survives which has plausibly been dated to

---

33 Peter Chrysologus, *Collectio Sermonum* no. 128, ed. by Olivar, iii, pp. 789–91.

34 For the extensive bibliography, Brown, 'The Church of Ravenna', p. 15 n. 3 and Carla, 'Milan, Ravenna, Rome', p. 248, who dates the work to the seventh century.

35 Dinkler, *Das Apsismosaik von S. Apollinare in Classe*.

36 E.g., Zattoni, 'La data del *Passio Sancti Apollinaris* di Ravenna'.

37 On this rivalry Verhoeven, *The Early Christian Monuments of Ravenna*, pp. 65–71. There is a recent discussion and English translation by Everett, *Patron Saints of Early Medieval Italy*, pp. 139–70, who raises the possibility at p. 151 that the text is late seventh century and thus was composed *after* the loss of Ravenna's *autocephalia*.

the sixth century, and perhaps the most remarkable church in Ravenna was built in his honour, a vast basilica almost as large as Sant'Apollinare, on which work commenced in the 570s and was completed in the 580s. The church later became part of a large monastic complex but was later abandoned after the community was incorporated in the basilica of Sant'Apollinare in 1455, and was finally destroyed in 1820. However, it has been the subject of extensive excavations in recent years, which have shown that the adjoining monastery became used as a palace by the Ottonians.[38] What is remarkable is that such a church should have been built at this turbulent time at all. The empire's hold over Italy was threatened by the Lombard invasions from 568 onwards; Classe itself was plundered in 579. The most likely explanation for the construction of this, the last of the major Ravenna churches, I would suggest, is that it was a deliberate assertion of the power and resilience of the empire in a period when it was under threat. Presumably, it was a joint project of the see and the exarchal government, and Severus may have been chosen as a symbol of opposition to the Arian Lombards, since he was a defender of orthodoxy in the fourth century.[39] The cult of Severus became one of the most important in Ravenna and, notoriously, the relics of this, one of the city's most eminent saints, were smuggled away to Mainz as a *furtum sacrum* by the Frankish cleric Felix in 836.[40]

Also important in Classe was the cult of Probus, another fourth-century bishop and possibly the figure who build the see's first cathedral, in Classe, not in Ravenna itself. This original church was rebuilt on a lavish scale in the time of Maximian but it later fell into ruin: only its plan can now be reconstructed. Probus's cult, however, flourished, as we know from a surviving saint's life, which emphasises the curative power of his relics. The *Vita Probi* can be dated to *c.* 963–974 and seem to be part of a great 'hagiographic renaissance' in that period to elevate the status of Ravenna as a historic imperial capital and to impress the new Ottonian rulers of Italy.[41]

Other prominent cults also seem to have developed for specific purposes. Many of the most popular have an association with Milan.[42] This may reflect either devotion among courtiers who moved from Milan to Ravenna in 402, or, more likely I think, a desire by Ravenna's elites to upstage its rival as an imperial seat and primary metropolitan in Northern Italy by appropriating some of its saints.

This particularly applies to the 'hagiographic family' of Vitalis and his associates. Vitalis was a wealthy citizen of Milan, married to Valeria, who had two sons Gervasius and Protasius, and who was supposedly martyred under Nero. However, Ravenna tradition placed his martyrdom in Ravenna and associated it with his support for

38 Augenti, Begnozzi, Bondi, Cirelli, Ferreri, Malaguti, Scozzari, 'Il monastero di San Severo a Classe'.
39 Racagni, ed., *La Basilica Ritrovata*. Augenti and Cirelli, 'San Severo and Religious Life in Ravenna'.
40 Geary, *Furta Sacra*, p. 48. Benericetti, *Il Pontificale di Ravenna: Studio Critico* p. 77. On the theft of these and other relics Augenti, 'Classe: Archaeologies of a Lost City'; Caroli, 'Culto e commercio delle reliquie a Ravenna nell' alto medievo'.
41 Schoolman, *Rediscovering Sainthood*, pp. 61–65.
42 Alan has recognised the importance of Milan as a centre for the 'export' of saints to other Italian cities, e.g. in Thacker, '*Loca sanctorum*'.

another local martyr, the physician St Ursicinus. There appears also to have been an element of confusion with another saint of the area called Vitalis, who converted his slave Agricola to Christianity and was martyred during the Diocletianic persecution.[43] All of these figures had prominent cults — a monastery of Saints Gervasius and Protasius was built in the fifth century and, of course, the church most famous for its mosaics was dedicated to Saint Vitalis in 548.

The 'vitality' of these cults is evident from the continued writing of lives and related texts as late as the tenth century. According to one such text, a *translatio* of Ursicinus:

> Ultra nongentos annos passionis eius quum Honestus antistes praesideret Ravennaticae Sedi, volens huius martyris sanctum corpum honorabilius collocare, suamque sedem sanctorum patrociniis facere meliorem, ac gloriosiorem, tempore caesareatus Ottonis maximi, omni reverentia sublevatum cum summa devotione ad Ursianam devexit Ecclesiam ... ibique in crypta sub avida usque modo crypta constat esse sepultum.

> > More than nine hundred years after his martyrdom, when the bishop Honestus was occupying the see of Ravenna, wishing to set the holy body of this martyr in a place of honor and to make his seat more noble and more glorious, through the protection of the saints, and in that time of the imperial rule of Otto the greatest, with every respect he brought [the body] now raised up to the Ursinian church with the greatest devotion ... and there in the crypt ... he was to be buried in that way.[44]

But perhaps the most interesting case is the cult of the fifth-century St Barbatianus which is the main focus of a recent study by Ned Schoolman. Barbatianus was a holy man from Syria who arrived in Ravenna in the fifth century and became confessor to Galla Placidia, the late Roman empress and mother of Valentinian III who played a prominent role in Agnellus's text and Ravenna traditions generally. The cult was clearly established early, since a church of St John and Saint Barbatianus is recorded in the sixth century and his supposed sarcophagus survives in the cathedral, the *Basilica Ursiana*.[45] Basing his study mainly on a text written as part of the hagiographical revival of the tenth Schoolman argues convincingly that the cult was resuscitated in the Ottonian period and a new *vita* produced which emphasised the saint's miracles and his closeness to the empress. Schoolman writes that,

> for Ravennate monks and nobles, the *vita* of Barbatianus became a tool by which the citizens of the city and region and the [Ottonian] emperors and their

---

43 Delehaye, 'L'hagiographie ancienne de Ravenne'; Carla, 'Milan, Ravenna, Rome', pp. 235–44; Verhoeven, *The Early Christian Monuments of Ravenna*, pp. 73–80.

44 *Passio Sancti Ursicini*, quoted from Schoolman, *Rediscovering Sainthood*, p. 58 (translation) and p. 73 n. 36 (text).

45 Schoolman, *Rediscovering Sainthood*, p. 140.

retinues may [have been] reminded of the importance of Ravenna as a locus of imperial political authority and … the city's urban monastic traditions. The tale of Barbatianus would have had a powerful attraction for the local Ravennate archbishops, clergy, monks, and even nobles, as at its core the life depicts the reliance of Galla Placidia on a holy man, his intercessions on her behalf, and his miraculous cures fashioned to suit the practical needs of Ravenna in affirming the authority and position of the city and its institutions becomes visible.[46]

However, the new-found prominence of Barbatianus was short-lived. In the eleventh century as antagonism to the empire grew, Barbatianus seems to have been eclipsed by new saints associated with the rapidly accelerating monastic reform such as the local monk Romuald, promoted by another local cleric, Peter Damian.[47] The established early saints, however, such as Apollinaris, Severus, and Probus continued to flourish and indeed, as we have seen, their relics were bitterly fought over.

One question remains: with this great panoply of saints was Ravenna a major pilgrimage centre? Of course, it was never a pilgrim magnet on the scale of Rome. In earlier writings I took a somewhat narrow view of pilgrimage as a long distance, often trans-Alpine, phenomenon, suggesting that Ravenna was somewhat of a backwater from the ninth century on, partly as a result of the conversion of the Lombard kingdom to Catholicism and the development of a new Western pilgrim route to Rome, the *Via Francigena*.[48] Certainly references to pilgrims are rare, but there is plenty of evidence of repairs to churches and the building of new crypts throughout the eighth, ninth and tenth centuries which would suggest some pilgrim traffic.[49] Also research on Ravenna in those centuries has shown that the city remained the metropolitan centre for a large area of north-eastern Italy. It may have attracted relatively few trans-Alpine pilgrims, but the large number of visitors from Emilia-Romagna and the Marche, the lordship of the archbishops, would have paid their respects to the prestigious saints of Ravenna, and the influence of these cults is reflected in their appearance in neighbouring centres such as Ferrara, Bologna, and Rimini. Ravenna was regularly visited by rulers, nobles, and ecclesiastics, some from across the Alps, for councils, court cases, and other activities, not to mention the clients, tenants and subordinates of the archbishop from all parts of the vast area over which the see exercised jurisdiction and held property. One should not confine one's approach to a narrow definition of specialist pilgrims, and all these

---

46 Schoolman, 'Engineered Holy Authority', abstract; Schoolman, *Rediscovering Sainthood*, especially c. 4 and 5, pp. 77–90; 91–124. I wish to record my gratitude to Ned Schoolman both for discussions on Ravenna and for his important published work, especially on local saints. On Barbatianus see also Verhoeven, *The Early Christian Monuments of Ravenna*, pp. 80–85.

47 Centro Studi Avellaniti, *San Romualdo. Storia, agiografia e spiritualità*; Centro Studi Avellaniti, *Ottone III e Romualdo di Ravenna. Impero, monasteri e santi asceti*. See also Schoolman, *Rediscovering Sainthood*, pp. 65–68.

48 Brown, 'The Background of Byzantine Relations with Italy'; Brown, 'The Interplay of Roman and Byzantine Traditions in the Exarchate of Ravenna'.

49 This is a major theme of the work of Verhoeven, *The Early Christian Monuments of Ravenna*.

figures would also have visited the shrines of Ravenna's saints.[50] Finally we know of the dissemination of manuscripts, columns, statues, and works of art from Ravenna to the North, both under the Carolingians and Ottonians. Otto I's new archbishopric of Magdeburg, for example, received columns, capitals and relics from Ravenna and further research might well confirm the diffusion of Ravenna cults to Northern Europe.[51] Certainly Ravenna saints such as Apollinaris have their cult centres in Germany, including Dusseldorf, Remagen and, fittingly, the imperial city of Aachen.[52] A particular role in this process may have been played by clerics such as Adalbert of Prague, who spent time in Ravenna, before performing missionary work in Eastern Europe.[53]

Two conclusions emerge from this preliminary study.

One is that feelings of local identity were very powerful determinants in the promotion of Ravenna's saints. Not only were local figures favoured, but outsiders were often given a dubious Ravenna pedigree. Saints from outside Ravenna, no matter how distinguished they were or how close to the city their place of origin was, as in the case of Peter Chrysologus, born in nearby Imola, were treated with a degree of suspicion. In addition, some of the greatest promoters of saints were outsiders, such as Archbishop Maximian in the sixth century, Archbishops Peter IV and Honestus in the tenth, eager to win the support of their clergy and their wider local congregations.

The second point is that the promotion of saints' cults generally had a specific purpose — to win more prestige for the Church, to advance its claims against rivals such as Rome, or to win the favour of potential benefactors, especially visiting rulers, whether Byzantine, Frankish, or Ottonian. Obviously most sees used their saints' cults to strengthen their power and prestige, but in the case of Ravenna we can see a particularly systematic, even brazen, case of such hagiographic promotion. Saints were an important element in the armoury of techniques which enabled Ravenna to become one of the most powerful sees in Italy between the fifth century and the eleventh. Only then did the see lose much of its power and wealth because it chose the wrong side in the Investiture Contest, to the extent of having an archbishop elevated as an antipope and rival to Pope Gregory VII: Wibert who became antipope Clement III.[54] That, however, is another chapter in the fascinating history of Ravenna.

---

50 These are major themes in my forthcoming work on Carolingian and Ottonian Ravenna and its hinterland. On attendance at councils and *placiti* in Ravenna, MacLean, 'Legislation and Politics in Late Carolingian Italy'.

51 On Magdeburg, Huschner, *Transalpine Kommunikation im Mittelalter*, pp. 624–794. The archbishopric of Magdeburg was instituted at a council held in Ravenna in 967.

52 Verhoeven, *The Early Christian Monuments of Ravenna*, pp. 71–72 suggest that the cult spread to Northern Germany in the late middle ages, but the case for much earlier adoption deserves investigration.

53 Novara, ed., *Missio ad gentes. Ravenna e l'evangelizzazione dell'Est europeo*. His friend St Romuald later dedicated a monastery to Adalbert's memory: Novara, *Sant'Adalberto in Pereo*.

54 Heydrich, *Ravenna unter Erzbischof Wibert (1073–1100)*.

Works Cited

Primary Sources

LPR   Agnellus of Ravenna, *Liber pontificalis ecclesiae Ravennatis*, ed. by Deborah M. Deliyannis, Corpus Christianorum Continuatio Mediaevalis, 199 (Turnhout: Brepols, 2006)

The Book of the Pontiffs of the Church of Ravenna, trans. by Deborah M. Deliyannis (Washington, DC: Catholic University Press, 2004)

Le Carte del Monastero di S. Andrea Maggiore di Ravenna, ed. by Giovanni Muzzioli, Storia e letteratura, 86 (Rome: Edizioni di Storia e Letteratura, 1961)

Passio Sancti Ursicini Martyris, in *Rerum Italicarum scriptores*, ed. by Ludovico Antonio Muratori (Milan: Typographia Societatis Palatinae, 1723), I.2, cols 560–62

Peter Chrysologus, *Collectio Sermonum*, ed. by Alexandre Olivar, Corpus Christianorum Series Latina, 24, 24A and 24B, 3 vols (Turnhout: Brepols, 1975–1982)

Ravennatis anonymi cosmographia, in *Ravennatis Anonymi Cosmographia et Guidonis Geographica*, ed. by Joseph Schnetz, Itineraria Romana, 2 (Leipzig: Teubner, 1940)

Venantius Fortunatus, *Vita S. Martini*, ed. by Friedrich Leo, *Monumenta Germaniae Historica: Auctores antiquissimi*, 15 vols (Hannover: Berolini, 1877–1919) IV.1 (1881), pp. 293–370

Secondary Studies

Augenti, Andrea, Ilaria Begnozzi, Mila Bondi, Enrico Cirelli, Debora Ferreri, Cecilia Malaguti, Paolo Scozzari, 'Il monastero di San Severo a Classe: risultati delle campagne di scavo 2006–2011', in *Atti del VI Congresso Nazionale di Archeologia Medievale, L'Aquila, 12–15 settembre 2012*, ed. by Fabio Redi and Alfonso Forgione (Florence: All'Insegna del Giglio, 2012), pp. 238–45

———, 'Classe: Archaeologies of a Lost City', in *Vrbes Extinctae: Abandoned Classical Towns*, ed. by Neil Christie and Andrea Augenti (Abingdon: Routledge, 2012), pp. 45–76

Augenti, Andrea, and Enrico Cirelli, 'San Severo and Religious Life in Ravenna during the Ninth and Tenth Centuries', in *Ravenna: Its Role in Earlier Medieval Change and Exchange*, ed. by Judith Herrin and Janet L. Nelson (London: Institute of Historical Research, 2016), pp. 297–322

Benericetti, Ruggero, *Il Pontificale di Ravenna. Studio Critico* (Faenza: Seminario Vescovile Pio XII, 1994)

Boesch Gaetano, Sofia, ed., *Agiografia altomedievale* (Bologna: Il Mulino, 1976)

Brown, Peter, *The Cult of the Saints: Its Rise and Function in Latin Christianity* (Chicago: University of Chicago Press, 1981)

———, 'Relics and Social Status in the Age of Gregory of Tours', in Peter Brown, *Society and the Holy in Late Antiquity* (London: Faber and Faber, 1982), pp. 222–50

Brown, T. S., 'The Church of Ravenna and the imperial administration in the seventh century', *The English Historical Review*, XCIV, CCCLXX (1979), 1–28

——, 'The Background of Byzantine Relations with Italy in the Ninth Century', *Byzantinische Forschungen*, 13 (1988), 27–45

——, 'The Interplay of Roman and Byzantine Traditions in the Exarchate of Ravenna', in *Bisanzio, Roma e l'Italia nell'Alto Medioevo: 3–9 aprile 1986*, Settimane di studio del Centro italiano di studi sull'alto medioevo, 34, 2 vols (Spoleto: Centro italiano di studi sull'alto medioevo, 1988), I, pp. 128–67

——, 'Ebrei e orientali a Ravenna', in *Dall'età bizantina all'età ottoniana: territorio, economia e società*, ed. by Antonio Carile, *Storia di Ravenna*, 2.1 (Venice: Marsilio, 1991), pp. 135–49

——, 'Culture and Society in Ottonian Ravenna: Imperial Renewal or New Beginnings?', in *Ravenna: Its Role in Earlier Medieval Change and Exchange*, ed. by Judith Herrin and Janet L. Nelson (London: Institute of Historical Research, 2016), pp. 322–46

Caroli, Martina, 'Culto e commercio delle reliquie a Ravenna nell' alto medievo', in *Ravenna tra Oriente e Occidente: storia e archeologia*, ed. by Andrea Augenti and Carlo Bertelli, I Quaderni di Flaminia, 8 (Ravenna: Angelo Longo, 2006), pp. 15–27

Carla, Filippo, 'Milan, Ravenna, Rome: Some Reflections on the Cult of the Saints and on Civic Politics in Late Antique Italy', *Rivista di Storia e Letteratura Religiosa*, 46 (2010), 197–272

Cavarra, Berenice, Gabriella Gardini, Giovanni Battista Parente, and Giorgio Vespignani, 'Gli archivi come fonti della storia di Ravenna: Regesto dei documenti', in *Dall'età bizantina all'età ottoniana: territorio, economia e società*, ed. by Antonio Carile, *Storia di Ravenna*, 2.1 (Venice: Marsilio Editrice, 1991), pp. 401–547

Centro Studi Avellaniti, *San Romualdo. Storia, agiografia e spiritualità. Atti del XXIII Convegno del Centro studi avellaniti (Fonte Avellana, 23–26 agosto 2000)* (Verona: Gabrielli, 2002)

Centro Studi Avellaniti, *Ottone III e Romualdo di Ravenna. Imperio, monasteri e santi asceti. Atti del XXIV Convegno del Centro Studi Avellaniti* (Verona: Gabrielli, 2003)

Corvisier, André, *Les saints militaires*, Bibliothèque d'histoire moderne et contemporaine, 20 (Paris: Champion, 2006)

Cirelli, Enrico, *Ravenna. Archeologia di una città* (Borgo S. Lorenzo: Edizioni All'Insegna del Giglio, 2008)

David, Massimiliano, *Eternal Ravenna: From the Etruscans to the Venetians* (Turnhout: Brepols, 2013)

Deichmann, Friedrich Wilhelm, *Ravenna, Hauptstadt des spätantiken Abendlandes*, 4 vols, (Wiesbaden: Steiner, 1969–1989)

Delehaye, Hippolyte, *Les légendes grécques des saints militaires* (Paris: Picard, 1909)

——, 'L'hagiographie ancienne de Ravenne', *Analecta Bollandiana*, 47 (1929), 5–30

Deliyannis, Deborah M., *Ravenna in Late Antiquity* (Cambridge: Cambridge University Press, 2010)

Demus, Otto, *The Church of San Marco in Venice*, Dumbarton Oaks Studies, 6 (Washington, DC: Dumbarton Oaks Research Library and Collection, 1960)

Dinkler, Erich, *Das Apsismosaik von S. Apollinare in Classe*, Wissenschaftliche Abhandlungen der Arbeitsgemeinschaft für Forschung des Landes Nordrhein-Westfalen, 29 (Cologne: Westdeutscher Verlag, 1964)

Efthymiadis, Stephanos, ed., *The Ashgate Research Companion to Byzantine Hagiography: Volume II, Genres and Contexts* (Farnham: Ashgate, 2014)

Everett, Nicholas, *Patron Saints of Early Medieval Italy AD c. 350–800: History and Hagiography in Ten Biographies*, Durham Medieval and Renaissance Texts and Translations, 5 (Toronto: Pontifical Institute of Mediaeval Studies, 2016)

Fasoli, Gina, 'Il dominio territorio degli arcivescovi di Ravenna fra l'VIII e l'XI secolo', in *I poteri temporali dei vescovi in Italia e in Germania*, ed. by Carlo Guido Mor and Heinrich Schmidinger, Annali dell'Istituto storico italo–germanico in Trento. Quaderno, 3 (Bologna: Mulino, 1979), pp. 87–140

——, 'Il patrimonio della chiesa ravennate', in *Storia di Ravenna, II.1. Dall'età bizantina all'età ottomana. Territorio, economia e società*, ed. by Antonio Carile (Ravenna: Marsilio, 1991), pp. 389–400

Follieri, Enrica, 'Vite e inni greci per i santi di Ravenna', *Rivista di Studi Bizantini e Neoellenici*, n.s., 2–3 (1965–1966), 193–203

Geary, Patrick, *Furta Sacra: Thefts of Relics in the Central Middle Ages* (Princeton: revised ed., Princeton University Press, 1991)

Gugliotta, Benedetto, 'L'evoluzione della proprietà ecclesiastica ravennate tra San Giovanni in Marignano e Cattolica nel Basso Medioevo', in *Archeologia e storia di un territorio di confine*, ed. by Christina Ravara Montebelli, Adrias, 4 (Rome: L'Erma di Bretschneider, 2008), pp. 99–110

Herrin, Judith, and Janet L. Nelson, eds, *Ravenna: Its Role in Earlier Medieval Change and Exchange*, (London: Institute of Historical Research, 2016)

Heydrich, Ingrid, *Ravenna unter Erzbischof Wibert (1073–1100): Untersuchungen zur Stellung des Erzbischofs und Gegenpapstes Clemens III. in seiner Metropole*, Vorträge und Forschungen Sonderband, 32 (Sigmaringen: Thorbecke, 1984)

Huschner, Wolfgang, *Transalpine Kommunikation im Mittelalter: Diplomatische, kulturelle und politische Wechselwirkungen zwischen Italien und dem nordalpinen Reich (9.–11. Jahrhundert)*, Monumenta Germaniae Historica: Schriften, 52, 3 vols (Hanover: Hahnsche, 2003)

MacLean, Simon, 'Legislation and Politics in Late Carolingian Italy: The Ravenna Constitutions', *Early Medieval Europe*, 18.4 (2010), 394–416

Markus, Robert A., *Gregory the Great and his World* (Cambridge: Cambridge University Press, 1997)

Mazzotti, Mario, 'La basilica di Santa Maria Maggiore in Ravenna', *Corso di cultura sull'arte ravennate e bizantina*, 7 (1960), 253–60

McLynn, Neil, B., *Ambrose of Milan: Church and Court in a Christian Capital*, Transformation of the Classical Heritage, 22 (Berkeley: University of California Press, 1994)

Morini, Enrico, 'Santi orientali a Ravenna', in *Storia di Ravenna, II.2. Dall'eta bizantina all'eta ottoniana*, ed. by Antonio Carile (Ravenna: Marsilio, 1992), pp. 283–303

Novara, Paolo, *Sant'Adalberto in Pereo e la decorazione in laterizio nel Ravennate e nell'Italia settentrionale (secc. VIII–XI)*, Documenti di Archeologia, 3 (Mantua: Editrice S.A.P, 1994)

——, ed., *Missio ad Gentes: Ravenna e l'evangelizzazione dell'Est europeo* (Ravenna: Fernandel Scientifica, 2002)

Orselli, Alba Maria, *L'idea e il culto del santo patrono cittadino nella letteratura latina cristiana* (Bologna: Zanichelli, 1965)

—————, 'Il santo patrono cittadino fra tardo Antico e Alto Medioevo', in *La cultura in Italia fra Tardo Antico e Alto Medioevo*. Atti del Convegno (Roma 12–16 Novembre 1979), 2 vols, (Rome: Herder, 1981), pp. 771–84

Penni Iacco, Emanuela, *La Basilica di Sant'Apollinare Nuovo di Ravenna attraverso i secoli* (Bologna: Ante Quem, 2004)

Picard, Jean-Charles, *Le souvenir des évêques: sépultures, listes épiscopales et culte des évêques en Italie du Nord des origines au Xe siècle*, Bibliothèque des Écoles françaises d'Athènes et de Rome, 268 (Rome: École française de Rome, 1988)

Pilsworth, Claire L., 'Representations of Sanctity in Milan and Ravenna, *c.* 400 – *c.* 900 AD' (Unpublished doctoral thesis, Cambridge University, 1999)

Pohl, Walter, and Ian Wood, 'Introduction: Cultural Memory and the Resources of the Past', in *The Resources of the Past in Early Medieval Europe*, ed. by Clemens Gantner, Rosamond McKitterick, and Sven Meeder (Cambridge: Cambridge University Press, 2015), pp. 1–12

Racagni, Paolo, ed., *La Basilica Ritrovata. I mosaici di San Severo a Classe* (Bologna: Ante Quem, 2010)

Ropa, Giampaolo, 'Agiografia e liturgia a Ravenna tra alto e basso Medioevo', in *Storia di Ravenna, iii. Dal mille alla fine della signoria polentina*, ed. by Augosto Vasina (Venice: Marsilio, 1993)

Sansterre, Jean-Marie, 'Monaci e monasteri greci a Ravenna', in *Storia di Ravenna, II.2. Dall'eta bizantina all'eta ottoniana*, ed. by Antonio Carile (Ravenna: Marsilio, 1992), pp. 323–30

Schoolman, Edward M., *Rediscovering Sainthood in Italy: Hagiography and the Late Antique Past in Medieval Ravenna* (New York: Palgrave, 2016)

—————, 'Engineered Holy Authority and the Tenth-Century *Vita* of St Barbatianus of Ravenna', in *Shaping Authority: How Did a Person Become an Authority in Antiquity, the Middle Ages and the Renaissance?* ed. by. Shari Boodts, Johan Leemans and Brigitte Meijns, Lectio, Studies in the Transmission of Texts and Ideas, 4 (Turnhout: Brepols, 2016), pp. 251–80

Sgarbanti, Romeo, *Ferrara: Nascita di una città (dopo la leggenda la storia)* (Ferrara: 2G Libri, 2008)

Spadoni, Claudio, and Linda Kniffitiz, eds, *San Michele in Africisco e l'età giustinianea a Ravenna atti del convegno 'La diaspora dell'arcangelo: San Michele in Africisco e l'età giustinianea': giornate di studio in memoria di Giuseppe Bovini. Ravenna, Sala dei Mosaici, 21–22 aprile 2005)*, Biblioteca d'arte, 12 (Milan: Silvana, 2007)

Sottocornola, Franco, *L'anno liturgico nei sermoni di Pietro Crisologo: Ricerca storico-critica sulla liturgia di Ravenna antica*, Studia Ravennatensia, 1 (Cesena: Centro studie ricerche sulla antica provincia ecclesiastica Ravennate, 1973)

Thacker, Alan, '*Loca sanctorum*: The Significance of Place in the Study of Saints', in *Local Saints and Local Churches in the Early Medieval West*, ed. by Alan Thacker and Richard Sharpe (Oxford: Oxford University Press, 2003), pp. 1–43

Thacker, Alan, and Richard Sharpe, eds, *Local Saints and Local Churches in the Early Medieval West* (Oxford: Oxford University Press, 2003)

Toffarella, Marcello, *Ferrara: La città rinascimentale e il delta del Po* (Rome: Istituto poligrafico e Zecca dello stato, 2005)

Trpimir Vedriš, 'Martyrs, Relics, and Bishops: Representations of the City in Dalmatian Translation Legends', *Hortus Artium Medievalium*, 12 (2006), 175–86

Verhoeven, Mariëtte, *The Early Christian Monuments of Ravenna: Transformations and Memory*, Architectural Crossroads. Studies in the History of Architecture, 1 (Turnhout: Brepols, 2011)

Zattoni, G., 'La data della *Passio s. Apollinaris* di Ravenna', in *Atti della R. Accademia delle scienze di Torino*, 32 (1904) 364–78 (reprinted in Zattoni, *Scritti storici e ravennati* [Ravenna: Libreria Tonini, 1975], pp. 113–128)

CATHERINE CUBITT

The Impact of the Lateran Council of 649 in Francia: The Martyrdom of Pope Martin and the *Life of St Eligius*

Rome in the 650s played host to an interesting collection of visitors. From England, the Northumbrians Benedict Biscop and Wilfrid probably arrived in *c.* 654 and *c.* 655–656 respectively.[1] They had just missed Bishop Taius of Zaragoza who was in Rome *c.* 651–653, but may have overlapped with delegates from the Frankish king, Clovis II, who obtained a privilege for the royal monastery of St Maurice d'Agaune in Burgundy from Pope Eugenius in 654.[2] This was a particularly tense time in papal Rome: Pope Martin had been arrested by imperial forces in June 653 after his convocation of the Lateran Synod in October 649, which had condemned the imperially-backed teaching of monotheletism. He was ignominiously transported to Constantinople, where he was tried and sentenced to death in December 653. The sentence was commuted to exile in the Cherson, where the pope died in miserable circumstances two years later.[3] Clearly things had not gone well: the first imperial exarch sent to arrest the pope had revolted, perhaps with Martin's support.[4] Further, faced with a prolonged vacancy through the pope's arrest and exile, the Roman clergy had selected a new pontiff, Eugenius, who was consecrated in August 654 in Martin's own lifetime. Conflict with Constantinople continued as Eugenius refused the *synodica* of the new patriarch of Constantinople, Peter.

Alan Thacker's work has shed a bright light on how visitors to Rome encountered the great city and the shrines and basilicas of its many saints and martyrs; he has demonstrated how Rome's emergence as 'custodian of the greatest deposit of holy remains … in the Christian world, a true *caput omnium*' took place gradually by the

---

1 Wood, 'The Continental Journeys of Wilfrid and Biscop', pp. 200–11.
2 See below pp. 76–77, and n. 3.
3 The dating of Martin's death is problematic, see Peeters, 'Une vie grecque', p. 249; I use the date of 16 September 655 from the earliest account of his death, see also Neil, *Seventh-Century Popes and Martyrs*, p. 249, n. 197.
4 Brandes, '"Juristische" Krisenbewältigung', pp. 141–212, and see below n. 22.

Catherine Cubitt • (Katy.Cubitt@uea.ac.uk) is Professor of Medieval History at the University of East Anglia.

Cities, Saints, and Communities in Early Medieval Europe, ed. by Scott DeGregorio and Paul Kershaw, SEM 46 (Turnhout: Brepols, 2020), pp. 71–103
BREPOLS PUBLISHERS   DOI 10.1484/M.SEM-EB.5.119623

second half of the seventh century.[5] His penetrating understanding of the textual and material evidence has illuminated the devotional effect of the city on men like Biscop, Wilfrid, and Taius.[6] But the sources are obstinately silent on the impact of the tumultuous events of the mid-seventh century on pilgrims to Rome. It is impossible to think, however, that they were either unaware or unmoved by the crises and conflicts attendant upon the monothelete controversy. This paper explores responses to the Lateran Synod and to Pope Martin's death in Francia, focusing on a contested passage in the *Vita Eligii* concerning these events.

The life of the seventh-century bishop, Eligius of Noyon, contains an important account of Pope Martin's outreach to the Frankish kingdom of Neustria and an intriguing description of the pope's cruel treatment at Byzantine hands and subsequent death. The significance of this material has been overshadowed by suspicion that it is a later interpolation into the original seventh-century text.[7] The *Vita*, composed in the late seventh century by Bishop Audoin of Rouen, is a source of exceptional interest.[8] However, like many Merovingian hagiographies, the *Vita Eligii* was deemed by its editor, Bruno Krusch, to have been partially rewritten and revised in the Carolingian period.[9] Krusch was followed in this judgement of the Martin narrative by its most recent editor, Isabelle Westeel,[10] but Walter Berschin and Clemens Bayer have defended the overall authenticity of the work as a seventh-century production by Audoin himself.[11] Further, Ian Wood noted the importance of the source for the seventh century, despite the fact that it only survives in a Carolingian redaction.[12] This article will demonstrate that, far from being a later and unreliable insertion, the account of Pope Martin is derived from contemporary sources probably dating to the 670s. The *Vita Eligii* is, therefore, a vital source for the reception of the monothelete conflict; it represents the sole western contemporary account outside Italy of these dramatic and important events, a vital reflection of the Lateran Synod and of the turmoil in Rome in the 660s and 670s.

This article consists of three sections. The first looks at what is known of western responses to the Lateran Synod in order to provide a context for the account in the

---

5   Thacker, 'Rome: The Pilgrims' City', pp. 89–139; and his, 'Rome of the Martyrs', pp. 19–20, quotation from p. 20.

6   Thacker, 'Rome of the Martyrs', pp. 19–20, and his 'Rome: The Pilgrims' City', pp. 122–31; Ó Carragáin and Thacker, 'Wilfrid in Rome', pp. 200–21.

7   *Vita Eligii episcopi Noviomagensis* (hereafter *VSE*), ed. by Krusch, pp. 634–760. On this edition see Westeel, 'Quelques remarques sur la *Vita Eligii*', pp. 33–47. Unfortunately, Westeel's edition has not been published.

8   See now also Sarti, 'The Digression on Pope Martin I'. I am most grateful to Dr Sarti for sharing this with me before publication. We have worked separately but arrived at similar conclusions.

9   See below, pp. 78–82. For a general critique of Krusch's judgments see Wood, 'Forgery in Merovingian Hagiography', pp. 369–84.

10   Westeel, 'Quelques remarques sur la *Vita Eligii*', pp. 39–40, and see van Uytfanghe, *Stylisation et condition humaine*, p. 11 states that the text is eighth century in its actual form. See also Scheibelreiter, 'Audoin von Rouen', pp. 195–216; Wood, *The Merovingian Kingdoms*, p. 150.

11   Berschin, 'Der heilige Goldschmied', pp. 1–7; Bayer, '*Vita Eligii*', pp. 461–524. For further discussion of Bayer's theory of later redaction, see below pp. 79–80.

12   Wood, *The Merovingian Kingdoms*, p. 150.

Vita Eligii. The second part focuses on the treatment of Pope Martin's death in that text. It will consider Krusch's claims of later forgery, raising questions about motivation and access to information. Having shown that the *Vita*'s account is unlikely to have been confected from the sources available in the early eighth century, this section will then compare it with seventh-century anti-monothelete texts and highlight their close kinship with the *Vita Eligii*. Given these significant similarities, the article will examine how a seventh-century Frankish writer might have had access to a dyothelete account, either in Francia or in Rome. I will argue that the discussion of Martin's death did derive from an eyewitness account as the *Vita Eligii* claims. The third and final section of the paper builds on the conclusion that the source of the Martin narrative in the *Vita Eligii* was anti-imperial propaganda probably encountered by Audoin in Rome. It then shows how the involvement of Eligius and Audoin in the Frankish response to the monothelete controversy arose directly out of their role in Frankish relations with the Empire and with Rome, and highlights the significance of their links to Columbanian monasticism.

The Lateran Synod of 649 and Western Responses

The bitter controversy over the teaching that Christ had one will drew the papacy into a conflict over religious and doctrinal authority with the Eastern emperor and patriarch of Constantinople. The convocation of the Lateran Synod in October 649 marked a real challenge to imperial authority prompting a harsh response in the trial and exile of Martin. Imperial and eastern reactions to the synod in the decades after 650 can be charted through a variety of documents, including the proceedings of the Council of Constantinople in 680 that condemned monotheletism as heretical.[13] But, for the western kingdoms, the impact is more difficult to trace. Pope Agatho responded to the Emperor Constantine's invitation to send Roman legates to the Constantinople Council by canvassing support in the West.[14] Archbishop Theodore of Canterbury, a former eastern refugee in Rome, was singled out for consultation because of his theological expertise. He did not attend but did convene a council at Hatfield in 679 which considered the question.[15] At Easter 680 a papal council convened by Agatho was attended by Bishops Wilfrid of York and Deodatus of Toul. Evidence from Spain also shows that the pope followed up on the ecumenical council and sent news at least to the Visigothic kingdom and probably elsewhere.[16] However, for the period before 679, evidence for the impact of the monothelete controversy in the West is scant and fragmentary.

---

13 See now Jankowiak, 'Essai d'histoire politique du monothéletisme', pp. 289–518.
14 *Concilium universal Constantinopitanum Tertium Concilii Actiones I–XI*, ed. by Riedinger, pp. 132–33, and see *Biblical Commentaries*, ed. by Bischoff and Lapidge, pp. 79–80.
15 Bede, *Historia ecclesiastica*, IV.17, ed. and trans. by Colgrave and Mynors, pp. 384–87; Cubitt, *Anglo-Saxon Church Councils*, pp. 252–58.
16 Cubitt, 'St Wilfrid', pp. 326–30; Wood, 'The Franks and Papal Theology', pp. 239–40; Jankowiak, 'Essai d'histoire politique du monothéletisme', pp. 509–10.

The christological controversy over the will of Christ that had been simmering since the 630s and 640s reached a climax in the pontificate of Pope Martin.[17] The theological policy of the patriarch and emperor, designed as a means of reconciling the long-standing and bitterly divisive doctrinal disagreement with the monophysites, taught that while Christ had two natures — one divine and one human — he possessed one will. The teaching was opposed in the Eastern Empire by those who saw it as a betrayal of the doctrinal settlement at the Council of Chalcedon and who therefore denounced it as heretical.[18] This group was spearheaded by a number of Palestinian monks, led initially by Patriarch Sophronius of Jerusalem and later by the theologian Maximus the Confessor.[19] The city of Rome provided a refuge, first for Sophronius and then for Maximus, from the political and religious upheaval in the East, beset by the Persian Wars and then, from the 630s, by Arab attacks.[20] Initially, the papacy had accepted the imperial position: Pope Honorius had sent a letter of support to the Patriarch Sergius, which included a statement that Christ possessed one will. However, as the controversy became more embittered, his successors seem to have been persuaded by the teachings of Maximus that the imperial position was in fact heretical. In 642 a pope of Palestinian extraction, Theodore, was elected and he began preparations for a major council in Rome to condemn the teaching, implicitly also condemning the faith of the emperors.[21] Since an imperial edict, the *Typos*, had in 647/648 prohibited any discussion of the question of wills, papal policy was now working in opposition to the emperor's express command. The council met in Rome in 649 under the presidency of Pope Martin, who succeeded Theodore in July of that year; it condemned monotheletism as a heresy and anathematized the current patriarch of Constantinople, two of his predecessors and a patriarch of Alexandria.

The Lateran Synod therefore represented an act of disobedience to the emperor. Moreover, Martin had been elected without imperial permission and was probably complicit in the revolt of Olympius. The imperial reaction was savage: Martin was treated brutally both on his lengthy passage to Constantinople and in the city itself. In exile, he was forced to send begging letters to Rome, pleading for food and assistance. His death on 16 September 655 was probably the result of these punishments.[22] Imperial suppression of resistance to its decrees continued after Martin's arrest:

---

17 See now *The Acts of the Lateran Synod*, trans. by Price, for a succinct account and reappraisal of these events.

18 The doctrinal issues have been clarified and reassessed by Richard Price in *The Acts of the Lateran Synod*, pp. 87–102. See also the important studies by Booth, *Crisis of Empire* and Jankowiak, 'Essai d'histoire politique du monothéletisme'.

19 Booth, *Crisis of Empire*.

20 Booth, *Crisis of Empire*, pp. 282–89; Sansterre, *Les Moines grecs et orientaux à Rome*, esp. I, pp. 1–31; Louth, 'Did John Moschus Really Die in Constantinople?', pp. 149–54; Thacker, 'Memorializing Gregory the Great', pp. 59–84.

21 *Le Liber pontificalis* ed. by Duchesne, I, pp. 331–35, and see *The Book of the Pontiffs*, trans. by Davis, pp. 67–68; Cubitt, 'The Roman Perspective', pp. 40–58.

22 For contemporary accounts of these events, see Neil, *Seventh-Century Popes and Martyrs*, pp. 167–265, and *Maximus the Confessor*, ed. by Allen and Neil, pp. 148–71.

Maximus and his follower, Anastasius Discipulus, were tried in 655 and sentenced to exile. Following the dyotheletes' continued resistance, Maximus and two followers, Anastasius Discipulus and Anastasius Apocrisiarius, were subject to a further trial and exiled to separate locations, where they died.[23]

The repercussions of these events are unclear: the *Liber pontificalis* reports that copies of the proceedings of the synod were sent to the East and West.[24] Martin's surviving correspondence reveals that he dispatched an encyclical letter and copies of the *acta* to the Church of Carthage and to Bishop John of Philadelphia, as well as other letters to eastern contacts.[25] In the West, only one letter of Martin survives, that to St Amandus, which was preserved at his monastery of Elnone/St Amand and appended to a ninth-century redaction of the saint's *Vita* by Milo, a monk of the house. This letter records that Martin sent the *acta* to Amandus, and documents his desire to win the support of the Austrasian Church and use it to defend his own position with the emperor. He asks Amandus to convene an episcopal council to confirm his decree and to send its proceedings (attested by the attending bishops) to him. Secondly, he asks that King Sigibert send a legation of bishops to Rome whom the pope can send on to the emperor.[26]

Unfortunately, although Amandus and his monastery took care to preserve the letter and the Lateran *acta*, it is not clear whether any further action was taken. But three further responses to the synod can be inferred. Ian Wood has argued that the presence in Rome between 651 and 653 of the Spanish bishop, Taius of Zaragoza should be linked to Martin's initiatives after the council.[27] Secondly, there is good evidence to suggest that Clovis II did convene a council of his bishops in Neustria and Burgundy in response to Martin's request. Thirdly, the privilege granted by Martin's successor, Eugenius, indicates continuing contacts between Burgundy and Rome at this crucial time.

The Council of Chalon-sur-Saône

The Council of Chalon-sur-Saône cannot be more precisely dated than to 647 × 653, but can plausibly be seen as a reaction to the Lateran Synod.[28] It was a very major council, attended by representatives from nine provinces, six metropolitans, a total of thirty-nine bishops and six episcopal proxies. Eligius and Audoin were among those present. It discussed the disciplinary cases of two bishops, whom it deposed,

---

23 *Maximus the Confessor*, ed. by Allen and Neil, pp. 23–25. Maximus and Anastasius Discipulus in 662, and Anastasius Apocrisiarius in 666.

24 *Liber pontificalis*, ed. by Duchesne, I, p. 337, and see *The Book of the Pontiffs*, trans. Davis, p. 69.

25 *The Acts of the Lateran Synod*, trans. by Price, cols. 394–97, usefully catalogues these; for the letters see Pope Martin, *Epistolae*, *Patrologia Latina*, ed. by Migne, LXXXVII, cols 145–91.

26 *Vita Amandi*, ed. by Krusch, pp. 425–56 (pp. 428–49), and see *The Acts of the Lateran Synod*, trans. by Price, pp. 408–12; Scheibelreiter, 'Griechisches-lateinisches-fränkisches Christentum', pp. 84–102.

27 Wood, 'Between Rome and Jarrow', pp. 310–12; *Chronica a. 754*, ed. by Mommsen, pp. 341–43.

28 *Concilia Galliae A. 511–A. 695*, ed. by de Clercq, pp. 302–10; Pontal, *Histoire des conciles mérovingiens*, pp. 216–20; Wood, 'Between Rome and Jarrow', p. 311.

and promulgated twenty canons.[29] While the council did not explicitly refer to the recent doctrinal controversy, it did affirm the faith defined by ecumenical tradition, by the Councils of Nicaea and Chalcedon:

> […] definiuimus, ut fidei normam, sicut in Niceno concilio pia est professione firmata uel a sanctis patribus tradita atque ab ipsis exposita uel in postmodum a sancto est Calcidonense concilio firmata, in omnibus et ab omnibus conseruetur.[30]

This statement must be read in the light of the Lateran Synod *acta* which denounced monotheletism as a betrayal of Chalcedon and as an innovation, substantiating their claim to represent the faith of the Fathers by the inclusion of a long patristic *florilegium*.

Pope Eugenius's Privilege for St Maurice d'Agaune

Pope Eugenius's privilege for St Maurice d'Agaune, obtained by delegates of King Clovis II, should be associated with Frankish-papal relations in the aftermath of the Lateran Synod. It contains an assertion of Roman authority unique amongst the surviving seventh-century papal privileges.[31]

> Eugenius humilissimus omnium seruorum dei et in sancta sede romana tocius orbis magistra, non meritis propriis sed intercessione beatissimi apostolorum principis Petri, ab omnipotenti deo in apostolatus arche electus. Quis dominus noster oues proprias quas suo sancto ac precioso sanguine adquisiuit beato Petro pascendas commisit, constat nimirum cunctos dei cultores ipsius subicione cuius nos ubique, non diffidimus protegi patrocinio.
>
> > Eugenius, most humble of all the servants of God and leader of the holy Roman seat of the whole world, elected by omnipotent God to the pinnacle of the of apostolate, not by my own merits but by the intercession of the most holy Prince of the Apostles, Peter. Our Lord who committed his own flock which

---

29   The provinces of Arles, Vienne, Lyons, Sens, Bourges, Tours, Besançon, Rouen and Rheims were represented. See Halfond, *Archaeology of Frankish Church Councils*, pp. 42–43, 190–91, 239, who suggests that the council was actually convened on the authority of the Mayor of the Palace, Erchinoald, since Clovis II was a teenager; Pontal, *Histoire des conciles mérovingiens*, pp. 216–20. Neither Halfond nor Pontal connect the council with the Lateran synod, but see the apposite comments on the council itself by Borias, 'Saint Wandrille', pp. 59–60. Borias argues that Wandregisil did in fact go to Rome with the conciliar proceedings. However, although the evidence for his journey is tantalising, it is also late. I intend to publish on this topic.

30   *Concilia Galliae A. 511–A. 695*, ed. by de Clercq, p. 303: 'We have determined that the rule of faith should be maintained in all things and by everyone, just as it was declared by the pious profession at the Council of Nicaea and handed down and expounded by the holy fathers and affirmed by the holy council of Chalcedon'.

31   The essential authenticity of this privilege has been established by Anton, *Studien zu den Klosterprivilegien*, who provides an edition of the text on pp. 12–23. He identifies some later tampering, chiefly in the relation to the royal donation of tithes, see *Studien zu den Klosterprivilegien*, pp. 148–49. On the pontificate of Eugenius and monotheletism, see Jankowiak, 'Essai d'histoire politique du monothéletisme', pp. 294–310.

he gained by his own holy and precious blood to the Holy Peter for feeding, it is certainly established that all the worshippers of God everywhere are subject to him, and we not hesitant to protect with our protection.[32]

Eugenius is here styled as *electus* so that the grant must have been issued before his consecration on 10 August 654.[33] The *arenga* belongs to a type emphasizing papal authority and his Petrine commission which is not recorded between the pontificate of Gregory the Great and that of Pope Sergius (687–701); its authenticity has been defended by Anton.[34] The unusual emphasis in this text on the pope's divine appointment and upon Petrine authority is surely a reflection of the conflict with Constantinople over monotheletism. The privilege may have been issued at a synod.[35] Was the privilege granted as a reward to Clovis for his support of the doctrinal position of the Lateran Synod? Did Pope Eugenius hope that such a grant would bind the monastery and king more closely to Rome? Whatever the underlying causes, the determination to underline papal legitimacy and power is indicative of the prominence of the doctrinal controversy at the papal court.

The *Vita Eligii*, Pope Martin, and the Lateran Synod

The account in the *Vita Eligii* of the Pope Martin's correspondence with the Frankish king and his response is of the first importance in our understanding papal outreach and western responses. The passage concerning the Lateran Synod and the death of Pope Martin occurs in the context of describing Eligius's involvement in a legation to Rome in response to the papal correspondence. Eligius was a leading bishop in the kingdom of King Clovis II (d. 657), having been a prominent member of the court of Dagobert, Clovis's father. Born in the Limousin, he had been apprenticed to a goldsmith in Limoges, before his reputation as a metalworker led to an invitation to work for the king. As a layman and royal courtier, he was famed for his exemplary piety, founding a monastery at Solignac with monks recruited from the Columbanian foundation of Luxeuil. He was a trusted royal servant, serving on a diplomatic mission to Brittany, with his fellow courtier, Audoin. In 641, both Eligius and Audoin were

---

32 Anton, *Studien zu den Klosterprivilegien*, p. 12, and see the detailed analysis on pp. 98–149 (especially at pp. 100–09).

33 *Liber pontificalis*, ed. by Duchesne, I, CCLVI, p. 341 n. 1 states that Eugenius was consecrated on 10 August 654. Anton, *Studien zu den Klosterprivilegien*, p. 103 dates the privilege between Eugenius's consecration in August and the date of Martin's death in September 655. However, the chronology of the *Liber pontificalis* as computed by Duchesne indicates that Eugenius was regarded as pope, not *electus* before Martin's death. In 655, during the trial of Maximus, papal apocrisiaries arrived in Constantinople, and Maximus's interrogators claimed that they would celebrate mass with the Patriarch, but by September 656 relations with the pope seem to have deteriorated, see, *Maximus the Confessor*, ed. by Allen and Neil, pp. 62–63.

34 Anton, *Studien zu den Klosterprivilegien*, pp. 106–09.

35 Anton, *Studien zu den Klosterprivilegien*, pp. 99–101.

consecrated as bishops of Noyon and Rouen respectively.[36] Eligius died in 660. The two men belonged to a network of former courtiers and churchmen that included Bishops Desiderius of Cahors and Sulpicius of Bourges.[37]

The original composition of the *Vita Eligii* can be attributed to Audoin of Rouen (also known as Dado).[38] This rests on the text itself where the author is explicit about his identity, most notably when recalling how he and Eligius were consecrated bishop in the same ceremony. Further, some manuscripts of the *Vita* also contain a letter exchange between Audoin and Bishop Chrodebert of Paris, in which the former sends the hagiography to the latter for emendation.[39] Finally, some manuscripts also identify Audoin as the author at the head of the text.[40] Audoin was a major political and ecclesiastical player in the Merovingian world, a member of the regency which governed the kingdom during the minority of Clovis II.[41] He must therefore have been a significant influence, for example, on the king's religious policy, including the convocation of the Council of Chalons. His biography therefore draws upon his first-hand understanding of his hero and of his political and religious world.

The *Vita Eligii* itself is a complex and intriguing text, dealing with the saint's secular and ecclesiastical careers. In its transmitted form, it consists of two books, the first numbering forty chapters and the second of eighty, each with their own separate prologues. It is one of the longest of Merovingian hagiographies, numbering forty-four pages in Krusch's *MGH* edition.[42] However, Krusch omitted many passages which he considered of little importance, cutting ruthlessly its lengthy passages of praise. Its latest editor, Isabelle Westeel, noted that roughly half of it is composed in rhymed prose, a style utilized by Audoin in his letter to Bishop Chrodebert and by others at Dagobert's court.[43]

The *Vita* contains symptoms of later revision, such as the designation of both Eligius and Audoin as *sancti viri* in II. c. 1 or the reference in II c. 2 to Audoin 'qui vocabatur Dado'.[44] Krusch argued that the *Vita* had been contaminated by interpolations and tampering in the Carolingian period. On the other hand, it is also important to note signs of continuity in the text, the use of rhyming prose mentioned above and the

---

36   *VSE* II.2, pp. 695–96; Wood, *The Merovingian Kingdoms*, pp. 150–52; Fouracre, 'The Work of Audoenus of Rouen', pp. 77–91.

37   Bayer, 'Vita Eligii', pp. 461–524; Wood, *The Merovingian Kingdoms*, p. 151; Wallace-Hadrill, *The Frankish Church*, pp. 68–69.

38   On Audoin, see Scheibelreiter, 'Audoin von Rouen', pp. 195–216; Wood, *The Merovingian Kingdoms*, pp. 150–52. See also Fouracre and Gerberding, *Late Merovingian France*, pp. 132–65.

39   *VSE*, p. 741. Westeel, 'Quelques remarques sur la *Vita Eligii*', considers that Chrodebert died in 674 and therefore sees this date as significant for the *VSE*'s date of composition, but see Bayer, 'Vita Eligii', p. 472 for a date of 682 or later.

40   Westeel, 'Quelques remarques sur la *Vita Eligii*', p. 38.

41   Fouracre and Gerberding, *Late Merovingian France*, pp. 137–52; Wood, *The Merovingian Kingdoms*, pp. 150–52.

42   Westeel, 'Quelques remarques sur la *Vita Eligii*', p. 35.

43   Westeel, 'Quelques remarques sur la *Vita Eligii*', pp. 43–46.

44   Introduction to *VSE*, pp. 646, 694–95; see Bayer, 'Vita Eligii', p. 473 and Sarti, 'The Digression on Pope Martin I'.

deployment of borrowings from Rufinus's translation of Eusebius's *Ecclesiastical History*.[45] Westeel suggests that the hagiography was revised by a monk at the monastery, St.-Eloi at Noyon, in order to advertise the merits of the saint.[46]

The dating of the *Vita* is therefore complex. Berschin dates the completion of the text to between 675 and 680.[47] Bayer's close analysis suggests that the text had been composed and revised in a number of stages. He postulates that Book 1 was completed after Eligius's death in 660 and before the second phase of composition by Audoin of Book II (and the preface to the *Vita*) which he dates to between 673 and 684. Two further stages, he argues, then occurred between 681 and a final redaction in the 690s.[48] One piece of internal evidence points to its composition in 673–675. In one chapter a prophecy made by Eligius concerning the reigns of the three sons of Clovis II and Balthild — Chlothar III, Theuderic III, and Childeric II — is recounted. Eligius foresaw the death of one of the three, presumably Chlothar who died in 673, the deposition of another, and the rule of the third over all three kingdoms of Austrasia, Neustria, and Burgundy. Theuderic III was deposed in 673 but restored to the throne in 675. This passage is likely to have been composed in 673–675, during Theuderic's imprisonment at St Denis, or shortly afterwards, since his restoration is not mentioned.[49] Audoin returned in 675 from a lengthy stay in Rome, so he may have written the *Vita* on his return.[50] The Martin narrative could therefore have been added to the *Vita* by a subsequent late seventh-century redactor but I will argue that there is a good case to be made that Audoin himself may have received the account in the 670s. It is transmitted in many manuscripts: the earliest — Brussels, Bibliothèque royale de Belge, MS no. 5374–5375 — dates from the second quarter of the ninth century.[51] It was also used in the *Vita sancti Lamberti*, composed between 743 and 745.[52] So, if any reworking occurred, it must have taken place by *c.* 825–850, possibly by the 740s. Krusch identified three key elements as indicative of later reworking: the description of a bishop's financial activities in Book I, Chapter 32, where the bishop of Tours gains fiscal rights at the expense of the count, the lengthy account of Pope Martin and his treatment at Byzantine hands (I, cc. 33–34), and two brief passages

---

45 Rufinus is used in the *Vita Eligii* in Book I, cc. 33–35, in the preface to Book II, in Book II, cc. 3–4, 6, 8, 10, 26, 31, pp. 689–92, 694, 696–97, 699, 700–01, 714, 716. And see also the use of his *Historia monachorum* at II.80, p. 740. On use of Rufinus in the seventh century see Lapidge, *The Anglo-Saxon Library*, pp. 88–90, 181, and his 'Rufinus at the School of Canterbury', pp. 119–30.

46 Westeel, 'Quelques remarques sur la *Vita Eligii*', pp. 40–41.

47 Berschin, 'Der heilige Goldschmied', pp. 1–7.

48 Bayer, '*Vita Eligii*', pp. 466–75.

49 See Bayer, '*Vita Eligii*', p. 472; Westeel, 'Quelques remarques sur la *Vita Eligii*', p. 39; *VSE* II.32, pp. 717–18 and for Theuderic III's deposition and reinstatement see Wood, *The Merovingian Kingdoms*, pp. 231–34.

50 Gerberding, *The Rise of the Carolingians*, p. 88.

51 On the manuscript transmission, see Krusch's list in *VSE*, pp. 656–59, and see Westeel, 'Quelques remarques sur la *Vita Eligii*', pp. 41–43; Bayer, '*Vita Eligii*', pp. 463–64.

52 See Krusch in the *VSE*, p. 656, and the *Vita Landiberti vetustissima*, ed. by Krusch, pp. 353–84; Westeel, 'Quelques remarques sur la *Vita Eligii*', pp. 46–47.

where the author is critical of the monastic order in Francia (II, c. 21).[53] It is worth noting that one of these elements at least — the bishop's assumption of financial authority — modern scholarship would no longer regard as anachronistic.[54] The material concerning Pope Martin and his opposition to the monothelete heresy is also positioned at the wrong place chronologically. Although it describes events after 649, it is positioned at the end of Book 1 which covers Eligius's secular career before his consecration as bishop in 641. Bayer, however, argues that this material is a digression by the narrator, rather than an interpolation.[55]

The Martin Narrative in the Vita Eligii

The section in the *Vita Eligii* concerning the monothelete teaching, Pope Martin's resistance and death in exile, and the Lateran Synod of 649, forms an extended digression, justified partly by Eligius's selection for the mission to Rome, and by the need, as its author tells us, to keep the memory of Martin's sanctity alive.[56] The Martin narrative occupies 58 lines of text, with 18 of those devoted to defending the pope's martyr status. Its preoccupation with Martin's martyrdom is unusual, as we shall see, and the passage contains a number of other unique or unusual features.

The Martin narrative is introduced by a comment concerning the death of the great king Dagobert and the succession of his son, Clovis II. This functions as a chronological marker — in the days of Clovis, a wicked heresy arose in the East and became widespread, meaning the teaching of monotheletism. The *Vita* then describes how this teaching was opposed by Pope Martin who summoned a great council — the Lateran Synod of 649 — to defend the faith and suppress this heresy. He sent the synodal *acta* with a letter to the king of the Franks, and with a request that the king would send a delegation of learned men to Rome in support of the pope. Eligius and a companion were to have gone but were prevented by an unspecified hindrance.

At this point, the text launches into a long excursus, describing the pope's sufferings and defending his martyr status. The devil was roused against the Church and hoped to win Martin over to the side of heresy by attacking him. Martin resisted steadfastly and refused to obey the imperial command to promulgate the monothelete teaching. Despite his many injuries, including a public beating in Rome before its lamenting people, the pope could not be turned from his defence of the faith. Martin was then taken to Constantinople, tried and exiled. In exile, he performed miracles, such as healing a blind person, and suffering many torments before he died. Martin's claims to be considered a martyr are vigorously defended in a passage of great interest where the author addresses an imaginary tirade to the heretics who denied this. The *Vita* says first that the heretics responsible for Martin's ill treatment and exile — ashamed

---

53 Krusch's introduction to *VSE*, pp. 647–49 and *VSE*, pp. 682, 685, 688–91.
54 See the useful discussion in Westeel, 'Quelques remarques sur la *Vita Eligii*', pp. 39–40. However, Westeel follows Krusch in seeing the Martin narrative as a later interpolation.
55 Bayer, '*Vita Eligii*', pp. 468–70.
56 *VSE* I.33, pp. 689–90; I.34, pp. 690–91.

that they had martyred him — claim that he died peacefully and absolve themselves of the responsibility for the punishment that led to his death. Then, the heretics are addressed and berated: although Martin did not die by the executioner's sword, he died in exile, defending the faith. Martin is worthy to be ranked with the martyrs for the faith because the glory of those who die in the cause of orthodoxy is greater than that of those who perish at the hands of pagans, refusing to sacrifice to idols. Those who defend the faith, suffer for the whole Church while those who are killed by pagans are protecting their own salvation. The passage is a passionate attack on the heretics responsible for the pope's punishment.

A number of aspects of this narrative require comment. Its take upon the course of the monothelete controversy is idiosyncratic — the focus of its hostility is upon the emperor, his decrees and those who punished the pope, with no explicit mention of the religious leaders involved. Its account of the synod itself is brief and it is notable that the description of the heretical teaching does not mention the questions of two wills or operations but portrays it as denying that Christ took the 'form of a servant' and that he took his human flesh from the Virgin. The passage is also remarkable for its detail, for example, in dating events to the reign of the Emperor Constantine, and in the wealth of information about Martin's mistreatment and his miracle.

The main outlines of this account can either be corroborated or are consonant with contemporary sources, although a couple of details are erroneous. The debate over the teaching of one will in Christ predated the reign of Constans II. Originating in the reign of Heraclius, the controversy did, however, come to a head after the Emperor Constans II issued the *Typos* prohibiting any discussion of the doctrinal question of wills. The *Vita* names Constans II as Constantine which was his formal name, and was used on official documents and coins.[57] Although the brief summary of the heresy does not accurately represent the doctrinal issues at stake, it does echo the words of Pope Leo's *Tome* on the natures of Christ, and, as I will argue below, there are reasons to think that contemporaries did consider that monothelete teaching denied Mary's status as *Theotokos*, mother of God. While the Martin narrative errs in describing him as publicly beaten and paraded in chains in Rome, he did suffer similar tribulations in Constantinople.

Krusch was impelled to question the authenticity of the Martin narrative because he felt that its strong pro-papal stance and assumption of close relations between Francia and Rome was not a feature of seventh-century Church politics, but rather reflected the Carolingian era. In particular, he singled out in a note the claim in the *Vita* that the pope was honoured by the author's fellows (*collegis*) in Rome, remarking that this claim referred more probably to the time of Boniface.[58] However, the relations of the Merovingian Church with Rome have been reevaluated by a number of scholars including Hallinger, Ewig, Wallace-Hadrill, and Wood, who point to significant

57   Peeters, 'Une vie grecque', p. 228.
58   *VSE* I.34, p. 691: 'Haec Pseudo-Audoini verba potius aevo Bonifatiano respondent'.

evidence of an early attachment to the papacy.[59] There is no longer any strong reason to see the close links to Rome in the Martin narrative as a sign of later tampering.

Moreover, Krusch's suggested time of tampering, the eighth century, raises more problems than it solves. Why would an early Carolingian author wish to insert a lengthy vehement passage concerning Pope Martin? It is hard to find evidence of active interest in the pope and the monothelete controversy in Francia between the late seventh and ninth centuries. The controversy was settled in 680 at the Council of Constantinople where it is notable that the proceedings only refer to Martin once, a hint that his fate was discreetly overlooked.[60] Monotheletism did enjoy a short-lived resurgence in the East under the Emperor Phillipikos Bardanes (711–713), an episode which is likely to have been the stimulus to the composition of a Greek *Life* of Martin, written possibly in Rome itself. This was dependent upon a late seventh-century Greek record of the pope's sufferings, the *Narrationes de exilio sancti papae Martini*, and lacks the passionate insistence on Martin as a martyr.[61] But Martin's cult does not seem to have attracted special attention from Boniface or his Carolingian contemporaries.[62]

If the Martin narrative is a later confection, where did its creator find his information?[63] Many of its details and its particular stance upon events cannot be easily paralleled in the surviving sources. Two key Latin texts come to mind: the *Liber pontificalis*, and the Lateran Synod *acta*. Neither of these works shares the polemical character of the *Vita Eligii* concerning Martin's death, not even the *Liber pontificalis*. The latter makes the claim that the pope worked posthumous miracles in Chersonnese, without providing any description of an individual miracle and moreover makes no explicit claim as to his status as a martyr: 'Then the oft-mentioned holy man was sent into exile to the place called Chersona, where, as it pleased God, the life of this confessor of Christ ended in peace; and he works many miracles even to the present day'.[64] The wrath of the *Liber pontificalis* is prudently focused upon the patriarchs of Constantinople and it is relatively muted in its criticism of the emperor. While imperial orders to impose the *Typos* and subsequently to arrest Martin are reported, blame for the *Typos* is reserved for the Patriarch Paul who is described as having deceived 'the clement emperor' into promulgating it.[65] It is notable that the *Liber pontificalis*

---

59 Hallinger, 'Römische Voraussetzungen', pp. 320–61; Ewig, 'Der Petrus- und Apostelkult im spätromischen und fränkischen Gallien', II, 318–54; Wallace-Hadrill, *The Frankish Church*, pp. 110–22; Wood, *The Merovingian Kingdoms*, pp. 243–46.
60 Jankowiak, 'Essai d'histoire politique du monothéletisme', p. 420.
61 Peeters, 'Une vie grecque', pp. 225–62; Neil, *Seventh-Century Popes and Martyrs*, pp. 105–09; Mango, 'La culture grecque', pp. 703–04.
62 See the records of Martin's commemorations collected by Neil, *Seventh-Century Popes and Martyrs*, pp. 93–121(where the VSE is omitted, as are the relic tags evidencing the pope's cult discussed here at pp. 91–92).
63 Introduction to *VSE*, p. 654, Krusch cites a letter of Martin's and other documents as sources.
64 *Liber pontificalis*, ed. by Duchesne, I, p. 338: 'Deinde directus est sepiusdictus sanctissimus vir in exilio, in loco qui dicitur Cersona, et ibidem, ut Deo placuit, vitam finivit in pace, Christi confessor; qui et mirabilia operatur usque hodiernam diem'. *The Book of the Pontiffs*, trans. Davis, p. 70. On the *Liber pontificalis* account, see now McKitterick, 'The Papacy and Byzantium', pp. 241–73.
65 *The Book of the Pontiffs*, trans. by Davis, pp. 68–69; *Liber pontificalis*, ed. by Duchesne, I, p. 336.

never gives the emperor's name. The biography of Martin does describe the Lateran Synod in a little detail, providing the number of bishops in attendance and recording its condemnation of Cyrus of Alexandria, and the patriarchs of Constantinople: Sergius, Pyrrhus, and Paul.[66] The *Liber pontificalis* was, therefore, not a source for the Martin narrative in the *Vita Eligii* since the hagiography has details not in the papal biographies and fails to draw upon information provided there.

It is also unlikely that the Lateran Synod *acta* underlie the hagiographical narrative. Like the *Liber pontificalis*, they concentrate their condemnations upon the patriarchs of Constantinople and avoid explicit censure of the emperors. The *Vita Eligii* certainly did not derive its summary of the doctrinal issues at stake from the complex doctrinal statements in the *acta* since it makes no mention of the fundamental questions of the operations and wills of Christ.

Here it is helpful to compare the *Vita Eligii* with the additional statement annexed to the *Vita sancti Amandi* by the monk Milo, who was working in the middle of the ninth century at the saint's own foundation, Elnone/St Amand.[67] He had the advantage of access both to Martin's letter to the saint, which he copied from its original papyrus copy, and the Lateran *acta*. These he drew upon directly, together with the *Liber pontificalis*. He explicitly cites the papal biography of Martin, describing how the pope convened 105 bishops to his council in the Lateran, and citing its condemnations of Cyrus of Alexandria and the patriarchs of Constantinople, and its statement about Martin's dissemination of the *acta* to the East and West. Milo's purpose was to magnify the reputation of his hero, Amandus, through his association with Martin and the council; he was not concerned with the pope's sanctity and mentions neither his arrest nor death in exile. Milo's account of the theological issues derived directly from the *acta* and included a concise statement about the Christological controversies over operations and wills. His augmentation of the *Life of St Amand* with a description of the monothelete controversy is very different to the account found in the *Life of Eligius*. Milo relied closely upon identifiable, extant sources and did not deviate or add to them in any significant way. This contrasts with the Martin narrative where it is not only difficult to trace a Latin source but which also relates a markedly different story from either the *Liber pontificalis* or the Lateran *acta*.

Comparison with Seventh-Century Dyothelete Texts

A third, and the most fruitful, set of sources with which to compare the Martin narrative are the polemical texts produced in the aftermath of the imperial clampdown on the dyothelete agitators after the Lateran Synod. These texts were composed by Maximus and his partisans in the 650s and 660s.[68] They consist of records of the trials, exile and sufferings of Maximus and his followers, Anastasius Discipulus,

---

66 *Liber pontificalis*, ed. by Duchesne, I, pp. 336–37; *The Book of the Pontiffs*, trans. by Davis, p. 69.
67 *Vita sancti Amandi*, ed. by Krusch, pp. 451–52. And see Wood, *The Missionary Life*, pp. 39–42.
68 *Maximus the Confessor*, ed. by Allen and Neil, pp. 21–22; Neil, *Seventh-Century Popes and Martyrs*, pp. 95–115.

Anastasius Apocrisiarius and others, and of Pope Martin, plus letters from Maximus and his followers written after their arrest and exile to stiffen dyothelete resistance to imperial policy.[69] The production of these texts started early, very soon after the first trials and condemnations of Martin and Maximus in 655 to 656. They evince a strong determination to position the persecuted dyotheletes as saintly opponents of imperial persecution and to circulate texts recording and commemorating their afflictions at the hands of Byzantine officials. Maximus and his followers maintained a dogged propaganda war against their oppressors: he and the two Anastasiuses, corresponded in 658 in an attempt to prevent a papal compromise with the emperor.[70] The imperial response to their continued pamphleteering was savage: both were sentenced in 662 to amputation of their hands and tongues and exile.[71] Other texts show continuing devotion in the 660s to the exiled dyotheletes, recording the attempted visit by two brothers, Theodore Spoudaeus and Theodosius of Gangra to the exiled Anastasius. Theodore Spoudaeus also seems to have been responsible for the collection of writings pertaining to Martin, his trial, and exile.[72]

It is these dyothelete propaganda texts, composed in the 650s and 660s, which provide the closest parallels to the Martin narrative of the *Vita Eligii*. However, the fact that they were composed in Greek makes it very unlikely that they were its sources. Indeed, they may have been unknown in the Latin West until Anastasius Bibliothecarius, the papal librarian, translated a selection of them into Latin in the 870s.[73] In comparing the dyothelete propaganda with the Martin narrative in the *Vita Eligii*, it is helpful to distinguish between the first wave of writings in defence of Maximus, Martin, and other victims of Byzantine persecution produced in the 650s and before the death of many of leaders in the 660s, and that written by Theodore Spoudaeus in 668/669. The former had a number of purposes: to memorialize and diffuse records of their persecution by the emperor, to defend their reputations from the charges of treason laid against them, to drum up support and to stiffen dyothelete resolve against the pressure to accept the imperial position, especially with regard to subsequent negotiations and compromises. Thus, a letter to the monks of Cagliari in Sardinia written by Anastasius (either Maximus's disciple or the papal apocrisiary) after 655 required them to lobby Rome to prevent it from capitulating to new imperial negotiations.[74] Records of the trials of Martin and Maximus were also quickly composed and distributed. In the case of Martin, this was written by Theodore Spoudaeus, probably a monk of the Church of the Resurrection in Jerusalem,

69 *Maximus the Confessor*, ed. by Allen and Neil.
70 *Maximus the Confessor*, ed. by Allen and Neil, pp. 12–123, 'Letter of Maximus to Anastasius (April, 658)'; pp. 124–31, 'Letter of Anastasius to the Monks of Cagliari (after 658)'.
71 *Maximus the Confessor*, ed. by Allen and Neil, pp. 22–26.
72 *Maximus the Confessor*, ed. by Allen and Neil, pp. 148–71, Neil, *Seventh-Century Popes and Martyrs*, pp. 104–05.
73 Neil, *Seventh-Century Popes and Martyrs*, pp. 48–51. Mango thinks that the Greek *Life of Martin* was composed in Rome.
74 *Maximus the Confessor*, ed. by Allen and Neil, pp. 124–31, where the letter is dated after 658. Brandes suggests after 655.

who had known Martin in Rome. It seems likely that this was initially composed before the pope's death in attempt to relieve his dire situation in the Chersonnese by winning assistance and supplies for him.[75] It was subsequently updated with a notice of Martin's death and burial at the church of St Mary Blachernes, Cherson; the pope is eulogized for his endurance in fighting for the faith and called a martyr.

The theme of martyrdom for the faith becomes much more pronounced in a second commemorative text composed by Theodore Spoudaeus in late 668 or early 669. This, the *Hypomnesticon*, is an account of his journey to succour two other dyothelete victims of imperial persecution. In the course of his travels, Theodore Spoudaeus learnt of the tribulations and ends of the other protagonists, Maximus, his two followers — Anastasius Discipulus and Anastasius Apocrisiarius — and of Martin. The *Hypomnesticon* is effectively a collection of martyr narratives about Maximus and his disciples and about Martin, asserting their sanctity, and recording personal items as relics of these men: books and writings of Maximus and Anastasius, including the twigs which they use continue to write after their hands had been amputated.[76] The *Hypomnesticon* also reported a miraculous display of lights at the tomb of Maximus.[77] Martin's sanctity and status is emphatically asserted: the exiled Theodore told Spoudaeus 'very many miracles of Martin', and gave him a piece of towel or handkerchief belonging to the pope and one of his papal boots.

> This was because Martin too had been exiled there after terrible sufferings while he was being conveyed from Rome. He handed himself over, eagerly desiring and longing passionately to be martyred for Christ's sake, both as an imitator and successor of holy Peter, chief of the Apostles, both during the sea voyage and in Byzantium itself. The upshot was that he was hit publicly by the enemies of God, who are worthy of their father the devil, and he was stripped of his clothes, and, too, heavy irons and chains were put around both his holy neck and the rest of his precious limbs. Then they lead him with the same irons in procession [...].[78]

The *Hypomnesticon* is a manifesto for the martyr status of those who had suffered in the fight against monotheletism. It is particularly insistent with regard to Martin, who had been subject to harsh and cruel treatment at the hands of imperial officials, but not the vicious and life-threatening punishment of mutilation. Martin died at least a year after his exile so the connection between Byzantine judicial brutality and his

---

75 On the identity of Theodore Spoudaeus, see Booth, *Crisis of Empire*, p. 302 n. 111, following Noret, 'À qui était destiné la lettre BHG 1233d d'Anastase Apocrisiaire?'; 'The *Narrationes de Exilio Sancti Martini Papae*', in Neil, *Seventh-Century Popes and Martyrs*, pp. 95–99, 166–233.

76 *Maximus the Confessor*, ed. by Allen and Neil, pp. 150–53, 154–55, 164–65.

77 *Maximus the Confessor*, ed. by Allen and Neil, pp. 162–63.

78 *Maximus the Confessor*, ed. by Allen and Neil, pp. 158–59: [...] διὰ τὸ καὶ αὐτὸν ἐκεῖσε ἐξόριστον γενέσθαι μετὰ τὸ πάνδεινα παθεῖν αὐτὸν ἐν τῷ παραπέμπεσθαι ἀπὸ Ῥώμης, ἑαυτὸν προδεδωκότα, ὀρεγόμενον καὶ ἐπιποθοῦντα πάνυ τὸ ὑπὲρ Χριστοῦ μαρτύριον, ὡς μιμητής τε καὶ διάδοχος τοῦ ἁγίου καὶ κορυφαίου τῶν ἀποστόλων Πέτρον, κατὰ τὸν πλοῦν τε καὶ ἐν αὐτῷ τῷ Βυζαντίῳ, ὥστε καὶ κατὰ πεδίον κοσσισθῆναι αὐτὸν παρὰ τῶν ἐχθρῶν τοῦ Θεοῦ, ἀξίων δὲ τοῦ πατρὸς αὐτῶν τοῦ διαβόλου, τῆς τε ἐσθῆτος αὐτοῦ γυμνωθέντος, καὶ βαρυσιδήρων καὶ ἀλύσεων περιτεθέντων τῷ τε ἁγίῳ αὐτοῦ τραχήλῳ καὶ τοῖς λοιποῖς αὐτοῦ τιμίοις μέλεσιν, εἶτα σὺν αὐτοῖς τοῖς σιδήροις πομπεύσαντος πᾶσαν τὴν μέσην[...].

demise was less direct than it had been for the mutilated Maximus and his followers. Describing how the death sentence on the pope was commuted to exile, he noted that Martin was eager for death in the cause of righteousness:

> In fact this [death] would already have happened as far as both his [Martin's] bold readiness and his purpose [were concerned], if the decisive intervention of God, who loves human beings and is supremely good, had not checked them, or the adversaries had not become ashamed by Martin's almighty bravery. I say this because even hard and inhuman tyrants are perhaps capable of experiencing even this, although they are excessively merciless and cruel in the manner of Satan who operated in them. Or they begrudged [him] martyrdom, in the manner of one similar to themselves, the apostate Julian, who was crazy about idols: that infamous man, truly wise in evil matters [...].[79]

It is likely that the Byzantine authorities were anxious not to give their enemies the charisma of martyrdom and therefore pulled back from the death penalty. Indeed, the prosecuting cases against both Martin and Maximus were not based upon their doctrinal views but rather upon activities indicative of treason.[80]

The Martin narrative in the *Vita Eligii* has significant points of contact with the *Hypomnesticon*, particularly with regard to its vehement insistence upon his place as a martyr. Like the *Hypomnesticon* and other polemical dyothelete texts — and unlike the *Liber pontificalis* and Lateran Synod *acta* — it vilifies the emperor and his officials as doing the work of Satan.[81] The Martin narrative provides a crude and over-simplified understanding of the teaching of one will and operation, equating it with a denial that Christ took human flesh, and a blasphemy against the Virgin Mary, a far cry from the complex writings of Maximus and the extensive theological discussions of the 649 *acta*. However, it may have reflected contemporary sensibilities. The statement that Christ did not take the form of a servant is a reference to the *Tome* of Pope Leo in the proceedings of the Council of Chalcedon, a touchstone of western orthodoxy.[82] The dyothelete case asserted and made much of the idea that the teachings of the patriarchs of Constantinople were innovations and a betrayal of Chalcedon. Moreover, any teaching that appeared to diminish or deny Christ's full humanity could be seen not only as an attack on his incarnation, but also on the Virgin Mary as the bearer

79 *Maximus the Confessor*, ed. by Allen and Neil, pp. 158–61: Ὁ καὶ ἤδη γέγονεν ἂν ὅσον τῇ εὐθάρσῳ αὐτοῦ προθυμίᾳ τε καὶ προθέσει, εἰ μὴ ἡ τοῦ φιλανθρώπου καὶ ὑπεραγάθου Θεοῦ ῥοπὴ τούτους ἀνέστειλεν, ἢ τῇ τούτου πολυ[α]σθενεῖ ἀνδρείᾳ αἰδεσθέντων τῶν καὶ ἀντιπάλων (οἴδασιν γὰρ καὶ τοῦτο πάσχειν πολλάκις καὶ τύραννοι ἀπηνεῖς καὶ ἀπάνθρωποι, εἰ καὶ λίαν εἰσὶν ἄσπλαγχνοι καὶ ὠμοὶ κατὰ τὸν ἐν αὐτοῖς ἐνεργοῦντα Σατᾶν), ἢ τῷ μαρτυρίῳ φθονησάντων κατὰ τὸν ὅμοιον αὐτῶν ἀποστάτην καὶ εἰδωλομανῆ Ἰουλιανὸν ἐκεῖνον τὸν περιβόητον καὶ ὄντως σοφὸν ἐν τοῖς κακοῖς [...].

80 Neil, *Seventh-Century Popes and Martyrs*, 'Letter of Martin', c. 9, pp. 181, 190–91, 200–05. See Booth, *Crisis*, pp. 300–06; Brandes, '"Juristische" Krisenbewältigung', pp. 141–212.

81 Neil, *Seventh-Century Popes and Martyrs*, e.g., 'Narrationes', p. 204, describing how Martin was mocked in Constantinople: 'Pauci autem ministrorum Satanae, gaudebant et subsannabant et capita transeuntes[...]', *Hypomnesticon*, p. 246: 'nimis immisericordes sint et crudeles secundum eum qui operatur in illis Satan[...]'.

82 *The Acts of the Council of Chalcedon*, trans. by Price and Gaddis, II.22, pp. 14–24 (p. 18).

of God. Indeed, Maximus himself was accused of 'blaspheming against the Mother of God' by soldiers in Selymbria in 656, suggesting that his complex Christological views were similarly misrepresented in a hostile fashion amongst the laity.[83]

While the Martin narrative is wrong in its claim that the pope was publicly beaten in Rome and paraded bound in chains, these details could ultimately derive from misunderstood depictions of Martin's sufferings such as those in the Greek sources, the *Narrationes* and the *Hypomnesticon*. The pope in fact was removed at night from the city to avoid a disturbance; however accounts of his time under arrest in Constantinople stress the callous way in which the suffering and sick pope was left exposed to public view, and how he was loaded with chains after his condemnation.[84] It is possible therefore that the description in the *Vita Eligii* ultimately derives from a report of Martin's humiliation and ill treatment in Constantinople, which was wrongly transferred to his removal from Rome.

The parallels between the seventh-century dyothelete texts, particularly the *Hypomnesticon*, and the Martin narrative are important. They alone provide the details of how shamefully he was treated when in Byzantine custody and describe him as a martyr. The *Vita Eligii*'s passionate defence of Martin as a martyr and haranguing against the heretics deemed responsible for his eventual demise fits much better with the tone of the dyothelete polemic. Moreover, the claim of the Martin narrative that some tried to deny his martyr status is matched only in the *Hypomnesticon* which, as we have seen, compares the pope's oppressors to Julian the Apostate who claimed that the Christian martyrs had been killed not for their faith but for their criminal activities.

It is very unlikely that either the *Hypomnesticon* itself or the *Narrationes* underlies the Martin narrative since they were composed in Greek. But what of the assertion of the *Vita Eligii* that the narrative is based upon an eyewitness account of a visitor from the East: 'Novimus quendam fratrem a partibus orientis venientem, qui ea quae narro se coram posito gesta esse testabatur'.[85] There is nothing inherently implausible about such a claim. The writings of Theodore Spoudaeus bear witness to the desire of the surviving dyotheletes to publicize their cause. The description of Martin's trial and tribulations in the *Narrationes*, probably initially composed to seek assistance for the pope in exile, describes itself as a letter 'sent to those orthodox fathers who are in the West or Rome or Africa', indicating that Maximus's followers sought a wider audience for their views than Rome and the Eastern Empire.[86] There were two possible ways in which a supporter might have told his tale to Audoin, or to the author of the Martin narrative. The first would see him as a traveller from the east encountered in Francia itself; the second possibility would be that such a contact could have taken place in Rome.

---

83 *Maximus the Confessor*, ed. by Allen and Neil, pp. 114–15.

84 Neil, *Seventh-Century Popes and Martyrs*, pp. 180–81, 191–93, 203–07.

85 *VSE* I.34, lines 19–20, p. 690: "We got to know a certain brother who came from eastern parts and who bore witness that the things which I am narrating took place in his presence".

86 Neil, *Seventh-Century Popes and Martyrs*, pp. 182–83, 'directam his qui sunt in Occidente seu Romae et Africa orthodoxis patribus'.

How did Audoin hear this Dyothelete Account?

Frankish Contacts with the Eastern Empire in the Seventh Century

Contacts with Constantinople and the East are well attested for the sixth century and reveal that the Byzantine emperors could act as a significant force in Frankish affairs. For example, the Merovingian royal claimant, Gundovald, took flight from Francia to Italy and thence eventually to Constantinople, where he remained in exile, plotting his return on one occasion with a visiting Frankish aristocrat. In 582/583 he launched a coup with imperial backing, arriving in Francia at Marseilles.[87] Such political connections took place within a broader context of contact and communications, especially Francia's involvement in a Mediterranean-wide exchange network.

The seventh century saw a decline in cross-Mediterranean contacts, particularly from the 630s, but commercial and cultural exchange did not cease altogether. Loseby's work on Marseilles, the key entrepôt for Mediterranean goods, charts a gradual deterioration.[88] The city's role in international trade and especially the import of eastern luxuries was closely controlled and exploited by Merovingian rulers. Dagobert I issued a privilege to the monastery of St Denis, granting an annual rent on royal tolls at Marseilles which was to be used to buy oil from the royal warehouse.[89] A similar grant was issued to Corbie by Chlothar III, and the St Denis privilege was by Clovis III and Chilperic in 691 and 716, although by the latter date, it may have become an empty letter. Numismatic evidence shows that Mediterranean trade at Marseilles continued to be profitable for Frankish rulers in the mid-seventh century. A special gold coinage was issued in the late sixth century at four cities, including Marseilles, and continued into the seventh century. Loseby associates it with the diffusion of goods via Marseilles.[90] The *Vita* of Eligius itself provides evidence of eastern contacts — in one miracle, the saint rescues a member of the household of the bishop of Uzés in difficulty with his camel; in another vignette, Eligius is praised for his redemption of foreign slaves, whose identity includes 'Mauros'. He invited the redeemed slaves to join his own household or to enter monasteries.[91]

Archaeological and numismatic evidence also shows a shift from an exchange network spread across the whole Mediterranean to one increasingly focused upon Africa. Excavations in Marseilles demonstrates that African amphorae dominate the

---

87   Wood, *The Merovingian Kingdoms*, pp. 93–96; Gregory of Tours, *Decem Libri Historiarum*, ed. by Krusch and Levison, VI, c. 24 and, VII, c. 36; Goffart, 'Byzantine Policy in the West', pp. 73–118. And for wider contacts, see Ewig, *Die Merowinger und das Imperium*.

88   Useful surveys by Loseby, 'The Mediterranean Economy', pp. 605–38; and his 'Post-Roman Economies', pp. 334–60.

89   *Gesta Dagoberti I regis Francorum*, ed. by Krusch, c. 18, pp. 406–07. See n. 117 for discussion of these.

90   Loseby, 'Marseille: A Late Antique Success Story?', pp. 175–77; Loseby, 'Marseille and the Pirenne Thesis I', pp. 203–30 (pp. 224–25); Loseby, 'Marseille and Pirenne Thesis II', pp. 167–94 (pp. 183–84); Loseby, 'The Mediterranean Economy', pp. 634–37. And see below p. 94.

91   *VSE* I.10, p. 677.

ceramic record in the sixth century, attaining a 'virtual monopoly' in the seventh.[92] North Africa could act as a hinge between the eastern and western Mediterranean. The *Doctrina Iacobi*, a Greek polemical text probably written in the early 640s, describes how a Jewish merchant, commissioned by a businessman in Constantinople to sell textiles, sold these in Carthage but also considered Gaul a likely market.[93] When Pope Martin was tried in Constantinople, his interpreter was named as Innocent the Consul, the son of Thomas, from Africa.[94] North Africa had been an important place of refuge for opponents of the imperial religious policy: it served as a base for Maximus and his followers in the 630s and 640s who seem to have stirred up resistance there.[95] In 645–646, two African councils condemned the imperial theological position. In July 645, a public disputation between Maximus the Confessor and the former patriarch of Constantinople, Pyrrhus, a leading monothelete, had taken place in Carthage. The revolt of the Exarch George in *c.* 647 against the emperor seems to have enjoyed the support of Maximus and Pope Theodore.[96]

It is therefore by no means impossible or implausible that a refugee or traveller from the Eastern Empire might have found his way to Francia in the seventh century. A possible route would have been from North Africa to Marseilles, and thence north up the Rhône. The Arab conquests of the 640s together with imperial persecution of dyotheletism may have led some to flee across the Mediterranean Sea. The hoarded wealth of one such refugee may have been deposited as an offering in the church foundations of St Vincent in Couladère (Cazères, Haute-Garonne). An excavation at the church revealed a deposit of over twenty bronze coins almost certainly minted at Carthage in the sixth and seventh centuries, including 3 coins of Heraclius and 6 of Constans II. These coins must have been collected in Carthage and hoarded after 660.[97] It is therefore possible that the Martin narrative represents an eyewitness report from an eastern émigré whom Audoin encountered in Francia.

A Roman Source for the Dyothelete Account of Martin?

However, Audoin could have received a report about the death of Martin when he visited Rome in the 670s, a possibility strengthened by the fact that Audoin was working on the *Vita* at exactly this time. Moreover, this was also a particularly difficult period in relations between Rome and Constantinople. Eugenius's hostile

92   Loseby, 'Marseille: A Late Antique Success Story?', at p. 172. See also Loseby, 'Marseille and the Pirenne Thesis I', p. 214; Loseby, 'The Mediterranean Economy', p. 616. See, for example, the shipwreck at Anse St-Gervais, Parker, *Ancient Shipwrecks*, no. 1001, pp. 372–73, dated *c.* 600–25, but Loseby gives a later date. Lafaurie and Morrisson, 'La penetration', pp. 38–98, esp. at p. 54.

93   Dagron and Déroche, 'Juifs et Chrétiens du VIIe siècle', pp. 17–273; *Doctrina Iacobi*, in 'Juifs et Chrétiens du VIIe siècle', V, 20, pp. 212–13, and p. 247 for the dating of the text.

94   Neil, *Seventh-Century Popes and Martyrs*, pp. 198–99.

95   Booth, *Crisis of Empire*, pp. 284–90; Jankowiak, 'Essai d'histoire politique du monothéletisme'.

96   *The Acts of the Lateran Synod*, trans. by Price, pp. 53–54.

97   Labrousse, 'La trouvaille de monnaies byzantines', pp. 99–108. See also the finds of seventh-century Byzantine coins catalogued by Lafaurie and Morrisson, 'La pénetration', pp. 54–55, and map 3 for finds at Gruisson, Boutenac, and also Mons, in Belgium.

stance had been moderated by his successor, Vitalian, who was reconciled to the emperor, receiving Constans II with honour in Rome in July 663.[98] However, the emperor used his sojourn in Rome to despoil it of valuable resources and sacred equipment.[99] In 666, Byzantine relations with Rome deteriorated when he confirmed a privilege of the Church of Ravenna, diminishing Rome's authority over its archbishops. Constans was assassinated in Sicily in 668, where he had moved his court. Despite Constans II's highhanded actions towards Rome, Pope Vitalian gave loyal support to his son, Constantine IV, when a revolt arose in the aftermath of the murder.[100]

Tensions between Rome and Constantinople manifest themselves in the 670s when Popes Vitalian and Adeodatus refused the *synodica* of the successive Patriarchs John and Constantine. These would have been dispatched after November 669 for John and September 675 for Constantine. This rift may have been caused by renewed opposition to imperial monotheletism or to the diminution of papal authority and dignity resulting from the imperial privilege to Ravenna.[101] Whatever the cause it is notable that these frosty relations occurred during Audoin's visit to Rome. Vitalian may have been careful to maintain support for the emperor, seen in his backing Constantine over the usurper Mezezius in 669, but there may have been wider hostility to the emperor in the city. The biography of Pope Vitalian in the *Liber pontificalis* denounced the depredations of Constans II in Sicily and, as Marek Jankowiak has suggested, the report (possibly erroneous) in the *Life of Deodatus* that the Roman bronze and booty removed to Sicily had fallen into the hands of the Arabs underlines the sacrilege of Constans' despoliations in Rome.[102] The flight of eastern monks to Rome in the seventh century had led to the establishment there of a number of Greek monasteries, some with affiliations to communities in Jerusalem. Members of these houses formed a core of opposition to monotheletism at the Lateran Synod of 649 and it is likely that many continued to oppose imperial doctrine.[103] The future archbishop of Canterbury, Theodore of Tarsus, is likely to have been a member of this circle and probably attended the Lateran Synod. He had fled to Rome and was probably a monk at St Sabas there: his theological prowess as a dyothelete expert was remembered in 678.[104] The friction in papal Rome over Ravennese autonomy and possibly over monotheletism may have intersected with the propaganda campaign waged by the partisans of Maximus the Confessor who were, at least in 668, proclaiming their heroes, Martin, Maximus, and the two Anastasiuses as martyrs. According to his *Vita*,

---

98 *Liber pontificalis*, ed. by Duchesne, I, p. 341; *The Book of the Pontiffs*, trans. by Davis, p. 71; Jankowiak, 'Essai d'histoire politique du monothéletisme', pp. 327–40.

99 *Liber pontificalis*, ed. by Duchesne, I, pp. 343–44, *The Book of the Pontiffs*, trans. by Davis, pp. 71–72.

100 Llewellyn, *Rome in the Dark Ages*, p. 158; Richards, *The Popes and the Papacy*, pp. 196–97; Jankowiak, 'Essai d'histoire politique du monothéletisme', p. 387.

101 Richards, *The Popes and the Papacy*, pp. 196–97, suggests that doctrinal differences were the cause, where Jankowiak, 'Essai d'histoire politique du monothéletisme', pp. 373–87, sees anger over Ravenna.

102 Jankowiak, 'Essai d'histoire politique du monothéletisme', p. 363.

103 Sansterre, *Les Moines grecs et orientaux à Rome*, I, pp. 13–39; Booth, *Crisis of Empire*, pp. 111, 290.

104 See above n. 103.

Audoin spent his time in Rome, visiting the shrines of the saints.[105] This devotional tour may have given rise to discussion of Martin's claims to sanctity, particularly if it took in the church of St Maria Antiqua where wall paintings depicted Popes Martin and Leo, and included texts from the Lateran Council *acta*.[106]

This scenario in which Audoin was in Rome when told about the tribulations and death of Martin, hearing this from partisans of the dyothelete cause, makes sense of the comment that concludes the Martin narrative, describing how the author included this within the *Vita* so that the memory of the pope would not fade:

> Ut tam eximii viri memoria, quia utique collegis meis in urbe Romana multa inpendit bona, quamvis in Oriente frequentetur, non usquequaque in Occidente oblivione tradatur.[107]

It is interesting to note that the author explicitly comments on the eastern commemoration of the pope in contrast with the western. Perhaps Audoin returned from Rome in 675 and felt impelled by his experiences there to insert this commemoration into his *Vita* of Eligius. This hypothesis for the origins of the Martin narrative and its passage into Audoin's hagiography is necessarily circumstantial but it is, I would argue, at least as plausible as a transmission of this account in the early eighth century. The case is strong for attributing the Martin narrative in the *Vita* to an eastern source, probably encountered by Audoin in Rome before 675.

The Cult of Pope Martin in Francia

Some support for this is provided by fragmentary evidence for devotion to Martin as a martyr in Francia. The relic collections surviving from the monastery of Chelles and from St Pierre Le Vif at Sens retained their early medieval tags recording the identity of the saints concerned. Roughly 150 labels survive from Chelles, the earliest from the eighth century. One amongst these bears the inscription 'Reliquias sancti Martini papa Romensis et marteres', dating to the first half of the eighth century. At Sens, the relic tags date from the late seventh or early eighth century: one dating from this time refers to a relic of St Martin the Martyr.[108] Not only do these two tags demonstrate culting of Martin as a martyr by the late seventh or early eighth century but they also point indirectly to the circle of Eligius and Audoin through Queen Balthild.

---

105 *Vita Audoini episcopi Rotomagensis*, ed. by Levison, pp. 536–67, esp. c. 10, pp. 559–60. Intriguingly, Audoin's biographer claims that he was inflamed by desire to visit Rome, 'semper eius mens ob amorem trinitatis in caelestibus anelaret'. And see Gerberding and Fouracre, *Late Merovingian France*, p. 151.

106 Rubery, 'Papal Opposition to Imperial Heresies', pp. 3–29.

107 *VSE* I.34, p. 691, 'so that the memory of so extraordinary a man — because assuredly he granted many good things in the city of Rome, although he is often commemorated in the East — should not be entirely consigned to oblivion in the west'. With thanks to Shelagh Sneddon for her advice on this and the other translations from the Latin.

108 McCormick, *Origins of the European Economy*, pp. 283–312. The tags have most recently been published by Atsma and Vezin in *Chartae Latinae Antiquiores* (hereafter *ChLA*), XVIII for Sens and XIX for Chelles. The Martin tags are *ChLA* XVIII, no. 38 and *ChLA* XIX, no. 80.

For Chelles was the refoundation and eventual refuge of Queen Balthild, the queen of Clovis II and, as widow, regent for his son Chlothar III and close associate of the two bishops.[109] Such was her reverence for Eligius that she attempted to obtain his holy corpse for veneration at Chelles; she had to content herself with ornamenting his shrine with her jewels.[110] She was a generous patron and devotee of relic cults. She and her monasteries, Chelles and Corbie, had close links with Columbanian foundations and, as we will see, so did Audoin and Eligius. Balthild also attempted to reform the religious life at a number of 'seniores basilicae' in the kingdom, imposing the monastic life and establishing immunities from episcopal control. One of these churches is likely to have been St Pierre le Vif at Sens.[111]

The Context of the Frankish Response

Audoin's use of an eastern dyothelete account can be contextualized with contemporary Frankish contacts with the Byzantine Empire, recently illuminated by Stefan Esders. In two detailed and penetrating studies of Fredegar's *Chronicle*, Esders has shown how its author had access to a contemporary Greek account critical of the Emperor Heraclius.[112] The *Chronicle*, which was first compiled *c.* 660, has long been famous for its early and detailed knowledge of events in the Byzantine Empire, including the earliest extant description of the Battle of Yarmuk in 636.[113] While Fredegar deploys his information cleverly to provide an implicit critique of the Frankish king, Dagobert, misunderstandings in his narrative indicate his close reliance on his underlying source. Esders shows that this was derived from a written Greek narrative, hostile to the emperor, which portrayed him in an eschatological framework and blamed the emperor's personal sin for the Arab conquests over imperial territory. Heraclius is castigated for his incestuous marriage to his niece, and for his adoption the heresy of Eutyches, a reference to his imperial support for monotheletism.[114] Esders concludes that this Greek account probably originated in dyothelete circles in Rome after the 649 Lateran Synod.

The Greek account of Heraclius embedded in Fredegar's Chronicle shares with the Martin narrative in the *Vita Eligii* a hostility to the Byzantine emperors whom both accounts portray as opposed to orthodoxy. But the two narratives are independent

109 Wood, *The Merovingian Kingdoms*, pp. 197–200; Nelson, 'Queens as Jezebels', pp. 32–34.
110 *VSE* II.41, p. 725.
111 *Vita sancti Balthildis*, ed. by Krusch, pp. 475–508; Nelson, 'Queens as Jezebels', pp. 38–41. Dierken, 'Prolégomènes à une histoire', II, p. 389 and Nelson, 'Queens as Jezebels', at p. 40 for the identification of Balthild's senior basilica of St Pierre as Sens; Wood, *The Merovingian Kingdoms*, is more cautious, p. 200.
112 Esders, 'The Prophesied Rule'; Esders, 'Herakleios, Dagobert und die "beschnittenen Völker"', pp. 239–311.
113 *The Fourth Book of the Chronicle of Fredegar*, ed. by Wallace-Hadrill; see Kaegi, *Byzantium and the Early Islamic Conquests*, p. 125; Wood, 'Fredegar's Fables', pp. 359–66.
114 Esders, 'The Prophesied Rule', p. 23. It is interesting to note here the suggestion of Wood that Fredegar might have had links with Columbanian monasticism, 'Fredegar's Fables', p. 360.

of each other — the final condemnation in Fredegar of Heraclius as an Eutychian is the only reference to imperial religion in that text and it lacks any mention of papal opposition. Moreover, Esders's extended arguments concerning Fredegar's account of Heraclius go beyond the provision of a parallel case of eastern borrowing to offer an important political context to *Vita*'s information about Martin's contacts with Francia in the aftermath of the Lateran Synod.

According to Fredegar, the Emperor Heraclius and Dagobert agreed a 'treaty of perpetual peace'.[115] Although, the Chronicler does not elaborate on the provisions of this alliance, Esders argues convincingly that it had a dual purpose. The two rulers seem to have agreed a joint policy towards the Slavs, Avars, and other pagan peoples living on the borders of their dominions. Dagobert was to extend his rule over the neighbouring peoples up to the western frontier of the empire. In 626 the Avars had joined with the Persians in besieging the city of Constantinople. After Heraclius's defeat of the Persians and the conclusion of the siege, the emperor turned his attention to his eastern frontier and to the Avars. It seems that his pact with Dagobert was part of this policy. But it was allied to militant Christianization of pagans and those who did not conform to orthodox Christianity. Heraclius proclaimed a policy of the forced conversion of the Jews which, according to Fredegar, Dagobert adopted within his kingdom. Dagobert's corresponding policy of enforced Christianization extended to all those outside the true faith. The *Vita sancti Amandi* describes how the saint successively applied to the king for permission to enforce baptism upon the lapsed Christian inhabitants of the Ghent region which in 629/630 he was proselytizing. Shortly after this, having completed his mission beyond the Scheldt, the saint departed for a mission to the Slavs beyond the Danube, a project which Esders connects to Dagobert's expansionist policy on the eastern borders of his kingdom. These endeavours collapsed in 633 when the Franks were defeated by the Wends and St Amandus — shaking the dust from his feet — moved on to work with the Basques. Christian mission was an integral part of a joint agreement between Dagobert and Heraclius aimed at expanding their Christian dominions; the work of Amandus in northern Francia and across the Danube was therefore motivated and facilitated by this shared vision of Christian universality. This vision moreover embraced not only Jews and pagans, but all outside the orthodox Christian community, including lapsed Christians and heretics.[116]

Esders's demonstration of the significant links between Francia and the Byzantine Empire in the period *c. 620–c. 660* underlines the endurance of close connections across the Mediterranean world, between Constantinople and the empire, Rome and Francia in the seventh century. Moreover, they emphasize that these were not limited to the exchange of luxury goods or of information but had profound implications for political and religious policy. They also place the involvement of Eligius and Amandus in the aftermath of the Lateran Synod in an important new light.

---

115   *The Fourth Book*, ed. by Wallace-Hadrill, c. 62, pp. 51, 'pacem perpetuam'.
116   Esders, '*Nationes quam plures nam conquiri*', pp. 285–91.

Eligius, Audoin, and Amandus and Imperial and Papal Policy

The report in the *Vita Eligii* that Martin sent the Lateran Synod *acta* to Francia with a letter asking for the support of the Frankish king and his learned men parallels the letter to Amandus requesting the convocation of a synod and the dispatch of an embassy to Rome which could also travel to Constantinople. The *Vita* states that Eligius (and probably Audoin) wished to be involved but was unable to participate. It is important to note that Eligius was already bishop of Noyon in 649 (the *Vita* displaces this episode to his previous lay career) so that his potential involvement agrees with Martin's request in the letter to Amandus for an episcopal legation. Why does the *Vita Eligii* single out this episode in relation to Eligius? The dramatic events surrounding the Lateran Synod are only rather nebulously linked to the saint by his desire to be involved in the Neustrian response. Why did Pope Martin write expressly to St Amandus about the synod? These are important questions concerning the intricate web of political and religious factors connecting Francia, Rome, and the Eastern Empire in the seventh century.

Eligius's involvement should be related to his experience and contacts not only as a prominent bishop but in also to his earlier roles as a lay counsellor and court goldsmith. His activities in Provence were not limited to the purchase of slaves or to networking trips that also facilitated the good behaviour of camels. As goldsmith at court, he acted as a moneyer and was one of those responsible for the exceptional issues of gold coins at Marseilles linked to Mediterranean trade which was mentioned above. Eligius's issues are distinctive in their maintenance of an unusually high gold content and, since these issues did not bear the name of a moneyer, in carrying his name.[117] The fiscal involvements of the saint suggest that he must have taken part in negotiations with both royal agents and visiting merchants in Provence. We should view him as a cosmopolitan figure, recruiting foreign slaves, including Moors, to his entourage and monasteries, and doing business with overseas traders. His Breton mission demonstrated his role as a diplomat.[118] His exemplary piety earned him an international reputation so that, according to the *Vita*, legations 'ex Romana vel Italica aut Gothica vel qualecumque provintia' sought his presence first before attending upon the king.[119] Does 'Romana' here signal Rome or the Eastern Empire? Eligius was in service at court in 629 and therefore could possibly have been involved in the king's negotiations with the Eastern Emperor. He was certainly directly involved in their outcome: Heraclius seems to have sent a relic of the True Cross to Dagobert which the king had enshrined at St-Denis, commissioning his court goldsmith to construct a special container for it.[120]

---

117 Loseby, 'Marseille and the Pirenne Thesis II', pp. 183–84; Lafaurie, 'Eligius monetarius', pp. 111–51.
118 VSE I, 13, p. 680 and see *The Fourth Book*, ed. by Wallace-Hadrill, c. 78, pp. 65–67, and Wood, *The Merovingian Kingdoms*, p. 160. On captives, see *VSE* I.10, p. 677.
119 VSE I.10, pp. 676–77.
120 Esders, '*Nationes quam plures nam conquiri*', p. 290; Vierk, 'Werke des Eligius', pp. 319–27, 368–78.

Columbanian Networks, the Papacy, and Mission

Like Eligius, Amandus was a politically prominent figure. Martin was adept in approaching him to lobby King Sigibert III to send a delegation since the saint was the king's godfather. Moreover, Amandus had been an essential agent in Dagobert's schemes for aggressive missionary work, a policy arising out of the king's treaty with Heraclius. Martin's choice of a go-between was therefore politically acute. Amandus was presumably known to the pope through his earlier visits to Rome. His *Vita* records that he owed his missionary vocation to a vision of St Peter on his first sojourn in Rome, sometime before 629. Amandus made a second visit to Rome, at some point before deciding to work beyond the Scheldt.[121] The missionary also enjoyed connections with Eligius and Audoin, since these men were responsible for persuading him to overcome his scruples about Dagobert's sexual misconduct in order to baptize his son, Sigibert III.[122] The links between these three men were probably also strengthened by a network of religious figures associated with the spread of Columbanian monasticism.[123] Amandus was assisted in the mission field beyond the Scheldt by Jonas, a former monk of Columbanus's Italian foundation of Bobbio and author of the *Vita sancti Columbani*.[124] Audoin's family had been inspired to found a number of important religious communities by an encounter with Columbanus himself; Audoin's own foundation was at Rebais.[125] Audoin's *Vita* of Eligius describes Luxeuil, Columbanus's major foundation in Francia, as the premier Frankish monastery noting the recruitment of its monks for the Solignac community.[126]

These Columbanian circles have been associated with the promotion of a distinctive ideology of mission that sought the conversion of all *gentes*.[127] Fritze linked these to papal ideas of mission initiated by Gregory the Great. Esders has shown how this idea of universal mission owed at least as much to eastern imperial ideas and activities under Heraclius, and was promoted by Pope Honorius under imperial impetus.[128] Amandus's own activities were motivated, as we have seen, both by papal and imperial stimuli.

The links between those involved in Columbanian monasticism and the papacy were strong. Columbanus's own relations with the papacy may have been tense since he rebuked the popes for their support of the imperial side in the Three Chapters

---

121 *Vita sancti Amandi*, ed. by Krusch, cc. 7–8, 10–12, pp. 434–36. Wood, *The Missionary Life*, pp. 39–40.
122 *Vita sancti Amandi*, ed. by Krusch, c. 17, pp. 440–41.
123 On Columbanian monasticism, see Prinz, *Frühes Mönchtum*, pp. 121–51, and now Fox, *Power and Religion in Merovingian Gaul*; also see Wood, 'The Irish in England and Continent, Part I', pp. 171–98 and p. 27; and his 'The Irish in England and Continent, Part II', pp. 189–214.
124 Wood, *The Missionary Life*, pp. 37–38; Wood, 'The *Vita Columbani*', pp. 63–80.
125 Wallace-Hadrill, *The Frankish Church*, pp. 68–69.
126 *VSE* I.21, p. 685.
127 Fritze, '*Universalis gentium confessio*'; Wood, *The Missionary Life*, pp. 39–42.
128 Esders, '*Nationes quam plures nam conquiri*', p. 297.

controversy.[129] But his own foundation of Bobbio petitioned Pope Honorius for an immunity to protect the community from episcopal interference and this set a precedent.[130] Bobbio may also have acquired a second privilege from Pope Theodore, an aggressive opponent of the imperial religious teaching.[131] Other Columbanian houses may also have sought papal privileges in the 640s: a cluster of forged texts recording privileges of John IV for Luxeuil, Rebais, and Remiremont. Wood has argued that genuine originals may underlie these later texts.[132] These privileges strengthened ties between Rome and the houses they benefited. They necessitated special delegations to the papal court and created special relationships: Honorius's Bobbio privilege placed the house directly under papal jurisdiction, removing it from the control of the diocesan bishop.[133] Eligius, Audoin, and Amandus all belonged to a network of individuals linked by an association with Columbanian houses, interests in Christian mission and a high regard for papal authority. Martin's outreach over the monothelete controversy operated at the intersection of these characteristics. Esders has argued that seventh-century Frankish mission was influenced by Roman law in equating paganism, heresy, and the Jewish faith.[134] A concern for correct belief lay at the heart of the evangelical activities of Amandus, Eligius, and Audoin as Martin may well have known. In seeking to draw the Frankish kingdoms into his conflict with the Eastern emperor and patriarch, he was reaching out to a group of men known to him for their activities in promoting true belief and orthodoxy.

Pope Martin's appeal to Amandus and to the Neustrian court for support against imperial monotheletism was therefore not made in a void. He had contacts who were politically prominent and informed about imperial policy. Although Dagobert's alignment with imperial religious and political policy had taken place over a decade earlier (and ended in failure with regard to the Slavs), it is nevertheless a nice question of how Martin's condemnation of Constantinople was received by the Frankish rulers, particularly as events unfurled in the 650s with the revolt of Olympius and the implication of Martin's involvement. Relations with the Eastern Empire remained important, with the imperial court based at Syracuse until the assassination of Constans II in 668. When Theodore of Tarsus was dispatched to Canterbury by Pope Vitalian in 668 as archbishop-elect, his companion, the African Hadrian of *Hiridanum*, was detained in Francia by Ebroin who suspected that he was on a mission from

---

129 See Wood, 'The Franks and Papal Theology', pp. 221–41; Gray and Herren, 'Columbanus and the Three Chapters', pp. 160–70; Bracken, 'Authority and Duty', pp. 168–213.
130 *Codice diplomatico*, ed. by Cipolla, pp. 100–03; Anton, *Studien zu den Klosterprivilegien*, pp. 55–57.
131 *Codice diplomatico*, ed. by Cipolla, pp. 108–11; Anton, *Studien zu den Klosterprivilegien*, pp. 58–59; Ewig, 'Bemerkungen zu zwei merowingischen Bischofsprivilegien', pp. 215–49. The extant privilege is probably interpolated.
132 *Diplomata, Chartae, Epistolae, Leges*, ed. by Pardessus, II, nos ccxci, cccii, ccciii, ccciv; Ewig, 'Bemerkungen zu zwei merowingischen Bischofsprivilegien'; Wood, 'Between Rome and Jarrow', pp. 307–09.
133 Ewig, 'Bemerkungen zu zwei merowingischen Bischofsprivilegien'.
134 Esder, '*Nationes quam plures nam conquiri*', p. 295.

the emperor to the English intended to damage his kingdom.[135] Hadrian had earlier twice served on missions to Gaul, possibly as an imperial delegate in connection with a Frankish-Byzantine alliance against the Lombards.[136] The evidence adduced above of trade contacts between the eastern Mediterranean, Africa, and southern France has highlighted the continued movement of people and goods across the Mediterranean, even if the volume of exchange was diminishing. The denunciation of imperial heresy in the *Vita Eligii* belongs in a context of imperial connections in Francia and economic activity in the Mediterranean.

Conclusion

The Martin narrative in the *Vita Eligii* opens up questions of the impact of the tumultuous events in Rome occasioned by the monothelete controversy. If accepted as genuine, it sheds important light on Roman religious affairs just before the imperial climbdown of the 680 Council of Constantinople. The testimony of the Martin narrative would suggest that dyotheletes in Rome, probably monks in eastern communities there, continued to agitate into the 670s. Moreover, its depiction of monotheletism as attacking both Pope Leo's *Tome* and the Council of Chalcedon, and undermining the status of the Virgin Mary, suggests the complexities of the doctrinal conflict were reduced by partisans to simple but powerful formulae designed to touch religious nerves in Rome and beyond. Tensions over imperial policy and eastern doctrinal teaching were manifest in the eternal city: Vitalian's care in appointing Abbot Hadrian to ensure that the Archbishop Designate of Canterbury, Theodore, did not introduce Greek customs contrary to the true faith, certainly indicates sensitivities.[137]

Rome in the two decades after the Lateran Synod is unlikely to have been a tranquil centre of saintly devotions. Alan Thacker has highlighted its dynamic promotion of saints' relics and martyr shrines in the city at this time, a vitality matched by its complex and often embittered responses to imperial policy and intervention. Visitors to the city such as Amandus, Audoin, Benedict Biscop, and Wilfrid came for spiritual nurture and religious guidance, encountering popes active in their support for universal mission, ready to provide them with immunities which safeguarded the purity of monastic life and which bound the churches of the western patriarchate to Rome at a time of great stress and vulnerability. These devout pilgrims brought home not only remembrances of long-dead saints and their sufferings but also fresh understandings of contemporary crises and world politics. The Martin narrative in the *Vita Eligii* is a testimony to the pull of Rome and its impact upon its pilgrims.

---

135   Bede, *Historia ecclesiastica*, ed. by Colgrave and Mynors, IV.1, pp. 332–33. Jankowiak, 'Essai d'histoire politique du monothéletisme', pp. 368–69.

136   Bede, *Historia ecclesiastica*, ed. by Colgrave and Mynors, IV.1, pp. 330–31; *Biblical Commentaries*, ed. by Bischoff and Lapidge, pp. 130–31; Ewig, *Die Merowinger und das Imperium*, p. 55.

137   Bede, *Historia ecclesiastica*, ed. by Colgrave and Mynors, IV.1, pp. 330–31; see the discussion by Booth, *Crisis of Empire*, pp. 298–99.

Works Cited

Primary Sources

The Acts of the Council of Chalcedon, trans. with introduction and notes by Richard Price
  and Michael Gaddis, 3 vols (Liverpool: Liverpool University Press, 2005)
The Acts of the Lateran Synod of 649, trans. by Richard Price, with contributions by Phil
  Booth and Catherine Cubitt (Liverpool: Liverpool University Press, 2014)
Bede, *Ecclesiastical History of the English People*, ed. by Bertram Colgrave and R. A. B.
  Mynors (Oxford: Oxford University Press, 1969)
Biblical Commentaries from the Canterbury School of Theodore and Hadrian, ed. by Bernhard
  Bischoff and Michael Lapidge (Cambridge: Cambridge University Press, 1994)
The Book of the Pontiffs (Liber Pontificalis), trans. by Raymond Davis (Liverpool: Liverpool
  University Press, 1989)
ChLA   *Chartae Latinae Antiquiores: Facsimile Edition of the Latin Charters Prior to the
  Ninth Century*, ed. by Albert Bruckner and Robert Marichal, 11 vols and supplement
  (Olten, Urs-Graf, 1954-), XIX (Dietikon-Zurich: Urs-Graf, 1987) and XVIII, ed. by
  H. Atsma and J. Vezin (Dietikon: Urs-Graf, 1990)
Chronica a. 754, ed. by T. Mommsen, in *Monumenta Germaniae Historica: Auctores
  antiquissimi*, 15 vols (Berlin: Weidmann, 1877–1919), XI (1904)
Codice diplomatico del monastero di S. Columbano di Bobbio fino all'anno MCCVIII, ed. by
  Carlo Cipolla (Rome: Tip. del Senato, 1918)
Concilia Galliae, 314–506, ed. by Charles Munier, in *Corpus Christianorum Series Latina*, 148
  (Turnhout: Brepols, 1963)
Concilia Galliae, A. 511–695, ed. by C. de Clercq, *Corpus Christianorum Series Latina*, 148A
  (Turnhout: Brepols, 1963)
Concilium universale Constantinopitanum Tertium Concilii Actiones I–XI, ed. by Rudolf
  Riedinger, *Acta Conciliorum Oecumenicorum* 2nd s., II, Pt. 1 (Berlin: ReInk, 1990)
*Diplomata, Chartae, Epistolae, Leges Aliaque Instrumenta ad res Gallo-Francicas Spectantia:
  Instrumenta ab Anno 628 ad Annum 751*, ed. by J. M. Pardessus, 2 vols (Paris:
  Imprimerie Royale, 1843–1849)
Doctrina Iacobi, edited in Gilbert Dagron and Vincent Déroche, 'Juifs et Chrétiens dans
  l'orient du VIIᵉ siècle', *Travaux et Mémoires*, 11 (1991), pp. 17–273
The Fourth Book of the Chronicle of Fredegar, ed. by J. M. Wallace-Hadrill (London: Thomas
  Nelson, 1960)
Gesta Dagoberti I regis Francorum, ed. by B. Krusch, in *Monumenta Germaniae Historica:
  Scriptores rerum Merovingicarum*, 7 vols (Hannover: Hahn, 1885–1920), II (1888),
  pp. 396–425
Gregory of Tours, *Decem Libri Historiarum*, ed. B. Krusch and W. Levison, in *Monumenta
  Germaniae Historica: Scriptores rerum Merovingicarum*, 7 vols (Hannover: Hahn,
  1885–1920), I. 1 (1951)
Le Liber pontificalis: Texte, introduction et commentaire, ed. by L. Duchesne, 3 vols 2nd
  edition (Paris: Boccard, 1981)
Maximus the Confessor and his Companions Documents from Exile, ed. and trans. by Pauline
  Allen and Bronwen Neil (Oxford: Oxford University Press, 2002)

Vita sancti Amandi, ed. by B. Krusch, in *Monumenta Germaniae Historica: Scriptores rerum Merovingicarum*, 7 vols (Hannover: Hahn, 1885–1920), V (1910), pp. 452–56

Vita Audoini episcopi Rotomagensis, ed. by W. Levison, in *Monumenta Germaniae Historica: Scriptores rerum Merovingicarum*, 7 vols (Hannover: Hahn, 1885–1920), V (1910), pp. 536–67

Vita sanctae Balthildis, ed. by B. Krusch, in *Monumenta Germaniae Historica: Scriptores rerum Merovingicarum*, 7 vols (Hannover: Hahn, 1885–1920), II (1888), pp. 475–508

VSE   *Vita Eligii episcopi Noviomagensis*, in, ed. by B. Krusch, in *Monumenta Germaniae Historica: Scriptores rerum Merovingicarum*, 7 vols (Hannover: Hahn, 1885–1920), IV (1902), pp. 634–760

Vita Landiberti vetustissima, ed. by B. Krusch, in *Monumenta Germaniae Historica: Scriptores rerum Merovingicarum*, 7 vols (Hannover: Hahn, 1885–1920), VI (1913), pp. 353–84

Secondary Studies

Anton, Hans Hubert, *Studien zu den Klosterprivilegien der Päpste im frühen Mittelalter* (Berlin: Gruyter, 1975)

Bayer, Clemens M. M., 'Vita Eligii', *Reallexikon der germanischen Alterstumkunde*, ed. by H. Beck, D. Guenich, and H. Steuer (Berlin: Gruyter, 1973–2008), pp. 461–524

Berschin, Walter, 'Der heilige Goldschmied: Die Eligiusvita – ein merowingisches Original?', *Mitteilungen des Instituts für Österreichische Geschichtsforschung*, 118 (2010), 1–7

Booth, Phil, *Crisis of Empire: Doctrine and Dissent at the End of Late Antiquity* (Berkeley: University of California Press, 2014)

Borias, A., 'Saint Wandrille et le crise monothélite', *Revue Bénédictine*, 97 (1987), 42–67

Bracken, Damian, 'Authority and Duty: Columbanus and the Primacy of Rome', *Peritia*, 16 (2002), 168–213

Brandes, Wolfram, '"Juristische" Krisenbewältigung im 7. Jahrhundert? Die Prozesse gegen Martin I. und Maximos Homologetes', *Fontes Minores*, 10 (1998), 141–212

Cubitt, Catherine, *Anglo-Saxon Church Councils c. 650–c. 850* (London: Leicester University Press, 1995)

——, 'St Wilfrid: A Man for his Times', in *Wilfrid: Abbot, Bishop, Saint, Papers from the 1300th Anniversary Conferences*, ed. by N. J. Higham (Donington: Shaun Tyas, 2013), pp. 311–47

——, 'The Roman Perspective', in *The Acts of the Lateran Synod of 649*, trans. by Richard Price, with contributions by Phil Booth and Catherine Cubitt (Liverpool: Liverpool University Press, 2014), pp. 40–58

Dagron, Gilbert, and Vincent Déroche, 'Juifs et Chrétiens dans l'orient du VIIe siècle', *Travaux et Mémoires*, 11 (1991), 17–273

Dierken, Alain 'Prolégomènes à une histoire des relations culturelles entre les Iles britanniques et le continent pendant le haut moyen age', in *La Neustrie Les Pays au nord de la Loire de 650 à 850, Colloque historique international*, ed. by H. Atsma, 2 vols (Sigmaringen: Thorkbecke, 1989), II, pp. 371–94

Esders, Stefan, 'Herakleios, Dagobert und die "beschnittenen Völker": Die Umwälzungen des Mittelmerraums im 7. Jahrhundert in der fränkischen Chronik des sog. Fredegar', in *Jenseits der Grenzen: Beiträge zur spätantiken und frühmittelalterlichen Geschichtsschreibung*, ed. by Andreas Goltz, Hartmut Leppin, and Heinrich Schlange-Schöningen (Berlin: De Gruyter, 2009), pp. 239–311

——, '*Nationes quam plures nam conquiri*: Amandus of Maastricht, Compulsory Baptism and "Christian Universal Mission" in Seventh-Century Gaul', in *Motions of Late Antiquity: Essays on Religion, Politics and Society in Honor of Peter Brown*, ed. by Jamie Kreiner and Helmut Reimitz (Turnhout: Brepols, 2016), pp. 269–307

——, 'The Prophesied Rule of a "circumcised people": A Travelling Tradition from the Seventh-Century Mediterranean', in *Barbarians and Jews: Jews and Judaism in the Early Medieval West*, ed. by Yitzhak Hen, Ora Limor, and Thomas F. X. Noble (Turnhout: Brepols, 2018), pp. 119–54

Ewig, Eugen, 'Bemerkungen zu zwei merowingischen Bischofsprivilegien und einem Papstprivileg des 7. Jahrhunderts für merowingische Klöster', in *Mönchtum, Episkopat und Adel zur Gründungszeit des Klosters Reichenau*, ed. by Arno Borst (Sigmaringen: Thorbecke, 1974), pp. 215–49

——, Der Petrus- und Apostelkult im spätrömische und fränkischen Gallien', in *Spätantikes und Fränkischen Gallien Gesammlte Schriften*, ed. by Hartmut Atsma (Munich: Artemis, 1976, 1979) 2 vols, II, pp. 318–54

——, *Die Merowinger und das Imperium*, Rheinisch-Westfälische Akademie der Wissenschaften Vorträge, 261 (Opladen: Westdeutscher, 1983)

Fouracre, Paul, 'The Work of Audoenus of Rouen and Eligius of Noyon in Extending Episcopal Influence from the Town to the Country in Seventh-Century Neustria', *Studies in Church History*, 16 (1979), 77–91

Fouracre, Paul and Richard A. Gerberding, *Late Merovingian France: History and Hagiography 640–720* (Manchester: Manchester University Press, 1996)

Fox, Yaniv, *Power and Religion in Merovingian Gaul* (Cambridge: Cambridge University Press, 2014)

Fritze, Wolfgang Hermann, '*Universalis gentium confessio*. Formeln, Träger und Wege universalmissionarischen Denken im 7. Jahrhundert', *Frühmittelalterliche Studien*, 3 (1969), 78–130

Gerberding, Richard, *The Rise of the Carolingians and the Liber Historiae Francorum* (Oxford: Oxford University Press, 1987)

Goffart, Walter, 'Byzantine Policy in the West under Tiberius II and Maurice: The Pretenders Hermenegild and Gundovald', *Traditio*, 13 (1957), 73–118

Gray, Patrick T. R., and Michael W. Herren, 'Columbanus and the Three Chapters Controversy – A New Approach', *Journal of Theological Studies*, n. s., 45, 1 (1994), 160–70

Halfond, Gregory I., *Archaeology of Frankish Church Councils, AD 511–768* (Leiden: Brill, 2010)

Hallinger, Kassius, 'Römische Voraussetzungen der bonifatianischen Wirksamkeit im Frankenreich', in *Sankt Bonifatius Gedenkgabe zum zwölfhundertsten Todestag* (Fulda: Parzeller, 1954), pp. 320–61

Jankowiak, Marek, 'Essai d'histoire politique du monothéletisme' (unpublished doctoral thesis, Ecole Pratique des Hautes Etudes, University of Warsaw, 2009)

Kaegi, Walter E., *Byzantium and the Early Islamic Conquests* (Cambridge: Cambridge University Press, 1992)

Labrousse, Michel, 'La trouvaille de monnaies byzantines de Saint-Vincent de Couladère (Cazères, Haute-Garonne)', *Revue numismatique*, 6th ser, 29 (1987), pp. 99–108

Lafaurie, Jean, 'Eligius monetarius', *Revue numismatique*, 6th ser, 19 (1977), 111–51

Lafaurie, Jean, and Cecile Morrisson, 'La penetration des monnaies byzantines en Gaule mérovingienne de visigothique du VIᵉ au VIIIᵉ siècle', *Revue numismatique*, 6th ser, 29 (1987), 38–98

Lapidge, Michael, 'Rufinus at the School of Canterbury', in *La Tradition vive: mélanges d'histoire des texts en l'honneur Le Louis Holtz*, ed. by Pierre Lardet (Turnhout: Brepols, 2003), pp. 119–30

——, *The Anglo-Saxon Library* (Oxford: Oxford University Press, 2006)

Llewellyn, Peter, *Rome in the Dark Ages* (London: Faber and Faber, 1971)

Loseby, Simon T., 'Marseille: a late antique success story?', *Journal of Roman Studies*, 82 (1992), 165–85

——, 'Marseille and the Pirenne Thesis I: Gregory of Tours, the Merovingian Kings and "un grand port"', in *The Sixth Century: Production, Distribution and Demand*, ed. by Richard Hodges and William Bowden (Leiden: Brill, 1998), pp. 203–30

——, 'Marseille and Pirenne Thesis II: "ville morte"', in *The Long Eighth-Century*, ed. by Inge Lyse Hansen and Chris Wickham (Leiden: Brill, 2000), pp. 167–94

——, 'The Mediterranean Economy', in *The New Cambridge Medieval History I c. 500–c. 700*, ed. by Paul Fouracre (Cambridge: Cambridge University Press, 2005), pp. 605–38

——, 'Post-Roman Economies', in *The Cambridge Companion to the Roman Economy*, ed. by Walter Scheidel (Cambridge: Cambridge University Press, 2012), pp. 334–60

Louth, Andrew, 'Did John Moschus Really Die in Constantinople?', *Journal of Theological Studies*, n. s., 49 (1998), pp. 149–54

Mango, Cyril, 'La culture grecque et l'occident au viiiᵉ siècle', *Settimane di Studio della Fondazione de studi all'alto mediovo*, 20 (1973), 683–721

McCormick, Michael, *Origins of the European Economy Communications and Commerce, A. D. 300–900* (Cambridge: Cambridge University Press, 2001)

McKitterick, Rosamond, 'The Papacy and Byzantium in the Seventh- and Early Eighth-Century Sections of the *Liber pontificalis*', *Papers of the British School at Rome*, 84 (2017), 241–73

Neil, Bronwen, *Seventh-Century Popes and Martyrs: The Political Hagiography of Anastasius Bibliothecarius* (Turnhout: Brepols, 2006)

Nelson, Janet, 'Queens as Jezebels: Brunhild and Balthild in Merovingian History', in Janet Nelson, *Politics and Ritual in Early Medieval Europe* (London: Hambledon, 1986), pp. 1–48

Noret, Jacques, 'À qui était destiné la lettre BHG 1233d d'Anastase Apocrisiaire?', *Analecta Bollandiana*, 118 (2000), 37–42

Ó Carragáin, Éamonn, and Alan Thacker, 'Wilfrid in Rome', in *Wilfrid: Abbot, Bishop, Saint, Papers from the 1300th Anniversary Conferences*, ed. by N. J. Higham (Donington: Shaun Tyas, 2013), pp. 212–30

Parker, A. J., *Ancient Shipwrecks of the Mediterranean and the Roman Provinces*, British Archaeological Reports: International Series, 580 (Oxford: Tempus Reparatum, 1992)

Peeters, Paul, 'Une vie grecque de Pape S. Martin I', *Analecta Bollandiana*, 51 (1933), 225–62

Pontal, Odette, *Histoire des conciles mérovingiens* (Paris: Cerf, 1989)

Prinz, Friedrich, *Frühes Mönchtum im Frankenreich* (Vienna: Oldenbourg, 1965)

Richards, Jeffrey, *The Popes and the Papacy in the Early Middle Ages* (London: Routledge and Kegan Paul, 1979)

Rubery, Eileen, 'Papal Opposition to Imperial Heresies: Text as Image in the Church of Sta. Maria Antiqua in the Time of Pope Martin (649–54/5)', *Studia patristica*, 50 (2011), 3–29

Sansterre, Jean-Marie, *Les Moines grecs et orientaux à Rome aux époques byzantine et carolingienne (milieu du VI*ᵉ *s. fin du IX*ᵉ *s.)*, Académie royale de Belgique, Mémoires de la classe des lettres 66, 2 vols (Brussels: Université de Bruxelles, 1982)

Sarti, Laury, 'The Digression on Pope Martin I in the *Life* of Eligius of Noyon (I. 33–34): A Testimony to Late Seventh-Century Knowledge Exchange between East and West', in *East and West in the Early Middle Ages: The Merovingian Kingdoms in Mediterranean Perspective*, ed. by Stefan Esders, Yaniv Fox, Yitzhak Hen and Laury Sarti (Cambridge: Cambridge University Press, 2019) , pp. 149–164

Scheibelreiter, Georg, 'Audoin von Rouen: Ein Versuch über den Charakter des 7. Jahrhundert', in *La Neustrie Les Pays au nord de la Loire de 650 à 850, Colloque historique international*, ed. by H. Atsma, 2 vols (Sigmaringen: Thorbecke, 1989), I, pp. 195–216

——, 'Griechisches-lateinisches-fränkisches Christentum: Der Brief Papst Martins I. an den Bischof Amandus von Maastricht aus dem Jahre 649', *Mitteilungen des Instituts Österreichische Geschichtsforschung*, 100 (1992), 84–102

Thacker, Alan, 'Memorializing Gregory the Great: The Origin and Transmission of a Papal Cult in the Seventh and Early Eighth Centuries', *Early Medieval Europe*, 7 (1998), 59–84

——, 'Rome of the Martyrs: Saints, Cults and Relics, Fourth to the Seventh Centuries', in *Roma Felix: Formation and Reflections of Medieval Rome*, ed. by Éamonn Ó Carragáin and Carol Neuman de Vegvar (Aldershot: Ashgate, 2007), pp. 13–49

——, 'Rome: The Pilgrims' City in the Seventh Century', in *England and Rome in the Early Middle Ages: Pilgrimage, Art, and Politics*, ed. by Francesca Tinti (Turnhout: Brepols, 2014), pp. 89–139

Uytfanghe, Marc van, *Stylisation biblique et condition humaine dans l'hagiographie mérovingienne* (Brussels: Koninklijke Academie voor Wetenschappen, 1987)

Vierk, Hayo, 'Werke des Eligius', in *Studien zu vor- und frühgeschichtlichen Archäologie Festschrift für Joachim Werner zum 65. Geburtstag*, ed. by G. Ulbert and G. Kossak (Munich: Beck, 1974), pp. 309–80

Wallace-Hadrill, J. M., *The Frankish Church* (Oxford: Oxford University Press, 1983)

Westeel, Isabelle, 'Quelques remarques sur la *Vita Eligii*, Vie de Saint Éloi', *Mélanges de science religieuse*, 56.2 (1999), 33–47

Wood, Ian, 'The *Vita Columbani* and Merovingian Hagiography', *Peritia*, 1 (1982), 63–80

——, 'Forgery in Merovingian Hagiography', in *Fälschungen im Mittelalter, Monumentia Germaniae Historica: Schriften*, 74 vols to date (Hannover: Hahn, 1938–) 33.5 (1988), V, pp. 369–84

——, 'Fredegar's Fables', in *Historiographie im frühen Mittelalter*, ed. by Anton Scharer and Georg Scheibelreiter (Vienna: Oldenbourg, 1994), pp. 359–66

——, *The Merovingian Kingdoms, 450–751* (Harlow: Longman, 1994)

——, *The Missionary Life: Saints and Evangelisation of Europe, 400–1050* (Harlow: Longman, 2001)

——, 'The Franks and Papal Theology, 550–660', in *The Crisis of the Oikoumene: The Three Chapters and the Failed Quest for Unity in the Sixth-Century Mediterranean*, ed. by Celia Chazelle and Catherine Cubitt (Turnhout: Brepols, 2007), pp. 222–41

——, 'The Continental Journeys of Wilfrid and Biscop', in *Wilfrid: Abbot, Bishop, Saint: Papers from the 1300th Anniversary Conferences*, ed. by N. J. Higham (Donington: Shaun Tyas, 2013), pp. 200–11

——, 'Between Rome and Jarrow: Papal Relations with Francia and England, from 597–716', *Settimane di Studio della Fondazione di studi sull'alto mediovo*, 61 (2014), 297–317

——, 'The Irish in England and on the Continent in the Seventh Century, Part I', *Peritia*, 26 (2015), 171–98

——, 'The Irish in England and on the Continent in the Seventh Century, Part II', *Peritia*, 27 (2016), 189–214

JENNIFER O'REILLY

Bede and Monotheletism

For Alan Thacker[1]

Charles Plummer remarked, 'There is hardly any form of heresy known in Bede's time which is not refuted in his writings', but in listing Bede's prodigious references to heresy and heretics, he provided only one reference to Monotheletism.[2] The low count may seem surprising, for Monotheletism was a seventh-century phenomenon, refuted by the Lateran Council of 649, and formally condemned, though not extinguished, by the Sixth Ecumenical Council (Constantinople III) in 680–681. It was condemned as contrary to the christological belief, articulated in the Tome of Pope Leo the Great and defined by the Council of Chalcedon (451), that the two natures of Christ, his divinity and humanity, were inseparably united in one person at the Incarnation, but remained distinct and unconfused, so that one and the same person was truly Son of God and truly Son of man.[3] In the West, and for the papacy, Chalcedon and the Tome had become a particular touchstone of tradition and orthodoxy, and the christology they characterised was at the centre of Bede's work. In the East, however, various Christian communities remained dissatisfied, including some Chalcedonians

---

1   Jennifer O'Reilly was working on this essay at the time of her sudden death in February 2016. She intended to include in it a tribute to Alan Thacker, whose friendship she valued and whose scholarship she admired. He was present in July 2013 at the International Medieval Congress in Leeds when she read a paper detailing the research on which the essay is based. He welcomed the paper warmly, and drew attention to its significance in his article, 'Why did Heresy Matter to Bede?' (p. 51, n. 34), which appeared the following year. The essay has been prepared for publication by Terence O'Reilly, who thanks Nicholas Madden, OCD, Éamonn Ó Carragáin, and Diarmuid Scully for their helpful comments on the text.
2   Bede, *Opera historica*, ed. by Plummer, p. lxii, n. 3. On Bede's references to heretics and heresies in his *Commentary on Luke*, see Brown, *A Companion to Bede*, p. 61, n. 126.
3   The Tome was cited in Chalcedon's definition of faith as being 'in agreement with great Peter's confession', a reference to St Peter's divinely inspired recognition of the identity of Christ in Matthew 16. 16, which is quoted in the Tome itself: see *Decrees of the Ecumenical Councils*, ed. by Tanner, vol. 1, pp. 80, 85.

Jennifer O'Reilly • (1943–2016) was Senior Lecturer in the School of History, University College Cork.

Cities, Saints, and Communities in Early Medieval Europe, ed. by Scott DeGregorio and Paul Kershaw, SEM 46 (Turnhout: Brepols, 2020), pp. 105-127
BREPOLS PUBLISHERS   DOI 10.1484/M.SEM-EB.5.119624

who wanted greater emphasis on the unity of Christ's two natures in one person, and those, known by their opponents as monophysites, who rejected Chalcedon's 'in two natures' formula and believed that the two natures of Christ were united in one nature at the Incarnation. In the reigns of Heraclius (610–641) and Constans II (641–668) a unifying theological solution was sought in a wider interpretation of Chalcedon, without resorting to another, potentially divisive, general council, and it was in this context that the debate about Monotheletism arose. Proponents accepted that Christ had two natures, but believed them to be united by a single energy (i.e. monoenergism, meaning a single principle of activity or mode of operation) and by one will, the divine will of the incarnate Word.[4] In the view of their opponents, this amounted to a denial of Christ's human will, and therefore of his manhood in its fullness. During the 640s the papacy and its theological advisers assembled a monumental refutation of those who declared 'there is only one operation and one will in Christ'.[5] In Constantinople, however, support for Monotheletism had emerged in the context of the crisis of empire and the attempt to reconcile the large monophysite populations in the eastern imperial provinces, which were vulnerable first to the Persians and then to the Arabs: between 635 and 642 Antioch, Jerusalem, and Alexandria had been taken. Monotheletism, and the debates about christology that it sparked, thus became central to the upheavals afflicting Church and Empire in the seventh century. My question, in the light of this, is twofold: what did Bede know about Monotheletism, and what was its significance for him?

The *Historia ecclesiastica*

From a reading of the *Historia ecclesiastica* it is not apparent that seventh-century papal Rome was subject to sometimes violent displays of imperial power to promote monotheletism or to prevent further discussion of the issues it had raised. The *Liber pontificalis* gives glimpses of such episodes, usually attaching blame to usurpers and exarchs or devious eastern patriarchs rather than to the emperors themselves. It selectively recounts Pope Martin I's summoning of the Lateran Synod in 649, which condemned the bishop of Alexandria and successive patriarchs of Constantinople for contriving innovations against the faith. The imperial exarch seized Pope Martin from the Lateran church; he was taken to Constantinople and rough-handled. The *Liber pontificalis* laconically notes, 'they failed to get his agreement'; Martin was sent into exile, 'where, as it pleased God, the life of this confessor of Christ ended

---

4   The distinct origins of monoenergism and monotheletism and their overlapping histories are traced in Hovorun, *Will, Action and Freedom*, pp. 5–51, 163–67; Booth, *Crisis of Empire*, pp. 188–96, 264–65; *The Acts of the Lateran Synod*, trans. by Price, pp. 18–27, 87–94.

5   This formula is the usual way of referring to monotheletism in papal documents, and in the *acta* of the Lateran Synod and of the Sixth Ecumenical Council. It is used in the same sense by Bede. Scholars currently differ about the extent to which the opponents of the monotheletes misunderstood, or misrepresented, their theology: see, for instance, *The Acts of the Lateran Synod*, trans. by Price, p. 92, and the contrasting approach of Hovorun, *Will, Action and Freedom*.

in peace, and he works many miracles to the present day'.[6] No mention is made of the pope's public humiliation and show trial for treason, nor of the brutal treatment from which he died in exile in the Crimea in 655, a fate later shared by his eminent theological adviser, Maximus the Confessor (662).

Pope Martin and the Lateran Synod are not mentioned in the *Historia ecclesiastica* until the account of the synod of Hatfield, held thirty years later in 679.[7] Archbishop Theodore, it is said, recorded that the bishops and learned men of the island of Britain assembled at Hatfield had united in declaring the orthodox faith and acknowledging all five universal councils of the Church. Bede then quotes their statement 'from a little further on' in Theodore's synodal book: 'And we acknowledge the council which was held in the city of Rome in the time of the blessed Pope Martin [...] in the ninth year of the reign of the most pious Emperor Constantine' (Constans II). They anathematized those whom the Lateran Council had anathematized and accepted those whom it had accepted.[8] In the following chapter, Bede briefly explains that the synod called by Martin was chiefly directed against those 'who declared only one operation and will in Christ' (*qui unam in Christo operationem et uoluntatem praedicabant*).[9] He further notes:

> Tales namque eo tempore fidem Constantinopolitanae ecclesiae multum contur-bauerant; sed Domino donante proditi iam tunc et uicti sunt. Vnde uolens Agatho papa, sicut in aliis prouinciis, ita etiam in Brittania qualis esset status ecclesiae, quam ab hereticorum contagiis castus, ediscere, hoc negotium reuerentissimo abbati Johanni Brittaniam destinato iniunxit.

>> Those who held this belief had greatly disturbed the faith of Constantinople at that time, but by the grace of God they were exposed and overwhelmed. Pope Agatho, therefore, wishing to know what was the state of the church in Britain as well as in other kingdoms, and how far it was free from the heretical contagion, entrusted the task to the reverend Abbot John (the Archcantor) who had already been appointed to go to Britain.[10]

Bede does not, however, present the Hatfield assembly (September 679) as a preparation for the synod that Agatho had summoned to Rome for March 680 in order to demonstrate the unity and orthodoxy of the western churches in refuting monotheletism. Agatho's synod is mentioned quite separately from Hatfield, and a whole book later, in the chapter devoted to Bishop Wilfrid (*Historia ecclesiastica* 5.19), who went to Rome to appeal against his unlawful expulsion by his enemies at home at the same time that Agatho had called a synod there 'to testify against those who

6   *Le Liber pontificalis*, ed. by Duchesne, vol. 1, pp. 336–40; *The Book of Pontiffs*, trans. by Davis, pp. 68–71.
7   Bede, *Historia ecclesiastica*, IV.17, ed. and trans. by Colgrave and Mynors, pp. 386–87.
8   *Historia ecclesiastica*, IV.17, ed. and trans. Colgrave and Mynors, pp. 386–87.
9   *Historia ecclesiastica*, IV.18, ed. and trans. by Colgrave and Mynors, pp. 388–91. Bede uses the full formula, as also in *HE* 5.19, though it is here translated by Colgrave and Mynors as 'those who declared that only one will operated in Christ' (pp. 390–91).
10 *Historia ecclesiastica*, IV.18, ed. and trans. by Colgrave and Mynors, pp. 390–91.

declared that there was only one will and operation in our Lord and Saviour'.[11] Wilfrid was ordered to sit among the bishops assembled for that purpose and to declare his own belief and that of the kingdom and island from which he had come. He made a confession of the catholic faith on behalf of 'the whole northern part of Britain and Ireland, together with the islands inhabited by the Angles and Britons, as well as the Irish and Picts', which was inserted into the acts of the synod.[12] Again, Bede gives no hint that Agatho's synod was itself in preparation for the Sixth Ecumenical Council (Constantinople III), already summoned by the emperor. It was to meet in Constantinople in November of the same year, 680, and formally condemn those who were 'sowing with novel speech among the orthodox people the heresy of one will and one operation in the two natures of the one member of the Holy Trinity, Christ our true God'.[13]

Such silences in the *Ecclesiastical History* might lead one to conclude that Bede was not well-informed about the progress, scale and seriousness of the controversy, and to question whether he understood much about monotheletism because of its Greek theological background. The absence from the work of a more complete account may be explained otherwise, however, notably in terms of the book's stated and implied objectives. Its story of conversion gives importance to the resolution of the Insular Paschal controversy, derived from a much older dispute within the Church but one which, unlike monotheletism, did not threaten schism between East and West or, in the view of moderate *Romani* such as Bede, question fundamental tenets of orthodox belief.[14] Bede's account of Hatfield and John the Archcantor's mission is unique and detailed but, presented without further reference to the monothelete controversy, it serves primarily to testify that the recently converted *Angli* at the ends of the earth were members of the universal Church, 'united in declaring the true and orthodox faith as our Lord Jesus Christ delivered it'.[15] It also affirms the continuing role of the papacy in safeguarding that tradition.

It can be readily shown, moreover, that Bede had access to considerably greater knowledge of monotheletism than, for whatever reason, he chose to use in the *Historia ecclesiastica*. There is, for instance his extensive use of the *Liber pontificalis* in the different context of the *Chronica maiora* within the *De temporum ratione* (*c.* 725). This contains information on the monothelete controversy from before, during and after the reign of Pope Martin, including the Sixth General Council in Constantinople, with the additional information of the names of those it had anathematised, among them

---

11 *Historia ecclesiastica*, V.19, ed. and trans. by Colgrave and Mynors, p. 522: 'eos qui unam in Domino Saluatore uoluntatem atque operationem dogmatizabant'.
12 *Historia ecclesiastica*, V.19, ed. and trans. by Colgrave and Mynors, p. 524; *The Life of Bishop Wilfrid*, ed. by Colgrave, Chapter 53, p. 14.
13 *Decrees of the Ecumenical Councils*, ed. by Tanner, p. 126: 'unius voluntatis et unius operationis in duabus naturis unius de sancta Trinitate, Christi veri Dei nostri, orthodoxae plebi novisone disseminando haeresim'.
14 Bede's views on this differ from those of extreme *Romani,* notably Wilfrid. See O'Reilly, "'All that Peter Stands For'".
15 *Historia ecclesiastica*, IV.17, ed. and trans. by Colgrave and Mynors, p. 385.

Pope Honorius.[16] There is also the fact that information concerning events in Rome at various points in the controversy would have been available in Northumbria, and especially in Bede's monastery, from returning visitors, among them senior ecclesiastics with contacts in Rome at the highest level. They included three of Bede's abbots, several monks from his monastery, and two local bishops. Two of the visitors, Acca and Nothelm, were closely involved with Bede's work.[17] The monastery had close links as well with two major figures, conversant with the monothelete controversy, who were sent to Britain from Rome by the papacy on particular missions, the Greek monk and learned theologian Theodore of Tarsus (602–690), and Abbot John, the Archcantor of St Peter's in Rome. When Pope Vitalian appointed Theodore to the see of Canterbury (668), he ordered Benedict Biscop, then visiting Rome from Lérins, to act as interpreter and guide to the new archbishop and all his associates. Benedict Biscop subsequently remained in Canterbury for two years in charge of the monastery of St Peter, of which Theodore's fellow monk Hadrian was in due course made abbot.[18] Theodore and Hadrian were Greek speakers by upbringing, and had direct knowledge of the christological debates of their time. Theodore had studied in Constantinople before arriving in Rome, where he appears to have become a seasoned 'Lateran professional',[19] familiar with the theological issues facing the papacy, and in particular with the thought of Maximus the Confessor, the leading opponent of monotheletism in Italy, who was instrumental in drafting the *acta* of the 649 Lateran Council.[20] The influence of Maximus on the Canterbury biblical commentaries, which reflect the teaching of Theodore and Hadrian, is clear.[21] Hadrian's successor

---

16 *Le Liber pontificalis*, ed. by Duchesne, vol. 1, pp. 350–59; *The Book of Pontiffs*, trans. by Davis, pp. 74–78; Bede, *De temporum ratione*, ed. by Jones, pp. 525–29.

17 Between 653 and *c.* 684 Benedict Biscop made six visits to Rome, five of them from Britain. One of these (*c.* 678–679) was with Ceolfrith (Bede, *Historia abbatum*, ed. and trans. by Grocock and Wood, pp. 24, 26, 30, 38, 44). Ceolfrith's successor, Hwaetbert, to whom Bede dedicated his commentary on the *Apocalypse*, had studied in Rome in the days of Pope Sergius (687–701) on 'a stay of no little duration' (*Historia abbatum*, ed, and trans. by Grocock and Wood, p. 66). Other unnamed monks from the monastery were also in Rome in 701 (*Historia abbatum*, ed. and trans. by Grocock and Wood, p. 59; *De temporum ratione*, p. 431; *The Reckoning of Time*, trans. by Wallis, p. 128). Bishop Wilfrid made three visits to Rome: the first, begun with Benedict Biscop, was probably at the time of the forced exile of Pope Martin (*c.* 653); Wilfrid was present later at Agatho's synod in 679, preparatory to the Sixth General Council, and at John VI's synod, 704. (*Historia ecclesiastica*, V.19, ed. and trans. by Colgrave and Mynors, pp. 518–21, 522–27; *The Life of Bishop Wilfrid*, ed. by Colgrave, pp. 10–13, 56–67, 102–21). On this last trip he was accompanied by Acca, future bishop of Hexham (709–732), Bede's bishop and correspondent, to whom he dedicated several of his exegetical works (*Historia ecclesiastica* V.20, ed. and trans. by Colgrave and Mynors, pp. 532–33). Nothelm, priest of the church of London, for whom Bede wrote *In Regum librum xxx quaestiones*, also visited Rome and supplied Bede with information from the papal registry (*Historia ecclesiastica*, Praefatio, ed. and trans. by Colgrave and Mynors, pp. 4–5).

18 *Historia abbatum*, ed. and trans. by Grocock and Wood, pp. 28–29.

19 Noble, 'Rome in the Seventh Century', p. 87.

20 *The Acts of the Lateran Synod*, trans. by Price, pp. 99–100; Ó Carragáin, *Ritual and the Rood*, pp. 266, 268 n. 27.

21 Bischoff and Lapidge, *Biblical Commentaries from the Canterbury School*; Lapidge, 'The Career of Archbishop Theodore', pp. 23–24.

as abbot in Canterbury, Albinus, who had been educated by Theodore and Hadrian, was later described by Bede as 'my principal authority and helper'[22] in the preparation of the *Historia ecclesiastica*.

John the Archcantor, similarly, travelled from Rome to Northumbria with Ceolfrith and Benedict Biscop, who had invited him to teach chant at Wearmouth. Charged by Pope Agatho with reporting on the faith of the English Church, and specifically its christology, he attended the synod of Hatfield called by Theodore, and received a copy of its proceedings to take back to the pope, while at Wearmouth he not only taught chant, but committed to writing 'all things necessary for the celebration of festal days throughout the whole year'. Bede notes the value accorded to his writings, which 'have been preserved to this day in the monastery, and copies have been made by many others elsewhere'. He then continues:

> [John the Archcantor] had also brought with him the decision made by the synod called by blessed Pope Martin [*synodum beati papae Martini* […] *secum veniens adtulit*] which had recently been held in Rome, which was chiefly directed against those who declared there was only one will and operation in Christ. He arranged for a copy of the decree to be made in the monastery of the holy abbot Benedict.[23]

The term employed by Bede to describe John's legacy (*synodum*), rendered here as 'the decision made by the synod',[24] is a formula used elsewhere to indicate not only the formal record of a council's decisions but its full proceedings or *acta*.[25] The Latin *acta* of Martin's Lateran synod of 649 constitute a very substantial dossier of varied materials, including papal speeches and episcopal testimonies, scriptural proof texts, and patristic *florilegia*, the condemnation of the imperial *Ecthesis* and *Typos*, the reading out and refutation of the views of named individuals who held there was only one will and one operation in Christ, contrary assertions of belief in Christ's two operations and two wills, supporting references to the role of Leo's

---

22   *Historia ecclesiastica, Praefatio*, ed. and trans. by Colgrave and Mynors, pp. 2–3.

23   *Historia ecclesiastica*, IV.18, ed. and trans. by Colgrave and Mynors, pp. 389–90. The translation has been modified here to include the reference to *unam operationem* omitted in the original. On this passage see Ó Carragáin, *Ritual and the Rood*, pp. 226, 268, n. 29.

24   The translation perhaps reflects Plummer's note, '"synodus" is here used loosely for "synodica *or* synodalis epistola"; i.e. the formal document containing the record of the resolutions of the council' (Bede, *Opera historica*, ed. by Plummer, p. 234).

25   As in the account of Pope Agatho's synod in 679 (*Historia ecclesiastica*, V.19, ed. and trans. by Colgrave and Mynors, p. 525), where Bede affirms that Wilfrid's acquittal 'was greatly assisted by the reading of the acts of the synod of Pope Agatho of blessed memory' (lectio synodi beatae memoriae papae Agathonis), when 'as the case required, the acts of this synod were read for some days in the presence of the nobility and a large crowd of people at the command of the pope' (cum ergo causa exigente synodus eadem coram nobilibus et frequentia populi, iubente apostolica papa, diebus aliquot legeretur). Similarly, the account of Pope Martin's council in the *Liber pontificalis* reads: 'Quem synodum hodie archivo ecclesiae continetur. Et faciens exemplaria, per omnes tractos Orientis et Occidentis direxit, per manus orthodoxorum fidelium disseminavit' (This synod is kept today in the church archive. He made copies and sent them through all the districts of East and West, broadcasting them by the hands of the orthodox faithful): *Le liber pontificalis*, ed. by Duchesne, vol. 1, p. 337; *The Book of Pontiffs*, trans. by Davis, p. 69.

Tome and the papacy in defending that belief, summaries of conciliar definitions, and a *symbolum*.[26] Bede and his community, in other words, had at their disposal a detailed record of the tenets of monotheletism as these were understood and contested in seventh-century Rome.

Walking on Water: Bede's Commentary on Mark 6. 48–50

While it is clear, however, that Bede had information about the monothelete controversy that is not used in the *Historia ecclesiastica*, and had likely access to far more than appears in his *Chronica maiora*, there remains the question of the degree of his understanding of monotheletism as this might be revealed in his works of biblical exegesis. Plummer long ago observed that Bede 'had no doubt often seen and used' John the Archcantor's transcript of the Lateran Synod, but in his separate listing of Bede's refutation of heresy and heretics the only example of monotheletism he cited, though without using that term and without further comment, was Bede's reference to Theodore of Pharan.[27] Some forty years later M. L. Laistner noted that the passage in which Bede cites Theodore, together with an extract from Dionysius the Pseudo-Areopagite to refute him, 'is drawn almost word for word from the Latin version of the Acts of the Lateran Council'.[28] How Bede used these texts, however, has not been discussed, yet it is of particular interest in trying to assess his knowledge of the Synod and his response to the heresy it had condemned.

The two items in question (the references to Theodore and Dionysius), and a summary of the brief comment linking them in the Lateran *acta*, appear in Bede's commentary on Mark's Gospel, generally dated between *c.* 721 and 731.[29] The context is his exposition of Mark's account of the miracle following the feeding of the five thousand, when the disciples were in a storm at sea at night, labouring against the winds, and Christ came, walking on the water: **And he would have passed by them. But they, seeing him walking upon the sea, thought it was an apparition and they cried out. For they all saw him and were troubled** (Mark 6. 48b–50a). Bede comments:

> Adhuc heretici putant fantasma fuisse dominum nec ueram assumpsisse carnem de uirgine. Denique Theodorus Pharanitanus quondam episcopus ita scripsit corporale pondus non habuisse secundum carnem dominum sed absque pondere et corpore super mare deambulasse. At contra fides catholica et pondus

---

26 Several scholars have remarked on features of the Lateran Synod that are echoed in the account of Hatfield in Theodore's synodal book, from which Bede quotes in *Historia ecclesiastica*, IV.17. It is possible that the Lateran *acta* brought by John the Archcantor were used in the framing of the Hatfield meeting, and that they were quoted or referred to there more fully than appears in Bede's summary and extracts from the synodal book.

27 Bede, *Opera historica*, ed. by Plummer, pp. lxii–lxiii, n. 3.

28 Laistner, 'The Library of the Venerable Bede', p. 259; Ganz, 'Roman Manuscripts in Francia and Anglo-Saxon England', pp. 617–45, n. 44.

29 Foley, 'Bede's Exegesis of Passages Unique to the Gospel of Mark', p. 108.

secundum carnem habere eum praedicat et onus corporeum et cum pondere atque onere corporali incedere super aquas non infusis pedibus. Nam Dionisius egregius inter ecclesiasticos scriptores in opusculis de diuinis nominibus hoc modo loquitur: *Ignoramus enim qualiter de uirgineis sanguinibus alia lege praeter naturalem formabatur et qualiter non infusis pedibus corporale pondus habentibus et materiale onus deambulabat in umidam et instabilem substantiam.*

> Up to the present time heretics have thought that [the body of] the Lord was a phantasm and that he did not assume true flesh from the Virgin. The latest, Theodore once bishop of Pharan, wrote that the Lord did not have in his flesh bodily weight but that he walked upon the sea without a body and weight. But against this, the catholic faith teaches that he has in his flesh both weight and bodily mass and that he walked upon the waters with bodily weight and mass without his feet sinking in. Now Dionysius, outstanding among ecclesiastical writers, in his work on the divine names, says the following: 'For we do not know how, in accord with a law other than the natural one, he was formed from a virgin's blood. We do not understand how with dry feet themselves having bodily weight and natural mass he walked onto a wet and unstable substance'.[30]

The quoted reference to Theodore of Pharan does not use the terminology of the one operation or one will of Christ or express a belief peculiar to monotheletism. Its inclusion in the list of arguments from Theodore's work condemned in the *acta* of the Lateran Synod may at first glance, therefore, seem surprising. This particular entry in the *acta*, however, in the third session of the Synod, is but a brief summary, recalling the tenth of eleven quotations from Theodore's treatise to Sergius, bishop of Arsinoe, which had appeared earlier in the same session. The *acta* describe how the eleven quotations — which ascribe one divine will and operation to Christ — had been read out by a papal notary and their teaching then reproved in a commentary delivered by Pope Martin.[31] There follow four brief summaries of points drawn from those extracts (including the summary quoted by Bede); all four concern the Lord's body, and each is compared with an appropriate passage from the teachings of the fathers of the Church, ending with an extract from the council of Chalcedon's definition of faith, which affirms that the distinctive character of each of Christ's two natures was 'ceaselessly preserved' and not destroyed at their 'coming together into one person and one hypostasis'.[32]

---

30 Bede, *In Marci evangelivm expositio*, ed. by Hurst, pp. 517–18, ll. 1128–141.

31 *Concilium Lateranense*, ed. by Riedinger, pp. 123–26; *The Acts of the Lateran Synod*, trans. by Price, pp. 204–09. The theological views of Theodore of Pharan are discussed in Hovorun, *Will, Action and Freedom*, pp. 58–59, 84, 118, 165, and in *The Acts of the Lateran Synod*, trans. by Price, pp. 191–92, where it is argued that the Synod's interpretation of them was flawed.

32 *Concilium Lateranense*, ed. by Riedinger, pp. 128, 130; *The Acts of the Lateran Synod*, trans. by Price, pp. 209–10, and n. 70. The text of the Chalcedon definition may be seen in *Decrees of the Ecumenical Councils*, ed. by Tanner, vol. 1, p. 86: 'nusquam sublata differentia naturarum propter unitionem magisque salva proprietate utriusque naturae et in unam personam atque subsistentiam concurrente'.

In the Tome Pope Leo had corrected Eutyches (a figure of monophysitism) for failing to see our human nature in Christ, and had instructed him on the two distinct natures of the incarnate Christ, stressing that at the Incarnation 'the proper character of both natures was maintained and came together in a single person'.[33] Leo's amplification of the statement, which was often quoted, appears in the Lateran *acta* in the *florilegium* of patristic texts on the natural operations of Christ: 'The activity of each form is what is proper to it in communion with the other: that is, the Word performs what belongs to the Word, and the flesh accomplishes what belongs to the flesh. One of these performs brilliant miracles, the other sustains acts of violence'.[34] Leo had cited familiar examples of what pertains to Christ's human and divine natures respectively: 'Hunger, thirst, weariness, sleep are patently human. But to satisfy five thousand people with five loaves [...], to walk on the surface of the sea with feet that do not sink, to rebuke the storm and level the mounting waves, there can be no doubt that these are divine'.[35] Leo was clear that the two natures of Christ acted 'in communion', but the rhetorical listing of what characterised each of them separately was open to interpretation, by a range of religious opinion, as insufficiently emphasising their union.[36] Bede's exposition of the gospel account of Christ walking on the water, perhaps reflecting this, affirms orthodox belief in the hypostatic union of the two distinct natures in Christ's person, and in doing so refutes Theodore's different account of the unity of Christ's two natures, already documented in the foregoing section of the *acta*. In the eleven extracts from his treatise read out in the Lateran Synod, Theodore asserts that not only miraculous acts of power but all the properties of the incarnation of Christ belong to one divine operation in which he took on such natural human 'passions' or movements as sleep, weariness, hunger, thirst, distress, and affliction.[37] In the tenth of the quoted passages, Theodore argues that human beings do not have the power to shed their natural bodily properties; Christ's shedding or suspension of human properties when he wished is an attribute of his 'divine and life-giving body', which is itself without any dimension at all: 'for without bulk and (so to say) bodilessly he came forth, without causing any separation, from the womb and the sepulchre and through doors, and walked on the sea as on

---

33 *Decrees of the Ecumenical Councils*, ed. by Tanner, vol. 1, p. 78: 'Salva igitur proprietate utriusque naturae et in unam coeunte personam'.

34 *Decrees of the Ecumenical Councils*, ed. by Tanner, vol. 1, p. 79: 'Agit enim utraque forma cum alterius communione quod proprium est, verbo scilicet operante quod verbi est, et carne exequente quod carnis est. Unum horum coruscat miraculis, aliud subcumbit iniuriis'. The Synod's repeated quotation of this passage is noted and discussed in *The Acts of the Lateran Synod*, trans. by Price, pp. 120–21, n. 46; 214, n. 95; 240–42; 333, nn. 253–54.

35 *Decrees of the Ecumenical Councils*, ed. by Tanner, vol. 1, pp. 79–80: 'Esurire sitire lassescere atque dormire evidenter humanum est, sed quinque panibus milia hominum satiare [...], supra dorsum maris plantis non desidentibus ambulare et elationes fluctuum increpata tempestate consternere sin ambiguitate divinum est'.

36 *The Acts of the Lateran Synod*, trans. by Price, p. 121, n. 47.

37 *Concilium Lateranense*, ed. by Riedinger, p. 122; *The Acts of the Lateran Synod*, trans. by Price, p. 205, extracts 5 and 7.

a floor'.[38] These words are repeated in the papal commentary that follows in the *acta* and are duly refuted:

> nam si 'absque tumore et incorporaliter ex utero processit et super dorsum maris deambulauit', hoc ipsud quod 'deambulabat et procedebat' ergo fantasma erat, non enim incarnatus substantialiter deus. unde nec miraculum iam cognoscebatur uirginitatis germen, neque magnum erat incarnati dei uerbi super mare deambulatio.
>
> > For if indeed 'without bulk and bodilessly he came forth from the womb' and as he walked trod 'on the back of the sea', then his walking and advancing was a mere illusion and not God incarnate in essence; nor again was the growth from a virgin recognised as a miracle, and nor was God the Word incarnate's walking on the sea a matter for astonishment.[39]

What Bede quotes from the Lateran *acta* is its brief summary highlighting Theodore of Pharan's explanation of how Christ was able to walk on water: he did so 'without a body and weight'. Understood in the context of the fuller quotation and examination of Theodore's views in the immediately foregoing pages of the *acta*, this argues that Christ was able to dispense with properties of his humanity (in the present case his bodily weight) by the exercise of his one divine will. The *fides catholica* voiced in the extract from the *Divine Names* of Dionysius quoted by Bede contends that, on the contrary, Christ walked on the water 'with his body's solid weight', but affirms that exactly *how* this was accomplished we cannot understand, because, like the mystery of the virginal conception and birth of Christ, the miracle was not in accordance with the known law of nature.[40] Underlying this is the orthodox belief that at the Incarnation the divine and human natures of Christ remained distinct but were indissolubly united in one person. It follows that on the occasions when Christ performed miracles through the power of his divinity, as when he walked on water, his humanity was not temporarily suspended, and he did not cease to have all his human properties (including bodily weight). What the terrified disciples saw walking on the sea in the storm was not, therefore, an apparition or a phantasm (Mark 6. 49).

Having at the outset refuted Theodore of Pharan's view that Christ's lack of bodily weight as he walked on the sea demonstrated that his humanity was not present, and having countered, through the words of Dionysius, that Christ *did* have bodily weight, but that the event recounted in the Gospel was not susceptible to explanation according to the customary laws of nature, Bede returns to his initial question by allusion to the new order brought about at the Incarnation. He says that when Christ walked on water he was teaching that 'haberet corpus ab omni peccatorum grauidine

---

38 *Concilium Lateranense*, ed. by Riedinger, p. 123; *The Acts of the Lateran Synod*, trans. by Price, p. 206, extract 10.

39 *Concilium Lateranense*, ed. by Riedinger, p. 127; *The Acts of the Lateran Synod*, trans. by Price, pp. 207–08.

40 Dionysius is further quoted on the mystery of this miracle in the fifth session in the *acta*: *Concilium Lateranense*, ed. by Riedinger, p. 303; *The Acts of the Lateran Synod*, trans. by Price, pp. 336–37.

liberum' (he had a body freed from every burden of sins).[41] The idea of bodily weight as one of the characteristic properties of the full humanity which Christ took on at his incarnation and retained, even when walking on water, is here dramatically contrasted with the image of the whole of humanity weighed down by the burden of sin, from which Christ alone was free. The orthodox belief that Christ in his humanity was without sin is a recurring theme in Bede's exegesis, though it is not elaborated here. The Chalcedon definition described Christ as consubstantial with the Father as regards his divinity, and at the same time 'consubstantialem nobis eundem secundum humanitatem, per omnia nobis simile absque peccato' (consubstantial with us as regards his humanity: like us in all respects *except for sin* [Hebrews 4. 15]).[42] Leo's Tome had emphasised that Christ was holy not only in his divine nature but in his humanity: 'His subjection to human weaknesses in common with us did not mean that he shared our sins'. By his 'unprecedented kind of birth' he had assumed human nature as it had been first formed by the Creator before the sin of Adam and Eve, that is, without inheriting the burden of original sin common to the rest of humanity. His virginal conception from the Holy Spirit, 'without stain of sin', was essential to human salvation from sin and death.[43] The canons of the Lateran Synod make the same point: because of the mode of Christ's birth, he was incorrupt and without sin in his humanity.[44] His human will was therefore not in conflict with his divine will; the two natures were in perfect accord in willing and bringing about human redemption and transformation. Bede's insistence, when discussing Theodore's views, on Christ's freedom from sin is thus fully in accord with the Synod's teaching.

Bede's Pastoral Concern

In his commentary on Mark 6. 48–50, Bede is not concerned with explicating the historical details of the monothelete controversy or the technical terms of operation and will; he does not identify the *acta* of the Lateran Synod as the source of his quoted extracts concerning Theodore and Dionysius, even though aspects of his commentary suggest his awareness of the *acta*'s substantial quotation and refutation of Theodore's views. He writes as an exegete and pastoral theologian, expounding sacred Scripture to reveal an essential aspect of the identity of Christ for the reader or listener. The opening sentence of his exposition declares, 'Adhuc heretici putant fantasma fuisse dominum nec ueram assumpsisse carnem de uirgine' (Up to the present time heretics have thought that [the body of] the Lord was a phantasm and

---

41 Bede, *In Marci evangelivm expositio*, ed. by Hurst, p. 518, ll. 1171–72.
42 *Decrees of the Ecumenical Councils*, ed. by Tanner, vol. 1, p. 86.
43 *Decrees of the Ecumenical Councils*, ed. by Tanner, vol. 1, p. 78: 'Nec quia communionem humanarum subiit infirmitatum, ideo nostrorum fuit particeps delictorum'; p. 79: 'nova autem nativitate generatus, quia inviolata virginitas concupiscentiam nescivit, carnis materiam ministravit'.
44 See Canon Three of the fifth session in *Concilium Lateranense*, ed. by Riedinger, pp. 370–71; *The Acts of the Lateran Synod*, trans. by Price, p. 377. The canon is discussed in Hurley, 'Born Incorruptibly'. See too O'Reilly, '"Know Who and What He is"', pp. 302–03, 313–14.

that he did not assume true flesh from the Virgin).[45] From the start, in other words, Bede indicates the serious implications of Theodore's teaching: denying the reality of Christ's human flesh denies the truth of the Incarnation. Theodore, once bishop of Pharan, is introduced as representing the most recent of such heretics, but the correction of his view offered by the text of Dionysius in the *acta* is quoted by Bede, not to address heretics, but rather to teach and sustain the faithful who, like the disciples in the Gospel episode, are vulnerable in their human weakness to occasions of fear and doubt. The exposition of Scripture by a great variety of means in order to reveal the true identity of Christ and its significance for the faithful is central to Bede's work.

This pastoral concern determines how Bede uses his knowledge of monotheletism in his teaching. Having considered the miracle of Christ walking on water, when his human nature was hard to see, Bede turns to 'the storms of the Passion', when Christ's humanity was evident. His human vulnerability to suffering put his human resolve to the test but, Bede explains, because his human and divine natures were united in his one person, his divinity was also present at the Passion, though it was not discernible according to previous expectations of how divine power might be manifested. Constantly moving between the literal text of the Gospel passage and its spiritual meaning, Bede shows the importance of right belief (the recognition of who Christ is) to the practice of the Christian life: 'Quia in tempestatibus passionum quae pro constantia fidei a perfidis ingeruntur talis non numquam prouisio divinitus ostenditur' (For the same plan is on occasion shown by God in the storms of the sufferings that are inflicted by enemies of the faith in proportion to (their victims') constancy in the faith).[46] He asks why the Lord, before reassuring the disciples and calming the storm (Mark 6. 50b–51), had first increased the terror of those he came to liberate by walking on the sea as if to pass them by like a stranger (Mark 6. 48b–50a). He shows that such a spectacular manifestation of Christ's divine nature had the effect of increasing their wonder at his power and their thanksgiving for deliverance from the storm, but, because they were still at a carnal or elementary stage in understanding, their hearts remained blinded to the truth that this was God. They failed to recognise the fullness of his divine majesty when he calmed the storm and showed that he was Lord of the elements, just as they had failed to recognise the continuing presence of his humanity when, through his divine power, he miraculously walked on water.

Bede then further extends the image of the storm to the experience of the faithful in times of trouble, remarking: 'Saepe enim ita fideles in tribulatione positos superna pietas deseruisse uisa est ut quasi laborantes in mari discipulos praeterire Iesus uoluisse putaretur' (Often, indeed, the divine mercy has appeared to have abandoned the faithful who are in tribulation, so that Jesus might be thought to have wished to pass by (the faithful) like the disciples labouring in the sea).[47] He cites the extreme example of the Church's martyrs, evoking their cries of desolation through the words of the psalmist, 'Why have you forgotten me? Why do I mourn

45 Bede, *In Marci evangelivm expositio*, ed. by Hurst, p. 517, ll. 1128–130.
46 Bede, *In Marci evangelivm expositio*, ed. by Hurst, p. 518, ll. 1145–147.
47 Bede, *In Marci evangelivm expositio*, ed. by Hurst, p. 518, ll. 1147–150.

whilst my enemies afflict me […] and say, "Where is their God?"' (Psalms 41. 10–11; Psalms 78. 10). The tribulation of the faithful is likened to that of the disciples who feared shipwreck in the storm, but their divine consolation is similarly assured: 'When you pass through the waters, I will be with you' (Isaiah 43. 2). Bede resumes the words of the Gospel, where Christ comforts the disciples in the storm: "'Have faith. It is I. Fear not". And he went up to them into the ship, and the wind ceased' (Mark 6. 50b–51). So too, Bede says, whenever the Lord enters a heart by grace, all evil, worldly and vicious spirits in conflict within the heart are suddenly stilled.[48] His spiritual interpretation of the Gospel text proceeds from the belief that Christ shares in the storms and troubles of the faithful since he shares our human nature. Bede elsewhere in his exegesis often explained that because the faithful are united with Christ, whose human nature is united to his divine nature, he enables them in their human weakness to share in his divine power to endure earthly tribulation and overcome inner turmoil and temptation.[49]

Telescoping Heresies: Eutyches and monotheletism

In the Lateran *acta*, Pope Martin notes that Theodore of Pharan's views, denying the full humanity of the Logos, showed him to be guilty of a whole range of heresies that had already been condemned in the work of the fathers and councils, including Arianism, Docetism, Manichaeism, and Apollinarianism. The argument is also used in the pope's analysis of other monotheletes, Sergius of Constantinople and Cyrus of Alexandria, whom he reproached for repeating old heresies, and for concealing this by pretending that their erroneous doctrines were in accord with the teachings of Chalcedon and the fathers.[50] Such telescoping of heresies from different periods of time appears in Bede's own exegesis, for example in his comment on Christ's words in Mark's account of the feeding of the four thousand,

> **I have compassion on the multitude, for behold they have now been with me three days and have nothing to eat … they will faint in the way** (Mark 8. 1):

Et in hac lectione consideranda est in uno eodemque redemptore nostro distincta operatio diuinitatis et humanitatis, atque error Eutichetis qui unam tantum

---

48 Bede, *In Marci evangelivm expositio*, ed. by Hurst, p. 518, ll. 1164–167: 'In quocumque enim corde Deus per gratiam sui adest amoris mox uniuersa vitiorum et aduersantis mundi siue spirituum malignorum bella compressa quiescunt'.

49 The belief is variously expounded in Bede's exegesis, for example in his Gospel homilies on the Incarnation: Bede, *Opera homiletica*, ed. by Hurst, pp. 34, ll. 84–91; 39, ll. 71–74; 50, ll. 165–67; Bede, *Homilies on the Gospels*, vol. 1, pp. 47, 54, 71.

50 *The Acts of the Lateran Synod*, trans. by Price, pp. 207, 223, 361, 401–02. Theodore, Sergius and Cyrus were also among those condemned in 680–81 at the Third Council of Constantinople for 'sowing with novel speech among the orthodox people the heresy of a single will and a single principle of action in the two natures of the one member of the holy Trinity, Christ our true God': *Decrees of the Ecumenical Councils*, ed. by Tanner, vol. 1, pp. 125–26.

in Christo operationem dogmatizare praesumit procul a christianis finibus expellendus. Quis enim non uideat hoc quod super turbam miseretur dominus ne uel inedia uel uiae longioris labore deficiat affectum esse et compassionem humanae fragilitatis? quod uero de septem panibus et pisculis paucis quattuor hominum milia saturauit divinae opus esse uirtutis?

> In this passage one should consider in the one and same Redeemer of ours the distinct operation of the divinity and humanity. The error of Eutyches, who presumed to affirm as a dogma only one operation in Christ, should be driven away, far beyond the limits of the Christian world. For who can fail to see in the fact that the Lord took pity on the crowd, lest it falter from lack of food or the effort of a prolonged journey, a fellow-feeling, a compassion for human weakness and, in his satisfying the hunger of four thousand men with seven loaves and a few fish, a work of divine power?[51]

The name of Eutyches is here related to the seventh-century monothelete doctrine of 'one operation in Christ'. The miraculous feeding of the crowd was the kind of miracle that Pope Leo had listed when showing Eutyches what pertained to Christ's divinity as distinct from what pertained to his humanity. Bede presents it in such a way as to emphasise that Christ's two distinct natures, fully divine and fully human, worked in communion. The implied argument of the passage is that Christ, having two natures, necessarily has two 'operations' or distinct kinds of activity proper to each nature; it might, therefore, be said that Eutyches, believing him to have only one nature, had already 'presumed to affirm as a dogma only one operation in Christ'.[52]

The tradition of designating heresy as an innovation, and at the same time as the manifestation of an old heresy already formally condemned by the fathers and councils of the Church, helps explain the opening statement of Bede's chapter on the synod at Hatfield in the *Historia ecclesiastica*, which has puzzled modern commentators: 'About this time Theodore [of Canterbury] heard that the faith of the church at Constantinople had been greatly shaken by the heresy of Eutyches. As he wished to keep the English churches over which he presided free from any such taint, he convened an assembly'.[53] The calling of the synod of Hatfield (679) is presented as a response to 'the heresy of Eutyches', yet Eutyches is named in the very same chapter

---

51 Bede, *In Marci evangelivm expositio*, ed. by Hurst, p. 527, ll. 1515-23.
52 The two complementary passages in the Marcan commentary that make a connection between the heresy of Eutyches and monothelete belief in one operation and one will in Christ are to be distinguished from the naming of Eutyches in Bede's earlier *Commentary on Luke*, which focuses instead on the denial of Christ's human nature for which Eutyches was condemned in Leo's Tome (*Decrees of the Ecumenical Councils*, ed. by Tanner, vol. 1, pp. 77–78). Bede's exposition of Luke 11:27 denounces the heresy of denying that the only begotten Son of God was born of the ever virgin Mary by the power of the Holy Spirit and drew his flesh from her. Bede enjoins the present faithful: 'Let us, therefore, lift up our voice against these statements of Eutyches in the company of the catholic Church'; he uses the condemnation of Eutyches as a means of reinforcing contemporary belief in the incarnate Christ's human nature, and the truth that Christ, born from the Virgin's womb, is true God and true man. Bede, *In Lucae evangelivm expositio*, ed. by Hurst, pp. 236–37, ll. 213–44.
53 *Historia ecclesiastica*, IV.17, ed. and trans. by Colgrave and Mynors, pp. 384–85.

as a heresiarch condemned at Chalcedon (451).[54] Leo the Great's Tome had been
directed against Eutyches specifically for his inability 'to recognize our [human]
nature in the only-begotten Son of God', and the name of Eutyches had come to
represent extreme monophysitism. The doctrinal definitions of general councils
were customarily identified in brief by the names of the particular heresiarchs each
council had condemned. This convention is followed in the *Historia ecclesiastica* in the
listing of the five general councils acclaimed in the Hatfield synod, and had already
been used in Bede's *Chronica maiora*.[55] In both lists the condemnation of Eutyches
helps characterise the Council of Chalcedon. The appearance of his name at the
beginning of Bede's chapter on Hatfield signals a perceived theological connection
between fifth-century monophysitism and seventh-century monotheletism, and the
role of the papacy in the refutation of both at Chalcedon and at the Lateran Synod
which affirmed Chalcedon.

A similar connection between the two heresies was made in Pope Agatho's weighty
letter to the Emperor, which was to be read out at the Sixth Ecumenical Council
at Constantinople (680–681). Agatho shows new heresy arising out of old, and he
presents testimonies from Greek and Latin fathers to vanquish 'the depraved dogma'
of those who threaten to split the unity of the Church by 'unam voluntatem, unamque
operationem duarum naturarum asserentes in uno Domino nostro Jesu Christo:
quod Ariani et Apollinaristae, Eutychianistae, Timotheani, Acephali, Theodosiani et
Gaianitae, et omnis omnino haereticus furor, sive confundentium, seu dividentium
Incarnationis Christi mysterium, docuit' (asserting one will, and one operation of
the two natures in the one Jesus Christ our Lord, a thing which the Arians and the
Apollinarians, the Eutychians, the Timotheans, the Acephali, the Theodosians and
the Gaianitae, and every heretical fury, taught, whether confusing or dividing the
mystery of Christ's incarnation).[56] The tradition was familiar to Bede, who in the
Chronica minora showed that he was aware (through Isidore) that the heresy of the
Acephali had been put down in the sixth century, yet in his *Chronica maiora* he could
refer to three prominent seventh-century monotheletes, Cyrus of Alexandria, Sergius
and Pyrrhus of Constantinople, as 'instigators of the Acephalite heresy' who 'taught
there was one operation of divinity and humanity in Christ and one will' and were
duly condemned at Pope Martin's synod in Rome.[57]

Assembling and documenting 'the tradition of the fathers' on this matter had
been carried out on an extraordinary scale in the preparation of the Lateran Synod of
649. A distinctive feature was the presentation in the fifth session of selected extracts

54   See the note on Eutyches in Bede, *Opera historica*, ed. by Plummer, p. 230.
55   *Historia ecclesiastica*, IV.17, ed. and trans. by Colgrave and Mynors, pp. 386–87; *De temporum ratione*,
     ed. by Jones, p. 528, ll. 1903–19; *The Reckoning of Time*, trans. by Wallis, pp. 231–32.
56   Agatho, *Epistola ad augustos imperatores*, col. 1172; *The Seven Ecumenical Councils*, ed. by Percival,
     p. 332.
57   *De temporum ratione*, ed. by Jones, pp. 525, ll. 1826–30; *The Reckoning of Time*, trans. by Wallis,
     pp. 229–30. Bede here follows the *Liber pontificalis: Le Liber pontificalis*, ed. by Duchesne, vol. 1, p. 337;
     The Book of Pontiffs, ed. by Davis, p. 69. On the Acephali (*Akephaloi*) see Herrin, *The Formation of
     Christendom*, p. 120.

from patristic writings, identified and arranged into *florilegia* on the natural wills and
operations of Christ. Pope Martin proclaimed them to be 'pious testimonies [...] for
the rebuttal of heretics'; through the fathers God had 'at many times and in many ways'
given enlightenment about the orthodox faith, which had been denied in the writings
of those now condemned.[58] After the *florilegia* were read out, the council members
affirmed that, in accordance with the holy councils, they believed and taught as the
fathers believed and taught, 'adding nothing and taking nothing away from what they
handed down to us'.[59] In such ways the Synod contrasted the recurrence of heresy in
the Church with continuity in its orthodox teachings. This concept of authority and
tradition is echoed in Bede's excerpts from the professions of faith made at Theodore's
synod at Hatfield. Those assembled there, in acclaiming the general councils and the
Lateran Synod, and condemning those whom the general councils had condemned,
showed that they were not adding to, or subtracting from, the fullness of revelation
and belief, 'as our Lord Jesus Christ delivered it in the flesh to the disciples who saw
Him face to face and heard His words, and as it was handed down in the creed of
the holy fathers and by all the holy and universal councils in general and the whole
body of the accredited fathers of the catholic Church'.[60]

Gethsemane: Bede's Commentary on Mark 14. 33–38

Christ's words in the garden of Gethsemane on the eve of his Passion were of particular
importance in the christological debate. They were central to the arguments against
monotheletism formulated by Maximus the Confessor,[61] and they feature strongly
in the *florilegium* of the fifth session of the Lateran Synod, devoted to patristic texts
on the natural wills of Christ. Some of these passages are also among the texts cited
in Pope Agatho's letter to the Emperor refuting the doctrines of the monotheletes.
There Agatho explained that in the Gospel accounts of the Gethsemane scene Christ
instructs the faithful that he is both true God and true man: 'Thus as man he prays
to the Father to take away the cup of suffering, because in him our human nature
was complete, sin only excepted: 'Father, if it be possible, let this cup pass from me;
nevertheless not as I will but as you will' (Matthew 26. 39; cf. Mark 14. 36); and in
another passage, 'Not my will but yours be done' (Luke 22. 42)'.[62] Agatho invoked
the testimony of the holy and approved fathers on what 'my will' and 'yours' signify,
using the customary practice of expounding the terms in the light of an additional

---

58 *Concilium Lateranense*, ed. by Riedinger, p. 253; *The Acts of the Lateran Synod*, trans. by Price, p. 304.
59 *Concilium Lateranense*, ed. by Riedinger, p. 319; *The Acts of the Lateran Synod*, trans. by Price, p. 346.
60 *Historia ecclesiastica*, IV.17, ed. and trans. by Colgrave and Mynors, pp. 386–87.
61 See Léthel, *Théologie de l'agonie du Christ*; Fédou, *La voie du Christ*, pp. 570–85; *The Acts of the Lateran
    Synod*, trans. by Price, pp. 96–99; *Scripta saeculi vii*, ed. by Allen and Neil, pp. xii–xxiii.
62 Agatho, *Epistola ad augustos imperatores*, col. 1173: 'Orat quidem ad Patrem ut homo, ut calicem
    passionis transageret, quia in eo nostrae humanitatis natura absque solo peccato perfecta est: *Pater,
    inquiens, si possibile est, transeat a me calix iste; verumtamen non sicut ego volo, sed sicut tu vis*. Et in alio
    loco: *Non mea voluntas, sed tua fiat*'; *The Seven Ecumenical Councils*, ed. by Percival, p. 333.

Gospel text, 'I came not to do my own will but the will of him who sent me' (John 6. 38). Quoting extracts from patristic texts used thirty years earlier in the Lateran *florilegium* of 649, Agatho cited not only Pope Leo, but also Ambrose,[63] Athanasius and other fathers from before Chalcedon, whose writings were seen as containing the means of refuting the seventh-century heresy. On the crucial words, *Yet not my will but yours be done*, he cited Athanasius: 'He shows that there are two wills, the one human which is the will of the flesh, but the other divine. For his human will, out of the weakness of the flesh, was fleeing away from the passion, but his divine will was ready for it.'[64] Recalling conciliar definitions of the two natures in Christ after their inseparable union, implying two natural wills, Agatho referred to 'most telling passages in other of the early venerable fathers, who speak clearly of the two natural operations in Christ, not to mention [...] those who afterwards conducted the laborious conflicts in defence of the venerable council of Chalcedon and of the Tome of St Leo against the heretics from whose error the assertion of this new dogma has arisen.'[65]

It is instructive to turn from the *florilegia* of the Lateran *acta* and Agatho's citations to Bede's exposition of the words of Christ in Gethsemane in his commentary on Mark. This makes clear once again his familiarity with the Synod's proceedings. Remarkably, he quotes or closely draws on several of the patristic texts assembled in the Synod's *florilegium* on Christ's natural wills. The manner in which he uses the material is also of interest. The modern edition of the commentary notes, for instance, that he uses a substantial quotation from Ambrose's *De fide* in his exposition of Mark 14. 33, 'Tristis est anima mea usque ad mortem' (My soul is sorrowful even unto death),[66] but the last few lines of the quotation had also been quoted in the *acta* of the Lateran Synod, in an extract which forms one of the first patristic texts in the *florilegium* on the natural wills of Christ.[67] Ambrose had used the first person voice of the faithful, affectively stressing that Christ at his passion 'assumed my will and my distress' because he had assumed human nature; it was as a man that he said [to the Father], 'Not as I will but

63 The passage from Ambrose, which includes the words, 'because he bears my sorrow as man, he spoke as a man, and therefore he says: "Not as I will but as you will"' (p. 333), had been quoted in the fifth session of the Lateran Synod: *Concilium Lateranense*, ed. by Riedinger, p. 274; *The Acts of the Lateran Synod*, trans. by Price, p. 316.

64 Agatho, *Epistola ad augustos imperatores*, col. 1176: 'duas voluntates hic ostendit, et unam quidem humanam, quae est carnis, aliam autem divinam. Quoniam humana propter infirmitatem carnis refugiebat passionem, divina autem ejus prompta'; *The Seven Ecumenical Councils*, ed. by Percival, p. 333. The passage (in fact from Pseudo-Athanasius, *De incarnatione et contra Arianos*) had been quoted in the Lateran Synod, and it was quoted again in the imperial confirmation of the decrees of Constantinople III: *Concilium Lateranense*, ed. by Riedinger, p. 282; *The Acts of the Lateran Synod*, trans. by Price, p. 323, n. 180.

65 Agatho, *Epistola ad augustos imperatores*, col. 1197: 'Non desunt autem et aliorum venerabilium Patrum probatissima testimonia, duas manifeste dicentium naturales operationes in Christo, ut silentio transeamus [...] quicumque postmodum pro rectitudine venerabilis concilii Chalcedonensis, et tomo sancti Leonis satisfaciendo, laboriosos conflictus adversus confundentium haereses pertulerunt, de quorum errore et novi dogmatis descendit assertio'; *The Seven Ecumenical Councils*, ed. by Percival, p. 335.

66 Bede, *In Marci evangelivm expositio*, ed. by Hurst, p. 615, ll. 797–812.

67 *Concilium Lateranense*, ed. by Riedinger, p. 274; *The Acts of the Lateran Synod*, trans. by Price, p. 316, extract 2.

as you will' (Mark 14. 36), and therefore, Ambrose says, "mea est tristitia quam meo suscepit affectu" (mine is the sorrow that he assumed from my state of mind). This leads Bede into a brief quotation from another work by Ambrose, his commentary on Luke, where the idea is repeated and extended: 'Therefore he suffered for me who had no reason to suffer on his own account'. While remaining unchanged in his eternal divinity, Christ was affected by 'the distress arising from my weakness' (that is, because he had become man).[68] This passage in the commentary on Luke (10. 56) is another of the patristic extracts cited in the same Lateran *florilegium* on the natural wills of Christ.[69]

Part of the preceding extract in the *acta*, also taken from Ambrose's commentary on Luke (7. 133), forms the next item in Bede's chain of quotations.[70] He includes the opening of the extract, which cites 'My soul is sorrowful, he says, unto death' (Matthew 26. 38; Mark 14. 34), and the explanation that Christ (in his divine nature) was not sorrowful because of death; rather, in his dread he was showing that he had assumed humanity, body and soul,[71] and with it the experience of hunger, thirst, distress, and all the emotions. Bede then comments on Mark 14. 36 with lines from Augustine's *Enarrationes in psalmos* (Psalms 100. 6), where Augustine cites the parallel Gospel text in Matthew 26. 39, and shows its application to the faithful. When under fear of death they too are to say what Christ said 'on our account', that is, 'Father, if it is possible, let this chalice pass from me'. But if this is not possible, they are to imitate Christ's human will further by saying, 'Not as I will but as you will, Father'. The few lines which Bede quotes are selected from a larger extract of Augustine's text in the same Lateran *florilegium*.[72]

At this point the Gethsemane prayer, 'Not what I will, but what you will' (Mark 14. 36), is repeated in Bede's commentary, and further illuminated by the juxtaposition of Christ's words from a different context, 'I came not to do my own will but the will of him who sent me' (John 6. 38). This Gospel text leads directly into the opening of Bede's brief quotation from the Second Tome of Leo the Great, drawn from an extract used in the *florilegium* of the Lateran *acta*, which cites John 6. 38 and emphasises that what Christ here called 'his own will' is the one he took in time from the Virgin, while 'the will of him who sent him' refers to what he possessed in common with the Father through all eternity.[73] The extract that directly follows Leo's in the Lateran *acta* is from a homily of Pseudo-Hippolytus, *In sanctam pascha*. It explains that Christ cried out for the chalice to pass, thereby showing that he was man, but, remembering why

68 Bede, *In Marci evangelivm expositio*, ed. by Hurst, pp. 615–16, ll. 812–15.
69 *Concilium Lateranense*, ed. by Riedinger, p. 274; *The Acts of the Lateran Synod*, trans. by Price, p. 317, extract 4.
70 Bede, *In Marci evangelivm expositio*, ed. by Hurst, p. 616, ll. 815–20; *Concilium Lateranense*, ed. by Riedinger, p. 274; *The Acts of the Lateran Synod*, trans. by Price, p. 317, extract 3.
71 Qualified in the *acta* by the words, 'apart from sin' (cf. Hebrews 4. 14), a phrase omitted by Bede.
72 Bede, *In Marci evangelivm expositio*, ed. by Hurst, p. 616, ll. 830–35; *Concilium Lateranense*, ed. by Riedinger, p. 280; *The Acts of the Lateran Synod*, trans. by Price, p. 321, extract 11.
73 Bede, *In Marci evangelivm expositio*, ed. by Hurst, p. 316, ll. 336–40 (the source of these lines in the Second Tome is not identified by the editor); *Concilium Lateranense*, ed. by Riedinger, p. 282; *The Acts of the Lateran Synod*, trans. by Price, p. 322, extract 13.

he had been sent, he cried out again, 'Father, not my will. The spirit is eager, but the flesh is weak'. Part of the extract is quoted by Bede, but he omits this final sentence and the abbreviated reference, 'Father, not my will', and instead reiterates the full text of Mark 14.36: 'Sed non quod ego uolo sed quod tu'.[74]

Mark's gospel next recounts Christ's exhortation to Peter to watch and pray that he might not enter into temptation: 'The spirit is willing but the flesh is weak' (Mark 14. 37–38). Instead of identifying this as an admonition to Peter concerning the inner struggle within all humanity between spirit and flesh (cf. Romans 7. 23), Bede relates it to Christ's own prayer in the previous verse, 'yet not what I will, but what you will' (Mark 14. 36), and the submission of his human will to the Father, with whom he shares the divine will. He then reflects on the significance of Mark's account, and, after the opening sentence referring to 'the Eutychians', his remarks are closely drawn from the extract ascribed to Athanasius which immediately follows that from Pseudo-Hippolytus in the Lateran *acta*:[75]

> Facit hic locus et aduersum Eutichianos qui dicunt unam in mediatore Dei et hominum domino et saluatore nostro operationem unam fuisse uoluntatem. Cum enim dicit, *Spiritus quidem promptus caro uero infirma*, duas uoluntates ostendit humanam uidelicet quae est carnis et diuinam quae est deitatis. Vbi humana quidem propter infirmitatem carnis recusat passionem diuina autem eius est promptissima quoniam formidare quidem in passione humanae fragilitatis est suscipere autem dispensationem passionis diuinae uoluntatis atque uirtutis est.

>> This passage also goes against the Eutychians who say that there was one operation and one will in our Lord and Saviour, 'the mediator between God and man' (1 Timothy 2.5). For when it says, 'the spirit indeed is willing, but the flesh is weak' (Mark 14. 38), it points to two wills: namely a human one, which is of the flesh, and a divine one, which is of God. Whence the human will, because of the infirmity of the flesh, shrinks from suffering, but his divine will accepts it most readily. For to dread suffering belongs to human weakness; but to accept suffering when it is given belongs to the divine will and power.[76]

Bede has at this stage quoted from at least seven of the extracts from patristic texts concerning the natural wills of Christ used in the Lateran *acta* specifically, and in almost the same order, as authorities against monotheletism. Only now, however, does he refer to the belief of those heretics, namely 'the Eutychians who say that there was one operation and one will in our Lord and Saviour'. The observation complements his reference earlier in the Marcan commentary to 'the error of Eutyches, who presumed to affirm as a dogma only one operation in Christ'. Just as Bede had

74 Bede, *In Marci evangelivm expositio*, ed. by Hurst, p. 616, ll. 840–43 (the source in Pseudo-Hippolytus is not identified); *Concilium Lateranense*, ed. by Riedinger, p. 282; *The Acts of the Lateran Synod*, trans. by Price, p. 323, extract 14.

75 *Concilium Lateranense*, ed. by Riedinger, p. 282; *The Acts of the Lateran Synod*, trans. by Price, p. 323, extract 15. This is the passage mentioned earlier that Pope Agatho also quoted.

76 Bede, *In Marci evangelivm expositio*, ed. by Hurst, pp. 617–18, ll. 881–90.

there insisted, 'in this passage (Mark 8. 1–2) one should consider in the one and same Redeemer of ours the separate operation of the divinity and humanity',[77] so now he shows that Mark 14. 38 'points to two wills: namely a human one, which is of the flesh, and a divine one, which is of God'. He then goes further by referring to 'our Lord and Saviour' as 'the mediator between God and man' (1 Timothy 2. 5), alluding to a Pauline text of great importance in christological debate and exegesis. Freely used by Augustine, and much quoted by Gregory the Great, it had a crucial role in Pope Leo's refutation of Eutyches in the Tome, where, expounding the inseparable union of Christ's truly divine and truly human natures at the Incarnation as necessary to human salvation, the pope proclaimed:

> Salva igitur proprietate utriusque naturae et in unam coeunte personam suscepta est a maiestate humilitas, a virtute infirmitas, ab aeternitate mortalitas, et ad resolvendum conditionis nostrae debitum natura inviolabilis est unita passibili, ut quod nostris remediis congruebat, *unus* atque idem *mediator dei et hominum homo Christus Iesus* et mori posset ex uno et mori non posset ex altero.

>> So the proper character of both natures was maintained and came together in a single person. Lowliness was taken up by majesty, weakness by strength, mortality by eternity. To pay off the debt of our state, invulnerable nature was united to a nature that could suffer; so that in a way that corresponded to the remedies we needed, *one* and the same *mediator between God and man, the man Christ Jesus* (1 Timothy 2:5) could both on the one hand die and on the other be incapable of death.[78]

Bede, similarly, uses the text of I Timothy 2. 5 throughout his writings to signal an orthodox faith in Christ.[79] The naming of Eutyches in the Marcan commentary, however, not only recalls the belief of the monophysites that there is only one nature in the incarnate Christ, but suggests the extension of that error among latter-day 'Eutychians', meaning monotheletes. Their belief that there is only one will in Christ denies his full human nature, and therefore his identity as the one mediator between God and man. Bede corrects such error in his exegetical and homiletic works in a variety of ways and contexts, but always consonant with the christological belief articulated by Pope Leo and Chalcedon, affirmed and clarified at the Lateran Synod of Pope Martin, and reiterated by Pope Agatho for the Sixth General Council.[80]

---

77 Bede, *In Marci evangelivm expositio*, ed. by Hurst, p. 527, ll. 1515–18.

78 *Decrees of the Ecumenical Councils*, ed. by Tanner, vol. 1, p. 78.

79 Examples include the description of Aidan in *Historia ecclesiastica*, III.17, ed. and trans. by Colgrave and Mynors, pp. 266–67; Bede, *In Lucae evangelivm expositio*, ed. by Hurst, p. 8, l. 160; p. 53, ll. 1365–66; p. 76, l. 2253;Bede, *De templo*, ed. by Hurst, p. 147, l. 13; p. 178, ll. 1257; p. 211, ll. 765–66; Bede, *De tabernaculo*, ed. by Hurst, p. 12, l. 294; p. 30, ll. 995–96; p. 35, l. 1201; p. 72, ll. 1208–9; p. 133, l. 1581; Bede, *In Ezram et Neemiam*, ed. by Hurst, p. 245, ll. 184–85; p. 311, ll. 938–39; p. 339, l. 10. Further instances are noted in Bede, *A Biblical Miscellany*, trans. by Foley and Holder, pp. 61, 64, 67, 92.

80 I am not arguing that Bede had seen Agatho's letter refuting monotheletism, but that he was familiar with the tradition its collection of texts and arguments presents, the rhetorical conventions it uses, and many of the patristic authorities it cites.

The foregoing examples do not exhaust the extent of Bede's allusions to monotheletism. Elsewhere he demonstrates a similar interest in questions of operation and will when expounding the divinity and humanity of Christ,[81] or the unity of the divine persons in the Trinity.[82] They are sufficient, however, to indicate his detailed understanding of the heresy, and his engagement with the theological issues it had brought to the fore. They also show his familiarity with the proceedings of the Lateran Synod, and his careful selection and use of their contents, though without identifying his source. This knowledge Bede used judiciously, in accordance with his artistic and pastoral aims. He was not concerned primarily with the historical details and contexts of past heresies, nor was he attempting to stem the mass conversion of Northumbria to monotheletism. Rather he made use of the way in which heresy and heretics can readily represent or encapsulate *continuing* challenges to the faith, understanding and behaviour of the teaching Church and its individual members. Like the fathers, he knew that the refutation of heresy can, by contradistinction, illuminate orthodox belief and practice.

Works Cited

Primary Sources

The Acts of the Lateran Synod of 649, trans. by Richard Price, with contributions by Phil Booth and Catherine Cubitt, Translated Texts for Historians, 61 (Liverpool: Liverpool University Press, 2014)

Agatho, Pope, *Epistola ad augustos imperatores*, in *Patrologiae cursus completus: series latina*, ed. by Jacques-Paul Migne, 221 vols (Paris: Migne, 1844–1864), LXXXVII (1863), cols 1162–1214

Bede, *A Biblical Miscellany*, ed. by W. Trent Foley and Arthur G. Holder, Translated Texts for Historians, 28 (Liverpool: Liverpool University Press, 1999)

---

81 Monotheletism probably left its mark, for example, on the emphasis on Christ's two wills in Homily II.3 on Christ's entry into Jerusalem before his Passion (Matthew 21. 1–9), where Bede mentions both Christ's descent from heaven and the prospect of his human suffering, yet shows that, because he is without sin, his human will is in accord with the divine will, and therefore ready to fulfil the Baptist's inspired prophecy that his suffering would take away the sins of the world: Bede, *Opera homiletica*, ed. by Hurst, p. 200, ll. 1–10. Homily I.6, on Luke 2. 1–14, uses the same device in demonstrating the communion of the divine and human wills when Christ was born: Bede, *Opera homiletica*, ed. by Hurst, p. 37, ll. 7–12.

82 In Homily I.20, on Peter's profession of faith in Christ (Matthew 16. 16), Bede affirms, 'una est uoluntas et operatio patris filii et spiritus sancti'. His concern is to show that since Christ shares his divine nature with the Father and the Holy Spirit, the will and operation of the Trinity is one and the same. Later he emphatically asserts the unity of the divine persons by describing the 'double procession' of the Holy Spirit from the Father and the Son as a reflection of their 'one will and operation': Bede, *Opera homiletica*, ed. by Hurst, p. 144, ll. 97–99, 108–11; Bede, *Homilies on the Gospels*, trans. by Martin, vol. 1, pp. 199–200. The Lateran Synod, similarly had affirmed its belief that in the Trinity there is 'one and the same […] will, operation': *Concilium Lateranense*, ed. by Riedinger, p. 369; *The Acts of the Lateran Synod*, trans. by Price, p. 377. See also Homilies I.5 and II.6: Bede, *Opera homiletica*, ed. by Hurst, p. 109, ll. 146–58; p. 290, ll. 9–23.

——, *De tabernaculo*, ed. by D. Hurst, Corpus Christianorum Series Latina, 119A (Turnhout: Brepols, 1969), pp. 1–139

——, *De templo*, ed. by D. Hurst, Corpus Christianorum Series Latina, 119A (Turnhout: Brepols, 1969), pp. 141–234

——, *De temporum ratione*, in *Bedae opera didascalia*, ed. by C. W. Jones, Corpus Christianorum Series Latina, 123A (Turnhout: Brepols, 1975–80), pp. 241–544

——, *Historia ecclesiastica gentis Anglorum*, ed. and trans. by Bertram Colgrave and R. A. B. Mynors, *Bede's Ecclesiastical History of the English People* (Oxford: Clarendon Press, 1969)

——, *Expositio Apocalypseos*, ed. by Roger Gryson, Corpus Christianorum Series Latina, 121A (Turnhout: Brepols, 2001)

——, *Historia abbatum*, in *Abbots of Wearmouth and Jarrow*, ed. and trans. by Christopher Grocock and I. N. Wood (Oxford: Clarendon Press, 2013), pp. 21–75

——, *Homilies on the Gospels*, trans. by Lawrence T. Martin and David Hurst, 2 vols (Kalamazoo: Cistercian Publications, 1991)

——, *In Ezram et Neemiam*, ed. by D. Hurst, Corpus Christianorum Series Latina, 119A (Turnhout: Brepols, 1969), pp. 235–392

——, *In Lucae euangelivm expositio*, ed. by D. Hurst, Corpus Christianorum Series Latina, 120 (Turnhout: Brepols, 1960), pp. 1–425

——, *In Marci euangelivm expositio*, ed. by D. Hurst, Corpus Christianorum Series Latina, 120 (Turnhout: Brepols, 1960), pp. 427–648

——, *On Ezra and Nehemiah*, trans. by Scott DeGregorio, Translated Texts for Historians, 47 (Liverpool: Liverpool University Press, 2006)

——, *On the Tabernacle*, trans. by Arthur G. Holder, Translated Texts for Historians, 18 (Liverpool: Liverpool University Press, 1994)

——, *On the Temple*, trans. by Seán Connolly, with an introduction by Jennifer O'Reilly, Translated Texts for Historians, 21 (Liverpool: Liverpool University Press, 1995)

——, *Opera historica*, vol. 1, ed. by Charles Plummer (Oxford: Clarendon Press, 1896)

——, *Opera homiletica*, ed. by D. Hurst, Corpus Christianorum Series Latina, 122 (Turnhout: Brepols, 1955), pp. 1–403

——, *The Reckoning of Time*, trans. by Faith Wallis, Translated Texts for Historians, 29 (Liverpool: Liverpool University Press, 1999)

The Book of Pontiffs (Liber pontificalis): The Ancient Biographies of the First Ninety Roman Bishops to AD 715, trans. by Raymond Davis, Translated Texts for Historians, 6 (Liverpool: Liverpool University Press, 1989)

Concilium Lateranense anno 649 celebratum, ed. by Rudolph Riedinger, Acta Conciliorum Oecumenicorum, series 2, vol. 1 (Berlin: De Gruyter, 1984)

Decrees of the Ecumenical Councils, ed. by Norman P. Tanner, 2 vols (London: Sheed and Ward, 1990)

Le Liber pontificalis, ed. by L. Duchesne, 3 vols (Paris: Boccard, 1981)

The Life of Bishop Wilfrid by Eddius Stephanus, trans. by Bertram Colgrave (Cambridge: Cambridge University Press, 1985)

Scripta saeculi vii vitam Maximi Confessoris illustrantia, ed. by Pauline Allen and Bronwen Neil, Corpus Christianorum Series Graeca, 39 (Turnhout: Brepols, 1999)

The Seven Ecumenical Councils of the Undivided Church, ed. by Henry R. Percival, *Nicene and Post-Nicene Fathers*, Second Series, 14 (Edinburgh: Clark, 1991)

Secondary Studies

Archbishop Theodore: Commemorative Studies on his Life and Influence, ed. by Michael Lapidge (Cambridge: Cambridge University Press, 1995)

Bischoff, Bernard, and Michael Lapidge, *Bible Commentaries from the Canterbury School of Theodore and Hadrian* (Cambridge: Cambridge University Press, 1994)

Booth, Phil, *Crisis of Empire: Doctrine and Dissent at the End of Late Antiquity* (Berkeley: University of California Press, 2014)

Brown, George Hardin, *A Companion to Bede* (Woodbridge: Boydell, 2009)

Fédou, Michel, *La voie du Christ, II: Développements de la christologie dans le contexte religieux de l'Orient ancien. D'Eusèbe de Césarée à Jean Damascène (1Vè – VIIIè siècle)* (Paris: Cerf, 2013)

Foley, W. Trent, 'Bede's Exegesis of Passages Unique to the Gospel of Mark', in *Biblical Studies in the Early Middle Ages*, ed. by Claudio Leonardi and Giovanni Orlandi (Florence: Galluzo, 2005), pp. 105–24

Ganz, David, 'Roman Manuscripts in Francia and Anglo-Saxon England', in *Roma fra oriente e occidente. Settemane di Studio del Centro Italiano di Studi sull'Alto Medioevo*, 49 (2002), 604–47

Herrin, Judith, *The Formation of Christendom* (Oxford: Blackwell, 1987)

Hovorun, Cyril, *Will, Action and Freedom: Christological Controversies in the Seventh Century* (Leiden: Brill, 2008)

Hurley, Michael, 'Born Incorruptibly: The Third Canon of the Lateran Council, AD 649', *The Heythrop Journal*, 2 (1961), 216–36

Laistner, M. L. W., 'The Library of the Venerable Bede', in *Bede: His Life, Times and Writings*, ed. by A. Hamilton Thompson (Oxford: Clarendon Press, 1935), pp. 237–66

Lapidge, Michael, 'The Career of Archbishop Theodore', in *Archbishop Theodore: Commemorative Studies on his Life and Influence*, ed. by Michael Lapidge (Cambridge: Cambridge University Press, 1995), pp. 1–29

Léthel, François-Marie, *Théologie de l'agonie du Christ. La liberté humaine du Fils de Dieu et son importance sotériologique mises en lumière par Saint Maxime Confesseur* (Paris: Beauchesne, 1979)

Noble, Thomas F. X., 'Rome in the Seventh Century', in *Archbishop Theodore: Commemorative Studies on his Life and Influence*, ed. by Michael Lapidge (Cambridge: Cambridge University Press, 1995), pp. 68–87

Ó Carragáin, Éamonn, *Ritual and the Rood: Liturgical Images and the Old English Poems of the Dream of the Rood Tradition* (London: The British Library, 2005)

O'Reilly, Jennifer, '"Know Who and What He is": The Context and Inscriptions of the Durham Gospels Crucifixion Image', in *Making and Meaning in Insular Art: Proceedings of the Fifth International Conference on Insular Art*, ed. by Rachel Moss (Dublin: Four Courts Press, 2007), pp. 301–16

———, '"All that Peter Stands For": The *Romanitas* of the Codex Amiatinus Reconsidered', in *Anglo-Saxon / Irish Relations before the Vikings*, ed. by James Graham-Campbell and Michael Ryan, Proceedings of the British Academy, 157 (Oxford: Oxford University Press, 2009), pp. 367–95

Thacker, Alan, 'Why did Heresy Matter to Bede? Present and Future Contexts', in *Bede and the Future*, ed. by Peter Darby and Faith Wallis (Farnham: Ashgate, 2014), pp. 47–66

FAITH WALLIS

Rectores at Risk: Erudition and Heresy in Bede's Commentary on Proverbs

In a characteristically perceptive essay on Bede's attitude towards heresy, Alan Thacker observed that Bede was on the whole less interested in the content of heretical doctrines, than in the threat heresy might pose to the moral fabric of the Christian community. Alan pointed to the crime of *perfidia* — treachery, betrayal — as the toxic heart of heresy. *Perfidia* encouraged Bede to roll schismatics and 'bad Catholics' who damaged the integrity of the faith by their vicious behaviour together with heretics *stricto sensu* into one damning category. The Church's bulwark against these traitors were its *doctores* and *praedicatores*, the learned teachers and preachers who could confront the twisted logic and specious rhetoric of heretics with the pure Gospel truth. These concerns became increasingly preoccupying as Bede reached the end of his life.

Tracing these themes across Bede's writings, however, Alan paused before the commentaries on Proverbs and the Song of Songs. He found in these works the same attention to the role of *doctores* and *praedicatores*, but not much concern with *perfidia*, at least in comparison to the other works surveyed. He noted the difficulty of dating these two commentaries, and then returned to his main theme.[1] The goal of my offering to this volume in honour of Alan is to pick up the hint he dropped: if *perfidia* is not the problem with heretics in the Proverbs commentary, then what is?

Bede's *Commentary on Proverbs* was one of his most widely read works of exegesis. There are at least eighty-eight manuscripts of the whole text, plus an additional fifteen copies of the extracted section from ch. 31 in praise of the Competent Woman (*De muliere forti*).[2] A late eighth-century copy of the Proverbs commentary possibly from Wearmouth and Jarrow survives as Oxford, Bodleian Library MS Bodley 819, and there are more Carolingian manuscripts of this text than of any other of Bede's Old

---

1 Thacker, 'Why did Heresy Matter to Bede?', p. 61. On the importance of the word *perfidia* for Bede and its association with heresy, see Alan Thacker, 'Bede, the Britons and the Book of Samuel'.
2 Laistner, *A Hand-List of Bede Manuscripts*, pp. 56–62, lists 86 copies of the full commentary, to which George Hardin Brown adds two (personal communication).

Faith Wallis • is Professor in the Department of History and Classical Studies at McGill University, jointly appointed to the Department of Social Studies of Medicine.

Cities, Saints, and Communities in Early Medieval Europe, ed. by Scott DeGregorio and Paul Kershaw, SEM 46 (Turnhout: Brepols, 2020), pp. 129-143
BREPOLS PUBLISHERS   DOI 10.1484/M.SEM-EB.5.119625

Testament commentaries. In the twelfth-century Bede revival, it was copied as often as his most widely diffused work, *On the Seven Catholic Epistles*.[3] The reason for this popularity is at once obvious and elusive. Obvious: because none of the Fathers, major or minor, had composed an exposition of this work.[4] Elusive: because we do not yet know why the book of Proverbs was so significant for Bede, his contemporaries and his later medieval readers, when it was apparently of marginal interest to the Fathers, at least as an integral work.[5]

Composing a full commentary on Proverbs was a challenge. It is not a book with an obvious structure or a unitary message, but rather a composite of several genres of ancient Near Eastern 'wisdom literature'. It contains instruction texts, and one in particular, covering chapters 1–9, where the instruction comes not from father or teacher, but from personified Wisdom herself. The central chapters of Proverbs, by contrast, are sentence collections — discrete maxims and adages of a moral character. Finally, chapters 25–31 comprise a suite of sayings structured around numbers (e.g. 'under three things the earth trembles; under four it cannot bear up...' [Proverbs 30. 21]), and the acrostic poem in praise of the Capable Woman.

Bede's *Commentary on Proverbs* is divided into three books that coincide with these three divisions. The first book covers chapters 1–9, whose theme is the praise of personified Wisdom and warnings about the danger posed by Wisdom's evil counterpart, the Harlot–Adulteress. The second book spans chapters 10–24, where, as Bede indicates, Solomon adopts a different rhetorical mode: not presenting an extended discourse on good and evil, but contrasting the actions of good and evil people in isolated maxims. Book 3 on the remainder of Proverbs is likewise, in Bede's view, marked by a stylistic change; Solomon is no longer addressing an audience, but recording private, interior reflections.

But the questions remain. Why did Bede elect to comment on a book that relates no narrative (such as one would find in the Gospels or the historical works of the Old Testament), conveys no argument (such as Bede would expound in the seven

---

3   Westgard, 'Bede and the Continent', p. 211. On Bodley 819, see Parkes, *The Scriptorium of Wearmouth-Jarrow*, p. 12.

4   The source apparatus of the edition by Hurst in *Corpus Christianorum Series Latina* 119B includes parallels in the commentary ascribed to Salonius, bishop of Geneva (fl. *c.* 440–451). However, the so-called Salonius commentary post-dates Bede, and may be based on Bede: Weiss, 'Essai de datation du Commentaire sur les Proverbes'; Flint, 'The True Author of the Salonii Commentarii' (arguing that the Salonius commentaries are by Honorius Augustodunensis). A major source for Bede's Proverbs commentary is Gregory the Great, whose *Moralia in Iob*, homilies on the Gospels and on Ezekiel, and *Regula Pastoralis* are frequently and largely silently quoted. Book 6 of Bede's commentary on another Solomonic text, the Song of Songs, is an anthology of extracts about the Song of Songs drawn from Gregory's writings. Since Bede did not know that Gregory had actually composed a commentary on this book, he constructed a Gregorian gloss for himself. It is not unlikely that he performed the same kind of indexing work as the foundation for the Proverbs commentary. *Regula Pastoralis* book 3 is particularly rich in references to Proverbs.

5   Proverbs 8. 22–30 was singled out as a proof-text in the controversy over Arianism: Doignon, 'Hilaire de Poitiers'. The praise of the Competent Woman was also a favorite locus: Maggazù, 'L'Elogio della "Donna forte" (*Prov.* 31. 10–31) nell'interpretazione patristica'.

Catholic Epistles), and displays no sustained theme (as does the Song of Songs)? The adages in the central portion of the book are particularly challenging. Most of them address themes of prudence and good morals, as proverbs are wont to do, often through contrastive examples. The wise, who are circumspect, virtuous, chaste, sober, discrete and careful managers of their wealth, are not like the fools, who are reckless, wicked, drunk, spendthrift, dissolute, and cannot control their tongues. Each proverb stands on its own, and Bede's exegesis in consequence turns each verse into a virtually self-contained 'bite'. Perhaps not surprisingly, he omits many verses without explanation. The expositions of each verse rarely exceed a dozen lines in Hurst's Corpus Christianorum Series Latina edition, which makes *In Proverbias* look more like Bede's early commentaries on Revelation (composed *c.* 703, perhaps earlier) or Acts (*c.* 710). The Proverbs commentary is also the only exegetical work of Bede other than the Revelation commentary to use the term *periocha* to denote the divisions of a text.[6] However, in the absence of any prologue or dedication, none of this provides a strong clue to the date of the Proverbs commentary.[7]

There is, however, one persistent motif in the Proverbs commentary which offers some insight into why Bede chose to expound this book: the role of learned clerics. Reading Proverbs with attention to this motif shows how Bede imagined the social and moral world depicted in the Old Testament text as a symbolic exposition of the values he felt appropriate for ecclesiastics, and perhaps particularly for monks; this latter category, of course, included himself.[8] In particular, the commentary extols the crucially important office of the teacher and preacher; but it also brings to the fore two interconnected dangers to which educated clerics would be particularly vulnerable: heresy, and intellectual vanity or snobbery. The man of learning — at once the prime candidate for the office of *rector* (teacher, preacher, leader of the Church) — was also the man who might pose the greatest risk for the Church's mission.

The exegesis on Proverbs 1. 1–4 (which Bede calls the *praetitulatio*) substitutes for the missing prologue. Here Solomon is presented as the type of Christ: in particular, he was the author of *parabolae* which foreshadow Christ's parables. *Parabolae* and *proverbiae* are in Bede's view interchangeable terms, because both convey truth under the guise of figures and symbols. Moreover (and here perhaps is a clue to Bede's purpose) both parables and proverbs are designed to be delivered

---

6 'Allegorice autem in hac periocha …': Bede, *In prouerbia Salomonis*, I, ed. by Hurst, p. 52. l. 5; 'Et haec periocha eadem …': Bede, *In prouerbia Salomonis*, I, ed. by Hurst, p. 56 line 1. On *periocha* in the commentary on Revelation, see Faith Wallis, *Bede: Commentary on Revelation*, pp. 59–64; on the concise, verse-by-verse commentary called *comaticum*, see pp. 23–25.

7 George Hardin Brown, who has led the field in studying the diffusion and reception of the Bede corpus, declines to hazard a guess at its date: *A Companion to Bede*, p. 14; I tend to concur. The date range of 709–716 has been cogently proposed by Arthur Holder, who argues that Bede's obsession with heresy and particularly Pelagianism is a surrogate for his real target, the 84-year Paschal cycle used by Iona and its dependents. Pelagianism ceased to be relevant to Bede after the conversion of Iona to Roman Paschal reckoning in 716; and hence, 716 is the *terminus ante quem* of the Proverbs commentary, which targets Pelagianism frequently: Holder, 'Hunting Snakes in the Grass', p. 347, n. 49; see also his 'Anti-Pelagian Character', pp. 101–03.

8 This is the theme of my 2016 Jarrow Lecture, *Bede and Wisdom*.

orally, and retained by the hearer in memory. What is to be spoken by one and remembered by the other is crisply defined in the exposition of Proverbs 1. 2: right belief, and right choices or actions.[9] In sum, Proverbs must be read allegorically; its message is didactic, intended to be delivered from a teacher to a hearer; and the substance of Proverbs concerns the relationship between correct understanding and virtuous action.

Bede's approach to allegorizing the book of Proverbs is twofold. The core of maxims is book-ended (so to speak) by two blocks of text which present symbolic figures: personified Wisdom is the protagonist of much of chs 1–9, and the Competent Woman is the subject of an encomium in ch. 31. Bede's method here is broadly typological: Wisdom is the Incarnate Christ (cf. I Corinthians 1. 24) but also the Church (particularly the *doctores* or teachers of the Church, of which more below), and the Competent Woman is a full-blown allegory the Church (analogous to the Bride in the Song of Songs). The two figures of Christ and the Church create the context for the interpretive strategy Bede adopts in dealing with this material.

Secondly, Bede turns the cast of characters portrayed in Proverbs into allegories of the estates of the Church. Read literally, the book of Proverbs depicts a lay society whose foundation is the patriarchal and biological family. But it is also an economically sophisticated world of merchants and landowners, inheritances and money-lending, business partnerships and contracts. It is an urban society of market squares and watchtowers, ruled over by kings who command armies and execute justice. The addressee is often the king himself, whose character determines his people's wellbeing, and who is the direct object of God's concern. There are no references to priests, and hardly a whisper of religious ritual or law. The wisdom (with a small 'w') of Proverbs is probity, justice, sobriety and prudence, and its reward is wealth, security, and good repute in this world. Bede's task was to re-imagine this world as a tissue of allusions to the values that define Christian ecclesiastics — particularly those of his own Anglo-Saxon milieu, who lived in dedicated communities, monasteries or minsters. This means he has to allegorize all the references to power, wealth, and sex in the Biblical text. What Bede has to say about wealth and sex is actually rather interesting,[10] but I wish to concentrate here on his reflections on power. Bede translates almost

---

9   Bede, *In prouerbia Salomonis*, I, ed. by Hurst, pp. 23–24, ll. 1–28.

10   The surface meaning of Proverbs is largely positive on the subject of wealth. But Bede makes it clear in his exposition of 10. 15 ('The substance of a rich man is the city of his strength; the fear of the poor is their poverty') that wealth can only be interpreted positively in an allegorical sense. He prefers to omit verses where wealth is too blatantly extolled, such as 14.20. Bede's reframing of Proverbs as a work addressed to ecclesiastics and perhaps especially monks is sealed by his treatment of marriage and family. References in Proverbs to children as the reward of virtue (13. 22, also 17. 6) must be read allegorically. However, verses which present women (especially harlots) in a negative light may be read literally as well as allegorically, and he furnishes several examples of how to do this (e.g. 7. 10a). With the exception of the praise of the Competent Woman, those verses in Proverbs which extol the virtues of a prudent wife (11. 22, 18. 22, 19. 14 …) are generally passed over in silence. On the other hand, he relishes commenting on verses which bemoan the quarrelsomeness of wives: celibacy is better than even the best of wives, to say nothing of the more common variety: Bede, *In prouerbia Salomonis*, II, ed. by Hurst, p. 108. ll. 20–25. His views on male sexuality are just as negative: as an

every reference to kings or secular rulership either into a reference to God himself (especially God as Judge at the end of time: e.g. Proverbs 19. 12, 20. 8, 22. 29), or into a symbol of the *rectores ecclesiae*, the leadership of the Church. The importance of these *rectores* to Bede's global understanding of the mission of the Church has been thoroughly exposed by Alan Thacker and Scott DeGregorio, although mainly in connection to Bede's later works.[11] The Proverbs commentary also places *rectores* at the forefront; indeed in the famous passage in Proverbs 8. 15–16 — 'By me kings reign and lawgivers decree just things. By me princes rule and the mighty decree justice' — 'kings' denotes the apostles and their successors, 'lawgivers' the evangelists and other ecclesiastical authors, and 'princes' the *praeceptores* and *rectores* of the Church.[12] For the most part when Bede conceives of government or leadership at all, he thinks of authority within the Church. Commenting on Proverbs 20 .21 ('The inheritance gotten hastily in the beginning, in the end shall be without a blessing'), Bede begins by quoting Gregory's *Regula Pastoralis* — a work which famously opens with the statement that the government *of souls* is the 'art of arts' — and then offers his own alternative reading: the person who is elevated to a position of authority before he has learned to serve will in the end not receive the blessing due to the *bonus rector*, and the same is true for anyone who rashly undertakes the ministry of the altar without sufficient training.[13]

Alan Thacker has drawn attention to Bede's intense concern with the role of preachers and teachers (*doctores, praedicatores, magistri*) as conduits of Christian truth to the community of the faithful as a whole.[14] In the Proverbs commentary, this theme is articulated with great insistence. At the very outset, commenting on 1. 6, Bede forges a link between Christ's expounding of his own parables to his disciples, and the extension of his instruction undertaken by the *magistri ecclesiae*, those 'wise men' who can understand and decode the mysteries of scripture.

> **Animaduertet parabolam et interpretationem uerba sapientium et enigmata eorum.** Hoc discipulis se humiliter audientibus ipsa quae eos in carne apparens erudiebat sapientia donauit ut et suas parabolas quae turbae nequibant intellegerent et prophetarum ac legis enigmata, id est obscura

---

example of hypocrisy (Prov. 20. 23) he cites a man who insists on taking revenge on another man who rapes his wife, but pleads for mercy when he himself violates a virgin dedicated to Christ: Bede, *In prouerbia Salomonis*, II, ed. by Hurst, p. 106, ll. 141–46.

11 Thacker, 'Bede and the Ordering of Understanding', pp. 43–45, and 'Bede's Ideal of Reform'; DeGregorio, '*Nostrorum socordiam temporum*', 'Bede's *In Ezram et Neemiam*'.

12 Bede, *In prouerbia Salomonis*, I, ed. by Hurst, p. 60, ll. 47–54.

13 Bede, *In prouerbia Salomonis*, II, ed. by Hurst, p. 106, ll. 121–33.

14 'For Bede, the *doctor* was essentially the initiate who had penetrated beyond the veil of the literal sense of Scripture to the *arcana* beneath. He (or indeed she) had to combine the active pursuit of learning with contemplative prayer and exemplary living in order to infuse the active pastorate not just with basic understanding but with right doctrine and true ideals. The *doctores* formed, so to speak, the intellectual powerhouse which inspired and instructed the practical preachers (*praedicatores*) who were to carry out the evangelizing work on the ground': Thacker, 'Bede and the Ordering of Understanding', p. 43.

dicta, spiritaliter animaduertere ac suis auditoribus dilucidare ualerent, sed
et sequentibus ecclesiae magistris eadem intelligentiae spiritalis archana pie
quaerentibus ac pulsantibus reserauit

> **... shall understand a parable and the interpretation, the words of the
> wise and their mysterious sayings.** Here Wisdom [i.e. Christ] gave to the
> disciples who listened humbly to the things that He taught them while He
> was in the flesh the ability both to understand His parables — something
> the crowds could not do — and to appreciate the enigmas of the law and the
> prophets (that is, their obscure sayings) and expound them to their listeners.
> But in addition, He unbarred the same arcana of spiritual understanding to
> the teachers of the Church who were to follow, and who asked and knocked
> in a pious spirit.[15]

Teachers are found at every turn in the Proverbs commentary.[16] The wise man so
frequently praised in the Scriptural text is the *doctor*,[17] and the one who undertakes
the *cura animarum*;[18] the father who does not spare the rod lest he spoil the child is
the *magister catholicus*.[19] God's creation of heaven and earth, evoked in Proverbs 3. 19
('The Lord God by wisdom has founded the earth, has established the heavens by
prudence') is an allegory of the Church and her *praedicatores*.[20] The rich man whose
barns are filled with abundance and whose presses run over with wine is the *doctor*
who gives the food of the word and the drink of spiritual grace.[21] The clouds thick

---

15 Bede, *In prouerbia Salomonis*, I, ed. by Hurst, p. 25, ll. 83–90.

16 This was noted by Jenkins back in 1935: 'Bede as Exegete and Theologian'.

17 E.g. 18.4: '**Aqua profunda uerba ex ore uiri, et torrens redundans fons sapientiae.** Verba
    sapientium aquae comparantur quia et lauant mentes audientium et inrigant ne uel peccatorum
    sorde deformes remaneant uel doctrinae caelestis inopia tabescant et quasi nociua ariditate
    deficiant. Et quia eadem doctorum uerba fidelium quaedam mystica latent et occulta quae sollertiore
    comprehendantur industria, quaedam uero aperta et cunctis audientibus facilia ad intellegendum
    profluunt, recte haec et aquam profundam et torrentem dicit esse redundantem. [**Words from the
    mouth of a man are as deep water: and the fountain of wisdom is an overflowing stream.** The
    words of wise men are compared to water because they both bathe the minds of those who hear
    them, and refresh them with water lest they remain deformed by the filth of sins and waste away
    from want of heavenly teaching, and suffer exhaustion, as it were, through an injurious drought. And
    because these words of faithful teachers conceal certain things which are mystical and hidden, and
    which can be comprehended with more resourceful effort, and abound in others which are evident
    and easy for everybody who hears them to understand, the water is rightly said to be both "deep"
    and the stream "overflowing."]'. Bede, *In prouerbia Salomonis*, II, ed. by Hurst, p. 97, ll. 7–15. This
    was a favorite verse of Bede's: it surfaces in his very first work of Biblical exegesis, the commentary
    on Revelation (Bede, *Expositio Apocalypseos*, ed. by Gryson, p. 545, ll. 239–40), in the middle of his
    career in the commentary on the Song of Songs (Bede, *In Cantica canticorum* III, ed. by Hurst, p. 262
    ll. 755–56), and close to the end, in the final prayer of the *Ecclesiastical History*, V.24, ed. and trans. by
    Colgrave and Mynors, pp. 570–71).

18 E.g. Bede's interpretation of Prov. 11.30 ('Et qui suscipit animas sapiens est') is an encomium of the
    pastoral role: Bede, *In prouerbia Salomonis*, II, ed. by Hurst, p. 74, ll. 162–68.

19 Bede, *In prouerbia Salomonis*, II, ed. by Hurst, p. 82, ll. 131–32.

20 Bede, *In prouerbia Salomonis*, I, ed. by Hurst, p. 42, ll. 155–58.

21 Bede, *In prouerbia Salomonis*, I, ed. by Hurst, p. 40, ll. 90–94.

with dew in Proverbs 3.20 are the *ecclesiae magistri* who by their contemplation and their lives (a significant pairing) irrigate the hearts of those below them.[22] Teachers are the gates of the city of the Lord (1.21).[23] 'Where there are no oxen, the crib is empty', says Proverbs 14.4, and who are the oxen but the *doctores catholici*?[24] The examples could be multiplied.

Bede's message about preaching and teaching has three points, which he hammers home again and again. First, it is a categorical imperative. This is rather strikingly set out in his exegesis of Proverbs 11. 25–26, which incorporates a silent quotation from Gregory's *Pastoral Care* (clearly a major inspiration here): those learned in the faith are laid under an obligation to pass it on to others, lest they incur the condemnation of the lazy and unprofitable servant.[25] Secondly, the *doctor* must walk the walk as well as talk the talk: indeed, to have genuine knowledge of spiritual things, one must live them as well as learn them.[26] But there is a third injunction, and this one is more ambiguous: the preacher must accommodate his message to the condition of his listeners, not speaking to weaker brethren as to spiritual men, but as to carnal men, lest he cast pearls before swine.[27] It raises the issue of the distance between the *doctores* and those they teach — a distance which could be a source of trouble. For over against the *ecclesiae magistri*, the worthy *doctores*, assiduous *praedicatores*, and the diligent *pastores* stand two opponents: the heretic, and the intellectually arrogant man of learning. The two are in fact quite closely linked, even identical, because intellectual vanity and elitism is one of the hallmarks of heresy.

Heresy is a major preoccupation of Bede in this commentary; the fool, the wicked, the unjust, the impious, the harlot and so forth are likened to heretics with almost monotonous predictability. Bede seizes on almost any occasion to introduce the subject. For example, in his exegesis of Proverbs 16. 21, 'The wise in heart shall be called prudent: and he that is sweet in words, shall attain to greater things', he says: 'Qui sapientiam catholicae fidei quam didicit illibatam suo in corde custodit merito prudentis nomen accipit, at qui eandem sapientiam etiam docte praedicare et contra hereticos defendere nouit maiora laboris amplioris praemia percipiet' (He who guards intact the wisdom of the Catholic faith which he has learned in his heart rightly receives the name of "prudent", but he who knows how to preach that wisdom *and defend it against heretics in a learned manner* will receive the reward of his greater labour).[28] In short, heresy seems to be something that Bede connects with the public act of teaching: we will return to this point in a moment.

What Bede has to say about heresy is at once predictable, and slanted in a distinctive direction. As Averil Cameron, Rebecca Lyman and others have astutely observed,

---

22 Bede, *In prouerbia Salomonis*, I, ed. by Hurst, p. 42, ll. 169–73.

23 Bede, *In prouerbia Salomonis*, I, ed. by Hurst, pp. 30–31, ll. 260–66.

24 Bede, *In prouerbia Salomonis*, II, ed. by Hurst, p. 83, ll. 18–19.

25 Bede, *In prouerbia Salomonis*, II, ed. by Hurst, pp. 72–73, ll. 123–32.

26 Bede, *In prouerbia Salomonis*, II, ed. by Hurst, p. 93, ll. 121–31.

27 Bede, *In prouerbia Salomonis*, II, ed. by Hurst, p. 77, ll. 111–13.

28 Bede, *In prouerbia Salomonis* II, ed. by Hurst, p. 93, ll. 117–20. cf. Thacker, 'Why did Heresy Matter to Bede?', p. 49, on the role of preachers in defending a Church perpetually under siege by heretics.

there was little 'live' heresy, either learned or popular, in western Europe during or prior to Bede's lifetime. On the other hand, there was a substantial literature about what Cameron calls 'remembered heresy'. This heritage from the patristic period took the form of polemical treatises, canons of councils, and catalogues and genealogies of heresies (Augustine, Filastrius, Gennadius …). Its cumulative effect was to objectify heresies (turning Pelagius and those who supported him into 'Pelagianism' for example), and thus to exaggerate both their coherence and their danger. The trope of genealogy found in the handbooks had a particularly powerful effect: heresies are depicted as doctrinally interbreeding, and like viruses, their doctrines were perennially mutating and re-emerging in more virulent form. Hence when real theological controversy broke out, for example Adoptionism in the Carolingian period, the instinct of men like Alcuin was to consult the nosologies of Augustine or Gennadius and identify *which* pre-existing heresy had re-appeared in their day.[29]

But heresiology also served a positive function, standing in for systematic theology by furnishing a sort of negative definition of what orthodox doctrine was *not*. One could say that even if Bede never met an Arian or a Sabellian, their alleged beliefs at least helped him to demarcate the boundaries of faith. This is perhaps best exhibited in the commentary on Proverbs 5. 6, where Bede presents a sweeping array of positions held by unspecified heretics as inversions of the clauses of the creed:

> **Vagi sunt gressus eius et inuestigabiles.** Vagi sunt sensus hereticae deceptionis quia alii Christum Deum, alii hominem esse negant, alii carnem accepisse, alii animam contradicunt, alii eum de uirgine natum, alii spiritum sanctum, alii patrem eum esse, alii paenitentibus ueniam dandam esse confiteri prohibent. Et in tam innumera haec pestis se findit itinera ut paenitus quot sint inuestigare nequeant. At catholica ueritas uaga et inuestigabilis non est quia una eademque cunctis est agnita totum per orbem fidelibus.
>
> > **Her steps are wandering and unaccountable.** The notions of heretical deception are 'wandering' because some deny that Christ is God, others that he is human; some object to [the doctrine] that he took flesh, others to [the doctrine] that he took a soul; some refuse to confess that he was born of a virgin, others that the Holy Spirit or the Father is God, and others that pardon is to be granted to penitents. And this plague has split itself into such an innumerable number of pathways that it is all but impossible to 'account' for how many of them there are. But Catholic truth is not 'wandering and unaccountable', because it is recognized as one and the same by faithful people throughout the world.[30]

---

29 Lyman, 'Heresiology: The Invention of "Heresy"'; Cameron, 'Heresiology', and 'How to Read Heresiology'; Brown, 'Pelagius and his Supporters'.

30 Bede, *In prouerbia Salomonis* I, ed. by Hurst, pp. 48–49 ll. 26–34. A similar catalogue appears in Bede's exegesis of II Peter 2.1 in *In epistolas VII catholicas*, pp. 268–69 ll. 11–12; cf. Holder, 'Hunting Snakes in the Grass', p. 109 and pp. 344–45 n. 20.

The Proverbs commentary mentions a few heresies by name: Arianism (four times), Origen's concept of universal salvation (twice),[31] Sabellianism and Donatism (once each), and Pelagianism explicitly twice and implicitly dozens of times, in comments on the futility of good deeds performed without grace, and repeated warnings against putting one's trust in one's own powers. Pelagianism of course had a special resonance for Bede. He saw it as a made-in-Britain heresy, vaguely linked to his other *bête noire*, the Insular form of the 84-year Paschal cycle.[32] But while I agree with Arthur Holder that Bede consciously or unconsciously uses heresy as a proxy for other issues that concern him, I see no evidence that in the Proverbs commentary that hidden concern was computus;[33] rather, it is a moral and ecclesial problem involving *doctores*.

However, instead of refuting the doctrinal positions of heretics,[34] Bede chooses to focuses his readers' attention on the moral failings associated with heresy. Here he was following in the footsteps of the Fathers, whose polemics and handbooks of heresies fused 'erroneous', 'demonic' and 'immoral' into a single damning package. Heretics could be immoral in a number of ways: they were 'deceptive, unfaithful, duplicitous and [sexually] promiscuous', but they were also 'superstitious, elitist, social climbing, [plagiarist, rebellious]'.[35] Bede chooses quite selectively from this list of vices; and his choices are dictated by his image of heretics as *intellectuals*. Heresy, for example, is frequently yoked with philosophy,[36] because heresy's *modus operandi* is

---

31 This was one of the rare heresies which had some purchase in Bede's immediately milieu: see Darby's essay in this volume, 'Heresy and Authority in Bede's *Letter to Plegwine*', p. 000. The relevant passages are: Bede, *In prouerbia Salomonis*, I, ed. by Hurst, p. 37, ll. 135–54, and II, p. 70, ll. 19–28.

32 Ó Cróinín, 'New Heresy for Old'. Bede tended to link the 84-year cycle to Quartodecimanism, but does pair it loosely with Pelagianism in *De temporum ratione* ch. 66, s.a. 4581, p. 525, ll. 1820–1825, and Wallis, *Bede: The Reckoning of Time* rev, p. 228. See also note 9 above, and Thacker's comments in 'Bede and the Irish', pp. 38–39. There are no fewer than twelve explicit references to Pelagianism in the commentary on the Catholic Epistles — more than in any other work by Bede including the commentary on the Song of Songs, which explicitly targets Julian of Eclanum.

33 See above, n. 7.

34 That the Proverbs commentary is not especially interested in heretical *doctrines*, is made evident by Bede's extremely jejune commentary on Proverbs 8. 22–30. This was a key proof–text in the fourth-century struggle against Arianism, because it depicts Wisdom (i.e. Christ) at the side of God before the creation of the world, but Bede is content to allude very briefly to nameless people who deny the coeternity of Son and Father, without mentioning Arianism explicitly: Bede, *In prouerbia Salomonis*, I, ed. by Hurst, p. 61, ll. 79–86.

35 Lyman, 'Heresiology: The Invention of "Heresy"', p. 298.

36 '**Lingua sapientium ornat scientiam, os fatuorum ebullit stultitiam**. Lingua catholicorum patrum ornat scientiam diuinorum eloquentiorum latius exponendo quae scriptura canonica aut obscure posuit aut historica tantum ratione scripta reliquit, et os hereticorum ebullit stultitiam dicta sacrae scripturae peruerse intelligendo suosque sensus eius auctoritati praeponendo. Potest et de paganorum philosophis intelligi quod ait, *os fatuorum ebullit stultitiam*, quales fuere Porphyrius et Iulianus qui contra ecclesiae doctores stultitiae suae fluenta fundebant' [**The tongue of the wise adorns knowledge: but the mouth of fools bubbles out folly**. The tongue of the Catholic fathers "adorns knowledge" of divine eloquence by expounding in detail those things which the canonical Scripture either expresses obscurely, or leaves exclusively on the historical plane. And the mouth of the heretics "bubbles out folly" by understanding the statements of holy Scripture in a perverse manner, and expounding it on the authority of their own notions. What he says — "the mouth of

to use perverse dialectic.[37] Their mastery of suave speech and specious logic means that it is harder to persuade heretics than to convert pagans,[38] and one should be wary when debating about Scripture with them.[39] Bede assumes that heretics communicate through books;[40] and have disciples and hearers just like the *doctores ecclesiae*. Indeed, heresy is particularly associated with learning, not lack of learning. 'Better the simple hearer of the word of God', says Bede, 'if he can put into action what he can understand of the Scriptures than any man of learning (*eruditus*) if he twists what he has so keenly understood into preaching heresy'.[41] Indeed, the heretic is the shadow side of the Catholic *eruditus* or scholar. It is the inordinate appetite for knowledge that leads to heresy,[42] and smart, ambitious minds are particularly susceptible. In his exposition of Proverbs 7. 26, Bede observes that the brilliant and talented Origen was lured into heresy, just as the mighty Samson, and the anointed kings David and Solomon, were led astray by women.[43]

In one telling passage, Bede paints a striking picture of how false but seductive teachings can be casually absorbed even when studying scripture with a *magister* or listening to *sermones*. The presence of the *magister* is no guarantee against harm, and the scholar must be vigilant: discerning the meaning of Scripture is like having a knife at your throat! Bede even insinuates that one's *magister* might himself be the problem.

Quando sederis ut comedas cum principe diligenter adtende quae posita sint ante faciem tuam et statue cultrum in gutture tuo, si tamen habes in potestate animam tuam. Per allegoriam cuncta dicuntur. Quando sederis ad legendum cum magistro ut pane uerbi reficiaris diligenter intellege quae scripta sunt et discretionem sacrae lectionis in tua locutione conserua, si tamen talis es

---

fools bubbles out folly" — can also be understood as pertaining to the philosophers of the pagans, such as Porphyry and Julian, who poured out the stream of their foolishness against the Church's teachers]. Bede, *In prouerbia Salomonis*, II, ed. by Hurst, pp. 86–87, ll. 5–13. Expounding Prov. 16. 14, 'The wrath of a king is as messengers of death', Bede ignores the king completely, focusing in on the messengers of death, who are the 'heretics and vain philosophers.' See Holder, 'Hunting Snakes in the Grass', p. 110, on the yoking of heresy and philosophy.

37 'Intexui funibus lectum meum, straui tapetibus pictis ex Aegypto. ... In tapetibus uero pictis ex Aegypto ornatus eloquentiae et dialecticae artis uersutia quae ab ethnicis originem sumpsit intelligitur per quam mens heretica sensum doctrinae pestilentis quasi meretrix thorum facinoris se texisse gloriatur'. [**I have woven my bed with cords; I have covered it with painted tapestry brought from Egypt**. ... By the "painted tapestry brought from Egypt" is meant the ornaments of eloquence and the craftiness of the art of dialectic derived from the pagans, and with which the heretical mind prides itself in clothing the notions of its pestilent teaching, as the Harlot clothes the couch of her scandalous behaviour.] Bede, *In prouerbia Salomonis*, I, ed. by Hurst, pp. 58, ll. 73–77.

38 Bede, *In prouerbia Salomonis*, II, ed. by Hurst, p. 95, ll. 25–29.

39 Bede, *In prouerbia Salomonis*, II, ed. by Hurst, p. 118, ll. 29–48.

40 Bede, *In prouerbia Salomonis*, I, ed. by Hurst, p. 52, ll. 149–51.

41 'Melior est pauper qui ambulat in simplicitate sua quam diues torquens labia insipiens. Melior est simplex auditor uerbi Dei, si ea quae intellegere in scripturis potuit operando perficit, quam eruditus quisque, si in illis quae acute intellexit ad heresim praedicandam labia retorquet.' Bede, *In prouerbia Salomonis*, II, ed. by Hurst, p. 99, ll. 1–5.

42 Bede, *In prouerbia Salomonis*, II, ed. by Hurst, p. 99, ll. 6–14.

43 Bede, *In prouerbia Salomonis*, I, ed. by Hurst, p. 59, ll. 97–101.

tantumque eruditus qui in potestate habeas animam tuam nec quasi indoctus mente tua circumferaris omni uento doctrinae. Guttur namque pro loquella posuit quia uox in gutture est, cultrum pro discretione quia cibos cum reficimur cultro secante praeparamus. Et sedens ut comedat cultrum in gutture suo statuit quando is qui diuina sedulus meditatur eloquia discreta ex ore uerba depromit nec alia saepius in lingua quam caelestis oraculi dicta reuoluit. Hoc autem eius est facere qui in potestate habet animam suam, id est immobilem inter errores fallentium sapientis animi statum seruare didicit. Vnde et recte subiungit: **Ne desideras de cibis eius in quo est panis mendacii**, quod est aperte dicere: Ne desideres eius auscultare sermonibus qui dulcedine mendaciorum dogmatum auditores suos fallere consueuit.

> **When you sit to eat with a prince, consider diligently what is set before your face: And put a knife to your throat, if it be so that you have your soul in your own power**. All this is said by way of an allegory. When you sit down to study with a teacher in order to refresh yourself with the bread of the word [of God], understand carefully what is written, and preserve the discrimination of the sacred text in your speech, if you be such (and so accomplished) a scholar who can hold your soul in [your own] power; and do not, like the uninstructed, let your mind be carried about by every wind of doctrine [cf. Ephesians 4.14]. By 'throat' he means 'speech', because the voice is in the throat, and the knife refers to discretion, because when we dine, we prepare the food by cutting it with a knife. And he determines to sit down to eat with a knife at his throat who assiduously meditates on the divine eloquence, utters discriminating words with his mouth, and revolves nothing else so often with his tongue as the sayings of the heavenly oracle. This is what he is to do who 'has his soul in his own power', that is, who has learned, amidst the errors of deceivers, to retain the steadfast state of a wise man's mind. Hence he rightly adds: [**23.3**] **Be not desirous of his meats, in which is the bread of deceit**. Which is clearly to say: Do not hanker to listen to addresses of one who is wont to deceive his listeners with the sweetness of false teaching.[44]

But what was the 'deception' these teachers and preachers might be purveying? It is tempting to say 'Pelagianism' simply because Bede is much exercised by this heresy, but I would like to suggest that it was not Pelagian doctrine, but the implication of spiritual pride in Pelagianism that was of concern to Bede. Just as Bede identifies heresy as an occupational hazard for the learned, so it is *intellectual* elitism and vanity that is the learned man's principal moral failing. And because heretics are elitist, exclusive, and arrogant, the reverse is also true: the intellectually arrogant are — if not actually heretics — as bad as heretics, and bad in the same way.

---

44 Bede, *In prouerbia Salomonis*, II, ed. by Hurst, p. 117, ll. 1–19. Bede may be alluding here to Augustine's *Letter to Deuterius* which describes a cleric who was caught teaching Manichean doctrines to 'students' (*discentibus*) at Hippo: see below, Darby, 'Heresy and Authority', at pp. 160-61.

It is remarkable how many references there are to this problem in the Proverbs commentary. Bede may have been sensitized to it because the text of Proverbs so often commends the wise man and contrasts him with the fool (*inspiens* or *stultus*). Hence his treatment of wisdom is informative, for he seems intent to avoid equating it to intelligence or learning. While he distinguishes true wisdom from *mundana sapientia* (e.g. commenting on 9. 4; 12. 11), he prefers to interpret wisdom as faith[45] or pious action.[46] What seems to trouble Bede most is when intellectual vanity crosses over into intellectual snobbery, and disdain for the less learned. Hence, deflating intellectual vanity is a major preoccupation. Proverbs 13. 20 reads: 'He that walks with the wise, shall be wise: a friend of fools shall become like to them'. For Bede, the one who becomes wise by walking with the wise is actually the *simplex* or *rusticus* (not identified, it should be noted, with the *stultus* or *insipiens*), who becomes wise by imitating the behaviour of wise men, even though he cannot grasp the *archana sapientiae*. The *stultus* by contrast is the man reputed for his intellect and learning, but who dissipates himself with frivolous entertainments.[47] Commenting on Proverbs 12. 9, Bede concludes: 'Melior est idiota et simplex frater qui bona quae nouit operans uitam meretur in caelis quam qui clarus eruditione scripturarum uel etiam doctoris functus officio indiget pane dilectionis' (Better the simple brother without book learning (*idiota et simplex frater*) who, doing the good that he knows, merits heaven, than the famous scholar of scripture (*clarus eruditione scripturarum*), even if he takes on the duty of teaching, who lacks the bread of charity).[48]

Intellectual arrogance seems to be a particular problem within religious communities. On two occasions, Bede goes out of his way to point out that a truly wise *doctor* should not think himself superior to less intellectually gifted *colleagues*. Expounding Proverbs 16. 20, Bede explains that the term *eruditus* refers to the preacher of God's word, but even one who is not competent to preach to others (*etiamsi ad praedicandum aliis idoneus non est*) will share the same beatitude with the preacher if he places his hope in the Lord.[49] The tone is sharper in the commentary on 20. 12: the *eruditus doctor* must never despise the simplicity of the well-meaning but less intellectually gifted *frater*.[50] Admittedly, Bede's use of the term *frater* is often quite loose, but I strongly suspect that the cleavage in this case runs between monk and monk, not between monk and layman. Intellectual elitism would have a particularly corrosive effect on the life of an enclosed community, exacerbating or substituting for other kinds of officially forbidden rivalries, such as those of birth and wealth.

Finally, there are some problematic verses which Bede elects to pass over in silence, notably Proverbs 17. 2, which predicts that the wise will rule over the foolish. Indeed, I think it would be a useful exercise to read the commentary on Proverbs

45 Bede, *In prouerbia Salomonis*, II, ed. by Hurst, p. 93, ll. 116–20.
46 Bede, *In prouerbia Salomonis*, II, ed. by Hurst, pp. 95–96, ll. 41–46.
47 Bede, *In prouerbia Salomonis*, II, ed. by Hurst, p. 81, ll. 87–96.
48 Bede, *In prouerbia Salomonis*, II, ed. by Hurst, p. 76, ll. 53–55.
49 Bede, *In prouerbia Salomonis*, II, ed. by Hurst, p. 92, ll. 111–15.
50 Bede, *In prouerbia Salomonis*, II, ed. by Hurst, p. 105, ll. 78–88.

as a diffuse meditation on the less well-publicized inner dramas of cenobitic life in Anglo-Saxon England.

To sum up, Bede's *Commentary on Proverbs* addresses ecclesiastics living in communities, who had responsibilities for the instruction of others as *doctores, praedicatores, and magistri.* Depending on the circumstances, these 'others' could be the children of the cloister, adult converts to the monastic life, members of the wider *familia,* the local gentry and tenantry — the Christian people at large. Bede's numerous quotations from Gregory's *Regula Pastoralis* are a harbinger of what was to become a major theme of his later works: namely, the lack of adequate numbers of adequately trained teachers. In the Proverbs commentary, however, he considers the problem from a different angle. There seems no lack of *eruditi* in the Proverbs commentary, and *eruditi* are the timber from which *doctores* are made. But *eruditi* are vulnerable — vulnerable as few others are to heresy, and vulnerable to inflated self-esteem, which can make them 'moral Pelagians' who behave like heretics by valuing their own notions above the common faith, and looking down on simple believers. A well-educated cleric carries a number of risk factors; he was constantly exposed to books and teachers, and his formation made him susceptible to those fine turns of phrase and clever arguments that could lead the vain and unwary astray. On the other hand, intellectual conceit and elitism might be used as an excuse by the *eruditus* to avoid preaching and teaching at all. In short, you could say that in the Commentary on Proverbs, Bede is using heresy as something that it is 'good to think with',[51] and what he is thinking about is the spectre of the *failure* of the *rectores* and *doctores* of the Church to spread the message of the faith to all people, simple as well as learned, women as well as men.

Works Cited

Primary Sources

Bede, *De temporum ratione,* ed. by Charles W. Jones, Corpus Christianorum Series Latina, 123B (Turnhout: Brepols, 1977)
——, *Historia ecclesiastica gentis Anglorum,* ed. and trans. by Bertram Colgrave and R. A. B. Mynors, *Bede's Ecclesiastical History of the English People* (Oxford: Clarendon Press, 1969)
——, *Expositio Apocalypseos,* ed. by Roger Gryson, Corpus Christianorum Series Latina, 121A (Turnhout: Brepols, 2001)
——, *In Cantica Canticorum,* ed. by David Hurst, Corpus Christianorum Series Latina, 119B (Turnhout: Brepols, 1983), pp. 167–375
——, *In epistulas septem catholicas,* ed. by David Hurst, Corpus Christianorum Series Latina, 121 (Turnhout: Brepols, 1983), pp. 181–342

---

51 The phrase is Claude Lévi-Strauss's, and is deployed to illuminating effect by Holder, 'Using Philosophers to Think With'.

————, *In prouerbia Salomonis*, ed. by David Hurst, Corpus Christianorum Series Latina, 119B (Turnout: Brepols, 1983), pp. 23–163

Bede: The Reckoning of Time, trans. with introduction and commentary by Faith Wallis (Liverpool: Liverpool University Press, 1999; rev. ed. 2004)

Secondary Studies

Brown, George Hardin, *A Companion to Bede* (Woodbridge: Boydell, 2009)

Brown, Peter, 'Pelagius and his Supporters: Aims and Environment', *Journal of Theological Studies*, n.s., 19 (1968), 93–114

Cameron, Averil, 'Heresiology', in *Late Antiquity: A Guide to the Postclassical World*, ed. by G. Bowersock, Peter Brown and Oleg Grabar (Cambridge, MA: Harvard University Press, 1999), pp. 488–90

————, 'How to Read Heresiology', *Journal of Medieval and Early Modern Studies*, 33 (2003), 471–92

Darby, Peter, 'Heresy and Authority in Bede's *Letter to Plegwine*', in *Cities, Saints and Communities in Early Medieval Europe: Essays in Honour of Alan Thacker*, ed. by Scott DeGregorio and Paul Kershaw (Turnhout: Brepols, 2020), pp. 145–69

DeGregorio, Scott, '*Nostrorum socordiam temporum*: The Reforming Impulse of Bede's Later Exegesis', *Early Medieval Europe*, 11 (2002), 107–22

————, 'Bede's *In Ezram et Neemiam* and the Reform of the Northumbrian Church', *Speculum*, 79 (2004), 1–25

Doignon, J., 'Hilaire de Poitiers commentateur de *Proverbes* 8, 26–30', in *Letture cristiane dei Libri Sapienziali. XX Incontro di studiosi della antichità cristiana 9–11 maggio 1991* (Rome: Institutum Patristicum 'Augustinianum', 1992), pp. 201–07

Flint, Valerie I. J., 'The True Author of the Salonii Commentarii in Parabolas Salomonis et in Ecclesiasten', *Recherches de théologie ancienne et médiévale*, 37 (1970), 174–86

Holder, Arthur, 'The Anti-Pelagian Character of Bede's Commentary on the Song of Songs', in *Biblical Studies in the Early Middle Ages*, ed. by Claudio Leonardi and Giovanni Orlandi (Florence: SISMEL, 2005), pp. 91–103

————, 'Using Philosophers to Think With: The Venerable Bede on Christian Life and Practice', *The Subjective Eye: Essays in Culture, Religion and Gender in Honor of Margaret R. Miles*, ed. by Richard Valantasis (Eugene: Pickwick, 2006), pp. 48–58

————, 'Hunting Snakes in the Grass: Bede as Heresiologist', in *Listen, O Isles, unto Me: Studies in Medieval Word and Image in Honour of Jennifer O'Reilly*, ed. by Elizabeth Mullins and Diarmuid Scully (Cork: Cork University Press, 2011), pp. 104–14

Jenkins, Claude, 'Bede as Exegete and Theologian', *Bede, his Life, Times and Writings*, ed. by A. H. Thompson (Oxford: Clarendon Press, 1935), pp. 152–200

Laistner, M. L. W., *A Hand-List of Bede Manuscripts* (Ithaca: Cornell University Press, 1943)

Lyman, Rebecca, 'Heresiology: The Invention of "Heresy" and "Schism"', in *The Cambridge History of Christianity Volume 2: Constantine to c. 600*, ed. by Augustine Casiday and Frederick W. Norris (Cambridge: Cambridge University Press, 2007), pp. 296–313

Maggazù, C. 'L'Elogio della "Donna forte" (*Prov.* 31, 10–31) nell'interpretazione patristica', in *Letture cristiane dei Libri Sapienziali. XX Incontro di studiosi della antichità cristiana 9–11 maggio 1991* (Rome: Institutum Patristicum 'Augustinianum', 1992) pp. 213–24

Ó Cróinín, Dáibhí, 'New Heresy for Old: Pelagianism in Ireland and the Papal Letter of 640', *Speculum*, 60 (1985), 505–16

Parkes, M. B., *The Scriptorium of Wearmouth–Jarrow* , Jarrow Lecture, 1982 (Jarrow: St Paul's Church, 1982)

Thacker, Alan, 'Bede's Ideal of Reform', in *Ideal and Reality in Frankish and Anglo-Saxon Society: Studies Presented to John Michael Wallace-Hadrill*, ed. by Patrick Wormald, Donald Bullough and Roger Collins (Oxford: Blackwell, 1983), pp. 130–53

——, 'Bede and the Irish', in *Beda Venerabilis: Historian, Monk, Northumbrian*, ed. by L. A. J. R. Houwen and A. A. MacDonald (Groningen: Egbert Forsten, 1996), pp. 31–59

——, 'Bede and the Ordering of Understanding', in *Innovation and Tradition in the Writings of the Venerable Bede*, ed. by Scott DeGregorio (Morgantown: West Virginia University Press, 2006), pp. 37–63

——, 'Bede, the Britons and the Book of Samuel', in *Early Medieval Studies in Memory of Patrick Wormald*, ed. by Stephen Baxter (Farnham: Ashgate, 2009), pp. 129–47

——, 'Why did Heresy Matter to Bede? Present and Future Contexts', in *Bede and the Future*, ed. by Peter Darby and Faith Wallis (Farnham: Ashgate, 2014), pp. 47–66

Wallis, Faith, *Bede and Wisdom*, Jarrow Lecture, 2016 (Jarrow: St Paul's Church, 2016)

Weiss, J. P., 'Essai de datation du Commentaire sur les Proverbes attribué abusivement à Salonius', *Sacris erudiri*, 19 (1969–1970), 77–114

Westgard, Joshua, 'Bede and the Continent in the Carolingian Age and Beyond', in *The Cambridge Companion to Bede*, ed. by Scott DeGregorio (Cambridge: Cambridge University Press, 2010), pp. 201–15

PETER DARBY

Heresy and Authority in Bede's *Letter to Plegwine*

Scholarly perceptions of the Northumbrian monk and scholar Bede underwent seismic changes at the turn of the twenty-first century as a variety of previously commonplace assumptions concerning the individual and his writings were dismantled one by one. Rarely is Bede now seen as a passive and uncritical transmitter of earlier texts. An important essay by this volume's honouree in 1983, 'Bede's Ideal of Reform', was a critically important stage in the realisation of these transitions. That essay explains that Bede's later writings were charged by a desire to influence the society in which he lived, and it does this by bringing a range of exegetical texts into dialogue with better-known parts of Bede's canon such as the prose *Life of St Cuthbert*, *Ecclesiastical History*, and *Letter to Ecgberht*. The reforming impulse highlighted in that essay of 1983 is now established as a cornerstone of modern interpretations of Bede's writings.[1] Many scholars would agree with the view expressed in Alan Thacker's subsequent contribution to an influential collection published in 2006, (which cemented many of the historiographical shifts described above), that Bede aspired to greatness within the Patristic tradition.[2]

This essay takes as its subject an extremely important but underappreciated letter of Bede's which documents his reaction to an accusation of heresy. Much of the letter concerns chronology, eschatology, and the six ages of the world, and

* This essay is offered in gratitude to Alan Thacker for the considerable effort that he has put into the mentoring of young scholars throughout his career. I would like to thank the anonymous reviewer, Máirín MacCarron and Faith Wallis for commenting on draft versions of this essay, and I wish to acknowledge the support of the British Academy for funding the period of postdoctoral research from which it has arisen.

1 e.g. Thacker, 'Bede and the Irish', pp. 34–38 and 'Bede and History', pp. 183–85; DeGregorio, '"*Nostrorum socordiam temporum*"', 'Bede's *In Ezram et Neemiam* and the Reform of the Northumbrian Church', 'Monasticism and Reform in Book IV of Bede's *Ecclesiastical History of the English People*', 'Bede's *In Ezram et Neemiam*: A Document in Church Reform?', and 'Visions of Reform: Bede's Later Writings in Context'; O'Brien, *Bede's Temple*, pp. 112–17.

2 Thacker, 'Bede and the Ordering of Understanding', pp. 54–63.

Peter Darby • is Lecturer in Medieval History at the University of Nottingham, author of *Bede and the End of Time* (Farnham: Ashgate, 2012), and co-editor of *Bede and the Future* (Farnham: Ashgate, 2014).*

Cities, Saints, and Communities in Early Medieval Europe, ed. by Scott DeGregorio and Paul Kershaw, SEM 46 (Turnhout: Brepols, 2020), pp. 145-169
BREPOLS PUBLISHERS   DOI 10.1484/M.SEM-EB.5.119626

it is an important source for the history of medieval apocalyptic thought because it describes Bede's interactions with contemporaries who wished to discuss the timing of the Last Judgement with him.[3] In the course of the *Letter to Plegwine* Bede recounts and dismisses several positions which he considered erroneous, revealing that two different apocalyptic target years and the concept of the thousand-year world age were current in early eighth-century Northumbria.[4] It is clear that the episode documented in the letter was a pivotal turning point in Bede's understanding of time and its end, but its full importance with regards to other aspects of Bede's intellectual development is yet to be fully realised. A close reading of the *Letter to Plegwine* will allow us to engage several themes pertinent to Alan Thacker's research. We will ask what the letter can tell us about Bede's understanding of heresy, a topic which Thacker has considered in one of his recent essays on Bede.[5] We will follow in the footsteps of his Jarrow Lecture by investigating aspects of the relationship between Bede and Augustine of Hippo.[6] The *Letter to Plegwine* is also important because it sheds light on Bede's relationship with a neighbouring monastic community led by Wilfrid, bishop of Hexham, a figure who has long interested Thacker and who has featured prominently in his recent publications.[7] Most importantly of all, by studying a text written in the midst of a significant controversy, we will encounter its author presenting himself as an authoritative figure, a side of Bede that Thacker has been encouraging us to see since 1983.

Bede's Letter to Plegwine

The *Letter to Plegwine* was written in the year 708, five years or so after Bede's ordination to the priesthood by John of Beverley, Wilfrid's predecessor in the see of Hexham.[8] Nothing is known of the addressee beyond what can be discovered from the letter itself. The letter explains that the allegation of heresy had been made against Bede two days before it was written. The fact that we have a clear timeframe for its composition (of around 48 hours from conception to execution) indicates that the patristic excerpts presented in the *Letter to Plegwine* (including lengthy citations from Augustine's *City of God* and Jerome's commentary on Isaiah) must have been available to Bede at very short notice.

---

3   Analysis of the letter's eschatological content is offered by: Jones, *Bedae opera de temporibus*, pp. 132–35; *Bede: The Reckoning of Time*, trans. by Wallis, pp. xxx–xxxi and 353–62; Darby, *Bede and the End of Time*, pp. 35–64; Palmer, *The Apocalypse in the Early Middle Ages*, pp. 95–105; Chazelle, 'Debating the End Times', pp. 219–27.
4   Bede, *Epistola ad Pleguinam*, 14–15, ed. by Jones, pp. 313–14.
5   Thacker, 'Why did Heresy Matter to Bede?'.
6   Thacker, *Bede and Augustine of Hippo*.
7   Thacker, 'Wilfrid, his Cult and his Biographer'; Thacker and Ó Carragáin, 'Wilfrid in Rome'; Thacker, 'Gallic or Greek? Archbishops in England from Theodore to Ecgberht', pp. 55–64.
8   Bede, *Historia ecclesiastica*, V.24, ed. and trans. by Colgrave and Mynors, pp. 566–67.

The accusation of heresy concerned the chronological framework presented in the world chronicle of the time-reckoning manual *On Times*.[9] Bede had extracted much of the data for the chronicle from the Vulgate Bible, a decision which led to the year of Christ's Incarnation being dated to *annus mundi* 3952.[10] According to the *Letter to Plegwine* Bede stood accused of denying that the Incarnation had taken place in the sixth age of the world.[11] However, in *On Times* the Incarnation is twice located at the beginning of Age Six.[12] Bede's accuser appears to have subscribed to the view that world ages and millennia were in some way linked (this position was afforded superficial credence in the early Middle Ages by chronologies that followed the Septuagint Bible in which the year of the Incarnation was calculated to *c.* 5199).[13] Bede's chronology severed any implicit link between millennia and the six *aetates saeculi* by locating Christ in the fourth millennium of historical time. In the eyes of the accuser (according to Bede's version of events) it seems that this somehow amounted to a denial of the Incarnation, an allegation which Bede dismisses in the second paragraph of the *Letter to Plegwine* by employing the following rhetorical question to point out that such a position would have led him towards an existential crisis: 'Quomodo enim christum uenisse negans christi in ecclesia potuissem esse sacerdos' (For if I had denied that Christ had come, how could I be priest in Christ's Church?).[14] Such caricaturing of opponents' positions as absurd was a tactic which was commonly employed in arguments about heresy in Late Antiquity.[15]

Bede believed that the defamatory remarks spoken against him had been made in the presence of Bishop Wilfrid.[16] By 708 Wilfrid was living out the last years of his eventful life in his home kingdom of Northumbria, the monasteries of Ripon and Hexham having been returned to him at the reconciliatory Synod of Nidd in 706.[17] The letter was sent to Plegwine to be passed on to a mutual acquaintance known as David, so that David could read it aloud in the presence of Wilfrid.[18] The fact that Bede felt the need to go through these channels to reach the incumbent bishop of Hexham in 708 is very interesting, especially in light of the direct access he would subsequently have to Acca when Acca succeeded Wilfrid as bishop upon the latter's death in 710.[19] The *Letter to Plegwine* mentions that *On Times* had been written five

---

9   Bede, *De temporibus*, 16–22, ed. by Jones, pp. 600–11.

10 Bede, *De temporibus*, 22, ed. by Jones, p. 607, ll. 3–4. The background to Bede's *annus mundi* chronology is explored by MacCarron, 'Bede, Irish Computistica and Annus Mundi'.

11 Bede, *Epistola ad Pleguinam*, 1, ed. by Jones, p. 307, ll. 6–8.

12 Bede, *De temporibus*, 16 and 22, ed. by Jones, p. 601, ll. 16–22 and p. 607, ll. 3–4.

13 E.g. the chronologies of Isidore and Eusebius-Jerome. See: Landes, 'Lest the Millennium be Fulfilled'.

14 Bede, *Epistola ad Pleguinam*, 2, ed. by Jones, p. 307, ll. 1–2. *Bede: The Reckoning of Time*, trans. by Wallis, p. 405.

15 Cameron, 'How to Read Heresiology', pp. 473–77.

16 Bede, *Epistola ad Pleguinam*, 17, ed. by Jones, p. 315, ll. 1–6.

17 Stephen of Ripon, *Vita Wilfridi*, 60, ed. and trans. by Colgrave, pp. 128–33; Bede, *Historia ecclesiastica*, V.19, ed. and trans. by Colgrave and Mynors, pp. 528–29.

18 David is a *cognomen* for a member of the bishop's inner circle who was known personally to Bede in some capacity. See further: Wallis, 'Why did Bede Write a Commentary on Revelation?', pp. 28–29.

19 For 710 as the date of Wilfrid's death see Stancliffe, 'Dating Wilfrid's Death and Stephen's *Life*'.

years previously, and the date of *On Times* can be securely assigned to the year 703 on account of internal evidence preserved within that text.[20] In terms of the chronology of Bede's writings, the *Letter to Plegwine* was therefore written after *On Times* and its companion pieces *On the Nature of Things* and the commentary on Revelation,[21] but before the completion of major commentaries on Acts, Luke, Mark, and 1 Samuel, the trilogy of works concerning the Jewish sanctuaries (*On the Tabernacle, On the Temple, and On Ezra-Nehemiah*), the longer treatise on computus *On the Reckoning of Time*, the prose *Life of St Cuthbert*, the *Ecclesiastical History*, and several other significant works.[22] At the time of the letter's composition, it is fair to say that the majority of the texts that would establish Bede's reputation as a prominent figure within the Western Patristic tradition were yet to be written.[23]

The *Letter to Plegwine* captures a significant moment in its author's career because it was one of the first works to have been written by Bede for an audience outside Wearmouth and Jarrow. *On Times* and *On the Nature of Things* were compiled for students within the monastery,[24] and the commentary on Revelation was dedicated to Hwætberht, a member of the community who would later serve as its abbot.[25] Two other works with claims to a date before 708 — the paired tracts *On the Art of Metre* and *On Schemes and Tropes* — were dedicated to a 'dulcissime fili et conleuita cuthberte' (beloved son and fellow deacon Cuthbert), a form of address which seems to hint at somebody in Bede's immediate circle.[26] I know of no evidence to

---

20 Bede, *Epistola ad Pleguinam*, 3, ed. by Jones, p. 307, ll. 1–4. Bede, *De temporibus*, 14, ed. by Jones, pp. 598–99, ll. 1–10; 22, p. 611, ll. 79–80.

21 For the view that these texts should be regarded as a coherent trilogy see Darby, 'Time Shift of 703'. On the dates of the individual works see: Wallis, *Bede: Commentary on Revelation*, pp. 39–57; Kendall and Wallis, *Bede: On the Nature of Things and On Times*, pp. 1–3.

22 An overview of the development of Bede's career is offered by Darby and Wallis, 'Introduction: The Many Futures of Bede'. Attempts to present Bede's writings in chronological order of composition have been made by Plummer, *Venerabilis Baedae opera historica*, I, pp. cxliii–clv; Brown, *A Companion to Bede*, pp. 13–15, and O'Brien, *Bede's Temple*, pp. xix–xx. Many of the issues surrounding the dates of individual works are set out by Lapidge, *Storia degli inglesi*, I, pp. xlviii–lviii.

23 On the circulation and dissemination of Bede's writings after his death see: Whitelock, *After Bede*; Bonner, 'Bede and his Legacy'; Pfaff, 'Bede Among the Fathers?'; Rollason, *Bede and Germany*; Hill, 'Carolingian Perspectives on the Authority of Bede'; Brown, *A Companion to Bede*, pp. 117–34; Westgard, 'Bede and the Continent'.

24 Bede, *De temporum ratione*, preface, ed. by Jones, p. 263, ll. 1–3.

25 Bede, *Expositio Apocalypseos*, preface, ed. by Gryson, p. 221, ll. 1–3 (addressing 'Eusebius'). Hwætberht is identified as Eusebius in *In primam partem Samuhelis*, IV, ed. by Hurst, p. 212, ll. 12–20.

26 Bede, *De arte metrica*, 25, ed. by Kendall, p. 141, ll. 26–36. For the view that the two grammatical treatises were early compositions of Bede's see: Plummer, *Venerabilis Baedae opera historica*, I, p. cxlv; Laistner and King, *Hand-list of Bede Manuscripts*, pp. 131–32; Blair, *The World of Bede*, pp. 249–50. The early dating rests upon how one interprets the form of words used by Bede to address Cuthbert. Several recent commentators have cast doubt upon the assumption that *De arte metrica* and *De schematibus et tropis* were early-career compositions, e.g.: Irvine, 'Bede the Grammarian', pp. 41–43; Holder, '(Un)Dating Bede's *De arte metrica*'; Franklin, 'The Date of Composition of Bede's *De schematibus et tropis* and *De arte metrica*'; Kendall, *Libri II De schematibus et tropis et De arte metrica*, pp. 28–29; Thacker, 'Ordering of understanding', pp. 50–51. A recent study by Neil Wright does not preclude an early date for *De arte metrica*: 'The Metrical Art(s) of Bede'.

suggest that the metrical *Life of St Cuthbert* and *On the Holy Places*, two further works which are sometimes assigned to the period before 708, were originally written with wide circulation in mind.[27] There is, admittedly, some uncertainty regarding the circumstances of composition for several of Bede's other writings, but the evidence so far as we have it identifies the *Letter to Plegwine* as the first text that Bede overtly addressed to the world beyond Wearmouth and Jarrow.[28]

There are contextual factors relating to format and delivery which undermine any attempts to treat the *Letter to Plegwine* in a straightforward and uncomplicated fashion. First of all, we must not forget that we only have Bede's account of what happened in 708. The letter is very clear about what Bede intended: he expected the letter to be read aloud in Wilfrid's presence by 'David', and also asked that Plegwine petition David to speak to the perpetrator of the accusation on a one-to-one basis.[29] Bede therefore presented his case before Wilfrid through a speech delivered by proxy; there would be (so far as we know) no trial, personal interrogation, or formal submission to a Church council. In assessing the content of the letter we must keep the occasion of its public reading in mind and be duly sensitive to the performative aspect of Bede's prose. But, as the following analysis will show, the *Letter to Plegwine* is rich in allusions to biblical and extra-biblical material which one could not realistically expect any listener to be fully attuned to in the course of a single reading. It is significant that the letter is included in the autobiographical list of writings offered in the *Ecclesiastical History's* final chapter because this suggests that posterity was also an important consideration for Bede.[30] We are therefore dealing with a document intended to serve two different purposes at once: it addresses the immediate problem of clearing Bede's name before the bishop, and it presents a version of record to be read by a wider audience after the controversy had been resolved. The historical circumstances and literary qualities of the *Letter to Plegwine* are closely entwined, and both of these aspects of the source must be considered in tandem.[31]

The aforementioned observation that the *Letter to Plegwine* was considered worthy of inclusion in Bede's autobiographical list of writings is additionally important because it suggests that he thought of the letter as part of his official canon. That list, which appears to present the various letters of Bede in their chronological order of composition, refers to a book of letters to different people, and records that the first of these concerned the six ages of the world — an unambiguous reference to the *Letter to Plegwine*. The entry for the *liber epistularum* describes four other letters

27 The circumstances surrounding the composition of the metrical *Vita Cuthberti* are discussed in some detail by Lapidge, 'Bede's metrical *Vita S. Cuthberti*', pp. 77–85. On *De locis sanctis*, four chapters of which were later excerpted in *Historia ecclesiastica* v.16–17, see: O'Loughlin, *Adomnán and the Holy Places*, pp. 188–97; Darby and Reynolds, 'Reassessing the "Jerusalem pilgrims"', pp. 28–31.

28 Darby and Wallis, 'Introduction: The Many Futures of Bede', pp. 9–11.

29 Bede, *Epistola ad Pleguinam*, 17, ed. by Jones, p. 315, ll. 1–6.

30 Bede, *Historia ecclesiastica*, V.24, ed. and trans. by Colgrave and Mynors, pp. 568–69.

31 Cf. Constable, *Letters and Letter Collections*, pp. 11–12.

but that group does not represent the sum total of Bede's correspondence.[32] Several epistolary prefaces to various exegetical and non-exegetical works have been preserved, and two further letters postdate the completion of the *Ecclesiastical History* and the compiling of Bede's list: one to Albinus of Canterbury and another to Ecgberht of York.[33] From his extensive knowledge of the Patristic tradition Bede knew that letters were an important part of a Christian writer's legacy, and he had access to epistolary writings by Gregory the Great, Leo the Great, and other popes, plus Augustine, Jerome, Dionysius Exiguus, and others.[34] Bede's understanding of the world was of course anchored by his thorough knowledge of the Bible, a self-contained library of sacred texts which includes a great deal of epistolary material, some of which, it will become clear, inspired certain features of the *Letter to Plegwine*.[35]

The Discourse of Heresy

It has long been recognised that heresy was a serious concern for Bede.[36] Indeed, his homily on Matthew 1. 18–25 makes it clear that he felt a responsibility to educate others on the subject.[37] Heresy was something to be avoided at all costs.[38] It involved a wilful separation from the unity of the Church, and it sprang from the dangerous impulses of obstinate individuals who compromised the collective faith of the Christian community through their foolish stubbornness.[39] Heretics were often highly intelligent and skilled in the art of rhetoric, qualities which made them all the more dangerous.[40] It is notable that Bede considered the accusation directed towards him to be serious enough to warrant a public letter of defence.[41] Allusions

---

32 Two of the letters were addressed to Acca and written *c.* 716: the first (*De mansionibus filiorum Israel*) discusses locations visited by the Israelites during the Exodus and the second (*De eo quod ait Isaias*) concerns Isaiah 24. 22. The remaining letters discuss technical aspects of time-reckoning: one to Helmwald on the leap year; the other to Wicthed on the equinox.

33 On the *Epistula ad Ecgbertum* see: Grocock and Wood, *Abbots of Wearmouth and Jarrow*, pp. l–lix. For the *Epistula ad Albinum*: Westgard, 'New Manuscripts of Bede's Letter to Albinus'.

34 Lapidge, *Anglo-Saxon Library*, pp. 191–228.

35 On the Bible as library see O'Reilly, 'Views from Vivarium and Wearmouth-Jarrow'.

36 Plummer, *Venerabilis Baedae opera historica*, I, pp. iii–iiii.

37 Bede, *Homiliarum euangelii libri II*, 1.5, ed. by Hurst, p. 35, ll. 103–25. See further the comments of Thacker, 'Why Did Heresy Matter to Bede?', p. 66: 'His [Bede's] very identity as a teacher and a scholar was bound up with keeping watch for heresy and bad practice'.

38 Bede, *De mansionibus filiorum Israel*, ed. by Migne, col. 699.

39 See Bede, *In epistulas septem catholicas, In epistolam II Petri*, ed. by Hurst, pp. 268–69, ll. 1–25 and the comments of Holder 'Hunting Snakes in the Grass', p. 109.

40 Bede, *In Cantica Canticorum*, preface, ed. by Hurst, p. 167, ll. 1–33. See: Ray, 'Bede and Cicero', pp. 6–8.

41 Jones (*Bedae opera de temporibus*, p. 132) thought that the charge was 'serious, and represented not a few *rustici* but a distinguished party of whom Bishop Wilfrid was one'. Thacker asserts that the controversy of 708 'rankled very deeply' for Bede and draws attention to the fact that the *Letter to Plegwine* was written for public dissemination: 'Why Did Heresy Matter to Bede?', p. 55. For Wallis 'the speed at which these events unfolded … bespeaks the urgency of the situation': 'Why Did Bede Write a Commentary on Revelation', p. 28.

made to the episode in the preface to Bede's *On the Reckoning of Time*, written for the benefit of his brethren some seventeen years after the *Letter to Plegwine*, suggest that he continued to regard it as a significant matter long after Wilfrid's death.[42]

Bede was acutely aware that the faintest whiff of heresy had the potential to taint his reputation for many years to come. In his commentary on the Seven Catholic Epistles, when tackling James 3. 5 (**the tongue is a small part of the body, but it makes great boasts; consider what a great forest is set on fire by a small spark**), Bede wrote:

> Sicut enim a modica scintilla ignis excrescens magnam saepe siluam incendit, ita incontinentia linguae suis nutrita leuitatibus magnam bonorum operum materiam, multos uitae spiritalis fructus, ubi adtaminauerit perdit sed et innumera plerumque optima quae uidebantur locutionis folia consumit.

> > Just as from a small spark a spreading fire often ignites a great forest, so an unrestrained tongue, feeding on its own trivialities, destroys the great substance of good works, the many fruits of a spiritual life, after it has spoiled them; but it also devours innumerable and countless folios of speech which appeared most excellent.[43]

That the danger posed by the words of others was one of the things on Bede's mind here is suggested by his response to the subsequent pericope: 'no one, however, is able to tame the tongue' (James 3. 8). This invites the comment that 'no learned good man can tame the tongue of those who neglect to restrain themselves from foolish outbursts' (*stulta uerbositate*).[44] It is tempting to relate these comments, and indeed certain other statements from Bede's collection of commentaries on the Catholic Epistles, to the events of 708 (not least a passage from the tract on 3 John which explains how to deal with slanderous babbling, and a discourse on false teachers from the commentary on 1 Peter which advocates patience in the face of insulting words from adversaries and recommends the reading of John Chrysostom to protect against the threat of heresy).[45] The adjective *stultus* (foolish, stupid) and the associated noun *stultitia* (foolishness, folly) are often used by Bede in connection with the subject of heresy. Indeed *stulta obstinatione* (foolish stubbornness) is described as a defining characteristic of heretics in Bede's commentary on 2 Peter.[46] *Stultitia* is also used in Paragraph 11 of the *Letter to Plegwine*, where Bede rejects any suggestion that a shorter reckoning of years was followed in the Old Testament era by rounding off a citation

---

42 Jones, *Bedae opera de temporibus*, pp. 132–35 (cf. *Bede: The Reckoning of Time*, trans. by Wallis, p. xxxi).

43 Bede, *In epistulas septem catholicas, In epistolam Iacobi*, ed. by Hurst, p. 204, ll. 99–103; trans. by Hurst, *The Commentary on the Seven Catholic Epistles*, pp. 38–39 (with modifications).

44 Bede, *In epistulas septem catholicas, In epistolam Iacobi*, ed. by Hurst, p. 206, ll. 157–61: 'nullus doctorum bonorum potest domare linguam eorum qui se ipsos a stulta uerbositate cohibere neglegunt'; trans. by Hurst, *The Commentary on the Seven Catholic Epistles*, p. 41.

45 Bede, *In epistulas septem catholicas, In epistolam III Iohannis*, ed. by Hurst, p. 333, ll. 67–74; *In epistolam I Petri*, ed. by Hurst, p. 245, ll. 69–93. The evidence for Bede's knowledge of the works of Chrysostom is examined by Love, 'Bede and John Chrysostom'.

46 Bede, *In epistulas septem catholicas, In epistolam II Petri*, ed. by Hurst, p. 268, ll. 1–4.

from Augustine's *City of God* with a rhetorical question which is designed to draw attention to the supposed absurdity of the position he disagreed with.[47]

A great deal of recent research on the subject of Bede and heresy has focused upon Bede's engagement with the subject on an intellectual level. That is not to say that the scholarship implies that Bede's statements about heresy are in any way abstract or detached from late seventh- and early eighth-century issues; indeed, quite the opposite is often true, especially in the biblical commentaries where statements about heresy connect to a wide range of important concerns. Alan Thacker has shown that Bede was very concerned about Pelagian writings circulating under Jerome's name, and he has also demonstrated that the issue of what to do with penitent heretics, which is addressed at considerable length in the commentary *On 1 Samuel*, had acute contemporary relevance for Bede.[48] Faith Wallis's contribution to this volume shows that many of the comments in Bede's exegesis of the Book of Proverbs regarding the pressing need for erudite teachers were written against a backdrop of concerns about heresy.[49] Several scholars have drawn attention to fact that the language of heresy was sometimes invoked during the Insular Paschal controversy,[50] and Arthur Holder has suggested that Bede's understanding of heresy was connected to concerns about the observance of Easter.[51] Jennifer O'Reilly and Éamonn Ó Carragáin have shown that the Northumbrians were closely entwined in the debates over Monotheletism which took place in the late seventh century, and that those debates were an important backdrop to the intellectual programme established at the monastery of Wearmouth and Jarrow.[52] Nevertheless, the *Letter to Plegwine* offers us something slightly different from the material which is currently at the heart of the scholarship concerning Bede and heresy; it affords a unique opportunity to see how Bede interacted with the subject when an immediate attack upon his personal integrity had been made.

The *Letter to Plegwine* reveals a great deal about Bede's understanding of heresy and its operation, and it describes the events of 708 in very interesting terms. Bede does not say that he stood accused of subscribing to an existing heresy; instead the second sentence of the letter's first paragraph expresses the belief that his accusers had placed him 'inter hereticos' (among the heretics).[53] The idea that heretics existed

---

47 Bede, *Epistola ad Pleguinam*, 11, ed. by Jones, p. 312, ll. 13–16.
48 Thacker, 'Why Did Heresy Matter to Bede?', pp. 53–54 and 56–61. On the matter of penitent heretics cf. Cubitt, *Anglo-Saxon Church Councils*, p. 63; Charles-Edwards, 'The Penitential of Theodore', pp. 164–67.
49 Wallis, '*Rectores* at Risk'.
50 E.g. Ó Cróinín, '"New Heresy for Old"'; Stancliffe, *Bede, Wilfrid and the Irish*.
51 Holder, 'Hunting Snakes in the Grass', pp. 113–14.
52 O'Reilly, '"Know Who and What He Is"', pp. 301–03, and 'Bede and Monotheletism'; Ó Carragáin, *The City of Rome*, pp. 15–18; Ó Carragáin, *Ritual and the Rood*, pp. 81–83 and 223–28.
53 Bede, *Epistola ad Pleguinam*, 1, ed. by Jones, p. 307, ll. 4–6. Cf. Bede, *De tabernaculo*, II, ed. by Hurst, p. 69, ll. 1071–85; *In primam partem Samuhelis*, IV, ed. by Hurst, p. 264, ll. 2220–28; *In Ezram et Neemiam*, III, ed. by Hurst, p. 356, ll. 683–85. Also pertinent are the occurrences of the phrase in: Augustine, *De haeresibus*, 57 and 81, ed. by Plaetse and Beukers, p. 326, ll. 4–8 and p. 336, ll. 1–3; and Cassiodorus, *Expositio Psalmorum*, 22, ed. by Adriaen, p. 211, ll. 92–93.

as a group of shady individuals who stood together in opposition to the Church is a common trope in Bede's writings. The letter's next sentence describes Bede's reaction to learning that his detractors considered him worthy of membership of this group, which was to ask which particular heresy he was accused of. This question demonstrates an awareness of what Averil Cameron has described as a 'family tree' approach to heresy in which divergent beliefs are categorised using pre-existing labels.[54] The categorising of opponents' beliefs as recurrences of existing heresies was commonly employed in the heresiological literature produced in Late Antiquity.[55] Also instructive is the statement which opens Paragraph 4 of Bede's letter:

> Ne autem me putes, dilectissime, post notam hereseos ad inficiandi malle subterfugere praesidium quam decorem recipere ueritatis, audi quae in libello memorato de aetatibus scripsi.

> > Lest you think, beloved, that now my heresy has been discovered, I prefer to make my escape under the protection of denial rather than receive the grace of truth, listen to what I wrote concerning the Ages in that little book I mentioned [i.e. *On times*].[56]

This passage, which employs a verb in the imperative mood to convey a sense of urgency (*audi*), describes the devious tactics that the perpetrator of a heresy would be expected to resort to upon the discovery of their error. Rather than hide behind a denial, as a duplicitous scheming heretic would, Bede assumes the mantle of a catholic *doctor* and tackles the accusation by proceeding to restate the words that he had written five years before. A further point of interest is the letter's use of the term 'heresiarch' to describe the author of a chronographical text which Bede had encountered in his youth.[57] This figure had devised a simplistic reckoning which was loosely based upon the parable of the workers in the vineyard (Matthew 20. 1–16).[58] The problem, in Bede's view, was that the text promoted *annus mundi* 6000 as a target year for the apocalypse in contravention of the Scriptural assertions that the hour of the Lord's coming is known to God alone.[59] The unusual categorisation of the proponent of this chronology as an arch-heretic adds further weight to the notion that Bede considered the matters at stake in the *Letter to Plegwine* to be serious. Bede used the term 'heresiarch' just eight times in his writings, and five of those are in the

---

54 Cameron, 'How to Read Heresiology', pp. 476–77; also Flower, 'Genealogies of Unbelief'. The way that Bede describes Monotheletism is a good example of this practice, on which see: Thacker, 'Why Did Heresy Matter to Bede?', pp. 51–52; and now O'Reilly, 'Bede and Monotheletism'.

55 Lyman, 'Heresiology'.

56 Bede, *Epistola ad Pleguinam*, 4, ed. by Jones, p. 308, ll. 1–3; *Bede: The Reckoning of Time*, trans. by Wallis, pp. 406–07.

57 Bede, *Epistola ad Pleguinam*, 14, ed. by Jones, p. 313, ll. 9–12.

58 For discussion: Darby, *Bede and the End of Time*, pp. 47–51.

59 E.g. Mark 13. 32 and Matthew 24. 36. Both of these verses are cited in paragraph 14 of the *Epistola ad Pleguinam*.

plural.[60] One of the two remaining singular usages is assigned to Arius of Alexandria, and the other to Diotrophes, a figure mentioned in 3 John, verse 9.[61]

Nearly three decades ago Roger Ray invoked the *Letter to Plegwine* in support of his view that Bede was familiar with the classical tradition of rhetoric, proposing that the letter was constructed according to guidelines for the construction of public speeches which (whether directly or indirectly) ultimately derive from Cicero.[62] The manuscript evidence for direct knowledge of Cicero's writings in early Anglo-Saxon England is problematic, as Ray himself acknowledges.[63] Nevertheless, Ray asserts that the *Letter to Plegwine* adheres to certain well-established rhetorical structures and devices. For example, he points out that the argument made by Bede towards the end of the letter — that the person who slandered him is in fact the one guilty of heresy and not himself — is a deployment of a rhetorical strategy known as *remotio criminis*, the act of turning the tables on one's accuser by accusing them of a crime to set aside the original charge.[64] Bede could have learnt about this tactic from reading the section on legal arguments in Book Two of Isidore of Seville's *Etymologies*, an important reference point for several of his pre-708 writings.[65] Ray suggests that Bede's attitude towards classical rhetoric owes a considerable debt to a position expounded by Augustine that it is acceptable to deploy pre-Christian eloquence in the service of the Church. Interestingly, Ray points out that Bede's views on this matter often intersect with his comments on the struggle against heresy. An example of this is a statement of Bede's regarding the council of Nicaea, which explains that Athanasius needed knowledge of classical eloquence to defeat Arius, an opponent who was himself a highly accomplished rhetorician.[66]

The Salutation

If rhetorical strategies help to ensure that the case for Bede's defence is suitably amplified, the case itself is ultimately grounded in the authority of Scripture and

---

60 Bede, *In prouerbia Salomonis*, II, ed. by Hurst, p. 123, ll. 88–91; Bede, *In Lucae euangelium expositio*, VI, ed. by Hurst, pp. 364–65, ll. 73–77; Bede, *In Marci euangelium expositio*, IV, ed. by Hurst, p. 596, ll. 47–50; Bede, *In primam partem Samuhelis*, IV, ed. by Hurst, p. 260, ll. 2053–59; Bede, *In Ezram et Neemiam*, III, ed. by Hurst, p. 356, ll. 695–702.

61 Bede, *Expositio actuum apostolorum*, ed. by Laistner, p. 13, ll. 206–09 (Arius); Bede, *In epistulas septem catholicas*, *In epistolam III Iohannis*, ed. by Hurst, p. 333, ll. 58–62 (Diotrophes).

62 Ray, 'Bede and Cicero', pp. 9–12. Cf. Knappe, 'Classical Rhetoric in Anglo-Saxon England', and the response to Knappe by Ray in his 'Who Did Bede Think He Was?', pp. 28–29.

63 'The internal evidence of Bede's writings compels me even though I cannot now claim that the surviving manuscripts of Cicero's works tell for my case'. Ray, 'Bede and Cicero', p. 14.

64 Ray, 'Bede and Cicero', pp. 10–11. See further: Murphy, *Rhetoric in the Middle Ages*, pp. 10–15.

65 Isidore of Seville, *Etymologiae*, II.5.6, ed. by Lindsay. On Bede's use of Isidore see Lapidge, *Anglo-Saxon Library*, pp. 212–15, and the comments of: Wallis in *Bede: The Reckoning of Time*, trans. by Wallis, pp. lxxx–lxxxii; McCready, 'Bede, Isidore and the *Epistola Cuthberti*'; Ray, 'Bede's *Vera lex historiae*', pp. 14–17; Kendall and Wallis, *Bede: On the Nature of Things and On Times*, pp. 13–20.

66 Ray, 'Bede and Cicero', p. 6, discussing *In primam partem Samuhelis*, IV, ed. by Hurst, pp. 262–63, ll. 2125–69. On the relationship between heresy and eloquence see further: Holder, 'Hunting Snakes in the Grass', p. 110 and Wallis, '*Rectores* at Risk'.

the world of patristic exegesis. Close study of the salutation and opening paragraph of the *Letter to Plegwine* reveals several interesting allusions to biblical and patristic themes and phrases which serve to establish Bede's credentials as an orthodox and knowledgeable authority figure. It is here, at the very beginning of his interaction with the letter's oral and textual audiences, that Bede establishes the pillars upon which his defence will be built. We begin with the curious salutation in which Bede addresses Plegwine by borrowing a phrase from Paul's epistle to the Philippians (identified in the citation that follows by italic type): 'Fratri dilectissimo et *in christi uisceribus* honorando Pleguinae, Beda in domino salutem' (To his brother Plegwine, beloved and deserving of honour *in the bowels of Christ*, Bede sends greeting in the Lord).[67] The Pauline expression complements the superlative adjective (*dilectissimo*) to communicate warmth and respect for the recipient. The suggestion is that Plegwine deserves to be recognised as embodying Christian values in a manner which is completely beyond reproach. It is unequivocally a warm greeting.

In his biblical commentaries Bede frequently aligned verses from different parts of the Bible to cast light on one another, a method which has been described as 'exegesis by concordance'.[68] A close examination of the wording of these citations occasionally reveals that Bede's phrasing does not correspond exactly with any of the versions of the Bible that he had access to, which gives the impression that Bede sometimes cited verses from memory in the course of his scriptural work.[69] The implication is that Bede and, one presumes, many of the men and women who read or listened to his works, had an extensive catalogue of memorised biblical verses at their disposal and were able to cross-refer across Scripture at will. Bishop Wilfrid committed the entire Psalter and several of the Bible's other books to memory, if the account of his biographer can be believed.[70] An echo of a verse, such as the one seen in Bede's greeting to Plegwine, would have steered an informed medieval reader through a series of connected scriptural verses and themes, bringing in patristic interpretations of those verses along the way. Close studies of Bede's writings reveal that a great deal of implied meaning often stands behind his carefully chosen citations.[71] Reading Bede's exegesis with the myriad allusions that lie beneath the surface in mind is not unlike working one's way through a succession of faith-related riddles. This process ultimately serves to underscore the unity of the Holy Scriptures because it repeatedly brings ideas, themes, and symbols from different parts of the Bible into dialogue with each other.

Bede's allusion to the 'bowels of Christ' should be approached in this way. Within the Bible the arresting phrase *viscera Christi* is used uniquely in Chapter 1 of

---

67 Bede, *Epistola ad Pleguinam*, ed. by Jones, p. 307, ll. 1–2.

68 Martin, *The Venerable Bede: Commentary on the Acts of the Apostles*, pp. xxix–xxx (citing Leclercq, *The Love of Learning*, pp. 82–83).

69 Marsden, *The Text of the Old Testament*, pp. 202–19. For an example of this practice from the *Epistola ad Pleguinam*, see note 99, below.

70 Stephen of Ripon, *Vita Wilfridi*, 2–3, ed. and trans. by Colgrave, pp. 4–9. Stephen's claims are repeated by Bede in *Historia ecclesiastica*, V.19, ed. and trans. by Colgrave and Mynors, pp. 518–19.

71 For example: O'Reilly, 'Bede on Seeing the God of Gods in Zion'.

Paul's Letter to the Philippians so there can be little doubt that Bede wanted to lead his audience to that particular passage. Paul regarded the Christian community at Philippi in Macedonia as faithful and supportive, and the tone of his letter to the Philippians is overwhelmingly positive even though it was written during a period of imprisonment.[72] The following citation displays the *viscera Christi* passage within the context of the verses either side of it (Philippians 1. 7–1.11):

> Sicut est mihi iustum hoc sentire pro omnibus vobis eo quod habeam in corde vos et in vinculis meis et in defensione et confirmatione evangelii socios gaudii mei omnes vos esse. Testis enim mihi est Deus quomodo cupiam omnes vos in visceribus Christi Iesu. Et hoc oro ut caritas vestra magis ac magis abundet in scientia et omni sensu; ut probetis potiora ut sitis sinceres et sine offensa in diem Christi; repleti fructu iustitiae per Christum Iesum in gloriam et laudem Dei.

> > It is right for me to think this for you all, since I have you in my heart; and that, in my chains and in the defence and confirmation of the gospel, you all are partakers of my joy. For God is my witness how I long after you all in the bowels of Christ Jesus. And this I pray: that your love may more and more abound in knowledge and in all understanding; that you may approve the better things; that you may be sincere and without offence unto the day of Christ, filled with the fruit of justice, through Jesus Christ, unto the glory and praise of God.[73]

Paul here speaks of justice and expresses hope that the recipient community's love, knowledge, and understanding might grow after the letter is read. There are obvious resonances here with the *Letter to Plegwine*.

Bede's echoing of a distinctive Pauline phrase draws attention to some surface-level similarities between the compositional contexts of Paul's letter to the Philippians and his own letter to the Wilfridians. Both letters attempt to persuade their recipients to align their views with the author's own, both authors were connected to the communities that they were addressing via personal messengers passing back and forth between them, and both were experiencing a degree of tribulation at the time of writing (although Paul's situation was admittedly more perilous than Bede's).[74] Although we must be cautious about taking the superlatives employed in epistolary salutations at face value because they are routinely formulaic and highly stylised,[75] a reading of the Pauline citation in its scriptural context confirms beyond any doubt that the greeting should be regarded as an expression of spiritual fraternity towards Plegwine. Bede's letter proceeds to cite work by a succession of individuals in support

---

72 Browning, *The Oxford Dictionary of the Bible*, p. 294.

73 The Latin is supplied from folio 976ʳ of the Codex Amiatinus (Florence, Biblioteca Medicea Laurenziana, MS Amiatino 1); translation: Douay-Rheims Bible (with minor modifications).

74 A messenger named Epaphroditus is mentioned in Philippians 2. 25 and 4. 18. The beginning of Bede's letter makes it clear that he had heard of the accusation made against him from a messenger sent by Plegwine: *Epistola ad Pleguinam* 1, ed. by Jones, p. 307, ll. 3–6.

75 Lanham, *'Salutatio' Formulas in Latin Letters to 1200*.

of the contested chronology, including Origen, Jerome, Augustine and Josephus as well as (revealingly) Bede himself, but these authorities are all brought in behind an eye-catching allusion to the writings of Paul, a figure revered as apostle to the Gentiles.[76]

Two further explanations as to why Bede chose to allude to this specific Pauline epistle in his greeting to Plegwine can be advanced. First, there are several occasions elsewhere in his corpus where the epistle to the Philippians is connected to the struggle against heresy. Two examples from the commentary *On Ezra-Nehemiah* will suffice: in an exposition of Ezra 4. 4, Bede draws upon Philippians 2. 21 when considering a series of figures from ecclesiastical history who suffered at the hands of heretics; in his exegesis of Nehemiah 4. 1–2 Bede echoes Philippians 3. 19 to castigate heretics and false Christians who block attempts to reform the Church because it could threaten their unholy lifestyles.[77] So it may be that Bede saw the epistle to the Philippians as providing useful ammunition in the fight against heresy, making its use as a framing device for the *Letter to Plegwine* entirely appropriate for the situation that had arisen in 708. Second, Bede would certainly have connected this particular Pauline epistle with important doctrinal issues on account of the famous Christological discourse at the beginning of its second chapter in which Paul reflects upon the relationship between Christ and God the Father (Philippians 2. 5–11).[78] At some point before 731 Bede assembled a volume of excerpts of interpretations of the Pauline epistles from Augustine's writings; in that collection Paul's Christological discourse is addressed with citations from *On the Trinity* and *Eighty-three Different Questions* which ruminate on Christ's human and divine natures.[79] This dimension to the letter to the Philippians is relevant because Bede characterised the allegation made against him in Christological terms. His understanding of the situation, as described in the *Letter to Plegwine's* opening paragraph, was that he stood accused of denying Christ's coming *in carne* in the sixth age of the world.[80] It is probably no coincidence that Bede framed the *Letter to Plegwine* with an allusion to the *viscera Christi*, a phrase drawn from an epistle renowned for its Christological content, and one which itself asserts a belief in the miracle of the Incarnation.

Additional layers of meaning are recoverable with reference to Patristic tradition. The salutation employed in the *Letter to Plegwine* reaches back to Paul but it does so through the letters of Augustine, a figure whose writings had a profound impact

---

76 E.g.: Bede, *Homiliarum euangelii libri II*, 2.22, ed. by Hurst, p. 347, ll. 178–204; Bede, *Expositio Actuum Apostolorum*, IV, ed. by Hurst, p. 28, ll. 80–82; Bede, *In Ezram et Neemiam*, I, ed. by Hurst, p. 283, ll. 1673–74; Bede, *De templo*, II, ed. by Hurst, p. 218, ll. 1035–41. See further the comments of O'Reilly, 'Introduction', pp. xxxiv–xxxv, and Heuchan, 'The Apostle Paul', especially pp. 427–28.

77 Bede, *In Ezram et Neemiam*, I, ed. by Hurst, p. 283, ll. 1670–86; 3, pp. 355–56, ll. 664–83.

78 This part of Paul's letter to the Philippians was invoked against Monotheletism in the *acta* of the Lateran Synod of 649; a copy of the acts was made at Wearmouth and known to Bede: O'Reilly, 'Know Who and What He is', pp. 313–14. See also MacCarron, 'Christology and the Future', p. 168.

79 *Collectio Bedae presbyteri ex opusculis sancti Augustini in epistulas Pauli Apostoli*, 344–45. On this work, which is yet to receive a critical edition, see: Wilmart, 'La collection de Bède le Vénérable sur l'Apôtre', and Fransen, 'Description de la collection de Bède le Vénérable sur l'Apôtre'.

80 Bede, *Epistola ad Pleguinam*, 1, ed. by Jones, p. 307, ll. 6–8.

upon Bede.[81] Bede's exegetical works and writings on time and nature demonstrate that he was familiar with a substantial body of Augustinian epistolary material.[82] It is notable, therefore, that Bede's salutation mirrors a formula used by Augustine:

> Fratri dilectissimo et in christi uisceribus honorando Pleguinae Beda in domino salutem (Bede, *Letter to Plegwine*).

> Fratri dilectissimo et in christi uisceribus honorando Consentio Augustinus in domino salutem (Augustine, *Letter 120*).

The two salutations are identical apart from the switching of the sender and recipient names: Bede for Augustine, and Plegwine in place of Consentius, the lay addressee of Augustine's *Letter 120*. The evidence for Bede's knowledge of the letter to Consentius is decisive. It is excerpted in his collection of Augustinian material on the Pauline epistles, and in his commentary on Luke Bede advises the reader to 'lege epistolam sancti augustini ad consentium de corpore domini post resurrectionem' (read the letter of St Augustine to Consentius concerning the body of the Lord after the resurrection).[83]

The phrase *in Christi visceribus* is additionally used in the salutations of a handful of other Augustinian letters, including the following two examples which were certainly known to Bede:

> Domino beatissimo et in christi uisceribus germanitus amplectendo, plus quam dici potest desiderabili fratri et coepiscopo paulino alypius et Augustinus (Augustine, *Letter 186*).

> Domino dilectissimo et in christi uisceribus honorando sancto fratri et conpresbytero hieronymo augustinus in domino salutem (Augustine, *Letter 82*).

The first example belongs to a letter from Augustine and his friend Alypius of Thagaste to Paulinus of Nola; this text, which outlines the dangers of the Pelagian heresy, makes two appearances in Bede's collection of Augustinian passages concerning the epistles of Paul.[84] The second is a letter from Augustine to Jerome which is drawn upon in Bede's commentary on Acts and excerpted several times in the Pauline epistles compendium.[85] There can be little doubt that Bede's greeting to Plegwine was deliberately chosen; not only does its use of a distinctive Pauline phrase conjure up thoughts of the apostle in

---

81   Thacker, *Bede and Augustine of Hippo*.

82   The following analysis draws upon the consolidated list of citations of Augustine's letters provided by Lapidge, *Anglo-Saxon Library*, p. 201.

83   Bede, *In Lucae evangelium expositio*, VI, ed. by Hurst, p. 419, ll. 2244–45; *Collectio Bedae presbyteri ex opusculis sancti Augustini in epistulas Pauli Apostoli*, 136, trans. by Hurst, p. 113.

84   *Collectio Bedae presbyteri ex opusculis sancti Augustini in epistulas Pauli Apostoli*, 205 and 267, trans. by Hurst, pp. 157 and 204. On Alypius and Augustine's letter to Paulinus see Lienhard, 'Paulinus of Nola', p. 628.

85   Bede, *Expositio Actuum Apostolorum*, ed. by Laistner, pp. 85–86, ll. 30–57 (cf. 18, p. 75, ll. 33–35); *Collectio Bedae presbyteri ex opusculis sancti Augustini in epistulas Pauli Apostoli*, 177, 263, 266, 292–93 and 299, trans. by Hurst, pp. 138–39, 201–02, 203, 218–19 and 222–23.

prison writing to the Philippians, it also serves to align Bede with Augustine through its use of a salutation formula which is recognisably Augustinian. Cumulatively these connections serve to situate the *Letter to Plegwine* within a Christian epistolary tradition which reaches all the way back to the New Testament.

Further Echoes of Augustine

It is worth citing in full the opening two sentences of the first paragraph of the *Letter to Plegwine* in which Bede describes his reaction to learning of the accusation made against him:

> Venit ad me ante biduum, frater amantissime, nuntius tuae sanctitatis, qui pacificae quidem salutationis a te laetissima uerba detulit. Sed haec tristi mox admixtione confudit, addendo uidelicet quod me audires a lasciuientibus rusticis inter hereticos per pocula decantari. Exhorrui, fateor, et pallens percunctabar, cuius hereseos arguerer.

> > Two days ago, beloved brother, a messenger from your Sanctity came to me bearing gladsome words of peaceful salutation from you. But thereafter he threw these into disorder by adding something very unfortunate, namely that you had heard it babbled out by lewd rustics in their cups that I was among the heretics. I confess I was terrified; blanching, I asked of what heresy I was accused.[86]

The statement 'exhorrui' (I was terrified) communicates the horror that Bede felt upon receiving the messenger's news. The verb *exhorreo* is a comparatively rare word in Bede's writings, and the statement in the *Letter to Plegwine* is the only instance in which Bede uses it in its first person singular form. It is used just four further times throughout his corpus, typically in connection with acts that Bede considered especially shocking: in a passage from the commentary on Luke (which is redeployed verbatim in the commentary on Mark) Bede employs this word in his discussion of the betrayal of Jesus by Judas;[87] it is also used in the *Ecclesiastical History*'s account of Adamnán, the Irishman at the monastery of Coldingham who was so horrified by a sin he had committed that he devoted himself to a life of extreme penance;[88] the fourth instance is found within a citation from Josephus which features in Bede's commentary on Acts.[89] Over two hundred and fifty uses of the various forms of this verb by Christian writers in the period up to and including Bede are recorded in the Brepolis Library of Latin Texts database, and more than half of these are found in

---

86 Bede, *Epistola ad Pleguinam*, 1, ed. by Jones, p. 307, ll. 3–7; *Bede: The Reckoning of Time*, trans. by Wallis, p. 405, with minor modifications.

87 Bede, *In Lucae evangelium expositio*, VI, ed. by Hurst, p. 374, ll. 457–60; Bede, *In Marci euangelium expositio*, 4, ed. by Hurst, p. 608, ll. 523–26.

88 Bede, *Historia ecclesiastica*, IV.25, ed. and trans. by Colgrave and Mynors, pp. 420–27.

89 Bede, *Expositio Actuum Apostolorum*, ed. by Laistner, p. 60, ll. 73–79.

the writings of St Augustine, a remarkably large proportion even allowing for the
sizeable nature of Augustine's output.[90] By way of contrast, Gregory the Great, the
next most prolific user of this verb from the period in question, employed *exhorreo*
just nine times. Bede's use of a word with distinct Augustinian resonances in the *Letter
to Plegwine* is worth investigating further, especially in light of the observations made
above concerning the letter's salutation formula and Alan Thacker's suggestion that
the bishop of Hippo was the most important reference point for Bede's understanding
of heresy.[91]

Two specific examples where Augustine also uses the verb *exhorreo* are instructive.
The first of these is in *On Heresies*, a text produced shortly before Augustine's death
at the behest of Quodvultdeus of Carthage. Significantly, the excerpt in question
is also featured in the anthology of excerpts from Augustine's writings compiled
by Eugippius.[92] Bede knew the Eugippian collection and used it in a variety of
different contexts, including for the assembling of his own collection of excerpts
from Augustine on the Pauline epistles.[93] The passage concerns Augustine's
response to the view ascribed to Origen that all Christians, including even the devil
and the damned, would ultimately be restored to the kingdom of God through a
lengthy process of purification after death. Augustine asks his reader: 'quis enim
catholicus christianus uel doctus uel indoctus non uehementer exhorreat eam
quam dicit purgationem malorum' (what catholic Christian, whether educated
or not, would not be exceedingly terrified at what he [Origen] calls the purgation
of the wicked?).[94] The rhetorical question asked by Augustine in *On Heresies*
connects the verb *exhorreo* to the discourse of heresy: the *catholicus christianus* is
expected to react to Origen's teachings on the fate of the damned with shock and
terror. A letter of Bede's written in response to a request from Acca concerning
the interpretation of Isaiah 24. 22 offers a carefully-prepared consideration of
this subject.[95]

A second Augustinian use of the term is worth considering because several
pervasive connections between the source in question and the *Letter to Plegwine*
are apparent. The text in question is a letter of Augustine's which was written after
the year 395 to Deuterius, bishop of Caesarea. The letter reports the actions taken
by Augustine against a member of the clergy who had been teaching Manichean
doctrines in Hippo. Augustine writes:

---

90 The search term 'exhorr*' yields 145 hits from Augustine's writings using the Brepolis cross-database
search tool (this total includes instances of the verb *exhorresco*, a synonym of *exhorreo*).

91 Thacker, 'Why Did Heresy Matter to Bede?', pp. 49–50.

92 Eugippius, *Excerpta ex operibus S. Augustini*, 19, ed. by Knöll, pp. 166–67.

93 Thacker, *Bede and Augustine of Hippo*, pp. 4 and 7–8.

94 Augustine, *De haeresibus*, 43, ed. by Plaetse and Beukers, pp. 310–11, ll. 14–16.

95 Bede, *De eo quod ait Isaias* (see also: Bede, *In primam partem Samuhelis*, III, ed. by Hurst, pp. 160–61,
ll. 998–1013; Bede, *Retractatio in Actus Apostolorum*, ed. by Laistner, p. 120, ll. 46–61; Bede, *In prouerbia
Salomonis*, II, ed. by Hurst, p. 70, ll. 19–28). For discussion of *De eo quod ait Isaias* see: Holder,
'Hunting Snakes in the Grass', p. 112; Foley and Holder, *Bede: A Biblical Miscellany*, pp. 35–38; Darby,
Bede and the End of Time, pp. 140–43.

Has cum illis intolerabiles blasphemias subdiaconus iste quasi catholicus non solum credebat, sed, quibus uiribus poterat, et docebat. nam docens patefactus est, cum se quasi discentibus credidit. rogauit me quidem, posteaquam se manichaeorum auditorem esse confessus est, ut eum in uiam ueritatis doctrinae catholicae reuocarem, sed, fateor, eius fictionem sub clerici specie uehementer exhorrui eum que coercitum pellendum de ciuitate curaui.

> This subdeacon, posing as a Catholic, not only believed but also taught, with all the energy he could, these intolerable blasphemies. For he was exposed as teaching them when he entrusted himself to people who posed as his students. After he confessed that he was a hearer in the Manichees, he in fact asked me to bring him back to the path of truth, which is Catholic doctrine. But, I admit, I was aghast at his pretense in the guise of a cleric, and I took measures to expel him from the city after chastising him.[96]

This excerpt shares much in common with the opening paragraph of Bede's *Letter to Plegwine*. First, Bede and Augustine both pair the deponent verb *fateor* (meaning 'I confess, I admit') with the first person singular, perfect tense form *exhorrui* (I shuddered, I was terrified).[97] Secondly, the two passages are preserved in letters, and thirdly, both of those letters concern the subject of heresy. As with the citation from Philippians in the salutation, Bede is channelling authority into his prose by using language carefully chosen to resonate with earlier epistolary material. When Bede came to express the extreme terror that he felt upon learning of the allegation made against him he chose to do so by drawing on a verb from Augustine's register which has specific connotations with the fight against heresy. This allowed Bede to place himself on the side of the righteous by casting his reaction to the controversy of 708 in a distinctly Augustinian mould.

Conclusions

The *Letter to Plegwine* reveals that Bede was a fluent and knowledgeable participant in the Christian discourse over heresy. The letter's prose is evidently rich and complex. It is clear that Bede wove biblical and patristic linguistic touchstones into the letter in order to align himself with major figures from the Christian tradition and add weight to the case for his defence. Additional investigation would no doubt reveal a great many further examples of this beyond those considered at length here. For example, Paragraph 3 invokes an interesting combination of Petrine authorities by alluding to Gregory the Great's repertoire of teachings on the active and contemplative lives

---

96 Augustine, *Epistulae*, 236, ed. by Goldbacher, vol. 4, p. 525, ll. 12–19; translation Teske, *Augustine: Letters*, II, p. 135.

97 Compare: 'Exhorrui, fateor, et pallens percunctabar, cuius hereseos arguerer' (Bede, *Epistola ad Pleguinam*, 1, ed. by Jones, p. 307, ll. 6–7) and 'sed, fateor, eius fictionem sub clerici specie uehementer exhorrui eum que coercitum pellendum de ciuitate curaui' (Augustine, *Epistulae*, 236, ed. by Goldbacher, vol. 4, p. 525, ll. 17–19).

whilst steering the reader's mind towards a statement concerning 'brotherly love' from the first epistle of Peter.[98] Likewise, Bede's letter ends with a pointed remark about snakes and charmers which echoes Ecclesiastes 10. 11, but the specific wording of the *Letter to Plegwine* appears to combine an uncommon usage twice found in the *Conferences* of Cassian with the Vulgate reading which had formerly been used by Augustine and Jerome.[99]

In conclusion, it is worth reflecting once again on the two-day timeframe for the composition of the *Letter to Plegwine*. Bede emerges from a microscopic investigation of the beginning of his letter as an extremely impressive figure: he seems to have been able to draw out multiple scriptural allusions and exegetical inferences at will, and he was able to execute those techniques in haste in the midst of a significant personal crisis. The *Letter to Plegwine* offers us a rare glimpse of an embattled Bede fighting to preserve his reputation. The intellectually sophisticated nature of the prose employed in the *Letter to Plegwine* underscores the extent of its author's learning, but the deft manner in which Bede self-consciously aligns himself with authority figures from the Christian tradition is also revealing. It is appropriate to finish this essay with an ending borrowed directly from Alan Thacker. Reflecting on Bede's career as a whole, Thacker remarked: 'Bede, I suspect, was aware of his eminence. He thought of himself as the Augustine of his age. And who is to say that he was not right?'[100] In 708 all but one of Bede's major works of biblical exegesis were yet to be issued, but in the *Letter to Plegwine* we encounter him as an assured figure who had no qualms about presenting himself as a commanding authority: not yet, perhaps, the Augustine of his age, but already showing many of the characteristics that in due course would establish him as such.

---

98   Bede, *Epistola ad Pleguinam*, 3, ed. by Jones, p. 308, ll. 12–16. The mention of 'the office of brotherly love (*fraterni amoris officium*)', which Bede felt had been compromised by the accusation of heresy, silently recalls 1 Peter 1.22. The subsequent reference to the 'darkness of blind error' (*Tenebras ... caecae falsitatis*) echoes the phrase 'darkness of blindness' (*caecitatis tenebras*) used a number of times by Gregory the Great (e.g. *Homiliae in Hiezechielem prophetam*, II.ii.12 ed. by Adriaen, p. 232, ll. 273–74).

99   Bede, *Epistola ad Pleguinam*, 17, ed. by Jones, p. 315, ll. 12–13: 'Vere enim dictum est quia si momorderit serpens in silentio, non est habundantia incantatori'. The Vulgate reading (as presented in Codex Amiatinus fol. 422ᵛ) is: 'si mordeat serpens in silentio nihil e[o] minus habet qui occulte detrahit' (cf. Augustine, *Speculum*, 8, ed. by Weihrich, p. 73, ll. 19–20; Jerome, *Commentarii in Isaiam*, 18, prologue, ed. by Adriaen, p. 742, ll. 69–71). Bede's wording more closely echoes Cassian's 'si momorderit serpens non in sibilo, non est abundantia incantatori' (Cassian, *Conlationes*, II.11 and XVIII.16, ed. by Petschenig, p. 51, ll. 10–11 and p. 529, ll. 19–20), although with the Vulgate's *'in silentio'* in place of Cassian's *'in sibilo'*.

100   Thacker, 'Bede and the Ordering of Understanding', p. 63.

Works Cited

Manuscripts and Archival Sources

Florence, Biblioteca Medicea Laurenziana, MS Amiatino 1 (Codex Amiatinus)

Digital resources

La Bibbia Amiatina: riproduzione integrale su CD-ROM del manoscritto Firenze, Biblioteca Medicea Laurenziana, Amiatino 1, ed. by Luigi G. G. Ricci, Lucia Castaldi, and Rosanna Minello (Florence: SISMEL, 2000)

Brepolis Library of Latin texts, http://brepolis.net

Primary Sources

Augustine of Hippo, *De civitate Dei*, ed. by Bernard Dombart and Alphonse Kalb, Corpus Christianorum Series Latina, 47 and 48 (Turnhout: Brepols, 1955)

——, *De haeresibus*, ed. by Roel Vander Plaetse and Clemens Beukers, Corpus Christianorum Series Latina, 46 (Turnhout: Brepols, 1969), pp. 286–345

——, *Epistulae*, ed. by Alois Goldbacher, Corpus Scriptorum Ecclesiasticorum Latinorum, 5 volumes (Vienna: Tempsky, 1895–1923)

——, *Augustine: Letters*, trans. by Roland J. Teske, 4 volumes, The works of Saint Augustine: a translation for the 21st Century. Part II (New York: New City Press, 2001–2005)

——, *Speculum*, ed. by Franz Weihrich, Corpus Scriptorum Ecclesiasticorum Latinorum, 12 (Vienna: Gerold, 1887), pp. 3–285

Bede, *De arte metrica*, ed. by Calvin B. Kendall, Corpus Christianorum Series Latina, 123A (Turnhout: Brepols, 1975), pp. 82–141

——, *De eo quod ait Isaias*, in *Patrologiae cursus completus: series latina*, ed. by Jacques Paul Migne, 221 vols (Paris: Migne, 1844–1864), 94 (1862), cols 702–10

——, *De locis sanctis*, ed. by Jean Fraipont, Corpus Christianorum Series Latina, 175 (Turnhout: Brepols, 1965), pp. 245–80

——, *De mansionibus filiorum Israel*, in *Patrologiae cursus completus: series latina*, ed. by Jacques Paul Migne, 221 vols (Paris: Migne, 1844–1864), 94 (1862), cols 699–702

——, *De schematibus et tropis*, ed. by Calvin B. Kendall, Corpus Christianorum Series Latina, 123A (Turnhout: Brepols, 1975), pp. 142–71

——, *De tabernaculo*, ed. by David Hurst, Corpus Christianorum Series Latina, 119A (Turnhout: Brepols, 1969), pp. 5–139

——, *De templo*, ed. by David Hurst, Corpus Christianorum Series Latina, 119A (Turnhout: Brepols, 1969), pp. 143–234

——, *De temporibus*, ed. by Charles W. Jones, Corpus Christianorum Series Latina, 123C (Turnhout: Brepols, 1980), pp. 585–611

——, *De temporum ratione*, ed. by Charles W. Jones, Corpus Christianorum Series Latina, 123B (Turnhout: Brepols, 1977)

———, *Epistola ad Pleguinam*, ed. by Charles W. Jones, *Bedae opera de temporibus* (Cambridge, MA: Mediaeval Academy of America, 1943), pp. 307–15

———, *Epistula ad Albinum*, ed. and trans. by Joshua A. Westgard, 'New manuscripts of Bede's letter to Albinus', *Revue Bénédictine*, 120 (2010), pp. 208–15

———, *Epistula ad Ecgbertum*, ed. and trans. by Christopher Grocock and Ian N. Wood in *Abbots of Wearmouth and Jarrow*, Oxford Medieval Texts (Oxford: Clarendon Press, 2013), pp. 123–61

———, *Epistula ad Helmuualdum*, ed. by Charles W. Jones, Corpus Christianorum Series Latina, 123C (Turnhout: Brepols, 1980), p. 629

———, *Epistula ad Wicthedum*, ed. by Charles W. Jones, Corpus Christianorum Series Latina, 123C (Turnhout: Brepols, 1980), pp. 635–42

———, *Expositio Actuum Apostolorum*, ed. by M. L. W. Laistner, Corpus Christianorum Series Latina, 121 (Turnhout: Brepols, 1983), pp. 3–99

———, *Expositio Apocalypseos*, ed. by Roger Gryson, Corpus Christianorum Series Latina, 121A (Turnhout: Brepols, 2001)

———, *Historia ecclesiastica gentis Anglorum*, ed. and trans. by Bertram Colgrave and R. A. B. Mynors, *Bede's Ecclesiastical History of the English People* (Oxford: Clarendon Press, 1969)

———, *Homiliarum euangelii libri II*, ed. by David Hurst, Corpus Christianorum Series Latina, 122 (Turnhout: Brepols, 1955), pp. 1–378

———, *In Cantica Canticorum*, ed. by David Hurst, Corpus Christianorum Series Latina, 119B (Turnhout: Brepols, 1983), pp. 167–375

———, *In epistulas septem catholicas*, ed. by David Hurst, Corpus Christianorum Series Latina, 121 (Turnhout: Brepols, 1983), pp. 181–342

———, *In Ezram et Neemiam*, ed. by David Hurst, Corpus Christianorum Series Latina, 119A (Turnhout: Brepols, 1969), pp. 237–392

———, *In Lucae euangelium expositio*, ed. by David Hurst, Corpus Christianorum Series Latina, 120 (Turnhout: Brepols, 1960), pp. 5–425

———, *In Marci euangelium expositio*, ed. by David Hurst, Corpus Christianorum Series Latina, 120 (Turnhout: Brepols, 1960), pp. 431–648

———, *In primam partem Samuhelis*, ed. by David Hurst, Corpus Christianorum Series Latina, 119 (Turnhout: Brepols, 1962), pp. 5–287

———, *In prouerbia Salomonis*, ed. by David Hurst, Corpus Christianorum Series Latina, 119B (Turnhout: Brepols, 1983), pp. 23–163

———, *Retractatio in Actuum Apostolorum*, ed. by M. L. W. Laistner, Corpus Christianorum Series Latina, 121 (Turnhout: Brepols, 1983), pp. 103–63

———, *Vita Cuthberti metrica*, ed. by Werner Jaager, *Bedas metrische Vita sancti Cuthberti*, Palaestra 198 (Leipzig: Mayer and Müller, 1935)

Bede: The Reckoning of Time, trans. by Faith Wallis, revised 2nd edition, Translated Texts for Historians, 29 (Liverpool: Liverpool University Press, 2004)

Cassian, *Conlationes*, ed. by Michael Petschenig, Corpus Scriptorum Ecclesiasticorum Latinorum, 13 (Vienna: Tempsky, 1888)

Cassiodorus, *Expositio Psalmorum*, ed. by Marc Adriaen, Corpus Christianorum Series Latina, 97 and 98 (Turnhout: Brepols, 1958)

Collectio Bedae presbyteri ex opusculis sancti Augustini in epistulas Pauli Apostoli, trans. by
David Hurst, *Bede the Venerable: Excerpts from the works of Saint Augustine on the
letters of the Blessed Apostle Paul*, Cistercian Studies Series, 183 (Kalamazoo: Cistercian
Publications, 1999)

Douay-Rheims Bible (Baltimore: John Murphy, 1899)

Eugippius, *Excerpta ex operibus S. Augustini*, ed. by Pius Knöll, Corpus Scriptorum
Ecclesiasticorum Latinorum, 9 (Vienna: Gerold, 1885)

Gregory the Great, *Homiliae in Hiezechielem prophetam*, ed. by Marc Adriaen, Corpus
Christianorum Series Latina 143 (Turnhout: Brepols, 1971)

Isidore of Seville, *Etymologiae*, ed. by Wallace Martin Lindsay, *Etymologiarum siue originum
libri XX* (Oxford: Clarendon Press, 1911)

Jerome, *Commentarii in Isaiam*, ed. by Marc Adriaen, Corpus Christianorum Series Latina,
73 and 73A (Turnhout: Brepols, 1963)

Stephen of Ripon, *Vita Wilfridi*, ed. and trans. by Bertram Colgrave, *The Life of Bishop
Wilfrid by Eddius Stephanus* (Cambridge: Cambridge University Press, 1927)

Secondary Studies

Blair, Peter Hunter, *The World of Bede*, revised 2nd Edition (Cambridge: Cambridge
University Press, 1990)

Bonner, Gerald, 'Bede and his legacy', *Durham University Journal*, 78 (1986), 219–30.

Brown, George Hardin, *A Companion to Bede* (Woodbridge: Boydell, 2009)

Browning, W. R. F., *The Oxford Dictionary of the Bible* (Oxford: Oxford University Press, 1996)

Cameron, Averil, 'How to Read Heresiology', *Journal of Medieval and Early Modern Studies*,
33 (2003), 471–92

Charles-Edwards, Thomas, 'The Penitential of Theodore and the *Iudicia Theodori*', in
Archbishop Theodore: Commemorative Studies on his Life and Influence, ed. by Michael
Lapidge, Cambridge Studies in Anglo-Saxon England, 11 (Cambridge: Cambridge
University Press, 1995), pp. 141–74

Chazelle, Celia, 'Debating the End Times with Bede', *Irish Theological Quarterly*, 80 (2015),
212–32

Constable, Giles, *Letters and Letter Collections*, Typologie des sources du Moyen Âge
occidental, 17 (Turnhout: Brepols, 1976)

Cubitt, Catherine, *Anglo-Saxon Church Councils c. 650–c. 850* (Leicester: Leicester
University Press, 1995)

Darby, Peter, and Reynolds, Daniel K., 'Reassessing the "Jerusalem pilgrims": The Case
of Bede's *De Locis Sanctis*', *Bulletin of the Council for British Research in the Levant*,
9 (2014), 27–31

Darby, Peter, and Faith Wallis, *Bede and the End of Time* (Farnham: Ashgate, 2012)

——, 'Bede's Time Shift of 703 in Context', in *Abendländische Apokalyptik. Kompendium
zur Genealogie der Endzeit*, ed. by Veronika Wieser, Christian Zolles, Catherine Feik,
Martin Zolles, and Leopold Schlöndorff (Berlin: Akademie, 2013), pp. 619–40

——, 'Introduction: The Many Futures of Bede', in *Bede and the Future*, ed. by Peter
Darby and Faith Wallis (Farnham: Ashgate, 2014), pp. 1–21

DeGregorio, Scott, '"*Nostrorum socordiam temporum*": The Reforming Impulse of Bede's Later Exegesis', *Early Medieval Europe*, 11 (2002), 107–22

——, 'Bede's *in Ezram et Neemiam* and the Reform of the Northumbrian Church', *Speculum*, 79 (2004), 1–25

——, 'Bede's *in Ezram Et Neemiam*: A Document in Church Reform?', in *Bède le Vénérable: entre Tradition et Postérité / The Venerable Bede: Tradition and Posterity*, ed. by Stéphane Lebecq, Michel Perrin and Olivier Szerwiniack (Lille: CEGES, Université Charles-de-Gaulle, 2005), pp. 97–107

——, 'Monasticism and Reform in Book IV of Bede's *Ecclesiastical History of the English People*', *Journal of Ecclesiastical History*, 61 (2010), 673–87

——, 'Visions of Reform: Bede's Later Writings in Context', in *Bede and the Future*, ed. by Peter Darby and Faith Wallis (Farnham: Ashgate, 2014), pp. 207–32

Flower, Richard, 'Genealogies of Unbelief: Epiphanius of Salamis and Heresiological Authority', in *Unclassical Traditions, volume II: Perspectives from East and West in Late Antiquity*, ed. by Christopher Kelly, Richard Flower, and Michael Stuart Williams (Cambridge: Cambridge Philological Society, 2011), pp. 70–87

Foley, William Trent, and Holder, Arthur G., *Bede: A Biblical Miscellany*, Translated Texts for Historians 28 (Liverpool: Liverpool University Press, 1999)

Franklin, Carmela Vircillo, 'The Date of Composition of Bede's *De schematibus et tropis* and *De arte metrica*', *Revue Bénédictine*, 110 (2000), 199–203

Fransen, Paul-Irénée, 'Description de la collection de Bède le Vénérable sur l'Apôtre', *Revue Bénédictine*, 71 (1961), 22–70

Heuchan, Valerie, 'The Apostle Paul in Anglo-Saxon England: All Things to All Men', in *A Companion to St Paul in the Middle Ages*, ed. Steven R. Cartwright (Leiden: Brill, 2012), pp. 425–47

Hill, Joyce, 'Carolingian Perspectives on the Authority of Bede', in *Innovation and Tradition in the Writings of the Venerable Bede*, ed. by Scott DeGregorio (Morgantown: West Virginia University Press, 2006), pp. 227–50

Holder, Arthur G., '(Un)Dating Bede's *De arte metrica*', in *Northumbria's Golden Age*, ed. by Jane Hawkes and Susan Mills (Stroud: Sutton, 1999), pp. 390–95

——, 'Hunting Snakes in the Grass: Bede as Heresiologist', in *'Listen, O isles, unto me': Studies in Medieval Word and Image in Honour of Jennifer O'Reilly*, ed. by Elizabeth Mullins and Diarmuid Scully (Cork: Cork University Press, 2011), pp. 105–14

Hurst, David, *The Commentary on the Seven Catholic Epistles of Bede the Venerable*, Cistercian Studies Series, 82 (Kalamazoo: Cistercian Publications, 1985)

Irvine, Martin, 'Bede the Grammarian and the Scope of Grammatical Studies in Eighth-Century Northumbria', *Anglo-Saxon England*, 15 (1986), 15–43

Kendall, Calvin B., and Wallis, Faith, *Bede: On the Nature of Things and On Times*, Translated Texts for Historians, 56 (Liverpool: Liverpool University Press, 2010)

Kendall, Calvin B., *Libri II De schematibus et tropis et De arte metrica: The Art of Poetry and Rhetoric* (Saarbrucken: AQ, 1991)

Knappe, Gabriele, 'Classical Rhetoric in Anglo-Saxon England', *Anglo-Saxon England*, 27 (1999), 2–29

Laistner, M. L. W., and Henry H. King, *A Hand-List of Bede manuscripts* (Ithaca: Cornell University Press, 1943)

Landes, Richard, 'Lest the Millennium be Fulfilled: Apocalyptic Expectations and the Pattern of Western Chronography 100–800 CE', in *The Use and Abuse of Eschatology in the Middle Ages*, ed. by Werner Verbeke, Daniël Verhelst, and Andries Welkenhuysen (Leuven: Leuven University Press, 1988), pp. 137–211

Lanham, Carol Dana, *'Salutatio' Formulas in Latin Letters to 1200: Syntax, Style and Theory*, Münchener Beiträge zur Mediävistik und Renaissance-Forschung, 22 (Munich: Arbeo-Gesellschaft, 1975)

Lapidge, Michael, 'Bede's Metrical *Vita S. Cuthberti*', in *St Cuthbert, his Cult and his Community to AD 1200*, ed. by Gerald Bonner, David Rollason, and Clare Stancliffe (Woodbridge: Boydell, 1989), pp. 77–93

———, *The Anglo-Saxon Library* (Oxford: Oxford University Press, 2006)

Lapidge, Michael, and Paolo Chiesa, *Storia Degli Inglesi (Historia ecclesiastica gentis Anglorum)*, 2 volumes (Rome: Mondadori, 2008–2010)

Leclercq, Jean, *The Love of Learning and the Desire for God: A Study of Monastic Culture*, trans. by Catharine Misrahi (New York: Fordham University Press, 1961)

Lienhard, Joseph T., 'Paulinus of Nola', in *Augustine through the Ages: An Encyclopedia*, ed. by Allan Fitzgerald (Grand Rapids: Eerdmans, 1999), pp. 628–29

Love, Rosalind, 'Bede and John Chrysostom', *Journal of Medieval Latin*, 17 (2008), 72–86

Lyman, J. Rebecca, 'Heresiology: The Invention of "Heresy" and "Schism"', in *The Cambridge History of Christianity Volume 2: Constantine to c. 600*, ed. by Augustine Casiday and Frederick W. Norris (Cambridge: Cambridge University Press, 2007), pp. 296–314

MacCarron, Máirín, 'Christology and the Future in Bede's *Annus Domini*', in *Bede and the Future*, ed. by Peter Darby and Faith Wallis (Farnham: Ashgate, 2014), pp. 161–80

———, 'Bede, Irish Computistica and *Annus Mundi*', *Early Medieval Europe*, 23 (2015), 290–307

Marsden, Richard, *The Text of the Old Testament in Anglo-Saxon England*, Cambridge Studies in Anglo-Saxon England 15 (Cambridge: Cambridge University Press, 1995)

Martin, Lawrence T., *The Venerable Bede: Commentary on the Acts of the Apostles*, Cistercian Studies Series, 117 (Kalamazoo: Cistercian Publications, 1989)

McCready, William D., 'Bede, Isidore and the *Epistola Cuthberti*', *Traditio*, 50 (1995), 75–94

Murphy, James J., *Rhetoric in the Middle Ages: A History of Rhetorical Theory from Saint Augustine to the Renaissance* (Berkeley: University of California Press, 1974)

Ó Carragáin, Éamonn, *The City of Rome and the World of Bede*, Jarrow Lecture, 1994 (Jarrow: St Paul's Church, 1994)

———, *Ritual and the Rood: Liturgical Images and the Old English Poems of the Dream of the Rood Tradition* (London: The British Library, 2005)

Ó Cróinín, Dáibhí, '"New heresy for old": Pelagianism in Ireland and the Papal Letter of 640', *Speculum*, 60 (1985), 505–16

O'Brien, Conor, *Bede's Temple: An Image and its Interpretation* (Oxford: Oxford University Press, 2015)

O'Loughlin, Thomas, *Adomnán and the Holy Places: The Perceptions of an Insular Monk on the Locations of the Biblical Drama* (London: Clark, 2007)

O'Reilly, Jennifer, 'Introduction', in *Bede: On the Temple*, trans. by Seán Connolly, Translated Texts for Historians, 21, (Liverpool: Liverpool University Press, 1995), pp. xvii–lv

————, 'The Library of Scripture: Views from Vivarium and Wearmouth–Jarrow', in *New Offerings, Ancient Treasures: Studies in Medieval Art for George Henderson*, ed. by Paul Binski and William Noel (Stroud: Sutton, 2001), pp. 3–39

————, 'Bede on Seeing the God of Gods in Zion', in *Text, Image, Interpretation: Studies in Anglo-Saxon Literature and its Insular Context in Honour of Éamonn Ó Carragáin*, ed. by Alastair Minnis and Jane Roberts (Turnhout: Brepols, 2007), pp. 3–29

————, '"Know Who and What He is': The Context and Inscriptions of the Durham Gospels Crucifixion Image', in *Making and Meaning in Insular Art: Proceedings of the Fifth International Conference on Insular Art*, ed. by Rachel Moss (Dublin: Four Courts Press, 2007), pp. 301–16

————, 'Bede and Monotheletism', in *Cities, Saints and Communities in Early Medieval Europe: Essays in Honour of Alan T. Thacker*, ed. by Scott DeGregorio and Paul Kershaw (Turnhout: Brepols, 2020)

Palmer, James T., *The Apocalypse in the Early Middle Ages* (Cambridge: Cambridge University Press, 2014)

Pfaff, Richard W., 'Bede among the Fathers? The Evidence from Liturgical Commemoration', *Studia Patristica*, 28 (1993), 225–29

Plummer, Charles, *Venerabilis Baedae opera historica*, 2 volumes (Oxford: Clarendon Press, 1896)

Ray, Roger, 'Bede and Cicero', *Anglo-Saxon England*, 16 (1987), 1–15

————, 'Bede's *Vera lex historiae*', *Speculum*, 55 (1980), 1–21

————, 'Who Did Bede Think he Was?', in *Innovation and Tradition in the Writings of the Venerable Bede*, ed. by Scott DeGregorio (Morgantown: West Virginia University Press, 2006), pp. 11–36

Rollason, David W., *Bede and Germany*, Jarrow Lecture, 2001 (Jarrow: St Paul's Church, 2001)

Stancliffe, Clare, *Bede, Wilfrid and the Irish*, Jarrow Lecture, 2003 (Jarrow: St Paul's Church, 2003)

————, 'Dating Wilfrid's Death and Stephen's *Life*', in *Wilfrid: Abbot, Bishop, Saint, Papers from the 1300th Anniversary Conferences*, ed. by Nicholas J. Higham (Donington: Shaun Tyas, 2013), pp. 17–26

Thacker, Alan T., and Ó Carragáin, Éamonn, 'Wilfrid in Rome', in *Wilfrid: Abbot, Bishop, Saint, Papers from the 1300th Anniversary Conferences*, ed. by Nicholas J. Higham (Donington: Shaun Tyas, 2013), pp. 212–30

Thacker, Alan T., 'Bede's ideal of reform', in *Ideal and Reality in Frankish and Anglo-Saxon Society: Studies Presented to J. M. Wallace-Hadrill*, ed. by Patrick Wormald, Donald Bullough, and Roger Collins (Oxford: Blackwell, 1983), pp. 130–53

————, 'Bede and the Irish', in *Beda Venerabilis: Historian, Monk and Northumbrian*, ed. by Luuk A. J. R. Houwen and Alasdair A. MacDonald. (Groningen: Forsten, 1996), pp. 31–59

————, *Bede and Augustine of Hippo: History and Figure in Sacred Text*, Jarrow Lecture, 2005 (Jarrow: St Paul's Church, 2005)

————, 'Bede and the ordering of understanding', in *Innovation and Tradition in the Writings of the Venerable Bede*, ed. by Scott DeGregorio (Morgantown: West Virginia University Press, 2006), pp. 37–63

————, 'Gallic or Greek? Archbishops in England from Theodore to Ecgberht', in *Frankland: The Franks and the World of the Early Middle Ages: Essays in Honour of Dame Jinty Nelson*, ed. by Paul Fouracre and David Ganz (Manchester: Manchester University Press, 2008), pp. 44–69

————, 'Bede and History', in *The Cambridge Companion to Bede*, ed. by Scott DeGregorio (Cambridge: Cambridge University Press, 2010), pp. 170–90

————, 'Wilfrid, his Cult and his Biographer', in *Wilfrid: Abbot, Bishop, Saint, Papers from the 1300th Anniversary Conferences*, ed. by Nicholas J. Higham (Donington: Shaun Tyas, 2013), pp. 1–16

————, 'Why Did Heresy Matter to Bede? Present and Future Contexts', in *Bede and the Future*, ed. by Peter Darby and Faith Wallis (Farnham: Ashgate, 2014), pp. 47–66

Wallis, Faith, *Bede: Commentary on Revelation*, Translated Texts for Historians, 58 (Liverpool: Liverpool University Press, 2013)

————, 'Why Did Bede Write a Commentary on Revelation?', in *Bede and the Future*, ed. by Peter Darby and Faith Wallis (Farnham: Ashgate, 2014), pp. 23–45

————, '*Rectores* at Risk: Erudition and Heresy in Bede's *Commentary on Proverbs*', in *Cities, Saints and Communities in Early Medieval Europe: Essays in Honour of Alan T. Thacker*, ed. by Scott DeGregorio and Paul Kershaw (Turnhout: Brepols, 2020)

Westgard, Joshua A., 'Bede and the Continent in the Carolingian Age and Beyond', in *The Cambridge Companion to Bede*, ed. by Scott DeGregorio (Cambridge: Cambridge University Press, 2010), pp. 201–15

————, 'New Manuscripts of Bede's Letter to Albinus', *Revue Bénédictine*, 120 (2010), 208–15

Whitelock, Dorothy, *After Bede,* Jarrow Lecture, 1960 (Jarrow: St Paul's Church, 1960)

Wilmart, André, 'La collection de Bède le Vénérable sur l'Apôtre', *Revue Bénédictine*, 38 (1926), 16–52

Wright, Neil, 'The Metrical Art(s) of Bede', in *Latin Learning and English Lore: Studies in Anglo-Saxon Literature for Michael Lapidge*, ed. by Katherine O'Brien O'Keeffe and Andy Orchard, 2 volumes (Toronto: University of Toronto Press, 2005), I, pp. 150–70

CLARE STANCLIFFE

Bede and Bishop Acca

Introduction

Bede's significance is now widely recognised, and not just as a historian, but also as an interpreter of the Bible and expounder of time. Although he lived in a monastery he was deeply concerned about the whole Northumbrian Church, and his later works often contain trenchant criticisms of its shortcomings. This makes one curious about his relationship with his diocesan bishop, Acca, who commissioned many of his biblical commentaries; and investigating this topic has the added advantage of shedding light on the formative period of Bede's career as a scholar, which is little studied.

Based on the warm language that Bede uses about him, both in his dedication letters and his *Ecclesiastical History*, Acca is traditionally seen as a close friend of Bede's; they shared a lively interest in Scriptural interpretation.[1] In 1988, however, this view was challenged by Walter Goffart. Goffart's revisionist views on the circumstances lying behind Bede's composition of his *Ecclesiastical History* led him to regard Bede as aligned with different political and religious factions from Acca.[2] He therefore questioned the close friendship generally posited between the two men. As regards Bede's effusive language when addressing Acca in his prefatory dedication letters, Goffart regarded this as formulaic.[3] As the sponsor of Bede's biblical commentaries, Acca 'was the equivalent to Bede of the granting agencies that foster our research with needed subsidies'. Bede's phrasing in his letters, calling Acca 'dearest of prelates', 'most lovable of bishops', and suchlike, must be read not as the expression of Bede's personal feelings towards Acca, but rather in the context of the conventions of the epistolary genre, much as our convention is to begin letters, 'Dear X'.[4]

---

1 Plummer, *Venerabilis Baedae Opera historica* II, 329; Whitelock, 'Bede and his Teachers', pp. 26–27; Wallace-Hadrill, *Bede's Ecclesiastical History of the English People: A Historical Commentary*, p. 195; Thacker, 'Acca [St Acca] (d. 740)'; Lapidge, 'Acca of Hexham', p. 66.
2 Goffart, *The Narrators of Barbarian History*, pp. 258–96, esp. 295–96; Goffart, 'Bede's Agenda', pp. 42–43.
3 Goffart, *The Narrators of Barbarian History*, p. 295, n. 261.
4 Goffart, 'Bede's History in a Harsher Climate', pp. 219–20.

Clare Stancliffe • is Honorary Reader in Ecclesiastical History in the departments of History, and of Theology and Religion, Durham University, UK.

Cities, Saints, and Communities in Early Medieval Europe, ed. by Scott DeGregorio and Paul Kershaw, SEM 46 (Turnhout: Brepols, 2020), pp. 171-194
BREPOLS PUBLISHERS   DOI 10.1484/M.SEM-EB.5.119627

There are many insights in Goffart's work, but it also leaves certain questions unanswered. For a start, he talks of 'the context of the epistolary genre', but gives no examples to establish the context. Again, while some of Bede's expressions, like 'dilectissimus' (most beloved), do appear formulaic, we occasionally get a phrase which is harder to explain in this way, as when he addresses Acca as 'dilectissime ac desiderantissime omnium qui in terris morantur antistitum Acca' (Acca, the most beloved and most longed for of all the bishops who dwell in the lands).[5] Finally, Goffart ignores Bede's fulsome portrait of Acca in his *Ecclesiastical History*. This last point has led some scholars to regard Goffart's views on the relationship between Bede and Acca as unconvincing.[6] Others, however, have been ready to follow his lead on the persistence of factionalism between Lindisfarne and the Wilfridians right up to 731. This raises the question of Bede's relationship with Acca in an acute form, which so far has been only summarily or speculatively dealt with.[7] The purpose of this paper, then, is to explore the topic more fully, and unconstrained by presuppositions.

The Traditional Evidence for Bede and Acca's Relationship

We begin with Bede's warm expressions about Acca in the prefaces to many of his biblical works. The evidence is given in the accompanying Tables 1–5 (see Appendix below), arranged according to category; and, within each category, according to approximate chronological order. For comparison's sake, Bede's address to others is also included. By setting out the evidence in this way, certain norms become apparent. Bede generally reserved 'dominus' for addressing bishops; he also uses it once for John, seemingly a priest, but in actuality probably a bishop.[8] 'Reuerentissimus' was reserved for bishops or priests. 'Dilectissimus' had a wide application, being used both for fellow religious who were not ordained (Helmwald, Plegwine, and an unnamed nun), and also for bishops and priests; with at least ten instances, it is the commonest adjective used. Superlative forms are normal, save for 'sanctus'.[9] Overall, the impression is that Bede enjoyed ringing the changes within a broad set of conventions. Adjectives applied to Acca like 'beatissimus', 'desiderantissimus', and (once) 'sanctus' can be paralleled elsewhere in Bede's address to Eadfrith and Albinus. The use of more elaborate expressions, however, is overwhelmingly focused

---

5 Bede, *In primam partem Samuhelis*, I, ed. by Hurst, p. 9, lines 34–35.

6 Bede, *Historia ecclesiastica* V.20, ed. and trans. by Colgrave and Mynors, pp. 530–33; Higham, *(Re-) Reading Bede*, pp. 63 and 230, n. 68.

7 Cf. Kirby, 'The Genesis of a Cult', pp. 395–97, esp. n. 67; Stancliffe, 'Disputed Episcopacy', pp. 24–39.

8 Lapidge, while originally seeing Bede's 'Johanni presbytero' as ruling out Bishop John of Beverley ('Bede's metrical *Vita*', p. 78 and n. 1), in 2008 accepted this identification without further comment: *Beda, Storia degli Inglesi* I, p. xlix n. 1 and p. liv. The close parallel with Augustine's address to bishop Sixtus of Rome, whom he addressed as 'conpresbytero' although both of them were bishops (below and n. 14) does make it plausible that Bede was mimicking Augustine in using 'presbytero' here for a bishop.

9 This tallies with general usage in epistolary salutation formulae: O'Brien, *Titles of Address in Christian Latin Epistolography*, pp. 116–19.

on Acca alone: 'nimium desiderantissimo'; 'et intima semper charitate venerando'; 'et cum omni semper honorificentia nominando'; and 'dilectissime ac desiderantissime omnium qui in terris morantur antistitum'. Note, however, 'in Christi visceribus honorando', addressed to Plegwine.[10]

Bede was not operating in a vacuum. He was following epistolary conventions, above all those found in the letters of Augustine, many of which he knew. This is clear with Bede's address to Plegwine, which exactly mirrors that of Augustine's epistle 120, known to Bede: 'Fratri dilectissimo et in Christi uisceribus honorando Consentio Augustinus in domino salutem'.[11] I have found no other instances as exact as this, and it may be relevant that this is probably the earliest of Bede's surviving letters (708), and was written at a time of emotional angst. These circumstances may have prompted him to adopt the wording of an unquestioned authority. But even if Bede generally preferred to make Augustine's style his own, his influence is palpable. Compare Bede's wording in the preface of *De eo quod ait Isaias* with Augustine's '*Domino beatissimo et* sincerissima *caritate uenerando sancto* fratri et consacerdoti papae Aurelio Augustinus in domino salutem'.[12] Or again, compare Augustine's address to Celestine, 'Domino uenerabili nimiumque desiderabili sancto fratri',[13] with Bede's address to Acca in his prefatory letter to *On Luke*, while the word play on 'dominus' in the preface to his metrical *Vita Cuthberti* echoes Augustine's letter to Sixtus of Rome, '*Domino in domino dominorum dilectissimo* fratri sancto et conpresbytero Sixto Augustinus in domino salutem'.[14]

Augustine was not the only model used; for instance, Augustine does not employ either 'reuerendissimus' or 'reuerentissimus', both found in Bede. These terms occur in continental usage for addressing bishops or the pope, and it might have been from papal correspondence that Bede became acquainted with them, as also with 'gloriosissimus'.[15] Whether there was any formal teaching at Wearmouth and Jarrow of epistolary conventions is unknown.[16] Wilfrid plausibly, and Benedict Biscop, possibly, could have learnt these on the continent, and passed on their knowledge (via Ceolfrith, in Wilfrid's case). Yet Bede's unusual use of 'reuerentissimus' not just for bishops but also for priests (in the cases of Albinus and Wicthed) does not appear to fit with epistolary conventions,[17] and may therefore indicate that he was

---

10 See the article by Peter Darby in this volume, pp. 155–59.

11 Augustine, *Epistulae* II, ed. by Goldbacher, p. 704. Lapidge, *Anglo-Saxon Library*, p. 201. For further discussion of the aptness of this phraseology, see Darby's contribution to this volume.

12 Augustine, *Ep.* 174, *Epistulae* III, ed. by Goldbacher, p. 650 (my italics); cf. also *Ep.* 209.

13 Augustine, *Ep.* 192, *Epistulae* IV, ed. by Goldbacher, p. 165.

14 Augustine, *Ep.* 194, *Epistulae* IV, ed. by Goldbacher, p. 176 (my italics).

15 Gregory I uses 'reuerentissimus' when addressing bishops in letters preserved in Bede's *Historia ecclesiastica*, I.24, 28, and 29, ed. and trans. by Colgrave and Mynors; and 'gloriosissimus' when addressing King Æthelberht in I. 32. For these terms in earlier correspondence, O'Brien, *Titles of Address in Christian Latin Epistolography*, pp. 113–14, 133–34.

16 For Bede's apparent knowledge of Latin rhetorical norms, see Ray, *Bede, Rhetoric, and the Creation of Christian Latin Culture*; cf. Lanham, 'Freshman Composition'.

17 I rely on O'Brien, *Titles of Address in Christian Latin Epistolography*, p. 114, although this only goes as far as AD 543.

self-taught. The same applies to his frequent use of 'antistes', which is apparently unknown in earlier salutation formulae, though Augustine occasionally uses it in the body of the letter.[18] Either way, Augustine appears to have been a formative influence, which fits well with Alan Thacker's demonstration of Augustine's significance for Bede.[19]

Given that Bede, like Augustine, was following epistolary conventions, it is relevant to note that Augustine could use effusive language even for those he had never met, and even for some one that he was critical of, as we see in his letter 40 to Jerome. Despite its address to 'domino dilectissimo et cultu sincerissimo caritatis obseruando atque amplectendo fratri et conpresbytero Hieronymo Augustinus', it was highly critical of Jerome's treatment of Paul's contretemps with Peter in Galatians 2. 11–14.[20] This would not have been lost on Bede, who knew this letter;[21] and we cannot therefore assume that Bede's effusive expressions to Acca imply intimate or uncritical friendship. When, in his *Ecclesiastical History*, he had occasion to express some one's real love for his bishop, he writes 'antistes meus amatus' (my beloved bishop), using a word that is found nowhere in epistolary conventions.[22]

Let us now turn to Bede's chapter on Acca in his *Historia ecclesiastica*. Bede starts by describing him as Wilfrid's priest, 'uir et ipse strenuissimus et coram Deo et hominibus magnificus' (a man of great energy and noble in the sight of God and man).[23] He tells how he embellished the church of Hexham and collected relics which he installed in various chapels. He built up a fine library, including many passions of martyrs. He was also a skilled musician, who invited an outstanding cantor from Kent to teach his community the musical traditions of Gregory's disciples, keeping him for twelve years. Bede then sums him up in a series of superlatives: 'Ipse episcopus Acca cantator erat peritissimus, quomodo etiam in litteris sanctis doctissimus et in catholicae fidei confessione castissimus, in ecclesiasticae quoque institutionis regulis sollertissimus extiterat' (Bishop Acca was himself a musician of great experience as well as a very learned theologian, untainted in his confession of the catholic faith and thoroughly expert in canon law).

This is a very odd chapter. It is unique in giving full-length treatment to some one who was still alive; and it praises Acca for precisely those aspects of Wilfrid's achievements that Stephen devoted space to, like his fine churches, but which Bede, despite knowing Stephen's account, omitted altogether from his lengthy appreciation of Wilfrid. Was it included because Acca expected it? Or because Acca had just been driven from his see, and Bede wished to affirm his good qualities at a time that he was perhaps being vilified? We must certainly bear in mind that Bede wrote it knowing that, in all probability, Acca would read it. Bede was therefore in a comparable position

18 O'Brien, *Titles of Address in Christian Latin Epistolography*, p. 79.
19 Thacker, *Bede and Augustine of Hippo*, esp. pp. 5–14.
20 Augustine, *Ep.* 40, *Epistulae* II, ed. by Goldbacher, pp. 69–81.
21 Lapidge, *Anglo-Saxon Library*, p. 201.
22 *Historia ecclesiastica*, V.6, ed. and trans. by Colgrave and Mynors, pp. 468–69. Cf. O'Brien, *Titles of Address in Christian Latin Epistolography*, p. 90: *amantissimus* is used in salutations, but not *amatus*.
23 *Historia ecclesiastica*, V.20, ed. and trans. by Colgrave and Mynors, pp. 530–31.

to someone today writing a reference for a person who would be likely to read their own reference — and who might also have some drawbacks. The picture given must be truthful, but at the same time the recipient must be prepared to read between the lines: to ponder the choice of words, and to note what is perhaps hinted at, or omitted. The first words to raise doubt are 'coram Deo et hominibus magnificus'. It is a good thing to be noble in the sight of the Lord; but in the sight of man? The Bible is full of reminders that God does not judge as man does, but rather sees into a person's inner being: think of Dives and Lazarus, or of Jesus's condemnation of 'hypocrites' who parade their religiosity to win human admiration.[24] *Magnificus* carries many of the same connotations as our 'magnificent': noble, yes, but also splendid, costly, sumptuous. This range of connotations is there in Bede's usage. Thus Cuthbert sought to merit eternal life *inter magnificos uiros* (amid [God's] mighty men), and Bede valued the *magnificos ... tractatus*, the 'splendid treatises' on the Bible written by the Fathers; he also mentioned the subscription of *magnifici regis Aldfridi* (splendid King Aldfrith).[25] In the present context a particularly interesting usage occurs in Bede's commentary *In Ezram*, written at much the same time as his *Ecclesiastical History*, adverting to those who build monasteries *magnifico opere* (with brilliant workmanship) without instituting *doctores* to exhort the people.[26] Here, there is no criticism of magnificent buildings in themselves; but there is an implicit contrast between the outward show of fine buildings, and the concurrent lack of what (Bede implies) really matters, well-instructed priests or other teachers.

This alerts us to an obvious omission: there is nothing about Acca's pastoral oversight of his diocese — and this within three years of Bede's excoriating criticisms of worldly bishops who neglected their pastoral duties in his letter to Bishop Ecgbert. Indeed, this letter's criticisms recall, or even echo, various passages in the Ezra commentary, including the one just cited.[27] Bede's chapter on Acca also raises an implicit contrast between Acca, *coram ... hominibus magnificus*, and Cuthbert, who seemed *quibusdam contemptibilis* (contemptible to some), in Bede's presentation of his deathbed speech.[28] Alan Thacker has cogently argued that Bede rewrote the Lindisfarne Life's portrayal of Cuthbert the bishop 'in such a way that it reads like a summary of the qualities later to be recommended in the letter to Egbert'.[29] Cuthbert, Bede wrote, had protected the people committed to his charge through

---

24   Cf. Luke 16. 19–31; Matthew 6. 1–6.

25   Bede, *Vita Sancti Cuthberti* (prose), ch. 4; ed. and trans. by Colgrave, pp. 166–67; Bede, *In Ezram et Neemiam*, III, ed. by Hurst, p. 377, line 1528; Bede, *Historia abbatum* II.15, ed. and trans. by Grocock and Wood, pp. 60–61. I owe these references to a word search on the Brepolis Library of Latin Texts database. A reference to Constantine constructing churches *magnifico et regio cultu* ('in magnificent and royal style') in Bede's *Historia ecclesiastica*, V.16 has been omitted from discussion as Bede is there reproducing the wording of Adomnán.

26   Bede, *In Ezram et Neemiam*, II, lines 600–04, trans. DeGregorio, p. 102, and, on the date, pp. xxviii–xlii. Bede was probably inspired by Jerome, *Ep.* 52. 10, ed. Hilberg, p. 431.

27   Bede, *Epistola ad Ecgbertum*, especially 11–12, ed. and trans. by Grocock and Wood, pp. 144–49; DeGregorio, trans., *Bede: Ezra*, p. 102 n. 1, and cf. pp. xxxii–xxxiii.

28   Bede, *Vita Sancti Cuthberti* (prose), ch. 39; ed. and trans. by Colgrave, pp. 284–85.

29   Thacker, 'Bede's Ideal', p. 141.

his prayers, had taught them about God, 'et quod maxime doctores iuuat, ea quae agenda docebat, ipse prius agendo praemonstrabat' (and — a thing which is a great help to teachers — he taught what ought to be done, after first showing them by his own example).[30] But of Acca as a teacher, preacher, exemplar, and shepherd to the people committed to his episcopal charge, Bede says nothing.

Thus none of the evidence usually adduced to demonstrate Bede's affection for Acca can be taken at face value. There exists a third body of evidence, strangely neglected, comprising the exchange of letters between Acca and Bede that prefaces Bede's commentary *In Lucam*, together with Bede's prefaces to other early commentaries dedicated to Acca. These are best viewed not in isolation but as part of an ongoing relationship between Bede and Acca. Since space is limited and the later years of Acca's episcopate have been discussed elsewhere,[31] the focus here will be on the formative years when their relationship was forged.

The Early Years of the Relationship and the Impact of the Heresy Accusation

Acca, a priest belonging to Wilfrid's *familia*, was probably much the same age as Bede.[32] Wilfrid had been unwilling to work with bishops trained at Whitby and Lindisfarne, whom he regarded as soft on 'heretics',[33] and had therefore found himself in exile for most of Bede's adult lifetime, being excommunicated *c.* 702–703.[34] Acca probably shared some or all of these periods of exile, and he definitely accompanied Wilfrid to Rome to appeal against their excommunication *c.* 703, by which time he was very close to Wilfrid.[35] The pope ordered the Northumbrian Church to make peace with Wilfrid, and this finally took place in 706. After a generation in which Wilfridians and non-Wilfridians had found each other impossible to work with, this must have been a difficult process. To accommodate Wilfrid, John of Beverley was moved sideways from Hexham to York while Wilfrid was installed at Hexham; Wilfrid thus became Bede's diocesan bishop. Relations between Wilfrid and Wearmouth and Jarrow will have been relatively straightforward: Bede's abbot, Ceolfrith, had once been a monk under Wilfrid and was ordained by him. It was presumably in these years that Bede came to know Wilfrid, and asked him the delicate question about Queen Æthelthryth's virginity.[36] It was probably in these same years that Bede first encountered Acca, like him, an able young priest, whom Wilfrid on his deathbed appointed as his successor at Hexham (710).

30   Bede, *Vita Sancti Cuthberti* (prose), ch. 26; ed. and trans. by Colgrave, pp. 242–43.
31   Stancliffe, 'Disputed Episcopacy'.
32   Lapidge, 'Acca of Hexham', p. 67 and n. 156.
33   Cubitt, 'Wilfrid's "Usurping Bishops"'; Stancliffe, *Bede, Wilfrid and the Irish*.
34   Cubitt, 'St Wilfrid', pp. 342–47.
35   Stephen, *Vita Wilfridi*, ch. 56, ed. and trans. by Colgrave, pp. 122–23; Lapidge, 'Acca of Hexham', p. 67; Thacker, 'Acca [St Acca] (d. 740)'.
36   Bede, *Historia ecclesiastica*, IV.19, ed. and trans. by Colgrave and Mynors, pp. 390–93.

One incident during these years proved traumatic for Bede. In 708 a monk of Wilfrid's community, Plegwine, sent word that Bede had been accused of heresy in the presence of Bishop Wilfrid. Bede was reproached with denying that the Incarnation had occurred in the sixth age of the world, and what survives is Bede's furious rebuttal of the charge, in a letter addressed to Plegwine. The problem arose from Bede's reassessment of the time that had elapsed since Creation in the chronicle in his *De temporibus* (703). Instead of reproducing the traditional chronology derived from the Septuagint, Bede, perhaps following an Irish source,[37] had given the dates of the six ages of biblical history using figures taken from Jerome's *Hebraica veritas* (Hebrew truth), his translation of the Old Testament direct from the Hebrew. The figures in the *Hebraica veritas* were considerably lower than those in the Septuagint, yielding a date for the Incarnation of 3952 years from Creation, rather than the customary 5199.[38] Bede's rebuttal includes detailed comparison of the number of years separating key biblical events as between the Septuagint and Jerome's *Hebraica veritas*, and discussion of the discrepancies. One detail that will concern us later is his noting that the Septuagint had (inaccurately) inserted an additional generation, that of Cainan, into its second age, and been followed in this by Luke's Gospel.[39] Bede further rejected the millenarian idea that each of the world's six ages would last approximately one thousand years, with the implication that one could calculate when the world would end. Such assumptions had lain behind the heresy accusation, since a rough equation of a thousand years per age was natural for those comparing the ages of the world to the days of Creation, and applying biblical passages about a thousand years being as a day in the Lord's sight.[40] Bede turned the tables on his unnamed accuser, and warned the 'ingenuous' Plegwine against being seduced by the erroneous popular view that one could work out the year of the Last Judgement, a view which Bede labels unambiguously as 'heretical'.[41] The accusation of heresy had stung him to the quick, and he ended the letter by asking Plegwine to present it to a learned monk named David, who was requested to read it out in the presence of Bishop Wilfrid. He wanted to be cleared in the bishop's presence, just as he had formerly been accused in his presence.

Does any of this have a bearing on the relationship of Bede and Acca? Faith Wallis has suggested that 'David' might have been a nickname for Acca, since his musical

---

37 Cf. *Laterculus Malalianus* 4, ed. by Stevenson, pp. 124–25, 177–78; Mc Carthy, 'Bede's Primary Source', pp. 159–79; Palmer, *The Apocalypse in the Early Middle Ages*, pp. 99–101.

38 Bede, *Epistola ad Pleguinam* §§ 1–5, ed. by Jones, pp. 307–09, trans. in Wallis, *Bede: The Reckoning*, pp. 405–08, and cf. pp. xxx–xxxi, 354–61. I use Jerome's and Bede's term *Hebraica veritas* for what later became known as the Vulgate, since both that terminology and its universal acceptance as the only authoritative version of the Bible still lay in the future.

39 Bede, *Epistola ad Pleguinam* §§ 5–6, ed. by Jones, p. 309; cf. Luke 3. 36 and Genesis 11. 13.

40 Psalm 89.4; I Peter 3. 8. Cf. Jones, 'Computistical Works', pp. 132–35; Darby, *Bede and the End of Time*, pp. 21–57.

41 Bede, *Epistola ad Pleguinam* § 14, ed. by Jones, p. 313. Bede's address of Plegwine as *tuam simplicitatem* is interesting as it is not a stock expression, occurring nowhere in O'Brien, *Titles of Address in Christian Latin Epistolography*. Wallis's translation as 'your simplicity' underplays the positive connotations of the term in early Christian discourse: cf. Matthew 10.16 and Romans 16.19.

ability and learning would tally with the qualities that Bede attributes to David.[42] This is speculative, but Acca will surely have known about the accusation, and might well have been present when it was made. Heresy was an extremely serious matter, and Wilfrid took a hard line against those he judged heretical on another chronological matter, the dating of Easter. The incident is in any case relevant for understanding Bede's relationship with Acca, since it raised key issues that continued to reverberate in the commentaries which Bede composed shortly afterwards, and sent to Acca.

The first direct evidence on Bede's relationship with Acca comes in his prefatory letter to his *Expositio Actuum Apostolorum*. This is explicitly addressed to 'Bishop Acca', so datable to after Acca's accession to the see of Hexham in 710. From this, we learn that, at Hwætberht's instigation, Bede had arranged to have his commentary on Revelation copied for Acca; and that Acca, apparently before he had even seen this, was urging Bede in 'very frequent letters' to comment on the Gospel of Luke. Bede, however, had felt unable to do this as yet, explaining 'et operis uidelicet immensitate perterritus et obstrepentium causarum, quas tu melius nosti necessitate praepeditus' (both because I was terrified by the immensity of the task, and also hindered by the demands of troublesome circumstances, of which you are very much aware).[43] Instead he had rushed off for his bishop the enclosed commentary on Acts, and he also enclosed a brief commentary on I John, based primarily on Augustine's work: presumably that which now forms part of his commentary *In epistolas VII catholicas*. None of these works can be dated with any precision, but Peter Darby has noted that there is some evidence that parts of the Acts commentary might antedate *De temporibus*, and that it and the commentary on Revelation, like *De temporibus* (703) and the letter to Plegwine (708), were written before Bede had developed his mature ideas about the seventh and eighth ages of the world. These ideas may appear first in his subsequent commentary on Luke, where initially they are tentatively expressed.[44] The commentaries on Revelation and Acts were therefore written at the latest in the very early years of Acca's episcopate,[45] followed by those on the Catholic Epistles

---

42 Wallis, 'Why Did Bede Write?', pp. 28–29.

43 *Expositio Actuum*, preface, ed. by Laistner, p. 3, ll. 1–12; I have adapted Martin's translation, *Commentary*, p. 3; cf. also Wallis, 'Why Did Bede Write?', pp. 27–28, and below n. 45.

44 Darby, *Bede and the End of Time*, ch. 3, esp. p. 80, n. 68, pp. 66–67, 77–83, and cf. 224–25. Plummer's discussion of the dating of Bede's works remains useful (*Venerabilis Baedae Opera historica* I, pp. cxlv–clix), but needs updating, for which see Darby and Wallis, 'Introduction: The Many Futures of Bede', pp. 6–20.

45 Wallis has argued (*Bede: Commentary on Revelation*, pp. 39–51, and cf. her 'Why Did Bede Write?') that the commentary on Revelation was written nearer to 701 than 710, but there is inadequate evidence to be sure either way. Perhaps the best argument for such an early date is that Bede prefaced it with a poem, as with his early *De natura rerum*, while his verse *Life of St Cuthbert* also originated early. I cannot follow her argument ('Why Did Bede Write?', pp. 25–27) that Bede's prefatory letter to his *Expositio Actuum* implies that Acca already had a copy of his Revelation commentary, since Bede there says that he has arranged for it to be copied for Acca, which he would scarcely have said if Acca already possessed it. Nor had Bede since been engaged in commenting on Luke, since the pair of letters prefacing the Luke commentary postdate Acca's reception of the Revelation commentary (Acca, *Ep.*, lines 68–75), but predate Bede's starting the Luke commentary (Bede, pref. *Ep.* to *In Lucam* lines 82–90). But none of this undermines her cogent argument that both the Revelation commentary

and on Luke, which themselves predated that on Samuel which Bede was working on in 716.

Bishop Acca was not to be fobbed off with the Acts commentary, but frequently continued to urge Bede 'et absens scribendo et conloquendo praesens' (both in writing when absent and in conversation when present) to turn now to Luke.[46] Bede carried on making excuses: he was apprehensive (*deterritus*) because of the difficulty of the task, and because the holy and learned Ambrose had already composed such a commentary. Acca countered that different audiences required different treatments; and as Ambrose's commentary was too lofty for the uncultured readers of their day, and the Fathers had seen nothing wrong in expounding the works of other Fathers in simpler terms, Bede should do the same. As for his shyness and protestations of inadequacy, Acca demanded that Bede should place his letter at the beginning of the commentary. Readers would then see that Bede had undertaken it solely in response to his request to expound Luke in a simpler style for less intelligent readers. He also urged Bede to comment on matters which Ambrose had omitted, saying that he believed that God would enlighten him, immersed as he was in meditating on the law of the Lord, day and night; and that it would be right to expect that Bede, 'qui neglectis ad integrum mundi negotiis aeternum uerumque sapientiae lumen indefessa mente persequeris et hic fructum intelligentiae purioris assequaris et in futurum ipsum *in quo sunt omnes thesauri sapientiae et scientiae absconditi regem in decore suo mundo corde contempleris*' (you who have sloughed off worldly concerns to pursue with tireless mind the full, true and eternal light of wisdom, should here attain the fruit of a purer understanding, and in the future would contemplate with a pure heart *the king in his beauty, in whom are hidden all the treasures of wisdom and knowledge*).[47] He then plunges straight into telling Bede that 'certain people' are asking why, in his commentary on Revelation, he has given a new interpretation of the four animals of Ezekiel's vision, identifying the lion with Matthew and the man with Mark, rather than vice versa. Further light is shed on the critical reception given in some quarters to his commentary on Acts by a comment in his later *Retractio in Actus Apostolorum*: Bede had been criticised by some for not being clear enough about how a certain biblical passage should be taken, when in reality the entire phrase was taken from an irreproachable source, Gregory Nazianzen.[48]

These remarks reveal an extraordinarily critical milieu for Bede's early exegetical work, and go some way to explain his reluctance to comment on Luke. Seemingly he

---

and that on I John are linked to Bede's desire to justify his views on chronology and the end times, and that the repercussions of the 708 contretemps between Bede and some Wilfridians continued to reverberate down to 725. This, in turn, undermines her attempt to close date the reference to 'obstrepentes causae' to 708 ('Why Did Bede Write?', esp. pp. 27–28, 31–34, 40–44), although I agree with her in interpreting these *obstrepentes causae* as linked to the heresy accusation of 708. My own view is that Bede remained embattled for some time after 708: cf. below pp. 180-83, 185 and n. 79.

46 Acca, *Ep.*, ed. by Hurst, p. 5.

47 Acca, *Ep.* to Bede, ed. by Hurst, p. 6, ll. 64–68, and cf. pp. 5–6. This letter and Bede's response comprise the prefatory material to Bede's *In Lucae evangelium expositio*.

48 Stansbury, 'Source-marks in Bede's Biblical Commentaries', pp. 384–85.

was being attacked as a plagiarist when his quotations were recognised, but sometimes also attacked for what he wrote when his critics thought that he had asserted a new interpretation (as with the Evangelist symbols), or that he had failed to make his meaning clear (even when this lack of clarity arose from his unrecognised source). To counter his critics, for his commentary on Luke Bede devised a system of marginal notations to demonstrate when and whom he was citing as an authority, while also devoting two-thirds of his epistolary preface to quotations taken from Augustine on the evangelist symbols, in response to the critics of his Revelation commentary.[49]

Three questions remain to be asked: Why was Acca pressing him to comment on Luke before he had even seen his commentary on Revelation? Why did Bede not produce the commentary on Luke for some years, but instead one on Acts? And where did Acca stand visà-vis the hostile reception given to Bede's early writings by at least some in Wilfridian circles?

A clue to the first two may arguably be found in Bede's changed wording as to why Luke followed the Septuagint in including Cainan between Sela and Arfaxat in Christ's genealogy, whereas Jerome's *Hebraica veritas* translation of Genesis omitted Cainan and represented Sela as Arfaxat's son, not grandson.[50] In his letter to Plegwine, Bede had noted Luke's inclusion of Cainan in the context of explaining how his own reckoning of the years between Creation and Christ's birth produced a shorter, more accurate chronology than had hitherto obtained. He explained that, in omitting Cainan, he had followed Eusebius who had omitted Cainan and erased 130 years, 'et evangelio Lucae et lxx pariter interpretibus fidem derogavit'.[51] Drawing attention to his view that the evangelist Luke had arguably set down something untrue proved to be unfortunate, as we can see from Bede's defensive comments in his (later) preface to his *Expositio Actuum*. There, after explaining that he did not yet feel ready to compose the commentary on Luke but was sending Acca one on Acts instead, he continued by quoting some of Jerome's comments on the evangelist Luke, including his greater familiarity with Greek than Hebrew, and then continued:

> Ex quo accidit quod maxime miror et propter ingenii tarditatem uehementissimo stupore perculsus nescio perscrutari qua ratione, cum in Hebraica ueritate a diluuio usque ad Abraham decem generationes inueniantur, ipse Lucas, qui spiritu sancto calamum regente nullatenus falsum scribere potuit, undecim generationes iuxta septuaginta interpretes adiecto Cainan in euangelio ponere maluerit.[52]

> It happens accordingly that I am very much amazed, and, struck with overpowering astonishment because of the slowness of my understanding,

49 Bede, pref. letter to *In Lucae evangelium expositio*, ed. by Hurst, pp. 6–10; Stansbury, 'Source-marks in Bede's Biblical Commentaries'.

50 Cf. Genesis 11. 10–14 and Luke 3. 35–36; cf. Bede, *Epistola ad Pleguinam* § 5, ed. by Jones, p. 309, lines 6–11.

51 'And called into doubt both the Gospel of Luke and the Seventy Translators.' Bede, *Epistola ad Pleguinam* § 6, ed. by Jones, p. 309, ll. 5–7; trans. Wallis, p. 408.

52 Bede, *Expositio Actuum Apostolorum*, preface, ed. by Laistner, p. 4; my translation, based on Martin, *The Venerable Bede: Commentary on the Acts of the Apostles*, p. 4.

do not know how to search for an explanation of why, when in the original Hebrew there are found ten generations from the Flood down to Abraham, Luke himself, whose pen, being controlled by the Holy Spirit, could in no way write anything false, preferred to set down eleven generations, having added Cainan in accordance with the Septuagint.

Note the change in tone between these two quotations. In both, Bede sticks to his argument that the Hebrew version was correct, and that Cainan was a later insertion. But in 708 he talked of how this cast doubt on Luke's version, whereas in his later *Expositio* he acknowledged that Luke's inspiration by the Holy Spirit precluded his writing anything false, and he professes himself unable to explain this. In regarding the Hebrew original as accurate, over against the New Testament version, Bede was following the general approach of Jerome. He knew his epistle 57,[53] where Jerome contended that the apostles and evangelists had sought to convey the general sense of Old Testament passages, without worrying about their precise wording. Jerome's adducing the discrepancy between Stephen's speech in Acts and the original Genesis account of the whereabouts of the patriarchs' burial place may have given Bede the confidence to tackle this in his Acts commentary, though he went further than Jerome.[54] But for Luke's inclusion of Cainan, Bede could not refer to rhetorical conventions, and Jerome had been silent: hence his confusion.

I would suggest that the Wilfridian critics who had accused Bede of being a heretic in 708, far from being mollified by his forthright rebuttal, had seized upon his words about how he had followed Eusebius, who had 'called into doubt both the Gospel of Luke and the Seventy Translators', and had raised the more serious issue of how Bede could square that view with the divine inspiration of the evangelist Luke. This, in turn, would explain why Acca was so urgently pressing Bede to comment on Luke's gospel, of all the seventy odd books in the Bible. After all, if he had simply wanted a useful gospel commentary, why had he not asked for one on Mark, which had not been the subject of any patristic commentary, whereas Ambrose's commentary on Luke was available in Northumbria, and, *pace* Acca's comments, does not seem to have been written in a particularly difficult style. Ambrose had, however, omitted any reference to Luke's inclusion of Cainan in Christ's genealogy — something that may have been in Acca's mind when he urged Bede to address questions which Ambrose had omitted.[55] This hypothesis cannot be proved, but it would explain why Acca was pressing Bede to comment specifically on Luke — and this before he had even seen Bede's commentary on Revelation; why Bede was so terrified at the demands laid upon him that he took the evasive course of commenting on Acts instead, which had the advantage of being by the same author, but raised no such fundamental questions about the inerrancy of the Gospel; and why he alludes to the Cainan question again in his preface to the Acts commentary, where it is not obviously relevant.

---

53 Cited in Bede, *Expositio Actuum Apostolorum*, XXVI.2, ed. by Laistner, p. 92, ll. 5–10.
54 Bede, *Expositio Actuum Apostolorum*, VII.16, ed. by Laistner, pp. 34–35, ll. 51–71; cf. Jerome, *Ep.* 57.10.1–3, ed. by Hilberg, pp. 521–22. See Ray, 'The Triumph of Greco-Roman Assumptions', pp. 76–77.
55 Acca, *Epistola*, ed. by Hurst, *In Lucae evangelium expositio*, prologus, p. 6, lines 55–59.

It is only recently that the chronological and eschatological issues raised by Bede's *De temporibus* have been properly explored, and the seriousness of the heresy charge against him has been grasped.[56] It has yet to be realised that Bede was also skating on thin ice when he apparently cast doubt on Luke's veracity. It is true that Eusebius had omitted Cainan when tallying up the years between the Flood and Abraham's birth, but he had done so silently, without mentioning Luke's Gospel.[57] The same might be said of Jerome, who had simply omitted Cainan both in his *Hebraica veritas* translation of Genesis and his *Hebrew Questions on Genesis*.[58] Indeed, Bede appears to be the first Latin author to address this issue.[59] Jerome and Augustine had engaged with the general chronological differences between the Septuagint and the *Hebraica veritas* versions of Genesis, and with the specific case of Methusaleh,[60] but had not discussed Cainan. What is noteworthy is that Bede selectively quotes from Augustine's discussion of Methusaleh, where Augustine notes that numerals are easily corrupted, and agrees that when the Septuagint and the Hebrew diverge, one should trust the text in the original language.[61] Yet Augustine's general position was very different: he accepted literally the story of the Holy Spirit's inspiration of the seventy translators, concluding that 'anything in the Septuagint that is not in the Hebrew manuscripts is something which the same Spirit preferred to say through the translators, thus showing that both were prophets'.[62] He had therefore included Cainan son of Arfaxat in his historical overview without any hint that his existence was controversial, and he had questioned the value of Jerome's project of retranslating the Old Testament direct from Hebrew, rather than focusing on a more accurate Latin translation of the Septuagint.[63]

Bede's concluding peroration to Plegwine that his computation was based on the *Hebraica veritas* 'per Originem prodita, per Hieronimum edita, per Augustinum laudata, per Iosephum confirmata', is reminiscent of the saw, 'argument weak: shout!'[64] Josephus was a Jew; Origen had been condemned as a heretic; Augustine, as we have seen, viewed the Septuagint as the authoritative version, not Jerome's *Hebraica veritas* — a fact largely obscured by Bede's selective quotations, but obvious to anyone

---

56 Darby, *Bede and the End of Time*, pp. 35–57; Wallis, 'Why Did Bede Write?'; Palmer, *The Apocalypse in the Early Middle Ages*, pp. 98–105.
57 Eusebius, *Chronicon*, Introduction, trans. Jerome, ed. by Helm, p. 15; cf. Bede, *Epistola ad Pleguinam*, § 6.
58 Jerome, *Hebraicae quaestiones*, 10.24–25, ed. Antin, p. 14; trans. Hayward, pp. 42, 145.
59 This is based on a word search under 'Cainan' on the *Patrologia Latina* database.
60 Cf. O'Loughlin, 'The Controversy over Methuselah's Death'.
61 Bede, *Epistola ad Pleguinam*, § 10, ed. by Jones, p. 311, ll. 6–18; Augustine, *De Civitate Dei*, XV.11–14, ed. by Dombart and Kalb, pp. 467–74.
62 Augustine, *De Civitate Dei*, XVIII.43, ed. by Dombart and Kalb, p. 640, ll. 55–57; my trans. based on *City of God*, trans. by Bettenson, p. 822. For the differing views of Jerome and Augustine see Williams, *The Monk and the Book*, pp. 64–94; Lössl, 'Shift'; Rebenich, 'Jerome', esp. pp. 63–65; Hayward, *Saint Jerome's Hebrew Questions*, pp. 7–23.
63 Augustine, *De Civitate Dei*, XVI.3 and 10, ed. by Dombart and Kalb, pp. 502–03 ll. 61–62 and p. 512, ll. 41–42; Augustine, *Ep.* 28.11, ed. by Goldbacher, vol. I (CSEL 34.i), p. 105, line 12 – p. 107 line 5.
64 Bede, *Epistola ad Pleguinam* § 16, ed. by Jones, p. 314, ll. 13–14; trans. Wallis, 'recorded by Origen, published by Jerome, praised by Augustine, confirmed by Josephus'.

who knew their Augustine. As for Jerome, he was indeed genuinely committed to the superior authority of the Hebrew; but contemporary criticism had led him at times to acknowledge the Hexaplaric revision and deny that he was critical of the Septuagint.[65] We must also recognise that Jerome's translation direct from the Hebrew had still not won universal acceptance as the only valid translation in Bede's day. It was not the version on which the Fathers had commented, and it was not the sole version used in Gregory the Great's Rome or Cassiodorus' monastery.[66] Wearmouth and Jarrow under Ceolfrith may have been unusual in the position they gave the *Hebraica veritas*; Hexham under Wilfrid and Acca might have thought differently — especially when the veracity of an evangelist was at stake. Small wonder, then, that Bede was initially 'terrified' at Acca's demand that he comment on Luke.

The Role of Acca

Although Bede faced critics at Hexham from 708 right through the early years of Acca's episcopate and beyond, we would arguably be wrong to regard Acca himself as their instigator. Certainly by the time of his surviving letter, Acca respected Bede's monastic calling and felt that God would enlighten him, perhaps drawing inspiration from Augustine's *De Trinitate*.[67] Again, when encouraging Bede to write by arguing that each should contribute what he could to adorning the Lord's house, he may have drawn his inspiration from Jerome, who had invoked the varied contributions that people brought for the tabernacle, Bede's own being his biblical works.[68]

One might even hazard the suggestion that Acca may have seen his relationship with Bede along the lines of Pope Damasus's relationship with Jerome: a busy bishop with a tame biblical expert, whose talents could be put to good use by requiring him to write. The prefatory letter to Bede's *Expositio Actuum* refers to Acca's letters urging him not to 'doze' (*obdormire*), but unwearyingly to search the scriptures and to write, following the Fathers' footsteps. Damasus had similarly accused Jerome of 'dozing' (*dormientem*) rather than replying to his biblical enquiries.[69] The classical citations in Acca's letter are striking for their period, and both in style and content the debt to Jerome is palpable.[70] Similarly Acca's questions to Bede *c.* 716 on the correct

---

65 Rebenich, 'Jerome', pp. 63–65.

66 Bogaert, 'The Latin Bible,' esp. pp. 69, 72–73; Marsden, *The Text of the Old Testament*, pp. 130–38.

67 Acca, *Epistola*, ed. by Hurst, *In Lucae evangelium expositio*, prologus, p. 6, ll. 59–68; cf. Augustine, *De Trinitate* III. 5, ed. by Mountain and Glorie, pp. 33–34, ll. 38–45: both cite Ps 1. 2, and Acca had quoted a nearby passage of Augustine at *Epistola*, p. 5, lines 30–32.

68 Jerome, *Prologus in libro Regum*, ed. by Weber, *Biblia Sacra*, p. 365, ll. 59–67.

69 Bede, *Expositio Actuum Apostolorum*, preface, ed. by Laistner, p. 3, ll. 3–9; Cain, *The Letters of Jerome*, pp. 53–67, esp. 57. Damasus's letter circulated with Jerome's reply (Jerome, *Ep.* 35.1.1 and *Ep.* 36); and the latter, at least, was known to Bede (Lapidge, *Anglo-Saxon Library*, p. 217), suggesting that both were known in early Northumbria. Acca's opening salutation, 'in domino salutem', would also fit with that seemingly used by Damasus: Cain, *The Letters of Jerome*, pp. 63–64.

70 Cain, *The Letters of Jerome*, p. 56; Acca, *Epistola* lines 17–20. Cf. Stephen of Ripon, *Vita Sancti Wilfridi*, preface (quoting Horace via Jerome; ed. by Colgrave, pp. 2, 151).

interpretation of two scriptural passages is reminiscent of Damasus's sending knotty biblical queries to Jerome. Bede had to break off from his commentary on Samuel to attend to them, and one of them posed a challenge to his tact since it was based on Acca's misinterpretation of something that Bede had written previously. The fact that he accomplished this successfully implies that Acca respected his judgement.[71]

What is noteworthy is that Acca encouraged Bede to make his contribution to the Church in the way that Bede adopted: through his writings. From his earliest commentary, that on Revelation, Bede showed awareness of the important role of 'teachers, that is, those who follow the footsteps of the apostles'.[72] Now Acca urged Bede himself to follow in the footsteps of the Fathers, to wrestle with biblical problems, and both to make the Fathers' insights available to a less cultured Northumbrian readership, and also to tackle questions which they had omitted. Above all, he demanded that Bede should overcome his reluctance and 'do it' (*age*)![73] He felt sure that Bede's rumination on the Scriptures, sequestered as he was from the pressures of the world, would enable him to be given fresh insights into their interpretation. This was the programme which Bede made his own. As Alan Thacker has emphasised, it also interlocked with Bede's whole conception of how the Northumbrian Church might be improved: those with the gifts and the leisure for higher contemplation should be *praedicatores* and *doctores*, preachers and teachers who benefited the less learned;[74] and Bede himself understood his role as a *doctor* who would not only render the Fathers' teachings more accessible, but would add to them.[75] Acca's conversations with Bede may have played a crucial role in restoring his self-confidence after the searing experience of the heresy accusation, thus enabling him to embark on his major run of biblical commentaries, beginning with the long deferred one on Luke.

Conclusion

Bede's relationship with Acca was more complex than has hitherto been realised, and our evidence is sometimes enigmatic, sometimes points in more than one direction. Bede's opening salutations in his letters to Acca accord with epistolary conventions and, generally, little weight should be attached to them.[76] His appreciative portrait of Acca

---

71   Bede, *De mansionibus*, ed. by Migne, col. 699A–B; *De eo quod ait Isaias*, ed. by Migne, cols 702B–D, 709C–710A. Darby, *Bede and the End of Time*, pp. 140–43.

72   Wallis, *Bede: Commentary on Revelation*, pp. 263–64.

73   Acca, *Epistola*, ed. by Hurst, *In Lucae evangelium expositio*, prologus, p. 5, ll. 22–68. Note also the echo of Acca's earlier letters which is caught in Bede's response, *Expositio Actuum Apostolorum*, pref. ed. by Laistner, p. 3, ll. 3–10.

74   Bede, *In Cantica canticorum*, I. ii. 8–10, II. iv. 1, III. v. 2, ed. by Hurst, pp. 218–21, especially p. 221, ll. 415–20; p. 244, lines 34–50; pp. 274–75, lines 127–44; Thacker, 'Bede's Ideal of Reform', pp. 130–34; DeGregorio, '"*Nostrorum socordiam temporum*"'.

75   Thacker, 'Bede and the Ordering of Understanding', esp. pp. 43–45; Ray, 'Who Did Bede Think?'.

76   See below, pp. 188–89.

in his *Ecclesiastical History* has glaring omissions when set against his contemporary ideals for the episcopate. The crucial evidence for the early years of their relationship reveals Acca as supportive of Bede's biblical exegesis, but at the same time needling him on controversial issues where his views appeared at variance with the Bible or its authoritative interpreters. The problems posed, however, are not insoluble, nor even surprising when we reflect on the unequal relationship between bishop and monk, and one lasting over twenty years; and on the difficult conditions of the early eighth-century Church in Northumbria, when a *modus vivendi* had to be worked out between the Wilfridians and their erstwhile critics, and between competing ideas about the role of the bishop that varied hugely as between the Wilfridians and Lindisfarne.[77] Nor should we assume that there was necessarily a monolithic view within each different church. Hexham in 708 held both Bede's critic and David, whose good offices Bede sought to enlist.

Our starting point is that in 708 Bede's chronological scholarship was sharply criticised by at least one educated and articulate member of Wilfrid's community. This precipitated Bede's outspoken rebuttal in his letter to Plegwine, which Jones read as a 'thinly veil[ed] ... attack' on Wilfrid himself.[78] It was scarcely couched in a way to mollify critics. Rather, I would suggest, his sharp criticism of those using the Bible to deduce when the world would end, while himself seeming to cast doubt on the veracity of an evangelist, stimulated renewed criticism at Hexham, and a demand that he should clarify his own position. This he did, in the first case through his commentary on Revelation,[79] and in the second by returning to the Cainan problem and rephrasing his conclusions in more diplomatic language. In the meantime Acca had succeeded Wilfrid as bishop of Hexham (710), and thus inherited the task of bridging the gap between Bede's views and those of his critic(s) there. He sought to do this by asking Bede to follow his commentary on Revelation, which defused the apocalyptic readings of that text, with one on Luke. A worthwhile enterprise in itself, this would also have the advantage of diluting the significance of the Cainan problem amidst other exegetical questions. Bede was initially scared of what Acca was demanding; but Acca had clearly discussed the issue with Bede,[80] and formed a favourable impression of his personal qualities and exegetical competence. He should probably be seen as a critical, but friendly mediator between Bede and his challenger(s) at Hexham. The eventual appearance of Bede's commentary on Luke justified his faith, and probably won Bede general recognition as a valuable interpreter of Scripture. On Luke's inclusion of Cainan (following the Septuagint), Bede noted both this and Cainan's absence from the *Hebraica veritas* Genesis, commenting

---

77 Stancliffe, 'Disputed Episcopacy'.

78 Jones, 'The Computistical Works of Bede', p. 135.

79 See Wallis, *Bede: Commentary on Revelation*, pp. 39–85. If this commentary was already written (cf. above, n. 45), it had simply to be copied and forwarded to Hexham. Alternatively, Hwætbert may have urged Bede to undertake it in 708: some of its content fits better with this dating, and it would explain why Bede tackled such a problematic book in his first exegetical venture: cf. Wallis, 'Why Did Bede Write?', pp. 24–25, 32–40.

80 Acca, *Epistola*, ed. by Hurst, *In Lucae evangelium expositio*, prologus, p. 5, ll. 2–5.

diplomatically: 'Sed quid horum sit uerius aut si utrumque uerum esse possit Deus nouerit'.[81]

All of this happened relatively early in Acca's episcopate, and certainly before 716. That is the year of Bede's commentary on Samuel, which marks a shift in his exegesis: from then on, he became more concerned at the imperfect standard of pastoral care in the Northumbrian Church, and the need for more and better *doctores* and *praedicatores* to remedy this.[82] Interestingly, the Samuel dedication also marks the high point of Bede's protestation of affection for Acca (cf. Tables 1–2).[83] Elsewhere I have argued that Acca embodied a different style of episcopacy from the monk–bishop tradition of Lindisfarne; and that as the second decade of the eighth century wore on, Lindisfarne came to feel threatened by Hexham, with Wilfridians belittling its paradigmatic saint, Cuthbert, and with Acca threatening its continuance as an episcopal see.[84] What is certain is that *c.* 720 Lindisfarne commissioned Bede to rewrite the Life of St Cuthbert. In that Life, Bede portrayed Cuthbert as the embodiment of his ideal of pastoral care, with the monk–bishop traversing the countryside to preach to people in scattered hamlets, and setting forth in his way of life the Christian ideal that he preached.[85]

In other words, Bede here reveals himself as implicitly critical of the Wilfridian view of episcopacy embodied by Acca.[86] There is a consistency between Bede's outspoken denunciation of his opponents at Hexham in 708 as drunken boors, who should rather have been focusing on their reading, and his denunciation in his letter to Ecgbert of bishops who surrounded themselves with companions given to gossiping, feasting and drinking, rather than with servants of Christ, and rather than focusing on the Scriptures.[87] There is also interesting evidence from his *De temporum ratione* of 725 that his adoption of Jerome's *Hebraica veritas* chronology was still a cause of friction.[88] He defended himself by quoting the very passage from Augustine's *De Trinitate* which Acca himself had used when urging Bede to comment on Luke. Augustine there argues for a variety of books by different authors, *diuerso stilo, sed non diuersa fide*, to cater for the needs of different readers.[89] Bede uses it deliberately

---

81 'But which of these may be more truthful, or if both may be true, God will have known.' Bede, *In Lucae evangelium expositio*, I. iii. 35–36, ed. by Hurst, p. 90, ll. 2806–7.

82 Thacker, 'Bede and the Ordering of Understanding', pp. 54–57; DeGregorio, '"Nostrorum socordiam temporum"', esp. pp. 112–14.

83 Above, p. 172; cf. Tables 1–2 in Appendix.

84 Stancliffe, 'Disputed Episcopacy'.

85 Thacker, 'Bede's Ideal of Reform'.

86 Stancliffe, 'Disputed Episcopacy', pp. 15–17, 27–32.

87 Bede, *Epistola ad Pleguinam* §§ 1 and 17, ed. by Jones, p. 307, lines 5–6, and p. 315, ll. 9–11; *Epistola ad Ecgbertum* §§ 3–4, ed. and trans. by Grocock and Wood, pp. 126–31 Cf. Goffart, 'Bede's History in a Harsher Climate', p. 219; DeGregorio, '"Nostrorum socordiam temporum"', pp. 112–13.

88 *De temporum ratione*, ed. by Jones, Pref. esp. p. 264, lines 35–37; also ch. 67. Cf. Jones, 'The Computistical Works of Bede', p. 135.

89 'Different in style, but not in faith', *De temporum ratione*, preface, ed. Jones, p. 265, lines 48–51; Acca, *Epistola*, ed. by Hurst, *In Lucae evangelium expositio*, prologus, p. 5, lines 30–32; Augustine, *De Trinitate*, III.5, ed. by Mountain and Glorie, p. 33, ll. 25–28. Note that Bede, like Acca, reads 'necesse' rather than Augustine's 'utile'.

to forestall any criticism from Hexham by citing the words of both Augustine and Acca himself! In the same work Bede restates the discrepancy between the *Hebraica veritas* and the Septuagint over Cainan, noting that Luke 'in this instance appears to have followed [the seventy's] translation', but making clear his own adherence to the chronology of the *Hebraica veritas*.[90] In other words he reaffirms the decision he made in his Luke commentary to note both traditions, but abandons his earlier neutrality in favour of whole-hearted endorsement of the *Hebraica veritas*'s chronology.

What conclusion, then, should we reach about Bede's relationship with Acca? It was not simply a friendly relationship between two individuals who shared an interest in theology and biblical exegesis. Acca, as Bede's bishop, appears to have been genuinely impressed by Bede's faith and intellectual abilities, and sought to harness these in the service of the Church. At the same time he did not use his episcopal authority to silence Bede's critic(s) at Hexham. He thus both encouraged and challenged Bede, simultaneously. Bede, for his part, doubtless enjoyed discussing biblical problems with someone interested in them, and each may have influenced the other in certain respects.[91] Yet Bede must have been acutely aware that he was talking to his diocesan bishop, and would not therefore have expressed everything that was in his mind. He regarded it as wrong to criticise Christian priests publicly, and his *Ecclesiastical History* has been aptly characterised as 'a gallery of good examples',[92] highlighting those facets of kings and churchmen that he wished to hold up for emulation. His chapter on Acca fits this neatly: Bede applauded what he found praiseworthy, and was silent over Acca's pastoral care of his diocese. As Bede's concern for the shortcomings of the Northumbrian Church grew after 716, he may have become more critical of Acca's failure to remedy these, while remaining appreciative of his good qualities, his lavish provision for his church, his library, and his care for music.

One significant corollary of this more nuanced view of the relationship between Bede and Acca should be noted. Bede's exegetical career was launched to a critical, and partially hostile audience at Hexham. He was challenged to go beyond his comfort zone and face intractable issues that the Fathers had passed over. This was the crucible out of which emerged his first major commentaries. Acca's mix of affirmation and challenge were the ideal forcing ground for Bede's maturation as a scholar.

Addendum: This paper was completed in December 2016, two years before the publication of Paul Hilliard, 'Acca of Hexham Through the Eyes of the Venerable Bede', *Early Medieval Europe*, 26.4 (2018), pp. 440–61. I have read this with interest, but do not feel the need to modify what I have written.

I would also like to take this opportunity to thank the anonymous referee for thoughtful comments.

---

90 Bede, *De temporum ratione*, ch. 66.23, ed. Jones and Mommsen, p. 468, lines 161–75, and cf. preface, ed. Jones, lines 13–37. Bede's wording in this section of his *Chronica maiora* is virtually the same as that in his commentary on Genesis: *Libri quattuor in principium Genesis*, III.xi.12, ed. Jones, lines 768–83; unfortunately the latter cannot be accurately dated.

91 Stancliffe, 'Disputed Episcopacy', p. 36.

92 Campbell, *Essays in Anglo-Saxon History*, pp. 19–20, 25.

Appendix: Tables

Table 1. Bede's Prefatory Letters with salutation formulae addressing Bishop Acca.

Domino in Christo desiderantissimo et uere beatissimo Accan episcopo Beda perpetuam in domino salutem	*Expositio Actuum*, p. 3
Domino beatissimo et nimium desiderantissimo Accae episcopo Beda humilis presbiter in Deo aeterno salutem	*In Lucam*, p. 6
Domino beatissimo et intima semper charitate venerando, sancto antistiti Accae, Beda, humillimus servorum Christi, salutem.	*De eo quod ait Isaias*, col. 702B
Domino in Christo dilectissimo et cum omni semper honorificentia nominando antistiti Accae, Beda fidelis tuus famulus	*De mansionibus filiorum Israel*, col. 699A
Dilectissimo ac reuerendissimo antistiti Acca humillimus famulorum Christi Beda salutem	*In principium Genesis*, p. 1

Table 2. Bede's Prefaces where the reference to Bishop Acca is embedded in the text.

Unde tuo crebro dilectissime ac desiderantissime omnium qui in terris morantur antistitum Acca prouocatus hortatu	*In Sam.* p. 9
In cuius euangelium tuo dilectissime antistitum Acca nec non et aliorum fratrum plurium commonitus hortatu	*In Marc.* p. 432
Quapropter reuerentissime antistes Acca tuis diligenter obsecundans hortamentis	*In Ezram*, p. 237

Table 3a. Bede's Prefatory Letters with salutation formulae addressing bishops.

Domino sancto ac beatissimo patri Eadfrido episcopo	Bede, *Vita Cuthberti* (prose), p. 142
Dilectissimo ac reuerentissimo antistiti Ecgberto Beda famulus Christi salutem	*Epistola* to Ecgbert, p. 124

Table 3b. Bede's Prefatory Letters with salutation formulae addressing priests (but cf. note 8).

Domino in domino dominorum dilectissimo Johanni presbytero Beda famulus Christi salutem	Bede, *Vita Cuthberti* (verse), p. 56
Dilectissimo fratri Nothelmo Beda salutem	*In Regum librum*, p. 293

Table 3c. Bede's Prefatory Letter with salutation formulae addressing a king.

Gloriosissimo regi Ceoluulfo Beda famulus Christi et presbyter	*Historia ecclesiastica*, p. 2

Table 4. Prefaces where the reference to another recipient, a monk or nun, is embedded in the text.

Apocalypsis sancti Iohannis ... septem mihi, frater Eusebi, uidetur esse diuisa periochis	*Expositio Apocalypseos*, p. 221
quod tibi exponi petististi, dilectissima in Christo soror	*In Canticum Abacuc*, p. 381

Table 5a. Letters with salutation formulae addressing other priests.

Reverentissimo ac sanctissimo fratri VVicthedo presbytero, Beda optabilem in domino salutem	*Epistola* to Wicthed, p. 319
Desiderantissimo et reuerentissimo patri Albino, Baeda Christi famulus salutem	*Epistola* to Abbot Albinus, ed. Plummer, I, 3

Table 5b. Letters with salutation formulae addressing other monks.

Fratri dilectissimo et in Christi visceribus honorando Pleguinae, Beda in domino salutem	*Epistola* to Plegwine, p. 307
Dilectissimo in Christo fratri Helmuualdo, Beda famulus Christi, Salutem	*Epistola* to Helmwald

Works Cited

Digital Resources

Brepolis, Library of Latin Texts, Series A http://clt.brepolis.net
Patrologia Latina Database, http://pld.chadwyck.co.uk/

Primary Sources

Acca, *Epistola* to Bede prefacing Bede's *In Lucae evangelium expositio*, ed. by D. Hurst, *Bedae Venerabilis Opera, pars 2, opera exegetica*, 3, Corpus Christianorum Series Latina, 120 (Turnhout: Brepols, 1960), pp. 5–6
Augustine, *City of God* trans. by Henry Bettenson, introduction by David Knowles, Penguin Classics (Harmondsworth: Penguin, 1972)
———, *De civitate Dei*, ed. by B. Dombart and A. Kalb, *Aurelii Augustini Opera, pars xiv, 1 and 2*; Corpus Christianorum Series Latina, 47–48 (Turnhout: Brepols, 1955)
———, *De Trinitate*, ed. by W. J. Mountain and F. Glorie, 2 vols, Corpus Christianorum Series Latina, 50–50B (Turnhout: Brepols, 1968)
———, *Epistulae*, ed. by A. Goldbacher (5 vols), vols I, II, III and IV, Corpus Scriptorum Ecclesiasticorum Latinorum, 34 i and ii, 44 and 57 (Wien: Tempsky, 1895, 1898, 1904, 1911)
Bede, *De eo quod ait Isaias: 'Et claudentur ibi in carcere et post dies multos visitabuntur'*, in *Patrologiae cursus completus: series latina*, ed. by Jacques Paul Migne, 221 vols (Paris: Migne, 1844–1864), 94 (1862), cols 702–10

————, *De mansionibus filiorum Israel*, in *Patrologiae cursus completus: series latina*, ed. by Jacques Paul Migne, 221 vols (Paris: Migne, 1844–1864), 94 (1862), cols 699–702

————, *De temporum ratione liber*, ed. C. W. Jones (incorporating Chronica maiora, ed. T. Mommsen), *Bedae venerabilis opera, pars vi: Opera didascalia, 2*; Corpus Christianorum Series Latina, 123B (Turnhout: Brepols, 1977)

————, *Epistola ad Helmvvaldum*, ed. by C. W. Jones, *Bedae venerabilis opera, pars vi: Opera didascalia, 3*; Corpus Christianorum Series Latina, 123C (Turnhout: Brepols, 1980), p. 629

————, *Epistola ad Pleguinam*, ed. by Charles W. Jones, *Bedae Opera de temporibus* (Cambridge, MA: The Mediaeval Academy of America, 1943), pp. 307–15

————, *Epistola ad VVicthedum*, ed. by Charles W. Jones, *Bedae Opera de temporibus* (Cambridge, MA: The Mediaeval Academy of America, 1943), pp. 319–25

————, *Epistola Bede ad Ecgbertum episcopum*, ed. and trans. by Christopher Grocock and I. N. Wood (Oxford: Clarendon Press, 2013), pp. 124–61

————, *Epistola to Albinus*, ed. by C. Plummer, *Venerabilis Baedae Opera Historica*, 2 vols (Oxford: Clarendon Press, 1896), I, p. 3

————, *Expositio Actuum Apostolorum*, ed. by M. L. W. Laistner, *Bedae Venerabilis Opera, pars 2, opera exegetica, 4*, Corpus Christianorum Series Latina, 121 (Turnhout: Brepols, 1983), pp. 1–99

————, *Expositio Apocalypseos*, ed. by Roger Gryson, *Bedae Opera, pars II, 5*, Corpus Christianorum Series Latina, 121A (Turnhout: Brepols, 2001)

————, *Expositio in canticum Abacuc prophetae*, ed. by J. E. Hudson, *Bedae Venerabilis Opera, pars 2, opera exegetica, 2B*, Corpus Christianorum Series Latina, 119B (Turnhout: Brepols, 1983), pp. 377–409

————, *Historia abbatum*, ed. and trans. by Christopher Grocock and I. N. Wood (Oxford: Clarendon Press, 2013), pp. 21–75

————, *Historia ecclesiastica gentis Anglorum*, ed. and trans. by B. Colgrave and R. A. B. Mynors, *Bede's Ecclesiastical History of the English People* (Oxford: Clarendon Press, 1969)

————, *In Cantica canticorum*, ed. by D. Hurst, *Bedae Venerabilis Opera, pars 2, opera exegetica, 2B*, Corpus Christianorum Series Latina, 119B (Turnhout: Brepols, 1983), pp. 165–375

————, *In Ezram et Neemiam*, ed. by D. Hurst, *Bedae Venerabilis Opera, pars 2, opera exegetica, 2A*, Corpus Christianorum Series Latina, 119A (Turnhout: Brepols, 1969), pp. 235–392

————, *In Lucae evangelium expositio*, ed. by D. Hurst, *Bedae Venerabilis Opera, pars 2, opera exegetica, 3*, Corpus Christianorum Series Latina, 120 (Turnhout: Brepols, 1960), pp. 1–425

————, *In Marci evangelium expositio*, ed. by D. Hurst, *Bedae Venerabilis Opera, pars 2, opera exegetica, 3*, Corpus Christianorum Series Latina, 120 (Turnhout: Brepols, 1960), pp. 427–648

————, *In primam partem Samuhelis libri IIII*, ed. by D. Hurst, *Bedae Venerabilis Opera, pars 2, opera exegetica, 2*, Corpus Christianorum Series Latina, 119 (Turnhout: Brepols, 1962), pp. 1–272

————, *In Regum librum xxx quaestiones*, ed. by D. Hurst, *Bedae Venerabilis Opera, pars 2, opera exegetica, 2*, Corpus Christianorum Series Latina, 119 (Turnhout: Brepols, 1962), pp. 289–322

————, *Letter to Plegwin*, trans. by Faith Wallis, in *Bede: The Reckoning of Time*, translated with introduction and commentary by Faith Wallis, Translated Texts for Historians, 29 (Liverpool: Liverpool University Press, 1999), pp. 405–15

————, *Libri quattuor in principium Genesis*, ed. C. W. Jones, *Bedae Venerabilis Opera, pars 2, opera exegetica, 1*, Corpus Christianorum Series Latina, 118A (Turnhout: Brepols, 1967)

————, *The Venerable Bede: Commentary on the Acts of the Apostles*, trans. with introduction and notes by Lawrence T. Martin, Cistercian Studies Series, 117 (Collegeville: Liturgical Press, 1989)

————, *Vita Sancti Cuthberti* (prose), ed. and trans. by B. Colgrave, *Two Lives of Saint Cuthbert* (Cambridge: Cambridge University Press, 1940)

————, *Vita Sancti Cuthberti* (verse), ed. by Werner Jaager, *Bedas metrische Vita sancti Cuthberti*, Palaestra 198 (Leipzig: Mayer & Müller, 1935)

Bede: Commentary on Revelation, translated with introduction and notes by Faith Wallis, Translated Texts for Historians, 58 (Liverpool: Liverpool University Press, 2013)

Bede: On Ezra and Nehemiah, translated with introduction and notes by Scott DeGregorio, Translated Texts for Historians, 47 (Liverpool: Liverpool University Press, 2006)

Bede: The Reckoning of Time, translated with introduction and commentary by Faith Wallis, Translated Texts for Historians, 29 (Liverpool: Liverpool University Press, 1999)

Eusebius, *Chronicon*, translated into Latin and expanded by Jerome, ed. by Rudolf Helm, *Die Chronik des Hieronymus*, Die griechischen christlichen Schriftsteller 47, *Eusebius Werke VII* (Berlin: Akademie, 1956)

Jerome, *Epistulae*, ed. by Isidore Hilberg (3 vols), vol. 1, Corpus Scriptorum Ecclesiasticorum Latinorum, 54, *S. Eusebii Hieronymi opera (sect. 1, pars 1), Epistularum pars 1* (Vienna: Tempsky, 1910)

————, *Hebraicae quaestiones in libro Geneseos*, ed. by P. Antin, *S. Hieronymi presbyteri opera, pars 1, opera exegetica, 1*; Corpus Christianorum Series Latina, 72 (Turnhout: Brepols, 1959)

————, *Prologus in libro Regum iuxta Hebraeos*, ed. by Robert Weber, *Biblia sacra iuxta vulgatam versionem*, 4th edn revised by Roger Gryson (Stuttgart: Deutsche Bibelgesellschaft, 1994, reprinted 2005), pp. 364–66

————, *Saint Jerome's Hebrew Questions on Genesis*, trans. with introduction and commentary by C. T. R. Hayward, Oxford Early Christian Studies (Oxford: Clarendon Press, 1995)

Laterculus Malalianus, ed. by Jane Stevenson, *The 'Laterculus Malalianus' and the School of Archbishop Theodore*, Cambridge Studies in Anglo-Saxon England, 14 (Cambridge: Cambridge University Press, 1995)

Stephen, *Vita Sancti Wilfridi*, ed. and trans. by B. Colgrave, *The Life of Bishop Wilfrid by Eddius Stephanus* (Cambridge: Cambridge University Press, 1927)

Secondary Studies

Bogaert, Pierre-Maurice, 'The Latin Bible, *c.* 600 to *c.* 900', in *The New Cambridge History of the Bible*, ed. by James Carleton Paget and others, 4 vols (Cambridge: Cambridge University Press, 2012–2015), II: *From 600 to 1450*, ed. by Richard Marsden and E. Ann Matter (2012), pp. 69–92

Cain, Andrew, *The Letters of Jerome: Asceticism, Biblical Exegesis, and the Construction of Identity in Late Antiquity*, Oxford Early Christian Studies (Oxford: Oxford University Press, 2009)

Campbell, James, *Essays in Anglo-Saxon History* (London: Hambledon Press, 1986)

Cubitt, Catherine, 'Wilfrid's "Usurping Bishops": Episcopal Elections in Anglo-Saxon England, c. 600–c. 800', *Northern History*, 25 (1989), 18–38

——, 'St Wilfrid: A Man for his Times', in *Wilfrid: Abbot, Bishop, Saint, Papers from the 1300th Anniversary Conferences*, ed. by N. J. Higham (Donington: Shaun Tyas, 2013), pp. 311–47

Darby, Peter, *Bede and the End of Time*, Studies in Early Medieval Britain (Farnham: Ashgate, 2012)

Darby, Peter, and Faith Wallis, 'Introduction: The Many Futures of Bede', in *Bede and the Future*, ed. by Peter Darby and Faith Wallis, Studies in Early Medieval Britain and Ireland (Farnham: Ashgate, 2014), pp. 1–21

DeGregorio, Scott, '"Nostrorum socordiam temporum": The Reforming Impulse of Bede's Later Exegesis', *Early Medieval Europe*, 11 (2002), 107–22

Goffart, Walter, *The Narrators of Barbarian History* (Princeton: Princeton University Press, 1988)

——, 'The *Historia Ecclesiastica*: Bede's Agenda and Ours', *The Haskins Society Journal*, 2 (1990), 29–45

——, 'Bede's History in a Harsher Climate', in *Innovation and Tradition in the Writings of the Venerable Bede*, ed. by Scott DeGregorio (Morgantown: West Virginia University Press, 2006), pp. 203–26

Hayward, C. T. R., *Saint Jerome's Hebrew Questions on Genesis*, trans. with introduction and commentary, Oxford Early Christian Studies (Oxford: Clarendon Press, 1995)

Higham, N. J. *(Re-)Reading Bede: The Ecclesiastical History in Context* (London: Routledge, 2006)

Jones, Charles W., 'The Computistical Works of Bede', in his *Bedae Opera de temporibus* (Cambridge, MA: The Mediaeval Academy of America, 1943), pp. 123–72

Kirby, D. P., 'The Genesis of a Cult: Cuthbert of Farne and Ecclesiastical Politics in Northumbria in the Late Seventh and Early Eighth Centuries', *Journal of Ecclesiastical History*, 46 (1995), 383–97

Lanham, Carol Dana, 'Freshman Composition in the Early Middle Ages: Epistolography and Rhetoric before the Ars Dictaminis', *Viator*, 23 (1992), 115–34

Lapidge, Michael, 'Bede's Metrical *Vita S. Cuthberti*', in *St Cuthbert, his Cult and his Community to AD 1200*, ed. by Gerald Bonner, David Rollason, and Clare Stancliffe (Woodbridge: Boydell, 1989), pp. 77–93

——, 'Acca of Hexham and the Origin of the *Old English Martyrology*', *Analecta Bollandiana*, 123 (2005), 29–78

——, *The Anglo-Saxon Library* (Oxford: Oxford University Press, 2006)

Lapidge, Michael, ed., Beda, *Storia degli Inglesi*, vol. 1, Scrittori greci e latini (no place given: Fondazione Lorenzo Valla, 2008)

Lössl, Josef, 'A Shift in Patristic Exegesis: Hebrew Clarity and Historical Verity in Augustine, Jerome, Julian of Aeclanum and Theodore of Mopsuestia', *Augustinian Studies*, 32 (2001), 157–75

Marsden, Richard, *The Text of the Old Testament in Anglo-Saxon England*, Cambridge Studies in Anglo-Saxon England, 15 (Cambridge: Cambridge University Press, 1995)

Mc Carthy, Daniel, 'Bede's Primary Source for the Vulgate Chronology in his Chronicles in *De temporibus* and *De temporum ratione*', in *Computus and its Cultural Context in the Latin West, AD 300–1200*, ed. by Immo Warntjes and Dáibhí Ó Cróinín (Turnhout: Brepols, 2010), pp. 159–89

O'Brien, Mary Bridget, *Titles of Address in Christian Latin Epistolography to 543 A.D.*, The Catholic University of America, Patristic Studies, 21 (Washington, DC: The Catholic University of America, 1930)

O'Loughlin, Thomas, 'The Controversy over Methuselah's Death: Proto-Chronology and the Origins of the Western Concept of Inerrancy', *Recherches de Théologie ancienne et médiévale*, 62 (1995), 182–225

Palmer, James T., *The Apocalypse in the Early Middle Ages* (Cambridge: Cambridge University Press, 2014)

Plummer, Charles, *Venerabilis Baedae Opera Historica*, 2 vols (Oxford: Clarendon Press, 1896)

Ray, Roger, 'The Triumph of Greco–Roman Assumptions in pre-Carolingian Historiography', in *The Inheritance of Historiography 350–900*, ed. by Christopher Holdsworth and T. P. Wiseman (Exeter: University of Exeter, 1986), pp. 67–84

——, *Bede, Rhetoric, and the Creation of Christian Latin Culture*, Jarrow Lecture, 1997 (Jarrow: St Paul's Church, 1997)

——, 'Who Did Bede Think he Was?', in *Innovation and Tradition in the Writings of the Venerable Bede*, ed. by Scott DeGregorio (Morgantown: West Virginia University Press, 2006), pp. 11–35

Rebenich, Stefan, 'Jerome: The "vir trilinguis" and the "hebraica veritas"', *Vigiliae Christianae*, 47 (1993), 50–77

Stancliffe, Clare, *Bede, Wilfrid, and the Irish*, Jarrow Lecture, 2003 (Jarrow: St Paul's Church, 2004)

——, 'Disputed Episcopacy: Bede, Acca, and the Relationship between Stephen's *Life of St Wilfrid* and the Early Prose Lives of St Cuthbert', *Anglo-Saxon England*, 41 (2013), 7–39

Stansbury, Mark, 'Source-marks in Bede's Biblical Commentaries', in *Northumbria's Golden Age*, ed. by Jane Hawkes and Susan Mills (Stroud: Sutton, 1999), pp. 383–89

Thacker, Alan, 'Bede's Ideal of Reform', in *Ideal and Reality in Frankish and Anglo-Saxon Society: Studies presented to J. M. Wallace-Hadrill* (Oxford: Blackwell, 1983), pp. 130–53

——, 'Acca [St Acca] (d. 740)', *Oxford Dictionary of National Biography*, ed. by H. C. G. Matthew and Brian Harrison (Oxford: Oxford University Press, 2004) http://www.oxforddnb.com/view/article/55, accessed 3 June 2011

——, *Bede and Augustine of Hippo: History and Figure in Sacred Text*, Jarrow Lecture, 2005 (Jarrow: St Paul's Church, 2005)

——, 'Bede and the Ordering of Understanding', in *Innovation and Tradition in the Writings of the Venerable Bede*, ed. by Scott DeGregorio (Morgantown: West Virginia University Press, 2006), pp. 37–63

Wallace-Hadrill, J. M., *Bede's Ecclesiastical History of the English People: A Historical Commentary* (Oxford: Clarendon Press, 1988)

Wallis, Faith, *Bede: Commentary on Revelation*, translated with introduction and notes, Translated Texts for Historians, 58 (Liverpool: Liverpool University Press, 2013)

——, 'Why Did Bede Write a Commentary on Revelation?', in *Bede and the Future*, ed. by Peter Darby and Faith Wallis, Studies in Early Medieval Britain and Ireland (Farnham: Ashgate, 2014), pp. 23–45

Whitelock, Dorothy, 'Bede and his Teachers and Friends', in *Famulus Christi*, ed. by Gerald Bonner (London: SPCK, 1976), pp. 19–39

Williams, Megan Hale, *The Monk and the Book: Jerome and the Making of Christian Scholarship* (Chicago: University of Chicago Press, 2006)

RICHARD SHARPE

King Ceadwalla and Bishop Wilfrid

The short career of King Ceadwalla in Wessex was a bloody business, perhaps right up to the point when he left England for Rome, where he was baptized by Pope Sergius on Holy Saturday, 10 April 689. Ten days later he was buried at St Peter's basilica, and Bede would publish his Roman epitaph.[1] Was this a great success-story for the Christian mission, a triumphant conversion, crowned by baptism at the hands of the pope and unblemished death in the white surplice of baptism? William of Malmesbury and Henry of Huntingdon in the twelfth century, both of them reading Bede as their chief witness, interpreted Ceadwalla's career in a heroic light.[2] They saw his life through his death *in albis* in Rome. Such a reading has endured. In commenting on his gifts of land made to churches, Dorothy Whitelock wrote, 'At the time when Ceadwalla made these grants he had not yet been baptized, but this was not out of hostility to the Christian faith, but because he wished his baptism to take place in Rome'.[3] Ceadwalla was not hostile to the faith when he yielded to Abbot Cyneberht's

---

1 Bede, *Historia ecclesiastica* V.7; *Inscriptiones Christianae Vrbis Romae*, vol. ii, pp. 288–89; Sharpe, 'King Ceadwalla's Roman epitaph'.
2 William of Malmesbury and Henry of Huntingdon both used the Anglo-Saxon Chronicle and Bede for what they say about Ceadwalla. William of Malmesbury, *Gesta Regum Anglorum*, I.34. 3, expressed the difficulty (*arduum memoratu*) of joining his career of blood-letting and his gifts to the church when still a pagan. His baptism in Rome, William says, was too well known to need repeating. In *Gesta Pontificum Anglorum*, III.102. 3, he adapts Stephen's chapter, even making Wilfrid provide Ceadwalla with horsemen and money. To William, however, Ceadwalla was primarily a benefactor of Malmesbury abbey. Henry of Huntingdon, *Historia Anglorum*, III.48–49, abridges Bede, *Historia ecclesiastica*, IV.13–14; at IV.3–5 he elaborates on the Chronicle before bringing in his baptism in Rome, *Historia ecclesiastica*, V.7; at IV.10 he recognizes Ceadwalla and Ine as holy men.
3 Whitelock, *Some Anglo-Saxon Bishops of London*, p. 8; influenced, no doubt, by F. M. Stenton, *Anglo-Saxon England*, p. 70, n. 3: 'Cædwalla's postponement of baptism does not imply that he had previously been in any hesitation between heathen and Christian beliefs, and gives no ground for describing him as a heathen. It is an illustration of the custom which in the seventh century still allowed an individual, unbaptized in infancy, to decide the circumstances of his formal admission into the church'. Twomey, 'Kings as catechumens', pp. 9–10, also accepts Ceadwalla's delayed baptism as a reflection of the Constantinian model in Bede's mind. Bede would not agree.

Richard Sharpe • was professor of diplomatic in the University of Oxford and a fellow of Wadham College.

Cities, Saints, and Communities in Early Medieval Europe, ed. by Scott DeGregorio and Paul Kershaw, SEM 46 (Turnhout: Brepols, 2020), pp. 195-222
BREPOLS PUBLISHERS   DOI 10.1484/M.SEM-EB.5.119628

persuasion, allowing two young boys, brothers of Arwald, king of the Isle of Wight, to be baptized before he put them to death, but his action was hardly that of a man converted in his heart yet delaying baptism till he could go to Rome to confess his faith. When, we ask, did he have his change of heart? If any person were responsible for his conversion, it would seem to have been Bishop Wilfrid, who for a time enjoyed a close relationship with King Ceadwalla. This is trumpeted in the contemporary Life of the bishop by his close associate Stephen. It shows through in the more discreet account provided by Bede. It becomes vivid through the witness-clause of the king's charter from the year 688.

Circumstances offer an explanation of how this conversion was achieved. Ceadwalla was a fighting man, thirty years old, when he went to Rome and died. Baptism does not kill a fit young man, but Bede has provided a clue: Cyneberht came to the king, 'qui tunc eisdem in partibus occultus curabatur a uulneribus quae ei inflicta fuerant proelianti in insula Vecta' ('who at the time lay in hiding in the same parts to be treated for wounds inflicted while he was fighting in the Isle of Wight') (*HE* IV.14). A front-line heathen king was susceptible to injury, perhaps to repeated injury, perhaps to sepsis. A dying king may be persuaded that even death, in the right circumstances, will add to his reputation. Bede's words, informing Whitelock's statement, again contain a clue: 'hoc sibi gloriae singularis desiderans adipisci, ut ad limina beatorum apostolorum fonte baptismatis ablueretur' ('desiring to obtain for himself the peculiar honour of being baptized at the portal of the blessed apostles') (*HE* V.7). Bede means us to understand that the dying king was motivated by special glory. Now, Stephen's *Vita S. Wilfrithi episcopi* says nothing of this: his Wilfrid was King Ceadwalla's high counsellor (*excelsum consiliarium*), uplifted by God in the king's triumphs whether in battle or by treaty (*aut acie gladii uictor aut foedere indultor pacis*).[4] Bede has much to say about Bishop Wilfrid and little about King Ceadwalla, but by focusing on them together we may improve our understanding of all three.

There are no simple facts from Ceadwalla's reign. It has usually merited a few pages in histories of Anglo-Saxon England, marking a stage in the rise of Wessex towards a position of power.[5] It is the nature of such books to gloss over difficulties for the sake of a clear narrative. In modern scholarship even his name varies: the West Saxon form Ceadwalla is here favoured over Bede's Northumbrian form Cædwalla.[6] Our

---

4 Stephen, *Vita S. Wilfrithi episcopi*, c. 42.

5 Stenton, *Anglo-Saxon England*, pp. 69–71; Kirby, *Making of Early England*, pp. 66–67; Sawyer, *From Roman Britain to Norman England*, pp. 42–48; Yorke, *Kings and Kingdoms of Early Anglo-Saxon England*, pp. 137–38, 145–46; Kirby, *Earliest English Kings*, pp. 98–104; Dutton, *Anglo-Saxon Kingdoms*, pp. 215–19; Higham, *An English Empire*, pp. 88, 121–22; Yorke, *Wessex in the Early Middle Ages*, p. 173. Sometimes Ceadwalla has barely a walk-on part, as in Higham, *The Convert Kings*, pp. 29, 276; Clay, 'Adventus, warfare, and the Britons in the development of West Saxon identity', pp. 191–92. The close relationship with Wilfrid figures in Gallyon, *The Early Church in Wessex and Mercia*, pp. 13–17.

6 Usual practice among historians is to follow Stenton, who writes Cædwalla like Cædmon. Cædmon was a Northumbrian, however, and Ceadwalla was a West Saxon. The pattern of readings in Bede manuscripts of the eighth century goes with that dialect difference — four from Northumbria have Cædwalla, one from Southumbria has Ceadwalla. Ceadual was the reading on his tomb in Rome, and his charter calls him Ceadwal. Now, though Stenton writes Cædwalla (in spite of his preference

sources are few, and we can never really understand his contemporary importance. He appears to have achieved wide power in southern England, laying the foundations of future West Saxon overlordship. A pagan, living according to pagan ways, he prospered without converting, and he got along with churchmen in a way that does not conform to the master-narrative of conversion. Most conspicuous among the churchmen around him was Bishop Wilfrid, despite the fact that his South Saxon diocese suffered the heel of oppression. Whatever the terms of their relationship, it has the appearance of an accommodation that might have brought opprobrium on the bishop. 'This murky episode', our friend Alan Thacker has written, 'which scarcely redounds to Wilfrid's credit, is treated with considerable circumspection by both Bede and Stephen of Ripon'.[7] As always we must read our sources with attention.

The nearest to a narrative comes from Bede's *Historia ecclesiastica*, following information supplied by Daniel, bishop of the West Saxons, who wrote to Bede about the church in his own kingdom and in the neighbouring kingdoms of the South Saxons and the Isle of Wight.[8] In recounting the episcopal succession among the West Saxons, Bede tells us that Bishop Hædde, Daniel's predecessor, was consecrated in London by Archbishop Theodore as their fifth bishop in succession from Birinus (*HE* IV.12). During Hædde's time the *subreguli*, who had divided the kingdom of the West Saxons between them after the reign of Cœnwalh, were defeated and killed by Ceadwalla, who:[9]

> suscepit imperium et, cum duobus annis hoc tenuisset, tandem superni regni amore compunctus reliquit, eodem adhuc praesule ecclesiam gubernante, ac Romam abiens ibi uitam finiuit, ut in sequentibus dicendum est.

> > took sovereignty upon himself, and when he had held it for two years, he relinquished it for love of the heavenly kingdom, all while the same bishop still governed the church, and, going away to Rome, he ended his life there, as shall be said more fully hereafter.

This skips lightly over his two-year reign and looks ahead to his death in Rome. We may wonder whether 'suscepit imperium' was meant to convey more than 'became king', but Bede's use of *imperium* is too various for us to be sure. There is no hint that the kingdom was not securely Christian. The key narrative comes at a point where Bede's text in our editions shows a rare degree of confusion. It straddles two chapters.

---

for West Saxon forms), Dorothy Whitelock, who never disagreed with Stenton except with much heart-searching and strong reason, writes Ceadwalla. So, in brief, both reason and authority support the form Ceadwalla. The spelling Cædwalla has remained standard because Bede is the most familiar point of contact for Latinists as Stenton is for historians.
7 Brief biography of Wilfrid by Thacker, 'Wilfrid [St Wilfrid] (*c*. 634–709/10)'.
8 Bede, *Historia ecclesiastica, Praefatio*. This is the same Daniel who kept up correspondence with the missionary Boniface in Germany and who, in particular, reflected on arguments to persuade heathens to reject their gods and receive Christianity (*Ep*. 23, ed. M. Tangl, *Die Briefe des heiligen Bonifatius und Lullus*, pp. 38–41).
9 Bede, *Historia ecclesiastica*, IV.12.

At the end of a chapter on how Wilfrid converted the South Saxons and, after he left, why they had no bishop of their own, we read:[10]

> Interea superueniens cum exercitu Caedualla, iuuenis strenuissimus de regio genere Geuissorum, cum exularet a patria sua, interfecit regem Aedilualch, ac prouinciam illam saeua caede ac depopulatione adtriuit; sed mox expulsus est a ducibus regiis Bercthuno et Andhuno, qui deinceps regnum prouinciae tenuerunt. Quorum prior postea ab eodem Caedualla, cum esset rex Geuissorum, occisus est, et prouincia grauiore seruitio subacta. Sed et Ini, qui post Caeduallan regnauit, simili prouinciam illam adflictione plurimo annorum tempore mancipauit. Quare factum est, ut toto illo tempore episcopum proprium habere nequiret, sed reuocato domum Vilfrido primo suo antistite, ipsi episcopo Geuissorum, id est Occidentalium Saxonum, qui essent in Venta ciuitate, subiacerent.

> > In the meantime, Ceadwalla, a most vigorous young man, of the royal lineage of the Gewisse, who was an exile from his own country, arrived with an army, slew King Æthelwalh, and wasted that kingdom with fierce slaughter and plundering; but soon he was expelled by Berhthun and Andhun, royal ealdormen, who afterwards held the government of the kingdom. The first of them was afterwards killed by the same Ceadwalla, when he was king of the Gewisse, and the [South Saxon] kingdom was subjected to harsh oppression. Ine, likewise, who reigned after Ceadwalla, kept that kingdom under similar servitude for several years. For this reason, during all that time, it happened that they were not able to have a bishop of their own; but their first bishop, Wilfrid, having been recalled home, they were subject to the bishop of the Gewisse, i.e. the West Saxons, who were in the city of Winchester.

If Bede's sequence of events is secure, Æthelwalh was killed and Sussex wasted with fierce slaughter even before Ceadwalla took power at home, after which he came again to kill Berhthun and enslave his people. Under Ceadwalla and his successor Ine, who ruled until 726, the South Saxons were oppressed by the West Saxons to such an extent that, during all that time, they were unable to have a bishop of their own but looked to the West Saxon bishop in Winchester. The chapter that follows is entitled, 'How the Isle of Wight received Christian inhabitants and how its two royal boys were put to death immediately after they received baptism':[11]

> Postquam ergo Caedualla regno potitus est Geuissorum, cepit et insulam Vectam, quae eatenus erat tota idolatriae dedita, ac stragica caede omnes indigenas exterminare ac suae prouinciae homines pro his substituere contendit, uoto se obligans quamuis necdum regeneratus, ut ferunt, in Christo quia, si cepisset

---

10 Bede, *Historia ecclesiastica*, IV.13, final paragraph. Plummer numbers the passage as chapter [15], Mynors as 15, and Lapidge (following LM) as 14. 7, but the chapter-headings in CKO (see below) show that it was composed as part of Chapter 13.

11 Bede, *Historia ecclesiastica*, IV.14. Plummer numbers the chapter as 14 [16] (giving priority to C), Mynors as 16 (14), and Lapidge as 14. 8-10, but it is clearly summarized by the heading of Chapter 14.

insulam, quartam partem eius simul et praedae Domino daret. Quod ita soluit, ut hanc Vilfrido episcopo, qui tunc forte de gente sua superueniens aderat, utendam pro Domino offerret. Est autem mensura eiusdem insulae iuxta aestimationem Anglorum mille ducentarum familiarum; unde data est episcopo possessio terrae trecentarum familiarum. At ipse partem quam accepit commendauit cuidam de clericis suis, cui nomen Bernuini, et erat filius sororis eius, dans illi presbyterum nomine Hiddila, qui omnibus qui saluari uellent uerbum ac lauacrum uitae ministraret.

Vbi silentio praetereundum non esse reor, quod in primitias eorum, qui de eadem insula credendo saluati sunt, duo regii pueri, fratres uidelicet Arualdi regis insulae, speciali sunt Dei gratia coronati. Siquidem imminentibus insulae hostibus fuga lapsi sunt de insula et in proximam Iutorum prouinciam translati, ubi cum delati in locum qui uocatur Ad Lapidem [*Stone, Hants*] occulendos se a facie regis uictoris credidissent, proditi sunt atque occidi iussi. Quod cum audisset abbas quidam et presbyter uocabulo Cyniberct, habens non longe ab inde monasterium in loco qui uocatur Hreutford [*Redbridge, Hants*], id est Vadum harundinis, uenit ad regem, qui tunc eisdem in partibus occultus curabatur a uulneribus quae ei inflicta fuerant proelianti in insula Vecta, postulauitque ab eo ut, si necesse esset pueros interfici, prius eos liceret fidei Christianae sacramentis imbui. Concessit rex, et ipse instructos eos uerbo ueritatis ac fonte saluatoris ablutos de ingressu regni aeterni certos reddidit. Moxque illi instante carnifice mortem laeti subiere temporalem, per quam se ad uitam animae perpetuam non dubitabant esse transituros.

After Ceadwalla had possessed himself of the kingdom of the Gewisse, he also took the Isle of Wight, which till then was entirely given over to idolatry, and by bloodthirsty slaughter endeavoured to destroy all the inhabitants and to introduce in their place people from his own kingdom. Having bound himself by a vow, though he was not yet, as they say, reborn in Christ, to give the fourth part of the land and of the booty to our Lord, if he took the island, he so fulfilled his promise by making this offering to our Lord to the use of Bishop Wilfrid, who was present, arriving just then by chance from his own nation. The measure of that island, according to the computation of the English, is twelve hundred hides, from which was given to the bishop possession of three hundred hides of land. This part that he received, he committed to one of his clerks called Beornwine, who was his sister's son, assigning to him a priest, whose name was Hiddila, who would administer the word and baptism of life to all who wanted to be saved.

Here I think it ought not to be omitted that, among the first fruits of the natives of that island who by believing gained their salvation, were two royal youths, brothers of Arwald, king of the island, who were crowned by the particular grace of God. For when the enemy approached, they made their escape out of the island and crossed over into the nearest province of the Jutes. Here, being brought to the place called At Stone, though they thought they could be hidden from the victorious king, they were betrayed and ordered to be killed. When this was heard by a certain abbot and priest, whose name was Cyneberht, who had a monastery not far from there at a place called Hreutford, that is, the Ford of Reeds, he came to the king, who at the time was hiding in the same parts to be treated for wounds inflicted while he was fighting in the Isle of Wight, and begged of him that, if the boys must inevitably be killed, it might be allowed that they be first taught the mysteries of the faith. The king consented, and Cyneberht, having taught them the word of truth and cleansed them by baptism, made them sure of their entry to the everlasting kingdom. Soon, the executioner being at hand, they joyfully underwent the temporal death, through which they did not doubt they were to pass to the life of the soul, which is eternal.

At one level the facts are allowed to speak for themselves. The word-order, 'stragica caede omnes indigenas exterminare', puts emphasis on Bede's neologism *stragicus* 'bloodthirsty' from CL *strages* 'bloodbath' and leaves no doubt over the sense of the verb *exterminare* 'exterminate'.[12] One can only wonder how many fighters Ceadwalla was able to ship across the Solent for this killing spree. Bede's *ut ferunt* ('as they say') is positioned in the phrase *necdum regeneratus in Christo* as if to doubt those who said that Ceadwalla was not yet baptized: it is meant rather to raise an eyebrow at those who claimed that an unregenerate pagan vowed a gift to God. His phrase *necdum regeneratus* is unambiguous.[13]

What Bede says of Wilfrid here is extremely limited. The South Saxons were left without a bishop of their own, 'reuocato domum Wilfrido primo eorum antistite' ('their first bishop, Wilfrid, having been recalled home'), and the bishop of the Gewisse in Winchester had oversight of their needs.[14] This sentence immediately precedes the passage quoted at length above, rendering Wilfrid's reappearance somewhat surprising, so that, when Ceadwalla butchered the inhabitants of the island, he was by chance on hand to accept a quarter share of the land and to appoint a priest to teach and baptize

---

12 Plummer, vol. ii, p. 229, knew no other example of *strāgicus*, which some later copies turned into 'trăgica'; cf. 'tragica caede' (*HE* III.1), on which the early copies agree. Piacente, 'Stragicus (Beda Hist. Eccl. 4, 16 [14])', pp. 81–85, made the case for emending against the early manuscripts in III.1 to the purely Bedan 'stragica'. The word also occurs in an eighth-century Mozarabic chronicle: 'illa minime recenseri tam stragica bella ista decreuit historia' (López Pereira, *Continuatio Isidoriana Hispana*, p. 270). This is more likely an independent coinage than evidence of early dissemination of Bede's *Historia* in Spain. Eadmer, *Vita S. Wilfridi*, c. 46 (ed. by Muir and Turner, p. 104), ignored the strong words and took the milder sense of *exterminare*, to exile or expel, 'expulsis indigenis'.

13 Compare, for example, 'conuersatio haec qua uiuitur inter gentes polluta est necdum his qui cathecizantur regenerationis fonte et gratia spiritus ablutis sanctificatis et iustificatis' (*In primam partem Samuhelis*, ed. by Hurst, p. 195, ll. 2498–2500); 'dum cotidie per lauacrum regenerationis regno diaboli auferuntur plures' (*In Ezram et Neemiam*, ed. by Hurst, p. 285, ll. 1768–70). Plummer, vol. ii, p. 229, pointed out the clause in a false charter in the name of King Ine, confirming a gift of land made by Bishop Hædde, 'Chedwalla annuente et propria manu *licet paganus* confirmante' (S 250 for Glastonbury); the act is a twelfth-century forgery, preserved, and perhaps composed, by William of Malmesbury.

14 Bede, *Historia ecclesiastica*, IV.13.

all who wanted to be saved. We may perhaps take this to refer to surviving women and children, taken over by the victors, rather than baptism before killing, such as befell the brothers of Arwald.[15] The story hardly lives up to what Bede's chapter heading advertised, 'how the island received Christian inhabitants', but Bede here wants to highlight the bright side. Wilfrid's being there is unexplained: 'qui tunc forte de gente sua superueniens aderat' ('who was present, arriving just then by chance from his own nation'). He arrived on the scene at the opportune moment to receive this pagan's thanksgiving generosity to the church. With no detailed chronology, this is impossible to make sense of. The sequel is the baptism and killing of the royal boys, who, when their executioner arrived, 'mortem laeti subiere temporalem' ('joyfully underwent temporal death'), knowing that they would pass to life eternal. In this way the last of the old heathen England was converted, as Bede sums up at the end of the passage quoted at length:[16]

> Hoc ergo ordine, postquam omnes Brittaniarum prouinciae fidem Christi susceperant, suscepit et insula Vecta, in quam tamen ob erumnam externae subiectionis nemo gradum ministerii ac sedis episcopalis ante Danihelem, qui nunc Occidentalium Saxonum est episcopus, accepit.

> > In this progression, therefore, after all the kingdoms of the island of Britain had embraced the faith of Christ, the Isle of Wight also received it; yet being under the affliction of foreign subjection, no one there has held the order or office of an episcopal see down to the time of Daniel, who is now bishop of the West Saxons.

And this is Bishop Daniel from whom Bede had his information. Bede appears to transmit a sense of Daniel's sympathy for people under the affliction of alien rule, rule to which the bishop was himself party.[17] He later expresses it that the diocese of the Isle of Wight was held by Daniel.[18] But if Wight was the last kingdom of the English to become Christian, the still unregenerate Ceadwalla, ruling in Wessex and beyond, stands out against the whole of Bede's historical argument. If the Gewisse had been converted by Birinus in the days of King Cynegisl (*HE* III.7), who died around 642, how did Ceadwalla, a member of the royal line, born about 659, remain unbaptized? Such questions point up how much we depend on believing what Bede tells us. He represents conversion as an event, bringing one kingdom after another into the faith of Christ, but here his own account discloses a different, more mixed, reality.

---

15 John Gillingham reads into Bede's verb *exterminare* the victor's taking control of the women and children of the defeated, 'Women, children, and the profits of war', pp. 65–66; 'A strategy of total war? Henry of Livonia and the conquest of Estonia, 1208–1227', pp. 209–10.

16 Bede, *Historia ecclesiastica*, IV.14. Henry of Huntingdon, *Historia Anglorum*, II.39, adds at this point: 'And so all the kings of England were made believers, and all parts of their kingdoms enjoyed the light and grace of Christ'.

17 Yorke, 'The Jutes of Hampshire and Wight', p. 89.

18 Bede, *Historia ecclesiastica*, V.23. The bishoprics of the Isle of Wight and of Sussex were held by Daniel but were not part of his West Saxon diocese.

If we seek to put his immediate story into its narrative context, something surprising emerges. At the start of Chapter 13 in Book IV, we learn that Bishop Wilfrid, exiled from his own diocese, had been to Rome and returned to Britain, where, unable to go back to Northumbria, he diverted to the kingdom of the South Saxons, whose king, Æthelwalh, had been converted years earlier with the encouragement of King Wulfhere of Mercia, himself a convert. Wulfhere had given the Isle of Wight and the kingdom of the Meonware to Æthelwalh, allowing the South Saxon king to take over two *prouinciae*, a word usually used by Bede for self-governing kingdoms, *in gente Occidentalium Saxonum* 'in the nation of the West Saxons'. The Wihtware and Meonware were, as Bede makes clear elsewhere, Jutish peoples, whom a Mercian overlord handed from West Saxon dominion to South Saxon dominion. Christianity had made little progress in Sussex until now. The Irish monk Dícuil and his few brethren at Bosham are said to have had no influence.[19] King Æthelwalh gave a great estate to establish Wilfrid as bishop at Selsey. Bede and Stephen agree on the figure of eighty-seven hides, but it was Stephen's text that supplied Bede with such detail.[20] Wilfrid remained here, 'merito omnibus honorabilis', 'deservedly honoured by everyone', says Bede (*HE* IV.13), for five years until the death of King Ecgfrith of Northumbria and his 'recall' to the north. Ecgfrith died in battle against the Picts on 20 May 685 (*HE* IV.24).[21] Any recall did not happen at once, but Wilfrid in due course went north. The five years between his return from Rome and his abandoning Selsey were roughly 682 to 686. Bede's 'annos quinque' may well mean more than four years but less than a full five.

Bede summarized the sequence of events in his long obituary of Wilfrid (*HE* V.19): Wilfrid came back to Britain, converted the South Saxons and sent priests into the Isle of Wight, and then, 'secundo anno Aldfridi, qui post Ecgfridum regnauit' ('in the second year of Aldfrith, who reigned after Ecgfrith'), he returned to his northern diocese at the new king's invitation. Here he follows Stephen, and the effect is to bring events in the Isle of Wight earlier to a time before his recall. The difference matters.

At this point, and before the chapter heading has been fulfilled with an explanation of why the South Saxons remained without a bishop of their own, a new chapter intervenes in our editions, for which there is no heading at the front of Book IV. In this chapter Bede tells how plague in a monastery in Sussex was miraculously ended through prayer and the death of one young convert, a boy lately called to the faith ('puerulus quidam de natione Saxonum, nuper uocatus ad fidem'). It is a story found in only one of the two branches of the textual transmission, and it has

19 The existence of this Irish settlement at Bosham on Portsmouth harbour must be one of the most unexpected facts recorded in the *Historia ecclesiastica*. Its later history begs a huge question. In the eleventh century Bosham appears to have been a royal minster with a 200-hide estate, better endowed than the episcopal see at Selsey. Was it really as insignificant at this date as Bede suggests?

20 Stephen, *Vita S. Wilfrithi episcopi*, c. 41. Eighty-seven hides is the total number represented in the forged charter of Ceadwalla in favour of Wilfrid at Selsey (S 232).

21 Eadmer, *Vita S. Wilfrithi*, c. 47, invents a story that Wilfrid in Sussex miraculously witnessed Ecgfrith's death in Pictland, imitating what he had no doubt read in the Lives of St Cuthbert (Colgrave, *Two Lives*, pp. 122, 244).

every appearance of being an afterthought, discontinuous in several ways from what precedes. First, a new source interrupts the information derived from Daniel. This is a story that Bishop Acca 'saepius referre et a fidelissimis eiusdem monasterii fratribus sibi relatum asserere solebat' ('used to tell rather often and to assert that it was told him by most trustworthy monks of the very same monastery').[22] Second, there is the dating, 'eodem ferme tempore quo ipsa prouincia nomen Christi susceperat, multas Brittaniae prouincias mortalitas saeua corripiebat' ('at almost the same time as that kingdom received the name of Christ, a terrible plague seized many of the kingdoms in Britain'). Wilfrid converted the South Saxons around 682, the plague was at its worst in 686. Wilfrid's five years in Sussex are telescoped. Third, the priest in whose monastery the miracle took place is introduced, Eappa, but no link is made to the preceding chapter, in which he was already named as one of four priests who baptized the people after Wilfrid baptized the *duces ac milites* of the South Saxons. The sick boy on whom the story is centred was lodged in the monastery, but it is not apparent why he was there. He had received the faith, but it is not said that he intended to become a monk. The story involves his being visited in a dream by SS. Peter and Paul, visually distinct, who explain to him what will happen and bid him tell Eappa to look up his calendar. By this means it was revealed that it was the feast of St Oswald, king of the Northumbrians, which was henceforth observed there, in accordance with the saints' instruction. After mass the sick boy received communion, and his death then proved the truth of his dream.[23] It is a curiously laboured story, and implicit in it is the notion that the calendar of saints in use was not in tune with actual local observance.

The story reflects the same obsessions on Acca's part with St Oswald and with the plague that Bede had recorded in Book III. There, Acca is cited as talking about miracles of St Oswald encountered when he, Acca, accompanied Bishop Wilfrid abroad and stayed with Willibrord among the Frisians in 704. And at that point, Bede inserted, in direct speech, one of the miracle-stories that Acca had told him from his own earlier pilgrim-life in Ireland, namely how he had induced the recovery of a plague-stricken Irishman by means of a fragment from the wood on which St Oswald's head had been stuck.[24] In the manuscripts that have it this new chapter

---

22   This comes across as emphatic, more so at least than Bede's saying that Acca 'is used to telling' ('solet referre', *HE* III.13) about his time with Wilfrid or Bede's teacher Trumberht 'used to tell me' ('referre solebat', *HE* IV.3); but Bede uses *saepius* quite lightly when referring to his own recurrent subjects, the Irish and Easter ('cuius saepius mentionem fecimus', *HE* III.3), St Æthelthryth ('cuius saepius mentionem fecimus', *HE* IV.17), and Ecgberht ('cuius superius memoriam saepius fecimus', *HE* V.22).

23   The story is discussed by Jesse Keskiaho with reference to Eappa's questioning the boy about the appearance of the saints and Bede's asserting the truth of the vision by reason of its fufilment, *Dreams and Visions in the Early Middle Ages. The reception and use of patristic ideas, 400–900*, 43–44.

24   Bede, *Historia ecclesiastica*, III.13. This must have happened during the period of pestilence *c.* 684–87, when Acca was young. Wilfrid was in Sussex then, but it is not apparent that Acca was already with him. The Sussex story came to Acca from trustworthy brethren, perhaps long after the event. We do not know when or where Acca became Wilfrid's priest. At *Historia ecclesiastica*, V.20 Bede says only that he started at York as a child in the household of Bishop Bosa (678–704/6) and thereafter (*deinde*) joined Wilfrid. His Irish sojourn is usually overlooked.

Table 6. Breakdown of *Historia Ecclesiastica*, IV. 13–15.

Book IV	CKO	Book IV	LMB	1896	1969	2010
XIII	*Vt Vilfrid episcopus prouinciam Australium Saxonum ad Christum conuerterit quae tamen illo abeunte propter aceruam hostium obpressionem proprium episcopum habere nequiuerit*	XIII	*Vt Vilfrid episcopus prouinciam Australium Saxonum ad Christum conuerterit*	13	13	13
13. 1	Pulsus autem ab episcopatu	13	Pulsus autem ab episcopatu			13. 1
13. 2	Erat autem ibi monachus	13	Erat autem ibi monachus			13. 2
13. 3	Euangelizans autem genti	13	Euangelizans autem genti			13. 3
13. 4	Quo tempore rex Aedliwalch	13	Quo tempore rex Aedliwalch			13. 4
			no chapter heading, XIIII against text	[14]	14	14
		14	In quo tunc monasterio			14. 1
		14	Eodem ferme tempore			14. 2
		14	Erat tunc temporis			14. 3
		14	Hac etenim die idem rex			14. 4
		14	Quae cum omnia			14. 5
		14	Quibus ita gestis			14. 6
13. 5	* Interea superueniens	14	Interea superueniens	[15]	15	14. 7
XIIII	*Vt Vecta insula christianos incolas susceperit, cuius regii duo pueri statim post acceptum baptisma sint interemti*	XIIII	*Vt Vecta insula christianos incolas susceperit, cuius regii duo pueri statim post acceptum baptisma sint interemti*	14 [16]	16 [14]	
14. 1	Postquam ergo Caedualla	14	Postquam ergo Caedualla			14. 8
14. 2	Vbi silentio praetereundum	14	Vbi silentio praetereundum			14. 9
14. 3	Sita est autem haec insula	14	Sita est autem haec insula			14. 10
XV	*De synodo facta in campo Haetfelda praesidente archiepiscopo Theodoro*	XV	*De synodo facta in campo Haetfelda praesidente archiepiscopo Theodoro*	15 [17]	17 [15]	15

* At the words *Interea superueniens* C has a later marginal note, 'Hic deest folium [[...]]'.

Roman numerals are used for chapters in the manuscripts, arabic for editorial numbering. Italics are used for chapter-headings; words in roman type identify the beginning of paragraphs. The text in CKO relates directly to its chapter headings. In LMB the number XIIII was added with the additional text; no corresponding addition was made to the chapter headings, but the heading to XIII was shortened to reflect the fact that its last section had now been cut off. Plummer aimed to retain the numbering of CKO while indicating that a new chapter 14 had been inserted; he inserted chapter headings for the added chapter 14 and the detached section, here 15, without early manuscript authority and therefore in brackets. Mynors, adhering to LMB, gave priority to their numbering of 14 but also introduced 15 for the section cut off from 13. Lapidge, who like Plummer repeated chapter headings at the start of each chapter, inserted the heading for 14 at the start of the added chapter, though it only becomes relevant at his 14. 8; this is clearly contrary to Bede's practice and intention. The number XIIII against the added chapter in the manuscripts was carried over from the unaltered chapter headings.

in Book IV has the number 14, and the remarks about how the South Saxons were left without a bishop of their own became detached from Chapter 13.[25] The heading of the chapter had said:

Vt Vilfrid episcopus prouinciam Australium Saxonum ad Christum conuerterit quae tamen illo abeunte propter aceruam hostium obpressionem proprium episcopum habere nequiuerit.

How Bishop Wilfrid converted the kingdom of the South Saxons to Christ, which, however, when Wilfrid left, was not able to have its own bishop on account of the cruel oppression by its enemies.

In the parent of the M- or μ-text of the *Historia*, that heading was reduced to the first statement without the relative clause.[26] Needed for consistency between chapter and heading, this had the effect also of removing what might have been read as an implicit criticism of the bishop who left his flock. No new heading was inserted to advertise the miracle of St Oswald, and the existing heading for Chapter 14 was not amended. Editors have recorded the words as added to the heading in the κ-text rather than deleted from the μ-text. Yet Mynors explicitly acknowledged the chapter as added, 'The addition in *m* of IV 14, which is clearly authentic, and would never have been removed by a reviser, stamps M as the later form'.[27] His policy was to adopt it as Bede's final text. Michael Lapidge makes a good case that the parent of the κ-text was improved in minor ways at Canterbury and that these few improvements were not authorial.[28] In line with a tenth-century marginal note in C, 'Hic deest folium [[...]]', he explained the absence of the episode as resulting from the accidental loss of a leaf. The fact of editorial changes in the κ-text does not mean that the μ-text at Jarrow necessarily remained untouched, and I disagree with his rejecting the view that this long passage was an addition made there. The insertion of an extra chapter in μ is proved by the disjunction between text and chapter-headings: those in the κ-text relate to the actual text, but in the μ-text the only provision made for the additional text intruded as IV 14 was to simplify the heading of Chapter 13. Lapidge's explanation for the supposed accidental loss of the story from κ is implausible: while a single lost folio would easily explain a lacuna of eighty-five lines of prose, the improbability that such an accident should happen so early in the tradition (before L and M were made) and yet remain unnoticed during the period of publication, that it should cause no disruption to syntax, should comprise a complete story, should coincide with what soon became a chapter-break, and should go against the relevance of the *capitula* is all too great to be plausible, nor did accidental loss cause the editing of the chapter-heading in the κ-text. The insertion can be dated. Two astronomical notes relating to events on 14 August 733 and 31 January 734 stand at the very end of the

---

25   Later manuscripts would make this detached paragraph into a self-standing Chapter 15.
26   Plummer, Plummer, p. 230 n. 1; Colgrave and Mynors, p. 324.
27   Comment by Plummer, p. xciv n. 1 and p. xcvi (whose instinct was sound even if his conclusion was not); Mynors, p. xli.
28   Lapidge, 'Author's variants in the textual transmission of Bede's *Historia ecclesiastica*'.

text in M itself; in κ they were added to the annalistic summary in *HE* V 24. While their positioning may be a perceived improvement at Canterbury, the sub-archetype κ cannot have lacked them and so was not written before 31 January 734. The added chapter was intruded after that date. Bede died on 26 May 735. The addition of seven hundred words is a far cry from authorial tinkering to improve a word here or there. Bede must have felt very strong reason for this substantive but botched alteration, the consequence of which is the messy chapter-divisions in our editions and the mismatch between text and headings.

These two episodes, in Book III and in the added chapter in Book IV, cite Acca before he has been properly introduced, and, in Wilfrid's long obituary, he appears again in the bishop's company as they return from Rome in 705. Wilfrid fell sick at Meaux, near Paris, and called for his priest Acca; Bede followed Stephen's *Vita* at this point.[29] After Wilfrid's death, Acca, Wilfrid's priest, was chosen to succeed him as bishop of Hexham, in which see he remained in 731, the formal end-date of Bede's *Historia*.[30] He was a friend of Bede and a long-term encourager of his writing, as we know from the prefatory letters to five of his biblical commentaries over a period of years.[31] Paul Hilliard has characterized Acca as a careful reader of Bede's writings, a co-worker, even a taskmaster.[32] The Moore manuscript of the *Historia ecclesiastica*, and no other copy, has annal-entries for the years 731 and 732, the first of which says that King Ceolwulf was captured and tonsured, and afterwards restored as king, while Bishop Acca was expelled from his see in 731.[33] The reference to the king's troubles appears also, in vaguer terms, in Bede's account of the state of the country when he ended his history.[34] Acca's expulsion is mentioned nowhere else, and its duration is uncertain. It invites one to ask whether Acca was at Jarrow between 731 and as late as 734, when Bede retouched his great work.[35] We might even imagine that he had read it and pressed the suggestion to insert his own story of the apostolic visitation on St Oswald's day in Sussex. Its effect is to break the trend of Bede's narrative, which

---

29   Bede, *Historia ecclesiastica*, V.19. Plummer showed that Bede derived this episode from Stephen's *Vita S. Wilfrithi episcopi*, c. 56 (Colgrave, 120–22), with which there is some direct verbal similarity.

30   Bede, *Historia ecclesiastica*, V.20, 23. Acca is described by Clare Stancliffe as 'the most influential Wilfridian after Wilfrid's death' ('Disputed episcopacy: Bede, Acca, and the relationship between Stephen's Life of St Wilfrid and the early prose Lives of St Cuthbert', p. 11).

31   The earliest dedication to Acca is likely to be the commentary on Luke (709 × 716), the last that on Ezra and Nehemiah (725 × publication of *Historia ecclesiastica*). The preface to the commentary on Genesis is difficult to date.

32   Bede's relationship with Acca is at the core of the discussion by Hilliard, 'Acca of Hexham through the eyes of the Venerable Bede', especially pp. 455–56, 459–60.

33   Plummer, p. 361; Colgrave and Mynors, p. 572.

34   Bede, *Historia ecclesiastica*, V.23.

35   The argument made here certainly indicates continuing close contact between Acca and Bede, and Acca's withdrawal to Jarrow may be supported by a further argument. Michael Lapidge has made the case that Acca wrote the Latin original underlying the Old English Martyrology, 'Acca of Hexham and the origin of the Old English Martyrology', pp. 29–78. The work draws on Bede's *Historia*, and, if the argument is correct, it is even possible that Acca worked on it at Jarrow after his expulsion from Hexham. Hilliard, 'Acca of Hexham through the eyes of the Venerable Bede', pp. 456–57, without these arguments, pictured Bede as 'deprived of his co-worker Acca since 731'.

was to say that Wilfrid had converted the South Saxons and then abandoned them to their fate under Ceadwalla. Even the shortening of the chapter-heading, necessitated by the splitting of the original chapter, served to remove Wilfrid's leaving his flock from the *capitulatio*. In the revised text of our editions, a dull miracle about an unnamed boy in an unnamed monastery now separates Wilfrid's mission to the South Saxons under King Æthelwalh from Æthelwalh's killing at the hands of Ceadwalla's men who ravaged the kingdom. It does not amount to the suppression of truth, but it is a sign that the tone of Bede's writing about Wilfrid was subject to scrutiny.

Acca had for many years been close to Wilfrid, and alongside Abbot Tatberht of Ripon he was named by Stephen as his master, urging him to write an account of Wilfrid's long life.[36] What the *Vita* says about Wilfrid's relationship with Ceadwalla reveals less about what happened than Bede does, but Stephen gives it a positive colour.[37] Ceadwalla, an exile of high lineage, emerged from the wilderness of the South Downs and the Weald (*e desertis Ciltine et Ondred*) and asked Wilfrid to teach him and help him, promising with a vow (*uouens uoto*) to be an obedient son.[38] The bishop helped him to overcome his enemies and win his kingdom. Now reigning over all the West Saxons, he called Wilfrid from his missionary work in Sussex (*gentilem populum in Suthsexum bene ad Deum conuertentem*) and made him 'his counsellor in all his realm'. Wilfrid became to Stephen's Ceadwalla as Joseph was to Pharaoh.[39] Ceadwalla kept the kingdom safe, 'whether victorious by the edge of the sword or making peace by agreement' (*aut acie gladii uictor aut foedere indultor pacis*). Just one phrase about Ceadwalla's coming to power reflects his methods, 'after killing and subduing his enemies' (*occisis et superatis inimicis eius*), and even that was expunged from one of the two manuscripts in which the *Vita* is preserved.[40] Stephen's Ceadwalla has shed his paganism and become well-behaved company for the bishop, albeit still with a sharp sword. The sequence of events, however, is different from Bede's main narrative. Stephen makes Wilfrid go from his ministry in Sussex directly into Ceadwalla's service, which Bede echoes in his obituary of Wilfrid (*HE* v. 19). Where he follows Daniel, however, Bede has Wilfrid 'recalled' from Sussex to Northumbria before his happening to turn up at Ceadwalla's side a year later.

We are distinctly short of a reliable chronological framework here. The Anglo-Saxon Chronicle only adds confusion. For this period it was written two centuries later,

---

36 Stephen, *Vita S. Wilfrithi episcopi*, Praefatio.

37 Stephen, *Vita S. Wilfrithi episcopi*, c. 42.

38 'Ondred' is no doubt the Weald of Kent and Sussex, forested and sparsely populated, into which the deposed West Saxon Sigeberht later fled, *Andred* in *ASC* (AE), 755, 892. 'Ciltine', rendered Chiltern by Colgrave (and often repeated), is better identified through two eighth-century charters, S 1612, S 106; Gelling, *Early Charters of the Thames Valley*, p. 99, suggests that the district-name *Ciltinne* is preserved in East and West Chiltington, more than twenty-five miles apart in the South Downs.

39 Stephen may hint here at Ceadwalla's paganism, as Sarah Foot points out to me, since Joseph worshipped the God of Israel, but Pharaoh worshipped the idols of Egypt. Joseph served as a very acceptable precedent.

40 These words appear in Salisbury Cathedral, MS 223 (Fell 3) (s. xii¹, Salisbury), but not in the slightly older northern witness to the text, BL MS Cotton Vespasian D. vi part 2 (s. xiᵉˣ, York or at least Yorkshire).

and Bede was one of its sources. Under 685 it has the phrase, *Her Ceadwalla ongan æfter rice winnan*, 'in this year Ceadwalla began to contend for the kingdom'. It adds reference to campaigns involving him and his brother Múl in Kent and, under 686, in the Isle of Wight. Ceadwalla's conquest of the island is often referred to 686 on this unreliable evidence. And then, under 688, it says that Ceadwalla went to Rome and received baptism from the pope, dying seven days later. The Chronicle has no doubt got this from Bede, whose annalistic summary (*HE* V.24) dates the king's departure to 688. His detailed text says that he went in the third year of Aldfrith's reign and died in 689 (*HE* v. 7). What Bede said was a reign of two years is thus extended by the Chronicle to three years with vague wording about when Ceadwalla began to win his kingdom.

Ceadwalla's one surviving charter that can be received as contemporary evidence adds another perspective. This 160-word act bears witness to the gift by 'Ceadwal dispensante Domino rex Saxonum' ('by God's providence king of the Saxons'), for the health of his soul, of sixty hides to establish a *monasterium* at Farnham in Surrey.[41] In passing we note that his Roman epitaph also names him 'Ceadual qui et Petrus rex Saxonum' ('Ceadwal, also called Peter, king of the Saxons'). The charter is dated to the first indiction, with the year of the incarnation also stated, 688, and the place at which the giving was done is named *Besingahearh* 'the sanctuary of the Besingas', a group whose name is preserved in the north-east Hampshire places of Old Basing and Basingstoke. The fact that the land given is in Surrey enlarges our sense of how far Ceadwalla's rule extended.[42] The king subscribed first and then, according to precedence, bishops, abbots, priests, and laymen. The bishops are Wilfrid, Eorconwald, and Hædde. Hædde was bishop of the West Saxons with his see in Winchester, Ceadwalla's own bishop, who took responsibility also for those Christians under his rule in Sussex and the Isle of Wight. With precedence over Hædde was Eorconwald, bishop of London and Essex, evidence that Ceadwalla's power embraced the only urban centre in the whole island. And with precedence above both was Bishop Wilfrid, the king's high counsellor. The charter bears out what Stephen has said. And below the bishops the leading abbot of the West Saxon kingdom attests, Aldhelm, abbot of Malmesbury, whose letter to Heahfrith shows that he knew something of heathen worship.[43] If the venue were still a pagan *hearg*, more than likely while Ceadwalla ruled, we must imagine these prelates as attending a public ceremony at, if not actually in, a heathen sanctuary, no doubt at the king's bidding.[44]

---

41 S 235, from the archive of the Old Minster at Winchester; translated by Whitelock, *English Historical Documents*, pp. 484–85 (no. 58).

42 Blair, *Early Medieval Surrey*, p. 8, points out that King Ine, Ceadwalla's successor, had authority as far east in Surrey as Bermondsey, just across the Thames from London, citing in evidence a privilege of Pope Constantine, 708 × 715 (JE 2148; Birch 133).

43 Aldhelm, *Epistola ad Heahfridum*, § 1, ed. by Ehwald, pp. 486–94; transl. Herren, pp. 160–64: 'ubi pridem eiusdem nefandae natricis ermula ceruulusque cruda fanis colebantur stoliditate in profanis' ('where once the crude pillars of the same foul snake and the stag were worshipped with coarse stupidity in profane shrines').

44 Blair, *Church in Anglo-Saxon Society*, p. 57 n. 181.

If the *hearg* were at Old Basing in Hampshire, the king would have commanded Bishop Eorconwald into his territory.[45] Excavation has revealed the possible site.[46] A second witness list shows the same bishops together. It is attached to two different documents, neither entirely secure as contemporary evidence. The Barking archive preserved as an incomplete single-sheet charter the gift by an East Saxon named *Hodilred* (Œthilred) of many hides of land to the abbess *Hedilburg* (Æthelburh); a hand thought to date from the late eighth century added the subscriptions of the East Saxon King Sæbbi, 'a man much devoted to God' (*HE* IV.11), and his two royal heirs Sigeheard and Suæbred, and of the three bishops, Eorconberht, Wilfrid, and Hædde.[47] Two other clergy appear to attest both acts.[48] An East Saxon venue, such as London, seems plausible though none is named; Ceadwalla did not attest, but the presence of his bishops Wilfrid and Hædde may mean that he was just off stage. The Barking charter is dated only to the month of March. The same witness list is attached to another problematic charter from Barking, so that one must suspect dependence.[49] Such a combination of names, closely datable, can hardly have been invented in the eighth century.

A few documents are enough to show that Ceadwalla's *imperium* was by no means confined to his own lands as king of the Gewisse and his conquered lands in Sussex and the Isle of Wight but reached across Surrey to London. In what Barbara Yorke has called 'his brief but spectacular period of overlordship', he had evidently seen off Mercian superiority.[50] For his wars in Kent we have the statement of the Anglo-Saxon Chronicle, apparently corroborated by a charter of King Suæbhard, which mentions his obtaining the kingdom of Kent 'a rege Mulo', named in the Chronicle

---

45 The place-name Basing appears denuded of any second element: perhaps *-hearg* was simply dropped after conversion.

46 John Blair, *Building Anglo-Saxon England*, p. 126, draws attention to the impressive pagan-period complex partially excavated at Cowdery's Down (now site of the Lynchpit housing development), on the hillside across the river Loddon from Basing minster (Millett and James, 'Excavations at Cowdery's Down, Basingstoke, 1978–81', pp. 151–279). He suggests that the *hearg* itself was defined by the old Roman enclosure juxtaposed to the Anglo-Saxon halls, whose layout reflects ceremonial practice.

47 S 1171, which survives as an original through the archive of Barking abbey; Whitelock, *English Historical Documents*, 486–88 (no. 60). The word-spacing in the uncial script was deemed incompatible with a contemporary date by Lowe, who declared it a single-sheet copy of the second half of the eighth century, appearing to introduce a new category into diplomatic practice. Chaplais, 'Some early Anglo-Saxon diplomas on single sheets: originals or copies?', pp. 327–32), disagreed but thought the charter as first written was left incomplete with the bounds and witnesses in a second hand at a later stage. He also observed that the number of hides had been altered at some time from LXXV to XL. Susan Kelly, to whom I am grateful for advice, raises the possibility that the transaction is earlier than appears in her forthcoming edition of the Barking charters. Its widely accepted dating has depended on the added witness list.

48 Guda *presbiter* is named in both; Hugon *abbas* in S 235 may be same as Hacona *presbiter et abbas* in S 1171 (copied as Hagona in S 1246).

49 S 1246, also from the Barking archive, was perceived as false by Whitelock, *Some Anglo-Saxon Bishops of London*, pp. 7–8, who thought it drew the names of its witnesses from the two seventh-century documents.

50 Yorke, *Kings and Kingdoms*, p. 48.

as Ceadwalla's brother.[51] In Bede's pages he came to power as *rex Geuissorum* but died as *rex Saxonum*.[52] His bishops Wilfrid and Hædde attested alongside Eorconwald in his own charter and alongside King Sæbbi in that for Barking. It may be added that after 688, King Ine would still refer to both Hædde and Eorconwald as 'my' bishops.[53]

Without sound dates, all this information leaves us unable to construct a sequential narrative.[54] Did Wilfrid play any part in Ceadwalla's rise to power? That appears to be Stephen's position but not Bede's. To answer the question, we need to know both when Wilfrid was recalled to Northumbria and when Ceadwalla became king. There has been a temptation to follow Bede, who says that for five years, 'usque ad mortem Ecgfridi regis' ('until the death of King Ecgfrith') (*HE* IV.13), Wilfrid laboured as bishop of the South Saxons. Now Ecgfrith was slain on 20 May 685. Ceadwalla's reign of just two years, a figure given twice by Bede, may be counted back from 688 to 686, and a gap opens up. This gap becomes longer if we mistrust Bede's annalistic summary and date Ceadwalla's departure just a few weeks before his death in April 689. His two-year reign fell mainly in 687 and 688.

Wilfrid's recall is itself tied in with the sequence of events in Northumbria, where we have too much information easily to set in order when few of our dates are precise. In all this we must be chary of integrating dates from different sources unless they are chronologically secure. It would be safer to establish the sequence of events as understood by Bede.

Bede has given us two relevant indicators. Wilfrid, he says, was recalled to Northumbria in the second year of King Aldfrith's reign (*HE* V.19), a date received from Stephen's *Vita* (c. 44). And Ceadwalla gave up his sceptre in the third year of King Aldfrith's reign (*HE* V.7). We know too that Ceolfrith was chosen abbot of Jarrow in the third year of the reign on 12 May in the first indiction, that is 688.[55] Bede had a clear sense of Aldfrith's regnal years. He reports that he reigned nineteen years (*HE* V.1) and died in 705 before completing the twentieth year of his reign (*HE* V.18). The northern DE-text of the Anglo-Saxon Chronicle adds precision: he died on 14 December 705 at Driffield, a royal estate of no small interest.[56] As Kenneth Harrison pointed out, this means that he was not yet king on that date in 685 but succeeded no later than 12 May 686.[57] For the purpose of argument, let us suppose he was recognized as king on the first day of 686. This means that Wilfrid did not

51 S 10; Kelly, *Charters of St Augustine's Abbey, Canterbury*, pp. 139–41 (no. 40). The text carries a date 1 March 689 in the king's second year, compatible with the killing of Múl in 687; there are difficulties over its composite character, but this information is too obscure to be interpolated. Kelly, pp. 143–44, discusses its testimony regarding Múl.

52 Yorke, 'The Jutes of Hampshire and Wight', p. 93.

53 *Laws of Ine*, Prologue, promulgated no later than 694; ed. by Liebermann, vol. i, p. 88; Whitelock, *English Historical Documents*, p. 399 (no. 32).

54 Much has been written in an effort to set dates on Wilfrid's mobile career. A recent point of reference is Cubitt, 'St Wilfrid: a man for his times', pp. 311-47 (chronology at pp. 342–47).

55 *Vita Ceolfridi abbatis*, c. 17, ed. by Plummer, p. 394.

56 [A. T. Thacker], VCH *East Riding of Yorkshire*, ix. 10–12; Yorke, *Rex doctissimus: Bede and King Aldfrith of Northumbria*, p. 16.

57 Harrison, 'The reign of King Ecgfrith', pp. 79–84; Yorke, *Rex doctissimus*, pp. 20–23.

return to Northumbria until 687. Up to five years back, he did not begin his ministry in Sussex before some time in 682.

Bishop Cuthbert in Northumbria died on 20 March 687. Bede does not make clear whether Wilfrid had already returned or arrived soon after: we do not know whether King Aldfrith called him to take Cuthbert's place, or, if he did, whether he did so following Cuthbert's withdrawal to the Inner Farne, straight after Christmas 686, or only following his death three months later. What Bede says is that, after Cuthbert was buried at Lindisfarne, Wilfrid administered (*seruabat*) the bishopric in that church during one year — not more than twelve months — until a successor was consecrated. Precisely that one year, from the saint's burial to Eadberht's consecration, was described in Bede's verse and prose Lives of St Cuthbert as a time of stormy troubles for the community, when some monks chose to leave the fold. Alan Thacker has joined these remarks with the one sentence in Bede's later *Historia* that points to Wilfrid as the cause, and drawn the inference, 'Bede was evidently determined that Wilfrid's role should be traceable, even if it was not made explicit'.[58] In other words Bede meant his reader to compare his two works and draw conclusions. Wilfrid's relations with this monastery began in his youth — Bede follows Stephen in writing about this — but they must have been broken long ago, when Wilfrid caused the community to split in 664, so that the Irish withdrew from the Northumbrian church. To judge from the verse Life, Bede depicted Cuthbert as recommending monks to leave rather than to stay and put up with Wilfrid's plans for Lindisfarne.

It is regrettable that we do not know exactly when Eadberht was consecrated, presumably in the early part of 688, and Wilfrid was cast out again. The second visit to King Aldfrith by the renowned Irish churchman, Adomnán, abbot of Iona, is best dated to the period around Easter 688, a year when the feast fell on 29 March by Roman reckoning and three weeks later by Irish reckoning.[59] We can guess that Adomnán would not have come at that time, if Wilfrid were still in authority at Lindisfarne. It would be convenient for our chronology, indeed, if Wilfrid had gone south to join Ceadwalla by March 688, witnessing Hodilred's charter for Barking: no other year fits so well. On this stage of his career both Stephen and Bede shed very little if any light. Stephen has stirred up the chronological sequence. He passed directly from describing Wilfrid's ministry in Sussex (c. 41) to his counselling Ceadwalla (c. 42).

---

58 Bede, *Vita metrica S. Cuthberti*, cc. 34 (prophecy), 37 (event) (ed. by Jaager, pp. 115, 119-20); id. *Vita S. Cuthberti*, c. 40 (Colgrave, *Two Lives*, p. 286 n. 357); Thacker, 'Shaping the saint: rewriting tradition in the early Lives of St Cuthbert' (pp. 410–11, 416–18, 419–20, quotation at p. 418).

59 Bede, *Historia ecclesiastica*, V.15, mentions that, during a visit to King Aldfrith, Adomnán saw the rites of the church canonically observed in a context that suggests he referred to the canonical Easter. The year 688 was the penultimate year of the 84-year cycle 606-89, and the date of Easter by Irish reckoning may be read off from the table in McCarthy and Ó Cróinín, 'The lost Irish 84-year Easter table rediscovered', pp. 227-42. Adomnán himself, *Vita S. Columbae*, ii. 46, says, 'on my first visit after Ecgfrith's battle and on my second two years later, though I walked in the midst of this danger of plague, the Lord delivered me'. A visit in the spring of 686 might well coincide with Aldfrith's accession, and the height of the plague, which carried off Abbot Eosterwine of Wearmouth on 7 March (*Vita Ceolfridi abbatis*, c. 13; Bede, *Historia abbatum*, c. 8). The second visit would fall in 688. He avoided a visit while Wilfrid was bishop at Lindisfarne during 687.

Next, however, he reports a meeting in London, at which Archbishop Theodore proposed, in the presence of Bishop Eorconwald, that Wilfrid should succeed him at Canterbury when the time came (c. 43). Wilfrid most properly thought such a decision should come from a synod, and Theodore sent letters to King Aldfrith, to Abbess Ælfflæd at Whitby, and to Wilfrid's patron in Mercia, King Æthelred, after which Wilfrid was restored to his property in Æthelred's kingdom. There follows a chapter on his reconciliation with Aldfrith (c. 44), 'in the second year of his reign' (the only interpretable date here), after which Wilfrid remained secure in his churches at Ripon and York for five years. Then there is the falling out with Aldfrith and the start of an eleven-year exile in Mercia (c. 45). Little of this is rooted in dates, but Stephen wants us to think that Wilfrid lived quietly in Northumbria for five years from 687 to 691.

On this whole period Bede appears to be completely silent, though in reality he was not. In his case too, the elusive sequence of the narrative was the means to discretion.

Only the charters speak to us with a year-date. In the first indiction, 688, Wilfrid is named in a charter by which the West Saxon king gave land in Surrey.[60] Here he attested as a superior bishop with precedence over the diocesan bishops Eorconwald and Hædde. He was fulfilling Stephen's role for him as high counsellor to King Ceadwalla. The fact that the venue was a place of heathen worship highlights the level of accommodation between the bishops and the king at this time.

With this in mind, we can return to what Bede says. At the end of *Historia ecclesiastica*, IV.13 he starts with Ceadwalla's defeating and killing Wilfrid's patron Æthelwalh and his ravaging of Sussex, while Wilfrid was still at Selsey. The South Saxon ealdormen took up arms to defend the kingdom and drove him off. In time Ceadwalla gained control of his own kingdom, the Gewisse, perhaps before the end of 686. He returned to Sussex, killed Ealdorman Berhthun, and began to oppress the kingdom. At just this point it was convenient for Wilfrid to go north early in 687 for what proved to be barely a year. Our sources say that he was called, not that he fled. None the less, the church he deserted in Sussex remained with no bishop of its own for decades, coming instead under the oversight of the bishop of the Gewisse. Going into Chapter 14, Bede allows a little overlap in his indicators of time. Already Ceadwalla, 'cum esset rex Gewissorum' ('when he was king of the Gewisse'), had taken over Sussex. Now Chapter 14 begins, 'Postquam ergo Caedualla regno potitus est Geuissorum' ('After Ceadwalla had possessed himself of the kingdom of the Gewisse'). At this point in Bede's account, he seized the Isle of Wight and massacred the inhabitants. By chance, Wilfrid had turned up from his own people. Without signalling the bishop's movements, Bede and Stephen both knew that Wilfrid had gone north in the second year of Aldfrith's reign and now, in what is surely the third year of Aldfrith's reign, he is back in the south of England, this time close enough to King Ceadwalla to be favoured with three hundred hides of land. If he had got out of Sussex when things became really uncomfortable, why is he back in Wessex, and

---

60   Gelling, *Thames Valley*, p. 150, plays with fire: 'It bears an incorrect incarnation date, 688, incompatible with the signature of Bishop Wilfrid. The indiction points to 687'. It does not.

in Ceadwalla's camp, a year later? Only Stephen tries to explain that and he does so, not only by eliding the sequence of events but also by leaving out all the sort of thing that Bede has told us about Ceadwalla. Wilfrid may have been drawn to Ceadwalla, because, within the space of a year, he had made himself the dominant king in southern England. Ceadwalla, perhaps seeing himself as moving from war to politics, from battle to treaty, wanted a grand representative to speak for him to Christian kings and their bishops. What Bishop Hædde thought of this is nowhere disclosed, but we shall suppose that some of what he knew passed to his successor Daniel. Yet we need not accuse Wilfrid of encroaching on his episcopal authority among the West Saxons and those under their power. Wilfrid was no more than a special adviser to the king, albeit in episcopal orders and taking precedence as such.

King Ceadwalla's brand of politics, however, required him to be *uictor* as well as *indultor pacis*. And the Wihtware were not doing well. Wight was perhaps strategically important to holding Sussex and Hampshire together. To weaken Wessex a Mercian king had long ago handed the Isle of Wight over to a South Saxon king, whom Ceadwalla had defeated and killed maybe two or three years before. What dealings he had had with the island in the meantime we are not told. The young King Arwald, whose brothers were still children, may have only recently inherited the throne. Now Ceadwalla's death-dealing attack in, as I should argue, 688, is the starkest instance of genocide in our sources.[61] The islanders were not Saxons but Jutes.[62] Bede presents them as the last stubborn outpost of paganism, 'eatenus erat tota [insula] idolatriae dedita' ('till then [the island] was entirely given over to idolatry'). That was not why Ceadwalla massacred them, and it is a fig-leaf to say that the pagan king already vowed (*ut ferunt*) to give a share of his conquest to the bishop. Wilfrid accepted his reward. Bede then tells the affecting story of how Abbot Cyneberht sought out the wounded Ceadwalla and secured his permission to baptize King Arwald's brothers, last heirs of the Jutish elite, before their execution. And at this point Bede reminds us that the island, like Sussex, came under West Saxon oppression, so that they had no bishop of their own, even as he wrote, when they were still looked after by the West Saxon bishop Daniel.

Daniel had surely known his predecessor Bishop Hædde, who died in 705, and he may well have channelled what Hædde told him. He may have had his own memories of life under Ceadwalla.[63] He appears to have instilled in Bede the idea that these territories should have had bishops of their own and not come under his, alien, supervision. He appears to have thought that Bishop Wilfrid abandoned his flock. Bede could no doubt have contributed a northern perspective here, but he chose not to explain Wilfrid's return to Bernicia in 687.

---

61 Fraser, 'Early Medieval Europe. The case of Britain and Ireland', p. 269. And p. 271: 'Bede's account of the genocide visited on the denizens of the Isle of Wight conveniently weds the purgation of elites with extermination'. He perhaps overstates the killing of the boys as 'its centrepiece'.

62 Bede, *Historia ecclesiastica*, I.15. At IV.14, Bede refers only to the Jutes in southern Hampshire, already under West Saxon control.

63 Consecrated bishop in 705, Daniel had by then no doubt reached the canonical age of thirty. He was therefore aged thirteen upwards at the time of the massacre of the Wihtware.

Table 7. Sequence of Events.

682?	Wilfrid is received in Sussex by King Aethelwalh and given land at Selsey, the beginning of nearly five years in Sussex
20 May 685	King Ecgrith's death during his invasion of Pictland; more than six months follow before a new king is installed
685?	Ceadwalla, not yet king of the Gewisse, attacks Sussex and kills King Aethelwalh. Berhthun and Andhun take over the kingdom
14 Dec 685	*terminus a quo* for King Aldfrith's accession, counting backwards twenty years before his death
12 May 686	*terminus ad quem* for King Aldfrith's succession, counting backwards from Ceolfrith's election as abbot of Jarrow, 12 May 688, in his third year
late 686	Ceadwalla becomes king of the Gewisse
25 Dec 686	After Christmas 686, Bishop Cuthbert retires from Lindisfarne and retreats to Farne Island
early 687	Wilfrid, recalled to Northumbria in the second year of King Aldfrith, leaves Sussex and travels north, a distance of 400 miles; allowing time for the summons to reach him and for him to travel north, perhaps three or four month elapse
20 Mar 687	Bishop Cuthbert's death on Farne Island
	Ceadwalla invades Sussex and kills Berhthun, beginning his rise to power
remainder of 687	Wilfrid at Lindisfarne as caretaker for nearly one year until a new bishop is installed
?Feb 688	Eadberht chosen and consecrated bishop in Lindisfarne; Wilfrid leaves Northumbria and returns to southern England
Mar 688	Wilfrid in London and attests the Barking charter with Bishop Eorcenwald and Bishop Hædde, perhaps at Easter 688, perhaps in Ceadwalla's invisible presence
29 Mar 688	Adomnán of Iona observes Easter in Northumbria, at a time when Wilfrid was in the south
spring 688	Wilfrid arrives in Wessex in the third year of King Aldfrith
?May 688	King Ceadwalla gives land to found Farnham minster in Surrey in a ceremony held at *Besingahearh* in the presence of the three bishops, Wilfrid, Eorcenwald, and Hædde, perhaps on an important date in his heathen ritual calendar
autumn 688	King Ceadwalla invades the Isle of Wight and massacres the Wihtware
late 688	Abbot Cyneberht intervenes with the wounded Ceadwalla to baptise the young brothers of King Arwald
very late 688	King Ceadwalla is persuaded to leave his kingdom to travel to Rome
10 April 689	Ceadwalla is baptised in Rome and died ten days later

There may have been talk of much worse.

If we may speak of charges against Wilfrid, they divide between his actions in Sussex and his conduct in Wessex as Ceadwalla's counsellor. Reading the two main passages from Bede, set out above, there is nothing to link Wilfrid with Ceadwalla's killing of Æthelwalh. The worst charge here would be that conditions in Sussex became frighteningly hostile and he thought it safer to return to Northumbria. The truth may be entirely innocent, that he was actually recalled by King Aldfrith. Anyone reading these paragraphs who remembered what Stephen had written, twenty years earlier, could draw a far worse inference. If Wilfrid helped Ceadwalla to his throne, he was already aligned with the pagan when his Christian patron Æthelwalh was killed and his Christian flock oppressed. This charge has been recognized by historians for more than a century. William Bright asked an awkward question: 'One cannot but wonder whether the apostle of Sussex was passive in such a crisis or whether his influence was used in vain'.[64] D. H. Farmer, trusting Stephen too far, wrote:[65]

> Wilfrid befriended an exiled Wessex prince, Cædwalla, and helped him regain his throne in 686. In the course of the fighting, Æthelwalh, Wilfrid's former patron, was killed. At this distance we do not know why Wilfrid apparently abandoned his former friend nor if his role in the whole affair was as important as Eddius [Stephen] made it.

Henry Mayr-Harting described the charge as one of 'the blackest treachery towards his trusting South Saxon patron'.[66] We are not the first to compare our sources. Bishop Acca knew what was written in Stephen's *Vita* — he was one of its patrons — and he may have known more behind it. In his mind, anyone knowing Stephen's version and reading Bede's chapters could well infer that Wilfrid helped Ceadwalla to destroy Æthelwalh, a truly appalling charge.[67] This is the reason why Acca persuaded Bede to interpolate a harmless but distracting chapter into his account of Wilfrid in Sussex. I am more inclined to think that the charge was unreal, arising only because Stephen had distorted the sequence of events in hope of boosting his subject — and without anticipating that someone closer to the events would gainsay him. In Bishop Daniel's mind Wilfrid left his diocese at the mercy of someone with no mercy. On the second charge, Wilfrid's choosing to serve a heathen king was hardly the worst of it. Other churchmen served Ceadwalla too, not least Bishop Hædde. But the slaughter in the Isle of Wight seems to have weighed on Daniel, with his apparent sympathy for those oppressed by his own king, and he conveyed his feelings to Bede. Wilfrid's quarter share of the island and its booty (*praeda*) was a blood-stained gift, albeit one

---

64 Bright, *Chapters of Early English Church History*, p. 392.
65 Farmer, 'St Wilfrid', *St Wilfrid at Hexham*, p. 50.
66 Mayr-Harting, 'St Wilfrid in Sussex', p. 7.
67 There is a comparison to be made here with Clare Stancliffe's asking whether Bede thought King Oswald was implicated in the murder of King Edwin's son Eadfrith (*HE* II.20); 'Oswald, most holy and most victorious king of the Northumbrians', pp. 73–74.

permitted by the law of the church.[68] None the less Acca was more concerned by the thought that Wilfrid betrayed a Christian king than that he was accessory to the genocide of the pagan Jutish Wihtware. Acca's strong partiality swayed Bede, who, in either case, wanted to avoid any direct accusations against Wilfrid.

For Bede, however, Ceadwalla represented a far larger problem in his historic vision for the ecclesiastical history of the English people. Lapses into paganism happened in the early days. Wessex, however, had had four bishops before Hædde. It was a converted kingdom. The conversion of Sussex and, such as it was, of the Isle of Wight marked the end of the whole process of conversion. How then was he to deal with Ceadwalla, *necdum regeneratus*, who paraded bishops at a site of animal-sacrifice while making a gift of land to found a minster? Nothing suggests that he was an apostate who renounced the faith. It is still less plausible to compare him to Constantine, a believer who postponed baptism because he could not rule without sin. Ceadwalla was quite simply a royal heathen, though born decades after his people received their first bishop. How Christian was the West Saxon aristocracy at this time? Bede can hardly have thought of him as a pagan king who led a band of murderous but Christian followers, but it was not Bede's way to focus on compromise.

Bede picked a careful path, saying enough but no more than enough. It was his use here and there of a few telling words that opened the door to our reconstruction of the likely sequence of events. What resolved the underlying problem for his master narrative was Ceadwalla's final conversion and baptism. The king had been injured in the fighting, and his hurt was so severe that he judged it better to hide away until it was on the mend. We are in the realm of guesswork to think that, whatever the injury, it was not healing well. Infection spelt death, and Bishop Wilfrid could teach lessons about death and beyond. In this way, we can envisage how Ceadwalla might be won over by a new grand plan. It would lead to honour, immortality indeed, for the king and an uplifting story that would wipe away any discredit that Wilfrid had earned from his joining Ceadwalla. The great uncertainty here was how long the plan would take. Would the ailing Ceadwalla survive the journey to the chief of cities? That was no doubt a gamble. If he gave up his sceptre and left his kingdom before the end of 688, as our sources say, then he was either taking the journey very slowly or he arrived in Rome with time to spare before Easter. There are strong reasons to think Abbot Aldhelm accompanied Ceadwalla on the journey to Rome and returned with a collection of verse inscriptions.[69] In one of his poems Aldhelm writes of the king's crossing the snowy Alps.[70] The implication is that

---

68 Theodore, *Iudicia*, I.7.2, 'De pecunia quae in aliena prouincia ab hoste superato rapta fuerit, id est rege alio superato, tertia pars ad ecclesiam tribuatur' ('Concerning livestock that has been taken from a defeated enemy in a foreign kingdom, that is when a king has been defeated, a third share shall be given to the church'); ib. II.14.7, 'Rex si alterius regis terram habet, potest dare pro anima sua'. ('If a king has the land of another king, he can make a gift of it for the sake of his soul').

69 Lapidge, 'The career of Aldhelm', pp. 59–61.

70 Aldhelm, *Carmina ecclesiastica* 3 (ed. by Ehwald, 14–18), on Bugga's church, lines 23–24, 'exin nimbosas transcendit passibus Alpes / aggeribus niueis et montis uertice saeptas' ('from there with steady pace he crossed the cloud-capped Alps hemmed in by heaps of snow and the mountain precipice'). The language may typify the mountains and need not signify a winter journey.

he followed the *iter Francorum*, where winter weather could have delayed his passage over the Great St Bernard pass.[71] Paul the Deacon suggests that he passed through Lombardy, where he was 'wonderfully' (*mirifice*) received by King Cunincpert. During the winter of 688–89, however, Cunincpert was excluded from his cities by the usurper Alahis, a problem that makes one wonder whether Paul had his facts right.[72] Aldhelm's poem relates that the king sickened a week after baptism, but given what we are told by Bede of his injury, we cannot believe he was in rude health until that moment.[73] Good luck, or providence, may have had to play its part in the timing of Ceadwalla's death.

Our sources are indeed circumspect. Stephen's role as propagandist for Wilfrid is plain to see. He has said so little about Wilfrid and Ceadwalla that we cannot even deduce how much he may have known. The fact that he mentions him at all, and in such positive terms, indicates that he knew there was a story and that he needed to counteract it. No one relying on Stephen would have learnt that Ceadwalla was not Christian. Bede reveals much more, but we have had to tease it out. What we see in his fractured narrative here makes sense as retelling the story from Bishop Daniel's point of view, modified to reflect other influences on Bede. His difficulties in portraying Wilfrid in the *Historia* have been the subject of remark since at least the days of James Raine and Charles Plummer.[74] Various ideas have come to the surface as to why Bede did not take wholeheartedly to that most energetic bishop. Discussion of Bede's views on Wilfrid naturally focused on those aspects of his career that feature in the larger story. Bede knew that Wilfrid was hated at Lindisfarne, but some of that resulted from what happened at Whitby in 664 and its aftermath: on the date of Easter Bede would have taken Wilfrid's side, but on his conduct at Lindisfarne Bede made

---

71 Earlier in the century the Rhône Valley route to Marseille and a voyage from there to Rome were favoured to avoid Lombard territory, though the sea crossing seems not to have been taken in winter. The *Iter Francorum*, much used in the eighth century and later, crossed the Alps by the Great St Bernard Pass and headed south through Ivrea and Pavia. Benedict Biscop's route through Vienne in 671 no doubt involved the long passage by sea (*Historia abbatum*, c. 4), but in 679 and 680 Wilfrid took the road over the Alps and met the Lombard king Perctarit (Stephen, *Vita S. Wilfrithi episcopi*, c. 12). Data on such matters are collected by Matthews, *Road to Rome*.

72 Paul the Deacon, *Historia Langobardorum*, VI.15, ed. by Waitz, p. 217: 'His diebus Cedoal rex Anglorum Saxonum, qui multa in sua patria bella gesserat, ad Christum conuersus Romam properauit. Qui per Cunincpertum regem ueniens ab eo mirifice susceptus est'. Paul, however, fits this into his sequence of event only in 698, too late by a decade, despite having the indiction in Ceadwalla's epitaph.

73 Lines 28–30, 'post albas igitur morbo correptus egrescit / donec mortalis clausit spiracula uitae' ('after Easter week his health failed and he took ill, till he closed the breath of mortal life').

74 J. Raine the Younger, *Historians of the Church of York* (1879-94), vol. i, p. xxxiv; Plummer, ii. 315–16. More recently Walter Goffart has stimulated debate by depicting Bede as a spokesman for those who were against Wilfrid, oversimplifying the complexities of Bede's position. The classic statement of Goffart's view is in the chapter, 'Bede and the Ghost of Bishop Wilfrid', *The Narrators of Barbarian History (AD 550–800). Jordanes, Gregory of Tours, Bede, and Paul the Deacon* (Princeton, NJ, 1988), pp. 235-329. Of the passages discussed above, he writes, 'Ostensibly naïve, Bede's entire treatment of Cædwalla in *HE* 4. 15–16 is ironic' (p. 319). His argument has been discussed by A. T. Thacker, 'Wilfrid, his cult and his biographer', and by N. J. Higham, 'Wilfrid and Bede's *Historia*', in *Wilfrid. Abbot, Bishop, Saint*, ed. by N. J. Higham (Donington, 2013), pp. 1–17; 54–66.

Cuthbert speak against Wilfrid. That was when he revised his Life of St Cuthbert. Years afterwards, preparing to write his *Historia*, he learnt Daniel's perspective on what happened in Wessex and Sussex, which may have made Bede very uncomfortable about Wilfrid. His virtues were well known, his prodigious striving for the cause of the church, and Bishop Acca was at hand to keep putting the case in favour, perhaps even after the stage when Bede had written out his views. Wilfrid's ambition and pride may always have been distasteful to Bede, who preferred monastic modesty; he could and did tone down Stephen's portrait. But Bede could not get out of his mind what Daniel had reported, that Wilfrid left Christians to a killer, that he later served the killer, turning a blind eye to carnage and accepting the victims' land as a gift from the killer. Of course, Cyneberht's story reflects the helplessness of a mere monk, able to persuade the king to permit instruction and baptism before his enemy's brothers were executed, saving souls but not lives. Yet Daniel saw them as victims, and he thought the king's high counsellor was complicit.

In the end, what Bede did was to redeem Ceadwalla's posthumous reputation while at the same time leaving enough hints for the truth to come out. Ceadwalla's conversion and baptism in Rome, prominently featured in Book V, saved the master-narrative. There is nothing to prove who persuaded Ceadwalla to think of his own soul, and there is no means of supporting the guess that Ceadwalla was open to such ideas only because death was near. Wilfrid was on the spot in 688 and had a prominent position.[75] Others may have played a part. Bishop Hædde and Abbot Aldhelm appear as close to Ceadwalla as Wilfrid. There was good reason for them all to want to turn the story into one of royal conversion at the threshold of the apostles. How this news was received by their fellow churchmen in 689 is now lost to us. Decades later, none of them received credit from Bede, who gave the halo to Ceadwalla himself. His sins were remitted in baptism, and he died unstained. Bede needed to do this to expunge the late pagan revival in Wessex in Hædde's time, and it worked on later medieval historians. The one whose reputation may have been tainted by the whole episode was Wilfrid. Writing his *Historia*, Bede could not shake off the idea, planted by Bishop Daniel but very likely not generally known in the north, that Wilfrid had blood on his hands.

What we learn from all this about Wilfrid is the clarification of the sequence of events in the 680s and the harmonization of what Stephen and Bede report. The factors staining the bishop's reputation have been recognized for a very long time. Ceadwalla on the other hand now emerges more visibly as a heathen who fought his way to power and, in enjoying his *imperium*, made prelates spectators and beneficiaries of his pagan conduct. The assembly at *Besingahearh* gives us vivid reason not to be swept along by the conversion narrative. There is doubt about the depth of real conversion in Wessex as late as 688 and, if in Wessex, then elsewhere too. More surprising, however, is the argument for the revision of Bede's *Historia* after its first circulation and in deference

---

75 Failing health and Wilfrid's influence were invoked by the Revd Charles Hole (1824–1906) in Smith's *Dictionary of Christian Biography*, vol. i, p. 373. More recently Wilfrid's likely role has been mentioned by Farmer, 'St Wilfrid', p. 51, and Stancliffe, 'Kings who opted out', pp. 170–71.

to Acca as guardian of Wilfrid's reputation. The unasked and surely unanswerable question here is who wrote the story of the apostolic visitation on St Oswald's day at a monastery in Sussex. We have supposed that, near the end of his life, Bede was persuaded to add it by Acca, something that makes us reflect on his own sense of the integrity of his text. Yet we cannot disprove the possibility that, though mentioning Acca in the third person, it was Acca's interpolation after Bede's death.

Works Cited

Primary Sources

Adomnán, *Vita S. Columbae*, ed. by A. O. Anderson and M. O. Anderson, Oxford Medieval Texts (Oxford, 1991); transl. R. Sharpe, *Adomnán of Iona. Life of St Columba* (London, 1995)

Aldhelm, *Carmina ecclesiastica* 3, ed. by R. Ehwald, *Aldhelmi opera, Monumenta Germaniae Historica, Auctores Antiquissimi*, 15 (1919), 14–18

——, *Epistola ad Heahfridum*, ed. by Ehwald, *Aldhelmi opera*, 486–94; transl. M. Lapidge and M. Herren, *Aldhelm. The Prose Works* (Cambridge, 1979)

ASC   *The Anglo-Saxon Chronicle*, transl. D. Whitelock with D. C. Douglas and S. I. Tucker (London, 1965)

Bede, *In Ezram et Neemiam*, ed. by D. Hurst, Corpus Christianorum Series Latina, 119A (Turnhout, 1969), pp. 235–392, transl. Scott DeGregorio in *On Ezra and Nehemiah*, Translated Texts for Historians, 47 (Liverpool, 2006)

——, *In primam partem Samuhelis*, ed. by D. Hurst, Corpus Christianorum Series Latina, 119 (Turnhout, 1962), pp. 1–272

——, *Historia abbatum*, ed. by C. Plummer, *Venerabilis Baedae opera historica* (Oxford, 1896), i. 364–87

——, *Historia ecclesiastica*, ed. by C. Plummer, *Venerabilis Baedae opera historica* (Oxford, 1896); ed. by R. A. B. Mynors, transl. B. Colgrave, *Bede's Ecclesiastical History of the English People*, Oxford Medieval Texts (Oxford, 1969); ed. by M. Lapidge, transl. P. Monat and P. Robin, *Bède le Vénérable. Histoire ecclésiastique du peuple anglais*, 3 vols, Sources Chrétiennes 489–91 (Paris, 2005); ed. by M. Lapidge, transl. P. Chiesa, *Beda. Storia degli inglesi*, 2 vols (Rome, 2010)

——, *Vita metrica sancti Cuthberti*, in *Bedas Metrische Vita sancti Cuthberti*, ed. by W. Jaager, Palaestra, 198 (Leipzig, 1935)

——, *Vita S. Cuthberti*, ed. by B. Colgrave, *Two Latin Lives of St Cuthbert* (Cambridge, 1940)

Boniface, *Epistulae*, ed. by M. Tangl, *Monumenta Germaniae Historica, Epistulae Selectae*, 1 (Berlin, 1916)

Eadmer, *Vita S. Wilfridi*, ed. by B. J. Muir and A. J. Turner (Exeter, 1998)

Henry of Huntingdon, *Historia Anglorum*, ed. by D. E. Greenway, Oxford Medieval Texts (Oxford, 1996)

Inscriptiones Christianae Vrbis Romae, ed. by G. B. de Rossi, 2 vols (Rome, 1857–61, 1888)

Laws of Ine, ed. by F. Liebermann, *Gesetze der Angelsachsen* (Halle, 1898-1916), i. 88–123

Paul the Deacon, *Historia Langobardorum*, ed. by G. Waitz, *Monumenta Germaniae Historica, Scriptores rerum Germanicarum in usum scholarum*, 48 (1878)

Stephen, *Vita S. Wilfrithi episcopi*, ed. by W. Levison, *Monumenta Germaniae Historica, Scriptores rerum Merovingicarum*, 6 (1913), 163–92 (editorial introduction), 193–263 (text); ed. by B. Colgrave (Cambridge, 1927)

Theodore, *Iudicia*, ed. by P. W. Finsterwalder, *Die Canones Theodori und ihre Überlieferungsformen* (Weimar, 1929), 239–334

Vita Ceolfridi abbatis, ed. by C. Plummer, *Baedae Venerabilis opera historica* (Oxford, 1896), i. 388–404

William of Malmesbury, *Gesta Pontificum Anglorum*, ed. by M. Winterbottom, Oxford Medieval Texts (Oxford, 2007)

——, *Gesta Regum Anglorum*, ed. by R. A. B. Mynors, M. Winterbottom, and R. M. Thomson, Oxford Medieval Texts (Oxford, 1998)

Secondary Studies

Blair, John, *Early Medieval Surrey* (Stroud, 1991)

——, *The Church in Anglo-Saxon Society* (Oxford, 2005)

——, *Building Anglo-Saxon England* (Princeton, NJ, 2018)

Bright, William, *Chapters of Early English Church History* (Oxford, 1897)

Chaplais, Pierre, 'Some early Anglo-Saxon diplomas on single sheets: originals or copies?', *Journal of the Society of Archivists* 3 (no. 7, April 1968), 315–36

Clay, John-Henry, 'Adventus, warfare, and the Britons in the development of West Saxon identity', in *Post-Roman Transitions: Christian and Barbarian Identities in the Early Medieval West*, ed. by W. Pohl and G. Herdemann (Turnhout, 2013), pp. 169–213

Colgrave, Bertram, *Two Lives of St Cuthbert* (Cambridge, 1940)

Cubitt, Catherine R. E., 'St Wilfrid: a man for his times', *Wilfrid. Abbot, Bishop, Saint*, ed. by N. J. Higham (Donnington, Lincs, 2013), pp. 311–47

Dutton, Leonard, *The Anglo-Saxon Kingdoms. The Power Struggles from Hengist to Ecgberht* (Hanley, Worcs, 1993)

Farmer, David Hugh, 'St Wilfrid', *St Wilfrid at Hexham*, ed. by D. P. Kirby (Newcastle, 1974), pp. 35–60

Fraser, James Earle, 'Early Medieval Europe. The case of Britain and Ireland', *The Oxford Handbook of Genocide Studies*, ed. by D. Bloxham and A. D. Moses (Oxford, 2010), pp. 259–79

Gallyon, Margaret, *The Early Church in Wessex and Mercia* (Lavenham, 1980)

Gelling, Margaret, *The Early Charters of the Thames Valley* (Leicester, 1979)

Gillingham, John B., 'Women, children, and the profits of war', *Gender and Historiography. Studies in the earlier middle ages in honour of Pauline Stafford* (London, 2012), 61–74

——, 'A strategy of total war? Henry of Livonia and the conquest of Estonia, 1208–1227', *Journal of Medieval Military History*, 15 (2017), 187–214

Goffart, Walter, 'Bede and the ghost of Bishop Wilfrid', in *The Narrators of Barbarian History (AD 550–800). Jordanes, Gregory of Tours, Bede, and Paul the Deacon* (Princeton, NJ, 1988), pp. 235–329

Harrison, Kenneth, 'The reign of King Ecgfrith of Northumbria', *Yorkshire Archaeological Journal*, 43 (1971), 79–84

Higham, Nicholas J., *An English Empire* (Manchester, 1995)

——, *The Convert Kings. Power and Religious Affiliation in Early Anglo-Saxon England* (Manchester, 1997)

——, 'Wilfrid and Bede's *Historia*', in *Wilfrid. Abbot, Bishop, Saint*, ed. by N. J. Higham (Donington, 2013), pp. 54–66

Hilliard, Paul C., 'Acca of Hexham through the eyes of the Venerable Bede', *Early Medieval Europe*, 26 (2018), 440–61

Kelly, S. E., *Charters of St Augustine's Abbey, Canterbury* (Oxford, 1995)

Keskiaho, Jesse, *Dreams and Visions in the Early Middle Ages. The reception and use of patristic ideas, 400–900* (Cambridge, 2015)

Kirby, David P., *The Making of Early England* (London, 1967)

——, *The Earliest English Kings* (London, 1991)

Lapidge, Michael, 'Acca of Hexham and the origin of the Old English Martyrology', *Analecta Bollandiana*, 123 (2005), 29–78

——, 'The career of Aldhelm', *Anglo-Saxon England*, 36 (2006), 15–69

——, 'Author's variants in the textual transmission of Bede's *Historia ecclesiastica?*', *Filologia mediolatina*, 16 (2009), 1–15

Lapidge, Michael, and Paolo Chiesa, *Beda. Storia degli inglesi*, 2 vols (Rome, 2010)

Lapidge, Michael, André Crépin, and others, *Bède le Vénérable. Histoire ecclésiastique du peuple anglais*, 3 vols, Sources Chrétiennes, 489–91 (Paris, 2005)

López Pereira, José Eduardo, *Continuatio Isidoriana Hispana. Crónica Mozárabe de 754* (León, 2009)

McCarthy, Daniel, and Dáibhí Ó Cróinín, 'The lost Irish 84-year Easter table rediscovered', *Peritia* 6/7 (1987-8), 227-42

Matthews, S. *The Road to Rome. Travel and travellers between England and Italy in the Anglo-Saxon centuries* (Oxford, 2007)

Mayr-Harting, Henry, 'St Wilfrid in Sussex', *Studies in Sussex Church History*, ed. by M. J. Kitch (London, 1981), 1–17

Millett, Martin, and Simon James, 'Excavations at Cowdery's Down, Basingstoke, 1978–81', *Archaeological Journal*, 140 (1983), 151–279

Mynors, R. A. B., and Bertram Colgrave, *Bede's Ecclesiastical History of the English People*, Oxford Medieval Texts (Oxford, 1969)

Piacente, Luigi, 'Stragicus (Beda Hist. Eccl. 4, 16 [14])', *Studi latini e italiani* (1986), 81–85

Plummer, Charles, *Venerabilis Baedae opera historica*, 2 vols (Oxford, 1896)

Raine, James, *Historians of the Church of York* (1879-94)

Sawyer, Peter H., *Handlist of Anglo-Saxon Charters* (London, 1968) [cited by no.]

——, *From Roman Britain to Norman England* (London, 1978)

Sharpe, Richard, 'King Ceadwalla's Roman epitaph', in *Latin Learning and English Lore. Papers for Michael Lapidge* (Toronto, 2005), i. 171–93

Smith, William, and Henry Wace, *A Dictionary of Christian Biography, Literature, Sects, and Doctrine*, 4 vols (London, 1877–87)

Stancliffe, Clare E., 'Kings who opted out', *Ideal and Reality in Frankish and Anglo-Saxon Society. Studies presented to J. M. Wallace-Hadrill* (Oxford, 1983), pp. 154–76

————, 'Oswald, most holy and most victorious king of the Northumbrians', *Oswald. Northumbrian King to European Saint*, ed. by C. E. Stancliffe and E. Cambridge (Stamford, 1995), pp. 33–83

————, 'Disputed episcopacy: Bede, Acca, and the relationship between Stephen's Life of St Wilfrid and the early prose Lives of St Cuthbert', *Anglo-Saxon England*, 41 (2012), 7–39

Stenton, Frank Merry, *Anglo-Saxon England* (Oxford, 1943, 1971)

Thacker, Alan T., 'Wilfrid [St Wilfrid] (*c.* 634–709/10)', *Oxford Dictionary of National Biography* (2004)

————, 'Great Driffield and its townships: early settlement', in *Victoria History of the County of York: East Riding* IX, ed. by Graham Kent with David Neave and Susan Neave (Woodbridge, 2012), pp. 5–13

————, 'Wilfrid, his cult and his biographer', in *Wilfrid. Abbot, Bishop, Saint*, ed. by N. J. Higham (Donington, 2013), pp. 1–17

————, 'Shaping the saint: rewriting tradition in the early Lives of St Cuthbert', in *The Introduction of Christianity into the Early Medieval Insular World. Converting the Isles I*, ed. by R. Flechner and M. Ní Mhaonaigh (Turnhout, 2016), pp. 399–429

Twomey, Carolyn, 'Kings as catechumens: royal conversion narratives, and Easter in the *Historia ecclesiastica*', *Haskins Society Journal* 25 (2013) [2014], 1–18

Whitelock, Dorothy, *Some Anglo-Saxon Bishops of London* (London, 1975)

————, *English Historical Documents* i *c. 500–1042* (London, 1979)

Yorke, Barbara A. E., 'The Jutes of Hampshire and Wight and the origins of Wessex', in *The Origins of Anglo-Saxon Kingdoms*, ed. by S. R. Bassett (Leicester, 1989), pp. 84–96

————, *Kings and Kingdoms of Early Anglo-Saxon England* (London, 1990)

————, *Wessex in the Early Middle Ages* (London, 1995)

————, *Rex doctissimus: Bede and King Aldfrith of Northumbria*, Jarrow Lecture (2009)

BARBARA YORKE

Bede's Preferential Treatment of the Irish

In 1996 Alan published a typically insightful and learned paper on 'Bede and the Irish' which has proved a starting point for subsequent discussions.[1] Alan had to steer his way between the extremes of two rather different interpretations of how Bede viewed the Irish that had been published in the decade before he wrote. On the one hand, there was the view of some historians of early medieval Ireland that Bede had been less than generous in acknowledging the Irish contribution to both his own work and to the development of the Church in Northumbria and beyond.[2] On the other, Bede was seen as being excessively favourable towards, and protective, of the Irish and their role in the Northumbrian Church in the context of contemporary rivalries within the Northumbrian Church establishment which had led to substantial attacks on the Irish legacy.[3] Alan's own interpretation was more nuanced and less polemical. He acknowledged that there were aspects of both criticism and favour within Bede's references to the Irish, but Alan stressed that there was no blanket treatment of Irish Church or churchmen, no virtues or failings that Bede viewed as specifically Irish. Bede placed the Irishmen about whom he wrote within the wider debates and concerns of western Christendom which they exemplified to different extents. When he praised Aidan and his disciples it was not because of peculiarly Irish elements of their way of life, but because they seemed to him to embody the ideal behaviours of religious men as delineated by one of Bede's great authorities, Pope Gregory the Great.

I found Alan's suggestion of approaching Bede's treatment of Aidan and his disciples as exemplars of supreme importance to Bede who happened to be Irish (rather than *because* they were Irish) very helpful when I was preparing a contribution in connection with the 2013 Paderborn conference *CREDO: Christianisierung*

---

1 Thacker, 'Bede and the Irish'.
2 Ó Cróinín, 'The Irish Provenance of Bede's Computus'; Picard, 'Bede, Adomnán and the Writing of History'; Thacker, 'Bede and the Irish', pp. 31–32.
3 Goffart, *The Narrators of Barbarian History*, pp. 235–328.

Barbara Yorke • is Emeritus Professor of Early Medieval History at the University of Winchester.

Cities, Saints, and Communities in Early Medieval Europe, ed. by Scott DeGregorio and Paul Kershaw, SEM 46 (Turnhout: Brepols, 2020), pp. 223–240
BREPOLS PUBLISHERS   DOI 10.1484/M.SEM-EB.5.119629

Europas im Mittelalter. This paper develops some ideas that were presented there.[4] It will begin by reasserting the importance to Bede of Aidan and of men and women trained by Aidan by considering the attribution of miracles within Northumbria in Bede's *Ecclesiastical History*. Subsequently it will consider Bede's portrayal of other Irish bishops of Lindisfarne, and address the issue of how one is to account for Bede's preferential treatment of Aidan and others closely associated with them. There are various avenues that will need to be explored including why Bede does not refer to Aidan in the chronicle in *On the Reckoning of Time*, and whether aspects of Bede's own biography need to be taken into account as well as his well-known concern for standards in the contemporary Northumbrian Church.

Northumbrian Miracles in Bede's *Ecclesiastical History*

An indication of whom Bede regarded with particular approbation in the Northumbrian Church can be reached by looking at the number of chapters and miracles in the *Ecclesiastical History* that he devoted to key individuals (Table 8). The rough numbering may be rather a crude approach, but it does delineate a striking contrast between those bishops and members of the royal house whose careers are discussed in some detail and with approbation, but to whom few or no miracles are ascribed, and those whose lives were endorsed before or after death, by many miracles. Although Bede does not himself describe the rationale that lay behind his use of miracles for recent historical figures, it is apparent that he uses them principally as external demonstrations of inward virtues.[5] So the individuals to whom most miracles are assigned can be recognised as those whom Bede most admired and whom he offered as models to his readers and listeners. Some of the same saints appear in two early eighth-century works the *Whitby Life of St Gregory* (written 704 × 714),[6] and Stephen's *Life of Bishop Wilfrid* (written 712 × 714),[7] and comparisons highlight further the idiosyncrasies of Bede's approach.

One striking contrast emerges in the treatment of Aidan and Paulinus. The former is one of the most noted miracle-workers in the *Ecclesiastical History*, but although the latter is praised, Bede assigns no miracles to Paulinus. To some extent this represents a trend in the Anglo-Saxon Church as a whole to put the emphasis on Pope Gregory as the apostle of the English rather than on Augustine and Paulinus who were seen as acting on his behalf.[8] The Whitby Life, for instance, concentrates on Gregory's miracles and does not assign any to Paulinus — although it does refer to his soul ascending to heaven in the form of a swan.[9] In Bede's *Ecclesiastical History* it was Aidan

4   Yorke, 'Heilige Männer, heilige Frauen'.
5   McCready, *Miracles and the Venerable Bede*, pp. 124–53.
6   Anon., *The Earliest Life of Gregory the Great*, ed. and trans. by Colgrave; Thacker, 'Memorializing Gregory the Great', p. 59.
7   Eddius Stephanus, *The Life of Bishop Wilfrid*, ed. and trans. by Colgrave.
8   Thacker, 'Memorialising Gregory the Great'.
9   Anon., *The Earliest Life of Gregory the Great*, ed. and trans. Colgrave, pp. 100–01.

Table 8. Bede's Northumbrian miracle-workers in the *Ecclesiastical History*.

	No. of chapters	No. of miracles (+ = more than one miraculous element in the same account)
Bishops		
Paulinus of York (d. 644)	6	o
Aidan of Lindisfarne (d. 651)	7	3+
Wilfrid of Hexham (d. 710)	5	1.5
Cuthbert of Lindisfarne (d. 687)	7	6+
Chad of York, (Lichfield) (d. 672)	2	3+
John of Hexham and York (d. 721)	5	5
Royals		
K. Edwin of Deira (d. 633)	8	o
K. Oswald of Bernicia (d. 642)	10	7
Hild, abbess of *Streanæshalch* (Whitby) (d. 680)	2	2 (+ Caedmon)

rather than Paulinus who provided the model of an ideal bishop and holy man for the Northumbrian Church, blessed through the ability to perform miracles.[10] Bede also clearly favoured Bishop Cuthbert, trained in Aidan's foundation of Lindisfarne over Wilfrid as a role model, something that is, of course, reflected in his composition of poetic and prose Lives of the former.[11] From the large number of miracles that Stephen provided in his *Life of Wilfrid*, which it is now generally agreed was known to Bede, he selected only one: the visitation of the Archangel Michael to Wilfrid at Meaux.[12] His other (partial) miracle for Wilfrid concerned the conversion of the South Saxons where Bede's account differs significantly from that of Stephen.[13] In Bede's account God sends rain after a drought that helps convince the South Saxons to convert, but it is presented as God's own decision rather than a request from Wilfrid as it is in Stephen's version.[14] Bede's chapters on Wilfrid make clear his admiration for many aspects of Wilfrid's career, and refer to him as 'the blessed Wilfrid', an attribution that is supported by the inclusion of the two (or one-and-a-half) miracles. But there

---

10 Bede, *Historia ecclesiastica*, III.3, 5, 15–17, ed. and trans. by Colgrave and Mynors, pp. 218–21, 226–29, 260–67.

11 Bede, *Vita metrica sancti Cuthberti*, ed. Jaager; Bede and Anon., *Two Lives of Saint Cuthbert*, ed. and trans. by Colgrave, pp. 142–359.

12 Eddius Stephanus, *The Life of Bishop Wilfrid*, ed. and trans. by Colgrave, pp. 526–29.

13 Bede, *Historia ecclesiastica*, IV.13, ed. and trans. by Colgrave and Mynors, pp. 370–77; Palmer, 'Wilfrid and the Frisians', pp. 236–38.

14 Eddius Stephanus, *The Life of Bishop Wilfrid*, ed. and trans. by Colgrave, pp. 80–85. See further Sharpe in this volume.

Table 9. Northumbrian miracle-workers and their links with Aidan.

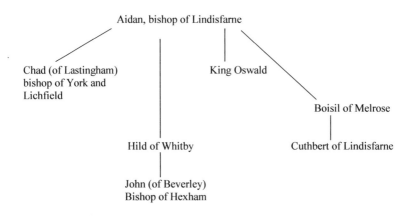

is no doubt that Wilfrid was a controversial and abrasive figure, and Bede carefully edits Stephen's fuller account.[15]

Two other Northumbrian bishops who score highly in the *Ecclesiastical History* for miracle accounts and approving accounts of their lives are Chad of Lastingham, who served briefly as bishop of York before being transferred to the Mercian see of Lichfield,[16] and John of Beverley, Bede's former diocesan at Hexham.[17] Both, like Cuthbert, can be seen as heirs of the Ionan tradition within Northumbria (Table 9). Chad had been trained by Aidan himself at Lindisfarne,[18] while John was one of five bishops who had been educated at *Streanæshalch* (Whitby) under Abbess Hild who had herself been instructed by Bishop Aidan.[19] Bede specifically writes of Hild passing on Aidan's teaching to future generations, and Bede's approval of her as a monastic leader is indicated by the number of chapters and miracles devoted to her. All the Northumbrian episcopal saints to whom Bede allocated most space and miracles can be traced directly or indirectly back to the teachings of Aidan, and so could be seen as his heirs (as shown in Table 9).

Bede's championing of the Irish tradition in such a marked manner is distinctive and idiosyncratic. Without the *Ecclesiastical History* we would scarcely have heard of Aidan and have known virtually nothing of the significance of the Ionan mission.[20] The author of the Anonymous *Life of Cuthbert* who was so closely associated with Lindisfarne, the monastery founded by Aidan, has only one brief reference to Aidan, when Cuthbert witnessed his soul being taken to heaven, and his significance is not

15 Higham, 'Wilfrid and Bede's *Historia*'.
16 Bede, *Historia ecclesiastica*, III.28 and IV.3, ed. and trans. by Colgrave and Mynors, pp. 316–17; 336–47.
17 Bede, *Historia ecclesiastica*, V.2, ed. and trans. by Colgrave and Mynors, pp. 456–59.
18 Bede, *Historia ecclesiastica*, III.28, ed. and trans. by Colgrave, pp. 316–17.
19 Bede, *Historia ecclesiastica*, IV.23, ed. and trans. by Colgrave and Mynors, pp. 404–15.
20 Higham, *(Re-)Reading Bede*, pp. 101–46.

explained.[21] Alcuin, who used the *Ecclesiastical History* as one of his main sources for his poem on the kings and bishops of York, has only one reference to Aidan.[22] He is described as *sanctissimus*, but there is no presentation of Aidan as an episcopal role model or of his legacy in the form of churchmen trained by him or his disciples (who included bishops of York).

Hild seems to have been airbrushed from the early history of *Streanæshalch* (Whitby) altogether, if the *Whitby Life of Pope Gregory* is a reliable guide, for the *Life* does not refer to her.[23] After the synod of Whitby, and the arrival in 669 of the *dirigiste* Archbishop Theodore, monasteries like Lindisfarne and *Streanæshalch* (Whitby)seem to have felt it advisable to distance themselves from their origins via the Ionan mission and any taint from the controversy over its calculation of Easter. While Bede was always measured in what he wrote on the issue, others were not. Stephen indicates that Wilfrid, following papal rhetoric, equated both the British and the Irish of Iona (inaccurately) as heretical Quartodecimans, and that anyone who remained in communion with them was suspect as well.[24] Stephen has Wilfrid say in a justificatory speech:

> Necnon et ego primus post obitum primorum procerum, a sancto Gregorio directorum, Scotticae virulenta plantationis germina eradicarem?

> Was I not the first, after the death of the first elders who were sent by St Gregory, to root out the poisonous weeds planted by the Irish.[25]

This speech implies that the true descent of the Northumbrian Church was from the Gregorian mission alone, something that was also promoted in the *Whitby Life of Pope Gregory*.[26] Bede, in contrast, in the *Ecclesiastical History* has the Irish missionaries of Lindisfarne complete in Northumbria what Paulinus from the Gregorian mission in Kent had begun. The numerous miracles attributed to Aidan and many of those whom he had trained can be seen as a statement by Bede that it was these people who should be regarded as the main apostles of Northumbria through whom God had performed miracles to aid the conversion of its people.

Aidan's work in Northumbria was achieved in partnership with King Oswald (634–642) and this association must go some way to explaining Bede's promotion of the cult of Oswald over that of King Edwin (616–633) who supported the mission of Paulinus. The attribution of miracles to the relics of Oswald, but not to those of Edwin is all the more surprising because Edwin's role in assisting Paulinus won him many favourable references in the *Ecclesiastical History* which were underpinned by complex biblical exegesis referencing the New Testament's fulfilment of Old

21 Bede and Anon., *Two Lives of Cuthbert*, ed. and trans. by Colgrave, pp. 70–71.
22 *Alcuin: Bishops, Kings, and Saints*, ed. and trans. by Godman, pp. 28–29.
23 Karkov, 'Whitby, Jarrow and the Commemoration of the Dead', pp. 129–35.
24 Charles-Edwards, *Early Christian Ireland*, pp. 391–415; Stancliffe, *Bede, Wilfrid and the Irish*.
25 Eddius Stephanus, *The Life of Bishop Wilfrid*, ed. and trans. by Colgrave, pp. 98–99.
26 Thacker, 'Memorializing Gregory the Great', pp. 61–71.

Testament prophecy.[27] In the *Ecclesiastical History* there are no references to the miracles at Edwin's tomb that are alluded to in the *Whitby Life of Pope Gregory* and that imply he was being promoted at *Streanæshalch* (Whitby) as a saint.[28] There are in fact many parallels between the cults of Edwin and Oswald, following their deaths in battle though this is not made apparent in the *Ecclesiastical History*. The Bernician royal family seems to have been much involved in the promotion of both cults. The head and arms of Oswald were retrieved by his brother and successor Oswiu (642–670); the head was given to Lindisfarne and the arm that had been blessed by Aidan became an important relic in the royal chapel at Bamburgh.[29] Edwin's head was a significant relic in the main church of York, but it is not known how it reached there. The bodies of both kings were subsequently retrieved from their respective battlefields by two daughters of Oswiu. Osthryth, queen of Mercia took Oswald's to her monastery of Bardney (Lincolnshire) and her sister Abbess Ælfflaed transferred that of her grandfather Edwin to her monastery of *Streanæshalch* (Whitby).[30] However, Bede stresses that Oswald joined the company of the saints because of a life well-lived in the promotion of Christianity, that is in the tradition of Christ and the apostles, and explicitly made a point of *not* presenting his death in battle as a martyrdom.[31] Through his deployment of miracles in the *Ecclesiastical History* Bede appears to be claiming that what was begun by Edwin and Paulinus was completed at a higher level by Oswald and Aidan. Miracle-working Northumbrian kings and bishops can be connected directly, or via another teacher, with Aidan himself. Even Bishop Wilfrid had begun his career at Lindisfarne and, though neither Bede nor Stephen specifically make this point, when he entered the community in 648 Aidan was still alive and in charge of the foundation.[32]

Bede's Portrayal of Other Irish Bishops of Lindisfarne

When we look at Bede's portrayal of other Irish bishops of Lindisfarne, it emerges clearly that it was the figure of Aidan and the standards he upheld that Bede particularly admired rather than Lindisfarne and its Irish background as such. It also shows that Bede was not indiscriminately supportive of the Irish mission or indiscriminately complimentary about the early bishops of Lindisfarne. The first candidate sent from Iona to become bishop of Lindisfarne, whom Bede does not name, is said to have made little headway, and was considered to be too harsh and unyielding in his approach. The description ascribed to this individual of the Northumbrian people as 'homines indomabiles et durae ac barbarae' (intractable, obstinate and uncivilised

---

27   Barrow, 'How Coifi Pierced Christ's Side'.
28   Anon., *The Earliest Life of Gregory the Great*, ed. and trans. by Colgrave, pp. 100–05.
29   Thacker, '*Membra disjecta*', pp. 100–04.
30   Thacker, '*Membra disjecta*', pp. 104–07.
31   Gunn, 'Bede and the martyrdom of Oswald'.
32   Eddius Stephanus, *The Life of Bishop Wilfrid*, ed. and trans. by Colgrave, pp. 6–7; Bede, *Historia ecclesiastica*, V.19, ed. and trans. by Colgrave and Mynors, pp. 518–19.

men) underlined his unsuitability. In contrast his replacement Aidan was endowed 'gratia discretionis, quae virtutum mater est' (with the grace of discretion, which is the mother of all virtues).[33]

Aidan's own successor was Fínán (651–661) in whose time monks from Lindisfarne, of both Irish and English origin, opened up important new areas of mission as a result of King Oswiu's wide-ranging overlordship. In 653 Peada, son of King Penda of Mercia and ruler of the Middle Angles, was converted to Christianity and a mission was dispatched from Lindisfarne to his kingdom. When Peada briefly became king of the southern Mercians in 655 priests from Lindisfarne extended their mission into that province as well.[34] This mission covered a large area from the Wash down to Oxfordshire where Diuma, one of the first wave of priests, was buried at Charlbury *in Feppingum*.[35] Fínán and Oswiu also oversaw the baptism of King Sigebert 'Sanctus' of the East Saxons, and sent him Cedd from the Lindisfarne mission to the Middle Angles to be their bishop in either 653 or soon after.[36] Bede dutifully reports the role of Fínán, but without any discernible enthusiasm or comment.

Elsewhere in the *Ecclesiastical History* Fínán's character was unfavourably contrasted by Bede with that of Aidan. Whereas Aidan was 'summae mansuetudinis et pietatis ac moderaminis virum' (a man of outstanding gentleness, devotion and moderation),[37] Fínán was 'homo ferocis animi' (a man of fierce temper).[38] When Rónán, an Irishman who had lived in Gaul and Italy, sought to persuade Fínán that the method of calculating Easter followed by Iona and Lindisfarne was incorrect, Fínán refused to listen to reason and became even more obdurate in his resistance to accepting what Bede believed to be the correct calendar.[39] To Bede, of course, the correct reckoning of Easter was a matter of supreme importance on which he had written at length.[40] Aidan had adhered to the same method of calculating Easter that Bede deplored for Fínán, but differences in their nature as religious men seems to have permitted Bede to excuse in Aidan what he explicitly condemned in Fínán.[41]

> Haec autem dissonantia paschalis obseruantiae uiuente Aidano patienter ab omnibus tolerabatur, qui patenter intellexerant quia, etsi pascha contra morem eorum qui ipsum miserant facere non potuit, opera tamen fidei pietatis et dilectionis iuxta morem omnibus sanctis consuetum diligenter exsequi curavit. Vnde ab omnibus, etiam his qui de pascha aliter sentiebant, merito deligebatur.

> This difference in the observance of Easter was patiently tolerated by all while Aidan was alive, because they had clearly understood that although

33 Bede, *Historia ecclesiastica*, III.5, ed. and trans. by Colgrave and Mynors, pp. 228–29.
34 Bede, *Historia ecclesiastica*, III.21, ed. and trans. by Colgrave and Mynors, pp. 278–81.
35 Blair, *Anglo-Saxon Oxfordshire*, 59.
36 Bede, *Historia ecclesiastica*, III.22, ed. and trans. by Colgrave, pp. 280–85.
37 Bede, *Historia ecclesiastica*, III.3, ed. and trans. by Colgrave, pp. 218–19.
38 Bede, *Historia ecclesiastica*, III.25, ed. and trans. by Colgrave, pp. 296–97.
39 Bede, *Historia ecclesiastica*, III.25, ed. and trans. by Colgrave and Mynors, pp. 294–97.
40 Bede, *The Reckoning of Time*, trans. by Wallis.
41 Bede, *Historia ecclesiastica*, III.25, ed. and trans. by Colgrave and Mynors, pp. 296–97.

he could not keep Easter otherwise than according to the manner of those who had sent him, he nevertheless laboured diligently to practice the works of faith, piety, and love, which is the mark of all the saints. He was therefore deservedly loved by all, including those who had other views about Easter.

Bede's preference for Aidan over Fínán may even have led Bede to adjust dates so that another favoured person could be more closely associated with the former rather than the latter. Bede records that the Deiran princess Hild, who later became abbess of Whitby, is said to have planned to join her sister Hereswith as a nun at Chelles, but was persuaded by Bishop Aidan to follow her religious vows in Northumbria instead.[42] The chronology Bede provides for Hild's life would place these events in 647, while Aidan was alive,[43] but there are significant problems with accepting this chronology, not least because Chelles was only founded as a nunnery by Queen Balthild in c. 657 (by which time Aidan who died in 651 cannot have been involved in influencing Hild's decision).[44] A date after the battle of the River Winwaed in 655, which left Oswiu victorious and the East Anglians and Deirans on the losing side, would provide a plausible context in which the Deiran princesses Hereswith (who was also an East Anglian widow) and her sister Hild might seek to flee England.[45] The offer which made Hild change her mind would have been the reconciliation with Oswiu that was implied in his entrusting his baby daughter Ælfflæd to her care with appropriate endowment for a nunnery, first at Hartlepool and, subsequently, at Streanæshalch (Whitby).[46] It may well be that Hild was first received and instructed as a nun by Aidan as Bede says,[47] but this further development of her career is more likely to have occurred while Fínán was bishop of Lindisfarne. In fact, Fínán is never mentioned by Bede in connection with Hild, and although in his long account of Hild's religious life in *Ecclesiastical History* IV.23 Bede refers to Whitby (*Streanæshalch*) — as he could hardly avoid doing — he does not mention the gift of Hartlepool or the guardianship of Ælfflæd. Reference to these is made only in an earlier chapter concerned with the battle of the river Winwaed and its aftermath.[48] Bede is concerned to play up Hild's links with Aidan and dismiss or obscure her connection with Fínán. He also seems to have wished to avoid any reference to her involvement with political compromise in his appraisal of her religious life which stresses the characteristics that had come from her training by Aidan.

Bede does not say whether Fínán advised Oswiu to achieve reconciliation with a surviving member of the Deiran royal house via support for her religious career, but

42 Bede, *Historia ecclesiastica*, IV.23, ed. and trans. by Colgrave and Mynors, pp. 406–07.

43 Bede, *Opera Historica*, ed. by Plummer, II, p. 244; Hunter Blair, 'Whitby as a Centre of Learning', pp. 4–8.

44 Wallace-Hadrill, *Bede's Ecclesiastical History*, pp. 163 and 232; Laporte, 'Grab und Reliquien'; Yorke, 'Queen Balthild's "monastic policy" and the origins of female religious houses'.

45 See below for further evidence of Oswiu's hostility to the Deirans in the murder of King Oswine of Deira and the foundation of the monastery of Gilling in atonement.

46 Bede, *Historia ecclesiastica*, III.24 and v. 15, ed. and trans by Colgrave and Mynors, pp. 290–93, 504–09.

47 Bede, *Historia ecclesiastica*, IV.23, ed. and trans. by Colgrave and Mynors, pp. 406–09.

48 Bede, *Historia ecclesiastica*, III.24, ed. and trans. by Colgrave and Mynors, pp. 290–93.

it was a way of dealing with a supplanted royal line with which he could have been familiar from his background in Ireland.[49] One also does not learn from Bede just how well-connected Fínán was, nor of his probable close links with Oswiu. For Irish genealogical traditions claim that Fínán was the son of the powerful Cenél nÉogain king Colmán Rímid and that his sister (or possibly another female relative) was the mother of Oswiu's son Flann Fína, better known in an Anglo-Saxon context as King Aldfrith of Northumbria (685/686–705).[50] Oswiu had spent time in his youth as an exile in Ireland and so his liaison is likely to have belonged to that period.[51] Bede is the only author who refers to his son Aldfrith as *nothus* 'illegitimate', a comment which in the context of the time would seem to disparage the status of his Irish mother.[52] Oswiu's acquaintance with Fínán may have gone back to this period in Ireland as well, and may be a reason why Fínán became bishop of Lindisfarne. The partnership of Oswiu and Fínán could have been presented by Bede as one that operated to the mutual benefit of Church and state like that of Edwin and Paulinus or Oswald and Oswine with Aidan, but he did not choose to do so and seems to have had reservations about both men.[53]

Fínán's successor as bishop of Lindisfarne was Colmán who had to defend the Ionan method of calculating Easter at the synod of Whitby in 664. Bede's recreation of the synod allows him to state his case, but the proponent of the English Easter, Wilfrid, has the best and, to Bede's mind, 'correct' lines.[54] Colmán withdrew after Whitby with some of the Anglo-Saxons of Lindisfarne who also could not accept the decision of the synod.[55] No character sketch of Colmán is given, though King Oswiu is said to have loved him 'pro insita illi prudentia' (on account of his innate prudence).[56] Bede wrote approvingly of how he had upheld the good practices at Lindisfarne established by Aidan, and of the high standards of monastic life established by his English followers at Mayo.[57] However, this separate English establishment is said to have been made because the English monks became annoyed by the Irish brethren leaving the monastery to travel in the summer and returning in winter to consume the fruits of Anglo-Saxon labour.

Colmán's immediate successor Tuda is said to have been educated among the southern Irish (and so would have followed the Roman Easter).[58] His accomplishments

49 Ó Corráin, 'Ireland *c.* 800', pp. 584–608.
50 Ireland, 'Aldfrith of Northumbria'; Lacey, *Cénel Conaill*, pp. 208–10; Yorke, *Rex Doctissimus*.
51 Moisl, 'The Bernician royal dynasty and the Irish', pp. 120–24.
52 Bede, *Vita metrica sancti Cuthberti*, ed. Jaager, pp. 98–99; Bede and Anon., *Two Lives of St Cuthbert*, ed. and trans. by Colgrave, pp. 238–39; Sarah McDougall, *Royal Bastards*, 22–65. However, in *Historia ecclesiastica*, IV.26, ed. and trans. by Colgrave, pp. 430–31, Bede uses 'dicebatur' 'it is said' for the claim that Aldfrith was son of Oswiu and brother of Ecgrith implying that he believed there was some doubt over his paternity.
53 Higham, *(Re-)Reading Bede*, pp. 156–58 (for reservations about Oswiu).
54 Bede, *Historia ecclesiastica*, III.25, ed. and trans. by Colgrave, pp. 294–309.
55 Bede, *Historia ecclesiastica*, III.26, ed. and trans. by Colgrave, pp. 308–09.
56 Bede, *Historia ecclesiastica*, III.26, ed. and trans. by Colgrave and Mynors, pp. 308–09.
57 Bede, *Historia ecclesiastica*, III.26 and IV.4, ed. and trans. by Colgrave and Mynors, pp. 308–09; 346–49; Orschel, 'Mag nEó na Sacsan'.
58 Bede, *Historia ecclesiastica*, III.26, ed. and trans. by Colgrave and Mynors, pp. 308–09.

are praised, but he died of plague soon after his appointment.[59] He was succeeded — after the complications of the appointments of Chad and Wilfrid — by Eata, and from his time all bishops of Lindisfarne were Anglo-Saxons.[60] Bede ended his discussion of Colmán's departure and of his successors by bringing the attention back to Aidan. Colmán took some of his bones with him to Ireland, but indicated that the rest should be buried in the sanctuary of the church at Lindisfarne. He also requested of the king that Eata should be appointed abbot of Lindisfarne (this was before the death of Tuda) as he was one of twelve boys who had been recruited and trained by Aidan.[61] The final section of the chapter is a paean of praise for the religious life of Colmán and his predecessors which further draws attention to the importance of the traditions established by Aidan. Even among the Irish of Lindisfarne Bede shows some reservations, especially of Fínán, and favoured those whose mode of life was closest to that of Aidan.

Bede and Aidan

Although Bede could not have known Aidan personally as he died in 651, over twenty years before Bede was born in *c.* 673, he did have personal links to him. Bede could have added himself to the list of those who had been trained by someone who had been trained by Aidan. In his account of the death of Chad at Lichfield Bede reveals that his source of information was 'frater quidam de his qui me in scripturis erudiebant, et erat in monasterio ac magisterio illius educatus, uocabulo Trumberct' (one of his brothers named Trumberct, a monk educated in his monastery [i.e. Lastingham or Barrow-on-Humber] and under his rule and one of those who taught me the Scriptures).[62] Bede says nothing else about Trumberct and his implication that he was at one time at Wearmouth or Jarrow (unless we are meant to understand that Bede travelled to study with him). Trumberct is not referred to in either of the histories of the abbots of Wearmouth and Jarrow.[63] But the connection of Trumberct with Chad links him with the Irish tradition, for not only had Chad been trained at Lindisfarne he had studied in Ireland at *Rath Melsigi*, in the company of the Anglo-Saxon religious exile Ecgbert, of whom Bede writes most approvingly and credits with the conversion of Iona to the Roman calculation of Easter.[64]

Trumberct's relatively unusual first name-element may suggest that he could have been related to Trumhere who became bishop of the Middle Angles and Mercians in the late 650s, and like Chad and Cedd was one of the Anglo-Saxon members of the Lindisfarne community who was sent to work further south during Oswiu's

59 Bede, *Historia ecclesiastica*, III.27, ed. and trans. by Colgrave and Mynors, pp. 312–13.
60 Cubitt, 'Wilfrid's "Usurping Bishops"', pp. 24–26.
61 Bede, *Historia ecclesiastica*, III.26, ed. and trans. by Colgrave and Mynors, pp. 308–09.
62 Bede, *Historia ecclesiastica*, IV.3, ed. and trans. by Colgrave and Mynors, pp. 342–43.
63 *Abbots of Wearmouth and Jarrow*, ed. and trans. by Grocock and Wood.
64 Stancliffe, 'British and Irish contexts', pp. 81–82; Ó Croínín, 'Rath Melsigi'.

overlordship.[65] If Trumberct was related to Trumhere he was very well-connected indeed, for Trumhere is said by Bede to have been a kinsman of Eanflaed, daughter of King Edwin of Deira (616–633) and of her cousin Oswine who also ruled in Deira (644–651).[66] After the latter had been murdered by Eanflaed's husband, King Oswiu, Gilling was founded in atonement and Trumhere was its first abbot. Aidan had worked closely with Oswine and died only twelve days after the king was murdered.[67] Bede does not actually say so, but there must be a possibility that the two deaths were connected.[68] His sympathies in the *Ecclesiastical History* are entirely with Oswine and Aidan.[69] Gilling was to have further connections with Bede for Abbot Ceolfrith of Jarrow began his career at Gilling when his brother Cynefrith was its abbot. When Cynefrith decided to travel to Ireland he appointed their kinsman Tunbert in his place. But in *c.* 660, Tunbert, Ceolfrith and other monks left Gilling to join Wilfrid's new foundation at Ripon (granted originally to Eata).[70] Bede says nothing about this in either the *Ecclesiastical History* or his *Lives of the Abbots*, and the information is to be found only in the Anonymous *Life of Ceolfrith*.[71] There was clearly a very disturbed period in the ecclesiastical history of Deira between 651 and 660 as the rapid change in abbots at both Gilling and Ripon suggests.[72] A potential period of crisis is the aftermath of the battle of the River Winwaed in 655 (referred to above as a possible crisis-point for Hild) in which Oswiu's nephew Oethelwald, who was subking in Deira, had initially supported Oswiu's enemy Penda of Mercia.[73] Oethelwald is not heard of again after the battle, and it may well be that he and others associated with him were additional victims of Oswiu's vengeance.

The selective use of material for the reign of Oswiu and the early history of Gilling provides a good example of how Bede might shape the presentation of events by suppressing some evidence and accentuating other information. While his decisions may have served some of his wider purposes, which will be considered further below, one can also see that they could be affected by Bede's personal history. Material that may not have been to the credit of the family of Abbot Ceolfrith of Jarrow, a man whom Bede clearly held in high regard, was omitted. Bede preferred to concentrate on evidence that rebounded to the credit and prestige of Anglo-Saxons trained by,

---

65 Bede, *Historia ecclesiastica*, III.22 and 24, ed. and trans. by Colgrave and Mynors, pp. 280–85 and 292–93. See also Trumwine, a monk of Whitby who for a period was bishop of the Picts: Bede, *Historia ecclesiastica*, IV.26, ed. and trans. by Colgrave and Mynors, pp. 428–31.

66 Bede, *Historia ecclesiastica*, III.24, ed. and trans by Colgrave and Mynors, pp. 292–95.

67 Bede, *Historia ecclesiastica*, III.15, ed. and trans. by Colgrave and Mynors, pp. 260–61.

68 Higham, 'Dynasty and Cult', pp. 96–100.

69 Bede, *Historia ecclesiastica*, III.14, ed. and trans. by Colgrave and Mynors, pp. 254–61; Higham, *(Re-) Reading Bede*, pp. 155–58.

70 *Abbots of Wearmouth and Jarrow*, ed. and trans. by Grocock and Wood, pp. 78–81.

71 *Abbots of Wearmouth and Jarrow*, ed. and trans. by Grocock and Wood, pp. xlvi–xlviii.

72 For the problems surrounding Ripon's early years see Eddius Stephanus, *The Life of Bishop Wilfrid*, ed. and trans. Colgrave, pp. 16–19; Bede, *Historia ecclesiastica*, III.25, ed. and trans. by Colgrave and Mynors, pp. 296–99; David Kirby,'Northumbria in the Time of Wilfrid', pp. 23–24.

73 Bede, *Historia ecclesiastica*, III.24, ed. and trans. by Colgrave and Mynors, pp. 290–91; see also his cryptic comment about Oethelwald as one of those who 'attacked' Oswiu in III. 14, pp. 254–55.

or in the tradition of Bishop Aidan, among whom Bede could include himself as the pupil of Trumberct.

In his continuing respect for a former teacher who had been trained in the Irish tradition Bede presents a contrast with the only other Anglo-Saxon to rival him in scholarship, Aldhelm of Malmesbury (late 630s–709). Aldhelm had probably been first educated by the Irishman Maildubh at Malmesbury and then in various schools in Ireland.[74] He then joined the school of Hadrian and Theodore at Canterbury, and was so impressed by their curriculum that he became highly critical of his previous Irish training and sought to discourage other Anglo-Saxons from studying there.[75] He was also strongly influenced by Theodore's condemnation of any aberrant religious practices among British or Irish clergy. Wilfrid too had received an initial education from Irish masters that was overlain by subsequent study in Francia and Rome. The personal educational experiences of Aldhelm, Wilfrid, and Bede may help to account for differences in attitude to the Irish, but it may also be significant that Aldhelm and Wilfrid were both bishops and actively involved in correcting and integrating British and Irish-trained Christians into the Anglo-Saxon Church. Bede shared their suspicion of the British,[76] but his loyalty to certain Irish and Irish-trained mentors seems exceptional.

Although Bede could not have met Aidan, he did have the opportunity to meet an abbot of Iona who was one of the foremost scholars of the day, namely Adomnán, the author of the *Life of St Columba*. Adomnán may have had a role in helping King Aldfrith of Northumbria (685/686–705) gain the throne, and soon after Aldfrith's accession he visited Northumbria twice, probably in 686 and 688,[77] with a third possible visit in *c.* 702.[78] At least one of these visits took him to Jarrow where Abbot Ceolfrith sought, ultimately successfully, to win him to the Roman calculation of Easter.[79] It is therefore likely that Bede had seen Adomnán in person, and, if Adomnán had indeed visited Jarrow in *c.* 702 to discuss the issue of Easter, as David Woods has suggested,[80] Bede could have played a role in the deliberations, for his work *On Times* is believed to have been completed in 703.[81] Bede certainly knew some of his books, and edited a version of Adomnán's *De Locis Sanctis* as well as quoting from it extensively in the *Ecclesiastical History* (a singular honour in this work).[82] Bede refers to Adomnán as 'uir bonus et sapiens et scientia scripturarum nobilissime instructus' (a good and wise man with an excellent knowledge of the scriptures).[83] But he may

---

74   Yorke, 'Aldhelm's Irish and British Connections'; Dempsey, *Aldhelm of Malmesbury*, pp. 31–63.

75   Lapidge, 'The Career of Aldhelm'; Dempsey, *Aldhelm of Malmesbury*, pp. 31–63.

76   Stancliffe, *Bede, Wilfrid and the Irish*, and 'British and Irish Contexts'.

77   Yorke, 'Adomnán at the Court of King Aldfrith'.

78   Woods, 'Adomnán, Plague and the Easter Controversy'.

79   Bede, *Historia ecclesiastica*, V.15 and 21, ed. and trans. by Colgrave and Mynors, pp. 504–09; 550–51.

80   Woods, 'Adomnán, Plague and the Easter Controversy'.

81   Bede, *The Reckoning of Time*, trans. by Wallis, p. xvi, n. 4.

82   O'Loughlin, *Adomnán and the Holy Places*; Bede, *Historia ecclesiastica*, V.16 and 17, ed. and trans. by Colgrave and Mynors, pp. 508–13.

83   Bede, *Historia ecclesiastica*, V.15, ed. and trans. by Colgrave and Mynors, pp. 506–07.

have gained more from a personal meeting with him including information about Columba and the organisation of Iona in which Bede seems to have been particularly interested,[84] and traditions about the foundation of Scottish Dál Riata by Reuda.[85] One does also wonder if Adomnán's presence at Jarrow might have had a significant impact on Bede himself. Adomnán embodied a monastic ethos that may have differed on several counts from what was practised at Wearmouth and Jarrow. His presence may have helped Bede envisage something of the effect that Aidan could have had on the Northumbrian court in the 630s and 640s.

Conclusion: The *Ecclesiastical History* in Context

Particularly in his attribution of miracles to Northumbrian royal and episcopal leaders Bede reveals his high regard for the standards promoted by Bishop Aidan of Lindisfarne that were maintained by those who followed and supported him. Bede's preferences are all the more surprising because they appear unheralded in his earlier writings. In his two *Lives* of St Cuthbert Bede undoubtedly praises and promotes the Lindisfarne bishop, but the Irish background of his training is understated, and in the prose *Life* in particular Cuthbert is portrayed as an exemplary monk and bishop in the Augustinian and Gregorian traditions.[86] The chronicle included by Bede in his *The Reckoning of Time* (725) recorded the role of Paulinus and Edwin in the conversion of Northumbria, but has nothing to say of Aidan and Oswald.[87] Such considerations may reflect what seems to have been an extremely tense and difficult period in the Northumbrian Church after the synod of Whitby of 664 when under Archbishop Theodore and Bishop Wilfrid any trace of association with Irish practices that had been branded as heretical had to be repudiated if not expunged.[88] Wilfrid caused considerable problems at Lindisfarne when he temporarily took over the bishopric after the death of Cuthbert in 687: 'tanta æcclesiam illam temptationis aura concussit, ut plures e fratribus loco magis cedere, quam talibus uellent interesse periculis' (so great a blast of trial beat upon that church that many of the brethren chose to depart from the place rather than be in the midst of such dangers).[89] Bede does not specify exactly what happened, and it may not only have been Cuthbert's own legacy that was attacked, but, as Clare Stancliffe has suggested, the relics of Aidan may have been a focus of Wilfrid's antagonism.[90]

---

84   Bede, *Historia ecclesiastica*, III.4, ed. and trans. by Colgrave and Mynors, pp. 222–25.
85   Bede, *Historia ecclesiastica*, I.1, ed. and trans. by Colgrave and Mynors, pp. 18–19; McSparron and Williams, '… And they Won Land Among the Picts' argue that Bede reproduced a reliable tradition also known to Adomnán.
86   Stancliffe, 'Cuthbert and the Polarity between Pastor and Solitary'.
87   Bede, *The Reckoning of Time*, ed. Wallis, p. 228; Cuthbert is also included p. 233.
88   Stancliffe, 'Bede, Wilfrid and the Irish', pp. 16–17, though as she points out, Theodore came to modify some of his initially harsh rulings on Irish who continued to follow the 'Celtic' Easter.
89   Bede and Anon., *Two Lives of St Cuthbert*, ed. and trans. by Colgrave, pp. 286–87.
90   Stancliffe, 'Bede, Wilfrid and the Irish', p. 25.

This was the discordant background against which Bede grew up in the Northumbrian Church, and in which his earliest writings were produced. The production of rival house histories within Northumbria in the late seventh and early eighth centuries can be seen as a product of these insecure times when reputations had to be protected and promoted.[91] The anonymous *Life of Cuthbert* was written between 698 and 705; the Whitby *Life of Pope Gregory* probably dates to between 704 and 714, and Stephen's *Life of Wilfrid* to between 712 and 714. Bede's metrical *Life of Cuthbert* may have been written around 705, not long after the anonymous *Life* was produced and perhaps intended as a twinned composition to it.[92] The prose *Life* though is somewhat later and is usually dated to around 720. By this time an important event had occurred which would allow Northumbria's Irish legacy to be viewed more objectively for in 716, apparently through the intervention of the Anglo-Saxon Ecgbert who had lived at *Rath Melsigi*, Iona had adopted the Roman method of calculating Easter.[93]

The adoption of the Roman Easter on Iona helps to explain why Bede was able to write so sympathetically about Aidan and the traditions he introduced to Lindisfarne. Although it has been claimed that the tensions caused by Wilfrid and his hardline views were still an issue that Bede needed to confront in the *Ecclesiastical History*,[94] his portrait of Wilfrid in that work seems conciliatory rather than overtly hostile.[95] Bede instead seems representative of a 'middle' party who believed in the correctness of the Roman Easter without feeling it necessary to castigate all aspects of the Northumbrian Irish tradition.[96] That there were rivalries within the Church hierarchy, leading, for instance, to the expulsion of Bishop Acca in 731, is undoubtedly the case, but the issues were not necessarily the same as in the post-Whitby period, and Bede does not explain them.[97] In part the tensions may well have been linked with political rivalries for the throne when following the death of Osred (son of Aldfrith) in 716 rival lines challenged the domination of the descendants of Oswiu.[98] Although Bede promoted the cult of Oswald in the *Ecclesiastical History*, it seems unlikely that he was motivated by the political disputes. Oswald is not known to have had any surviving descendants, and Bede's treatment of his brother Oswiu who did was less than favourable and his discussion of the reigns of Aldfrith and Osred limited and reserved.[99]

The contemporary issue to which Bede draws the reader's attention in the *Ecclesiastical History*, is one which, as Alan Thacker and Scott DeGregorio have indicated,[100] is also highlighted in his later biblical commentaries and the *Letter to*

---

91   Rollason, 'Hagiography and Politics'; Goffart, *The Narrators of Barbarian History*, pp. 262–71.
92   Thacker, 'Lindisfarne and the Origins of the Cult', pp. 115–22.
93   Bede, *Historia ecclesiastica*, v. 22, ed. and trans. by Colgrave and Mynors, pp. 552–55; Charles-Edwards, *Early Christian Ireland*, pp. 308–26.
94   Goffart, *The Narrators of Barbarian History*, pp. 307–28.
95   Stancliffe, 'Bede, Wilfrid and the Irish'; Higham, *(Re)-Reading Bede*, pp. 58–69.
96   Charles-Edwards, *Early Christian Ireland*, pp. 336–37.
97   Stancliffe, 'Disputed Episcopacy'.
98   Kirby, 'Northumbria in the Time of Wilfrid', pp. 20–29.
99   Higham, *(Re-) Reading Bede*, pp. 187–209.
100 Thacker, 'Bede's Ideal of Reform'; DeGregorio, '"Nostrorum socordiam temporum"'; DeGregorio, 'Bede's *In Ezram et Neemiam*'.

Ecgbert, also written in 731, namely, the quality of Northumbria's bishops. Aidan is promoted as a model bishop in the traditions laid down by Augustine of Hippo and Gregory the Great and the reader is invited to reflect on how those same qualities seem to be lacking in the current day:

> In tantum autem uita illius a nostri temporis segnitia distabat, ut omnes qui cum eo incedebant, siue adtonsi seu laici, meditari deberent, id est aut legendis scripturis aut psalmis discendis operam dare ... Numquam diuitibus honoris siue timoris gratia, siqua deliquissent, reticebat, sed aspera illos inuectione corrigebat. Nullam potentibus saeculi pecuniam, excepta solum esca, siquos hospitio suscepisset.

> > Aidan's life was in great contrast to our modern slothfulness all who accompanied him, whether tonsured or laymen, had to engage in some form of study, that is to say, to occupy themselves either with reading the scriptures or learning the psalms ... Neither respect nor fear made him keep silence about the sins of the rich, but he would correct them with a stern rebuke. He would never give money to powerful men of the world, but only food on such occasions as he entertained them.[101]

It was a model of episcopal behaviour and way of life which conformed to impeccable Romanist standards, but which contrasted, as Clare Stancliffe has argued, with some aspects of that favoured by Bishop Wilfrid and his followers.[102]

By 731 the discord over the Easter controversy and the tensions of its aftermath had cleared and Bede was free, or at least freer, to write what he wished on the topic. Perhaps too as a senior and well-established theologian he felt better able to follow his own inclinations than when he was a younger man. In choosing which Northumbrian individuals he deemed to be most significant, and the best role models, Bede seems to reveal his own preferences. The achievements and qualities of Aidan were not recorded in any of the surviving texts so, as Bede says, his information came 'ab eis qui illum nouere' (from those who knew him).[103] These included his own teacher Trumberct, Abbot Ceolfrith of Jarrow, and the diocesan who ordained him as deacon and priest, John of Beverley, bishop of Hexham. Bede himself was part of a network of exemplary individuals who could trace their religious standards back to Aidan. In many ways the *Ecclesiastical History* is Bede's most personal work and he ended it with a brief account of his life and a list of his written works.[104] In choosing to put so much emphasis on Aidan and his connections, Bede not only reveals his own high standards, but perhaps alerts us to the individuals who were most significant to him in making him the man that he was.[105]

---

101 Bede, *Historia ecclesiastica*, III.5, ed. and trans. by Colgrave and Mynors, pp. 226–29.
102 Stancliffe, 'Disputed Episcopacy'.
103 Bede, *Historia ecclesiastica*, III.17, ed. and trans. by Colgrave and Mynors, pp. 266–67.
104 Bede, *Historia ecclesiastica*, V.24, ed. and trans. by Colgrave and Mynors, pp. 566–71.
105 I would like to record my thanks to Scott DeGregorio and to the anonymous referee who both helped me to improve the paper though their observations and corrections, though, of course, they bear no responsibility for any problems remaining.

Works Cited

Primary Sources

Alcuin: The Bishops, Kings, and Saints of York, ed. and trans. by Peter Godman (Oxford: Clarendon Press, 1982)

Anon., *The Earliest Life of Gregory the Great*, ed. and trans. by Bertram Colgrave (Lawrence; University of Kansa Press, 1968)

Bede, *Historia abbatum*, ed. and trans. by Christopher Grocock and Ian N. Wood in *Abbots of Wearmouth and Jarrow*, Oxford Medieval Texts (Oxford: Clarendon Press, 2013), pp. 22–75

——, *Historia ecclesiastica*, ed. and trans. by Bertram Colgrave and R. A. B. Mynors (Oxford: Clarendon Press, 1969)

——, *Opera Historica*, ed. by Charles Plummer, 2 vols (Oxford: Clarendon Press, 1895)

——, *The Reckoning of Time*, trans. Faith Wallis (Liverpool; Liverpool University Press, 2004)

——, *Vita metrica sancti Cuthberti*, in *Bedas Metrische Vita sancti Cuthberti*, ed. by W. Jaager, Palaestra, 198 (Leipzig: Mayer & Müller, 1935)

Bede and Anon., *Two Lives of St Cuthbert*, ed. and trans. by Bertram Colgrave (Cambridge: Cambridge University Press, 1940)

Eddius Stephanus, *The Life of Bishop Wilfrid*, ed. and trans. by Bertram Colgrave (Cambridge: Cambridge University Press, 1927)

Secondary Studies

Barrow, Julia, 'How Coifi Pierced Christ's Side: A Re-Examination of Bede's *Ecclesiastical History* II, Chapter 13', *Journal of Ecclesiastical History*, 62 (2011), 693–707

Blair, John, *Anglo-Saxon Oxfordshire* (Stroud: Sutton, 1994)

Charles-Edwards, Thomas, *Early Christian Ireland* (Cambridge: Cambridge University Press, 2000)

Cubitt, Catherine, 'Wilfrid's "Usurping Bishops": Episcopal Elections in Anglo-Saxon England, *c.* 600–*c.* 800', *Northern History*, 25 (1989), 18–38

DeGregorio, Scott, '"Nostrorum socordiam temporum": The Reforming Impulse of Bede's Later Exegesis', *Early Medieval Europe*, 11 (2002), 107–22

——, 'Bede's *In Ezram et Neemiam* and the Reform of the Northumbrian Church', *Speculum*, 79 (2004), 1–25

Dempsey, George, *Aldhelm of Malmesbury and the Ending of Late Antiquity*, Studia Traditionis Theologiae (Turnhout: Brepols, 2015)

Goffart, Walter, *The Narrators of Barbarian History (A.D. 550–800): Jordanes, Gregory of Tours, Bede and Paul the Deacon* (Princeton: Princeton University Press, 1988)

Gunn, Vicky, 'Bede and the Martyrdom of Oswald', *Studies in Church History*, 30 (1993), 57–66

Higham, Nicholas, 'Dynasty and Cult: The Utility of Christian Mission to Northumbrian Kings between 642 and 654', in *Northumbria's Golden Age*, ed. by Jane Hawkes and Susan Mills (Stroud: Sutton, 1999), pp. 95–104

————, (Re-)Reading Bede: The Ecclesiastical History in Context, (London: Routledge, 2006)

————, 'Wilfrid in Bede's *Historia*', in *Wilfrid: Abbot, Bishop, Saint, Papers from the 1300th Anniversary Conferences*, ed. by Nicholas Higham (Donington: Shaun Tyas, 2013), pp. 54–66

Hunter Blair, Peter, 'Whitby as a Centre of Learning in the Seventh Century', in *Learning and Literature in Anglo-Saxon England*, ed. by Michael Lapidge and Helmut Gneuss (Cambridge: Cambridge University Press, 1985), pp. 3–32

Ireland, Colin, 'Aldfrith of Northumbria and the Irish Genealogies', *Celtica*, 22 (1991), 64–78

Karkov, Catherine, 'Whitby, Jarrow and the Commemoration of the Dead', in *Northumbria's Golden Age*, ed. by Jane Hawkes and Susan Mills (Stroud: Sutton), pp. 126–35

Kirby, David, 'Northumbria in the Time of Wilfrid', in *Saint Wilfrid at Hexham*, ed. by David Kirby (Newcastle upon Tyne: Oriel, 1974), pp. 1–34

Lacey, Brian, *Cénel Conaill and the Donegal Kingdoms A.D. 500–800* (Dublin: Four Courts, 2006)

Lapidge, Michael, 'The Career of Aldhelm', *Anglo-Saxon England*, 36 (2007), 15–69

Laporte, Jean-Pierre, 'Grab und Reliquien der Königin Balthilde in Chelles-sur-Marne', in *Königinnen der Merowinger. Adelsgräber aus den Kirchen von Köln, Saint-Denis, Chelles und Frankfurt am Main*, ed. by Egon Wamers and Patrick Périn (Regensburg: Schnell und Steiner, 2013), pp. 126–44

McCready, William D., *Miracles and the Venerable Bede*, Studies and Texts, 118 (Toronto: Pontifical Institute of Mediaeval Studies, 1994)

McDougall, Sarah, *Royal Bastards: The Birth of Illegitimacy, 800–1230* (Oxford: Oxford University Press, 2017)

McSparron, Cormac and Williams, Brian, '"…and they won land among the Picts by friendly treaty or the sword": How a Re-Examination of Early Historical Sources and an Analysis of Early Medieval Settlement in North Co. Antrims Confirms the Validity of Traditional Accounts of Dál Riatic Migration to Scotland from Ulster', *Proceedings of the Society of Antiquaries of Scotland*, 141 (2011), 145–58

Moisl, Herman, 'The Bernician Royal Dynasty and the Irish in the Seventh Century', *Peritia*, 2 (1983), 103–26

Ó Corráin, Donnchadh, 'Ireland *c.* 800: Aspects of Society', in *A New History of Ireland: I Prehistoric and Early Ireland*, ed. by Dáibhí Ó Cróinín (Oxford: Oxford University Press, 2008), pp. 549–608

Ó Cróinín, Dáibhí, 'The Irish Provenance of Bede's Computus', *Peritia*, 2 (1983), 229–47

————, 'Rath Melsigi, Willibrord and the Earliest Echternach Manuscripts', *Peritia*, 3 (1984), 17–42

O'Loughlin, Thomas, *Adomnán and the Holy Places: The Perceptions of an Insular Monk on the Location of the Biblical Drama* (London: Clark, 2007)

Orschel, Vera, 'Mag nEó na Sacsan: An English colony in Ireland in the Seventh and Eighth Centuries', *Peritia*, 15 (2001), 81–107

Palmer, James, 'Wilfrid and the Frisians', in *Wilfrid: Abbot, Bishop, Saint, Papers from the 1300th Anniversary Conferences*, ed. by Nicholas Higham (Donington: Shaun Tyas, 2013), pp. 231–42

Picard, Jean-Michel, 'Bede, Admonán and the Writing of History', *Peritia*, 3 (1984), 50–67

Rollason, David, 'Hagiography and Politics in the Early Northumbria', in *Holy Men and Holy Women: Old English Prose Saints Lives and Their Contexts*, ed. by Paul Szarmach (Albany: State University of New York Press, 1996), pp. 95–114

Stancliffe, Clare, 'Cuthbert and the Polarity between Pastor and Solitary', in *St Cuthbert, His Cult and Community*, ed. by Gerald Bonner, David Rollason, and Clare Stancliffe (Woodbridge: Boydell Press, 1989), pp. 21–44

——, *Bede, Wilfrid and the Irish*, Jarrow Lecture, 2003 (Jarrow: St Paul's Church, 2003)

——, 'British and Irish Contexts', in *The Cambridge Companion to Bede*, ed. by Scott DeGregorio (Cambridge: Cambridge University Press, 2010), pp. 69–83

——, 'Disputed Episcopacy: Bede, Acca, and the Relationship between Stephen's *Life of St Wilfrid* and the Early Prose Lives of St Cuthbert', *Anglo-Saxon England*, 41 (2013), 7–40

Thacker, Alan, 'Bede's Ideal of Reform', in *Ideal and Reality in Frankish and Anglo-Saxon Society. Essays Presented to J, M. Wallace-Hadrill*, ed. by Patrick Wormald, Donald Bullough, and Roger Collins (Oxford: Basil Blackwell, 1983), pp. 130–53

——, 'Lindisfarne and the Origins of the Cult of St Cuthbert', in *St Cuthbert, His Cult and Community*, ed. by Gerald Bonner, David Rollason, and Clare Stancliffe (Woodbridge: Boydell, 1989), pp. 103–22

——, '*Membra disjecta*: The Division of the Body and Diffusion of the Cult', in *Oswald: Northumbrian King to European Saint*, ed. by Clare Stancliffe and Eric Cambridge (Stamford: Paul Watkins, 1995), pp. 97–127

——, 'Bede and the Irish' in *Beda Venerabilis: Historian, Monk and Northumbrian*, ed. by L. A. J. R. Houwen and A. A. MacDonald (Groningen: Forsten, 1996), pp. 31–60

——, 'Memorializing Gregory the Great: The Origin and Transmission of a Papal Cult in the Seventh and Early Eighth Centuries', *Early Medieval Europe*, 7 (1998), 59–84

Wallace-Hadrill, J. M., *Bede's Ecclesiastical History of the English People: A Historical Commentary* (Oxford: Clarendon Press, 1985)

Wilfrid: Abbot, Bishop, Saint, Papers from the 1300th Anniversary Conferences, ed. by Nicholas Higham (Donington: Shaun Tyas, 2013)

Woods, David, 'Adomnán, Plague and the Easter Controversy', *Anglo-Saxon England*, 40 (2012), 1–14

Yorke, Barbara, *Rex Doctissimus: Bede and King Aldfrith of Northumbria* (Newcastle upon Tyne: Jarrow lecture, 2009)

——, 'Adomnán at the Court of King Aldfrith', in *Adomnán of Iona: Theologian, Lawmaker, Peacemaker*, ed. by Jonathan Wooding (Dublin: Four Courts, 2010), pp. 36–50

——, 'Aldhelm's Irish and British Connections', in *Aldhelm and Sherborne: Essays to Celebrate the Founding of the Bishopric*, ed. by Katherine Barker and Nicholas Brooks (Oxford: Oxbow, 2010), pp. 164–80

——, 'Heilige Männer, heilige Frauen und die Christianisierung Northumbriens', in *CREDO: Christianisierung Europas im Mittelalter*, ed. by Christoph Stiegemann, Martin Kroker and Wolfgang Walter (Petersberg: Michael Imhof, 2013), 2 vols, I, pp. 214–21

——, 'Queen Balthild's 'monastic policy' and the Origins of Female Religious Houses in Southern England', in *Early Medieval Monasticism in the North Sea Zone*, ed. by Gabor Thomas and Alexandra Knox, Anglo-Saxon Studies in Archaeology and History, 20 (Oxford: Oxbow, 2017), pp. 7–16

SCOTT DEGREGORIO

Bede's Midlife Crisis: The Commentary on First Samuel

The date of AD 716 is hardly a conspicuous one in the grand sweep of the early medieval west. But it is one that looms large in that very best of sub-periods of early Anglo-Saxon England's history, the Age of Bede, for which Alan Thacker has long been so perceptive a guide. I recall first encountering Alan's scholarship on Bede when I was starting my graduate work on Anglo-Saxon literature at the University of Toronto in the mid-1990s. Bede, I had previously come to think, was boring. Of course till that point I had not read much at all, only a few obligatory bits of the *Ecclesiastical History* (i.e. Coifi's sparrow, Caedmon's Hymn, etc.), and had not the least idea about the frameworks in which the man himself, as author, monk or whatever, should be studied. All that changed in a flash when I read 'Bede's Idea of Reform' and 'Monks, Preaching and Pastoral Care in Early Anglo-Saxon England'. Suddenly both Bede's oeuvre and the landscape of his cultural world were dense with compelling issues to consider. This led me to devote a chapter of my dissertation to his exegesis, something wholly inconceivable when I had arrived at Toronto.[1] Alan was extremely kind to receive this chapter when I asked him to read it, even though he hardly knew me at all, and to return it with generous and insightful recommendations for improvement. Much of the work I have since done on Bede I owe to the inspiration of his scholarship and the collegial guidance of his conversation, as the following chapter will no doubt show. And with that, let's return to AD 716.

All too often, in Bede's times or any other distant past, dates and the events associated with them remain elusive and conjectural, but 716 is a rare exception as its eventfulness is well documented. We know of the big events on the scene that year: the death — perhaps even murder, as some have speculated — of King Osred, and the conversion of Iona from its own insular customs to the Roman Easter and tonsure, thanks to the teaching of Ecgberht, a monk from Lindisfarne.[2] But closer to Bede's own

---

1 DeGregorio, 'Explorations of Spirituality'.
2 Bede mentions these together at *Historia ecclesiastica*, V.22, ed. and trans. by Colgrave and Mynors, pp. 552–53. On the complexity of Ecgberht's mission, see Herbert, *Iona, Kells, and Derry*, pp. 57–60.

Scott DeGregorio • is Professor of English and College-Wide Programs at the University of Michigan — Dearborn.

Cities, Saints, and Communities in Early Medieval Europe, ed. by Scott DeGregorio and Paul Kershaw, SEM 46 (Turnhout: Brepols, 2020), pp. 241-263
BREPOLS PUBLISHERS   DOI 10.1484/M.SEM-EB.5.119630

sphere we know too about the departure of his beloved Abbot Ceolfrith for Rome, an event that, in his biography of Ceolfrith, he dates precisely to 4 June 716, and in a different work pointedly associates with 'inopinata mentis anxietas' (unexpected mental anguish) — in no small part, as he makes a point of indicating, because of its 'subitus' (suddenness).

> …discessu abbatis mei reuerendissimi qui post longam monasterialis curae obseruantiam subitus Romam adire atque inter loca beatorum apostolorum ac martyrum Christi corporibus sacra extremum senex reddere halitum disponendo non parua commissorum sibi animos et eo maiore quo improuisa conturbatione stupefecit.

>> …the departure of my very reverend abbot, who, after his long service caring for the monastery, by suddenly arranging to go to Rome and to give out his last breath as an old man among the places made holy by the bodies of the blessed apostles and martyrs of Christ, stunned the minds of those entrusted to him with no small confusion, made all the greater for the fact that it was unforeseen.[3]

These words are from the prologue to the fourth book of Bede's *In primam partem Samuhelis*, the long work of exegetical commentary he wrote on 1 Samuel. Thanks to these famous remarks concerning Ceolfrith's dash Rome-ward, we have something usually unattainable in the study of Bede's exegesis — relatively firm grounds for dating this commentary. That is, we can place this one commentary fairly securely in historical time, and thus begin to explore the relation of its date to its contents with something besides rampant speculation. The writing of *On First Samuel*, as I shall refer to it hereafter, is thus another event that can be confidently linked to AD 716, a year of self-admitted crisis for Bede. And so I want to argue that *On First Samuel* itself is a work forged of crisis, very apparent in the text itself, and that this aspect too is something that makes the commentary a distinctive work, indeed a pivotal one in Bede's exegetical corpus.

First, some chronological points of orientation should be laid down for context. The commencement of Bede's authorial career is usually placed sometime around between 695–700, with the composition of the textbooks *De arte metrica*, *De schematibus et tropis*, and *De orthographia*.[4] Following in the early 700s are *De locis sanctis*, *De natura rerum*, *De temporibus*.[5] Here also belongs his first attempt at biblical commentary, the *Expositio Apocalypseos*, dated by Wallace to shortly before 710.[6] This commentary, we can say with reasonable certainty, was succeeded by other attempts to treat the New Testament, first the commentaries on Acts and First John, and then on Luke's

3 Bede, *In primam partem Samuhelis*, IV, ed. by Hurst, p. 212, ll. 7–12; *Bede: On First Samuel*, trans. by DeGregorio and Love, p. 433.
4 Laistner, *Hand-List*, pp. 132, 137.
5 Laistner, *Hand-List*, pp. 83, 139, 145; and Kendall and Wallis, 'Introduction', pp. 1–3.
6 Wallis, 'Introduction', pp. 39–57.

gospel.[7] While the first instalment of the commentary on Genesis was, on rather fragile grounds, set by Laistner sometime between 703 and 709, Calvin Kendall has now confidently redated it to no earlier than 718, thus removing it from the flurry of Bede's earliest exegetical activity.[8] This means that Bede's first exegetical engagements, so far as we know, concerned the New Testament. We can, therefore, speak about a shift that he makes to the Old Testament as denoting a separate stage — and a most significant one at that, since it would, when Bede was done, end up encompassing material from every major section of the Old Testament except the major prophets, indeed even the Apocrypha.[9] But the central point for our purpose is that we can just about pinpoint when that stage began in earnest, and here too we find ourselves again at AD 716. Bede's first real sustained attempt at Old Testament allegorical exegesis, that is to say, may well have been his commentary on the first book of Samuel.

To be sure, AD 716 can hardly be the date for the whole work. It is important to emphasize that the reference to Ceolfrith's departure, which allows us to grasp that date, occurs in the prologue to Book 4, the last book of the commentary.[10] As a chronological marker, then, Ceolfrith's departure in June 716 is at best the *terminus post quem* for the final book of *On First Samuel*, but not for the three that precede it. The text is massive; at nearly 300 pages in Hurst's edition, it comes in as Bede's longest Old Testament commentary.[11] It is unlikely if not impossible that it was knocked out in one year. For one thing, all too easily forgotten, we would have to account for the pace of monastic routine and other such daily interruptions that could have been a drag on Bede's work schedule. But for another, we have evidence that this was already a rather frenetic period for Bede, what with his work on the *tres pandectes nouae translationis* that was undoubtedly going on at this same time, or else his reply to Nothhelm's queries in *Thirty Questions on the Book of Kings*, dated to 715 by Paul Meyvaert. Indeed Meyvaert has demonstrated that parts of this letter devoted largely to explicating the historical sense of certain difficult passages in the Book of Kings appear to have been drawn from work Bede had already done in *On First Samuel*.[12]

Thus as one of several projects afoot at this time, Bede's long work on 1 Samuel surely must be seen as unfolding over not one but perhaps a few years. Indeed, evidence internal to *On First Samuel* suggests that it was perhaps begun sometime after 710. The prologue refers to its dedicatee Acca as bishop, and moreover refers to

---

7 See Bede, *Expositio Actuum Apostolorum, Praefatio*, ed. by Laistner, p. 5, lines 76–77, where he mentions having just completed an exposition of the Epistle to 1 John, which later would form one section of the commentary he devoted to the Seven Catholic Epistles. Because the letter Acca wrote to Bede, which now forms part of the preface to the Luke commentary, speaks of Bede's work on Acts as now completed, it would appear that Bede worked through these texts in the following order: Seven Catholic Epistles first, then the Acts of the Apostles, finally Luke's Gospel. See Laistner, *Hand-list*, pp. 20, 25–20, and 44–49.
8 Kendall, 'Introduction', pp. 45–53.
9 DeGregorio, 'Bede and the Old Testament'.
10 Bede, *In primam partem Samuhelis*, IV, ed. by Hurst, p. 212, ll. 1–28.
11 The text runs to 268 pages in Hurst's edition, topping Bede's commentary on the Song of Songs, which comes in at 208 pages.
12 Meyvaert, '"In the Footsteps of the Fathers"'.

the commentary he had written on the Gospel of Luke, recently completed.[13] Given all this, Paul Meyvaert's guess was that *On First Samuel* was begun around 713 and was completed by 717.[14] We have no way of confidently affirming this exact range of dates, but it is probably not that far off. A period of a few years sounds about right for a commentary of this size and complexity.

So we have a good idea of when Bede was writing *On First Samuel*. The other thing we know is that this was not the happiest of times in Bede's Northumbria. In the fifth and final book of the *Ecclesiastical History*, he made a point of pausing to make note of the eventfulness of AD 716, writing that

> Siquidem anno ab incarnatione Domini DCCXVI, quo Osredo occiso Coenred gubernacula regni Nordanhymbrorum suscepit, cum uenisset ad eos de Hibernia Deo amabilis et cum omni honorificentia nominandus pater ac sacerdos Ecgberct, cuius superius memoriam saepius fecimus, honorifice ab eis et multo cum gaudio susceptus est.

> > In the year of our Lord 716, when Osred was killed and Cenred became ruler of the Northumbrian kingdom, Ecgberht, beloved of God (a father and priest to be named with all honour and he whom I have often spoken of), came to Iona from Ireland and was most honourably and joyfully received.[15]

The rest of this chapter celebrates a jubilant fact, namely that, as Bede goes on to say, 'Susceperunt autem Hiienses monachi docente Ecgbercto ritus uiuendi catholicos sub abbate Duunchado, post anno circiter LXXX ex quo ad praedicationem gentis Anglorum Aidanum miserant antistitem' (The monk of Iona accepted the catholic ways of life under the teaching of Ecgberht, while Dúnchad was abbot, about eighty years after they had sent Bishop Aidan to preach to the English).[16] But this is not what has caught the attention of scholars; their eyes have drifted rather to the three words buried in the introductory subordinate clause: 'quo Osredo occiso'. This boy king, the son of King Alchfrith, came to the throne in 705 at the tender age of 8. He ruled for just over a decade, thanks in no small part to assistance from Northumbria's most powerful churchman, Bishop Wilfrid, who adopted Osred as his son. In another work, the *Letter to Ecgberht*, Bede associates Northumbrian monasticism's precipitous decline with the start of Osred's reign,[17] though in his verse life of St Cuthbert, written much earlier, he alluded to him in quite favourable terms: '...utque nouus Iosia fideque animoque magis quam annis maturus, nostrum regit inclitus orbem' (like a new Josiah, more mature in faith and spirit than in years he rules our world with distinction).[18] Of him

13 Bede, *In primam partem Samuhelis*, IV, ed. by Hurst, pp. 9–10, ll. 34–47. In 710, upon the death of Wilfrid, Acca succeeded him as bishop of Hexham: see Bede, *Historia ecclesiastica*, V.20, ed. and trans. by Colgrave and Mynors, pp. 530–31.
14 Meyvaert, '"In the Footsteps of the Fathers"', p. 275.
15 Bede, *Historia ecclesiastica*, V.22, ed. and trans. by Colgrave and Mynors, pp. 552–53.
16 Bede, *Historia ecclesiastica*, V.22, ed. and trans. by Colgrave and Mynors, pp. 554–55.
17 Bede, *Epistola ad Ecgbertum Episcopum*, § 13, ed. by Grocock and Wood, pp. 148–49.
18 Bede, *Vita metrica sancti Cuthberti*, ed. by Jaager, pp. 99–100; *Bede's Latin Poetry*, ed. and trans. by Michael Lapidge.

elsewhere in his voluminous writings, Bede said no more. But David Kirby, some time ago, surmised that Osred's death must have been accompanied by a sense of insecurity in the kingdom, since with it came the end of the long hegemony that Æthelfrith's descendants had enjoyed since the accession of Oswald in 634.[19] The instability of things appears to be confirmed, as Peter Darby more recently has noted, by the fact that Osred's successor Cenred was of a different lineage and the further certainly more dire fact that his reign lasted only a mere two years.[20] This much, at least, is plain enough. The more elusive question, of course, is how this unstable political climate may have affected Wearmouth and Jarrow and, more specifically, its prodigious house author.

More recent work has answered this question with a strong yet admittedly speculative thesis, and here Thacker's voice has led the way. In a brief yet intrepid piece written in 2009, entitled 'Bede, the Britons and the Book of Samuel', Thacker argues first that Bede viewed the Britons as a problem, settled not already in the distant past but much alive in his own present day. Discussing various episodes concerning the British in the *Ecclesiastical History*, Thacker observes: 'Nothing in Bede's treatment of these episodes suggests that he viewed the Britons as a problem that was remote or in any way confined to the past. Indeed, he speaks at least three times of them in unmistakably hostile terms as a contemporary issue, still burning in his mind at the time the *Historia Ecclesiastica* was being written'.[21] He added weight to this claim, mid-discussion, with a fascinating analysis of Bede's use of the word *perfidia* 'faithlessness' as he used it in *On First Samuel*, some 62 times by Thacker's count.[22] There Bede applies the word especially to those enemies of the faith who exhibit the trait of 'faithlessness' — heretics, Jews, false brethren and bad Catholics, and schismatics chief among them. Thacker drew special attention to Bede's treatment of faithless Jews and heretics, noting that they 'offer an obvious parallel to the Britons',[23] and insisting again that such a focus resulted not merely from theological interests, but rather because 'Bede had present-day *perfidia* on his mind'.[24] A final section concludes Thacker's chapter, which begins with this admirably honest sentence: 'This highly speculative paper will conclude with one last especially wild speculation'.[25] In a few short paragraphs, intended to raise questions rather than provide answers, Thacker concludes by wondering whether the wider political events of 716 involving the slaying of Osred had something to do with Ceolfrith's quick departure for Rome in that year and so, by extension, also with the sudden mental anguish that caused Bede 'to lay down his pen at the completion of the third book of the commentary'.[26] He asked, 'Could the Britons have been implicated in his death?' and, even more boldly whether 'some of the brethren of Wearmouth–Jarrow had been involved in

19 Kirby, *Earliest English Kings*, p. 147.
20 Darby, *Bede and the End of Time*, p. 168.
21 Thacker, 'Bede, the Britons and the Book of Samuel', p. 134.
22 Thacker, 'Bede, the Britons and the Book of Samuel', p. 136.
23 Thacker, 'Bede, the Britons and the Book of Samuel', p. 141.
24 Thacker, 'Bede, the Britons and the Book of Samuel', p. 141.
25 Thacker, 'Bede, the Britons and the Book of Samuel', p. 144.
26 Thacker, 'Bede, the Britons and the Book of Samuel', p. 144.

the plotting which led to the killing of Osred and the departure of Ceolfrith'. Of Bede himself Thacker wrote:

> Almost certainly, the violent death of the king — probably through treachery — and the — perhaps enforced — resignation of his abbot were important factors in Bede's preoccupation with *perfidia* in his commentary. There can be little doubt that as he wrote Bede had his own times much in mind, and through discourse on heresy, false brethren and the unfaithful Jews sought to express his feelings about contemporary events. He understood, it seems to me, the ambivalence of the biblical text itself and endorsed its picture of the fall of kings.[27]

As applied to Bede's own day, this 'picture', Thacker believed, in fact included a veiled reference to Osred's untimely death, in Book 2 of the commentary, in the midst of Bede's comments on 1 Samuel 15. 27–28, where Samuel forecasts the rejection of King Saul: '**The Lord has rent the kingdom of Israel from you this day, and will give it to your neighbour who is better than you**'. Here is the key sentence:

> Sed et hodie quisque sacra eloquia quibus eruditus est et ad quaerendum regnum caeleste imbutus improba mente contempserit quia uestem sacrosanctam ungentis se in regnum maculat ablatam sibi regni beatitudinem proximo meliori relinquit.

>> But also today everyone who has been educated in the sacred words and instructed to seek the kingdom of heaven but has scorned those words with wicked mind, because he dishonours the sacrosanct garment of the one anointing him for the kingdom, leaves for his neighbour, who is better than him, the blessedness of the kingdom that has been taken from him.[28]

Osred, of course, is not mentioned here, but it struck Thacker that such an image as that of the kingdom being torn from Saul and given to David, since Bede 'was writing it during a crisis of kingship of his own Northumbria', must surely mean that 'Almost certainly Bede had contemporary political implications in mind'.[29]

These are of course brilliant insights, typical of Thacker's ability to tease out deeper meanings, and his understanding of Bede as always engaged.[30] If they are correct, then *On First Samuel* was indeed very much a text forged in the crucible of crisis, both personally for the author, given what was afoot at Wearmouth and Jarrow, and more widely for the Northumbrian kingdom at large. Ian Wood has recently echoed Thacker in articulating a similar view of the work: 'The British threat, the murder of Osred and the division of the Wearmouth–Jarrow community surely impinged on Bede's thought as he wrote the Commentary on Samuel — a choice of subject, like

---

27 Thacker, 'Bede, the Britons and the Book of Samuel', p. 146.
28 Bede, *In primam partem Samuhelis*, II, ed. by Hurst, pp. 134, ll. 2765–69; *Bede: On First Samuel*, trans. by DeGregorio and Love, p. 314.
29 Thacker, 'Bede, the Britons and the Book of Samuel', p. 146.
30 In addition to Thacker, 'Bede's Ideal of Reform', see Thacker, 'Bede and the Ordering of Understanding', esp. pp. 39–46, and 'Bede and History', pp. 183–88.

the Book of Ezra, that was unique to Bede in the late and post-Roman period'.[31] Two
of these points — the British threat and divisions at Wearmouth and Jarrow — strike
me as most plausible indeed;[32] but the third must, it seems to me, remain conjectural,
as Thacker himself was quick to concede (recall his own caveat: 'one last especially
wild speculation'). Of course, we cannot be sure that a reference to Osred lies behind
the one passage to which Thacker points. Contextually, the meaning of the sentence
is quite straightforward when it is viewed within its larger textual frame. Here it may
be helpful to say something about the organization and technique of *On First Samuel*,
given Bede's novel approach to it, before coming back to the question of King Osred.

Structurally, *On First Samuel* differs from Bede's other commentaries in two ways.[33]
First, each of the four books begins with its own unique prologue. Usually Bede has
a single prologue for the entire work; having four individual prologues thus marks
a significant departure from his usual practice. These four prologues vary in length
as well as in theme. The prologue to Book 1, as we would expect, explains Bede's
overall approach to the text of 1 Samuel, namely his hugely ambitious attempt to
read every last detail of the literal Old Testament story in a capaciously allegorical
yet coherent way:

> hunc sanctissimum domino ex matris utero nazareum non minus suis in scriptis
> euangelistae quam historici functum officio probare satagam quippe qui et ipse
> omnia mediatoris Dei et hominum hominis Iesu Christi sacramenta figurato
> fidelis historiae sed plenissimo designarit eloquio.

>> I shall take pains to show that also this Nazarene [sc. Samuel], very holy to the
>> Lord from his mother's womb, fulfilled the role of evangelist in his writings
>> no less than he did of an historian; in fact he has represented all the sacred
>> mysteries of the mediator between God and men, the man Jesus Christ, in
>> the figural, yet very laden, language of faithful historical narrative.[34]

While Bede turns to allegory in all his commentaries, there is something different
at work here, both in the level of scrutiny that he brings to each word and phrase
of each biblical lemma, but also in the almost obsessive way that he tries to map
the events and personages of the Old Testament narrative onto New Testament
realities. Book 2 has the longest of the four prologues, which runs close to two
and a half pages in Hurst's edition, on the question of the chronology of Saul's
reign.[35] Book 3 meanwhile contains the briefest prologue, which functions mainly

---

31 Wood, 'Who are the Philistines?', 179.
32 On these topics, see further Stancliffe, *Bede and the Britons*, and 'British and Irish Contexts'; Foley
    and Higham, 'Bede on the Britons'; Wood, *The Most Holy Abbot Ceolfrid*, and 'The Foundation of
    Wearmouth–Jarrow'.
33 For a discussion of the style of these four prologues, see Brown, 'Bede's style in his Commentary *On 1
    Samuel*'.
34 Bede, *In primam partem Samuhelis*, II, ed. by Hurst, pp. 10, ll. 42–47; *Bede: On First Samuel*, trans. by
    DeGregorio and Love, p. 103.
35 Bede, *In primam partem Samuhelis*, II, ed. by Hurst, pp. 68–70, ll. 1–95.

to enact the transition from Saul's reign to David's,[36] while the fourth prologue, as already noted, describes the interruption and effects caused by Ceolfrith's sudden departure for Rome.[37] These prologues make it clear that Bede worked through the text of 1 Samuel chronologically: the prologue to Book 3 begins by acknowledging the completion of Books 1–2, and the very raison d'être of the fourth prologue is to explain the delay between the completion of Book 3 and the commencement of the fourth and final book.

In addition to these four consecutive prologues, *On First Samuel* has another curious structural feature, this one pertaining to the way Bede sought to compartmentalize the whole of it. While he proceeds chronologically through the biblical text, as he normally would, he departs from the strategy typically utilized in the commentaries he had produced so far — that is, commenting on individual verses, often quite briefly, but with no necessary link from one comment to another. Instead, Bede carves the full text of 1 Samuel into 42 distinct allegorical units which form the backbone of the four consecutive books (these, incidentally, are to be distinguished from the 43 capitula that come at the beginning of the text). To emphasize again, this is not a practice Bede adopts elsewhere. These 42 units do vary in the number of verses they contain, but oftentimes they match or are very close to the subheadings found in the modern text of 1 Samuel, i.e. the birth of Samuel, the Song of Hannah, David's battle with Goliath, etc. The one unifying feature of these units is found at the first verse of each: each time a unit begins, Bede offers a brief thematic summary of the allegory, before proceeding to unpack it in greater detail as he works through the relevant verses. To select a single example, here is the brief thematic summary found in the first thematic unit of Book 1:

> **Fuit uir unus de Ramathaim–sophim de monte Efraim et nomen eius Helcana**, et cetera usque ad id quod ait Annae Helcana uir suus, **Numquid non ego melior sum tibi quam decem filii**.
> Prima beati Samuhelis lectio typice designat unum eundemque dominum Iesum Christum sinagogae pariter et ecclesiae redemptorem semper rectoremque credendum unius de iustitia se legis suaeque credulae prolis ubertate iactantis alterius suae longae desolationis iniurias humili apud eiusdem sui redemptoris misericordiam deuotione deflentis ideoque redamantis et redemptoris sublimi consolatione respirantis.

>> **There was one man of Ramathaim–Sophim, of Mount Ephraim, and his name was Elkanah**, etc. [1 Samuel 1. 1], up to the verse in which Elkanah her husband says to Anna, '**Am I not more to you than ten sons**' [1 Samuel 1. 8]. This first passage of blessed Samuel symbolically represents one and the same Lord Jesus Christ who must be believed in as redeemer and ruler forever of both the Synagogue and the Church equally: the one, boasting of the justice of the Law and of the abundance of its believing offspring; the

36   Bede, *In primam partem Samuhelis*, II, ed. by Hurst, pp. 137, ll. 1–25.
37   Bede, *In primam partem Samuhelis*, II, ed. by Hurst, pp. 212, ll. 1–28.

other, bewailing the injuries of its long desolation with humble supplication to the mercy of that same redeemer, and therefore loving him in return and refreshed by the sublime consolation of that redeemer.[38]

Bede's grouping of verses like these into allegorically coherent units achieves a few things. It puts readers on notice to the larger thematic designs to be traced by his exegesis. Given how much Bede has to say in this very long commentary, such thematic summaries do provide a handy portrait of the forest through the trees as it were, allowing us to see the bigger picture that Bede is trying to paint. But equally, they do shed considerable light on the trees themselves, to continue the image, as each individual verse, or often this or that detail within a given verse that Bede might choose to dwell upon, can be seen to find its place within a pre-announced framework of Christian meanings and interrelationships.

Now, to come back to Osred, and the passage from Book 2 under question. It belongs to a long thematic section, found at the end of Book 2 of the commentary, that corresponds to the whole of the fifteenth chapter of 1 Samuel in a modern Bible. Following the technique that we just noted above, Bede commences his discussion of this section of verses with a clear statement of the thematic arc he aims to trace:

> **Et dixit Samuhel ad Saul: Me misit dominus ut unguerem te in regem super populum eius Israhel**, et cetera usque ad id quod **lugebat Samuhel Saul quoniam dominum paenitebat quod constituisset regem Saul super Israhel**. Haec lectio sub Saulis et Dauid specie Iudaeorum regnum ob culpam perfidiae ad gentes transferendum immo omnes qui peccata cum suis auctoribus perfecto odio non oderint extirpandos docet a regno fidei et hoc melioribus proximis dato nihilominus eos **qui operantur iniquitatem** cum suis operibus esse perdendos.

> **And Samuel said to Saul: 'The Lord sent me to anoint you king over his people Israel'** [1 Samuel 15. 1], and so on down to where it says, **Samuel mourned for Saul, because the Lord repented that he had made him king over Israel** [1 Samuel 15. 35]. This passage teaches under the image of Samuel and David that the kingdom of the Jews, because of faithlessness, ought to pass to the gentiles, or rather that all who have not hated sins with perfect hatred along with those who commit them ought to be removed from the kingdom of faith and, once it has been given to better neighbours, that those **who are workers of iniquity** ought to be destroyed along with their works.[39]

Thus he announces the typological paradigm according to which he reads the events of 1 Samuel 15 and, with it, the decidedly spiritual meaning with which he imbues the image of the transferal of the kingdom — it holds, on its face, a purely spiritual meaning, having to do with what is perhaps the major theme of Bede's commentary,

---

38 Bede, *In primam partem Samuhelis*, I, ed. by Hurst, pp. 11, ll. 1–10; *Bede: On First Samuel*, trans. by DeGregorio and Love, pp. 104–05.

39 Bede, *In primam partem Samuhelis*, II, ed. by Hurst, pp. 130, ll. 2425–33; *Bede: On First Samuel*, trans. by DeGregorio and Love, p. 302.

namely the passage of the covenant from the Jews to the Gentiles. When he breaks from this figural paradigm in this section, he informs his reader that he has done so, as he does when commenting on 1 Samuel 15. 11 ('**And Samuel was grieved, and cried to the Lord all night**'):

> Non haec per allegoriam exponenda sed ad imitationem potius sunt trahenda uirtutis ut pro fratrum erratis quae ipsi in se intellegere nondum queunt non solum contristemur in animo sed et omni ad dominum pro eis intentione clamemus nec non et ipsos mox ut locus tempusque arriserit ad agnitionem correptionemque reuocare curemus.
>
>> These words are not to be expounded allegorically but rather to be taken as a model of virtue for imitation, that we should grieve in mind over the errors of our brothers which they cannot yet perceive in themselves, but also cry out to the Lord on their behalf with all our effort and also take care to recall them to recognition and correction, as soon as circumstances and time permit.[40]

Now importantly, just prior to commenting on 1 Samuel 15. 27–28, the passage to which Thacker points, we should note that Bede says the following when he comes to 1 Samuel 15. 23, 26:

> Sicut cetera lectionis huiusce sic et haec reprobati Saulis abiectio iuxta allegoriam quidem sinagogae iuxta uero leges tropologiae cuiuslibet falso christiani uel magistri uel discipuli primo fideli ac postmodum damnabili possunt conuenire statui...
>
>> Just as with the rest of this passage so also here the rejection of the condemned Saul, according to an allegorical interpretation can refer indeed to the Synagogue, but according to the principles of tropological interpretation to the false condition of any Christian, whether teacher or pupil, who begins by being faithful and thereafter becomes worth of condemnation... [41]

Very plainly, then, Bede is setting himself up for a tropological, in addition to an allegorical, reading of the text. Specifically, he draws a parallel between the waywardness of the Jews of old and any Christian today who exhibits the same kind of wilful intransigence that the Jews do. Hence when he comes to 1 Samuel 15. 27–28, it is that comparison which he develops, in the scope of his full comment, and particularly with regard to issue of scriptural understanding — like Old Testament Jews, Christians today have the words of Scripture open before them, but they fail to read them aright according to their true spiritual sense. Here is what Bede says:

> Conuersa gratia prophetali ut propter peccata discederet a Iudaeis apprehendere illi non totum propheticae lectionis indumentum quo animam calefacere fide

---

40 Bede, *In primam partem Samuhelis*, II, ed. by Hurst, pp. 130, ll. 2625–30; *Bede: On First Samuel*, trans. by DeGregorio and Love, p. 309.

41 Bede, *In primam partem Samuhelis*, II, ed. by Hurst, pp. 133, ll. 1746–50; *Bede: On First Samuel*, trans. by DeGregorio and Love, p. 313.

uel ornare possent operibus sed extremam solummodo summitatem quae est in parte litterae quam et ipsam a soliditate sensus spiritalis abstrahentes quasi a propheticae uestis integritate sciderunt ideoque quoniam prophetas scindere non timuerunt scindi a se regnum Dei et gentibus tradi meruerunt. Sed et hodie quisque sacra eloquia quibus eruditus est et ad quaerendum regnum caeleste imbutus improba mente contempserit quia uestem sacrosanctam ungentis se in regnum maculat ablatam sibi regni beatitudinem proximo meliori relinquit.

> As the prophet's grace turned so as to go away from the Jews on account of their sins, they did not grasp the whole of the prophetic text's raiment, by which they could have kept the soul warm by faith or adorned it by works, but pulling at only the outermost edge, which is the literal meaning, they tore it away from the solidity of the spiritual meaning, from the integrity of the prophet's garment, as it were, and therefore, since they were not afraid to tear at prophets, they deserved to have the kingdom of God torn from them and handed over to gentiles. But also today everyone who has been educated in the sacred words and instructed to seek the kingdom of heaven but has scorned those words with wicked mind, because he dishonours the sacrosanct garment of the one anointing him for the kingdom, he leaves for his neighbour, who is better than him, the blessedness of the kingdom that has been taken from him.[42]

If this last sentence was indeed written by Bede both to make this plain surface point about the dire consequences of scorning Scripture's dictates, and to drop an allusion to Osred's murder, we must admit that the remark is impressive as much for its stealth as it is in and of itself. Indeed, given the long sweep of this prodigious commentary, we might equate it to something like a needle in a haystack.

In the words of James Campbell, another great reader of Bede, our monk from Jarrow is famous for nothing if not his 'usual discretion'.[43] Surely it is not hard to see why an allusion to such a delicate contemporary matter, if that is truly what it is, would have to be veiled, covert in the extreme. All the same, it is precisely this reticence that is notable. While Bede clearly had few qualms about using the word *perfidia* so frequently throughout the commentary, such that it can be traced, as Thacker has done so illustratively, any further allusions to a contemporary crisis of kingship are scarcely to be found in *On First Samuel*, even though the text of 1 Samuel afforded Bede countless more opportunities to make such allusions. There is an interesting point to make here, again pertaining to the way Bede has structured the commentary as a whole in terms of the 42 allegorical units discussed above. That point is this — there is but one place in the commentary where Bede varies from this structural pattern, and in light of the foregoing I think it is conspicuous. It comes in Book 2 of *On First Samuel* and concerns 1 Samuel 12, the famous chapter wherein Samuel gives way to

42 Bede, *In primam partem Samuhelis*, II, ed. by Hurst, pp. 133–34, ll. 2758–65; *Bede: On First Samuel*, trans. by DeGregorio and Love, p. 314.
43 Campbell, 'Bede', p. 176.

Saul, and rule by kingship comes at last to Israel. Now Bede does, to be sure, mark
off this chapter as a thematic unit, as follows:

> **Dixit autem Samuhel ad uniuersum Israhel: Ecce audiui uocem uestram** et
> cetera usque ad id quod ait, **Quod si perseueraueritis in malitia et uos et rex
> uester pariter peribitis**. In hac lectione Samuhel proprie statum Israhelitici regni
> describit. Contestatus namque populum quod et se innoxio et domino semper
> saluatore abiecto regem sibi male petierint sub eiusdem regis figura uariantia
> totius eorum regni tempora comprehendit.

> **And Samuel said to all Israel: 'Behold I have hearkened to your voice'**
> [1 Samuel 12. 1], and so on down to where it says, **'But if you will still do
> wickedly, both you and your king shall perish together'** [1 Samuel 12. 25].
> In this passage Samuel specifically describes the position of Israel's kingdom.
> For having testified against the people that they have cast aside both what
> was harmless to them and the Lord who was always their saviour and have
> wickedly sought a king for themselves, he includes under the figure of their
> same king the fluctuating times of the whole kingdom.[44]

But his usual practice everywhere else in the commentary, namely to proceed through
the whole unit verse by verse, commenting as he goes, is not followed here. In this
one instance, he does no such thing. Rather he passes over all but a mere two verses
of the twenty-five that make up this section. He comments only on verses 14–15,
which echo the oft-heard generic statement articulated above all in Deuteronomy,
namely that serving the Lord results in prosperity, disobeying him in punishment.[45]
All the rest he ignores, as if he wishes to avoid having to say anything about the
problems of kingship in theory, or the vices of this or that particular (Anglo-Saxon?)
king. There are certainly options here in how we might read this omission. But one
would be to take it as a deliberate silence, as if Bede thought it best to keep mum. If
On First Samuel is, then, in any way a response to, or product of, the political crisis
of 716 with its violent overthrow of a king, it would seem that it is remarkable for its
elusiveness, or perhaps better its restraint — not unlike the tactic Bede would later
employ in writing the *Ecclesiastical History*.[46]

I now want to turn to a different yet related issue, also much concerned with
crisis, but in this case the marks it has left on the commentary are a bit easier to
trace. It too is a theme that Thacker led the way in identifying, as the very impulse
behind much that Bede wrote. I speak here of the reform of Church and society, as
outlined in his 1983 essay, 'Bede's Idea of Reform'. The seminal insight of this piece,

---

44   Bede, *In primam partem Samuhelis*, II, ed. by Hurst, p. 98, ll. 1277–84; *Bede: On First Samuel*, trans. by
     DeGregorio and Love, pp. 257–58.

45   Bede, *In primam partem Samuhelis*, II, ed. by Hurst, pp. 99–101, ll. 1285–1398.

46   Cf. Thacker's own comments, in 'Bede and History', p. 178–79, on Bede's delicate handling of events
     connected with another eventful date, namely 731, at which point he chose to end his narrative
     account in the *Ecclesiastical History* – 'Bede, it seems, deliberately chose to draw a veil over the
     presumably unseemly manoeuvrings of a period of significant change'.

so basic yet so far-reaching, is that Bede was 'concerned about the world in which he lived'.[47] By this he meant not just that Bede was aware of specific problems that were plaguing religious life in his own day, but more profoundly that in his writings he sought to articulate a programmatic agenda for solving them. Bede's vision as Thacker characterized it highlighted the key role to be played by teachers and preachers both in the Church as well as in society at large:

> Bede saw these men as charged with the transmission of the Church's intellectual heritage; they were to be faithful interpreters of the Scriptures and a bulwark against heresy. Equally important, they were *custodes animarum*, guardians of souls, who were to exhort and instruct the faithful and convert the heathen. Such men had of necessity to be of superior education and intellect, initiates into the higher mysteries of the faith which the common crowd of ordinary believers could not understand. They were the 'eyes' of the Church who penetrated the *superficies litterae* of Holy Writ to the heavenly arcana beneath. Above all (and this was a theme to which Bede constantly returned), they were to set a holy example, to show in deed what they taught by word. In short, they were to be an intellectual and moral elite.[48]

This was, Thacker would go on to note, an essentially monastic vision of the pastorate, given equally to the twinned idea of action and contemplation, and so one very much formed by Bede's own lived experience. Thacker claimed that this vision was 'a key to all of Bede's later works, not only the commentaries and homilies, but the hagiography and histories as well', and that his preoccupations there 'have to be seen in the context of Bede's growing anxiety about the state of the Church and society in his day'.[49] In the limited scope of his essay, he chose to devote his attention almost exclusively to showing how those concerns shaped Bede's later hagiographical and historical writings, in particular the prose *Life of Saint Cuthbert* and the *Ecclesiastical History*. But in passing he did note that such anxieties do appear to have left their trace 'As early as 716, in his commentary on 1 Samuel …'.[50] It is this perceptive insight that Thacker did not have the leeway to pursue there that I should like finally to develop here.

Any discussion about Bede's views on reform must still begin, however, not with 716 but with 5 November 734, the date on which he sat down to distil his reformist views within the remit of one brief writing, *The Letter to Bishop Ecgberht*.[51] This letter is notable for other reasons — it is Bede's latest extant work, his death coming just six short months later, on 26 May 735.[52] The letter provides Ecgberht with three things: a reminder of the duties that he, as archbishop, must be ever solicitous to

---

47 Thacker, 'Bede's Ideal of Reform', p. 130.

48 Thacker, 'Bede's Ideal of Reform', p. 131.

49 Thacker, 'Bede's Ideal of Reform', pp. 131, 132.

50 Thacker, 'Bede's Ideal of Reform', p. 132.

51 Bede, *Epistola ad Ecgbertum Episcopum*, § 17, ed. by Grocock and Wood, pp. 160–61.

52 The date is given in the first-hand account of his death written by his pupil Cuthbert; the text is printed in Colgrave and Mynors' Oxford Medieval Texts edition of the *Historia ecclesiastica – Epistola de obitu Bedae*, ed. and trans. by Colgrave and Mynors, pp. 580–81.

perform; a list of key problems in the Northumbrian Church, corruption of clerical standards foremost of all, that Ecgberht must assiduously seek to correct; and finally some suggested remedies that Bede wished to see Ecgberht implement forthwith, before the situation deteriorated beyond repair.[53] Because Bede took care in his letter to give such concentrated expression to all this, we thus have a very clear sense of what the issues are. That is, the letter itself can form something like a baseline for identifying many of Bede's reforming ideas, and from that later point we can attempt to move backwards to see how much earlier such ideas might have appeared on Bede's radar.[54] Such a method has already proven fruitful with regard to the work Bede did on Ezra-Nehemiah, another long seminal commentary that, like *On First Samuel*, he devoted to an Old Testament book virtually ignored by previous commentators.[55] There can be little doubt that some of the very same issues that he would flag up in the letter were already strong motivations for the way Bede read the Ezra story. Hence there is his startling comparison of the appointment of priests and Levites in the reconstructed temple (as mentioned in Ezra 6. 18) to 'eis qui monasteria magnifico opere construentes nequaquam in his statuunt doctores qui ad opera Dei populum cohortentur sed suis potius inibi uoluptatibus ac desideriis seruiunt' (those who, though founding monasteries with brilliant workmanship, in no way appoint teachers in them to exhort the people to God's work but rather those who will serve their own pleasures and desires there),[56] or perhaps even more significantly, his reading of the unjust tax imposed on the returnees mentioned in Nehemiah 5. 4:

> Quod apud cotidie eodem ordine fieri uidemus. Quanti enim sunt in populo Dei qui diuinis libenter cupiunt obtemperare mandatis sed ne possint implere quod cupiunt et inopia rerum temporalium ac paupertate et exemplis retardantur eorum qui habitu religionis uidentur esse praediti cum ipsi ab eis quibus praeesse uidentur et immensum rerum saecularium pondus ac uectigal exigunt et nihil eorum saluti perpetuae uel docendo uel exempla uiuendi praebendo uel opera pietatis impendendo conferunt. Atque utinam aliquis in diebus nostris Neemias, id est consolator a domino, adueniens nostros compescat errores nostra ad amorem diuinum praecordia accendat nostras a propriis uoluptatibus ad constituendam Christi ciuitatem manus auertens confortet.

> We see that this occurs among us in the same manner every day. For how many are there among God's people who willingly desire to obey the divine commands but are hindered from being able to fulfil what they desire not only by a lack of temporal means and by poverty but also by the examples of those who seem to be endowed with the garb of religion, but who exact an immense tax and weight of worldly goods from those whom they claim to be

---

53 For an overview of the whole with discussion of its larger relevance within Bede's writings and general outlook, see DeGregorio, 'Visions of Reform'; and Grocock and Wood, 'Introduction', esp. pp. l–lix.

54 For an example of this approach, see DeGregorio, '"Nostrorum socordiam temporum"'.

55 DeGregorio, 'Bede's *In Ezram et Neemiam*', and 'Footsteps of his Own'.

56 Bede, *In Ezram et Neemiam*, II, ed. by Hurst, p. 303, ll. 601–04; trans. by DeGregorio, p. 102.

in charge of while giving nothing for their eternal salvation either by teaching them or by providing them with examples of good living or by devoting effort to works of piety for them? Would that some Nehemiah (i.e. a 'consoler from the Lord') might come in our own days and restrain our errors, kindle our breasts to love of the divine, and strengthen our hands by turning them away from our own pleasures to establishing Christ's city![57]

Passages such as these in the Ezra commentary have made it possible to view this work and the Ecgberht letter as of a piece when it comes to the question of Bede's ideal of reform. Some uncertainty has, however, surrounded the dating of this commentary: does its genesis lay near to the Codex Amiatinus with its famous Ezra miniature, and thus not too far away from AD 716, or does it belong to the following decade, with *On the Tabernacle* and *On the Temple*, and thus to a later phase of Bede's career?[58] Uncertainty over dating is fortunately something we need not worry about in the case of *On First Samuel*. Any reform ideas it may contain we can confidently say were in Bede's mind during the years around AD 716. Now there are two things worth noting in this connection: first, *On First Samuel* does contain passages that resonate strongly with Bede's letter; but second, and perhaps more tellingly, the letter itself makes explicit mention of the prophet Samuel — a strong indication that, to Bede's mind, this Old Testament prophet was a figure of special relevance to his thinking about reform.

Bede's reference to the prophet Samuel in the *Letter to Ecgberht* is especially tellingly precisely because of when it occurs. It comes as a peroration of sorts to his fierce attack on episcopal avarice, in the form of the tax levied in return for pastoral ministrations which often were poorly dispensed or omitted altogether in more remote areas. Bede summed up the situation this way:

> Audiuimus enim — et fama est — quia multae uillae ac uiculi nostrae gentis in montibus sint inaccessis ac saltibus dumosis positi, ubi nunquam multis transeuntibus annis sit uisus antistes qui ibidem aliquid ministerii aut gratiae caelestis exhibuerit; quorum tamen ne unus quidem a tributis antistiti reddendis esse possit immunis; nec solum talibus locis desit antistes, qui manus impositione baptizatos confirmet, uerum etiam omnis doctor, qui eos uel fidei ueritatem uel discretionem bonae ac malae actionis edoceat, absit. Sicque fit, ut episcoporum quidam non solum gratis non euangelizent uel manus fidelibus imponant; uerum etiam, quod grauius est, accepta ab auditoribus suis pecunia, quam Dominus prohibuit, opus uerbi quod Dominus iussit exercere contemnant.

> For I have heard and it is common gossip, that many of our race's villages and hamlets are located in out-of-the-way, hilly places and thick woodland, where in the passage of many years a bishop has never been seen who might have

---

57 Bede, *In Ezram et Neemiam*, III, ed. by Hurst, pp. 359–60, ll. 825–37; *Bede: On Ezra and Nehemiah*, trans by DeGregorio, p. 184. For discussion of this and the foregoing quotation, see DeGregorio, 'Bede's *In Ezram et Neemiam*', pp. 11–13.

58 See DeGregorio, 'Bede's *In Ezram et Neemiam*', pp. 21–23, and 'Introduction', pp. xxxvi–xlii; and, Meyvaert, 'In the Footsteps of the Fathers', pp. 284–86, and 'Date of Bede's *In Ezram*', pp. 1093–96.

set forth any kind of ministry or heavenly grace, and yet not one of them is able to be exempt from paying tribute to the bishop; not only may there be no bishop for such places, who can confirm those baptizied by the laying on of hands, but there is also total absence of any teacher who might teach them the truth of the faith or the difference between food and bad conduct. So it is that some of the bishops not only do not evangelize without payment or lay hands on the faithful, but they also — a far more serious matter — receive money from their hearers, which the Lord forbids, and then refuse to carry out the work of preaching, which the Lord commands![59]

In offering a solution to this dire situation, quite strikingly Bede thought it efficacious not to continue in his own words but to let the power of exempla do the talking, and specifically in the form of the actions of Samuel. In this very next sentence he continues thus:

cum Deo dilectus pontifex Samuel longe aliter fecisse omni populo teste legatur. 'Itaque conuersatus', inquit, 'coram uobis ab adolescentia mea usque ad diem hanc, ecce praesto sum, loquimini de me coram Domino et coram Christo eius, utrum bouem alicuius tulerim, an asinum, si quempiam calumniatus sum, si oppressi aliquem, si de manu cuiusquam munus accepi; et contemnam illud hodie, restituamque uobis. Et dixerunt: Non es calumniatus nos, neque oppressisti, neque tulisti de manu alicuius quippiam'.

> For it is said that the priest Samuel, beloved of God, behaved far differently, with all the people as witnesses: '"I have behaved thus towards you", he said, "from my youth right up to this day; see, here I am; speak of me in the presence of the Lord in the presence of his anointed, where I have taken anyone's ox, or their ass, if I have slandering anyone, if I have oppressed anyone, if have received any gifts from anyone's hand and I will condemn it today and will restore it to you". And they said, "you have not slandered us, nor have you oppressed us, nor have you received anything from the hands of anyone"'.[60]

Unlike the corrupt ecclesiastics of Bede's Northumbrian Church, the priest and prophet Samuel demanded no compensation for his pastoral services. Accordingly, Bede could see him as the antithesis and a potent counter-example to the very clergy whom he was decrying in the letter. 'Cuius innocentiae ac iustitiae merito', so Bede says of Samuel, highlighting his priestly virtues, 'inter primos populi Dei duces et sacerdotes annumerari, atque in precibus suis superno auditu atque alloquio dignus existere meruit' (He deserved to be reckoned amongst the foremost leaders and priests of the people of God by the merit of his innocence and honesty, and showed himself worthy in his prayers to be heard and to converse with heaven).[61]

---

59 Bede, *Epistola ad Ecgbertum Episcopum*, § 7, ed. and trans. by Grocock and Wood, pp. 134–37.
60 Bede, *Epistola ad Ecgbertum Episcopum*, § 7, ed. by Grocock and Wood, pp. 136–37; the cited verses are I Samuel 12. 2–4.
61 Bede, *Epistola ad Ecgbertum Episcopum*, § 7, ed. by Grocock and Wood, pp. 136–37.

Moving back from the letter to *On First Samuel* itself, we would be inclined to think that the figure of Samuel, and the larger outlines of the Old Testament story itself, were linked in Bede's mind to issues of priestly conduct that had relevance to his own day. We cannot be so bold as to claim to have found Bede's sole reason for devoting a commentary to 1 Samuel; all the same it is unlikely that the topical force of Samuel's example dawned upon him only at the end of his career, when he wrote to Ecgberht. A reading of the commentary as a whole leaves little doubt that, at least to some degree, concerns about a crisis in pastoral care along the lines of the letter to Ecgberht were already something Bede thought needing voicing at this earlier point.

Consider for example how he treats the corrupt sons of the priest Eli, who are mentioned early on in 1 Samuel and whose wicked mistreatment of the people is precisely the raison d'être for the replacement of their priestly house by the young Samuel. Of them Bede observes that they

> … suum diuino cultui praeferrent obsequium dicentes miseris auditoribus ut suae quisque concupiscentiae carnalis illecebras non aetheriae caritatis flamma Deo dignae consumerent sed in conditoris iniuriam minus castigatas pro libitu carnalium impenderent praeceptorum. Haec autem suis auditoribus improbi non uerbis sed rebus ipsis dicebant. Quorum simillima hodieque per magistros et sacerdotes ecclesiae fieri utinam nesciremus.

> … put their own service before the worship of God, telling their wretched listeners that they, each one of them, should not consume the enticements of their own lust in the flame of a heavenly love worthy of God, but, to the Creator's harm, should use them, less cleansed, according to the pleasure of fleshly precepts. These wicked men were in the habit of saying these things to their hearers not in words but rather in their very behaviour. If only we did not know that things like this are done even today by teachers and priests of the Church![62]

What makes this passage so resonant with the *Letter to Ecgberht* is not just the nod to the present at the end, but also the specific crimes of Eli's sons: they are greedy, take more from the people than is due, and in this way defile their sacrosanct office in precisely the same way as do the Northumbrian clerics who 'accepta ab auditoribus suis pecunia, quam Dominus prohibuit, opus uerbi quod Dominus iussit exercere contemnant' (receive money from their hearers, which the Lord forbids, and then refuse to carry out the work of preaching, which the Lord commands!).[63]

Elsewhere in *On First Samuel* it is precisely this awareness that, on the one hand, Bede is concerned to allude to the present, and that, on the other, he is doing so with regard to vices that he later singles out as problems in need of reform when he writes to Ecgberht, that should make us pause to take stock of a potential contemporary edge of his exegesis. And so we sense this again when Bede takes up 1 Samuel 15. 22,

62 Bede, *In primam partem Samuhelis*, I, ed. by Hurst, pp. 26–27, ll. 644–48; *Bede: On First Samuel*, trans. by DeGregorio and Love, p. 133.
63 Bede, *Epistola ad Ecgbertum Episcopum*, § 7, ed. by Grocock and Wood, pp. 136–37.

a verse that comes in the midst of the famous scene where Samuel announces Saul's rejection. It is the moment when Samuel reminds Saul that what God wants from his servants is an obedient heart, not material offerings such as 'the fat of rams'. After applying the verse 'Iudaeis...qui neglecto iudicio misericordia et fide ceterisque talibus' (to the Jews who abandoning judgement, mercy, and faith and other such things), Bede once again hastens to point out that 'Sed et nunc in ecclesia sunt non pauci diuitiis pariter et criminibus aggrauati qui peccata quibus adhaerere non desistunt elemosinis se cotidianis abluere confidant' (But even now in the Church there are not a few, weighed down by wealth and sins alike, who trust that they can wash away the sins to which they do not cease from clinging, by daily almsgiving).[64] While again the temporal marker — *Sed et nunc in ecclesia* — is sufficient to catch the eye of any reader of Bede's letter, it is the point about the inefficacy of alms when unaided by a clean conscience that strengthens the parallel since Bede concludes the letter by reminding Ecgberht of the foolishness of those who are 'per eleemosynas, quas inter concupiscentias quotidianas ac delicias pauperibus dare videbantur, criminibus absolui posse credendi sunt' (thought to be capable of receiving absolution from their wicked behaviour because of the alms which they were seen to give to the poor in the course of their daily self-indulgence and gluttony).[65] Or consider Bede's handling of 1 Samuel 13. 20, 'Descendebat ergo omnis Israhel ad Philisthiim ut exacueret unusquisque uomerem suum et ligonem et securem et sarculum' (So all Israel went down to the Philistines, every man to sharpen his ploughshare, and his spade, and his axe, and his rake). Picking up the image of 'going down' or 'descent', Bede observes, once again with reference to the present, that

> Descendunt et hodie non nulli relicta altitudine uerbi Dei ad quod audiendum ascendere debuerant auscultantque fabulis saecularibus ac doctrinis daemoniorum et legendo dialecticos rethores poetasque gentilium ad exercendum ingenium terrestre quasi ad fabros Philisthiim pro exacuendis siluestris siue ruralis culturae ferramentis inermes, hoc est spiritali scientia priuati, conueniunt.

>> Today too some descend, having abandoned the height of God's word which they ought to have ascended to hear, and they listen to secular tales and devilish doctrines, and by reading pagan dialecticians, rhetoricians, and poets in order to exercise their earthly ability, it is as if they go unarmed (i.e. deprived of spiritual knowledge) to the blacksmiths of the Philistines, so to speak, to sharpen tools for use in the woods or fields.[66]

Early on in the letter, Bede laments a similar 'descent', this one concerning those Northumbrian clerics 'qui risui, iocis, fabulis, commessationibus et ebrietatibus, ceterisque vitae remissioris illecebris subigantur' (who are steeped in mockery and

---

64 Bede, *In primam partem Samuhelis*, II, ed. by Hurst, p. 133, ll. 2727–29; *Bede: On First Samuel*, trans by DeGregorio and Love, p. 312.

65 Bede, *Epistola ad Ecgbertum Episcopum*, § 17, ed. by Grocock and Wood, pp. 158–59.

66 Bede, *In primam partem Samuhelis*, II, ed. by Hurst, p. 112, ll. 1853–59; *Bede: On First Samuel*, trans. by DeGregorio and Love, p. 279.

pranks, made-up stories, feasting together, and drunkenness and other wanton pursuits of a rather lax way of life).[67] It should not be overlooked that in both commentary and letter Bede chooses to include the word *fabulae* in his list of specific vices. Nor should it be overlooked that Bede's point in both works is virtually the same: such frivolities are unbefitting for teachers who should prefer to listen to God's word instead. It is a good example of how a small detail from the letter might be able to shed some light on what lies beneath a passage from the commentary, with its deliberate *et hodie*.

On its own, the evidence we have been considering so far from *On First Samuel*, however tantalizing it may be, would not be enough to build a conclusive case for the presence of a reform agenda to the commentary. It is rather the addition of those echoes to passages such as the following that makes the cumulative case stronger. Here Bede is commenting on 1 Samuel 14. 31–32, the scene where the Israelites, exhausted after their victory over the Philistines at Michmash, commit a ritual fault when they slaughter the Philistine flocks and eat the meat with blood. Though Bede does offer a brief comment of literal meaning of the episode, his attention turns quickly to a rather different reading:

> Significat autem magistros inertes qui sicut hodie cernimus longo saepe cathecizandi labore defatigati non nullos quos daemonicis erroribus praedicando eruerant a gentilibus quidem ritibus erudiendo mactant imitari conati illum cui destinatis de caelo cuncti generis animantibus dictum est: **Macta et Manduca** [Acts of the Apostles 10. 3]. Sed quasi in terra mactant et cum sanguine manducant quos a terrenis sensibus carnisque et sanguinis illecebris minus perfecte uel docendo uel ipsi uidendo non subtrahunt assuetosque adhuc uitiis necdumque agendis uirtutibus institutos accelerant ecclesiae membris incorporare contra exemplum primi pastoris ecclesiae qui in caenaculo, hoc est in summa uiuendi uel docendi arce, locatus mactare oblata et a Deo purgata manducare praecipitur.

> This refers to lazy teachers who, just as we see today, wearied by the time-consuming task of frequent catechizing, slaughter through their teaching some of those whom they have by their preaching rescued from demonic errors, indeed from the rituals of pagans; in this they tried to imitate him to whom it was said, when living things of every species were shown to him from heaven: **Slaughter and eat** [Acts of the Apostles 10. 3]. But these teachers slaughter on the ground and eat with the blood, as it were, those whom they do not draw away from earthly senses and the allurements of flesh and blood, being less perfect either in their teaching or their own living and hasten to incorporate them among the members of the Church when they are still accustomed to vices and not yet well grounded in performing virtues, contrary to the example of the first pastor of the Church who, placed in the upper room, that is, at the highest citadel of living and teaching, was ordered to kill and eat offerings purified by God.[68]

---

67 Bede, *Epistola ad Ecgbertum Episcopum*, § 4, ed. by Grocock and Wood, pp. 128–29.

68 Bede, *In primam partem Samuhelis*, II, ed. by Hurst, p. 122, ll. 2254–59; *Bede: On First Samuel*, trans. by DeGregorio and Love, p. 295.

The contemporary import of these remarks is indeed hard to miss. Bede's whole point in writing to Ecgberht is to underline the damage that has been done to the Northumbrian populace through poorly-trained indolent teachers, and to urge the archbishop to correct them: 'Haec tuae sanctitati, dilectissime antistes, paucis de calamitate qua nostra gens miserrime laborat insinuans, obsecro sedulus ut haec quae peruersissime agi conspicis, quantum uales, ad rectam uitae normam reuocare contendas' (In these few words I set before your holiness, most beloved bishop, these examples of the disastrous state in which our people most wretchedly labor and urge you earnestly to strive to recall these things which you see being done most wickedly to the correct standards of conduct as far as is in your power).[69] In the commentary, it is therefore most striking that, in his comments on the very next verse (1 Samuel 14. 33–34), Bede moves on to make that very point, namely that it is the ultimate prerogative of 'rulers' (*rectores*) to see to it that such correction is indeed dispensed:

> Cognita perfecti quique rectores desidia neglegentium doctorum quod peccent domino baptizantes eos quos a carnali contagione necdum plena fidei institutione purgarint continuo tales praeuaricationis reos arguunt et catholica auctoritate uitae caelestis regulam palam proponi iubent magistrisque inertibus quos uulgaris eatenus imperitia uexarat imperari ut adductis usque ad eam quam ipsi a patribus didicerant uitae formulam cunctis quos imbuendos susceperint super firmissimum catholicae perfectionis exemplar eos cathecizando a pristina conuersatione paternae traditionis occidant et baptizando ecclesiae membris incorporent neque ultra peccent domino fidei et uitae caelestis ignaros unitati sui corporis, hoc est ecclesiae Christi, nectentes.

> All perfect rulers, when they learn of the indolence of negligent teachers — namely the fact that they sin against the Lord when they baptize those whom they have not yet cleansed of their fleshly corruption by full instruction in the faith — they immediately rebuke those guilty of this violation; and by their catholic authority they order that the rule of heavenly life be set forth openly, and that it be enjoined upon those lazy teachers whom ordinary ignorance has hitherto afflicted, that, having led all those whom they have undertaken to teach to that standard of life which the negligent teachers themselves learned from the fathers, they should, by catechizing them upon the soundest model of catholic perfection, cut them off from their former way of life handed down to them by their ancestors, and they should, by baptizing them, incorporate them in the members of the Church; and the negligent teachers should no longer sin against the Lord in binding those who are ignorant of the faith and heavenly life into the unity of his body, that is, Christ's Church.[70]

---

69   Bede, *Epistola ad Ecgbertum Episcopum*, § 9, ed. by Grocock and Wood, pp. 138–39.

70   Bede, *In primam partem Samuhelis*, II, ed. by Hurst, pp. 122–23, ll. 2281–94; *Bede: On First Samuel*, trans. by DeGregorio and Love, p. 297.

As Thacker himself and others have noted, the Latin noun *rector* is a loaded word for Bede.[71] While it could refer to a secular ruler, he often uses it to mean an ecclesiastical leader, as is clearly the case in this instance — hence the reference to 'catholic authority'. Here then is a passage, and one that we know was written around AD 716, in which Bede is not only alarmed by the damaging influence of *rectores inertes*, but also keen to underline the duty of *perfecti rectores* to use their sacral authority to bring some remedy to the problem. If this does not ring loudly of the missive he would send to Ecgberht some 15 years later, one wonders what else should be made of it. But it will have to be left to another discussion to say just who, in AD 716, Bede might have had in mind.

There would appear to be good reason, then, to see in this long commentary on Samuel some evidence of concerns that had weighed on Bede's mind, be they about the perfidiousness of the Britons, the violent overthrow of Osred and the political instability that would follow it, or the breakdown in pastoral standards that we know Bede felt were enervating the Northumbrian Church in his day. While the emotional outpouring that comes in the fourth prologue was first and foremost directed at the sudden news of Ceolfrith's departure, we may suspect that other matters played a hand in working up Bede's state of mind. He spoke candidly of the 'sweat' (*sudor*) that the writing of *On First Samuel* wrung from him,[72] and one can see why. By virtue of its sheer length, its obsessive fascinating with *allegoresis*, and its apparent attempt to engage with pressing issues in the turbulent social atmosphere of early eighth-century Northumbria, this commentary, perhaps Bede's very first attempt to say something meaningful about the Old Testament, might well be seen as the product of a crisis in the life of the prolific monk of Jarrow.

Works Cited

Primary Sources

Bede, *Epistula ad Ecgbertum Episcopum*, ed. and trans. by Christopher Grocock and Ian N. Wood in *Abbots of Wearmouth and Jarrow*, Oxford Medieval Texts (Oxford: Clarendon Press, 2013), pp. 123–61

——, *Expositio Actuum Apostolorum*, ed. by M. L. W. Laistner (Cambridge MA: The Medieval Academy of America, 1939, reprinted 1970)

——, *Historia ecclesiastica*, ed. and trans. by Bertram Colgrave and R. A. B. Mynors (Oxford: Clarendon Press, 1969)

——, *In Ezram et Neemiam*, ed. by D. Hurst, Corpus Christianorum Series Latina, 119A (Turnhout: Brepols, 1969), pp. 235–392

---

71 Thacker, 'Bede's Ideal of Reform', pp. 132–34; 'Monks, Preaching and Pastoral Care', pp. 152–54; also Markus, 'Gregory the Great's *rector*'.

72 Bede, *In primam partem Samuhelis*, III, ed. by Hurst, p. 137, ll. 1; *Bede: On First Samuel*, trans. by DeGregorio and Love, p. 319.

————, *In primam partem Samuhelis*, ed. by D. Hurst, Corpus Christianorum Series Latina, 119 (Turnhout: Brepols, 1962), pp. 1–272

————, *Vita metrica sancti Cuthberti*, in *Bedas Metrische Vita sancti Cuthberti*, ed. by W. Jaager, Palaestra, 198 (Leipzig: Mayer & Müller, 1935)

Bede: Commentary on Revelation, trans. by Faith Wallis, Translated Texts for Historians, 58 (Liverpool: Liverpool University Press, 2013)

Bede's Latin Poetry, ed. and trans. by Michael Lapidge (Oxford: Oxford University Press)

Bede: On Ezra and Nehemiah, trans. by Scott DeGregorio, Translated Texts for Historians, 47 (Liverpool: Liverpool University Press, 2006)

Bede: On First Samuel, trans. by Scott DeGregorio and Rosalind Love, Translated Texts for Historians, 70 (Liverpool: Liverpool University Press, 2019)

Bede: On Genesis, trans. by Calvin Kendall, Translated Texts for Historians, 48 (Liverpool: Liverpool University Press, 2008)

Secondary Studies

Brown, George Hardin, 'Bede's Style in his Commentary *On 1 Samuel*', in *Text, Image, Interpretation: Studies in Anglo-Saxon Literature and its Insular Context in Honour of Éamonn Ó Carragáin*, ed. by Alastair Minnis and Jane Roberts, Studies in the Early Middle Ages, 18 (Turnhout: Brepols, 2007), pp. 233–51.

Campbell, James, 'Bede', in *Latin Historians*, ed. by T. A. Dorey (London: Routledge, 1966), pp. 159–90

Darby, Peter, *Bede and the End of Time* (Farnham: Ashgate, 2012)

DeGregorio, Scott, 'Explorations of Spirituality in the Writings of the Venerable Bede, King Alfred, and Aelfric of Eynsham' (unpublished doctoral thesis, University of Toronto, 1999)

————, '"*Nostrorum socordiam temporum*": The Reforming Impulse of Bede's Later Exegesis', *Early Medieval Europe*, 11 (2002), pp. 107–22

————, 'Bede's *In Ezram et Neemiam* and the Reform of the Northumbrian Church', *Speculum*, 79 (2004), pp. 1–25

————, 'Footsteps of his Own: Bede's *Commentary on Ezra-Nehemiah*', in *Innovation and Tradition in the Writings of the Venerable Bede*, ed. by Scott DeGregorio (Morgantown: West Virginia University Press, 2006), pp. 143–68

————, 'Bede and the Old Testament', in *The Cambridge Companion to Bede*, ed. by Scott DeGregorio (Cambridge: Cambridge University Press, 2010), pp. 127–41

————, 'Visions of Reform: Bede's Later Writings in Context', in *Bede and the Future*, ed. by Peter Darby and Faith Wallis (Farnham: Ashgate, 2014), pp. 207–32

Foley, William Trent, and Nicholas J. Higham, 'Bede on the Britons', *Early Medieval Europe*, 17.2 (2009), 154–85

Grocock, C., and I. N. Wood, 'Introduction', in *Abbots of Wearmouth and Jarrow*, ed. and trans. by C. Grocock and I. N. Wood, Oxford Medieval Texts (Oxford: Oxford University Press, 2013), pp. xiii–cxx

Herbert, M., *Iona, Kells, and Derry* (Oxford: Oxford University Press, 1988)

Kendall, Calvin, 'Introduction', in *Bede: On Genesis*, trans. by Calvin Kendall, Translated Texts for Historians, 48 (Liverpool: Liverpool University Press, 2008), pp. 1–61

Kendall, Calvin B., and Faith Wallis, 'Introduction', in *Bede: On the Nature of Things and On Times*, trans. by Calvin B. Kendal and Faith Wallis, Translated Texts for Historians, 56 (Liverpool: Liverpool University Press, 2010), pp. 1–68

Kirby, D. P., *The Early English Kings* (London: Unwin Hyman, 1991)

Laistner, M. W. L., *A Hand-list of Bede Manuscripts* (Ithaca: Cornell University Press, 1943)

Markus, Robert, 'Gregory the Great's *rector* and his genesis', in *Grégoire le Grand*, ed. by J. Fontaine and others (Paris: CNRS, 1986), pp. 137–46

Meyvaert, Paul, '"In the Footsteps of the Fathers": The Date of Bede's *Thirty Questions on the Book of Kings* to Nothelm', in *The Limits of Ancient Christianity: Essays on Late Antique Thought and Culture in Honour of R. A. Markus*, ed. by W. E. Klingshirn and M. Vessey (Ann Arbor: University of Michigan Press, 1979), pp. 267–86

——, 'The Date of Bede's *In Ezram* and his Image of Ezra in the Codex Amiatinus', *Speculum*, 80 (2005), 1087–1133

Stancliffe, Clare, *Bede and the Britons*, Whithorn Lecture (Whithorn: Friends of the Whithorn Trust, 2007)

——, 'British and Irish Contexts', in *The Cambridge Companion to Bede*, ed. by Scott DeGregorio (Cambridge: Cambridge University Press, 2010), pp. 69–83

Thacker, Alan, 'Bede's Ideal of Reform', in *Ideal and Reality in Frankish and Anglo-Saxon Society: Studies Presented to J. M. Wallace-Hadrill*, ed. by Patrick Wormald with Donald Bullough and Roger Collins (Oxford: Basil Blackwell, 1983), pp. 130–53

——, 'Monks, Preaching and Pastoral Care in Early Anglo-Saxon England', in *Pastoral Care before the Parish*, ed. by John Blair and Richard Sharpe (Leicester: Leicester University Press, 1992), pp. 137–70

——, 'Bede and the Ordering of Understanding', in *Innovation and Tradition in the Writings of the Venerable Bede*, ed. by Scott DeGregorio (Morgantown: West Virginia University Press, 2006), pp. 37–63

——, 'Bede, the Britons and the Book of Samuel', in *Early Medieval Studies in Memory of Patrick Wormald*, ed. by Stephen Baxter (Farnham: Ashgate, 2009), pp. 129–47

——, 'Bede and History', in *The Cambridge Companion to Bede*, ed. by Scott DeGregorio (Cambridge: Cambridge University Press, 2010), pp. 170–90

Wallis, Faith, 'Introduction', in *Bede: Commentary on Revelation*, trans. by Faith Wallis, Translated Texts for Historians, 58 (Liverpool: Liverpool University Press, 2013), pp. 1–96

Wood, Ian, *The Most Holy Abbot Ceolfrid*, Jarrow Lecture (Jarrow: St Paul's Church, 1995)

——, 'The Foundation of Wearmouth–Jarrow', in *The Cambridge Companion to Bede*, ed. by Scott DeGregorio (Cambridge: Cambridge University Press, 2010), pp. 84–97

——, 'Who are the Philistines? Bede's Readings of Old Testament Peoples', in *The Resources of the Past in Early Medieval Europe*, ed. by Clemens Gantner, Rosamond McKitterick, and Sven Meeder (Cambridge: Cambridge University Press, 2015), pp. 172–87

ARTHUR HOLDER

Bede's *perfecti*, the Vision of God, and the Foretaste of Heaven

More than thirty years ago now, Alan Thacker's seminal article on 'Bede's Ideal of Reform' set the direction for much subsequent scholarship by identifying Bede's reformist agenda as a key to understanding all of his later works, the biblical commentaries and homilies as well as the historical and hagiographical writings.[1] We have come to understand Bede as the avid proponent of a pastoral strategy, largely derived from his reading of Gregory the Great, aimed at the formation of an elite group of pastors and teachers for the Northumbrian Church. Like his mentor, Bede acknowledged the ultimate superiority of the contemplative life, which will alone persist into eternity when this present age passes away and the saints enter with joy into their heavenly reward. But for those still toiling here below, both Gregory and Bede expressed a preference for the mixed life combining contemplative prayer with active service. Thus Bede was constantly exhorting the Church's spiritual leaders to devote themselves to the ministry of preaching. The ideal was for them to practice what they preached, and to do so with unfailing zeal.

As Thacker noted, Bede's reformist vision was in many ways essentially monastic. Life ordered according to the monastic *regula* was, in his view, the best possible preparation for those called to be teachers, preachers, pastors, and inspiring examples for lay Christians in a country only recently converted from its pagan past. Singing the daily office, celebrating the sacraments, and keeping the appointed vigils and fasts would train the Church's leaders in humility and the other virtues necessary for their work. Studying Holy Scripture and meditating upon it night and day would nourish them with the riches of divine wisdom, which they could then share with those in their charge. Fervent prayer would prepare them to receive God's grace, without which they would never be able to accomplish anything at all. We might say that Bede's emphasis was on the ascetic theology that formed leaders for the Church and the pastoral theology that would guide them in the exercise of their ministerial vocation. But he did not entirely ignore

---

1 Thacker, 'Bede's Ideal of Reform'.

Arthur Holder • is Professor of Christian Spirituality in the Graduate Theological Union, Berkeley, California.

Cities, Saints, and Communities in Early Medieval Europe, ed. by Scott DeGregorio and Paul Kershaw, SEM 46 (Turnhout: Brepols, 2020), pp. 265-285
BREPOLS PUBLISHERS
DOI 10.1484/M.SEM-EB.5.119631

what later ages have called mystical theology, understood in accordance with Bernard McGinn's identification of the mystical element in Christianity as that which concerns 'the preparation for, the consciousness of, and the reaction to what can be described as the immediate or direct presence of God'.[2] It is true that Bede did not expand upon these topics with the philosophical sophistication of an Augustine or the psychological perspicacity of a Gregory the Great, but they do appear rather frequently in his biblical commentaries, and occasionally in other genres as well. Paying attention to the mystical aspects of Bede's theology should not obscure the energetic reform agenda that Alan Thacker and others have identified as his primary concern, but it may help to provide some additional depth and shadow to the picture that has developed in recent years.

Our subject here will be Bede's teaching on the vision of God in this life as a foretaste of heaven enjoyed by some (but not all) of those he called the *perfecti*.[3] According to Bede in agreement with the central tradition of Western Christianity, the full vision of God in his essence is reserved for the saints in the life to come. Intimations of that vision in the present life are brief and rare, given by divine grace only to a few select souls among the perfect. Delightful though such experiences may be, they must not be allowed to distract the Church's spiritual leaders from the ministry of preaching and the care of souls. Granted that Bede's primary focus was on the mixed life of contemplation and action with its attendant imperative for preaching, what role did the possibility of a limited divine vision in this life play in his theology? Was it simply a legacy from his patristic sources that he had to acknowledge, however grudgingly? Or did it in fact serve a purpose as an integral part of his theological project and reform agenda? How did he adopt and modify his sources on this topic — especially Augustine and Gregory,[4] but to some extent Ambrose and John Cassian as well? In order to investigate these questions, we will consider Bede's identification of both the *perfecti* in the Church and the biblical exemplars who were said to have seen God. We will also need to understand what, in Bede's view, the chosen few actually saw, and how they saw it. To do so, we will consider his appropriation of the language of ecstasy or *excessus mentis*, as well as his notion of the heavenly foretaste. Finally, we will try to determine if there were any among the saints of his own time that Bede considered to have had such mystical experiences, and whether he might have counted himself among them.

Bede's *perfecti*

When Bede discusses mystical experiences granted to a select few among the faithful, he often identifies the recipients of such gifts as the *perfecti*. His use of this term does

2 McGinn, *The Foundations of Mysticism*, p. xvii.

3 For previous studies see Carroll, *The Venerable Bede*, pp. 211–15; DeGregorio, 'The Venerable Bede on Prayer and Contemplation', 26–34; O'Reilly, 'Bede on Seeing the God of Gods', 18–29; and O'Brien, *Bede's Temple*, 177–79.

4 On Augustine's influence, see Thacker, 'Bede and Augustine of Hippo'; on Gregory's, see Meyvaert, 'Bede and Gregory the Great', and DeGregorio, 'The Venerable Bede and Gregory the Great'.

not imply that persons in this category are morally without fault; indeed, intense compunction for sin is one of their distinguishing characteristics. Naturally it is to be expected that the perfect are more virtuous in their behaviour than ordinary Christians and more loving toward their neighbours. While beginners in the faith may think it suffices for them to demonstrate the virtues of faith, hope, and love, the perfect go on to perform works of supererogation by preaching the word and by devoting themselves to vigils, fasts, liturgical singing, and *lectio divina* while enduring persecution for the sake of the gospel.[5] But above all, the perfect are notable for the fervour of their devotion. They can be identified simply as 'qui se sincera ac fixa intentione Deo seruire meminerint' (those who remember to serve God with sincere and rapt attention).[6] In both the tabernacle of Moses and the temple of Solomon they were represented by the altar of incense in front of the oracle, where the offerings made were not fleshly sacrifices for remission of sins but the fragrant smoke of prayer and heavenly desires. The outer altar of holocaust was covered in bronze because its resonance suggested the sound of preaching, but the altar of incense was covered in more precious gold in order to represent those who are 'minus aliis quae in secreto de interna suauitate gustent dicentes aperiunt minus eructare proloquendo sufficiunt quanta ipsi intus dulcedine in abdito uultus Dei reficiantur' (less open about telling others of the inner pleasures they taste in secret, and less able to give utterance by declaring how much they have been interiorly refreshed with sweetness in the hidden face of God).[7]

Bede's typical contrast is between the *perfecti* and the *carnales* as two classes of people in the Church. The carnal are by no means to be despised; they are counted among the faithful and can anticipate sharing in heavenly joys if they persist in the Christian way of life. However, they are only beginners who should not presume to aspire to contemplation before they have attained perfection of the active life.[8] Sometimes Bede made a further distinction by naming three categories: the beginners who are just starting out, the *proficientes* who are still making progress, and the perfect who have reached maturity, but he never offered any specific distinguishing marks for the middle group; his purpose in delineating the categories seems to have been to encourage all Christians to keep moving forward rather than to provide a measuring stick for gauging the precise extent of their progress.[9] As Bede had learned from Gregory the Great, 'Nemo enim repente fit summus sed

---

5 On compunction among the *perfecti*, see Bede, *De tabernaculo*, III ed. by Hurst, p. 138, ll. 1746–47; on their virtue, Bede, *De templo*, I, ed. by Hurst, p. 168, ll. 834–48; on love of neighbour, Bede, *De tabernaculo*, III, ed. by Hurst, pp. 126–27, ll. 1307–16; on works of supererogation, Bede, *De templo*, I, ed. by Hurst, p. 196, ll. 166–71.

6 Bede, *In Cantica canticorum*, III, ed. by Hurst, p. 272, l. 24; *The Venerable Bede: On the Song of Songs and Selected Writings*, trans. by Holder, p. 140.

7 Bede, *De tabernaculo*, III, ed. by Hurst, p. 125, ll. 1242–75; for the quotation see ll. 1273–75, *Bede: On the Tabernacle*, trans. by Holder, p. 146; see also Bede, *De templo*, I, ed. by Hurst, p. 172, ll. 1008–18; p. 176, ll. 1181–93.

8 Bede, *In primam partem Samuhelis*, I, ed. by Hurst, p. 56, ll. 1879–88.

9 Bede, *In Cantica canticorum*, III, ed. by Hurst, p. 261, ll. 662–65.

gradatim necesse est a minoribus ad perfectiora tendamus' (No one attains to the highest place all of a sudden, but it is necessary for us to move gradually from the lesser things to the more perfect).[10] The *perfecti* may be few in number, but they are the engine that drives the Church forward toward its ultimate goal, which is the vision of God.

Although Bede often seems to equate the *perfecti* with monks and members of the clergy, he sometimes goes out of his way to say that lay people can be among the perfect and that some priests are unworthy. When he came to write in *De tabernaculo* about the bronze basin in which the Old Testament priests were to wash their hands, Bede explained that this symbolized the greater degree of compunction incumbent upon 'omnibus perfectis in quocumque gradu positis' (all the perfect in whatever rank they may be stationed) since in the New Testament the mystical name of priest applies to all members of the Church.[11] On the other hand, even if someone has the name and status of a Christian priest, he will lose his authority to preach if he strays into heresy or falls into the depravity of wicked deeds.[12] Whether clergy or laity, the *perfecti* can only be perfect within the limits of human perfection. They are not completely sinless, but they are far advanced on their way to the state of true perfection enjoyed by the saints in heaven.[13] In the life to come, all the faithful will rejoice to see the vision of God. Here on earth, says Bede, only a very few of the *perfecti* are granted a preliminary glimpse of that divine vision. Just as their perfection is possible only within the constraints of human frailty, so is their vision of God limited so long as they are living here below. But since it was apparently important to Bede that some of the perfect do attain this vision while on earth, let us consider how he understood their mystical state of bliss.

The Vision of God

Like his patristic predecessors, Bede had to deal with an apparent contradiction in the biblical record concerning the possibility of seeing God in this life. Even within a single chapter in the book of Exodus, we read that 'the Lord used to speak to Moses face to face, as one speaks to a friend' (33. 11) and then a few verses later we hear God saying, 'You cannot see my face, for no human being shall see my face and live' (33. 20). What then are Christians to make of Jesus's promise in the Beatitudes that 'the pure in heart shall see God' (Matthew 5. 8)? And how are they to understand Paul's oblique testimony about his own experience of being caught up to the third heaven or to Paradise — whether in the body or out-of-body, he professed not to know — where

---

10   Bede, *De tabernaculo*, II, ed. by Hurst, p. 89, ll. 1877–88; cf. Gregory the Great, *Homiliae in Hiezechihelem*, II.III.3, ed. by Adriaen, p. 238, ll. 53–55.

11   Bede, *De tabernaculo*, III, ed. by Hurst, p. 138, ll. 1748–65; for the quotation see ll. 1762–63, trans. by Holder, p. 161; see also Bede, *De templo*, I, ed. by Hurst, pp. 193–94, ll. 76–94.

12   Bede, *De tabernaculo*, III, ed. by Hurst, p. 95, ll. 77–82.

13   Bede, *De tabernaculo*, II, ed. by Hurst, p. 52, ll. 406–14; Bede, *De templo*, I, ed. by Hurst, p. 165, ll. 735–43.

he had heard things that no mortal is permitted to repeat (II Corinthians 12. 2–4)? In his own wrestling with this problem, Augustine had explained that at the time when they saw God in that form (*species*) by which he is God, Moses and Paul were in a sense dead because they were in ecstasy and thus completely separated from their bodily senses.[14] Gregory the Great's usual position on the issue was that in this life the divine vision is possible only 'in aenigmate' (in obscurity, as in I Corinthians 13. 12) and not 'in species' (by sight), but there is one passage in the *Moralia* where he seems to accept Augustine's interpretation.[15] Thus both of Bede's principal authorities believed that it was possible for a few people in this life to have an intellectual vision of God that is direct and immediate, although Gregory was generally more cautious than Augustine about the clarity of that vision.

Following his predecessors, Bede affirmed that the vision of God in this life is both possible and desirable, but quite limited in several different ways. Although the future delight of seeing God in heaven was his more frequent theme, he noted that when Scripture says that 'God had made them joyful with great joy' (Nehemiah 12. 43), this can also be understood with reference to a rare form of earthly happiness:

> Potest haec dedicatio etiam in hac uita typice in quibusdam electis coepta intellegi qui purificato cordis oculo ea quae in futuro cuncta perceptura est ecclesia non nulla ex parte gaudia contemplari merentur ut Esaias Iezechiel Danihel ceterique prophetae ut apostoli qui clarificatum in monte sancto dominum uidere gaudebant ut Paulus qui in paradisum atque in tertium rapi caelum meruit ut in apocalipsi sua Iohannes.
>
> > This dedication can be interpreted typologically as having begun even in this life for certain people of the elect who, having purified the eye of the heart, deserve to contemplate in some part all those joys that the Church is to gain in the future, as did Isaiah, Ezekiel, Daniel and other prophets; as did the apostles who rejoiced to behold the Lord when he was glorified on the holy mountain; as did John in his Apocalypse.[16]

For Christians in later times as for these biblical worthies, the vision of God is made possible only by an extraordinary effusion of divine grace.[17] Such a vision is not only limited in being restricted to a few select persons among the *perfecti*, but it is also limited in frequency and duration, and in never being full or complete.[18] Whoever

---

14 Augustine, *De Genesi ad litteram*, XII.27, ed. by Zycha, pp. 420–22; Augustine, *Epistula* CXLVII.31, ed. by Goldbacher, pp. 305–06.

15 Gregory the Great, *Homiliae in Hiezechihelem*, I.VIII.30, ed. by Adriaen, p. 120, ll. 660–70; Gregory the Great, *Moralia in Iob*, XVIII.XL.89, ed. by Adriaen, p. 952, ll. 59–69.

16 Bede, *In Ezram et Neemiam*, III, ed. by Hurst, p. 385, ll. 1830–37: *Bede: On Ezra and Nehemiah*, trans. by DeGregorio, p. 217.

17 Bede, *In Cantica canticorum*, I, ed. by Hurst, p. 219, ll. 333–42; p. 281, ll. 379–98; p. 300, ll. 33–39; Bede, *In primam partem Samuhelis*, ed. by Hurst, p. 57, ll. 1918–29.

18 Limited to a few: Bede, *De tabernaculo*, I, ed. by Hurst, pp. 8–9, ll. 143–50; Bede, *In Cantica canticorum*, I, ed. by Hurst, p. 220, ll. 376–82. Limited in frequency and duration: Bede, *Homiliae euangelii*, I.24, ed. by Hurst, pp. 171–72, ll. 57–61; Bede, *In primam partem Samuhelis*, ed. by Hurst, pp. 58–60, lines

sees God in this life can never see God's essence, which is the lesson Bede derives from a verse in the Song of Songs in which he understands Christ the bridegroom to be admonishing the Church as bride: 'Turn away your eyes from me, for they have made me flee away' (Song of Songs 6. 5 [6. 4]). Bede's explanation conveys the apophatic message that to see God is to know that he is invisible:

> Auertere ergo iubemur in praesenti a cognoscenda Dei substantia oculos nostrae inquisitionis quia ipsi eum auolare fecerunt a nobis, non quod ille quaesitus longius recedat qui promittit dicens: **Quaerite et inuenietis**, sed quod nos illo reuelante discamus quia quo altius puro corde quaeritur eo certius quam sit incomprehensibilis comprehenditur.

> > In the present time, therefore, we are commanded to turn our searching eyes away from knowing God's essence because they make him flee away from us. This does not mean that he withdraws very far away when he is being sought, for he has made a promise to us in saying, '**Seek and you will find**' (Matthew 7. 7), but rather that when he appears we should learn that the higher he is sought by the pure in heart, the more certainly is he comprehended as being incomprehensible.[19]

The final limitation that Bede places on the divine vision to a few *perfecti* is that it should always inspire the recipient with an increased zeal for pastoral ministry, especially preaching.[20]

Although Bede's treatment of the divine vision is for the most part congruent with that of Augustine and Gregory, he differs from them in one important aspect. As Bernard McGinn has observed, when Augustine and Gregory discuss the progressive stages of contemplation, they describe a threefold movement derived from the neo-Platonic philosophy of Plotinus: 1) a withdrawal of the senses from all that is exterior to the soul, 2) a focused concentration of the soul upon itself, and 3) an ecstatic upward movement of the soul toward God.[21] What is missing in Bede is the second step of interiorization, which is precisely the step that might imply some sort of meditative technique. For Bede, the gift of the divine vision is always instantaneous, passive, and without any sort of intentional preparation. As he describes it in his commentary on Tobit:

> Et dominus ac saluator noster curam agit eorum quos in bonorum operum incolumitate perstare cognouerit. Ipse intuitum cordis eorum a praesentis uitae delectatione claudens ad contemplationem perpetuae lucis adtollit, ipse illos post huius uitae terminum ad caelestia perducit.

1977–94. Limited in never being full or complete: Bede, *In Regum librum XXX quaestiones*, ed. by Hurst, p. 307, ll. 37–41.

19 Bede, *In Cantica canticorum*, IV, ed. by Hurst, p. 303, ll. 165–70; *The Venerable Bede: On the Song of Songs and Selected Writings*, trans. by Holder, p. 180.

20 Bede, *In Cantica canticorum*, I, ed. by Hurst, p. 221, ll. 406–20.

21 On Augustine, see McGinn, *The Foundations of Mysticism*, p. 233. On Gregory, see McGinn, *The Growth of Mysticism*, pp. 56–57.

Our Lord and Saviour also takes care of the ones he knows have persisted in the health of good works. For by closing the heart's eye to the allure of this present life he lifts them to contemplation of the perpetual light and leads them to heavenly things after this life is over.[22]

There is never any clear direction in Bede's writings that the *perfecti* should take some specific action designed to acquire the vision of God in this life. Certainly they should persevere in both the works of mercy that characterize the active life and the 'intentio mentis' (concentration of the mind) that belongs to the contemplative life. But for Bede that *intentio mentis* was to be focused not on the soul's introspective self-reflection but on the ultimate goal of eternal life.[23] For the vast majority even of the perfect, their desire to see God will be fulfilled only in the age to come. For the very few who are granted a preliminary glimpse, everything depends on God's initiative.

While brief references to the divine vision are scattered throughout Bede's exegetical works, there are several passages in which the theme is treated at some length. Two such passages appear in the commentary on I John, which was one of Bede's earliest works of exegesis, written *c.* 709–716. Commenting on I John 3. 2 ('For we shall see him as he is'), Bede avers that only in heaven will the elect be able to contemplate God 'in ipsa deitatis suae substantia' (in the very substance of his deity). Quoting Augustine's *Epistula* 147 without attribution, he goes on to explain that Moses and the others who have seen God in this life were able to behold him 'in specie qua uoluit' (in the appearance that he chose) but in the life to come the saints will comprehend him 'in natura qua in semet ipso etiam cum uideretur latuit' (in that nature in which he is hidden within himself even when he is seen).[24] When he comes to I John 4. 12 ('No one has ever seen God'), Bede quotes again from the same letter of Augustine, and from Ambrose's commentary on Luke as well, to assert once again that bodily eyes can never see the invisible God as he is in himself.[25] In these passages Bede's emphasis is on denying that God can be fully comprehended in this life.

In another commentary from the same early period before 716, however, Bede does discuss the possibility of some sort of limited vision of God even in this life. Commenting on Song of Songs 2. 8 ('The voice of my beloved!'), he writes of the soul's joy at hearing God's voice:

> Nam etsi necdum faciem dilecti nostri licet intueri iam multum nobis est praestitum in eo quod in scripturis sanctis interim eloquiorum eius dulcedine reficimur, multum praestatur eis quibus altiori dono conceditur ut subleuato ad caelestia purae mentis intuitu non nullam futurae uitae suauitatem etiam in praesenti praegustent.

> For although we are not yet permitted to gaze upon the face of our beloved, much has already been given to us in that we are refreshed from time to time

---

22 Bede, *In Tobiam*, ed. by Hurst, p. 19, ll. 35–39; *Bede: A Biblical Miscellany*, trans. by Foley, p. 78.

23 Bede, *In Ezram et Neemiam*, II, ed. by Hurst, p. 305, ll. 711–14.

24 *In epistolas septem catholicas*, ed. by Hurst, p. 302, ll. 47–48, 59–61; *Bede the Venerable: Commentary on the Seven Catholic Epistles*, trans. by Hurst, pp. 185–86.

25 *In epistolas septem catholicas*, ed. by Hurst, pp. 314–15, ll. 136–85.

by the sweetness of his words in the Holy Scriptures, and much is given to those who are allowed the even greater gift of having a pure mind's gaze lifted up to heaven so that while still in the present time they might have a not inconsiderable foretaste of the sweetness of the life to come.[26]

Here we should note that Bede clearly distinguishes between the relatively common refreshment 'given to us' that comes by hearing God's voice in Scripture and the rare gift 'given to those' whose contemplative vision constitutes a foretaste of heaven. The few perfect souls who receive such a gift are like mountains and hills because in their purity of mind they rise above the rest of the Church's members and say, 'For if we are out of our mind it is for God' (II Corinthians 5. 13) and 'we have been beholders of his greatness' (II Peter 1. 16).[27] Examples of such sublime contemplatives favoured with divine grace include Isaiah who saw the Lord high and lifted up in the temple (Isaiah 6. 1–3) and Paul who was caught up to Paradise and the third heaven (II Corinthians 12. 2–4).[28] A little further on in the same commentary, Bede speaks again of these visionary mountains when he imagines the Church as Christ's bride beseeching her Lord: 'Obsecro a generali instructione reuertaris saepius ad illustranda sublimius corda perfectorum et [...] precor ut dulcedinem uitae immortalis [...] aliquibus etiam in itinere quamuis a longe speculandam reueles' (I entreat you, then, to turn from instructing all in general in order to enlighten the hearts of the perfect to a higher degree, and [...] I pray that you will allow some who are still on the way to see, even if only from afar, the sweetness of immortal life).[29] Although Bede does not elaborate on the reasons why the Church is so eager for some of her members to have a foretaste of celestial joy, the implication is that their special blessing is in some way for the benefit for all.

An Advent homily probably preached some time in the 720s provided another occasion for Bede to consider how the biblical assertion that 'No one has ever seen God' (this time taken from John 1. 18) can be reconciled with the divine appearances to the patriarchs like Abraham and Jacob and to prophets like Isaiah. Employing language largely borrowed from Gregory the Great, Bede explained:

Sed recte intellegendum in cunctis huiusmodi uisionibus homines sanctos Deum non per ipsam naturae suae speciem sed per quasdam imagines esse contemplatos. Viderunt ergo sancti Deum per subiectam creaturam, uerbi gratia, ignem angelum nubem electrum; [...] quia fragili adhuc uasculo carnis inclusi per circumscriptas rerum imagines uidere possunt quem per incircumscriptum aeternitatis suae lumen nequaquam ualent intueri.

---

26 Bede, *In Cantica canticorum*, I, ed. by Hurst, p. 218, ll. 280–85; *The Venerable Bede: On the Song of Songs and Selected Writings*, trans. by Holder, pp. 72–73. For the dating of this commentary before 716, see Holder, 'The Anti–Pelagian Character of Bede's Commentary', pp. 100–03.

27 Bede, *In Cantica canticorum*, III, ed. by Hurst, pp. 218–19, ll. 289–325.

28 Bede, *In Cantica canticorum*, III, ed. by Hurst, p. 219, ll. 326–42.

29 Bede, *In Cantica canticorum*, II, ed. by Hurst, pp. 229–30, ll. 719–26; *The Venerable Bede: On the Song of Songs and Selected Writings*, trans. by Holder, p. 87.

> In all visions of this sort holy men contemplated God not through the very
> form of his nature, but through certain images. Therefore the holy ones saw
> God through a subordinate creature, for example, fire, an angel, a cloud, or
> lightning; [...] for those who are still contained within the weak vessel of
> the flesh can see him through circumscribed images of things, although they
> are by no means capable of looking at him through the uncircumscribed
> radiance of his eternity.[30]

From this passage we can understand how Bede could consider the divine theophanies
of the Old Testament as true — but limited — visions of God himself. Such visions
did not disclose 'the very form of his nature', but they did convey 'images' of his
majesty. As he went on to explain, only through the revelatory instruction of the
incarnate Christ, who came from the Father's lap (John 1. 18) to teach the faithful
about the mystery of the Trinity, can Christians learn the path by which after death
they may at last come to the 'uisionem incommutabilis et aeterni luminis' (the vision
of the unchangeable and eternal radiance).[31]

Patristic authors had recognized Moses as the paradigmatic mystic visionary
in the Old Testament, as Paul was in the New. Thus it is not surprising that Bede's
commentary on the tabernacle (*c.* 721–725) should treat Moses' ascent of Mount
Sinai to meet the Lord in the midst of a cloud as an allegory about those few chosen
souls who, having perfected the active life, are able to ascend to divine contemplation
'qualiscumque et quantulacumque' (after a fashion and to some slight degree) while
still clothed in flesh.[32] Like Augustine and Gregory before him, Bede can be classified
as a theologian of the Divine Light, which is evident in his interpretation of the
mysterious cloud in Exodus 24. 16:

> Medium namque caliginis unde uocatus esse dicitur non inesse Deo tenebras ullas
> significat sed quia lucem habitat inaccessibilem, et sicut item dicit apostolus, **Quem
> uidit nullus hominum sed nec uidere potest**. Caligo namque illa obscuritas
> est archanorum caelestium terrenis quidem cordibus inaccessibilis sed Moysi et
> ceteris mundo corde beatis diuina reserante gratia penetrabilis quibus dicitur in
> psalmo: **Accedite ad eum et illuminamini**.

> Surely the midst of the darkness, from which [Moses] is said to have been
> called, does not signify that there are any shadows in God, but rather that he
> dwells in light inaccessible. As the Apostle also says (I Timothy 1. 16), '**No
> human being has seen him, or ever can see him**'. For that darkness is the

---

30 Bede, *Homiliae euangelii*, ed. by Hurst, I.2, p. 11, ll. 159–68; *Bede the Venerable: Homilies on the Gospels*,
    I, trans. by Martin and Hurst, p. 14; cf. Gregory the Great, *Moralia in Iob*, XVIII.LIV.88, ed. by Adriaen,
    pp. 951–52, ll. 35–58. Commenting on Hagar's vision of an angel, Bede affirms that whether she had
    recognized him as the living God or only as God's representative, she had received a divine vision;
    Bede, *In principium Genesis*, ed. by Jones, p. 201, ll. 261–65.

31 Bede, *Homiliae euangelii*, I.2, ed. by Hurst, pp. 11–12, ll. 169–86; *Bede the Venerable: Homilies on the
    Gospels*, I, trans. by Martin and Hurst, pp. 15–16.

32 Bede, *De tabernaculo*, I, ed. by Hurst, p. 8, ll. 143–47; *Bede: On the Tabernacle*, trans. by Holder, p. 5.

obscurity of the heavenly mysteries. It is indeed inaccessible to earthly hearts, but when disclosed by divine grace it can be penetrated by Moses and the rest of the blessed who are pure in heart, to whom it is said in the psalm, '**Come to him and be illuminated**' (Psalm 34. 5 [33. 6]).[33]

That the 'rest of the blessed' here refers to a select few of the perfect on earth is clear from Bede's subsequent observation that the children of Israel at the foot of the mountain, who behold the glory of the Lord only from afar, are like the majority of Christians who are unable to follow the perfect in comprehending divine mysteries due to human frailty but can at least stay close to them by believing, hoping, and loving while keeping their mind's eye fixed on the recollection of eternal splendour.[34]

Bede's commentary on Genesis (*c.* 722–725 for Books III and IV) discusses a number of divine appearances to Abraham and his wives Hagar and Sarah, but the visitation of three men at the vale of Mambre is said to be *sacratior* ('holier') than all the rest. Bede gives an allegorical interpretation to many of the details in the story: Abraham sat at the door of his tent because he was a stranger in this world always ready to enter the world to come, and it was hot that day because he was inflamed with the love of divine contemplation. The three men represented the Holy Trinity but Abraham addressed them as 'Lord' (in the singular) because Father, Son, and Holy Spirit are one God. He lifted up his eyes at their approach because those who long to see the citizens of heaven and the glory of the divine majesty must raise their gaze from base desires to the light of the Sun. As Abraham ran to meet the angels and begged them not to go away, so also 'necesse est ut quotiescumque gustum aliquem internae dulcedinis animo concipimus, mox omnibus uotis ac promptis bonorum operum gressibus satagamus, ne nos citius eadem dulcedo relinquat' (whenever we acquire in our heart any taste of inward sweetness, it is necessary that we immediately busy ourselves with every form of prayer and step promptly with good works, lest that sweetness desert us too quickly).[35] Bede is keen to note that Abraham was eager to show hospitality to the strangers and to command his wife and servant to do so as well, which shows that all the recipients of divine grace should encourage themselves and their followers to carry out the Lord's commands.[36] In all of this, there is no direct reference to the ecstatic vision of God in this life on the part of the *perfecti*, but Bede is using the theophany to Abraham as a teaching opportunity to direct the intention of the faithful to their ultimate goal.

33 Bede, *De tabernaculo*, I, ed. by Hurst, p. 9, ll. 156–63; *Bede: On the Tabernacle*, trans. by Holder, p. 6. In his commentary on Genesis, Bede explains that the creation narrative refers to three different forms of light: the inaccessible light in which God dwells, the primordial light created on the first day, and the heavenly lights of sun, moon, and stars created on the fourth day. Bede, *In principium Genesis*, ed. by Jones, pp. 7–8, ll. 162–68, and p. 15, ll. 415–22.
34 Bede, *De tabernaculo*, I, ed. by Hurst, pp. 9–10, ll. 176–91.
35 Bede, *In principium Genesis*, ed. by Jones, pp. 209–11, ll. 556–636; for the quotation see p. 211, ll. 629–32, *On Genesis: Bede*, trans. by Kendall, p. 289.
36 Bede, *In principium Genesis*, ed. by Jones, p. 213, ll. 680–89.

Excessus mentis

Although Bede did not show much interest in the psychological or physiological aspects of mystical experiences, he was familiar with the conventional terminology for describing them, especially the language of *exstasis* (from the Greek, 'ecstasy') and *excessus mentis* (literally, 'going out of one's mind'). The definition of the phenomenon that appears in his commentary on Habakkuk follows the conventional line: 'Siue autem stupor siue alienatio siue excessus mentis dicatur, unum idemque significat cum quis repentino miraculo turbatus ac stupefactus, a sensu suae mentis redditur alienus' (But whether it is called *stupor* or *alienatio* or *excessus mentis*, one and the same thing is meant when, agitated and rendered speechless by a sudden astonishing occurrence, one is left cut off from one's mental faculties).[37] These terms could have either positive or negative connotations depending on the context. Bede noted, for example, that the Greek text of Acts uses the term εκσταςις with reference to Peter's vision of being called to preach to the gentile Cornelius, but he was also aware that Simon Magus could be said to have thrown people into an ecstasy by putting them in a stupor with his magic tricks.[38] In his commentary on Genesis, Bede reproduced Augustine's textual note to the effect that the Old Latin version of Genesis 2. 21 had characterized the deep sleep that befell Adam as an *exstasis*, that is to say, a *mentis excessus*. Still following Augustine, Bede went on to explain that Adam's ecstasy was actually a prophetic trance in which he had been taken up to join the angels in heaven, given a vision of his final end, and inspired to declare upon his return to the body that the woman taken from his side was 'bone of my bones and flesh of my flesh'.[39]

In fact, Bede believed that all the prophets had received their revelations while in a contemplative state.[40] As we have seen, he often alluded to the prophets as prototypes of the perfect Christian souls who receive the divine vision in this life. His account of the prophet Habakkuk's experience describes a mystical event from the perspective of the one undergoing the experience:

> Raptus ad contemplationem caelestium arcanorum propheta se quodammodo super se esse uidit eleuatum; et quo altior efficitur lumine contemplationis eo se inperfectiorem conspicit merito actionis. Subleuatus enim ad intuenda superna, iure de his quae in infimis gesserat conturbatur. Turbata est autem uirtus prophetae,

---

37 Bede, *Expositio Bedae presbyteri in Canticum Habacuc*, ed, by Hudson, p. 400, ll. 527–30; *Bede: On Tobit and on the Canticle of Habakkuk*, trans. by Connolly, pp. 85–86.

38 Bede, *Retractatio in Actus Apostolorum*, ed. by Laistner, p. 136, ll. 77–80, and p. 159, ll. 10–15, where Bede noted that the Greek word for ecstasy could be translated into Latin as *stupor mentis* (mental amazement), *mentis excessus, pauor* (fear), or *alienatio* (delirium). See also p. 118, ll. 6–9, for *exstasis* or *excessus mentis* as *admiratio* (wonder).

39 Bede, *In principium Genesis*, ed. by Jones, pp. 57–58, ll. 1833–42, quoting from Augustine, *De Genesi ad litteram*, IX.19, ed. by Zycha, p. 294.

40 Bede, *In epistolas septem catholicas*, ed. by Hurst, p. 228, ll. 139–40. Note, however, that Bede did not believe that the prophets were still in ecstasy when they delivered their prophecies in oral form; see Bede, *In primam partem Samuhelis*, II, ed. by Hurst, p. 80, ll. 1 l. 509–19.

et contremuerunt ossa, expauit uenter, non solum quia minus perfectum se actione cognouit, uerum etiam quia omnes qui pie uellent uiuere in Christo, persecutiones passuros dicit; sed et ipsum Christum qui sine peccato intraret in mundum, non sine poena peccati exiturum uidit esse de mundo.

> When rapt in contemplation of the heavenly mysteries, the prophet saw himself raised somehow or other above himself; and the higher he rose in the light of contemplation, the more imperfect he saw himself in merit of action. For when raised aloft to gaze on heavenly things, he was with good reason deeply perturbed about the things he had done in this life. But the prophet's strength was troubled and his bones shook violently, his belly trembled with terror [Habakkuk 3. 16], not only because he knows he was less perfect in conduct, but also because he says that all who devoutly wished to live in Christ would suffer persecutions; but he saw too that Christ who entered the world, would not leave the world without the punishment of sin.[41]

Bede's explanation that the prophet's bodily distress following his ascent to the height of contemplation had resulted from a heightened awareness of his own sinfulness is an example of what Augustine and Gregory called *relapsus* ('sinking back') or *reuerberatio* ('being beaten back').[42] The earlier writers had often spoken of the falling back that occurred after a contemplative had seen the Divine Light; here Bede understands Habakkuk as having had a vision of the Church's coming tribulations and its eventual salvation through the incarnation, passion, and ascension of Christ.

Another reference to ecstatic vision comes in Bede's commentary on the *fenestrae obliquae* ('slanting windows') in the temple of Solomon, which he understood as a type of Christian teachers and other spiritual people who catch a glimpse of the secrets of heavenly mysteries while being 'out of their minds for God' (another allusion to II Corinthians 5. 13). They are like windows because they fill the Church with the light of what they have seen in secret, and those windows are slanted because 'quisquis iubar supernae contemplationis uel ad momentum perceperit mox sinum cordis amplius castigando dilatet atque ad maiora capessenda sollerti exercitatione praeparet' (whoever receives a ray of heavenly contemplation even for a moment must immediately expand the bosom of his heart more fully by mortification and prepare it by skilful training to strive for greater things.)[43] Leslie Alcock once supposed that Bede's interpretation of the slanting windows had been prompted by direct observation of the properties of double-splayed windows in Anglo-Saxon stone churches, but the more likely inspiration was a passage in a homily by Gregory the Great that Cuthbert Butler called 'the most scientific and formal exposition of his doctrine of mysticism'. As

---

41 Bede, *Expositio Bedae presbyteri in Canticum Habacuc*, ed. by Hudson, p. 403, ll. 610–19; *Bede: On Tobit and on the Canticle of Habakkuk*, trans. by Connolly, p. 89.

42 See McGinn, *The Growth of Mysticism*, p. 68 and his references to some relevant passages in Gregory's writings on p. 449, n. 245.

43 Bede, *De templo*, I, ed. by Hurst, p. 162, ll. 615–25; for the quotation see ll. 622–25; *Bede: On the Temple*, trans. by Connolly, p. 25 (translation slightly modified).

was his custom, Bede has condensed Gregory's teaching and omitted the explicit references to interiorization while preserving the moral exhortation directed to pastors and teachers.[44]

The Foretaste of Heaven

There are seven instances in Bede's writings where he uses some form of the word *praegustare* ('to have a foretaste') to describe the perfect soul's anticipatory experience of celestial delights.[45] Interestingly, he seems to have used the term in that sense more than any previous Latin patristic author. Augustine never used *praegustare* to refer to the foretaste of heaven, but it does appear in that context in two other writers well known to Bede. In Abba Isaac's famous conference 'On Prayer', John Cassian writes about union with God in perfect love as the goal for a monk, who must aspire to have a foretaste of heaven while still in the body. The word also appears three times in the writings of Gregory the Great, once in the *Moralia* and twice in the pope's homilies on Ezekiel — each time in relation to contemplative experience.[46]

Although Gregory once uses the term when he is talking about being filled with God's love at the banquet of Holy Scripture, in Bede's usage *praegustare* seems always to refer to an experience of the divine presence that is direct and unmediated. This more restricted usage was evident in the passage in the Song commentary quoted above, where he distinguished between the general refreshment granted to many faithful Christians through their reading of Scripture and the particular foretaste given to those whose 'pure mind's gaze' is lifted to heaven.[47] The same association of 'foretaste' with unmediated vision is implied in Bede's interpretation of the additional half cubit in the height of the table in the tabernacle. The table itself signifies Holy Scripture, but the extra half cubit stands for the beginning of contemplation that some saints enjoy while still in the flesh. Like Isaiah and Micah and the other prophets, like Peter, James, and John on the mountain of Transfiguration, and like Paul caught up to Paradise and the third heaven, some of the saints are permitted 'non solum

---

44 Alcock, 'Fenestrae obliquae'; Butler, *Western Mysticism*, p. 72; Gregory the Great, *Homiliae in Hiezechihelem*, II.v.17–18, ed. by Adriaen, pp. 289–90, ll. 460–93. There is nothing in Bede's comment on the slanted windows similar to Gregory's identification of the contemplative as *qui cor intus habet* ('the one who has his heart within himself').

45 Bede, *De tabernaculo*, I, ed. by Hurst, p. 22, l. 683; p. 62, l. 780; Bede, *De Cantica canticorum*, I, ed. by Hurst, p. 218, l. 285; p. 327, l. 439; p. 363, l. 176 (in an excerpt from Gregory the Great, *Homiliae in Hiezechihelem* II.iv.15, ed. by Adriaen, pp. 269–70, ll. 414–33); Bede, *Homiliae euangelii* I.9, ed. by Hurst, p. 64, l. 169; Bede, *Vita metrica sancti Cuthberti*, XXXVI, ed. by Jaager, p. 118. All references to the number of times that Bede and his sources used particular Latin words are derived from searches of the Library of Latin Texts Series A and B (http://clt.brepolis.net/llta/Default.aspx; http://clt.brepolis.net/lltb/Default.aspx).

46 John Cassian, *Conlationes* X.7, ed. by Petschenig, p. 293, l. 27; Gregory the Great, *Moralia in Iob*, XVI. xix.23, ed. by Adriaen, p. 813, l. 28; Gregory the Great, *Homiliae in Hiezechihelem* I.v.12 and II.iv.15, ed. by Adriaen, p. 63, l. 226 and p. 269, l. 426.

47 Bede, *In Cantica canticorum*, I, ed. by Hurst, p. 218, ll. 280–85.

sperare caelestia praemia uerum etiam ex parte uidendo praegustare…raptim et in transitu' (not only to hope for heavenly rewards but also to have a foretaste [of them] by seeing in part…fleetingly and only in passing).[48] Thus the foretaste of heaven is distinguished not only by the content of the anticipated vision (and note the synaesthesia of a foretaste that comes by seeing) but also by the mode of its communication. In heaven where the faithful at last see God as he is, there will be no scriptures, no teachers, and no sacraments, ('cum inhabitans in electis suis Deus omnipotens interius sicut lux uitae illustrat et sicut panis uitae satiat quos introducens in gaudium regni sui perpetua beatitudine sublimat') (when God Almighty, dwelling internally in his elect, shines upon them as the Light of life, satisfies them as the Bread of life, and raises them up to perpetual blessedness, leading them into the joy of his kingdom).[49] In Bede's mystical theology, an earthly foretaste of this heavenly bliss is just as direct and unmediated, though of course much less intense and never sustained for very long.

Mystical Experience in Bede's England

If Bede was convinced that some *perfecti* are able to see God in this life by ecstatic vision, and that the favour shown to them is in some way beneficial to the whole Church, we might expect him to have included some accounts of mystical experience in his historical and hagiographical works. No mystical experiences are described in Bede's history of the abbots of his own monastery, which is, after all, notorious for not even containing any miracle stories.[50] The *Historia ecclesiastica*, however, contains several accounts of people who are visited by angels, have visions of a dying saint being taken to heaven by angels, or see visions of a saintly departed companion.[51] The out-of-body visions of Fursa and Dryhthelm, famous for their place in a long tradition of otherworldly journeys to heaven and hell, included the sight of angels — but so too did the story of the unrepentant Mercian man whose vision only showed him the torments he would soon have to endure.[52] Caedmon was inspired in a dream in which 'someone' (presumably an angel) instructed

---

48 Bede, *De tabernaculo*, I, ed. by Hurst, pp. 22–23, ll. 680–98; *Bede: On the Tabernacle*, trans. by Holder, 22–23.

49 Bede, *De tabernaculo*, II, ed. by Hurst, p. 73, ll. 1230–39; *Bede: On the Tabernacle*, trans. by Holder, 81–82, slightly altered.

50 Bede, *Historia abbatum*, ed. and trans. by Grocock and Wood; but see McCready, *Miracles and the Venerable Bede*, pp. 51–52, for the possibility that Eostorwine's foreknowledge of his own death in I.8 (p. 42) and the coincidence of Benedict Biscop's death with the recitation of Psalm 83 (82) in II.14 (p. 54) might be considered minor miracles.

51 In Bede, *Historia ecclesiastica*, ed. and trans. by Colgrave and Mynors, see angelic visitations at i.19 (pp. 60–61), III.8 (pp. 238–39), IV.3 (pp. 340–43); visions of dying saints taken to heaven at III. 8 (pp. 238–39), IV.9 (pp. 360–61), IV.23 (pp. 412–15); visions of departed saints at IV.3 (pp. 340–41), IV.9 (pp. 362–63).

52 Bede, *Historia ecclesiastica*, III. 19, V.12 and V.13, ed. and trans. by Colgrave and Mynors, pp. 268–77, 488–99, 498–503.

him to compose English songs in praise of the Creator, and Adomnán likewise heard from 'someone' that the monastery at Coldingham would be destroyed by fire, but both of those experiences are in a somewhat different category from the vision of God.[53]

The English saint whom Bede seems to have most clearly identified as having been granted the divine vision while still in the flesh was (not surprisingly) Cuthbert. Some of Cuthbert's supernatural experiences are perhaps better classified as miracle stories (like having his knee cured by a poultice prepared according to the instructions of an angel on horseback) or stories of divine vocation (such as the vision of Saint Aidan's soul being taken to heaven by a choir of angels in heavenly light that inspired Cuthbert to become a monk).[54] But there are three episodes in Cuthbert's life that in Bede's treatment definitely present the marks of mystical experience of the kind we have been discussing. The first is when Cuthbert as guestmaster in the monastery at Ripon unknowingly provides hospitality to an angel who vanishes into thin air but leaves behind three warm loaves of bread so white in colour, fragrant in smell, and sweet in taste that the saint realizes they must have come from the *paradiso uoluptatis* ('paradise of joy').[55] In the anonymous life that was Bede's principal source, the author had compared the angel's appearance to Cuthbert to that of the three angels to Abraham at Mambre and noted that from that time on Cuthbert used to tell the story to his brethren not to boast but to edify others, as the Apostle Paul had done.[56] Bede drops the reference to Abraham at the beginning of the story but expands the comparison to Paul at the end by noting that Cuthbert would relate this and other such stories about himself with humility, as the teacher of the Gentiles had done, 'sub praetextu alterius personae loquitur dicens, "Scio hominem in Christo ante annos quattuordecim raptum usque ad tertium coelum"' (under the guise of another person, saying: 'I knew a man in Christ above fourteen years ago, such an one caught up even to the third heaven').[57] The implication is that Cuthbert's experiences had been similar to that of the Apostle.

In the second episode, also from the prose life, Cuthbert, now bishop of Lindisfarne, was sitting at table with abbess Ælfflaed on an estate belonging to her monastery at Whitby. In the midst of dinner,

> Subito [...] Cuthbertus auersam a carnalibus epulis mentem ad spiritualia contemplanda contulit. Unde lassatis ab officio suo membris corporis, mutato

---

53   Bede, *Historia ecclesiastica*, IV.24, ed. and trans. by Colgrave and Mynors, pp. 414–21.

54   Bede, *Vita sancti Cuthberti*, II and IV, ed. and trans. by Colgrave, pp. 158–61 and 164–67, although Cuthbert's vision of the heavenly translation of Aidan is reported in language reminiscent of Benedict's famous vision in Gregory the Great's *Dialogi*, II.xxv.2–8, ed. by de Vogüé, pp. 236–42; for discussion see DeGregorio, 'The Venerable Bede on Prayer and Contemplation', p. 30, n. 128.

55   Bede, *Vita sancti Cuthberti*, VII, ed. and trans. by Colgrave, pp. 175–79.

56   *Vita sancti Cuthberti auctore anonymo*, II, ed. and trans. by Colgrave, pp. 76–79.

57   Bede, *Vita sancti Cuthberti*, VII, ed. and trans. by Colgrave, pp. 178–79. On Bede's thoroughgoing revision of the anonymous author's biblical allusions, see Shockro, 'Bede and the Rewriting of Sanctity'.

colore faciei et quasi attonitis contra morem oculis, cultellus quoque quem tenebat decidit in mensam'.

> Cuthbert suddenly turned his mind from the carnal banquet to contemplate spiritual things. The limbs of his body relaxed and lost their function, the colour of his face changed, and his eyes were fixed against their wont as if in amazement, while the knife which he was holding fell to the table.[58]

Prompted by an attendant priest, Ælfflaed asked Cuthbert what he had seen in his vision. At first he demurred, joking, 'Can I eat all day? I must rest sometimes'. But finally he was persuaded to reveal that he had seen the soul of a holy man from the abbess's monastery being taken to heaven by angels, and he predicted that the abbess herself would tell him the man's name while he was celebrating mass the next day. That is of course exactly what happened, after Aelfflaed learned that a shepherd named Hadwald had fallen to his death while climbing a tree.

The third episode in which Cuthbert is apparently portrayed as having a mystical experience is when he is on his deathbed before receiving the viaticum. In Bede's prose life of the saint, Cuthbert is said to have 'quietum expectatione futurae beatitudinis diem duxit ad uesperam, cui etiam peruigilem quietis in precibus continuauit et noctem' (passed a quiet day in the expectation of future bliss, until the evening; and he also continued quietly in prayer through a night of watching).[59] But in the metrical life written some years earlier, Bede had described him on that same occasion as 'suae praegustans gaudia palmae' (foretasting the joys of his triumph).[60] Remembering how 'foretaste' functions as something as a technical term for Bede, we may be justified in supposing that Cuthbert's quiet prayer in the night was answered with a preview of the Divine Light. In any case, it is certain that Bede believed that Cuthbert did not have long to wait for the fullness of heavenly joy because he reported that when Cuthbert and Hereberht the hermit died on the same day, 'spiritus eorum, mox beata inuicem uisione coniuncti sunt, atque angelico ministerio pariter ad regnum celeste translati' (their spirits were straightway united in the presence of the blessed vision and together they were borne to the heavenly kingdom by the ministry of angels).[61]

And what of Bede himself? We can safely assume that he considered himself among the *perfecti*, but did he believe that he was one of the very few who see God in the present life? As Bernard McGinn has noted, explicit first-hand accounts of

58 Bede, *Vita sancti Cuthberti*, XXXIII, ed. and trans. by Colgrave, pp, 262–63. Bede has elaborated on the description of Cuthbert's physical transformation in his source, which had simply said that Ælfflaed saw Cuthbert go into a trance and drop his knife; *Vita sancti Cuthberti auctore anonymo*, X, ed. and trans. by Colgrave, pp. 126–27.

59 Bede, *Vita sancti Cuthberti*, XXXIX, ed. and trans. by Colgrave, pp. 284–85.

60 Bede, *Vita metrica sancti Cuthberti*, XXXVI, ed. by Jaager, p. 118. Cf. Bede, *Historia ecclesiastica*, IV.8, ed. and trans. by Colgrave and Mynors, pp. 358–59, where a nun of Barking has a vision of a bright light that filled the room where she lay dying.

61 Bede, *Vita sancti Cuthberti*, XXVIII, ed. and trans. by Colgrave, pp. 250–51; the same story is told in Bede, *Historia ecclesiastica*, IV.29, ed. and trans. by Colgrave and Mynors, pp. 440–41.

mystical experience are exceedingly rare in Christianity's first millennium; the autobiographical narratives of visions and auditions found in Augustine's *Confessions* were widely read but seldom emulated by other authors in late antiquity or the early medieval period.[62] Scholars eager to determine if those authors could claim to have had mystical experiences themselves are usually forced to rely on indirect evidence such as the intensity of an author's language or the detailed nature of any expositions of mystical phenomena. On that basis, there is widespread agreement that Gregory the Great believed himself to have had the kind of limited (but genuine) vision of God that he described with such great enthusiasm and in considerable detail. Comparable passages in Bede's works are less frequent, not as fully developed, and more restrained in tone. Perhaps the closest he comes to indicating that he, like Gregory, understood what it was like to be torn away from the pleasures of contemplation by the demands of other people in his community is when he explains that the Lord's admonition 'Do not arouse or awaken the beloved before she wishes' (Song of Songs 2. 7) means that no one should disturb the minds of the elect while they are praying or meditating on Holy Scripture.[63] Who at Wearmouth and Jarrow would have been more subject to such importunities than Bede? But he never suggests that he was the contemplative soul whose meditations were being interrupted, and his reflections on the earthly fulfilment of the divine vision are only occasionally charged with emotional energy.

What engaged Bede's most passionate eloquence was the theme of desire and longing, more than that of satisfaction and fulfilment. In a homily comparing the active and contemplative lives, he speaks of the person in the contemplative life who turns the eye of the mind from worldly affairs toward love alone and begins even now 'gaudiumque perpetuae beatitudinis quod in futura percepturus est uita etiam in praesenti coeperit ardenter desiderando praegustare et aliquando etiam quantum mortalibus fas est in excessu mentis speculando sublimiter' (to gain a foretaste of the joy of the perpetual blessedness he is to attain in the future, by ardently desiring it, and even sometimes, insofar as is permitted to mortals, by contemplating it sublimely in mental ecstasy).[64] Notice how Bede says that it is possible to have a foretaste of heaven by ardent desire, even if the contemplative stops short of *excessus mentis*. His commentaries are replete with references to what Gregory the Great had called the compunction of love, as distinct from the compunction of fear.[65] A typical example is when Bede explains that although the perfect are confident that their sins have been forgiven, they are still never without tears because they continually say, 'Quo diutius a uidenda facie Dei ad quem ardenter sitio differor eo dulcius pane lacrimarum quas in eius memoriam fundo reficior' (The longer I am delayed from seeing the face of God for which I thirst so ardently, the more sweetly am I refreshed with the bread

62 McGinn, *The Foundations of Mysticism*, pp. xiv–xv.
63 Bede, *In Cantica canticorum*, I, ed. by Hurst, p. 217, ll. 246–50; see also pp. 276–77, ll. 206–45.
64 Bede, *Homiliae euangelii*, I.9, ed. by Hurst, p. 64, ll. 163–71; *Bede the Venerable: Homilies on the Gospels*, I, trans. by Martin and Hurst, p. 91.
65 Gregory the Great, *Moralia in Iob*, XXIV.VI.10–11, ed. by Adriaen, p. 1194, l. 1 – p. 1196, l. 40; Gregory the Great, *Homiliae in Hiezechihelem*, II.x.20–21, ed. by Adriaen, pp. 395–96, ll. 531–74.

of the tears that I pour out in memory of him).[66] Bede's best-known prayer — at the end of the *Historia ecclesiastica* — asks that he might come to Jesus, the fountain of all wisdom, and appear before his face forever; here his desire was not so much to see as to be seen.[67] But in the prologue to the prose life of Cuthbert, Bede asked Bishop Eadfrith and the brethren at Lindisfarne to pray that he 'quatinus et nunc pura mente desiderare, et in futuro perfecta beatitudine merear *uidere bona Domini in terra uiuentium*' (may be worthy, now, with a pure heart to long for, and hereafter, in perfect bliss, 'to see the goodness of the Lord in the land of the living' [Psalms 26. 13]).[68] According to the other Cuthbert's account of Bede's death, he was still filled with ardour near the end, saying, 'Tempus uero absolutionis meae prope est; etenim anima mea desiderat Regem meum Christum in decore suo uidere' (The time of my departure is at hand, and my soul longs to see Christ my King in all His beauty [Isaiah 33. 17]).[69] And if Bede (following Gregory once again) was correct about the life of the angels and saints in heaven, he is still longing now, and will continue to long for God eternally, since the celestial citizens who contemplate the divine presence are so happy 'ut ineffabili nobis ordine et semper eius uisa gloria satientur et semper eius dulcedinem quasi nouam insatiabiliter esuriant' (that in an ordering to us ineffable they are both satisfied at seeing his glory always and always insatiably hunger after his sweetness as if it were new).[70]

Conclusion

Although Bede was less interested than Augustine or Gregory the Great had been in describing what happens to the soul in experiences of divine vision, such experiences still had a significant role to play in his pastoral strategy. As Conor O'Brien has noted, Bede's works are filled with expressions of longing for the heavenly homeland, 'but such longing only makes sense if its fulfilment proves reasonable and possible'.[71] Stories about people in the Bible or in the history of the English Church who had seen God helped Bede keep his audience's attention on the temporal horizon where earthly existence fades into eternal joy. The few perfect souls who see God while still in this present life stand at the vanishing point on that far off horizon, and Bede persistently pointed his readers in their direction as a way of intimating what lies beyond.

---

66 Bede, *De tabernaculo*, III, ed. by Hurst, p. 137, ll. 1720–22; *Bede: On the Tabernacle*, trans. by Holder, p. 160. See also in the same commentary p. 132, ll. 1510–18, as well as Bede, *De templo*, II, ed. by Hurst, pp. 224–25, ll. 1278–99 and Bede, *In Cantica canticorum*, III, ed. by Hurst, p. 280, ll. 367–73.

67 Bede, *Historia ecclesiastica*, V.24, ed. and trans. by Colgrave and Mynors, pp. 570–71.

68 Bede, *Vita sancti Cuthberti*, prol., ed. and trans. by Colgrave, pp. 146–47.

69 Cuthbert of Wearmouth–Jarrow, *Epistola de obitu Bedae*, ed. and trans. by Colgrave and Mynors, pp. 584–85.

70 Bede, *In epistolas septem catholicas*, ed. by Hurst, p. 230, ll. 177–81; *Bede the Venerable: Commentary on the Seven Catholic Epistles*, trans. by Hurst, p. 76. Bede goes on to quote Gregory the Great, *Homiliae euangelia*, II.xxxvi.1, col. 1266 on the way in which the satisfaction of spiritual pleasures only serves to increase desire.

71 O'Brien, *Bede's Temple*, p. 177.

Works Cited

Primary Sources

Augustine, *De Genesi ad litteram*, in *Sancti Aureli Augustini: De Genesi ad litteram libri duodecim eiusdem libri capitula; De Genesi ad litteram imperfectus liber; Locutionum in Heptateuchum libri septem*, ed. by Joseph Zycha, Corpus Scriptorum Ecclesiasticorum Latinorum, 28 (Vienna: Tempsky, 1894), pp. 1–456

———, *Epistula CXLVII*, in *S. Aureli Augustini Hipponiensis episcopi Epistulae*, vol. 2: *Epistulae CXXIV–CLXXXIVA*, ed. by Alois Goldbacher, Corpus Scriptorum Ecclesiasticorum Latinorum, 44 (Vienna: Tempsky, 1904), pp. 274–331

Bede, *De tabernaculo*, ed. by D. Hurst, Corpus Christianorum Series Latina, 119A (Turnhout: Brepols, 1969), pp. 1–139

———, *De templo*, ed. by D. Hurst, Corpus Christianorum Series Latina, 119A (Turnhout: Brepols, 1969), pp. 141–234

———, *Expositio Bedae presbyteri in Canticum Habacuc*, ed. by J. E. Hudson, Corpus Christianorum Series Latina, 119B (Turnhout: Brepols, 1983), pp. 377–409

———, *Historia abbatum*, in *Abbots of Wearmouth and Jarrow*, ed. and trans. by Christopher Grocock and I. N. Wood (Oxford: Clarendon Press, 2013), pp. 21–75

———, *Historia ecclesiastica*, ed. and trans. by Bertram Colgrave and R. A. B. Mynors (Oxford: Clarendon Press, 1969)

———, *In Cantica canticorum*, ed. by D. Hurst, Corpus Christianorum Series Latina, 119B (Turnhout: Brepols, 1983), pp. 165–375

———, *In epistolas septem catholicas*, ed. by D. Hurst, Corpus Christianorum Series Latina, 121 (Turnhout: Brepols, 1983), pp. 179–342

———, *In Ezram et Neemiam*, ed. by D. Hurst, Corpus Christianorum Series Latina, 119A (Turnhout: Brepols, 1969), pp. 235–392

———, *In primam partem Samuhelis*, ed. by D. Hurst, Corpus Christianorum Series Latina, 119 (Turnhout: Brepols, 1962), pp. 1–272

———, *In principium Genesis*, ed. by Charles W. Jones, Corpus Christianorum Series Latina, 118A (Turnhout: Brepols, 1967)

———, *In Regum librum XXX quaestiones*, ed. by D. Hurst, Corpus Christianorum Series Latina, 119 (Turnhout: Brepols, 1962), pp. 289–322

———, *In Tobiam*, ed. by D. Hurst, Corpus Christianorum Series Latina, 119B (Turnhout: Brepols, 1983), pp. 1–19

———, *Homiliae euangelii*, ed. by D. Hurst, Corpus Christianorum Series Latina, 122 (Turnhout: Brepols, 1955), pp. 1–378

———, *On Ezra and Nehemiah*, trans. by Scott DeGregorio, Translated Texts for Historians, 47 (Liverpool: Liverpool University Press, 2006)

———, *On Genesis: Bede*, trans. by Calvin B. Kendall, Translated Texts for Historians, 48 (Liverpool: Liverpool University Press, 2008)

———, *Retractatio in Actus Apostolorum*, ed. by M. L. W. Laistner, Corpus Christianorum Series Latina, 121 (Turnhout: Brepols, 1983), pp. 101–63

————, *Vita metrica sancti Cuthberti*, in *Bedas Metrische Vita sancti Cuthberti*, ed. by
   W. Jaager, Palaestra, 198 (Leipzig: Mayer & Müller, 1935)

————, *Vita sancti Cuthberti*, in *Two Lives of Saint Cuthbert: A Life by an Anonymous Monk
   of Lindisfarne and Bede's Prose Life*, ed. and trans. by Bertram Colgrave (Cambridge:
   Cambridge University Press, 1940), pp. 141–307

Bede: A Biblical Miscellany, trans. by W. Trent Foley and Arthur G. Holder, Translated Texts
   for Historians, 28 (Liverpool: Liverpool University Press, 1999)

Bede: On the Tabernacle, trans. by Arthur G. Holder, Translated Texts for Historians, 18
   (Liverpool: Liverpool University Press, 1994)

Bede: On the Temple, trans. by Seán Connolly, Translated Texts for Historians, 21
   (Liverpool: Liverpool University Press, 1995)

Bede: On Tobit and on the Canticle of Habakkuk, trans. by Seán Connolly (Dublin: Four
   Courts, 1997), pp. 65–95

Bede the Venerable: Commentary on the Seven Catholic Epistles, trans. by David Hurst,
   Cistercian Studies Series, 82 (Kalamazoo: Cistercian Publications, 1985)

Bede the Venerable: Homilies on the Gospels, trans. by Lawrence T. Martin and David Hurst,
   2 vols (Kalamazoo: Cistercian Publications, 1991)

Cuthbert of Wearmouth–Jarrow, *Epistola de obitu Bedae*, in *Bede's Ecclesiastical History of
   the English People*, ed. and trans. by Bertram Colgrave and R. A. B. Mynors (Oxford:
   Clarendon Press, 1969, repr. with corrections, 1991), 579–87

Gregory the Great, *Dialogi,* in *Grégoire le Grand: Dialogues*, ed. by Adalbert de Vogüé, trans.
   into French by Paul Antin, 2 vols (Paris: Éditions du Cerf, 1978–1980)

————, *Homiliae euangelia*, in *Patrologiae cursus completes: series latina*, ed. by Jacque-Paul
   Migne, 221 vols (Paris: Migne, 1844–1864), LXXVI (1857), cols 1075–1312C

————, *Homiliae in Hiezechihelem,* ed. by Marcus Adriaen, Corpus Christianorum Series
   Latina, 142 (Turnhout: Brepols, 1971)

————, *Moralia in Iob,* ed. by Marcus Adriaen, Corpus Christianorum Series Latina, 143,
   3 vols (Turnhout: Brepols, 1979–85)

John Cassian, *Conlationes*, ed. by Michael Petschenig, Corpus Scriptorum Ecclesiasticorum
   Latinorum, 13 (Vienna: Gerold, 1886)

Vita sancti Cuthberti auctore anonymo, in *Two Lives of Saint Cuthbert: A Life by an
   Anonymous Monk of Lindisfarne and Bede's Prose Life*, ed. and trans. by Bertram
   Colgrave (Cambridge: Cambridge University Press, 1940), pp. 59–139

The Venerable Bede: On the Song of Songs and Selected Writings, trans. by Arthur Holder,
   Classics of Western Spirituality (New York: Paulist Press, 2011), pp. 35–249

Secondary Studies

Alcock, Leslie, '*Fenestrae obliquae*: A Contribution to Literate Archaeology', *Antiquity*, 48
   (1974), 141–43

Butler, Cuthbert, *Western Mysticism: Augustine, Gregory, and Bernard on Contemplation
   and the Contemplative Life*, 2nd edn (London: Dutton, 1926; repr. Mineola: Dover
   Publications, 2003)

Carroll, Sister M. Thomas Aquinas, *The Venerable Bede: His Spiritual Teaching*, Studies in Mediaeval History, new ser., 9 (Washington, DC: Catholic University of America Press, 1946)

DeGregorio, Scott, 'The Venerable Bede on Prayer and Contemplation', *Traditio*, 54 (1999), 1–39

——, 'The Venerable Bede and Gregory the Great: Exegetical Connections, Spiritual Departures', *Early Medieval Europe*, 18 (2010), 43–60

Holder, Arthur, 'The Anti-Pelagian Character of Bede's Commentary on the Song of Songs', in *Biblical Studies in the Early Middle Ages*, ed. by Claudio Leonardi and Giovanni Orlandi (Florence: SISMEL, 2005), pp. 91–103

McCready, William, *Miracles and the Venerable Bede*, Studies and Texts, 18 (Toronto: Pontifical Institute of Mediaeval Studies, 1994)

McGinn, Bernard, *The Foundations of Mysticism: Origins to the Fifth Century*, The Presence of God: A History of Western Christian Mysticism, 1 (New York: Crossroad, 1991)

——, *The Growth of Mysticism: Gregory the Great through the 12th Century*, The Presence of God: A History of Western Christian Mysticism, 2 (New York: Crossroad, 1994)

Meyvaert, Paul, 'Bede and Gregory the Great', Jarrow Lecture, 1964, repr. in *Bede and His World*, ed. by Michael Lapidge, vol. 1: 1958–1978 (Aldershot: Variorum, 1994), pp. 103–32

O'Brien, Conor, *Bede's Temple: An Image and its Interpretation* (Oxford: Oxford University Press, 2015)

O'Reilly, Jennifer, 'Bede on Seeing the God of Gods in Zion', in *Text, Image, Interpretation: Studies in Anglo-Saxon Literature and its Insular Context in Honour of Éamonn Ó Carragáin*, ed. by Alastair Minnis and Jane Roberts, Studies in the Early Middle Ages, 18 (Turnhout: Brepols, 2007), pp. 3–29

Shockro, Sally, 'Bede and the Rewriting of Sanctity', *The Haskins Society Journal*, 21 (2010), 1–19

Thacker, Alan, 'Bede's Ideal of Reform', in *Ideal and Reality in Frankish and Anglo-Saxon Society: Studies Presented to J. M. Wallace-Hadrill*, ed. by Patrick Wormald with Donald Bullough and Roger Collins (Oxford: Basil Blackwell, 1983), pp. 130–53

——, *Bede and Augustine of Hippo: History and Figure in Sacred Text*, Jarrow Lecture, 2005 (Jarrow: St Paul's Church, 2005)

JULIA BARROW

Bede's Wise and Foolish Virgins: *Streanæshalch* and Coldingham

Bede was first and foremost a biblical exegete — he was probably the greatest expert on the Bible writing in the eighth century — and the Bible was never far from his thoughts, even when he was trying to sort out the course of events in seventh- and eighth-century Anglo-Saxon England in his *Ecclesiastical History of the English People*. Scholarship on Bede's biblical studies has, however, lagged some way behind scholarship on Bede's historical works. It is easy to understand why. On the one hand, Bede's *Ecclesiastical History* is our only narrative source for many events of the seventh and eighth century, and more specifically it is often the closest in time to them. On top of that it is a monumental but also a very subtle work: readers can go back to it again and again and always notice something new. On the other hand, Bede's Bible scholarship can be dry and has been slow to find enthusiasts. Over the last twenty years, however, that has changed dramatically. Alan Thacker has opened up many lines of enquiry in Bede's theological writings and Scott DeGregorio and W. Trent Foley, amongst others, have undertaken studies of Bede's biblical exegesis.[1] A comparison of the volume of essays on Bede and his writings edited by A. Hamilton Thompson and published by Oxford in 1935 (*Bede, His Life, Times, and Writings*) with the Cambridge handbook on Bede edited by Scott DeGregorio in 2010 (*The Cambridge Companion to Bede*) shows a significant shift: most of the essays in the 1935 volume focused on Bede's historical writings, overwhelmingly on the *Ecclesiastical History*, whereas the range of interests in the Cambridge volume is much wider.[2] Bede's computational writings and his schoolroom textbooks get proper attention and his exegesis is much more fully dealt with than in the 1935 collection. The shift is spelled out by the editor

---

1 Thacker, *Bede and Augustine of Hippo*; DeGregorio, "'Nostrorum socordiam temporum'";
   DeGregorio, 'Bede, the Monk, as Exegete'; DeGregorio, 'The Venerable Bede and Gregory the Great';
   Foley, 'Bede's Exegesis of Passages Unique to the Gospel of Mark'; *Bede: On Ezra and Nehemiah*,
   trans. by DeGregorio.
2 Thompson, ed., *Bede: His Life, Times, and Writings*; DeGregorio, ed., *Cambridge Companion to Bede*.

Julia Barrow • FBA (j.s.barrow@leeds.ac.uk) is Professor in Medieval Studies at the
University of Leeds.

Cities, Saints, and Communities in Early Medieval Europe, ed. by Scott DeGregorio and Paul Kershaw,
SEM 46 (Turnhout: Brepols, 2020), pp. 287-307
BREPOLS PUBLISHERS   DOI 10.1484/M.SEM-EB.5.119632

in his preface: 'Scholarship has always privileged the *Ecclesiastical History*, and it is now time to see Bede's works in a more integrated and holistic way'.[3]

Even so, in spite of a newly developing interest in Bede's biblical exegesis there has so far been relatively little exploration of how Bede used the Bible in his historical writings. Work has been done on which version of the Bible he was using (chiefly the Vulgate, but partly the *Itala*), but analysis of the exegesis has been slower.[4] However, scholars have noted several parallels. The sparrow motif in *HE* II. 13 was compared with the sparrow in Psalm 83. 4 as long ago as 1979 by D. K. Fry and its parallels with Matthew 10. 29 have been noted more recently by Danuta Shanzer.[5] Similarly, in 1994 Henry Mayr-Harting noted that Bede's account of King Oswine of Deira's submission to his more powerful opponent Oswiu of Bernicia paralleled Luke 14. 31 where Christ says that a ruler with smaller forces will try to make peace with a ruler with bigger forces. Unfortunately for Oswine, Oswiu took advantage of the opportunity to kill him, but Oswine's dismissal of his forces had saved lives among his own followers.[6] Eric Knibbs has examined Bede's use of exegesis in his Prose *Life of St Cuthbert*.[7] Alheydis Plassmann has commented briefly on Bede's use of exegesis in *HE*.[8] Ian Wood in his study of Bishop Chad's monastery at Lastingham has noted Bede's use of Isaiah.[9] Recently Thomas Rochester has demonstrated how Bede made use of Luke's Gospel in explaining his method of writing history.[10] The present author has re-examined Bede's account of how Edwin of Northumbria converted to Christianity in *HE* II. 9–14 in the light of the Gospel of St John. The sequence of chapters about Edwin's conversion culminates in a dramatic scene where Edwin's 'high priest' Coifi mounts a stallion and rides to a pagan temple at Goodmanham to throw a spear into it and thus pollute it. In spite of some wise words of caution by Ray Page about the dangers of reading Bede as a trustworthy source on non-Christian religion, it has been a very popular passage for people trying to find out about pre-Christian Anglo-Saxon belief systems.[11] However, the word used by Bede to describe Coifi's spear is not the standard Latin word *hasta* but the rather scarcer *lancea*, which just happens to be the term used in the Vulgate for the lance that pierced Christ's side in John 19. 34: since for Bede the wound in Christ's side was foreshadowed by the doorway allowing access into the Temple this suggests that he saw Coifi as opening the way towards the salvation of the Northumbrians.[12]

---

3   DeGregorio, 'Preface', p. xvi.
4   *Baedae Opera Historica*, ed. by Plummer, II, pp. 392–94 (Appendix II); Marsden, *The Text of the Old Testament*, pp. 206–09.
5   Fry, 'The Art of Bede', esp. 194–200; Shanzer, 'Bede's Style', p. 332.
6   Mayr-Harting, 'Bede's Patristic Thinking as an Historian', pp. 368–69.
7   Knibbs, 'Exegetical Hagiography'. Note also, on one of Bede's contemporaries, Laynesmith, 'Stephen of Ripon and the Bible'.
8   Plassmann, *Origo Gentis*, pp. 55, 74–75; see also her 'Beda Venerabilis – *Verax historicus*'.
9   Wood, *Lastingham in its Sacred Landscapes*, pp. 2–4.
10   Rochester, 'Sanctity and Authority', 77–78, 86–91.
11   Page, 'Anglo-Saxon Paganism', p. 129.
12   Barrow, 'How Coifi pierced Christ's Side'.

The current article undertakes another case study of Bede's tacit use of biblical parallels in *HE*, in this case *HE* IV. 23–26, in which Bede describes two double monasteries headed by abbesses in the later seventh century and then goes on to comment on the defeat and death of King Ecgfrith of Northumbria in battle against the Picts in 685. By tacit biblical parallels, I mean without direct quotations of two words or more. Bede was able to create parallels simply through the use of motifs and story-lines, but he could also quote single words from the Vulgate (like *lancea* in *HE* II. 13) in order to give his readers a clue to his line of thought. He could also quote phrases from appropriate passages in his own biblical commentaries. While doing all of this, he was able simultaneously to insert obvious and direct scriptural quotations, citing books of the Bible other than the one he was using for his underlying parallel, as a sort of Bachian counterpoint. The direct quotations can supply a clue to what is going on: for example, Bede uses words from Paul that are adjacent to passages from Paul that he had cited in his Luke commentary in a passage of *HE* where he is tacitly making use of Luke.[13] Occasionally, additional layers of counterpoint can be supplied through quotations from books other than the Bible, for example Eusebius, whose *Ecclesiastical History* was Bede's principal model, and also Vergil. We will be coming back to Vergil later.

Before looking for biblical parallels in the story Bede tells in Book IV chapters 23–26 it would be helpful to reflect on his open use of the Bible in *HE*, basing this examination on the biblical quotations identified by three sets of editors: Charles Plummer, Bertram Colgrave and R. A. B. Mynors, and Michael Lapidge.[14] Discussion here will be limited to the parts of *HE* that are Bede's own text, for his work contains numerous, in some cases very lengthy, quoted sources, notably the treatise made up of Gregory I's letters to Augustine on penance and issues of purity, the *Libellus Responsionum*; excerpts from Adomnán of Iona's treatise *On the Holy Places*; and the letter of Abbot Ceolfrid to the Pictish king Nechtan on the correct dating of Easter.[15] All of these authors use biblical quotations much more frequently than Bede does. With these sections omitted, and restricting our survey to quotations of two words or more, we can observe how Bede made direct use of the Bible in *HE*.

Bede was relatively sparing in his use of direct biblical quotations. If the papal letters are omitted, Book I of *HE* barely quotes the Bible at all. Bede did not cite the Bible in a stream-of-consciousness manner: he was as deliberate in his use of Scripture as he was about everything else in his prose. Sometimes he noted the source of his quotations — one of the Jonah quotes is introduced as 'prophetic';[16] one of the Isaiah quotes is attributed;[17] the Gospel quotations are occasionally

---

13   See below, notes 53, 55–56.

14   *Baedae Opera Historica*, ed. by Plummer; *Bede's Ecclesiastical History of the English People*, ed. by Colgrave and Mynors; *Bède le Vénérable*, *Histoire ecclésiastique du peuple anglais*, ed. and trans. by Crépin, Lapidge, Monat and Robin. For a list of the biblical quotations of two words or more identified by these editors, see Appendix.

15   *HE* I. 27; V. 16–17, 21.

16   *HE* V. 9 citing Jonah 1. 12 with the words 'Tum ipse quasi propheticum illud dicens'.

17   *HE* III. 23, citing Isaiah 35. 7 ('iuxta prophetiam Isaiae').

introduced with 'the Lord says' or an equivalent phrase;[18] Pauline quotations are sometimes introduced with 'as the Apostle says' (*sicut Apostolus ait*) or 'according to the Apostle' (*iuxta Apostolum*) or a similar phrase;[19] Hebrews 12. 6 is introduced with 'as scripture witnesses' (*scriptura teste*).[20] Bede's use of biblical citations is varied. Sometimes they provided useful stock phrases that described what his characters were doing — Archbishop Theodore died 'old and full of days', like David; King Eadbald of Kent 'died and was buried with his fathers'.[21] (But even in these apparently straightforward instances the reader is sometimes being provoked into a reaction: for example, Eadbald was buried in a church where only one of his predecessors had previously been laid to rest). Sometimes biblical quotes are placed in the invented speeches Bede gives some of his characters, and above all in the speeches given to Wilfrid in the great showdown at the Synod of Whitby in 664, when Wilfrid comprehensively demolished Bishop Colmán on the issue of Easter dating. Here, Bede is building quotes into his development of personality and drama. On occasion, he inserted quotations to underline a moral point.[22] Bede made surprisingly little direct use of the historical books of the Old Testament, even though one would expect them to provide plenty of parallels for his Anglo-Saxon kings. Where he did, he did not necessarily quote the most obvious source: one very striking example of his choice of a less obvious source comes in his comparison of the pagan King Æthelfrith of Northumbria with Saul, where, instead of using I Samuel, Bede cited the Genesis passage about Benjamin as a ravenous wolf and told his readers that this refers to Saul as a descendant of Benjamin.[23] In terms of frequency of quotation, the New Testament wins hands down. If we look at the biblical quotations so far identified by editors, the most frequently cited books of the Bible are, in order: Acts (19), Matthew (16), Psalms (14), Luke (10), I Corinthians (8) and II Corinthians and John (7 each).

Now, to our case study. In 685 King Ecgfrith of Northumbria went north to attack the Picts. Somewhere in northern Scotland he was defeated and killed by the forces of the Pictish king, Nechtan.[24] From this point onwards the fortunes of Northumbria began 'to ebb and flow away', according to Bede, using a quotation

---

18   *HE* II. 2, citing Matthew 11. 29–30 ('Dominus inquit'); III. 19, citing Matthew 25. 13 ('dicente Domino'); IV. 23, citing John 5. 24 ('ut verbis Domini loquar'); V. 19, citing Mark 10. 29–30 and Luke 18. 29–30 ('propter Christum et propter Evangelium').

19   *HE* II. 1, citing I Cor. 9. 2 ('apostolicum sermonem'); II. 5, citing I Cor. 5. 1 ('apostolus testatur'); II. 9, citing II Cor 4. 4 ('sicut apostolus ait'); III. 4, citing Philippians 3. 15 ('iuxta promissum apostoli'); III. 5 citing I Cor. 3. 2 ('iuxta apostolicam disciplinam'); IV. 9, citing II Cor. 12. 9 ('iuxta Apostolum'); IV. 23, citing II Cor 12. 9 ('iuxta exemplum apostoli'); V. 22, citing Romans 10. 2 ('apostolicum […] sermonem').

20   *HE* II. 1, describing how Gregory I was scourged by illness.

21   *HE* V. 8, citing I Chron. 23. 1; II. 7, citing II Kings 14. 20.

22   See below notes 53, 55.

23   *HE* I. 34, citing Gen. 49. 27.

24   *HE* IV. 26. Currently there is debate as to where the defeat occurred: traditionally the site has been identified as Dunnichen Moss, but recently Alex Woolf has suggested that the site was probably north of the Mounth: 'Dún Nechtain'.

from Vergil's Æneid.[25] The decline was relative, not absolute: what seems to have happened was that Northumbria lost the ability to threaten its neighbours into absolute submission by carrying out long-distance raids, which had been a normal feature of seventh-century warfare.[26] To the south, Mercia, which itself had inflicted a heavy defeat on Northumbria in 679, began to build up defences; to the north, the Picts secured Abercorn on the southern side of the Firth of Forth. Bede records Ecgfrith's defeat in *HE* IV. 26, and since it is a pivotal moment it is worth thinking about how it is positioned in relationship to other events in the book. Bede's organisation of events in Book IV was essentially chronological, but he did not always have precise dates for them.[27] The book starts with the death of Archbishop Deusdedit in 664 and the process by which Theodore came to be appointed as archbishop of Canterbury, and it ends with the miracles following the death of Cuthbert. Theodore was selected by Pope Vitalian in late 667, consecrated in March 668, and arrived in England in May 669; Cuthbert died on 20 March 687. Within this sequence, Chapter 23 takes as its starting point Hild's death in 680, but then backtracks to cover her whole life and to say a little about her monastic foundation, a double house of men and women, at *Streanæshalch* (Whitby).[28] Next come two chapters with no dating, Chapter 24 on the poet Caedmon, which effectively adds to the description of Hild's community in Chapter 23, and Chapter 25 on another Northumbrian double house, the monastery of Coldingham. Chapter 25 begins by saying 'at about this time Coldingham burned down through carelessness'. It too backtracks to explain how an ascetic Irishman called Adomnán living in the community urged the abbess, Æbbe, to make the inmates lead less worldly lives, and added that she would be spared experiencing the destruction of her monastery by being allowed to die before it happened. Accordingly, Æbbe corrected her flock, but then died, whereupon everyone returned to worldly living and Coldingham burned down.[29] The only precise dating we have for Æbbe's death is late, provided by Reginald of Durham in the *Life* he wrote of her in the twelfth century. Here, Reginald said that Æbbe died in 683, a date almost certainly worked out from Bede.[30] Outside Bede's writings, Æbbe's last datable appearance can be

25 Vergil, *Æneid*, II. 169: 'ex illo fluere ac retro sublapsa referri'.
26 Yorke, *Kings and Kingdoms*, pp. 85, 91; Rollason, *Northumbria, 500–1100*, pp. 41–42. Stancliffe, *Bede and the Britons*, pp. 21–22, notes the threat posed by Strathclyde to Northumbria after 685.
27 For a different interpretation of how Bede organised *HE* IV see Higham, 'Bede's Agenda in Book IV'.
28 This backtracking technique is frequent in *HE*, occurring also, for example, in II.12 (Edwin's vision while at Raedwald's court, included in the account of Edwin's conversion) and III. 4 (the history of Iona inserted after the account of Aidan arriving in Northumbria and settling at Lindisfarne).
29 Much earlier, Æbbe had invited Cuthbert, then an inmate of Melrose, to her community, according to both the Anonymous *Life of Cuthbert* II. 3 and Bede's *Prose Life*, ch. 10, *Two Lives of Saint Cuthbert*, pp. 80, 189. In the Bedan version, this was to preach to her community and to set a good example to them, material that is not repeated in *HE*. Bede places the event after Boisil had died (664) and Cuthbert had succeeded him as prior.
30 Reginald of Durham's *Vita et Miracula Sanctae Ebbae* is unpublished; for discussion of the date, see Thacker, 'Æbbe'. More than one Æbbe existed in the later seventh century: Æbbe, a laywoman who became an abbess, occurs in Stephanus' *Vita Sancti Wilfridi* and is described as still alive at the time Stephanus was writing ('adhuc vivens illa, nunc sanctimonialis materfamilias nomine Æbbe'), *Vita*

traced to *c.* 681, since Stephanus in his *Life of Wilfrid* explains that it was Æbbe who persuaded Ecgfrith and his queen to release Wilfrid on his return from Rome.[31] Bede presumably placed the undated Coldingham story in relation to the neighbouring chapters because he had some idea of its relative chronology even if he did not have precise knowledge of the dates. However, it was his choice to include the Coldingham story in his narrative, and the aim of this paper is to argue that, whether or not the positioning of Chapter 25 is correct in chronological terms (it may well be) this was not Bede's sole aim in placing it where he did. Instead, I wish to argue that the symbolic significance of the Coldingham story may be just as important.

Chapter 24 on Caedmon is placed where it is because it fits in with the account of Hild, since it provides an example of how inspirational she was as leader of her monastery. Caedmon, a cowherd, always shy about singing songs to his friends at feasts, was taught how to compose and sing sacred song in Old English by a figure appearing to him in a dream, and was then encouraged by Hild to develop his talent. Chapter 25 on Coldingham, by contrast, may owe its position in part to Bede's desire to create a more powerful and dramatic plot for Book IV. After a description of the wise and devout Hild and her spiritually flourishing monastery with its talented poet, Bede continues with the theme of double houses (the particular significance of these for Bede, who grew up in an all-male religious house, was that they contained nuns as well as monks) by moving to Coldingham, but this entails a significant shift in mood as he switches from describing a well-organised double house to one that was poorly managed and suffered a disastrous fire, which led to the dispersal of many of the inmates. This prepares the reader for the bigger calamity awaiting Northumbria in Chapter 26 when Ecgfrith goes north to meet the Picts.

Before seeing how Bede introduces his biblical exegesis into his accounts of Hild's community and Æbbe's community, we need to consider his treatment of both houses in full. To do this, we need to take note of the earlier references to both monasteries in *HE*, and to reflect on the topography of the sites, a matter of great importance to Bede. Coldingham lies on the coast about ten miles north of Berwick. Recent excavations suggest that the middle Anglo-Saxon monastery probably lay under the later medieval priory in Coldingham itself, a low-lying settlement at the mouth of a stream,[32] though the remains of fortifications on the cliffs just to the north have

---

Sancti Wilfridi, chap. 37, p. 76. He differentiates her from Æbbe of Coldingham, whom he describes as the sister of Oswiu and for whom he uses the past tense, *Vita Sancti Wilfridi*, ch. 37, pp. 74–77; ch. 39, pp. 78–79, at 78: 'ad coenobium, quod Colodaesburg dicitur, pervenerunt, cui praesidebat sanctissima materfamilias nomine Æbbae, soror Oswiu regis sapientissima.' Colgrave also (p. 174) notes an Ebba (Ælfthryth, abbess of Repton in the late seventh century) depicted in one of the roundels of the Guthlac Roll of *c.* 1200, British Library, Harley Roll Y 6. The Whitby cross-head whose inscription has sometimes been read as ABBAE is in fact AHHAE, either Edwin's sister Acha, or a namesake: Higgitt, 'Monasteries and Inscriptions', at pp. 231, 233 and fig. 4; see also Okasha, *Hand-list of Anglo-Saxon Non-Runic Inscriptions*, p. 122 no. 125 (Whitby IV), and, on the function of the Whitby stones, Okasha, 'Memorial Stones or Grave Stones', p. 97.

31 Stephanus, *Vita Sancti Wilfridi*, ch. 39, pp. 78–97, and notes on pp. 174–75. Stephanus does not supply the date but it can be worked out from the events in Wilfrid's life: see Thacker, 'Æbbe'.

32 Stronach, 'The Anglian Monastery and Medieval Priory of Coldingham'.

sometimes been interpreted as the monastery itself.[33] A not dissimilar association of a fortified high-status hall and monastic houses can be found elsewhere in Northumbria: *Arbeia*, a former Roman fort at South Shields, near the monasteries of *Donemutha* and Jarrow, seems to have been a high-status site in the Middle Saxon period, for example.[34] Coldingham is first mentioned in *HE* IV. 19, when Bede recounts the life of Æthelthryth of Ely, who had first taken the veil at Coldingham *c.* 672 under Æbbe 'in loco, quem Coludi urbem nominant' (in the place, which they call the citadel of Coludi). *Streanæshalch* (Whitby), Hild's principal monastery, is first mentioned in *HE* III. 24.[35] In this chapter we are told how King Oswiu dedicated his daughter Eanflæd to the monastic life and entrusted her to Hild (Bede compares his action to that of Jephtha sacrificing his daughter in Judges 11. 30–40). Oswiu also provided a very generous endowment of twelve estates each of ten hides for monks, and one of these properties may have been the ten-hide estate at *Streanæshalch* (Whitby) acquired by Hild, who constructed a monastery there.[36] Immediately after this, in *HE* III. 25, comes Bede's account of the meeting held at *Streanæshalch* in 664 to decide on the correct date for Easter, better known as the Synod of Whitby. Here Bede provides an explanation for the name *Streanæshalch* (Whitby) — 'quod interpretatur Sinus Fari' (which means the Bay of the Lighthouse). This is an impossible etymology, as many scholars have pointed out; *halh* really means 'nook' or 'corner' rather than bay, while the first part of the name relates to OE *gestreon* and refers to gain or acquisition, so the name probably describes what archaeologists term a 'productive site' — the sort of place where people would agree to meet to buy and sell. *Streanæshalch*-type names were not infrequent in Anglo-Saxon England; there were two (now lost) sites in Anglo-Saxon Worcestershire, and Strensall in Yorkshire, about sixteen miles north-east of York, is another example.[37] Although a case has been made for identifying Bede's *Streanæshalch* with this latter site,[38] it seems likely that Bede himself was using the name for what is now Whitby, because when he describes Hild's death in IV. 25 he says it took place in her monastery thirteen miles from another house that she had founded at Hackness, and Whitby is indeed thirteen miles from Hackness.[39] The name Whitby is Scandinavian and could not have been applied to the site until the later ninth century at the earliest; Carole Hough argues that a Strensall-type name

---

33 Alcock, Alcock and Forster, 'Reconnaissance Excavations on Early Historic Fortifications'. See also *The Miracles of Saint Æbbe*, ed. and trans. by Bartlett, esp. pp. xii–xv.

34 Wood, 'The Foundation of Bede's Wearmouth-Jarrow' at p. 92.

35 On Hild's career see Thacker, 'Hild'; Yorke, *Nunneries*, esp. pp. 162–65, and also 17, 25, 32, 51, 106, 111, 123–24, 126–27, 147–48, 198. See *Abbots of Wearmouth and Jarrow*, ed. and trans. by Grocock and Wood, p. xxvi, on the likelihood that Hild's first monastery, on the north bank of the River Wear, was taken over by Benedict Biscop for his foundation of Wearmouth.

36 Cubitt, 'Wilfrid's "usurping bishops"', p. 37.

37 For discussion of the etymology, see Styles, 'Whitby Revisited'; Hough, 'Strensall, *Streanaeshalch* and Stronsay'.

38 Butler, 'Church Dedications and the Cult of Anglo-Saxon Saints', p. 49 n. 11; Styles, 'Whitby Revisited'; Barnwell, Butler and Dunn, 'The Confusion of Conversion' esp. pp. 316–21.

39 Fell, 'Hild, Abbess of Streonæshalch', esp. pp. 79–81; see also Thacker, 'Hild'; Pickles, '*Streanæshalch* (Whitby), its Satellite Churches and Lands', pp. 267–69.

might have been possible for the mouth of the River Esk just below Whitby's dramatic headland;[40] another, less likely, possibility is that Hild had another monastery at Strensall and that its name might have been applied to Whitby as well.[41]

Bede's consciousness that he was dealing with two communities of nuns probably led him to reflect on the parable of the Wise and Foolish Virgins in Matthew 25. 1–13, in which Christ warns his listeners to be prepared for the Second Coming by telling the story of how a group of young women waited as bridal attendants for the bridegroom's arrival with their lamps lit, and how some brought extra oil with them and some did not, so their lamps went out and while they went off to buy new oil the bridegroom appeared and the doors were locked, shutting them out. This is the main Gospel parallel Bede intended his readers to note for *HE* IV. 23–25, but a more elaborate set of Gospel allusions can be spotted in *HE* IV. 25 as well, on which more shortly. In the parable of the Wise and Foolish Virgins, the Vulgate uses two separate adjectives to describe the wise virgins: they are *prudentes*, or prudent, in Matthew 25. 2–4 when they take their lamps to wait for the homecoming of the bridegroom and the bride, remembering to take extra oil with them, but *sapientes* in verse 8, where the foolish (*fatuae*, Matthew 25. 2–3, 8) virgins ask the wise virgins if they could spare some of their oil, and the wise ones explain that they cannot do this because they do not have enough to share, and tell the foolish ones to go out and buy more for themselves.[42]

First of all, Hild herself is described as possessing wisdom (Aidan admired her for her *sapientia*) and prudence ('so great was her *prudentia*' that kings sought her advice).[43] This mirrors the qualities of the wise virgins in the Vulgate (*prudentes*; *sapientes*). Admittedly, Hild is not termed a virgin by Bede — he prefers to call her a handmaid of Christ (*Christi famula*; *Christi ancella*) and a mother of all of her nuns (*matrem illarum omnium*) — but her fellow-nuns are described as virgins.[44] On at least three occasions Bede connects Hild with light.[45] Her monastery's name is explained as 'the bay of the lighthouse'; her mother Breguswith had a dream of a shining necklace filling all Britain with its splendour when she was an infant; when Hild died the nun Begu at Hackness had a vision in which she saw the roof being pulled off and the building filling with light.[46] Hild's monastery was so well-run, so

40 Hough, 'Strensall, *Streanaeshalch* and Stronsay'. For discussion of the Whitby site, see Cramp, 'A Re-consideration of the Monastic Site of Whitby', p. 3; Rahtz, 'Anglo-Saxon and Later Whitby'.

41 Barnwell, Butler and Dunn, 'The Confusion of Conversion', p. 323.

42 In the Greek original, only one adjective, *phronimoi*, is used for the wise virgins, but the Latin translation required two adjectives to cover the range of meanings.

43 *HE* IV. 23.

44 *HE* IV. 23, where Begu is described as having dedicated her virginity to the Lord, and Frigyd is a *virgo*. Fell perceptively argued that Bede's reluctance to term Hild a *virgo* suggests that she had probably been married and had a family before becoming a nun: Fell, 'Hild, Abbess of Streonæshalch', pp. 79–81, and also Thacker, 'Hild'.

45 Light-allusions and light-miracles are commonly provided by Bede in his accounts of holy men and women in *HE*, but the co-relation of the accounts of Streanæshalch and Coldingham in *HE* IV. 23–25 suggests that a particular emphasis is intended here.

46 *HE* III. 25 and IV. 23.

full of spiritual activity, that it trained up no fewer than five future bishops and in addition the singing cowherd, Caedmon, who, with Hild's encouragement, became the first author of Christian verse in Old English.[47] Bede openly compares Caedmon, who ruminated over his verses, with the clean animal who chews the cud in Leviticus and Deuteronomy, a very suitable allusion for a cowherd.[48] But there may be a hidden Gospel allusion too: possibly the Caedmon story (*HE* IV. 24) was intended to remind the reader of the parable of the talents, which follows immediately on from the parable of the Wise and Foolish Virgins in Matthew (Matthew 25. 14–30). In contrast to Hild and her nuns, the inmates of Coldingham are careless; their monastery burns down through 'negligence' and they spend most of their nights feasting, sleeping, or weaving elaborate clothes to adorn themselves as brides, or to win the friendship of men from outside the community (rather than waiting for their spiritual bridegroom).[49] They fail to store up spiritual oil, in other words.

However, Bede had another range of biblical parallels in mind when he described the inmates of Coldingham. Thinking about the parable of the wise and foolish virgins would have put him in mind of the companion passages in Luke 12. 35–40 and 12. 43–48 in which Christ, after commanding his followers to keep their loins girded and their lamps lit, says that servants who stay awake waiting for their master to return from his wedding are blessed and then talks about the special responsibilities of stewards placed in charge of servants for making sure that they do not spend their time feasting and getting drunk. In fact much of Luke 12 is echoed in the Coldingham narrative.

Here is how Bede does it: Coldingham burned down through carelessness, and those who knew the community blamed its leaders for not controlling the wickedness of those who lived there. As it happened, the inmates had received a warning: an ascetic Irishman called Adomnán, living in the community, told Æbbe that he had had a dream in which a stranger had told him that he had inspected the community and found them not performing vigils and prayers but either asleep or else feasting, drinking, gossiping and making elaborate garments and that the cells or *domunculae* built for prayer have become *cubilia* (lairs) of allurements (*inlecebrarum*). There is some similarity here to Christ's warning to his disciples to avoid the leaven of the Pharisees in Luke 12. 1, and even more so to the passage where Christ says that the things which are covered will be uncovered and the things hidden in bedchambers (*in cubiculis*) will be made known from house-tops in Luke 12. 2–3.[50] The house-tops may be hinted at in a description of Adomnán returning

---

47 On the debate on the transmission of Caedmon's hymn see, among others, O'Brien O'Keeffe, 'Orality and the Developing Text of Caedmon's *Hymn*'; Orchard, 'Poetic Inspiration and Prosaic Translation'; Cavill, 'Bede and Cædmon's *Hymn*'.

48 'At ipse cuncta, quae audiendo discere poterat, rememorando secum et quasi mundum animal ruminando': cf. Leviticus 11. 3 and Deuteronomy 14. 6.

49 I am very grateful to Máirín MacCarron for pointing out this allusion to me. See also MacCarron, 'The Adornment of Virgins', esp. pp. 151–52, for further biblical allusions in this passage.

50 Bede's use of *cubilia* rather than *cubicula* is probably to echo Romans 13. 13 'non in cubilibus et impudicitiis' (not in chambering or wantonness): see also text shortly before n. 53 below.

to Coldingham with a colleague and seeing the 'high buildings' and weeping over the idea that they could be destroyed. The 'allurements' in Bede echo his own use of the phrase *saeculi illecebris* ('the allurements of the world') in his commentary on Luke 12. 45.[51] Adomnán himself has adopted a strict manner of life (*districtio vitae artioris*), eating only on Thursdays and Sundays, as the result of a penance imposed on him by a confessor who had gone back to Ireland and died before Adomnán could be released from his burden. Bede uses the phrase *artioris vitae status* when commenting on Luke 12. 49;[52] he may also be suggesting that Adomnán has accepted the advice in Luke 12. 4–5 about not fearing those who kill the body but fearing those who can send him to hell. There are no close parallels between *HE* IV. 25 and Luke 12. 13–21, in which Christ refuses to advise on dividing up an inheritance and then tells the story of what happened to the rich man who decided to build bigger barns, though the rich man's sudden death is not too distant from the main theme of *HE* IV. 25. However, there are close parallels between *HE* IV. 25 and Luke 12. 22–49, and also with Bede' commentary on Luke. Christ's command to his disciples not to care about what they ate or what they wore is echoed in Bede's critique of the inmates of Coldingham, who loved feasting and were very interested in what they wore. Bede makes Adomnán's visionary speaker say 'even the virgins who are dedicated to God put aside all respect for their profession and, whenever they have leisure, spend their time weaving elaborate garments with which to adorn themselves as if they were brides, so imperilling their virginity, or else to make friends with strange men. So it is only right that a heavy vengeance from heaven should be preparing for this place and for its inhabitants in the form of raging fire'. Or, to quote Christ as reported by Luke (12. 27–28), 'Consider the lilies how they grow: they toil not, neither do they spin; yet I tell you that Solomon in all his glory was not arrayed like one of these. Wherefore, if God so clothe the grass of the field, which today is, and tomorrow is cast into the oven, shall he not much more clothe you, o ye of little faith?' Equally, the feastings and drinking-bouts (*commessationum, potationum*) in HE IV. 25 are close to the phrase *edere et bibere et inebriari* ('to eat and drink and be drunk') in Luke 12. 45, though here Bede avoids Luke's exact wording and instead fits in a verbal reference to Romans 13.13 *non in comessationibus et ebrietatibus* ('not in feasting and drunkenness'), a passage to which he has also alluded slightly earlier in his choice of *cubilia* rather than *cubicula*. Bede is suggesting to his readers to reflect on the whole of Romans 13. 11–14, with its demand that it is now time to wake from sleep, put off the works of darkness and put on the armour of light. He quotes Romans 13.11 'that it is now time to awake from sleep' in his commentary on Luke 12. 37 ('Blessed are those servants, whom the Lord when he cometh shall find watching').[53]

---

51   Bede, *In Lucam Evangelium Expositio*, IV, ed. by Hurst, p. 259, ll. 1141–42.
52   Bede, *In Lucam Evangelium Expositio*, IV, ed. by Hurst, p. 261, ll. 1189–91 on Luke 12. 49: 'Haec ad interrogationem beati Petri sciscitantis an artioris uitae status sit ab omnibus expetendus specialiter sententia respondit'.
53   Bede, *In Lucam Evangelium Expositio*, IV, ed. by Hurst, p. 256, ll. 1019–25.

Æbbe was much moved when she heard Adomnán's warning, and he assured her that the disaster would not occur until after her death. Here Bede quotes from the promises made to Solomon and to Ahab that evil things would not come in their time (I Kings 11.12 and 21.29). Adomnán described the punishment to come as a *plaga*, a wound or weal from being struck ('stripe'), a single-word quotation from Luke 12. 48, which states that servants knowing the will of their master but failing to prepare will be beaten with many stripes, while the ones who did not know what their master wanted will be beaten with few stripes.[54] The community, shaken by news of the vision, did penance, but their change of heart was not permanent:

> Qua diuulgata uisione, aliquantulum loci accolae paucis diebus timere, et se ipsos intermissis facinoribus castigare coeperunt. Uerum post obitum ipsius abbatissae redierunt ad pristinas sordes, immo sceleratiora fecerunt. Et cum dicerent, 'Pax et securitas', extimplo praefatae ultionis sunt poena multati.
>
> > Those who lived in the monastery were somewhat afraid for a few days and began to give up their sins and do penance. But after the death of the abbess, they returned to their old defilement and committed even worse crimes; and when they said 'peace and security', suddenly the predicted punishment and vengeance fell upon them.[55]

This passage parallels the description of the servants not necessarily watching for their lord's arrival, which comes like a thief in the night, in Luke 12. 37–40. The phrase 'peace and security' is a quote from I Thessalonians 5. 3, and it is noticeable that Bede in his commentary on Luke 12. 45 (in which the wicked servant says his lord is delaying) quotes from I Thessalonians 5. 2: 'For the day of the Lord will come as a thief in the night'.[56] The fire at Coldingham, which Bede puts at the start of *HE* IV. 25: 'About this time, the monastery of virgins at Coldingham, which has previously been mentioned, was burned down through carelessness' is intended to remind the reader of Luke 12. 49: 'Ignem veni mittere in terram, et quid volo nisi ut accendatur?' (I am come to send fire on the earth, and what will I, unless it be kindled?).

And then, in the following chapter, as we have seen, Ecgfrith of Northumbria was killed in 685. Bede starts *HE* IV. 26 by saying that in 684 Ecgfrith had unjustly sent an army to Ireland to wreak havoc on a people who had always been friendly to the English. Although Bede does not identify the part of Ireland that was attacked, we know from the Annals of Ulster that Ecgfrith campaigned against the kingdom of Brega, lying between the Liffey and the Boyne.[57] He was advised in 684 not to attack the Irish and in 685 not to fight the Picts but went ahead and did so, 'and

---

54 Another 'code word' linking *HE* IV. 25 with Luke 12 is *vigilia* (Luke 12. 38, with *vigilantes* in the preceding verse) *HE* IV. 25, ed. by Colgrave and Mynors, p. 422: *peruigil, uigiliis*; p. 424: *uigiliis, uigilant*.

55 *HE* IV. 25.

56 Bede, *In Lucam Evangelium Expositio*, IV, ed. by Hurst, p. 260, ll. 1150–51. For more comment on Bede's use of I Thessalonians in *HE* IV. 25, see Darby, *Bede and the End of Time*, p. 214.

57 See discussion by Yorke, 'Adomnán at the Court of King Aldfrith', at pp. 37, 39.

the punishment for his sin was that he would not now listen to those who sought
to save him from his own destruction'. Next, Bede quotes Vergil, *Aeneid*, II. 169:
'From this time the hopes and strength of the English kingdom began to "ebb and
fall away" — *fluere ac retro sublapsa referri*'. Here we can reflect on another set of
parallels underlying the chapters on Hild's *Streanæshalch* (Whitby) and Æbbe's
Coldingham. There seems to be a recurring sea motif in Bede's accounts of the two
monasteries, which were, of course, both coastal. Hild, full of light, is compared to
a lighthouse, but the parallel for the less competent Æbbe is surely the receding
tide. Her name in the *Ecclesiastical History* is a shortened form (hypocoristic), a
sort of pet-name, and Bede does not supply her full name at any point, though
it was probably Ælfburh or Æthelburh.[58] The Æbbe form, close in sound to the
words *ebbian*, to ebb, and *ebba*, the ebb, may be intended to make readers think
of the tide.[59] This makes the quotation from Vergil especially apposite. Curiously,
however, the echo was not picked up in the ninth-century Old English translation
of Bede, which renders 'fluere ac retro sublapsa referri' as 'toflowan 7 gewanad
beon'.[60] The sea motif continues through most of the remaining chapters of Book
IV, which deal with St Cuthbert, much of whose life was spend on Inner Farne
and on Lindisfarne.

One final feature of the Coldingham story needs to be noted before we can conclude.
The holy man Adomnán who advised Æbbe to correct her unruly community was,
obviously, not the same man as his much more famous namesake and contemporary
Adomnán, abbot of Iona and biographer of St Columba (?627/628–704). But the
occurrence of the name at this point in the narrative is surely not coincidental. The
more famous Adomnán was much involved in sorting out the political situation in
Northumbria after Ecgfrith's death. Ecgfrith was eventually succeeded by his half-
brother, Aldfrith, who was half-Irish and had spent his life in Ireland and on Iona,
from which he travelled to Northumbria; Barbara Yorke suggests that he did not in
fact become king until either late in 685 or early in 686.[61] Adomnán himself visited
Northumbria in 687 to redeem a group of Irish hostages and escort them back to
Ireland; he also paid another visit in 688 and on one of these occasions he gave a
copy of his *De Locis Sanctis* to Aldfrith, who was a friend of his.[62] Bede admired this

---

58   For Æbbe's occurrence in the Durham *Liber Vitae* see *The Durham Liber Vitae*, ed. by Rollason
      and Rollason, I, p. 93 (16ʳ, 36ᵗʰ in a list of abbesses and queens); for comment on her name see
      The Durham Liber Vitae, ed. by Rollason and Rollason, II, p. 166. On Hild's name see Fell, 'Hild,
      Abbess of Streonæshalch', pp. 76–78. According to Fell, the name Hild, which means 'battle', may
      in its fuller form have been Hildigyð, Hildiðryð, or Hildeburh. Anglo-Saxon abbesses with these
      names are commemorated in the Durham *Liber Vitae*, see *The Durham Liber Vitae*, ed. by Rollason
      and Rollason, I, p. 93 (16ʳ, no. 59; 16ᵛ, no. 12); p. 94 (17ʳ, no. 24); see III, p. 83 for some caution in
      identifying any of these three with Hild. On the name Hild, see Redin, *Studies on Uncompounded
      Personal Names*, p. 40.

59   *Anglo-Saxon Dictionary*, ed. by Bosworth and Toller, p. 8 (*s.v. a-ebbian; æbbung*), pp. 237–38 (*s.v. ebba;
      ebbian*).

60   *The Old English Version of Bede's Ecclesiastical History*, ed. by Miller, I, p. 358.

61   Yorke, 'Adomnán at the Court of King Aldfrith', p. 40.

62   Yorke, 'Adomnán at the Court of King Aldfrith', pp. 40–41.

work greatly and included extracts from it in *HE* V. 16–17; moreover, Bede praised Adomnán for having accepted the correct dating of Easter (*HE* V. 15). Might the inclusion of the ascetic Adomnán in *HE* IV. 25 be intended to represent the Irish faction backed by *Streanæshalch* (Whitby) (Aldfrith was backed by Abbess Ælfflæd of Whitby, and Hild of Whitby had backed the Ionan side in the Easter dispute down to the Synod of Whitby in 664), showing their moral superiority to the pro-Wilfrid faction backed by Æbbe?

We may conclude by thinking of the various layers of interpretation Bede was establishing in the *Ecclesiastical History*. As a good exegete, he wanted his readers to explore the literal, allegorical, tropological, and anagogical interpretations. The literal interpretation is the narrating of events — Hild died in 680, Caedmon began to compose sacred verse while Hild was abbess, Æbbe was unable to maintain discipline at Coldingham. The allegorical interpretations are the lighthouse, the clean animal chewing the cud, and the weakness of the receding tide. The tropological interpretations are the direct Bible quotations, especially the Pauline passages proposing correct modes of behaviour. Surely, however, the anagogical interpretations are the hidden parallels linking up Bede's Northumbrians with the events and the parables in the Gospels.

Appendix: Biblical Quotations in the *Historia Ecclesiastica*

Quotations listed below are those identified by Charles Plummer, Bertram Colgrave, R. A. B. Mynors and Michael Lapidge. This list excludes biblical quotations present in passages from other authors' works cited by Bede.

Genesis
1. 4 (*HE* V. 14)
35. 29 (*HE* I. 8)
49. 27 (*HE* I. 34)

Exodus
3. 8 (*HE* I. 1)
14. 5 (*HE* II. 12)

Leviticus
11. 3 (*HE* IV. 24)
19. 18 (*HE* I IV. 28)

Deuteronomy
6. 5 (*HE* IV. 28)
14. 6 (*HE* IV. 24)

Judges
11. 30–38 (*HE* III. 34)

I Kings
11. 12 (*HE* V. 25)
21. 29 (*HE* V. 25)

II Kings
14. 20 (*HE* II. 7)
17. 24 (*HE* II. 15)
17. 41 (*HE* II. 15)
25. 9–10 (*HE* I. 15)

I Chronicles
23. 1 (*HE* V. 8)

Ezra
6. 22 (*HE* II. 12)
8. 31 (*HE* I. 19)

Judith
14. 6 (*HE* I. 26)

Job
12. 24 (*HE* II. 12)
29. 11–17 (*HE* II. 1)
31. 16–18 (*HE* II. 1)
42. 16 (*HE* II. 20)

Psalms
9. 9 (*HE* III. 22)
17. 13–14 (*HE* IV. 3)
29. 5 (*HE* V. 23)
31. 1 (*HE* V. 13)
65. 5 (*HE* IV. 23/25)
67. 7 (*HE* II. 2)
83. 3 (*HE* IV. 13)
83. 8 (*HE* III. 19)
94. 2 (*HE* IV. 25)
95. 13 (*HE* III. 22)
96. 1 (*HE* V. 23)
97. 8 (*HE* III. 22)
106. 34 (*HE* IV. 23/25)
111. 9 (*HE* II. 1)

Proverbs
26. 11 (*HE* II. 5)

Ecclesiastes
3. 5 (*HE* IV. 3)

Ecclesiasticus
44. 14 (*HE* V. 8)

Isaiah
35. 7 (*HE* III. 23)
43. 2 (*HE* III. 19)
44. 9–19 (*HE* III. 22)

Daniel
9. 16 (*HE* I. 25)

Jonah
1. 12 (*HE* V. 9)
3. 5–10 (*HE* IV. 25)

Matthew
2. 16 (*HE* V. 10)
3. 7 (*HE* IV. 25)
3. 8 (*HE* IV. 27)
7. 22–23 (*HE* III. 25)
8. 14–15 (*HE* IV. 4)
9. 37 (*HE* I. 29)
10. 8 (*HE* IV. 24)
10. 16 (*HE* II. 6)
11. 29–30 (*HE* I. 14)
11. 29–30 (*HE* II. 2)
12. 45 (*HE* II. 15)
16. 18–19 (*HE* III. 25)
19. 29–30 (*HE* V. 19)
22. 37 (*HE* IV. 28)
22. 39 (*HE* IV. 28)
25. 13 (*HE* III. 19)
28. 20 (*HE* IV. 19)

Mark
1. 30–31 (*HE* V. 4)
10. 29–30 (*HE* V. 19)

Luke
1. 23 (*HE* II. 3)
3. 7 (*HE* IV. 25)
3. 8 (*HE* IV. 27)
4. 38–39 (*HE* V. 4)
10. 2 (*HE* I. 29)
10. 3 (*HE* II. 6)
11. 26 (*HE* II. 15)
18. 29–30 (*HE* V. 19)
21. 27 (*HE* IV. 3)
24. 39 (*HE* II. 1)

John
5. 24 (*HE* IV. 23)
Cf. 8. 56 (*HE* IV. 3)
8. 56 (*HE* V. 22)
10. 12 (*HE* II. 6)
13. 1 (*HE* IV. 3)

18. 18 (*HE* III. 14)
Cf. 21. 15–17 (*HE* II. 6)

Acts
2. 44–45 (*HE* IV. 23)
2. 44–45 (*HE* IV. 27)
3. 2–8 (*HE* V. 2)
4. 22 (*HE* III. 12)
4. 32–34 (*HE* IV. 23)
4. 32 (*HE* IV. 27)
7. 56 (*HE* V. 14)
8. 5 (*HE* V. 19)
10. 11 (*HE* IV. 7)
11. 28 (*HE* I. 3)
13. 48 (*HE* II. 14)
16. 3 (*HE* III. 25)
17. 21 (*HE* I. 36)
18. 18 (*HE* III. 25)
19. 11–12 (*HE* IV. 17)
20. 19 (*HE* IV. 9)
21. 20 (*HE* III 25)
21. 26 (*HE* III. 25)
26. 18 (*HE* II. 1)

Romans
10. 2 (*HE* III. 3)
10. 2 (*HE* V. 22)
10. 18 (*HE* II. 8)
11. 2 (*HE* I. 22)

I Corinthians
3. 2 (*HE* III. 5)
3. 13–15 (*HE* II. 19)
5. 1 (*HE* II. 5)
5. 5 (*HE* IV. 25)
6. 10 (*HE* IV. 26)
9. 2 (*HE* II. 1)
15. 6 (*HE* V. 11)
15. 50 (*HE* IV. 26)

II Corinthians
1. 12 (*HE* I. 17)
4. 4 (*HE* II. 9)
5. 1 (*HE* IV. 3)
11. 2 (*HE* II. 9)

11. 3 (*HE* II. 5)
12. 9 (*HE* IV. 9)
12. 9 (*HE* IV. 23)

Galatians
1. 1 (*HE* IV. 24)
1. 14 (*HE* V. 19)
2. 2 (*HE* III. 25)
2. 4 (*HE* III. 7)

Ephesians
2. 2 (*HE* II.7)
2. 20–22 (*HE* IV. 3)
3. 14 (*HE* II. 2)
3. 14 (*HE* V. 1)

Philippians
2. 8 (*HE* II. 6)
3. 15 (*HE* III. 4)

I Thessalonians
5. 3 (*HE* IV. 25)

I Timothy
2. 5 (*HE* III. 17)

II Timothy
4. 1 (*HE* IV. 3)
4. 6 (*HE* IV. 9)

Hebrews
12. 6 (*HE* II. 1)

James
1. 12 (*HE* I. 7)

I Peter
1. 18 (*HE* V. 22)
2. 5 (*HE* IV. 3)
4. 5 (*HE* IV. 3)

II Peter
1. 14 (*HE* IV. 29)
2. 21 (*HE* III. 30)
2. 22 (*HE* II. 5)
3. 12 (*HE* IV. 3)

Revelation
1. 7 (*HE* IV. 3)

Works Cited

Manuscripts and Archival Sources

Reginald of Durham, *Vita et Miracula Sanctae Ebbae*, Oxford, Bodleian Library, MS Fairfax 6, fols 164^r–173^v

London, British Library, MS Harley Roll Y 6

Primary Sources

Anonymous Life of St Cuthbert in Two Lives of Saint Cuthbert: A Life by an Anonymous Monk of Lindisfarne and Bede's Prose Life, ed. by Bertram Colgrave (Cambridge: Cambridge University Press, 1940), pp. 59–139

Baedae Opera Historica, ed. by Charles Plummer, 2 vols (Oxford: Clarendon, 1896)

Venerabilis Baedae, Opera Historica, ed. by Charles Plummer (Oxford: Clarendon, 1896)

Bede, *Historia Abbatum*, in *Abbots of Wearmouth and Jarrow: Bede's 'Homily' i.13 on Benedict Biscop; Bede's 'History of the Abbots of Wearmouth and Jarrow'; The Anonymous 'Life of Ceolfrith'; Bede's 'Letter to Ecgbert, Bishop of York'*, ed. and trans. by Christopher Grocock and Ian N. Wood (Oxford: Clarendon Press, 2013), pp. 21–76

——, *Historia Ecclesiastica*, in *Bede's Ecclesiastical History of the English People*, ed. and trans. by Bertram Colgrave and Roger Aubrey Baskerville Mynors (Oxford: Clarendon Press, 1969)

——, *In Lucae euangelium expositio*, in *Bedae Venerabilis Opera*, II, 3, ed. by David Hurst, Corpus Christianorum Series Latina, 120 (Turnhout: Brepols, 1960), pp. 5–425

——, *In Marci euangelium expositio*, in *Bedae Venerabilis Opera*, II, 3, ed. by David Hurst, Corpus Christianorum Series Latina, 120 (Turnhout: Brepols, 1960), pp. 431–648

——, *On Ezra and Nehemiah*, trans. by Scott DeGregorio (Liverpool: Liverpool University Press, 2006)

——, *Prose Life of St Cuthbert*, in *Two Lives of Saint Cuthbert: A Life by an Anonymous Monk of Lindisfarne and Bede's Prose Life*, ed. and trans. by Bertram Colgrave (Cambridge: Cambridge University Press, 1940), pp. 141–307

Bède le Vénérable, *Histoire ecclésiastique du peuple anglais*, ed. and trans. by André Crépin, Michael Lapidge, Pierre Monat, and Philippe Robin, 3 vols, Sources chrétiennes, 489–91 (Paris: Cerf, 2005)

Cartularium Saxonicum. A Collection of Charters Relating to Anglo-Saxon History, ed. by Walter de Gray Birch, 3 vols (London: Whiting, 1885–1893)

Durham Liber Vitae, in *The Durham Liber Vitae: London, British Library, MS Cotton Domitian A. VII: Edition and Digital Facsimile with Introduction, Codicological, Prosopographical an Linguistic Commentary, and Indexes, including the Biographical Register of Durham Cathedral Priory (1083–1539)*, ed. by David Rollason, Lynda Rollason, Elizabeth Briggs, and A. J. Piper, 3 vols (London: British Library, 2007), I, pp. 81–294

The Miracles of Saint Æbbe of Coldingham and Saint Margaret of Scotland, ed. and trans. Robert Bartlett (Oxford: Clarendon Press, 2003)

The Old English Version of Bede's Ecclesiastical History of the English People, ed. by Thomas Miller, 2 vols in 4, Early English Texts Society, original series, 95–96, 110–11 (London: Trübner, 1890–1898)

Stephanus, *Vita Sancti Wilfridi*, in *The Life of Bishop Wilfrid by Eddius Stephanus*, ed. and trans. by Bertram Colgrave (Cambridge: Cambridge University Press, 1927)

Vergil, *Aeneid*, Book II, in *P. Vergili Maronis Aeneidos Liber Secundus*, ed. by R. G. Austin (Oxford: Clarendon Press, 1964)

Secondary Studies

Alcock, Leslie, Elizabeth A. Alcock, and Sally M. Forster, 'Reconnaissance Excavations on Early Historic Fortifications and Other Royal Sites in Scotland, 1974–84: 1. Excavations near St Abb's Head, Berwickshire, 1980', *Proceedings of the Society of Antiquaries of Scotland*, 116 (1986), 255–79

An Anglo-Saxon Dictionary, ed. by Joseph Bosworth and Thomas Northcote Toller (London: Oxford University Press, 1898)

Barnwell, Paul S., Lawrence A. S. Butler, and C. J. Dunn, 'The Confusion of Conversion: *Streanæshalch*, Strensall and Whitby and the Northumbrian Church', in *The Cross Goes North: Processes of Conversion in Northern Europe, AD 300–1300*, ed. by Martin Carver (Woodbridge: Boydell, 2003), pp. 311–26

Barrow, Julia, 'How Coifi pierced Christ's Side: A Re-examination of Bede's *Ecclesiastical History*, II, chapter 13', *Journal of Ecclesiastical History*, 62 (2011), 693–706

Butler, Lawrence A. S., 'Church Dedications and the Cult of Anglo-Saxon Saints in England', in *The Anglo-Saxon Church: Papers on History, Architecture and Archaeology in Honour of Dr H. M. Taylor*, ed. by Lawrence A. S. Butler and Richard K. Morris, CBA Research Report, 60 (London: Council for British Archaeology, 1986), pp. 44–50

Cavill, Paul, 'Bede and Cædmon's *Hymn*', in *'Lastworda Betst': Essays in Memory of Christine Fell, with her Unpublished Writings*, ed. by Carole Hough and Kathryn A. Lowe with Ray I. Page (Donington: Shaun Tyas, 2002), pp. 1–17

Cramp, Rosemary, 'A Re-consideration of the Monastic Site of Whitby', in *The Age of Migrating Ideas: Early Medieval Art in Northern Britain and Ireland*, ed. by R. Michael Spearman and John Higgitt (Edinburgh: National Museums of Scotland, 1993), pp. 64–73

Cubitt, Catherine, 'Wilfrid's "Usurping Bishops": Episcopal Elections in Anglo-Saxon England, *c.* 600-*c.* 800', *Northern History*, 25 (1989), 18–38

Darby, Peter, *Bede and the End of Time* (Farnham: Ashgate, 2012)

DeGregorio, Scott, '"Nostrorum socordiam temporum": The Reforming Impulse of Bede's Later Exegesis', *Early Medieval Europe*, 11 (2002), 107–22

——, 'Bede, the Monk, as Exegete: Evidence from the Commentary on Ezra-Nehemiah', *Revue bénédictine*, 115 (2005), 343–69

——, ed., *The Cambridge Companion to Bede* (Cambridge: Cambridge University Press, 2010)

——, 'Preface', in *The Cambridge Companion to Bede*, ed. by Scott DeGregorio (Cambridge; Cambridge University Press, 2010), pp. xv–xvii

———, 'The Venerable Bede and Gregory the Great: Exegetical Connections, Spiritual Departures', *Early Medieval Europe*, 18 (2010), 43–60

Fell, Christine, 'Hild, Abbess of Streonæshalch', in *Hagiography and Medieval Literature: A Symposium, Proceedings of the Fifth International Symposium organized by the Centre for the Study of Vernacular Literature in the Middle Ages held at Odense University on 17–18 November 1980*, ed. by Hans Bekker-Nielsen, Peter Foote, Jørgen Højgaard Jørgensen, and Tore Nyberg (Odense: Odense University Press, 1981), pp. 76–79

Foley, William Trent, 'Bede's Exegesis of Passages Unique to the Gospel of Mark', in *Biblical Studies in the Early Middle Ages: Proceedings of the Conference on Biblical Studies in the Early Middle Ages*, ed. by Claudio Leonardi and Giovanni Orlandi, Millennio medievale, 52 (Florence: SISMEL, 2005), pp. 105–24

Fry, Donald K., 'The Art of Bede: Edwin's Council', in *Saints, Scholars, and Heroes: Studies in Medieval Culture in Honor of Charles W. Jones*, ed. by Margot H. King and Wesley M. Stevens, 2 vols (Collegeville: Saint John's Abbey and University, 1979), I, pp. 191–207

Higgitt, John, 'Monasteries and Inscriptions in Early Northumbria: The Evidence of Whitby', in *From the Isles of the North: Early Medieval Art in Ireland and Britain, Proceedings of the Third International Conference on Insular Art held in the Ulster Museum, Belfast, 7–11 April 1994*, ed. by Cormac Bourke (Belfast: HMSO, 1995), pp. 229–36

Higham, Nicholas J., 'Bede's Agenda in Book IV of the "Ecclesiastical History of the English People": A Tricky Matter of Advising the King', *Journal of Ecclesiastical History*, 64 (2013), 476–93

Hough, Carole, 'Strensall, *Streanaeshalch* and Stronsay', *Journal of the English Place-Name Society*, 35 (2003), 17–24

Knibbs, Eric, 'Exegetical Hagiography: Bede's Prose *Vita Sancti Cuthberti*', *Revue bénédictine*, 114 (2004), 233–52

Laynesmith, Mark D., 'Stephen of Ripon and the Bible: Allegorical and Typological Interpretations of the *Life of St Wilfrid*', *Early Medieval Europe*, 9 (2000), 163–82

MacCarron, Máirín, 'The Adornment of Virgins: Æthelthryth and her Necklaces', in *Listen, O Isles, unto me: Studies in Medieval Word and Image in Honour of Jennifer O'Reilly*, ed. by Elizabeth Mullins and Diarmuid Scully (Cork: Cork University Press, 2011), pp. 142–55

Marsden, Richard, *The Text of the Old Testament in Anglo-Saxon England*, Cambridge Studies in Anglo-Saxon England, 15 (Cambridge: Cambridge University Press, 1995)

Mayr-Harting, Henry, 'Bede's Patristic Thinking as an Historian', in *Historiographie im frühen Mittelalter*, ed. by Anton Scharer and Georg Scheibelreiter, Veröffentlichungen des Instituts für Österreichische Geschichtsforschung 32, (Vienna: Oldenbourg, 1994), pp. 367–74

O'Brien O'Keeffe, Katherine, 'Orality and the Developing Text of Caedmon's *Hymn*', *Speculum*, 62 (1987), 1–20

Okasha, Elizabeth, *Hand-list of Anglo-Saxon Non-Runic Inscriptions* (Cambridge: Cambridge University Press, 1971)

———, 'Memorial Stones or Grave Stones?', in *The Christian Tradition in Anglo-Saxon England: Approaches to Current Scholarship and Teaching*, ed. by Paul Cavill (Woodbridge: Brewer, 2004), pp. 91–101

———, *Women's Names in Old English* (Farnham: Ashgate, 2011)

Orchard, Andy, 'Poetic Inspiration and Prosaic Translation: The Making of *Cædmon's Hymn*', in *Studies in English Language and Literature: 'Doubt Wisely': Papers in Honour of E. G. Stanley*, ed. by M. J. Toswell and Elizabeth M. Tyler (London: Routledge, 1996), pp. 402–22

Page, Ray I., 'Anglo-Saxon Paganism: The Evidence of Bede', in *Pagans and Christians: The Interplay between Christian Latin and Traditional Germanic Cultures in Early Medieval Europe, Proceedings of the Second Germania Latina Conference held at the University of Groningen, May 1992*, ed. by Tette Hofstra, L. A. J. R. Houwen, and Alistair A. MacDonald, Germania Latina, 2 (Groningen: Forsten, 1995), pp. 99–129

Pickles, Thomas, '*Streanæshalch* (Whitby), its Satellite Churches and Lands', in *Making Christian Landscapes in Atlantic Europe: Conversion and Consolidation in the Early Middle Ages*, ed. by Tomás Ó Carragáin and Sam Turner (Cork: Cork University Press, 2016), pp. 267–69 and 500–04

Plassmann, Alheydis, *Origo Gentis: Identitäts- und Legitimitätsstiftung in früh- und hochmittelalterlichen Herkunftserzählungen*, Orbis mediaevalis. Vorstellungswelten des Mittelalters, 7 (Berlin: Akademie 2006)

——, 'Beda Venerabilis – *Verax Historicus*. Bedas *Vera lex historiae*', in *Wilhelm Levison (1876–1947). Ein jüdisches Forscherleben zwischen wissenschaftlicher Anerkennung und politischem Exil*, ed. Mathias Becher and Yitzhak Hen, Bonner historische Forschungen, 63 (Siegburg: Franz Schmitt, 2010), pp. 123–43

Rahtz, Philip, 'Anglo-Saxon and Later Whitby', in *Yorkshire Monasticism: Archaeology, Art and Architecture from the 7th to 16th Centuries*, ed. by Lawrence R. Hoey, British Archaeological Association Conference Transactions, 16 (Leeds: Maney, 1995), pp. 1–11

Redin, Mats, *Studies on Uncompounded Personal Names in Old English* (Uppsala: Akademiska, 1919)

Rollason, David, *Northumbria, 500–1100: Creation and Destruction of a Kingdom* (Cambridge: Cambridge University Press, 2003)

Sawyer, Peter H., *Anglo-Saxon Charters: An Annotated List and Bibliography*, Royal Historical Society Guides and Handbooks, 8 (London: Royal Historical Society, 1968)

Shanzer, Danuta, 'Bede's Style: A Neglected Historiographical Model for the Style of the *Historia Ecclesiastica*', in *Source of Wisdom: Old English and Early Medieval Latin Studies in Honour of Thomas D. Hill*, ed. by Charles D. Wright, Frederick D. Biggs and Thomas N. Hall (Toronto: University of Toronto Press, 2007), pp. 329–52

Stancliffe, Clare, *Bede and the Britons* (Whithorn: Friends of the Whithorn Trust, 2007)

Stronach, Simon, 'The Anglian Monastery and Medieval Priory of Coldingham: *Urbs Coludi* Revisited', *Proceedings of the Society of Antiquaries of Scotland*, 135 (2005), 395–422

Styles, Tania, 'Whitby Revisited: Bede's Explanation of *Streanaeshalch*', *Nomina*, 21 (1998), 133–48

Thacker, Alan T., 'Æbbe', in *Oxford Dictionary of National Biography*, ed. by Henry Colin Grey Matthew and Brian Harrison, 60 vols and index (Oxford: Oxford University Press, 2004)

——, 'Hild', in *Oxford Dictionary of National Biography*, ed. by Henry Colin Grey Matthew and Brian Harrison, 60 vols and index (Oxford: Oxford University Press, 2004)

————, *Bede and Augustine of Hippo: History and Figure in Sacred Text*, Jarrow Lecture, 2005 (Jarrow: St Paul's Church, 2005)

Thompson, Alexander Hamilton, ed., *Bede: His Life, Times and Writings. Essays in Commemoration of the Twelfth Centenary of His Death* (Oxford: Clarendon Press, 1935)

Wood Ian N., *Lastingham in its Sacred Landscapes*, Fifth Lastingham Lecture, 2008 (Lastingham: Lastingham Publications, 2009)

————, 'The Foundation of Bede's Wearmouth–Jarrow', in *The Cambridge Companion to Bede*, ed. by Scott DeGregorio (Cambridge: Cambridge University Press, 2010), pp. 84–96

Woolf, Alex, 'Dún Nechtain, Fortriu and the Geography of the Picts', *Scottish Historical Review*, 85 (2006), 182–201

Yorke, Barbara, *Kings and Kingdoms of Early Anglo-Saxon England* (London: Seaby, 1990)

————, *Nunneries and the Anglo-Saxon Royal Houses* (London: Continuum, 2003)

————, *Rex Doctissimus: Bede and King Aldfrith of Northumbria*, Jarrow Lecture, 2009 (Jarrow: St Paul's Church, 2009)

————, 'Adomnán at the Court of King Aldfrith', in *Adomnán of Iona: Theologian, Lawmaker, Peacemaker*, ed. by Jonathan M. Wooding with Rodney Aist, Thomas Clancy, and Thomas O'Loughlin (Dublin: Four Courts, 2010), pp. 36–50

Unpublished Dissertations

Rochester, Thomas, 'Sanctity and Authority: Documenting Miracles in the Age of Bede' (unpublished doctoral thesis, University of Birmingham, 2017)

PAUL FOURACRE

Risano Revisited: A Step Too Far for Charlemagne?

In the year 804 a *placitum* or meeting was held at Risano in Istria at the head of the Adriatic Sea. The *placitum* had been called to address the grievances of the Istrians against their ruler, Duke John.[2] The Franks had taken control of Istria in the later eighth century and John was in effect the governor of the region. Istria, which had formerly been under Byzantine influence, lay at the very margins of the Carolingian Empire. It was strategically important in terms of control over the northern Adriatic into which the Franks had been drawn after the collapse of the Lombard kingdom in 774.[3] It lay at the junction of Frankish and Byzantine influence and it provided a counter-balance against the rising power of Venice. It had also been crucial as a recruiting ground in the wars against the Avars and bordered the dangerous and unstable region of Friuli. A duke of Istria, who may well have been John, is first mentioned in a unique letter from Charlemagne to his wife Fastrada.[4] In this letter, written in September 791, Charlemagne reports the success of an initial raid against the Avars, commending the service of a duke of Istria who came along with his men. Unfortunately the letter survives only in a copy in which all personal names have been removed, so we cannot be sure that the duke was 'our' John.

The Franks had recently raised the bishopric of Grado at the head of the Adriatic to the status of a patriarchate, so that the patriarch, one Fortunatus, was the metropolitan of Istria. Grado was in competition with neighbouring Aquileia, another patriarchate,

---

1 I am grateful to Jinty Nelson for discussion of the Risano case, and to Peter Štih for sending me the most recent edition of the text and the relevant volume of *Acta Histriae*.
2 The *placitum* has the name form 'Riziano'. 'Risano' is the Italian form, and 'Rižana' the form in Slavonic languages. On John's identity and career, *Placitum Rizianense*, ed. by Krahwinkler, pp. 111–14.
3 For this background, Brown, *Gentlemen and Officers*. References to Istria and the Risano dispute are scattered throughout this work.
4 *Caroli Magni epistolae*, ed. by Dümmler, no. 20, pp. 528–29, trans. King, *Charlemagne: Translated Sources*, pp. 309–10.

Paul Fouracre • (paul.j.fouracre@manchester.ac.uk) is Professor Emeritus of Medieval History at the University of Manchester.[1]

Cities, Saints, and Communities in Early Medieval Europe, ed. by Scott DeGregorio and Paul Kershaw, SEM 46 (Turnhout: Brepols, 2020), pp. 309-323
BREPOLS PUBLISHERS   DOI 10.1484/M.SEM-EB.5.119633

which also had lands and rights in Istria.[5] In 827 at the Synod of Mantua Grado lost its metropolitan status which reverted to Aquileia.[6] In 804, however, Grado was still in the ascendant, having been granted an immunity by Charlemagne in the previous year.[7] Fortunatus, the Patriarch of Grado, is a colourful and controversial figure.[8] His predecessor and relative, also named John, had been murdered (probably in 802) by two Venetian dukes. Fortunatus received the *pallium* from Pope Leo III in March 803, being addressed as *patriarcha*, whereas his predecessor had been addressed as *archiepiscopus*. The see of Aquileia seems to have been vacant at this point. Fortunatus was clearly reliant on Frankish support and immediately made his way to Charlemagne at his residence of Salz. It was then that Grado received the immunity that guaranteed Fortunatus's position. It seems likely that arrangements to hold a *placitum* at Risano were made at this meeting, perhaps as a response to Fortunatus outlining the problems he faced in Istria. Those problems grew worse for Fortunatus after the Franks and the Venetians came to an accommodation. Fortunatus was excluded from Grado in 806. When the Byzantines re-established overlordship over the Venetians, Fortunatus again fled to Charlemagne, and he was reassigned to the bishopric of Pula in Istria, returning to Grado only upon the Franco–Byzantine peace of 812, and this only with a reduction of his powers over coastal regions. Fortunatus was addressed as patriarch in a confirmation of the Risano settlement issued sometime between 814 and 821, but in the early 820s he joined in the revolt of the Slav leader Liudevit.[9] As a result he was forced to flee again, this time through Dalmatia to Constantinople. Finally he returned to Francia with a Byzantine embassy in 824, but died in the course of this mission. In 804, however, Duke John and Fortunatus were working together to build up Frankish influence in the region. This was bitterly resented by the Istrians who appealed to Charlemagne on the basis that John was daily oppressing them. 'We have therefore fallen into poverty and are mocked by our kinsmen and neighbours of Venice and Dalmatia, and even by the Greeks under whose power we were formerly'.[10] The complaint ended in time-honoured dramatic fashion: 'If the lord emperor Charles will help us, we can escape. If not, it is better for us to die rather than to live'.[11] Despite this

---

5   In a charter of 792 Aquileia's status was confirmed and those serving it in Istria were given fiscal privileges and exemption from the payment of tithes: *Die Urkunden Pippins, Karlmanns und Karls des Grossen*, ed. by Mühlbacher, no. 174, pp. 233–34.

6   *Concilia Aevi Karolini*, I.2, ed. by Werminghoff, no. 47, pp. 583–89. This gives a history of Aquileia versus Grado. The partriarchate was said to have been returned to Aquileia at the request of the Istrians.

7   *Die Urkunden Pippins, Karlmanns und Karls des Grossen*, ed. by Mühlbacher, no. 200, pp. 269–70.

8   On Fortunatus's career, see Krahwinkler, 'Patriarch Fortunatus'.

9   A copy of the confirmation is in *Codex Trevisaneus*, fol. 27ʳ. There is now a printed edition: *Urkunden Ludwigs des Frommen*, ed. by Kölzer, no. 82, p. 202.

10 'Unde omnes devenimus paupertatem, et derident nostros parentes et convicini nostri Venetias et Dalmatias, etiam Greci, sub cuius antea fuimus potestate': *Urkunden Ludwigs des Frommen*, ed. by Kölzer, no. 82, p. 202.

11 'Si nobis sucurrit domnus Carolus imperator, possumus evadere, sin autem, melius est nobis mori quam vivere.': *Urkunden Ludwigs des Frommen*, ed. by Kölzer, no. 82, p. 202.

sense of doom we can see from events of the next two decades, and especially from Fortunatus's career, that Frankish control in Istria was somewhat fleeting and always subject to challenge from the Venetians, the Byzantines and the Slavs. Perhaps 804 was the high-water mark of Frankish influence, and the concessions made at Risano may indicate that despite Duke John's best efforts, the Franks were never in a position properly to integrate Istria into their empire.

Charlemagne did help the Istrians, sending in a priest, Izzo, and two counts, Cadalao and Aio to hold an inquiry, and this is what the *placitum* of Risano records. It basically upheld the complaints of the Istrians. We have a copy of the record in a sixteenth-century Venetian codex, the *Codex Trevisaneus* which also contains the charter that confirms concessions made to the Istrians as a result of the inquiry.[12] The language of the *placitum* is in accord with the language of the other documents of the period, and the confirmatory charter is good evidence that the hearing did indeed take place. There is therefore no reason to doubt the authenticity of the record which the Venetians copied centuries later as they themselves came to agreement with the towns of Istria and wished to emphasize the former independence of those towns. The *placitum* is even today regarded as a kind of charter of rights for the Slovenes and its 1200th anniversary was celebrated in print in 2004–2005, the document receiving attention from Slovenian, Italian, and German scholars.[13] There is little to be added to this detailed scholarship, but the document has rarely been discussed in the English language. It has also been discussed very much in terms of what it can tell us about Istria itself. In what follows I too shall comment on the *placitum* of Risano, but with a greater emphasis on its significance for a wider understanding of the Carolingian Empire.

As we have seen, up to the late eighth century Istria had been nominally under Byzantine rule. Architecture, sculpture and cemetery archaeology show a considerable Byzantine presence there, including troops. A study by Michael McCormick has drawn attention to the cultural markers which expressed identity in these Western Byzantine enclaves, that is, in language, naming fashions, dress, travel, and title, all of which tied the enclaves to the metropolis, and has also noted that this Byzantine presence has left a genetic imprint in the prevalence of type B Thalassemia.[14] The gene for the latter is carried largely by people of East Mediterranean origins, so the prevalence could indicate significant population movement from East to West in the Mediterranean region, although this migration could surely have taken place at a much earlier time. Istria looks as if it might have been very much like the cities of coastal Dalmatia that are mentioned in Constantine Poryphrogenitus's *De administrando imperio* which describes the regions notionally subject (or once subject) to the Byzantine Empire in the mid-tenth century. Chapter 29 of this work

---

12   The text of the *placitum* comes from *Codex Trevisaneus*, fols 21[r]–23[r]. The edition used here is *Placitum Rizianense*, ed. by Krahwinkler, pp. 67–81.

13   In 2004 Krahwinkler's edition of the text and commentary was published. In 2005 there was a special edition of the journal *Acta Histriae* containing fourteen papers on Risano and the background to the dispute. Online at: http://zdjp.si/en/acta-histriae-13-2005-1.

14   McCormick, 'The Imperial Edge'.

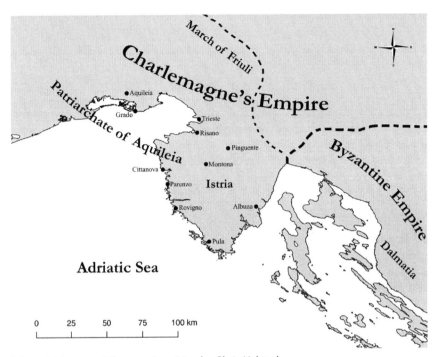

Map 1. Istria around the year 800. Map by Chris Halsted.

lists the cities of Decatera, Ragusa, Spalato, Tetrangourin, Diadora, Arbe, Vekla and Opsara 'the inhabitants of which are called *Romani* to this day'.[15] If the *De administrando* had continued up the coast to include Zara, the Istrian towns, and Grado, then no doubt these would have been treated in similar terms, as Venice had been in Chapter 28.[16] As Francesco Borri has pointed out, these towns share the same *origo gentis* myths with the towns of the Dalmatian *Romani*, that is to say as refuges from the barbarians — be they Hun, Slav, Avar, or Lombard — who took advantage of crumbling Roman power.[17] It is striking how locals sought Byzantine titles through which to demonstrate their social status, travelling to Constantinople to get the title of *ypatus*, or consul. In 807, for example, the Venetian *dux* Beatus travelled to Constantinople in order to acquire the title *ypatus*, even though, interestingly, he had visited Charlemagne at the end of 805.[18] Was there a bidding war between the two empires? Our source for Beatus's visit, John the Deacon's early eleventh-century *Historia Veneticorum*, is strong testimony for the web of contacts with Constantinople. The gravity of the palace there was still strong enough to

15 Constantine Porphyrogenitus, *De administrando imperio*, 29, p. 125.
16 Constantine Porphyrogenitus, *De administrando imperio*, 28, pp. 118–21.
17 Borri, '"Neighbors and Relatives"', pp. 23–25.
18 John the Deacon, *Historia Veneticorum*, II. 26.

draw in the locals of distant provinces who sought to shore up their privileges. And when the Franks threatened to ignore that source of privilege and to realign the local hierarchy around their own customs, they met resistance. They were beaten out of Venice and in Istria they climbed down in the face of local resentment. It is this climbdown which is recorded in the Risano *placitum*.

That the emperor should send special representatives to inquire into injustice was an established way of proceeding. The term *iustitia*, the plural of *iustitium*, had a threefold meaning of justice in the abstract sense, concrete rights, and the judicial process in general; 'doing justice' meant, inter alia, sorting out claims to rights, and complaints against officials. As such it was at the heart of the Carolingian notion of 'correction' (*correctio*), that is, bringing a divinely sanctioned order to the world. Charlemagne's capitularies returned to this theme again and again, promoting the idea that agents of the king, *missi*, check up on officials to make sure that justice was done.[19] There is in particular a run of capitularies from Italy that dealt with abuses by officials, and a letter from Charlemagne to his son Pippin, king of Italy, in which the emperor said that it had come to his notice that officials in Italy, including dukes, had been abusing rights of hospitality and had been imposing labour services and other 'oppressions' on communities.[20] Though this letter post-dates the Risano hearing, it might, along with the Italian capitularies, suggest that the 'oppressions' the Istrians complained of were widespread south of the Alps. Outside of the capitularies, close analysis of court-case records, most recently by Marios Costambeys, suggests that in a more general social sense, justice was generally not done. Invariably judgements in court cases went in favour of those with the most powerful interests, to the extent that the supposedly equitable system of justice could in practice be used as a tool of subjugation.[21] But things were different with sworn inquests such as we see at Risano. The *missi* in cases of inquest had a direct brief to stick to centrally agreed rules and laws and reported back to the ruler. At this moment, as Stefan Esders has remarked, *Adelsherrschaft* (rule by the powerful over sectional interests) gave way to *Königsherrschaft* (rule by king over all other interests).[22] The poem known as 'On Judges' by Theodulf of Orléans, from the end of the eighth century, presents an image of the ideal judge that is based in part on Theodulf's own experiences as a *missus*.[23] It reads as naïvely optimistic about the judge's ability to support the weak against the powerful, but the Risano episode suggests that Theodulf was perhaps not too wide of the mark when it came to sworn inquests. We know, for instance, of an inquiry that took place two years earlier when Theodulf's rival Alcuin had been accused of incorrect procedure in a case of sanctuary: he had wrongly given sanctuary to a man fleeing

---

19 On Carolingian attitudes towards justice, see Fouracre, 'Carolingian Justice'.

20 The Italian capitularies are *Karoli Magni capitularia*, I, ed. by Boretius, nos 89–103, pp. 187–212. Charlemagne's letter to Pippin is no. 103, pp. 211–12.

21 Costambeys, 'Disputes and Documents'.

22 Esders, 'Regionale Selbstbehauptung', p. 103.

23 In the *Monumenta Germaniae Historica* edition, *Poetae Latini*, I, ed. by Dümmler, no. 28, pp. 493–517. Theodulf's poem is titled *contra iudices*. Its proper title is *Paraenesis ad Iudices*.

Theodulf, and a riot broke out when Theodulf's men came for him.²⁴ The inquest, which had the power to coerce witnesses, found Alcuin clearly in the wrong. That Alcuin, an author of *correctio*, should be the subject of an inquest, suggests that the regime was prepared to look seriously at misconduct even by it most loyal supporters.

Let us now turn to the Risano text itself. Two counts and a priest had been sent as *missi* to Istria *pro causis* concerning the property of the holy churches and of our lords, and the *violentia* exercised against the people, the poor, widows, and orphans.²⁵ The patriarch Fortunatus and five other bishops, plus other *primates*, were assembled. Then 172 'leading men' (*homines capitanei*) from the cities and fortified towns were sworn in to tell the truth about the *res* of the Church, the *iustitia* of the lords and the abuses of the people. The *capitanei* brought with them records (*breves*) from each city and fort. These documents had been drawn up in the time of the Greeks, that is, under the *magistri militum* Constantine and Basil. They brought along the *breves* because they had had no help from the churches and, it seems to mean, no other record of their customs. Fortunatus was first in the firing line. There was no complaint against him, as long as his *familia* continued to observe the ancient custom of honouring the local bishop, *iudices*, and people when he did the rounds as patriarch. Basically, it seems, there was not much to be said about Fortunatus, for he was a recent appointment. But then the *iudices* from across Istria laid complaints against the other bishops. They enumerated nine grievances plus some others. The bishops used to pay half of any dues to the emperor, imperial agents used to be put up in the bishop's house. In the time of the Greeks documents of exchange and lease were not destroyed. Force had been used to extract pig dues from the villagers. The proportion of vines taken had gone up from quarter to a third. The *familia* of the Church should not commit outrages against free men, that is beat them or sit down in front of them. They had pursued the free men with swords. The people were too fearful to complain to their lord, that is, to their duke, John. Those leasing land from the Church were never before evicted after three generations. Sea fishing had been prevented. They, and the subject is still the *familia* of the church, beat people up and cut their nets. The *capitanei* then answer about the *iustitia* that their *domini* had had in the time of the Greeks, that is, up to the day they came into the hands of their present lords (a phrasing which might tell us something about how power changed hands in Istria). Listed are the dues from nine places, which amounted to 344 silver mancuses (an equivalent in gold coin, 344 *solidi* is given). Even if this amount should be doubled to include the half no longer paid by the Church, it does seem to be a rather small sum. The grievance is that in the old days this money went straight to the palace, but now Duke John holds on to it. Besides which, various olive groves and lands which yielded income for the fisc are now in John's hands and he again keeps the income for himself.

---

24 For a discussions of this case see Wallach, *Alcuin and Charlemagne*, pp. 103–26; Meens, 'Sanctuary, Penance, and Dispute Settlement'; Bidu, 'Alcuin, Charlemagne et le droit d'asile'; Kramer, 'The Exemption that Proves the Rule'.

25 'pro causis sanctarum Dei ecclesiarum dominorum nostrorum, seu et de violentia populi, pauperorum, orfanorum et viduarum', *Placitum Rizianense*, ed. by Krahwinkler, p. 67.

Thus far one can see Fortunatus being tolerated as long as he maintained local customs of *adventus* and visitation and thus did not upset the local hierarchy. But it seems that the other bishops had already done this, humiliating free people, raising dues, not respecting documents, evicting tenants, monopolising fishing, and so on. They were riding roughshod over local customs and privileges. It seems that the Istrians had a strong sense of their rights and customs in the time of the Greeks, and that they trusted their Greek governors to maintain their rights and to get the revenues to the palace. Taxation was clearly important in maintaining a sense of community based on loyalty to the palace. Frankish lordship was by comparison harsh, corrupt and humiliating. The local leader was not a conduit to the palace. As we shall see, he actually blocked access to it. These passages suggest that it was in fact the Church, and especially the bishops, who were in the vanguard of 'Francification', as we would also see in Saxony and Bavaria. This is yet another side to Carolingian *correctio*. But the attack on Duke John was even fiercer than that on the *familia* of the Church.

The next section of the document opens with the phrase 'regarding the *forcia* which duke John does to us'.[26] He had taken away pig pasture in the woods from which the complainants' forefathers had raised *herbaticum* and *glandaticum*, that is, pasture and pannage dues. These are two terms found widely throughout Northern Italy and Francia. If they were also terms long in use in Istria, as opposed to a translation of local terms by the drafters of the document, then one might see here a sub-Roman heritage common to Istria, Francia, and Italy. The difference would be that the Frankish rulers were excluding the natives from customary rights which they were appropriating for themselves. A further exclusion was the settlement of Slavs on *terras nostras*, the point being that these settlers now paid rent to John. Not only this, but the Istrians had been instructed to pay their tithes to the Slavs. Oxen and horses had also been taken. The Istrians claim that if they say anything they are threatened with death. The Franks have, moreover, disregarded the 'ancient custom' (*antiquam consuetudinem*) by which boundaries were fixed. Next we hear of the destruction of the local hierarchy. From 'ancient times' (*antiquo tempore*), that is, 'under the rule of the empire of the Greeks' (*sub potestate Grecorum imperii*) the custom was that local titularies, the *actus tribunati, domesticos, vicarios,* and *locoservator* each sat in place according to their *honor*, i.e., office, when they went to meetings. Those who wished to have a title higher than that of *tribunus* would travel to the Empire to be ordained *hypatus* (consul). Anyone who was an *imperialis hypatus* then had the right to proceed directly after the *magister militum*, giving their superiority ceremonial recognition. One cannot see on what basis these titles were granted, whether they reflected or somehow created the precedence they conferred, but it is clear that the local hierarchy had a certain imperial definition. Now, however, Duke John 'has taken the tribunate from us'.[27] In its place he has established *centarchi* over the people, the term probably referring to military command. Everyone has been assigned to the service of John's sons, daughters and son-in-law, and the people, meaning presumably

---

26 'De forcia … quas Ioannes dux nobis fecit', *Placitum Rizianense,* ed. by Krahwinkler, p. 74.
27 'Tribunatus nobis abstulit', *Placitum Rizianense,* ed. by Krahwinkler, p. 76.

people like the *capitanei*, have to join the poor in building palaces. The same people do military service but they can no longer take free men with them, only *servi*. John has further taken away their freedmen and billeted foreigners on them, and over these foreigners they have no control. Each tribune had in the time of the Greeks been allowed to have five *excusati*, presumably men not liable to military service or fiscal obligation, although a more common Frankish meaning is men who have moved from one lord to another. Anyway, these have now gone. The people, and we cannot tell how far up the social scale this goes, now have to supply *fodrum*, fodder, to work on the lord's estate (*curtis*), to tend vines, bake lime, build houses, feed dogs, and make *tegorias*. The latter has been translated as 'bricks', but I would prefer to read it as *tuguria*, shelters, as this term crops up in Frankish charters of immunity as an obligation to the count. In fact all of these burdens can be found elsewhere in polyptychs (estate surveys) and immunities, which suggests that the Istrians were being brought into line with obligations in Francia generally, rather than being singled out for harsh treatment.

New dues were said to be being raised on sheep. The people have been forced, as they never were before, to sail to Venice, Ravenna, and Dalmatia for John and his family. People are made to transport goods by road, with their own horses, which are then taken from them, forcing the carriers to walk home. Worse, John gathers gifts for the emperor as had been done in the time of the Greeks, but the duke takes the gifts to Francia himself, claiming to be the Istrians' interlocutor with the emperor, and then gives the gifts on his own account in return for office for himself and his sons. In the time of the Greeks, if the need arose one in a hundred sheep was taken as imperial dues. Now one is taken from anyone who had more than three sheep. The point here is not only that dues and services had gone up, but also that John was keeping the income for himself. The Greek *magistri militum* never did that, and the coming and going of the imperial *missi* had been monitored by the tribunes. Finally, the complaint was that for three successive years pagan Slavs had been settled on church and other lands and the people had been forced to pay their tithes to them — are these military settlers, one wonders? With all of the burdens imposed upon them, the Istrians had fallen into poverty and were, as we saw earlier, now mocked by their kinsmen and neighbours of Venice and Dalmatia, 'and even by the Greeks'. It was the phrase 'kinsmen and neighbours' which persuaded Borri that there remained a sense of community in the Northern Adriatic.

John's defence was that he believed these were normal public obligations. Now he was prepared to honour the Istrians' customs and to drop the carriage and sailing obligations. The people, presumably those of tribune level, could now have free men in the commendation as was allowed to lords elsewhere. Foreigners would be controlled and the Slav settlers checked to make sure they were doing no damage, and they would be made to pay dues themselves. So what John had promised was to lower the charges, reduce the level of obligations and to restore something of the dignity of the local elite. The document ends with John giving pledges on these issues, the people instructed to give up their complaints, and John being warned on pain of penalty to fulfil everything he had promised. Carolingian legislation warns those visited by *missi* in cases such as this not to wait until the agents had gone and then to resume their wicked ways.[28] If the confirmation charter is genuine, it would seem that the agreement made at Risano did stick. How do we interpret this extraordinary document?

The first point to make is that the Risano inquest was unique. Whereas other inquests, such as that at Tours over Alcuin's misconduct, tackled specific events or misdemeanours, this one set out to inquire into the customs of an entire province, hence the large number of people who testified to it.[29] The view from the end of the nineteenth century was that Istria saw the clash of two systems or principles, that is, between the privatised feudal arrangements of the Franks and the bureaucratic and public power of the Byzantines.[30] When the Franks tried to replace the communal, fiscal and hierarchical traditions of the Istrians with their own customs of personal dependence and 'unpaid' military obligations there was bound to be a clash. In more recent scholarship the hard and fast division between the two principles has been considerably weakened as both the Byzantines and the Franks have been seen to have been working from a common heritage of late Roman laws, customs, and taxes. As the very process of the inquest shows, the Franks did have a form of central government that did on occasion intervene against its own officers. Conversely, provincial elites in the Byzantine world have been seen to have united civil and military functions, so that society was dominated by military leaders, as it was north of the Alps, although power was expressed through a complex of offices rather than in terms of lordship and dependence.[31] The difference in the north was that kings took over those powers formerly exercised under the aegis of the Roman emperors, whereas in the former Byzantine areas of the west, and especially after the disappearance of the exarchate of Ravenna, local leaders exercised such powers in an essentially acephalous state. Stefan Esders argues that what we see in Istria is a situation comparable with the inception of the so-called 'successor states' centuries earlier in which Germanic rulers took over rights formerly exercised by Roman government.[32] He goes on to argue that some of the hated labour obligations in Istria had their origins in the *sordida munera* of the later Roman period, that is, common building and defensive obligations levied on all communities. That may be pressing the continuity argument too far in the sense that traceability may not necessarily indicate social continuity, but the operative term is 'communities'. At stake here was the right of the community to collect taxes and pay them directly to the ruler, and for the elite to have a privileged position within the community and to have circumscribed military obligations. There is a strong sense of city identity here, and when the Istrians thought about how conditions had deteriorated, they compared their situation with that of other communities. It has even been said that this determination to hang on to a measure of self-government is

---

28 This is in a letter sent by *missi* to counts in preparation for a visitation: *Karoli Magni capitularia*, ed. by Boretius, no. 85, pp. 183–84, trans. by King, *Charlemagne: Translated Sources*, pp. 258–59.
29 Esders, 'Regionale Selbstbehauptung', pp. 64–65.
30 For the work of L. M. Hartmann discussed here see the succinct summary in English in Hartmann, *The Early Medieval State: Italy, Byzantium and the West.*
31 Brown, *Gentlemen and Officers*, pp. 61–143.
32 Esders, 'Regionale Selbstbehauptung', pp. 77–78.

the root of the much later commune movement in Italy.[33] That is unprovable because nearly three centuries separate Risano from the first communes. What John and the Franks seem to have been doing was to attempt to reorganize the province around the provision of military service and the resources for military activity. They, were, for example taking horses from Istria for use in the north, as well as increasing the levels of military obligation.

Peter Štih saw John's regime in Istria as exceptional: he thought in terms of emergency measures to counter the Avar threat, but a more general feeling is that John's *forcia* were typically Frankish.[34] This we can also see from the immunity granted to Fortunatus in 803. In it Grado was given judicial rights and exemptions from payments that are identical to those given to churches in Francia proper. An earlier privilege given to Aquileia (in 792 when Aquileia was the patriarchate for the area) excused those who served the Church in Istria from paying for pasture (*herbaticum*), from providing lodging (*mansionaticos*), or providing fodder (*fodrum*), unless there was a military emergency.[35] These are precisely some of the dues that the Risano *capitanei* complained about, and they are dues found all over Francia. Perhaps the Istrians were also unfamiliar with immunities, that is, with favoured institutions and their dependants being excused certain public obligations, which might explain the hostility towards the bishops that we see in the Risano document. It is, however, unwise to draw too strong contrast between new Frankish ways and Istrian custom. Traditional scholarship, such as Hartmann's, contrasted an East that still taxed and a West in which taxation had withered and had been replaced by dues paid to lords rather than to the state. In the words of Matthew Innes, in their complaint 'the Istrians were contrasting a fiscal system, albeit one in which payments were long divorced from any regular process of assessment or registration, but fossilized as customary imposts, with an array of corvées and exactions that rested on an interpersonal calculus of public and political status'.[36] These payments may have been 'fossilized' in terms of amount, but as political custom they were very much alive as recorded in the *breves* the *capitanei* brought to the inquests. They were fiercely defended, possibly because, at 344 mancuses of silver for the whole province, they were rather small. The 'array of corvées and exactions' imposed by John were apparently larger.

The terms of the complaint about the 'oppressions' of Duke John are strikingly similar to those made in Francia about 'evil customs' (*malae consuetudines*) from the later tenth century onwards. In both cases there was resentment around the imposition of new dues and labour services and the loss of traditional privileges. The imposition of the *malae consuetudines* in the later period has often been understood as the result of a breakdown of the Carolingian system of public justice, and in particular as the consequence of the demise of the court of the count (*mallus publicus*) and the rise of

33 Esders, 'Regionale Selbstbehauptung', p. 108.
34 Štih, 'Istria at the Beginning of Frankish Rule'. This article is in Slovenian, with English and Italian summaries.
35 See above, no. 5.
36 Innes, 'Framing the Carolingian Economy', p. 45.

seigneurial lordship. The *mallus* was supposedly a bulwark against the oppression of the free, and its decline was said to have led to an increase in serfdom.[37] Should it be true that the rise of complaints about *malae consuetudines* were indicative of the decline of the *mallus*, then the fact that similar complaints were made in Istria would suggest that this region too was undergoing a collapse of public justice and the rise of arbitrary powers, but a good one hundred and fifty years earlier than in the north. Yet, if we see John as acting on behalf of the Carolingian regime, such powers in Istria were anything but arbitrary, and we must also remember that by sending in the *missi* and solemnly recording their findings, the regime was effectively the impresario of the Istrian complaint. More recent thinking about the later *malae consuetudines* is that complaint came via the Church which was trying to define its rights and customs and to defend its property against lords who were similarly struggling to maximise their resources.[38] The demise of the count's court was in this view not the cause of enserfment, for as we have seen, 'public justice' in those courts was more likely to favour the interests of the powerful than those of the weak. In the late tenth century, one person's dues and services of Carolingian (or even older) origins were another person's unjust exactions, because they were seen to be in the 'wrong' hands. That view would certainly capture the atmosphere of the Risano complaints. The complaints, therefore, cannot be said to indicate the 'seigneurialisation' of Istria. One can indeed argue that rising tide of complaint came along with the growing power, not the decline, of the Carolingian regime there. The comparison is in an important one because it invites us to think again about why people complained at different times, and in different circumstances, about unjust exactions.

If the Risano hearing came when the Carolingian regime was at the height of its powers, having recently crushed the Avars and ended conflict with the Saxons, one must ask why the Carolingians seemed to back down over Istrian customs and privileges. There is a range of possible answers, though a dearth of evidence ensures that none of them is compelling. If we follow Štih's view that arrangements in Istria were in effect emergency measures, then there may have been no reason to stick to them in more settled times. Or, there could have been reasons why Charlemagne wished to curtail the power of John and his family. John may have been genuinely oppressive, and the *missi* may have seen justice done, just as the capitularies asked that it be done. John might have been becoming too independent. Or, in the light of their eventual retreat from the region, it could be that Istria was just too remote for the Franks to control without the full cooperation of the native elites. The document gives the distinct impression that those elites felt that things had been better when they were ruled (significantly very lightly) by the 'Greeks'. Venetian

---

37 This is the view of the so-called 'French School' modelled on the work of Georges Duby on the decline of the *mallus publicus*. There was lively debate about the 'feudal crisis' in *Past and Present* in the 1990s. The most sophisticated critique of the Duby model and of the false dichotomy of 'public' and 'private' justice is White, 'Tenth-Century Courts at Mâcon' which has a very useful bibliography on the debate. On serfdom, see Fouracre, 'Marmoutier and its Serfs'.

38 For a discussion on why complaints about *malae consuetudines* were made see Barton, *Lordship in the County of Maine*, pp. 112–45; Cushing, *Reform and the Papacy*.

ties with Byzantium, the practice of going to Constantinople to receive the title of *hypatus*, reference to kinsmen and neighbours in other Byzantine regions, the communal collection and payment of taxes, and ceremonies of *adventus* in which Byzantine officials played a part, all suggest that the Franks would have found that Byzantine influence in the area remained strong, despite the fact that Constantinople did not have the military power to defend it. The enduring strength of that influence we may describe as 'soft power' in the region. In this light, the *De administrando imperio* looks less like a prime example of archaic and wishful thinking, and more like a practical handbook on the way to handle communities that continued to be receptive to overtures from the 'Greeks'. By comparison, the Carolingians seemed to have had no such 'soft power'. *Correctio* may have been a call to universal salvation, but it was presented as a demand for conformity and obedience. Power to the Franks meant conquest and domination, and Istria may simply have been beyond the range of domination. In other words, the Franks under the early Carolingians may have had the power to annex, but not the means to colonise. Let us close by returning to the villain of the piece, Duke John.

The Risano *placitum* comes down heavily on Duke John, his sons, his daughters, and his son-in-law. It is fear of John that prevents the Istrians from resisting the *familia* of the Church even when they were being beaten up. John is oppressive. It is he personally who has broken with the customs of the Istrians, raised dues, stolen horses, placed foreigners in houses, settled Slavs in the area, made people do undignified and humiliating labour services, and perform carting services, all under the threat of violence. John, moreover, has tricked the Istrians out of giving gifts to the emperor, giving them on his own behalf in return for favours for himself and his sons. So he is not only violent and oppressive, but also mendacious. John is not recorded as having defended himself, except to say that he thought that some of the lands he had taken were actually fiscal lands, that is, ultimately belonging to the emperor. But even here he adds that if the Istrians say under oath they were not fiscal lands, he will not contradict them. Finally, John is made to give pledges (*vadia*) 'to amend everything'. If he now commits further oppressions, he will be penalized. One wonders how John could have continued in office after such a dressing down. It could be that the *missi* were preparing a document that enabled Frankish rule in Istria to continue, and that the price of staying in power for John, his family, and his associates, was to take the blame for a reorganization that no doubt they had been asked to carry out. John may have been persuaded that his climbdown was a price worth paying, especially if he was given assurances that this document would not affect his standing in Charlemagne's regime, or in other words, that no dishonour be attached to his conduct in Istria. An important point to remember here is that in early medieval writing in general, when things went wrong, blame was either widespread and collective (due to the sins of the people) or individual and personal (due to abuse of power and other injustices committed by a named person). There is no hint in our document that anyone had offended God. Although the Church is prominent as an (oppressive) institution, God is not mentioned at all. There was no vocabulary for a clash of systems, or for systemic malfunction. All that had gone wrong was put down to the *forcia* of Duke John.

The Risano *placitum* is unique in terms of the number of people before the inquiry, the attack on Frankish practices, and, as we have just seen, the widespread criticism of a high-status leader, a duke. Because it is unique, we must be wary of reading out from the document to make more general statements about how Charlemagne's regime treated distant provincials. It is nevertheless possible to say that in the Northern Adriatic region the Franks were surprisingly tentative in feeling their way towards control. One gets the same impression about the war against the Avars, long prepared, and long a focus of anxiety. The Franks were similarly cautious when it came to dealing with the Byzantines. This was the corner of their empire in which they seem to have been at their least confident. We may infer that here was the limit of their power, perhaps a buffer zone to protect their interests in Lombardy and Bavaria. The Risano affair shows that they were capable of drawing back and of making compromises, just as they were in Benevento where intervention also went badly wrong. The inquest demonstrates that there was a mechanism for bringing complaints against officials, and the charter of confirmation indicates that that mechanism could be effective in providing remedies. The *placitum* shows yet again the use and importance of writing in Carolingian government. Overall, the climbdown at Risano presents the regime in a favourable light but, as Esders suggests, it is at precisely such moments that a regime could show itself as capable of being just. Away from the margins of the Empire, in Saxony, say, Charlemagne's subjects might have seen quite a different side to the regime.

Works Cited

Primary Sources

Caroli Magni epistolae, ed. by Ernst Dümmler, in *Epistolae Merowingici et Karolini aevi (III)*, in *Monumenta Germaniae Historica: Epistolae*, 8 vols (Hannover: Weidmann, 1887–1939) IV (1892), pp. 528–32; 546–48; 555–66

Codex Trevisaneus, Archivio di Stato di Venezia, Secreta, fols 21^r–23^r & fol. 27^r

Concilia Aevi Karolini, I.1, ed. by Albert Werminghoff, *Monumenta Germaniae Historica: Concilia*, 8 vols to date (Hannover: Hahn, 1893–) II.1 (1906)

Constantine Poryphrogenitus, *De administrando imperio*, ed. by Gyula Moravcsik and trans. by Romilly J. H. Jenkins, Dumbarton Oaks Texts, 1 (Washington, DC: Dumbarton Oaks Center for Byzantine Studies, 1967)

John the Deacon, *Historia Veneticorum*, in *Giovanni Diacono, Istoria Veneticorum*, ed. and Italian trans. by Luigi Andrea Berto, Fonti per la Storia Dell'Italia Medievale. Storici italiani dal Cinquecento al Millecinquecento ad uso delle scuole, 2 (Bologna: Zanichelli, 1999)

Karoli Magni capitularia, ed. by Alfred Boretius, *Monumenta Germaniae Historica: Capitularia regum Francorum*, 2 vols (Hannover: Hahn, 1883–1897) I (1883), pp. 44–185

King, P. D., *Charlemagne: Translated Sources* (Lambrigg: King, 1987)

Placitum Rizianense, ed. by Harald Krahwinkler, *…in loco qui dicitur Riziano…, Zbor v Rižani pri Kopru leta 804. Die Versammlung in Rižana/Risano bei Koper/Capodistria im Jahre 804*, Knjižnica Annales, 40 (Koper: Univerza na Primorskem – Zgodovinsko društvo za južno Primorsko, 2004), pp. 67–81

Theodulf of Orléans, 'Paraenesis ad Iudices', in *Poetae Latini aevi Carolini*, ed. by Ernst Dümmler, in *Monumenta Germaniae Historica: Antiquitates*, 6 vols (Hannover: Weidmann, 1881–) I (1881), pp. 493–517

Die Urkunden Ludwigs des Frommen, ed. by Theo Kölzer and others, *Monumenta Germaniae Historica: Diplomata Karolinorum*, 4 vols (Wiesbaden: Harrassowitz, 1906–2016), II, 3 vols (2016)

Die Urkunden Pippins, Karlmanns und Karls des Grossen, ed. by Engelbert Mühlbacher, *Monumenta Germaniae Historica: Diplomata Karolinorum*, 4 vols (Wiesbaden: Harrassowitz, 1906–2016), I (1906), 1–478

Secondary Studies

Barton, Richard, E., *Lordship in the County of Maine c. 890–1160* (Woodbridge: Boydell, 2004)

Bidu, Maxence, 'Alcuin, Charlemagne et le droit d'asile', *Médiévales*, 71 (2016), 109–36

Borri, Francesco, '"Neighbors and Relatives". The Plea of Rižana as a Source for Northern Adriatic Elites', *Mediterranean Studies*, 17 (2008), 1–26

Brown, T. S., *Gentlemen and Officers: Imperial Administration and Aristocratic Power in Byzantine Italy A.D. 554–800* (Rome: British School at Rome, 1984)

Costambeys, Marios, 'Disputes and Documents in Early Medieval Italy', in *Making Early Medieval Societies: Conflict and Belonging in the Latin West 300–1200*, ed. by Kate Cooper and Conrad Leyser (Cambridge: Cambridge University Press, 2016), pp. 125–54

Cushing, Kate, *Reform and the Papacy in the Eleventh Century: Spirituality and Social Change* (Manchester: Manchester University Press, 2005)

Esders, Stefan, 'Regionale Selbstbehauptung zwischen Byzanz und dem Frankenreich. Die *inquisitio* der Rechtsgewohnheiten Istriens durch die Sendboten Karls des Grossen und Pippins von Italien', in *Eid und Wahrheitssuche. Studien zu rechtlichen Befragungspraktiken im Mittelalter und früher Neuzeit*, ed. by Stefan Esders and Thomas Scharff (Frankfurt: Peter Lang, 1999), pp. 49–112

Fouracre, Paul, 'Carolingian Justice: The Rhetoric of Improvement and Contexts of Abuse', in *La Giustizia nell'Alto Medioevo (Secoli V–VIII)*, Settimane di Studio del Centro Italiano di Studi Sull'Alto Medioevo, 42, 2 vols (Spoleto: Centro Italiano di Studi Sull'Alto Medioevo, 1995), pp. 771–803, reprinted in Paul Fouracre, *Frankish History: Studies in the Construction of Power* (Farnham: Ashgate, 2013), no. XI, with the same pagination

——, 'Marmoutier and its Serfs in the Eleventh Century', *Transactions of the Royal Historical Society*, sixth series, 15 (2005), 29–49, reprinted in Paul Fouracre, *Frankish History. Studies in the Construction of Power* (Farnham: Ashgate, 2013), no. XV, with the same pagination

Hartmann, Ludo Moritz, *The Early Medieval State: Byzantium, Italy and the West*, Historical Association General Series, 14 (London: Historical Association, 1960)

Innes, Matthew, 'Framing the Carolingian Economy', *Journal of Agrarian Change*, 9.1 (2009), 42–58

Krahwinkler, Harald, 'Patriarch Fortunatus of Grado and the *Placitum* of Riziano', *Acta Histriae*, 13.1 (2005), 63–78

Kramer, Rutger, 'The Exemption that Proves the Rule: Autonomy and Authority between Alcuin, Theodulf and Charlemagne (802)', *Medieval Worlds*, 6 (2017), 231–61

McCormick, Michael, 'The Imperial Edge: Italo–Byzantine Identity, Movement and Integration', in *Studies on the Internal Diaspora of the Byzantine Empire*, ed. by Hélène Ahrweiler and Angeliki E. Laiou (Washington, DC: Dumbarton Oaks Research Library and Collection, 1998), pp. 17–52

Meens, Rob, 'Sanctuary, Penance, and Dispute Settlement under Charlemagne: The Conflict between Alcuin and Theodulf of Orléans over a Sinful Cleric', *Speculum*, 82.2 (2007), 277–300

Štih, Peter, 'Istra na začetku frankovske oblasti in v kontekstu razmer med severnim Jadranom in srednjo Donavo /Istria at the Beginning of Frankish Rule and in the Context of the State of Affairs in the Wider Region Between the Northern Adriatic and the Central Danubian Area', *Acta Histriae*, 13.1 (2005), 1–20

Wallach, Luitpold, *Alcuin and Charlemagne: Studies in Carolingian History and Literature*, Cornell Studies in Classical Philology, 32 (Ithaca: Cornell University Press, 1959)

White, Stephen. D., 'Tenth-Century Courts at Mâcon and the Perils of Structuralist History: Re-reading Burgundian Judicial Institutions', in *Conflict in Medieval Europe: Changing Perspectives on Society and Culture*, ed. by Warren Brown and Piotr Górecki (Aldershot: Ashgate, 2003), pp. 37–68

JINTY NELSON

Hincmar of Reims meets Bede

The purpose of the present paper is to claim that Hincmar's citing of Bede in his *De divortio* is a feature of special interest, not just within that work itself and in its immediate context of political and legal dispute, but in terms of the effect on Hincmar's thinking of his intellectual encounter with some of Bede's exegetical works. Alan Thacker is one of those who in recent decades have been transforming appreciation of Bede's biblical exegesis and its impact not only in Anglo-Saxon England but also far beyond. This paper is offered in Alan's honour, and in gratitude for his learning, his friendship, and his lively presence as a colleague in the University of London.

In terms of authorial energy and output, 860 was Hincmar of Reims' *annus mirabilis*. In 859, the regime of his royal lord and patron, Charles the Bald, had been 'restored' to full strength, and Hincmar's political position had accordingly become stronger.[1] His largest theological work, completed in 860, was a third and very large treatise on Predestination which had lasting influence.[2] His treatise *De divortio* was a *pièce d'occasion*, sparked by the scandalous divorce case of King Lothar II and his queen, Theutberga. Its impact was intended to be immediate. It survives in a single ninth-century copy.[3] Its opening sentence declares its intended audience: 'the glorious lord kings, the venerable fellow-bishops and everyone in the bosom of the catholic church'. Though it met the demands of 860 and a particular historical moment, later citations from it show that it was not just consigned to a Reims book-cupboard

---

1 For the 'restoration' of January 859, see Nelson, *Charles the Bald*, pp. 190–95.

2 Devisse, *Hincmar Archevêque de Reims*, I, pp. 224–69. See also Stratmann, *Hinkmar von Reims als Verwalter*, a pioneering study of a crucial area of Hincmar's concerns and, more recently, Gillis, 'Heresy in the Flesh'.

3 The exemplary edition of Böhringer, *De divortio Lotharii regis et Theutbergae Reginae*, has generated enhanced interest in the work and its author, and her 'Introduction' is a model of *Monumenta* scholarship. The unique manuscript of *De divortio*, BNF Lat. 2866, is available online at http://gallica. bnf.fr/ark:/12148/btv1b9078140k. The text is now published in an English translation by Stone and West, *The Divorce of King Lothar*. I supply page references to the Stone/West translation below, and in places have amended the initial version of this paper in light of their excellent 'Introduction', pp. 1–81, and cut some material which is far better dealt with by them.

Jinty Nelson • (jinty.nelson23@gmail.com) is Emeritus Professor of Medieval History, King's College London.

Cities, Saints, and Communities in Early Medieval Europe, ed. by Scott DeGregorio and Paul Kershaw, SEM 46 (Turnhout: Brepols, 2020), pp. 325-343

BREPOLS PUBLISHERS   DOI 10.1484/M.SEM-EB.5.119634

but was read later in the ninth century and after. In recent years, the *De divortio* has attracted more, and more wide-ranging, scholarship than ever before.[4] Before writing it, Hincmar had become well-acquainted with some of the exegetical works of Bede, including the mighty *Commentary on the Gospel of Luke*.[5] It looks as if the acquaintance deepened in the very process of Hincmar's writing the *De divortio*. In his legal opinion on the *cause célèbre* of Lothar II's divorce, Hincmar used a great deal of patristic biblical exegesis, especially in citations of the works of Augustine, Gregory the Great, and Jerome. Bede was named as author only seven times.[6] Letha Böhringer, who produced the fine MGH edition of the *De divortio*, commented that 'Hincmar seems to have assigned Bede little authority as an individual, for compared with the large number of [other] citations [of named authors] this author is only seldom named'.[7] Böhringer evidently thought that Bede's being seldom named, or present *stillschweigend*, 'silently', that is, unnamed, implied that Hincmar did not rate Bede very highly. I will argue that Hincmar did indeed value Bede highly, not so much for the quantity of citations from Bede's works, whether or not he was named, but for their quality, in the sense that the precise contexts in which citations occur suggest the significance of Bede's exegesis for Hincmar's thinking. I will discuss the seven citations of Bede's work where the author is named by Hincmar, and end by a consideration of 'silent' citations.

De divortio is a large and complicated work, whose structure is worth outlining by way of preliminary. It starts with a preface (pp. 107–14), and thereafter is divided into 23 sections of Question and Response which vary a good deal in length. The basic structure consists of, first, the historical context of the divorce case of Lothar II (sections 1, pp. 114–25; 2, pp. 125–29; and 3, pp. 129–32: roughly nineteen pages, with section 1 the longest at eleven pages), then discussions of canon law on marriage, the use of the ordeal, matters of legal process, and incest (sections 4, pp. 132–35; 5, pp, 135–46; 6, pp. 146–60; 7, pp. 161–62; 8. pp. 163–64; 9, pp. 164–67; 10, pp. 168–74; 11, pp. 174–76; and 12, pp. 177–96: roughly sixty-four pages in all, with the sections 5, on canon law, and 12, on incest, substantially longer than the rest), followed by more elaborate treatments of Lothar's context, conduct, and prospects as Hincmar saw

---

4 Airlie, 'Private Bodies and the Body Politic', is the starting-point for any consideration of the *De divortio* in the context of Carolingian politics; see further the illuminating monograph of Heidecker, *The Divorce of Lothar II* and the contributions (not least those of the editors themselves) to Stone and West, ed., *Hincmar of Rheims.*

5 Hincmar is absent from the indexes of DeGregorio, ed., *The Cambridge Companion to Bede*, and Brown, *A Companion to the Venerable Bede* (see below, p. 327, nn. 9 and 10), and Bede is absent from the indexes of Heidecker, *The Divorce of Lothar II*, and the invaluable edited work of Stone and West ed., *Hincmar of Rheims.* There is a sense in which Bede and Hincmar haven't yet met.

6 See Devisse, *Hincmar Archevêque de Reims*, III, pp. 1366–67; Hincmar, *De divortio*, ed. by Böhringer, 'Quellen' [Sources], p. 277.

7 Hincmar, *De divortio*, ed. by Böhringer, 'Einleitung' (Introduction), p. 76: 'Der Person Bedas scheint Hinkmar wenig Autorität beizumessen, denn verglichen mit der großen Zahl der Zitate wird der Autor nur selten genannt.' Here the editor adds that when Bede is cited without being named, as in *Responsio 6, Divorce*, trans. by Stone and West, p. 150, or *Responsio 21, Divorce*, trans. by Stone and West, p. 268, he is being cited 'stillschweigend' (silently).

them in 860 (sections 13, pp. 196–203; 14, pp. 203–05; 15, pp. 205–13; 16, pp. 213–14; 17, pp. 214–17; 18, pp. 217–18; 19, pp. 218–19; 20, pp. 219–20; 21, pp. 220–26; 22, pp. 26–32; and 23, pp. 232–34: some nineteen pages in all, with sections 15 and 17, on magic and witchcraft, occupying over twelve pages).[8] The citations of Bede by name come in the Preface, and sections 1, 5, 9, 13, 14 and 15. There is a rough correlation between the distribution of Bede-citations and lengthier thematic discussions in particular chapters. Citations of Bede, whether he is named or 'silent', come from a small number of his many works: the *Commentary on Luke* has pride of place, then come the *Gospel Homilies*, the *Commentary on Mark*, the *Commentary on the Seven Catholic Epistles*, the *Commentary on Proverbs*, and the *Thirty Questions on the Book of Kings*. The *Commentary on Luke* was by far Bede's largest work — it consists of 425 pages, with 15,841 lines, in the Corpus Christianorum edition — and it is the most often cited by Hincmar, 'silently' or otherwise.[9] In what follows, I will discuss the references to Bede in turn, and then assess their overall significance within Hincmar's treatise.[10]

I. *De divortio*, Preface. In the wide-ranging preface to *De divortio*, Hincmar set out the high offices of the Church, starting with the papacy, which was responsible for cases of universal interest and concern, such as those involving the sacraments, and hence the salvation of all. To this case of the king and queen, 'kings of the earth and all the people, princes and judges of the earth, young men and maidens, old men and younger ones' (Psalms 148. 11–12), ought to give consideration, as they also should to the truthfulness of judgement and episcopal consensus, and to the study of a king's 'mercy, patience and love' (I Timothy 6. 11) with regard to his honour, for 'the king's honour loves justice' (I Timothy 3. 10).[11] Hincmar's next three citations concerned impartial judgement, and the requirement that a magistrate put eternal grace before temporal glory.[12] In the last section of the Preface, Hincmar addressed judges. He quoted Gregory the Great: 'I see some men who are so ready to accept the importance of someone powerful that when he requires them to do something

---

8   See Hincmar, *De divortio*, ed. by Böhringer, 'Einleitung', esp. pp. 28–31; Heidecker, *The Divorce of Lothar II*, pp. 78–86. I regard Böhringer's 'Anhang' (Appendix), or Heidecker's 'Part 2', as a separate thing, and, for the purposes of the present paper, irrelevant because Bede is not cited in it.

9   For statistics, see Brown, *A Companion to the Venerable Bede*, pp. 59–61. The *Commentary on Luke* remains untranslated. The *Gospel Homilies*, happily, are translated, *Bede the Venerable: Homilies on the Gospels*, trans. by Martin and Hurst. See Brown, *A Companion to the Venerable Bede*, pp. 73–76, and Martin, 'Bede and Preaching', pp. 156–69, at 162–67. Fundamental to understanding the purposes of these homilies remains Thacker, 'Bede's Ideal of Reform'.

10 For assessments of Bede's influence on the Continent in the ninth century, see McKitterick, 'Kulturelle Verbindungen'; Hill, 'Carolingian Perspectives'; Westgard, 'Bede and the Continent'. For Bede's influence on Hincmar, see Devisse, *Hincmar Archevêque de Reims*, III, pp. 1366–67: these pages inspired the present paper, and also provoked my enquiry into exactly where and why in the *De divortio* Hincmar met Bede.

11 Hincmar, *De divortio*, ed. by Böhringer, *Praefatio*, p. 108, ll. 5–8, and cf. p. 110; Airlie, 'Private Bodies and the Body Politic', p. 3, quoting 'Anhang', *Responsio* 1, p. 236. The 'Anhang', pp. 235–61, 'has little to do with marriage as such', Heidecker, *The Divorce of Lothar II*, p. 85; cf. above, n. 7.

12 Psalm 25. 3–7; Gregory the Great, *Moralia* I. 7–17, ed. by Adriaen, with an allusion to John 12. 43.

to get his favour they have no hesitation in denying the truth in the case of someone they are close to. And what is Truth but He who said, "I am the Way, the Truth and the Life"?'. Then Hincmar quoted a longer passage from Bede without identifying the work, which was in fact the *Commentary on Luke*:

> *Et beatus Baeda.* Today, many affect horror at Judas's crime of selling his Lord and Teacher for money, a crime so immense in its criminality, and yet they are heedless of the warning. For they themselves give false testimony and sell truth for money, which, since the Lord said "I am Truth" is tantamount to selling the Lord. When they collude to stain an association of brotherhood by some kind of pestilence of discord, they betray the Lord because God is love; and even if no one gives money, they "sell their Lord for thirty pieces of silver" because they take upon themselves the image of the prince of this world, that is, they follow the example of the ancient Enemy, after neglecting the image of their maker, in which they were created. The man who, neglecting love and fear of the Lord, is instead persuaded to love and care for earthly and temporary and even criminal things does indeed sell his Lord.[13]

The latter part of the preface set out moral instructions for king, bishops, and 'everyone', with reminders of the Last Judgement.[14] From the viewpoint of 'today', Hincmar castigated mendacity and betrayal, hypocrisy and greed, drawing the lesson that ecclesiastical and civil judges alike must give judgement under the eyes of the eternal judge. Judas's crime of 'selling his Lord for money' was worse than any other, and hence Judas was the worst of sinners. Hincmar's placing of the Bedan passage at the heart of the preface indicated, by sketching what the antithesis of a just 'association of brotherhood' could look like, how it might be possible for Christians, guided by good kings and bishops, and recalling the inevitability of Judgement, to value truth in a social world and set their sights on the life hereafter.[15]

II. A series of Questions (*Quaestiones*, *Interrogationes*) and Answers (*Responsiones*) provided the structure of the main part of the *De divortio*. The first Question rehearsed material already gathered on the case by Lothar II's leading counsellors, clerical and lay.[16] Two sets of *capitula* (numbered points) had been produced at successive councils at Aachen, the first in January 860, and the second in February/March 860, and now

---

13 Hincmar, *De divortio*, ed. by Böhringer, *Praefatio*, p. 109, quoting, Bede, *In Lucam Evangelium Expositio*, IV, ed. by Hurst, pp. 374 and 379. The translation, like all the others in this paper, is mine. See *The Divorce of King Lothar*, trans. by Stone and West, p. 88.

14 Of kings, Hincmar writes: 'God has set them in so very lofty a place so that they can be seen by all their subjects and be held as if they were a mirror (*ad speculi vicem haberi*) to inspire terror into the wicked and love into the good'. *De divortio*, ed. by Böhringer, *Praefatio* p. 110; *The Divorce of King Lothar*, trans. by Stone and West, p. 89.

15 To my mind, Hincmar's Augustinian leanings are evident here: cf. Nelson, 'The Intellectual in Politics', esp. pp. 162–63, 168.

16 Hincmar, *De divortio*, ed. by Böhringer, pp. 114–25. On the importance of laymen as 'secular judges', see Airlie, 'Private Bodies and the Body Politic', p. 16, with n. 40, and Nelson, '"Hunnish Scenes"/ Frankish Scenes', at p. 176, pp. 183–86.

sent to Hincmar. In Cap. XVI was the Lotharingian elite's account of how the king grieved (*doluit*) on first hearing of Theutberga's confession and how her conduct had displeased him.[17] Lothar had subsequently repeated his performance of grief with tearful sighs and groans.[18] After considering all the evidence, Lothar's churchmen had decreed public penance for the queen. Hincmar's response to all this was to point out that Theutberga had not, as the churchmen said, given her evidence to bishops but bared her crimes to the king and to laymen: the king had made a legal judgement and, according to law and justice, married laymen had judged the wife of the lay king.[19]

Hincmar then turned to the report of the king's grief and sadness. Lothar should beware, wrote Hincmar, lest such grief should be, not the washing-away of a crime, but — *quod absit* — a confession of crime. At this point, after mentioning without naming other *doctores ecclesiae*, Hincmar cited verbatim thirteen lines of the second of Bede's *Gospel Homilies*:

> *Venerabilis presbiter Baeda, illorum* [i.e., *doctores ecclesiae*] *sequens sententiam dicit*, 'This is indeed the justice of the supernal judgement: the damned often recognize and admit that they have erred, and do the statutory penance for their error, yet do not cease from their erring, with the result that in confession and penance they give testimony against themselves, for they do not commit crimes in ignorance when they refuse to restrain themselves from the sin which they condemn — and therefore they perish the more justly when they fail to turn aside from the pit of perdition which they could have foreseen'.[20]

Grief and remorse were false, then, if the sinner persisted in sin. Hincmar's citation of Bede's *Gospel Homily* II continued with the example of Herod, who according to Matthew 14. 9, was 'made sad' when he heard Herodias's request that she be brought the head of John the Baptist:

> The sadness of Herod was like the repentance of Pharoah and of Judas, each of whom, when his conscience called him to account, reluctantly made known his crimes, and then insanely made them even greater. Thus Herod after being asked for John's head actually put a look of grief on his face, damning himself, therefore, by openly showing to everyone that he had known the man whom he was now handing over to die to be innocent and holy. But in truth if we look more closely into that execrable heart, it was secretly rejoicing, because it was previously intending, had it been possible to get away with this, the very thing that that woman was requesting. If it had been the head of Herodias that was

---

17 Hincmar, *De divortio*, ed. by Böhringer, *Responsio* 1, p. 121, ll. 32–33.

18 Hincmar, *De divortio*, ed. by Böhringer, *Responsio* 1, p. 122, ll. 7–8. Airlie, 'Private Bodies and the Body Politic', pp. 29–30, rightly stresses the theatricality of political communication and the emotional temperature of the Aachen hearings.

19 Heidecker, *The Divorce of Lothar II*, pp. 74–76.

20 Hincmar, *De divortio*, ed. by Böhringer, *Responsio* 1, p. 123, ll. 11–15, picking up on p. 121, ll. 32–33, cites Bede, *Homiliarum euangelii libri II* , 23, ed. by Hurst, p. 122, ll. 134–52. The translation is my own, and slightly differs from that of Martin and Hurst, *Bede the Venerable: Homilies on the Gospels*, II, p. 234. Cf. *The Divorce of King Lothar*, trans. by Stone and West, p. 111.

being asked for, no one could doubt that he would not have been willing to give it, nor in refusing to do so that he would have been truly sad.[21]

Hincmar commented:

> Thus this king of ours, looking into the eyes of the supernal inspector, who looks into all hearts and to whom the thoughts of every person are known, should weigh up most carefully whether he could accept with equal grief from, and gaze back with an equally calm face at, Him from whom he might perhaps hear at that moment: 'Because you have detached this woman from yourself, may you never permit this woman or the other woman to come near you in any way ever again.'[22]

In bracketing Lothar with the tyrant Herod as well as Pharaoh and Judas, Hincmar indicated both the hypocrisy of Lothar's contrition and his false dealing with God as well as with man.[23] Infinitely worse than condemnation through canon law was the awesome finality of divine judgement by the *supernus spectator*, the Heavenly Inspector, whose eyes bored into the human soul. It was not long since Hincmar had fired off in Advent 858 a letter to Lothar's uncle Louis the German in which he evoked the terrible plight of the king after death, face to face with the Almighty, bereft of friends, supporters, wife, and family, naked and alone.[24] In the closing paragraphs of *Responsio* I Hincmar warned Lothar to think hard about the Heavenly Inspector, reminding him that he had admitted knowingly receiving 'a false judgement instead of a truthful examination' when he falsely accused Theutberga of incest, then acknowledged the verdict of innocence resulting from the ordeal undergone by Theutberga's representative (*vicarius*, p. 114, l. 9) in 858 (citing Matthew 4. 7, and Proverbs 3. 34), and yet subsequently refused to take her back.[25]

Just as the very recent past supplied the context for episcopal judgement on Lothar, so the placing of the citation from Bede in Hincmar's Response I gave it a special impact. The citation, the last in Response I, comes very near its end. It was here that Hincmar rehearsed, and criticized, the evidence proffered by the Lotharingian elite in the divorce case, and set the scene for his own responses in the rest of the

---

21 Hincmar, *De divortio*, ed. by Böhringer, *Responsio* 1, p. 123, ll. 16–23. Once again, my translation differs from that of Martin and Hurst, *Bede the Venerable: Homilies on the Gospels*, II, p. 234. Cf. *The Divorce of King Lothar*, trans. by Stone and West, pp. 111–12.

22 Hincmar, *De divortio*, ed. by Böhringer, *Responsio* 1, p. 123, ll. 23–27: 'Unde et hic domnus noster rex superni spectatoris intendens oculos, qui corda omnium conspicit et cui cogitatio hominis confitetur, [Psalm 75. 11] diligentissime ponderet, si aequo dolore acciperet et aequa vultus serenitate eum respiceret, a quo tunc forte audiret: Quia a te feminam istam absolvis nec illam talem vel talem tibi quocunque modo ulterius umquam adproximare permittas'.

23 Airlie, 'Private Bodies and the Body Politic', p. 30.

24 See the letter sent by Hincmar, on behalf of the bishops of the provinces of Reims and Rouen, from the palace of Quierzy, to King Louis the German, Hincmar of Reims, *Epistola ad regem Hludicum*, ed. Hartmann, c. 4, p. 410, ll. 6–16. Hincmar later told Charles the Bald that the letter had also been destined for him, *Epistolae* 126, ed. by Perels, p. 64.

25 See *Annales Bertiniani*, ed. by Grat, Vieiliard and Clémencet *s.a.* 857, 858, pp. 74, 78, trans. by Nelson, *The Annals of St-Bertin*, pp. 84, 87. For the ordeal and the use of a *vicarius*, see also Hincmar, *De divortio*, ed. by Böhringer, *Interrogationes* and *Responsiones* 6 and 7, and also 9, as below, pp. 334–37.

De divortio. It was at this point that Hincmar chose to place Bede's reading of the story of Herod in Matthew 14: a terrible warning of the consequences of duplicity. Hincmar knew well Jerome's *Commentary on Matthew*;[26] but here he preferred to draw on one of the *Gospel Homilies* of Bede, another *doctor ecclesiae*. To remind *hic domnus noster* of the worst of biblical bad exemplars — Herod, Pharaoh, and Judas — was to warn him and his supporters in the strongest terms of the dangers of his present situation, to remind him of the inadequacy of lay judgement, and of the responsibility of bishops to render account to God for their legal rulings. At the same time, and with characteristic probing of this particular king's psychology and susceptibilities, Hincmar offered an interim but potentially damning moral judgement on Lothar himself.

III. Question and Response 5, among the lengthiest in the *De divortio*, focused on the key issue of what grounds justified the separation of married couples.[27] Hincmar reeled off a string of *doctores catholici*: Innocent I, Leo I, Gregory I, the bishops of 'the African Council', alias Carthage (419), Ambrose (*sc.* Ambrosiaster), John Chrysostom, and Origen in Rufinus's Latin translation. Finally, at the end of this list of authorities, though not actually citing or quoting the works of any of them, Hincmar named *Będa presbiter venerabilis*.[28] The reference, though the relevant work is not named, is to Bede's *Commentary on Mark*. Nearing the end of Response 5, Hincmar quoted and commented on I Corinthians 7. 10–11: 'Iis autem qui matrimonio iuncti sunt, praecipio non ego sed Dominus, uxorem a viro non discedere… Et vir uxorem non dimittat' (Now to the married I command, yet not I but the Lord: a wife is not to depart from her husband… And a husband is not to divorce his wife). 'The Lord's command' is that of Christ in Mark 10. 11–12: 'Quicumque dimiserit uxorem suam, et aliam duxerit, adulterium committit super eam. Et si uxor dimiserit virum suum … moechatur' (Whosoever shall put away his wife, and marry another, committeth adultery against her. And if a woman shall put away her husband … she committeth adultery). These coupled commands were at the heart of the *De divortio*'s teaching on marriage. Though Bede was not quoted here, his *Commentary on Mark* earned him a place on Hincmar's muster-roll of *doctores catholici*.

IV. Response 9 centred on magic, a subject of great interest to Hincmar. The king's divorce case had raised concerns about possible use of witchcraft, especially as practised by women.[29] After citing Gregory's *Moralia in Iob* on fraudulent judgements

---

26 Jerome, *Commentarius in Mattheum*, ed. by Adriaen, II. 14. 9, p. 118, ll. 1155–59.

27 Hincmar, *De divortio*, ed. by Böhringer, pp. 135–46.

28 Hincmar, *De divortio*, ed. by Böhringer, p. 143, l. 11. Hincmar evidently referred to Bede, *In Marci Evangelium expositio*, ed. by Hurst, III, 10, 10–12, pp. 558–59, where at p. 559, ll. 665–70, Bede also cited and briefly commented on Matthew, 19. 9 to the effect that only if the husband entered the religious life could he leave his wife, and otherwise as long as she lived he could not leave her and marry another.

29 Hincmar's interest, exceptionally well-evidenced in the *De divortio*, raises questions about representativeness and the effects of antique written culture, thought-provokingly discussed by Flint, *The Rise of Magic*, pp. 51–58, 254–328, to be taken with the critical and sympathetic review by Murray,

through the machinations of the Devil, Hincmar quoted Augustine's *De doctrina Christiana* on various forms of superstition. He then cited *venerabilis presbiter Beda in commento libri Samuhelis*:

> If someone is moved [to ask] how a woman can, by demonic art, disturb and raise up a prophet [i.e. Samuel] after his death, let him know for certain that either the Devil showed therein a false semblance to the seekers, or, if Samuel truly did stand there, only so much was being allowed to the Devil in such doings as the Lord would have permitted. Nor was it such a wonder that such things were being allowed to a malign spirit for certain more secret causes, when he even stood the Saviour on the pinnacle of the Temple [Luke 4. 9] and when Job asked to be tempted and accepted that [cf. Job 1. 9–12]. If we believe that what appeared was instead a fantasm of an unclean spirit, then [the question of] how such a spirit might foretell true and prophetical things ought not to throw anyone into confusion. For we have come to know that the Devil is often capable of foreknowing or foretelling many future things which he would have learned of from holy angels; but all the less should any attention be paid to those sayings of his when every word he speaks and all he performs with regard to human beings, is said and done out of his keenness to lead them astray.[30]

In Lothar's divorce, Hincmar and his contemporaries perceived the Devil and his minions at work in the world, and working disproportionately through the agency of women. In responding to the question of the meaning of diabolical acts, and why and how they occurred, Hincmar quoted Bede's forthright statement of the omnipotence of God, who permitted the Devil to tempt human beings, including Christ Himself, but could always thwart the Devil's designs. To drive home this crucial point, Hincmar chose among his patristic citations the pre-eminently clear one of Bede.

V. In Question and Response 13, Hincmar had to respond to a series of questions: whether the king had committed adultery by having intercourse with his 'concubine' after he had been 'suspended' from sexual relations with his wife; whether it might be true, 'as some people say', that 'there are women who create irreconcilable hatred between a man and his wife through the use of witchcraft and also unspeakable love

---

'Review Article: Missionaries and Magic', esp. p. 189, on 'forces' that reflect 'not literary influences but the age-old emotional geometry of social situations involving love, death, jealousy…', and p. 203, on the co-existence of 'magical and non-magical' modes of thinking in the heads of both intellectuals (Hincmar and Bede for instance) and rustics.

30 Hincmar, *De divortio*, ed. by Böhringer, p. 166, ll. 13–22, 'Et venerabilis presbyter Beda in commento libri Samuhelis dicit…'; see *In primam partem Samuheli libri* IV, ed. by Hurst, 28, pp. 256–57, ll. 1890–1904. For the two Books of Samuel as Books 1 and 2 of the four Books of Kings, see Bede, *Thirty Questions on the Book of Kings*, in *Bede: A Biblical Miscellany*, trans. by Trent Foley, 'Introduction', p. 81. Cf. *The Divorce of King Lothar*, trans. by Stone and West, p. 175. For the *Commentary on Samuel*, still untranslated, see Brown, *A Companion to the Venerable Bede*, pp. 47–48; also Brown, 'Bede's Neglected Commentary on Samuel', and Thacker, 'Bede and the Ordering of Understanding', esp. p. 54. The forthcoming translation of the *Commentary on Samuel* by Scott DeGregorio and Rosalind Love is eagerly awaited. See also Bede's *In Lucae evangelium expositio*, ed. by Hurst, II, iv, 29–30, pp. 108–09.

between a man and another woman'; and 'why God, so it is said, often permits such things to occur in a lawful marriage; and if such male witches and female enchanters have been found, what should be done about this'.[31]

Hincmar's Response to the first part of the question is that if the king has had intercourse with 'the other woman' after a legal marriage has been formed, he cannot deny having committed adultery. A string of scriptural, canonistic, and patristic passages are offered in support of this view.[32] Hincmar says that it is for bishops to reconcile husband and wife 'after due satisfaction', that is, penance. A passage from Gregory's *Gospel Homilies* follows, denouncing bishops who misuse their powers to bind and to loose, citing Ezechiel 13. 19: 'they killed souls which should not die, and saved souls alive which should not live'. Those who have neither been purified nor received absolution yet presume to take the sacraments of the Saviour's body and blood have been deceived by 'the kind of "shepherds" of whom the prophet Ezekiel 13. 18, said [quoting the words of the Lord, as reported in the King James Version], "Woe to the women that sew pillows to all armholes, and make kerchiefs upon the head of every stature to hunt souls. Will ye hunt the souls of my people, and will ye save the souls alive that come unto you?" The unabsolved are unworthy to take the sacraments: "He that eateth and drinketh unworthily eateth and drinketh damnation to himself, not discerning the Lord's body [I Corinthians 11. 29]"'.

It is at this point that Hincmar brings in Bede as a 'holy author', quoting Christ's words in Luke 22. 21:

'But behold, the hand of him that betrayeth me is with me on the table'. They say,[33] today too, and for all eternity: Woe to that man who comes to the Lord's table with evil intent, and who, with hidden plots in mind and a heart polluted by some crime, does not fear to take part in the secrets of Christ's mysteries [i.e. the Sacraments]. This person follows the example of Judas in betraying the Son of Man not to those sinners the Jews, but to sinners who are his own members, for whose sake he dares to violate the inestimable and inviolable body of the Lord. That person who neglects love and fear and is convinced instead to love and cherish earthly and fleeting things and even crimes, is selling the Lord. Woe to that man, I say, concerning whom Jesus, indubitably present at the holy altars and about to consecrate the sacrifice as set out, is compelled to ask the heavenly ministers who are standing in his presence, 'Behold, the hand of him that betrayeth me is on this table'.[34]

The betrayer at the Lord's table is Judas; and anyone who takes the sacraments at the Lord's table 'with a mind and a heart polluted' betrays the Lord again. The person

---

31 Hincmar, *De divortio*, ed. by Böhringer, *Responsio* 13, p. 196, ll. 13–23.

32 Hincmar, *De divortio*, ed. by Böhringer gives details in the notes to pp. 197–98.

33 'Dicunt' is an interpolation of Hincmar's.

34 Hincmar, *De divortio*, ed. by Böhringer, *Responsio* 13, p. 199, ll. 6–18: Hincmar alludes to I Corinthians 11. 29, and then says: 'sicut auctores sancti, ut demonstrat venerabilis presbiter Beda in commento evangelii Lucae, exponentes sententiam dicentis domini ...'. For the *Commentary on Luke*, cf. above, n. 9. The translation is mine. Cf. *The Divorce of King Lothar*, trans. by Stone and West, pp. 225–26.

who neglects love of the Lord and instead cherishes worldly things sells the Lord again. The leitmotif in Response 13, as in Responses 1 and 9, is the individual's personal responsibility: a polluted mind and heart are transparent to God's piercing gaze.[35]

VI. In Response 14, Hincmar cites Bede by name, as he had done in Response 1, whereas in Response 6, Bede had been cited 'silently'.[36] The Bedan passage was *Gospel Homilies*, II. 23, on Matthew 5. 34. The brevity of Response 14 on oaths presumably resulted from the very lengthy treatment of this subject earlier in *De divortio*, in Response 6. Its relevance to Lothar's divorce hinged on the function of oaths in disputes and in specifically in marital cases. A more pressing problem was perjury. In his first capitulary (Herstal, 779), Charlemagne had decreed the penalty for a perjurer, even if he was a free man, of having his right hand cut off.[37] Rachel Stone comments that this crime was castigated with notable rigour in 802, adding that Jonas of Orléans' *De institutione laicali* II. 26, quotes Bede's *Commentary on Luke* at this point: those who bear false witness in return for small gifts 'sell God', as Judas did.[38]

VII. In Response 15, Hincmar returns with a vengeance to the question of women's magic and its power to cause irreconcilable hatred between man and wife. Hincmar starts with a few Old Testament examples in point, describes a recent case in a neighbouring diocese, plunders Isidore of Seville for details of the many forms of witchcraft as practised, inserts a lengthy miracle-story in which St Basil puts paid to the marriage-destroying efforts of the Devil himself, and ends with a third citation, the longest and the most precisely-located, '*in tertio libro* of the venerable priest Bede's

---

35 Hincmar, *De divortio*, ed. by Böhringer, *Responsio* 13, p. 202, ll. 22–25, ends with a barely-veiled threat to Lothar: 'if someone perhaps emerges — may this not happen — puffed up by the arrogance of earthly power who scorns obedience and breaks the rein of Christianity and rushes forth to fall headlong into the abyss of damnation, the bishop, following the prophet Ezechiel [4. 3] will have his iron pan for his own liberation.' (My translation.) Cf. *The Divorce of King Lothar*, trans. by Stone and West, p. 231.

36 Hincmar, *De divortio*, ed. by Böhringer, *Responsio* 14, pp. 203–04, and *Responsio* 1, pp. 123–24, above, pp. 329–30. Cf. *The Divorce of King Lothar*, trans. by Stone and West, p. 111; compare *Responsio* 6, pp. 148–49, cf. *The Divorce of King Lothar*, trans. by Stone and West, pp. 149–50.

37 *Capitularia*, I, ed. by Boretius, no. 20, c. 10, p. 49; also no. 33 (*Capitulare missorum generale*, 802), c. 36, p. 98: 'Et usum periurii omnino non permittant [missi nostri], qui hoc pessimum scelus christiano populo auferre necessae est'; no. 34 (*Capitulare missorum specialia*, 802), c. 7, p. 100; no. 44 (*Capitulare missorum*, Thionville, late 805), c. 11, p. 124 (with provision for those accused of perjury to be isolated and interrogated); no. 51 (*Capitulare cum primis conferenda*, 808), c. 3, p. 138; no. 52 (*Capitula cum primis constituta*, 808), c. 4, p. 139; no. 53 (*Capitulare missorum*, 808), c. 3, p. 140; no. 65 (*Capitulare missorum*, 810), c. 10, p. 154; *Concilium Turonense* (813), c. 34, in *Concilia Aevi Karolini* I.2, ed. by Werminghoff, no. 38, p. 291. For the late antique legal context of the penalty of cutting-off the hand for counterfeiting coin, viewed as equivalent to treason, see Hendy, *Studies in the Byzantine Monetary Economy*, noting, p. 327, the presence of this penalty in the Emperor Leo III's *Ekloga* XVII. 18 (726 × 741).

38 Jonas of Orléans, *De institutione laicali*, col. 226; Bede, *In Lucae evangelium expositio* VI, 22, 5–6, p. 374. See Stone, *Morality and Masculinity*, pp. 169–70.

Commentary on Luke'. Bede starts from Luke 8. 30, the story of 'a certain man which had devils long time and ware no clothes' [King James Version]:

'And Jesus asked him, saying: What is thy name? But he said: Legion, because many devils were entered into him'.

He (Jesus) does not ask for the name as one who is ignorant, but so that, once the affliction which the raving man was suffering had been publicly confessed, the power of the healer might shine out in a way yet more deserving of thanks. But priests of our own period, who know how to drive out demons by the grace of exorcism, regularly say that sufferers cannot be cured unless they openly reveal by confession, so far as they can appreciate it, everything that they have suffered at the hands of unclean spirits, by sight or hearing or tasting [*Hincmar adds*] and by smell,[39] or touching or any perception of body or mind, awake or asleep. And most of all when the demons whom the Gauls call *dusii*, appearing to men in the guise of women or to women in the character of men, pretend that, by an unspeakable wonder-working, they, being incorporeal spirits, have both sought and obtained sexual intercourse with a human body, do they (the priests) require both the name of the demon, by which he said he should be recorded, and the ways of making an oath, by which they agreed a bond of love one to the other, to be acknowledged. This business is very like a fabrication and yet it is very true and very well-known from the testimony of many people, so that (for example) a priest who is a neighbour of mine reported that he had begun to cure a nun from a demon, but that as long as the matter remained hidden he had not been able to do her any good; yet, once the phantasm by which she was harmed was confessed, he had soon put it to flight by means of prayers and other appropriate forms of purification, and by medical care, with the help of blessed salt, he had cured that woman's body from the sores which it had contracted from the demon's touch. However, while he was in no way able to close up one of the sores which he had found more deeply embedded in her side, but rather it promptly opened up again, he had accepted a plan through which it might be healed from the woman herself whom he wanted to cure. 'If', she said, 'you sprinkled oil that has been blessed for use on the sick on it as a remedy and in that way anointed me, I shall promptly be restored to health. For on one occasion I saw, being placed by means of the spirit in a city very far off that I have never seen with the eyes of the body, a girl suffering from a similar affliction who was cured in that way by a priest'. He did as she had suggested, and at once the sore agreed to accept the remedy that it had previously scorned. I have taken care to explain in a few words these measures against the deceptions of demons, so that you may understand that it was not uselessly that the Lord asked for the name of the spirit that he was about to expel'.[40]

---

39 Hincmar adds 'smell' to Gregory the Great's list of the senses.

40 Hincmar, *De divortio*, ed. by Böhringer, *Responsio* 15, pp. 205–13, with the passage from Bede, *In Lucae evangelium expositio*, III, on Luke 8. 30, pp. 184–85, ll. 714–50. Cf. *The Divorce of King Lothar*, trans. by Stone and West, pp. 247–48. See further Stone and West's Introduction, *The Divorce of King Lothar*,

This exceptionally lengthy citation of Bede closes Response 15.

What moved Hincmar to quote this passage? Bede reflected here on the most spectacular case of demonic possession in Scripture (see Luke 8. 27–33, for the whole story). Similar cases, familiar in Bede's world, were also familiar in Hincmar's, and Hincmar, like Bede, sometimes used the present tense in such contexts. Hincmar, like Bede, was interested in making connexions between Scriptural times and his own.[41] In his *Commentary*, Bede responded to Luke 8. 27–33 by offering two contemporary instances, one about 'the bishops of our time' in general, the other about a particular case about which he had learned from a local priest. In Response 15, Hincmar described a case of a bewitched husband in 'one of our suffragan sees', where the bishop's intervention had re-established married love persisting *nunc usque*.[42] Bede had regarded medicine and supernatural power as complementary, an approach endorsed by Hincmar when he chose the story of the sick nun's cure as the finale of Response 15.

VIII. Three 'silent' citations of Bede help in reconsidering Hincmar's purpose in using them at all. Response 6 addresses the meaning of ordeals by hot or cold water. These ordeals divided good from bad, wrote Hincmar, but in different ways. The hot water 'cooked' the guilty but 'freed' the innocent 'uncooked' whose scalded flesh was healing well. Hincmar saw a problem in the reverse apparently happening in the ordeal by cold water, where the innocent were submerged and the guilty floated, yet, in the Flood, those in the ark were lifted out but the guilty drowned. Using I Peter 3. 21 and 20 (in that order), Bede in his *Commentary on the Seven Catholic Letters*, made a typological connexion between the Ark in the Flood and baptism, which Hincmar drew on, making small interpolations [here italicised], but without mentioning Bede by name: 'it is not by different waters but by the same waters that heretics *and bad Christians* are submerged in the depths, while *those who are orthodox and just* are raised up to heavenly kingdoms'.[43] The citation from Bede's commentary clarified a difficult passage, but its brevity may have led Hincmar to omit Bede's name, and he had already enlisted anyway the authority of *patres catholici*, further clarifying the *figura* by his added phrases. This was the only time Hincmar cited Bede's

pp. 64–69. Rightly commenting, p. 69, that Hincmar 'treats magic in a fairly matter-of-fact way', they note, p. 67, that in 834, according to the Astronomer, *Vita Hludowici imperatoris*, ed. by Tremp, c. 52, p. 496, 'Lothar I had arranged for Gerberga, sister of the highly placed nobleman Bernard of Septimania, to be drowned *tamquam venefica*' (perhaps better translated 'as a witch', than 'as if a witch', and noting the phrase *aquis praefocata est*), cf. Nithard, *Historiarum Libri IIII*, ed. by Lauer, I. 5, p. 24, '*more maleficorum … mergi praecepit*'; but they omit the evidence of Thegan, *Gesta Hludowici imperatoris*, ed. by Tremp, c. 52, p. 244: '[*Hlutharius*] … *extinxit eam iudicio coniugum impiorum consiliariorum eius*', where the gender of the judges and the toxicity of the verb are equally suggestive.
41 Cf. Hincmar, *De divortio*, ed. by Böhringer, *Praefatio*, p. 109, 'hodie'; *Responsio* 13, p. 199, 'hodie'.
42 Hincmar, *De divortio*, ed. by Böhringer, *Responsio* 15, pp. 205–06.
43 Bede, *In Epistolas Septem Catholicas*, ed. by Hurst, pp. 249, l. 221, and 250, ll. 256–57: 'Et ipsius [i.e. Peter] epistolae sententiam de figura baptismatis in arca diluvii exponentes patres catholici dicunt, quia *non aliis, sed ipsis aquis haeretici* et mali Christiani *ad inferna merguntur, quibus* orthodoxi et iusti quique *ad caelestia regna sublevantur*'.

Commentary on the Seven Catholic Letters.[44] Perhaps he was not very familiar with it, or he may have been quoting by memory to produce an embroidery of I Peter 3. 20–21: 'In qua pauci, id est, octo animae, salvae sunt per aquam. Quod et vos nunc similis *formae* salvos facit baptisma', picking up 'ad caelesti secum regna perduxit', and further stitching in: 'Quos ergo aquae diluvii non salvavit extra archam positos sed occidit, sine dubio praefigurabat omnem hereticum licet habentem baptismatis sacramentum non aliis'.[45] Perhaps it was just a case of Hincmar's being, as Jean Devisse put it in another context — his apparent discovery of the idea of a universal contract — 'déconcertant'.[46] Bede's reflections on Peter's Epistle fascinated him. Yet, with characteristic tenacity, he never lost sight of the main point in Response 6, which was to justify the use of ordeals.

Response 13 consists of a lengthy discussion of how bishops should impose penance. Near the end, Hincmar includes a longer citation from Bede's *Commentary on the Proverbs of Solomon*, again not naming Bede.[47] He introduced the citation with a warning about the application of *episcopalis cura*. The first five verses of Proverbs constitute a single sequence each part of which is one by one supplied by Bede with a brief explanation geared to explaining the duty of an ecclesiastical superior to care for souls. Proverbs 6. 1, is a difficult passage for exegetes in every period. What Bede made of this verse: 'If you pledge yourself to your neighbour, you have pledged yourself for a stranger', intrigued Hincmar, who added a phrase to Bede's comment [here in italics] so as to make it explicit that for Christian readers, the superior is a bishop:

> ... if you have accepted the soul of your brother [even] to the risk of your way of life, you have now bound your mind to the duty of care which you had not previously got *before you assumed pastoral office*.[48]

For Bede, the interpretation of this puzzling verse in its historical context was Solomon's teaching that the duty of care should be exercised properly by someone who stood surety to a neighbour; the surety had to advise the making of repayment to the creditor thus freeing the debtor, and the surety, from obligation. Bede gave as the allegorical meaning, that a teacher must instruct someone how to behave correctly, and the 'open' meaning, that the surety, though he risked inability to carry out his

44 As pointed out by Böhringer, *De divortio*, pp. 152–53, n. 43, adding that Bede himself may well have been drawing on Fulgentius.

45 Hincmar, *De divortio*, ed. by Böhringer, *Responsio 6*, p. 249, l. 240; p. 249, l. 221; p. 250, ll. 254–56.

46 Devisse, *Hincmar*, II, p. 1135: 'Déconcertant Hincmar, moderne par tant d'aspects, préoccupé de questions qui sont encore brûlantes pour nous, si irrémédiablement carolingien par tant d'autres'.

47 Hincmar, *De divortio*, ed. by Böhringer, *Responsio 5*, p. 201, Hincmar's introduction, ll. 3–12, Bede's rehearsing of the Scriptural text, with his comments, ll. 12–24.

48 Bede, *In Proverbia Salomonis*, ed. by Hurst, I, c. 6, vv. 1–6, p. 52, ll. 2–10, l. 25: 'In promptu est litterae sensus quia suadet ei qui spopondit pro amico ut ipsum sollicitus ammoneat quatenus reddita pecunia quam debet creditori et se ipsum liberet. Allegorice autem in hac periocha doctorem, porro in sequente uacantem quemlibet ut se gerere debeat instruit. Dicitur enim praeceptori: Si spoponderis ... tuam, quod est aperte dicere: Si animam fratris in periculo tuae conuersationis acceperis, iam ligasti mentem apud curam sollicitudinis quae ante deerat'.

responsibilities, must recognize himself being bound in a new way to administer care. Scott DeGregorio points out that Bede 'was breaking new ground' in this and many of his other Old Testament commentaries because there were simply 'no earlier commentaries to transmit'.[49]

Hincmar added to Bede's interpretation of Proverbs 6 words that left no doubt as to how the text must be applied in the contemporary context of *De divortio*: a bishop assumed *ex officio* a new responsibility to deliver pastoral care effectively. It may be said that the passage suited Hincmar's book; but it looks to me as if he was impressed by Bede's groundbreaking work. Beyond Bede, of course, was Solomon himself. If Hincmar did not mention Solomon in reference to Proverbs 6, he did so a little earlier in Response 13, and a little later, in the very brief Response 14, he asserted the difficulty of finding anyone more wise than Solomon.[50] That is the nearest I can get to answering why Hincmar quoted Bede's *Commentary on Solomon's Proverbs* without citing Bede by name.

In Response 21, Hincmar wrapped up the central question of *De divortio*, namely, whether Lothar II could reject Teutberga, do penance, and make his concubine his wife. The answer on every canonical ground was 'no'.[51] Near the end of the Response, came a 'silent' and very brief citation from Bede that Hincmar took from the *Commentary on Luke* 11. 31–32: so briefly, indeed, as to provide a clue to the omission of Bede's name: 'Kings, bishops and secular judges ought to fear what is said in the Gospel [Matthew 12. 41–42, and Luke 11. 31], about "the Ninevites and the queen of the South", that "they shall rise in judgement with this most wicked generation and shall condemn it"'. He continues immediately with this from Bede's *Commentary on Luke* 11. 31: 'They [*recte* "She"] shall condemn, not by the power of judgement but by the comparing of a better deed'.[52] The 'comparison' was between notions of judgement in the Old Testament and the New, as Bede made clear at length, and as Hincmar went on, in his own words, 'if those kings [of the Medes and Persians], and idolatrous judges served the order of judgement, are we, under Christ, the judge of the living and the dead, to deviate less dutifully on any consideration whatsoever from the order of judgement?' Hincmar had immediately before this cited at some length from Augustine, *De adulterinis coniugiis*. Devisse suggested that Hincmar was quoting Augustine's text in haste.[53] Devisse did not spell out the tendency for haste to produce a faulty rendering, nor did he suggest that the next-door citation might

---

49 DeGregorio, 'Bede and the Old Testament', p. 131.

50 Hincmar, *De divortio*, ed. by Böhringer, *Responsio* 13, p. 200, l. 3, à propos Proverbs 26. 11, and *Responsio* 14, p. 204, l. 15.

51 Hincmar, *De divortio*, ed. by Böhringer, *Responsio* 21, pp. 220–26.

52 Hincmar, *De divortio*, ed. by Böhringer, *Responsio* 21, p. 225, ll. 34–35: 'Condemnabunt [*recte* Condemnabit] utique non potestate iudicii, sed comparatione melioris facti [*recte* facti melioris]', citing Bede's *Commentary on Luke*, p. 238, ll. 285–86. The *Commentary* on these verses pp. 238–39, ll. 285–320, ran to 35 lines.

53 Devisse, *Hincmar Archevêque de Reims*, III, p. 1484, n. 2: 'Il est invraisemblable qu'Hincmar ai eu le manuscrit… Peut-etre a-t-il emprunté le *De adulterinis coniugiis* pour lecture rapide en 860?' Hincmar quoted it at length in *De coercendo et exstirpando raptu viduarum, puellarum et sanctimonialium*, written in 876: see Stone, 'The Invention of a Theology'.

also be slightly flawed. Hincmar's own consciousness of some flaw seems the likeliest reason for his decision not to credit Bede by name, even when he was citing the Bedan work he knew best of all, the *Commentary on Luke*. In any case, having given the gist of Bede's exegesis on this point, Hincmar may well have thought there was little more to say. What might be suspected here, and this is no very dark suspicion, is some intellectual collusion between Hincmar and Bede.

My conclusion can be brief too. Hincmar knew some of Bede's exegetical works, and manuscripts of several (on *Kings, Psalms, Proverbs, Song of Songs, Tobit*) belonged to the Reims library in Hincmar's time.[54] The *Commentary on Luke* is not among them: nevertheless, in light of the passages discussed above, it is safe to infer that the *Commentary on Luke* was one work Hincmar knew very well. His knowledge was not turned on like a tap in 860, but it was then, and not before, that Hincmar needed to write the *De divortio*. First and foremost, for this commission, and this task, Hincmar needed legal and historical arguments, but he also needed exegetical ones. The evidence of *De divortio* shows Hincmar reading Bede's exegesis very attentively, imitating, and sharing, Bede's methods. Both scholars were, and situated themselves as, heirs to earlier Fathers, especially Augustine and Gregory. It is sometimes alleged that medieval people had no sense of historical specifics, nor of anachronism. A churchman who was a contemporary of Hincmar's, and, like Hincmar, a master-exegete, was Hrabanus Maurus. This is not the place to attempt a comparison of the oeuvres of these two, but I think it can be said that despite a good deal of overlap, their priorities as exegetes were different. Hrabanus's admonitory use of Old Testament history belonged in what Mayke de Jong has called 'a teleological perspective' and 'a typological drama of good and evil': fundamentally this was a moralizing genre, educative rather than offering 'an intelligent approach to contemporary events'.[55] Hincmar's aim in his *pièces d'occasion* was to apply exegetical understandings to particular contemporary political issues. Hrabanus's readings of biblical history generated a transposition of Old Testament models to be imitated by Carolingian rulers. His intended audience, royals apart, consisted of clergy. Hincmar's aims were more complicated: legalistic, pragmatic, politically instrumental, and *à jour*. In the ninth century, he was one of a kind.

I have come to think that Hincmar perceived Bede's 'today' as more like his own than either Hincmar or Bede felt was the case with the late antique worlds of Augustine and Gregory. In 860, there was, or there grew to be, a likeness, a rapport, between the ways Hincmar worked and the ways he found that Bede had worked. Their social worlds were similar. Their interests in exegetical meanings, linkages between Old and New Testaments, between Scriptural time and 'modern times', were not only typological or allegorical but literal, and topical. Bede the monk, like

---

54 See Carey, 'The *Scriptorium* of Reims', esp. pp. 51, 52, 56. See further the works cited in n. 11, above. On the Reims *scriptorium* in Hincmar's time, see the critical comments of McKitterick, 'Carolingian Book Production', pp. 12–13.

55 De Jong, 'The Empire as *ecclesia*', esp. pp. 198, 222. See also the short but penetrating paper of Le Maitre, 'Les methods exégétiques de Raban Maur'; and Heydemann and Pohl, 'The Rhetoric of Election', pp. 26–27 (Hrabanus, relying heavily on Bede, offered original touches of his own).

Hincmar the bishop, took a latitudinarian view of I Peter I 2.9. Bede as well as Hincmar wrote for their own times, and sometimes in similar genres. True, Hincmar stood out as different, both from the Fathers, the admired exegetes of the past, and any of his own contemporaries: he wrote political *pièces d'occasion* in the style of *Gutachten*, legal opinions. *De divortio*, uniquely large scale as it was, could be compared with other pieces such as the Quierzy letter (858), *De fide Carolo regi servanda* (875), *De iure metropolitanorum* (876), and *De villa Noviliaco* (also 876): all of these were interventions in the public arena, replete with legal and prudential arguments. But what Hincmar (*c.* 805–882) and Bede (*c.* 673–735) shared was the medium and message of exegesis. Of course these two missed meeting by a long chalk, and there could be only one-way, not mutual, influence of one on the other. It is possible, though, in the *De divortio* more than anywhere else, for the modern reader to imagine, even to sense over the many decades that divided their *actual* lives, a meeting of two minds.

Works Cited

Primary Sources

Annales Bertiniani, ed. by Félix Grat, Jeanne Vieillard and Susanne Clémencet, with notes by Léon Levillain (Paris: Librairie C. Klincksieck, 1964)

The Annals of St-Bertin, trans. by Janet L. Nelson, Ninth-Century Histories, I (Manchester: Manchester University Press, 1991)

Astronomer, *Vita Hludowici Imperatoris*, ed. by Ernst Tremp, in *Monumenta Germaniae Historica: Scriptores rerum Germanicarum in usum scholarum separatim editi*, 78 vols (Hannover: Hahn, 1871–), LXIV (1995), pp. 279–558

Bede, *In Epistulas Septem Catholicas*, ed. by David Hurst, Corpus Christianorum Series Latina, 121 (Turnhout: Brepols, 1983), pp. 181–342

——, *In Lucae Euangelium Expositio*, ed. by David Hurst, Corpus Christianorum Series Latina, 120 (Turnhout: Brepols, 1960), pp. 5–425

——, *In Marci Euangelium Expositio*, ed. by David Hurst, Corpus Christianorum Series Latina, 120 (Turnhout: Brepols, 1960), pp. 431–648

——, *In Prouerbia Salomonis*, ed. by David Hurst, Corpus Christianorum Series Latina, 119B (Turnout: Brepols, 1983), pp. 23–163

——, *In Regum Librum XXX quaestiones*, ed. by David Hurst, Corpus Christianorum Series Latina, 119 (Turnhout: Brepols, 1962), pp. 89–138

Bede: A Biblical Miscellany, trans. by W. Trent Foley (Liverpool: Liverpool University Press, 1999), pp. 81–143

Bede the Venerable, Homilies on the Gospels, trans. by Lawrence T. Martin and David Hurst 2 vols (Kalamazoo: Cistercian Publications, 1991)

Ecloga: das Gesetzbuch Leons III und Konstantinos V, ed. by Ludwig Burgmann, Forschungen zur byzantinischen Rechtsgeschichte, 10 (Frankfurt am Main: Löwenklau, 1983)

Hincmar of Reims, *De divortio Lotharii regis et Theutbergae reginae*, ed. by Letha Böhringer, *Monumenta Germaniae Historica: Concilia*, 8 vols to date (Hannover: Hahn, 1893–), IV (1992), *Supplementum* 1

————, *Epistola ad regem Hludowicum* (November, 858), in *Die Konzilien der karolingischen Teilreiche 843–59*, ed. by Wilfried Hartmann, *Monumenta Germaniae Historica: Concilia Aevi Karolini*, 8 vols to date (Hannover: Hahn, 1893–), III (1984), no. 41, pp. 405–27

————, *Epistolae*, ed. by Ernst Perels, *Monumenta Germaniae Historica: Epistolae*, 8 vols (Hannover: Weidmann, 1887–1939), VIII (1939, reprinted 1975)

————, *The Divorce of King Lothar and Queen Theutberga: Hincmar of Rheims's De divortio*, translated, with introduction and commentary, by Rachel Stone and Charles West (Manchester: Manchester University Press, 2016)

Homiliarum euangelii libri II, ed. by David Hurst, Corpus Christianorum Series Latina, 122 (Turnhout: Brepols, 1955), pp. 1–378

Gregory the Great, *Moralia*, ed. by Marcus Adriaen, Corpus Christianorum Series Latina, 143, 143A and 143B (Turnhout: Brepols, 1979–85)

In primam partem Samuhelis, ed. by David Hurst, Corpus Christianorum Series Latina, 119 (Turnhout: Brepols, 1962), pp. 5–287

Jerome, *Commentarium in Mattheum libri IV*, ed. by David Hurst and Marcus Adriaen, Corpus Christianorum Series Latina 77 (Turnhout: Brepols, 1969)

Jonas of Orléans, *De institutione laicali*, in *Patrologiae cursus completus: series latina*, ed. by Jacques-Paul Migne, 221 vols (Paris: Migne, 1844–1864), CVI (1864), cols 121–278

Karoli Magni capitularia, ed. by Alfred Boretius, *Monumenta Germaniae Historica: Capitularia regum Francorum*, 2 vols (Hannover: Hahn, 1883–1897), I (1883), pp. 44–185

Nithard, *Historiarum Libri IIII*, ed. by Philippe Lauer (Paris: Les Belles Lettres, 1926), revised by Sophie Glansdorff, Les classiques de l'histoire au Moyen Âge, 51 (Paris: Les Belles Lettres, 2012)

Thegan, *Gesta Hludowici imperatoris*, ed. by Ernst Tremp, in, *Monumenta Germaniae Historica: Scriptores rerum Germanicarum in usum scholarum separatim editi*, 78 vols (Hannover: Hahn, 1871–), LXIV (1995), 167–259

Secondary Studies

Airlie, Stuart, 'Private Bodies and the Body Politic in the Divorce Case of Lothar II', *Past and Present*, 161 (1998), 3–38

Brown, George Hardin, 'Bede's Neglected Commentary on Samuel', in *Innovation and Tradition in the Writings of the Venerable Bede*, ed. by Scott DeGregorio (Morgantown: West Virginia University Press, 2006), pp. 121–42

————, *A Companion to the Venerable Bede* (Woodbridge: Boydell, 2009)

Carey, Frederick M., 'The *Scriptorium* of Reims during the Archbishopric of Hincmar', in *Classical and Mediæval Studies in Honor of Edward Kennard Rand*, ed. by Leslie W. Jones (New York: Jones, 1938), pp. 41–60

DeGregorio, Scott, ed., *Innovation and Tradition in the Writings of the Venerable Bede* (Morgantown: West Virginia University Press, 2006)

————, ed., *The Cambridge Companion to Bede* (Cambridge: Cambridge University Press, 2010)

————, 'Bede and the Old Testament', in *The Cambridge Companion to Bede*, ed. by Scott DeGregorio (Cambridge: Cambridge University Press, 2010), pp. 127–41

Devisse, Jean, *Hincmar Archevêque de Reims 845–82*, 3 vols (Geneva: Droz, 1975, 1976)

Flint, Valerie, *The Rise of Magic in Early Medieval Europe* (Oxford: Clarendon Press, 1991)

Gillis, Matthew B., 'Heresy in the Flesh: Gottschalk of Orbais and the Predestination Controversy in the Archdiocese of Rheims', in *Hincmar of Rheims. Life and Work*, ed. by Rachel Stone and Charles West (Manchester: Manchester University Press, 2015), pp. 247–67

Heidecker, Karl, *The Divorce of Lothar II: Christian Marriage and Political Power in the Carolingian World* (Ithaca: Cornell University Press, 2010)

Hendy, Michael F., *Studies in the Byzantine Monetary Economy, c. 300–1450* (Cambridge: Cambridge University Press, 1985)

Heydemann, Gerda, and Walter Pohl, 'The Rhetoric of Election: I Peter 2. 9 and the Franks', in *Religious Franks: Religion and Power in the Frankish Kingdoms, Studies in Honour of Mayke de Jong*, ed. by Rob Meens, Dorine van Espelo, Bram van den Hoven van Genderen, Janneke Raaijmakers, Irene van Renswoude, and Carine van Rhijn (Manchester: Manchester University Press, 2016), pp. 13–31

Hill, Joyce, 'Carolingian Perspectives on the Authority of Bede', in *Innovation and Tradition in the Writings of the Venerable Bede*, ed. by Scott DeGregorio (Morgantown: West Virginia University Press, 2006), pp. 227–49

de Jong, Mayke, 'The Empire as *ecclesia*: Hrabanus Maurus and Biblical *historia* for Rulers', in *The Uses of the Past in the Early Middle Age*, ed. by Yitzhak Hen and Matthew Innes (Cambridge: Cambridge University Press, 1999), pp. 191–226

Le Maitre, Philippe, 'Les methods exégétiques de Raban Maur', in *Haut Moyen-Âge. Culture, Éducation et Société. Études offertes à Pierre Riché*, ed. by Michel Sot (Paris: Éditions Européennes ERASME, 1990), pp. 343–52

Martin, Lawrence T., 'Bede and Preaching', in *The Cambridge Companion to Bede*, ed. by Scott DeGregorio (Cambridge: Cambridge University Press, 2010), pp. 156–69

McKitterick, Rosamond, 'Carolingian Book Production: Some Problems', The Library, 6th series, 12 (1990), 1–33, repr. in her *Books, Scribes and Learning in the Frankish Kingdoms, 6th–9th Centuries* (Aldershot: Variorum, 1994), chapter XII, with the same pagination

———, 'Kulturelle Verbindungen zwischen England und den fränkischen Reich in der Zeit der Karolinger', in *Deutschland und der Westen Europas im Mittlelalter*, ed. by Joachim Ehlers, Vorträge und Forschungen, 56 (Stuttgart: Thorbecke, 2002), pp. 121–48

Murray, Alexander, 'Review Article: Missionaries and Magic in Dark-Age Europe', *Past and Present*, 136 (1992), 186–205

Nelson, Janet L., *Charles the Bald* (London: Longman, 1992)

———, 'The Intellectual in Politics: Context, Content and Authorship in the Capitulary of Coulaines, November 843', in *Intellectual Life in the Middle Ages: Essays Presented to Margaret Gibson*, ed. by Leslie Smith and Benedicta Ward (London: Hambledon, 1992), pp. 1–14, repr. in Janet L. Nelson, *The Frankish World* (London: Hambledon, 1996), pp. 155–68

———, '"Hunnish Scenes"/Frankish Scenes: A Case of History that Stands Still?', in *Gender and Historiography: Studies in the Earlier Middle Ages in Honour of Pauline Stafford*, ed. by Janet L. Nelson, Susan Reynolds, and Susan Johns (London: University of London Press, 2011), pp. 175–90

Stone, Rachel, 'The Invention of a Theology of Abduction: Hincmar of Rheims on *raptus*',
    Journal of Ecclesiastical History, 60 (2009), 433–48
———, *Morality and Masculinity in the Carolingian Empire* (Cambridge: Cambridge
    University Press, 2012)
Stone, Rachel, and Charles West, eds, *Hincmar of Rheims: Life and Work* (Manchester:
    Manchester University Press, 2015)
Stratmann, Martina, *Hinkmar von Reims als Verwalter von Bistum und Kirchenprovinz*,
    Quellen und Forschungen zum Recht im Mittelalter, 6 (Sigmaringen: Thorbecke, 1991)
Thacker, Alan T., 'Bede's Ideal of Reform', in *Ideal and Reality in Frankish and Anglo-Saxon
    Society*, ed. by Patrick Wormald, Donald Bullough, and Roger Collins (Oxford:
    Blackwell, 1983), pp. 130–53
———, 'Bede and the Ordering of Understanding', in *Innovation and Tradition in the
    Writings of the Venerable Bede*, ed. by Scott DeGregorio (Morgantown: West Virginia
    University Press, 2006), pp. 37–63
Westgard, Joshua A. 'Bede and the Continent in the Carolingian Age and Beyond', in *The
    Cambridge Companion to Bede*, ed. by Scott DeGregorio (Cambridge: Cambridge
    University Press, 2010), pp. 201–15

FRANCESCA TINTI

The English Presence in Rome in the Later Anglo-Saxon Period: Change or Continuity?*

The importance of Rome in early medieval England and, more specifically, the Anglo-Saxons' pilgrimages to and presence in the Eternal City have attracted the attention of many scholars, including Alan Thacker, who has produced some of the most significant publications on this topic.[1] With few exceptions, most of the attention has concentrated on the seventh, eighth, and, to some extent, the ninth centuries; scholarly interest in the presence of the English in Rome seems to be significantly less pronounced for the later Anglo-Saxon period.[2] This is at least partly due to patterns of source survival and distribution. For instance, the collection of papal biographies known as the *Liber pontificalis*, which is one of the most informative texts on the presence of the English in Rome in the eighth and ninth centuries, stopped being compiled in the late ninth century, and detailed recording only started again in the twelfth century. Similarly, the evidence provided by the graffiti left by the English pilgrims on the walls of the Roman catacombs only casts light on the earlier period, for visits to the catacombs seem to have declined sharply in the second half of the eighth century when the bodies of saints and martyrs began to be moved on a large scale into the churches within the

---

* For help with various matters related to this chapter I am grateful to Robert Gallagher, Edward Roberts, Rory Naismith, and the late Letizia Ermini Pani. I also wish to thank Scott DeGregorio and Paul Kershaw for their patience and valuable editorial work. This chapter is part of the activities conducted by the University of the Basque Country Research Group GIU17/006 within the research project HAR2017-86502-P funded by the Spanish Ministerio de Ciencia e Innovación.

1 Thacker, 'In Search of Saints'; Ó Carragáin and Thacker, 'Wilfrid in Rome'; Thacker, 'Rome: The Pilgrims' City'. See also Moore, *The Saxon Pilgrims to Rome*; Levison, *England and the Continent*, pp. 14–44; Colgrave, 'Pilgrimages to Rome'; Howe, 'Rome: Capital of Anglo-Saxon England'; Lapidge, 'The Career of Aldhelm', pp. 52–64; Matthews, *The Road to Rome*; Story, 'Aldhelm and Old St Peter's'.

2 Noticeable exceptions include: Ortenberg, 'Archbishop Sigeric's Journey'; Ortenberg, *The English Church*; Treharne, 'The Performance of Piety'; and Tinti 'The Archiepiscopal Pallium'. For a more detailed discussion of the development of scholarship in this area, see Tinti, 'Introduction'.

Francesca Tinti • (francesca.tinti@ehu.eus) is Ikerbasque Research Professor at Universidad del País Vasco UPV/EHU.

Cities, Saints, and Communities in Early Medieval Europe, ed. by Scott DeGregorio and Paul Kershaw, SEM 46 (Turnhout: Brepols, 2020), pp. 345-371
BREPOLS PUBLISHERS   DOI 10.1484/M.SEM-EB.5.119635

walls.[3] As for the sources which originated in England, it can be noted that no later Anglo-Saxon narrative text contains reports comparable to those of Bede or Stephen of Ripon on the multiple journeys to Rome of such pilgrims as Benedict Biscop, Ceolfrith, or Wilfrid. In the later Anglo-Saxon period the evidence for the relations between England and Rome and for the English presence in the city seems to be more dispersed, and one has to gather it piecemeal by consulting a wide variety of sources, including chronicles, charters, liturgical manuscripts, miscellaneous collections, correspondence, and archaeological finds.[4] This is what this chapter will attempt to do, building on the fundamental work that Alan has produced for the earlier period, in order to assess whether the evidence for an English presence in Rome during the tenth and eleventh centuries points towards divergence from or continuity with earlier patterns of practice. This will be done by concentrating on three main questions: who went to Rome in the later Anglo-Saxon period; what the reasons were for their journeys; and where travellers stayed and which sites they visited while in Rome.

Who?

Most of the categories of the men and women who are known to have gone to Rome in the seventh to ninth centuries can also be found travelling to the Eternal City in the later Anglo-Saxon period: kings, nobles, bishops, abbots, priests, and wealthy landowners. As for kings, however, the only one who is known to have gone to Rome in the tenth or eleventh century is Cnut, who was there in 1027 to attend the imperial coronation of Conrad II.[5] No other king from England appears to have gone there after 874 — the year when Burgred of Mercia was deposed by the Vikings and set off for Rome, where he died shortly afterwards.[6] In the earlier period several English kings' journeys to Rome had followed the voluntary relinquishing of their thrones and the decision to go and finish their days in the Eternal City, a drastic and definitive change of life and environment which clearly no longer held the same appeal in later times.[7]

---

3 Surviving graffiti would seem to indicate that the Anglo-Saxons were the largest 'ethnic' group of foreign visitors to the catacombs; see Izzi, 'Anglo-Saxons Underground'.

4 The one source which records most of the journeys to Rome undertaken by various members of the late Anglo-Saxon ecclesiastical and secular elites is the *Anglo-Saxon Chronicle*, which, however, given its annalistic nature, rarely provides much detail about any such trip.

5 Bolton, *The Empire of Cnut the Great*, pp. 181–83, 237, 294–300; Treharne, *Living through Conquest*, pp. 28–47; Treharne, 'The Performance of Piety'.

6 Burgred was buried in the church of St Mary in the *Schola Saxonum*, the English quarter in Rome; see further discussion below, pp. 360–61. A couple of decades earlier, in 855, King Æthelwulf of Wessex had also gone to Rome, accompanied by his son Alfred. According to *Asser's Life of Alfred*, ed. by Stevenson, cc. 8, 11–12, pp. 7–9, Alfred had also been in 853. See *Alfred the Great*, trans. and introduction by Keynes and Lapidge, pp. 69–70, 234, and Keynes, 'Anglo-Saxon Entries in the *Liber Vitae* of Brescia', pp. 112–14.

7 Caedwalla of the West Saxons went in 688 and his example was followed by his successor, Ine, who went in 726. Coenred of Mercia also gave up his kingdom in 709 and travelled to Rome to finish his days at the thresholds of the apostles; see Colgrave, 'Pilgrimages to Rome', pp. 164–66, and Stancliffe, 'Kings Who Opted Out'.

Another departure from the earlier period concerns the presence of consecrated women among the groups of pilgrims who headed towards Rome. Reservations about the practice of female pilgrimage had been expressed by a number of prominent churchmen in the eighth century, including Boniface and Alcuin.[8] In voicing such preoccupations, however, they and their correspondents affirm that abbesses and nuns were participants in such journeys, whereas in the tenth and eleventh centuries consecrated women are never mentioned in this context. This could be explained by the general meagreness of references to religious women in late Anglo-Saxon England, but also by taking into account the restrictions on movement, the emphasis upon *stabilitas*, and the cloistered life imposed by the Benedictine reform, especially on female communities.[9] It must be acknowledged that such restrictions were also imposed on monks, but exceptions for abbots, though not abbesses, were clearly made. In 1022 Abbot Leofwine of Ely accompanied Archbishop Æthelnoth, who went to Rome to fetch his pallium, the white woollen band marked with crosses which constituted the main symbol of archiepiscopal authority, while Abbot Æthelsige of St Augustine's, Canterbury was there in 1063.[10]

The women who did go from England to Rome in the tenth and eleventh centuries were normally accompanying their kinsmen, especially husbands or fathers, and their participation in the journey is generally referred to in relation to that of their male companions.[11] A famous example is that of Judith, the Flemish wife of Earl Tostig, who went to Rome with her husband and a number of other magnates in 1061.[12] Among the less famous examples is an unnamed woman, married to a certain Wiohstan. Both of them are known to have gone to Rome with their son in the first half of the tenth century thanks to a charter preserved in the Selsey archive, confirming the lands that Wiohstan had sold to Bishop Wulfhun for 2000 silver pence and a horse before setting out on his pilgrimage.[13] A rare case of a female pilgrim who seems to have been acting without the involvement of any male relative is that of Siflæd, who lived between the late tenth and the early eleventh century and for whom two different

---

8   Halpin, 'Anglo-Saxon Women', pp. 100–01.
9   On the evidential problems which characterize the study of religious women in the later Anglo-Saxon period see Foot, *Veiled Women*, pp. 1–34.
10   Leofwine, whose journey to Rome is said to have followed his having been unjustly driven from Ely, is mentioned in two versions of the *Anglo-Saxon Chronicle* recording Æthelnoth's trip: *The Anglo-Saxon Chronicle, vol. VII: MS E*, ed. by Irvine, p. 75 and *The Anglo-Saxon Chronicle, vol. VIII: MS F*, ed. by Baker, pp. 11–12. On Æthelsige see Goscelin, *Historia Translationis S. Augustini*, col. 33.
11   Incidentally, this has also been suggested by Simon Keynes as a possible interpretation for the arrangement of the ninth-century male and female Anglo-Saxon names entered on fol. 31ᵛ of the *Liber Vitae* of Brescia: Keynes, 'Anglo-Saxon Entries in the *Liber Vitae* of Brescia', pp. 109–10.
12   This embassy is referred to in a number of sources, including the anonymous *Life of King Edward*, ed. and trans. by Barlow, I.5, pp. 52–53. On Judith see Dockray-Miller, *The Books and the Life of Judith of Flanders*. It has also been suggested that Æthelswith, wife of the above-mentioned Burgred of Mercia, accompanied him to Rome in 874. She is said in the *Anglo-Saxon Chronicle* to have died in 888 and to have been buried in Pavia; her name also appears next to that of Burgred in the *Liber Vitae* of Brescia: *Alfred the Great*, trans. and introduction by Keynes and Lapidge, pp. 113, 281; Keynes, 'Anglo-Saxon Entries in the *Liber Vitae* of Brescia', pp. 109–10.
13   S 1206; *Charters of Selsey*, ed. by Kelly, no. 16.

vernacular wills have been preserved in the Bury St Edmunds archive. The relative chronology of the two documents is uncertain, but one of them, possibly the later one, is introduced by a sentence declaring 'in this document it is made known how Siflæd granted her possessions when she went across the sea', a common way of referring to a pilgrimage to Rome.[14] No reference is made in either will to a husband or children. She may have been a widow, as is often the case with female testators acting on their own, and this may obviously explain why, unlike other female contemporaries, she is not described as going to Rome with a husband.

Will-making was one of the most common of the activities which characterized the organization of a journey to the thresholds of the apostles.[15] Throughout the Anglo-Saxon period there must have been a clear awareness of the dangers that one could encounter on the way to or from Rome, and indeed in Rome itself, where several English people are known to have died. One cannot fail to mention the Saracens' attacks to which Flodoard of Rheims refers in his *Annals* under the years 921 and 923, when many English people, who were on their way to Rome, were killed in the Alps.[16] That these two tragic events should have taken place within just two years of each other testifies to the popularity that the journey still enjoyed in the tenth century. The Exeter guild statutes, dating to the middle of the same century, also suggest that the pilgrimage to Rome was a fairly common practice, as they asserted that individual guild members had to pay five pence to supply the needs of any member desiring to go 'æt suþfore' (on the southern pilgrimage).[17] Furthermore, the prominence which the needs of travellers to Rome are given in Cnut's letter to the English of 1027 confirms that the journey was still popular in the first half of the eleventh century, despite the fact that for this period we lack the testimony of a history like Bede's, attesting explicitly to the attraction of the practice. In the letter, which Cnut wrote after having attended the coronation of Conrad II in Rome, the king says that he had spoken to both the emperor and King Rudolf III of Burgundy 'about the needs of all the people of my entire realm, both English and Danes, that they concede fairer law and securer peace to them on the road to Rome, and that they

---

14 '[H]er Switeleþ on þis write ihu Sifled vthe hire aihte þo sche ouer se ferde': S 1525a; *Anglo-Saxon Wills*, ed. and trans. by Whitelock, no. 38. Cf. S 1490; *Anglo-Saxon Wills*, ed. and trans. by Whitelock, no. 28. This is the will of Ældric Modercope (probably of AD 1042 × 1043), which uses the same phrase to refer to his pilgrimage to Rome. Another mid-eleventh-century will from Bury St Edmunds, of a man named Ketel, refers to his going to Rome with his stepdaughter: S 1519; *Anglo-Saxon Wills*, ed. and trans. by Whitelock, no. 34.

15 Although wills survive in greater numbers for the later Anglo-Saxon period, it would seem that already in the eighth century pilgrims had begun to make bequests prior to their departure. See, for instance, S 1182; *Charters of St Augustine's Abbey*, ed. by Kelly, no. 12. This charter of 762 was issued when Dunwald, thegn of the late King Æthelberht of Kent, was about to leave for Rome, taking with him money that was to be dispensed there for Æthelberht's soul. Dunwald bequeathed to the church of SS Peter and Paul (i.e., the later St Augustine's) a small piece of land in Canterbury.

16 *Les Annales de Flodoard*, ed. by Lauer, pp. 5, 19. In 958 Ælfsige, archbishop-elect of Canterbury, died in the Alps while on his way to collect the pallium; see Tinti, 'The Archiepiscopal Pallium', pp. 312, 314.

17 Conner, *Anglo-Saxon Exeter*, pp. 168–69; *English Historical Documents*, ed. by Whitelock, no. 137, p. 605.

should not be hindered by so many barriers along the road and vexed by unjust tolls; [...] and all the princes confirmed with edicts that my people, both merchants and others who journey to make their prayers, might go to and return from Rome without any hindrance of barriers and toll-collectors, in firm peace and secure in a just law'.[18]

Why?

A category of travellers to Rome which is particularly well attested both in the earlier and in the later Anglo-Saxon periods consisted of members of the Church, and bishops in particular, since ecclesiastical business had been and continued to be one of the main reasons which took the Anglo-Saxons to Rome. However, as will emerge more clearly in the next few pages, every journey to Rome at this time is likely to have entailed also some aspects of a pious pilgrimage.[19] This is what is attested, for instance, in the only surviving detailed itinerary of an Anglo-Saxon in Rome, that of Archbishop Sigeric of Canterbury, who went there in 990 to collect his pallium, and whose itinerary shows that while in Rome, Sigeric took this opportunity to visit many prominent churches in the city. In what follows, therefore, the aim is not so much to identify the specific reasons behind every known late Anglo-Saxon trip to Rome in the tenth and eleventh centuries, as to examine what key conditions or circumstances demanded such a journey, bearing in mind that many such trips may have been motivated by a combination of different reasons and activities.

The Archiepiscopal Pallium

The collection of the archiepiscopal pallium in person probably represents the main novel feature of the later Anglo-Saxon period in terms of what motivated the journey to Rome. Before the tenth century, the pallium had normally been sent from the pope after having been formally requested through a legate, as was the case in 780–781, when Alcuin was sent to Rome in such a capacity to collect the pallium for Eanbald of York.[20] Already in 634 Pope Honorius I had explained in a letter to Honorius of Canterbury that he had sent the pallium to the bishops of Canterbury and York in order to spare them a long journey by sea and land.[21] However, from

---

18 Treharne, *Living through Conquest*, pp. 30–31. For the Latin text of the letter see *Die Gesetze der Angelsachsen*, ed. by Liebermann, I, p. 276. On Bede's comments about the popularity of the practice in the seventh and eighth centuries see Thacker, 'Rome: The Pilgrims' City', p. 124.

19 This was also the case for Cnut's journey to Rome of 1027, which, although mainly intended to allow him to attend the imperial coronation of Conrad II, gave rise to a number of representations of the king as a pious penitent pilgrim. See Bolton, *The Empire of Cnut the Great*, pp. 294–95; Treharne, *Living through Conquest*, pp. 28–47; Treharne, 'The Performance of Piety'.

20 Bullough, *Alcuin*, pp. 333–36.

21 Bede, *Historia ecclesiastica*, II.18. Before the tenth century two only English bishops are known to have gone to Rome in person to fetch the pallium: Wigheard in 667 or 668 and Berhtwald in 692. In both cases the journey seems to have been necessary to reinforce their authority and preempt possible disputes. See Brooks, *The Early History of the Church of Canterbury*, p. 134.

the pontificate of Archbishop Wulfhelm (926–941) onwards, the archbishops of
Canterbury began to go regularly to Rome shortly after their election to fetch the
pallium in person; in the second half of the tenth century their colleagues at York
also started to do the same, though apparently not as assiduously.[22] The reasons for
the new practice are not entirely clear, and it should be stressed that it started at a
time when the papacy was not yet expecting archbishops to go to Rome in person
for this purpose.[23] In other words, the English prelates seem to have anticipated a
requirement which would be actively enforced by the reforming popes of the second
half of the eleventh century.[24] Nicholas Brooks has suggested that these journeys
may have been related to the need to obtain papal approval for the translation to
Canterbury of bishops who had previously held other bishoprics, a practice which
in principle was not allowed by canon law.[25] Episcopal transfer, however, was far from
unusual in western Christendom, and although the motivation for the regularity of
the archiepiscopal trips from Canterbury to Rome is never spelt out in surviving
sources, the enthusiasm with which such a long and dangerous journey was embraced
at the southern archiepiscopal see can be linked with the interest in Rome and the
papacy detectable in various sources which originated at Canterbury in the period
under investigation.

A relevant example is provided by a section of a well-known miscellaneous manuscript of the first half of the eleventh century: London, British Library, MS Cotton
Tiberius B V, fols 2–73, 77–85. As various scholars have maintained, fols 19^v–24^r are
most likely to derive from an exemplar dating from the time of Archbishop Sigeric
(990–994), not least because they contain the only surviving copy of his itinerary,
together with various other catalogue texts displaying a special interest in Rome.[26]
As well as a list of Roman emperors (fol. 20^r), they include a catalogue of popes
in two parts; the first one, on fol. 19^v, ends with Hadrian III (884–885), while the
second (fol. 23^v) lists the popes who held the Roman see between 914 and 996. This
second list is especially interesting for a number of reasons. First of all, unlike the
earlier catalogue of popes, it provides details about the duration of their respective
pontificates, going down to days and months, as well as the office they held before
acceding to the Roman see; secondly, the first pope on the list is John X (914–928),
i.e., the one that Archbishop Wulfhelm would have met in 927, while the last one
is John XV (985–996), the pope who held the Roman see at the time of Sigeric's
journey. Most interestingly, the duration of this last pontificate is given as 'annos .iv.

---

22 Tinti, 'The Archiepiscopal Pallium'.
23 For significant exceptions see Tinti, 'The Archiepiscopal Pallium', pp. 313–16.
24 Schoenig, 'Withholding the Pallium'; see also Schoenig, *Bonds of Wool*.
25 Brooks, *The Early History of the Church of Canterbury*, pp. 239–40 and 244.
26 Dumville, 'The Catalogue Texts'. It should be noted that the list of the churches which Sigeric saw in
    Rome is followed on the same folio by a list of the localities he went through on the way back from
    Rome to the Channel, before crossing to England. The second part of his diary, which will not be
    discussed here, has traditionally attracted more attention than the Roman section because of the early
    evidence it provides for the history of the *Via Francigena*.

mensem unum et dimidium'.[27] This would in fact bring one only to the year 989 or 990 rather than the actual end of John XV's reign.[28] If Stubbs's interpretation of the word 'dimidium' as half a year rather than half a month is correct, the duration given for John XV's pontificate would cover the time up to Sigeric's visit in 990. Moreover, as the archbishop's itinerary follows immediately on from this papal chronology on the same folio, a link between these two items is most likely. It seems very probable that the detailed information on the tenth-century papacy preserved in this second catalogue was collected by Sigeric himself while in Rome.

Sigeric's list has been discussed alongside other, similarly scant, surviving catalogues of tenth-century popes by a number of scholars who have tried to reconstruct the history of the papacy through this particularly 'dark' period.[29] The relations between these various texts are not entirely clear and it is not possible to identify any direct source for Sigeric's catalogue; however, it may be significant that among all the surviving catalogues this is the only one starting with the pontificate of John X,[30] which leaves a gap of thirty years after the end of Hadrian III's pontificate, i.e., the last one to be mentioned in the earlier list contained in the same manuscript. In other words, comprehensiveness was not the intended goal for Cotton Tiberius B V. However, the fact that the catalogue should begin with John X, the pope whom Archbishop Wulfhelm met in 927, deserves further attention. As mentioned above, Wulfhelm was the first of a series of Canterbury archbishops-elect to go to Rome in person to fetch the pallium, while Sigeric was the sixth.[31] It is therefore tempting to see in this tenth-century list of popes and its relationship with Sigeric's itinerary the fruit of an initiative taken to preserve a record of papal history through a period in which successive archbishops of Canterbury enjoyed a close — and immediate — relationship with the Roman pontiffs, thanks to the journey to Rome which marked the beginning of their episcopates. Links with the papacy had been strong at Canterbury since the time of the mission sent by Gregory the Great in the late sixth century, but they had probably acquired greater tangibility by the end of the tenth century because of the new tradition which had been established in the earlier decades. The pallium represented the most eloquent symbol of an authority derived directly from Rome and the journey that every archbishop-elect since Wulfhelm would make to fetch it in person amplified its significance.[32]

---

27 The manuscript can be accessed at http://www.bl.uk/manuscripts/Viewer. aspx?ref=cotton_ms_tiberius_b_v!1_fo02r.

28 Cf. *Memorials of St Dunstan*, ed. by Stubbs, p. 391 and Pesci, 'L'itinerario romano di Sigerico', pp. 59–60.

29 Le '*Liber Pontificalis*', ed. by Duchesne (hereafter *LP*), II, pp. ix–xx; Piazzoni, 'Biografie dei papi del secolo X', p. 372.

30 *LP*, II, pp. xiii–xx.

31 See Tinti, 'The Archiepiscopal Pallium', p. 314.

32 For the relations between Canterbury and Rome throughout the Anglo-Saxon period see Brooks, 'Canterbury and Rome', and Brooks, 'Canterbury, Rome and the Construction of English Identity'. In the eleventh century the new practice of the archiepiscopal journey to Rome to fetch the pallium also resulted in liturgical developments at Canterbury. While tenth-century pontificals include prayers and rubrics which match a context in which the pallium was still being sent from Rome, later

Ecclesiastical Politics

While travelling to collect the pallium constitutes a novel element in the tenth and eleventh centuries, continuity from the earlier period can certainly be seen in the numerous trips undertaken by English ecclesiastics in times of crisis. Wilfrid of York's repeated journeys between the later seventh and early eighth century to appeal to the pope against his deprivation of the vast Northumbrian see and the confiscation of his possessions possibly represent the most dramatic Anglo-Saxon precedent, but in the later period too it is possible to witness several other bishops embarking on such a trip because of issues concerning their episcopal authority.[33] For instance, in 801–802 Æthelheard of Canterbury travelled to Rome following the crisis generated by 'the rise and fall of the archbishopric of Lichfield' (to use Thomas Noble's phrase) in order to have his authority restored over the territory that had been previously reassigned to the Lichfield province.[34]

Several of the journeys undertaken by the Anglo-Saxon bishops were planned so that they could attend the synods which had been summoned in Rome, and their missions often seem to have combined ecclesiastical business with diplomatic matters. This is particularly evident in the eleventh century, when reforming popes began to hold annual Easter synods.[35] In 1050, according to the C manuscript of the *Anglo-Saxon Chronicle*, Bishops Herman of Ramsbury and Ealdred of Worcester were in Rome on a mission for the king. Although the object of the mission is unclear, the E manuscript of the *Chronicle* specifies that they were sent so that they could participate in a 'great synod' and that they arrived on Easter Eve.[36] Possibly the most remarkable of the late Anglo-Saxon missions which also involved participation in an Easter synod is that of 1061, when a substantial party made its way to Rome. This again included Ealdred of Worcester, who had recently been appointed to the archbishopric of York, as well as Earl Tostig and his wife, the above-mentioned Judith of Flanders. The source which provides most information about this mission is the anonymous *Vita Ædwardi regis*, which also mentions the presence in Rome at the same time of two royal priests, Giso

---

manuscripts, like the mid-eleventh century Canterbury pontifical which is now Cambridge, Corpus Christi College, MS 44 (available online at https://parker.stanford.edu/parker), include innovative features such as an enthronement rite introduced by the rubric 'Ad processionem archypresulis de Roma uenienti palliumque offerenti responsum' (p. 274a). This rite was explicitly designed to provide a liturgical setting for the return of an archbishop from Rome, as the procession would take him to various parts of the cathedral, including the altar of Christ, where he had to offer the pallium by placing it on the altar before retrieving it and then wearing it. After proceeding to the chapel of the Blessed Virgin for further prayers, he was then led 'ad pontificalem cathedram' where the actual enthronement took place. Tinti, 'The Archiepiscopal Pallium', pp. 319–29.

33   The literature on Wilfrid's journeys to Rome is vast; see, most recently, Wood, 'The Continental Journeys of Wilfrid and Biscop', and Ó Carragáin and Thacker, 'Wilfrid in Rome'.

34   Noble, 'The Rise and Fall of the Archbishopric of Lichfield'.

35   Stroll, *Popes and Antipopes*, p. 46. See also di Carpegna Falconieri, 'Roma e Leone IX', pp. 328–29.

36   *The Anglo-Saxon Chronicle, vol. V: MS C*, ed. by O'Brien O'Keeffe, p. 111; *The Anglo-Saxon Chronicle, vol. VII: MS E*, ed. by Irvine, p. 80.

and Walter, who had gone all the way there to be consecrated bishops by the pope.[37] The most problematic business which the party had to deal with concerned Ealdred, who had embarked on the trip to fetch the pallium in person, as many other English archbishops-elect had done for more than a century. Things, however, were changing in Rome, and whereas transfers from one episcopal see to another had not apparently been a problem for earlier archbishops-elect, Pope Nicholas II was not prepared to allow Ealdred to get away with his irregular situation and decided to deny him the pallium. However, on its way back to England the party was attacked and robbed and had to return to Rome, where the pope, moved by compassion, agreed to grant Ealdred the pallium, on condition that he renounced Worcester.[38]

Gifts and Payments

Ecclesiastical politics was a major motivation behind the journey to Rome both in Wilfrid's and Ealdred's time. As we have seen, however, it is often difficult and probably misdirected to try to identify the single major reason which took any traveller or groups of travellers to Rome, as ecclesiastical and secular business was often intertwined with pilgrimage both in the early and the later period. The mixed nature of many such trips becomes most apparent when considering the role played by money and other forms of pious gifts. In some cases it would seem that the delivery of payments from England to Rome may have been the principal aim of a number of visits such as those recorded in the *Anglo-Saxon Chronicle* between the years 883 and 890, when the task of taking alms to Rome was entrusted to ealdormen or leading ecclesiastics.[39] The regularity of the payments at this time is confirmed by the *Chronicle* entry for the year 889, which explicitly states that alms were not sent that year. It is also interesting that payments are described in these entries as being sent not only by King Alfred but also by the West Saxon people.[40]

Alms and gifts had been an important part of many Anglo-Saxons' journeys before Alfred's time, starting with those of the kings who in the seventh and eighth centuries had gone to Rome to finish their days there.[41] One could say that in many ways all such pious donations formed part of the same sentiment of devotion to Rome, the

---

37 *The Life of King Edward*, ed. and trans. by Barlow, pp. 54–55. Giso and Walter thus avoided having to be consecrated by the irregular Stigand of Canterbury. While in Rome, Giso also secured a privilege from the pope confirming and protecting the possessions of his see (Jaffé 4457). See further Tinti, 'The Pallium Privilege of Pope Nicholas II for Archbishop Ealdred of York'.

38 *The Life of King Edward*, ed. and trans. by Barlow, pp. 52–57; Tinti, 'The Pallium Privilege of Pope Nicholas II for Archbishop Ealdred of York'. For a discussion of how the election of reforming popes such as Leo IX and Nicholas II affected the relations between England and the papacy, especially in the matter of appointments to episcopal sees, see Barlow, *The English Church 1000–1066*, pp. 301–08.

39 *Two of the Saxon Chronicles Parallel*, ed. by Plummer, pp. 31–35.

40 It would seem that during Offa of Mercia's reign payments had also been sent to Rome annually, at least for some time, as it appears to be confirmed by a letter sent by Pope Leo III to Offa's successor, King Coenwulf. See Naismith, 'Peter's Pence and Before', p. 221, and Naismith and Tinti 'The Origins of Peter's Pence'.

41 Bede, *Historia ecclesiastica*, V.7, V.19.

papacy and what both represented, even though the payments of the 880s look more routinized than those of the earlier kings who left their country for good. In the later Anglo-Saxon period the institutionalization of payments from England to Rome became firmer, especially from the mid-tenth century, when legal codes began to provide precise instructions on a tribute alternatively called *Romscot, Rompenincg* or *Romfeoh*, known in the later Middle Ages as Peter's Pence.[42] This consisted of a penny which had to be paid annually by each household by St Peter's day (29 June). It should be noted, however, that while in the ninth century and before the *Chronicle* occasionally identifies the people in charge of taking alms to Rome, that is no longer the case in later times, and the latest person known to have played such a role is Archbishop Plegmund of Canterbury, who, according to Æthelweard's *Chronicle*, took alms to Rome on behalf of King Edward the Elder and the *populus* in 908.[43] In other words, just when our sources begin to provide more prescriptive information on the gathering of the money to be sent to Rome, it ceases to be possible to identify the individuals charged with taking the payments there. One wonders whether such payments ceased to be explicitly associated with specific individuals because of the development of a more institutional approach to tributes owed to the papacy.

We do know, however, that money kept being sent from England in the later tenth and eleventh centuries, and not just because of the references to Peter's Pence in the late Anglo-Saxon law codes just discussed. Tenth-century numismatic findings are particularly telling, as several major hoards of English coins from Rome (together with further single or stray finds) date from this period.[44] The largest of these, containing more than 800 coins, is the famous Forum Hoard found during the excavations of the House of the Vestal Virgins. Its significance is not simply due to the sheer number of coins it contains but, more importantly, to the silver tags which were found with them and which name Pope Marinus II (942–946) as the intended recipient of the payment.[45] Numismatic evidence must obviously be treated with caution because it depends heavily on chance findings, but as Rory Naismith has demonstrated, in the period from *c.* 920 to *c.* 970, Anglo-Saxon coin finds in Rome are more numerous than any other coinage, including Roman and Italian ones. This is comparable to the relative ratios of coins recovered for the period *c.* 780–850, though in absolute terms the Anglo-Saxon coin finds of the later period are much more numerous. It should be stressed, however, that none of these findings, not even the Forum Hoard coins, can be directly or unequivocally related to a Peter's Pence delivery.[46] In fact, *Romfeoh* represents only one aspect of the long history of Anglo-Saxon payments to Rome.

---

42   Naismith and Tinti, *The Forum Hoard of Anglo-Saxon Coins*, pp. 38–44, and Naismith and Tinti 'The Origins of Peter's Pence'.

43   *The Chronicle of Æthelweard*, ed. by Campbell, p. 52.

44   Naismith, 'Peter's Pence and Before'.

45   Naismith and Tinti, *The Forum Hoard of Anglo-Saxon Coins*.

46   See Naismith and Tinti, *The Forum Hoard of Anglo-Saxon Coins* for a discussion of the significance of this hoard, including the possibility that it may have been taken to Rome by Bishop Theodred of London (909 × 926–951 × 953).

A significant novel element in our eleventh-century sources is the occasional unease when discussing payments due to or expected by the papacy. The most remarkable of all these is a letter of protest to the papacy against the convention of archbishops travelling to Rome to collect the pallium, which is likely to have been drafted by Archbishop Wulfstan of York (d. 1023). Although it was probably never sent, its contents are very interesting as they provide a stark contrast to the enthusiasm with which, as shown above, the practice of the journey to Rome appears to have been embraced at Canterbury. The letter's last section is particularly pertinent, as it refers to the payments required in exchange for the pallium, almost directly accusing the papacy of simony.[47] That payments were by this time being required in such a context is further confirmed in Cnut's letter of 1027. Here too reference is made to the fact that 'archbishops were so much constrained by the immense amount of money which was demanded of them when they journeyed to the apostolic seat, according to custom, to receive the pallium'.[48] Cnut states that he had complained to Pope John XIX about this practice, and that it had been agreed that it should cease. In the first decades of the eleventh century the English therefore appear to have developed a somewhat more critical attitude towards the financial burden of their relations with the papacy, something which we certainly do not see in the earlier period with reference to the gifts and money taken to Rome.

One last point which should be noted in this connection is that while evidence exists for the later period that substantial sums of money were being taken from England to Rome, there is none to suggest other types of gifts were also sent. This may simply be another aspect of the different patterns of source survival and distribution mentioned at the beginning of this chapter, since it is only because of the evidence provided by the *Liber pontificalis* for the earlier period that we know of a number of valuable objects which were sent to Rome by the English in the eighth and ninth centuries. The most interesting account of the donations made by a single English traveller to St Peter is probably that concerning the gifts of King Æthelwulf, recorded within the biography of Benedict III (855–858).[49] The list includes several golden and silver objects, including four 'gabathe saxisce de argento exaurate' (silver-gilt Saxon bowls), as well as precious liturgical vestments, but while the latter were probably purchased in Rome rather than brought from England, the four silver-gilt Saxon bowls are most likely to have been produced in England. Richard Gem has recently conducted a detailed analysis of the references to these objects which can be encountered in the *Liber pontificalis*, noting that this collection of papal biographies refers to forty-six different groups of *gabatae* of different size and shape, for a total of c. 277 objects.[50] In six out of these forty-six cases, for a total of about nineteen objects, the word *gabata* is followed by the adjective *saxisca*, indicating their English origin. These probably

---

47 Tinti, 'The Archiepiscopal Pallium', and Tinti, 'The Preservation, Transmission and Use of Papal Letters in Anglo-Saxon England'.

48 Treharne, *Living through Conquest*, p. 31; *Die Gesetze der Angelsachsen*, ed. by Liebermann, I, p. 276.

49 *LP*, II, p. 148; *The Lives of the Ninth-Century Popes*, trans. by Davis, pp. 186–87.

50 Gem, 'Gabatae Saxiscae'.

represent gifts obtained from English travellers which the popes then proceeded to redistribute to various Roman churches. The objects in question are most likely to have been bowls used as lamp fittings or ornaments placed in the vicinity of altars. As Gem has noted, it is probable that their patterned decoration distinguished the Saxon (i.e., English) bowls from the others also mentioned in the *Liber pontificalis*. This is extremely interesting because it points towards a clear awareness of the English presence in Rome in the earlier period thanks to a number of objects which could be found in the most sacred areas of several Roman churches. For the tenth and eleventh centuries, however, available sources do not permit identification of the presence in Rome of objects of English origin. Pious gifts and payments, whether entirely voluntary or actively solicited, kept arriving from England, as we have seen above, but by this point they seem to have consisted almost entirely of money, or, if they also included valuable objects, these did not make their way into either surviving written texts or the archaeological record.[51]

Penance

As has been reiterated throughout this chapter, every Anglo-Saxon journey to Rome was likely to entail some aspects of a pious pilgrimage within which offerings and payments played an important role; however, it should also be noted that over the tenth and eleventh centuries it is possible to identify the development of a specific type of pilgrimage to Rome, namely that of very serious sinners. Evidence for this is provided by various sources, including the *Liber Eliensis*, which refers to an early eleventh-century episode when a thegn named Leofwine, after having killed his mother, was advised by 'priests and wise men' to go to Rome and seek penance from the pope.[52] Surviving late tenth- and early eleventh-century correspondence, including letters of introduction drawn up by English bishops for departing penitents and papal letters assigning penance, similarly indicates that such journeys were prescribed for people who had committed particularly heinous crimes, such as the killing of a cousin, brother, father, or even a child. These sinners would have gone to Rome to receive their penance directly from the pope.[53] The correspondence survives in various manuscripts of Archbishop Wulfstan's so-called commonplace book, and it is likely that Wulfstan was the initiator of the collection at a time, during King Æthelred's reign, when penance

---

51   However, though not concerning Rome directly, it may be worth noting that Eadmer of Canterbury refers to the bishop of Benevento as the recipient of an opulent vestment from Cnut and Emma in return for a relic of St Bartholomew: Eadmer, *Historia novorum in Anglia*, ed. by Rule, pp. 107–08.

52   *Liber Eliensis*, ed. by Blake, II. 60. See Cubitt, 'Individual and Collective Sinning', pp. 61–62.

53   Aronstam, 'Penitential Pilgrimages to Rome'; Tinti, 'The Preservation, Transmission and Use of Papal Letters in Anglo-Saxon England'. As mentioned above, King Cnut's journey to Rome also had an important penitential dimension as he himself made clear in the letter that he wrote to his subjects in 1027: 'I make it known to you that I have recently gone to Rome and have prayed for the redemption of my sins and for the salvation of the kingdoms whose people are subject to my rule': Treharne, *Living through Conquest*, p. 30. Cnut had apparently also committed a serious crime by ordering the killing of his brother-in-law Úlfr Þorgilsson, and the penitential nature of his pilgrimage might be understood in this context. See Bolton, *The Empire of Cnut the Great*, pp. 219, 237.

was being promoted on a national scale.[54] It would seem that evidence for penitential pilgrimage to Rome in this period is more ample for England than it is for Continental regions and, perhaps more significantly, that the English Church encouraged such a practice without fearing a possible reduction of local episcopal jurisdiction, something about which Continental bishops were apparently more anxious.[55]

Where?

The one obvious reference for anyone interested in identifying the sites that the English travellers would have visited while in Rome in the tenth or eleventh century is the above-mentioned Roman itinerary of Archbishop Sigeric. It should be borne in mind, however, that the archbishop's activities were not necessarily replicated by the other late Anglo-Saxon visitors to Rome. We do not know, for instance, whether seventy years later Earl Tostig and his wife would have embarked on a similar tour of major churches and holy sites, or what less prominent and probably less wealthy lay visitors, such as the above-mentioned Siflæd or Wiohstan, would have done after reaching Rome. As will emerge further below, the archbishop's experience was entirely focused on churches, and even involved a lunch with the pope at the Lateran. Sigeric's diary, however, remains the most important source for any study of the English presence in Rome in the later Anglo-Saxon period and for this reason, even though it has already been examined by numerous scholars, it will be drawn upon in what follows in order to compare the archbishop's itinerary with what is known about the sites visited by earlier English pilgrims.

St Peter's on the Vatican

The Petrine focus of the English pilgrimage to Rome, already clearly established by the late seventh century, was also at the heart of later Anglo-Saxon pilgrims' experiences. As Alan Thacker has noted, the biographers of Boniface, Willibald, and Wynnebald specify that these pilgrims went directly to St Peter's when arriving in Rome and indicate that they spent a lot of time at the Vatican.[56] Sigeric's itinerary shows continuity in this respect as he is said to have first gone 'ad limitem beati Petri apostoli'.[57] One would obviously like to know what in particular Sigeric paused to observe within the Basilica and more generally in the Vatican complex, as well as all the other sites he visited; such information however is not provided by the itinerary.[58] In fact, if its contents are to be taken at face value, Sigeric visited twenty-three sites in

---

54 Cubitt, 'The Politics of Remorse' and Cubitt, 'Individual and Collective Sinning'.
55 Aronstam, 'Penitential Pilgrimages to Rome', p. 69.
56 Thacker, 'Rome: The Pilgrims' City', p. 127.
57 For a transcription of Sigeric's diary see Ortenberg, 'Archbishop Sigeric's Journey', pp. 199–200.
58 For a useful discussion of what Sigeric could have seen in the old Basilica of St Peter as well as the other churches he visited in Rome, see Ortenberg, 'Archbishop Sigeric's Journey', pp. 210–25. On Old St Peter's see most recently the essays in *Old St Peter's, Rome*, ed. by McKitterick, Osborne, Richardson, and Story.

two days, or, possibly, two and a half days, thus probably leaving little time to linger around each of the churches mentioned.[59] In any case, the archbishop would have had to go back to St Peter's to collect his pallium, a ceremony which is unlikely to have taken place on his first visit to the Basilica, as Pope John XV would have had to have been informed of Sigeric's arrival.[60] The ceremony would have resembled closely another one which had occurred thirty years earlier and which was described in Dunstan's Pontifical (Paris, Bibliothèque nationale de France, MS fonds latin 943, fol. 7ʳ).[61] The rite took place at the altar of St Peter, which stood above the Petrine shrine that had been redesigned by Gregory the Great. The rubric that in the Pontifical introduces the letter of privilege through which Pope John XII (955–964) granted Dunstan the pallium in 960 specifies that he did not receive it from the hands of the pope, but took the pallium directly from the altar, thus emphasizing the significance of his archiepiscopal authority, which derived directly from St Peter.[62]

The schola Saxonum/Anglorum

From St Peter's Sigeric moved 'ad sanctam Mariam scolam Anglorum'. This is the church which, following the fire of 847, had been built or rebuilt by Leo IV 'supra schola Saxonum'.[63] The origin, nature, and purpose of the *schola Saxonum*, like those of the other *scholae peregrinorum* (of the Franks, Lombards, and Frisians), which were situated near the Vatican Basilica and were particularly active in the eighth and ninth centuries, cannot be identified with certainty, though it is clear that one of their main functions was to provide assistance and hospitality to visiting fellow countrymen.[64] This is where Sigeric is most likely to have resided while in Rome in 990, as can be inferred from the position of the passage in his itinerary which refers to his going back home ('deinde reuersi sunt in domum') after visiting the church

---

59 Ortenberg, 'Archbishop's Sigeric Journey to Rome', pp. 207–08. At one point the itinerary mentions that Sigeric and his companions went home at the end of the day ('reuersi sunt in domum'), a piece of information which is then followed by what they did on the following day ('Mane ad sanctam Mariam rotunda'). An extra half day can be deduced bearing in mind that after visiting St Peter's at their arrival, they went 'ad sanctam Mariam scola Anglorum', where they could have then stopped to spend the night. For a sceptical view on such a short duration for Sigeric's visit see Pesci, 'L'itinerario romano di Sigerico', pp. 50–51, 56.

60 The itinerary also mentions a lunch that Sigeric and the pope had together at the Lateran after the archbishop had visited S. Giovanni. At this meeting they could have also arranged a date and time for the pallium ceremony. It should be noted, however, that in the case of Archbishop Æthelnoth, who went to Rome in 1022, the D version of the *Chronicle* says that Æthelnoth feasted with the pope after receiving the pallium. See Tinti, 'The Archiepiscopal Pallium', pp. 320–21.

61 The manuscript is available online at http://gallica.bnf.fr/ark:/12148/btv1b6001165p.

62 Tinti, 'England and the Papacy', pp. 171–72.

63 *LP*, II, p. 128; *The Lives of the Ninth-Century Popes*, trans. by Davis, p. 148: 'over the Schola Saxonum'.

64 The literature on the *scholae peregrinorum* is vast; see, most recently, Stocchi, 'San Michele dei Frisoni', Santangeli Valenzani, 'Hosting Foreigners in Early Medieval Rome', and Ermini Pani, 'Per un organico funzionamento della corte papale'.

of San Pancrazio at the end of a long day of sightseeing.[65] If there was continuity in the provision of hospitality and assistance, the same cannot be said for the military function that the *scholae* had performed in the earlier period, and which still applied in 846 when, according to the *Liber pontificalis*, they were sent to Portus to defend the city against the Saracens.[66] No hint of any military role can be found in tenth- and eleventh-century sources, though of course, if the *Liber pontificalis* had not stopped being compiled in the late ninth century, we might have known more. As Riccardo Santangeli Valenzani and others have recently observed, it is important to bear in mind that the term *schola* could encompass a number of different meanings, as it indicated both the institution and the people who resided there, as well as the physical buildings.[67]

While the entry in Sigeric's itinerary does not say much about the nature and function of the *schola* in the late tenth century, it does signal a significant change in the ethnic description of those who resided there: instead of *Saxones*, they are now called *Angli*. At first sight, this may seem to be a Roman confirmation of the developments in the ethnic labelling of the Anglo-Saxons that can be observed in England in the period between the ninth and the tenth century; these have been explained as the ultimate result of King Alfred's military, political, cultural, and linguistic achievements, which led to the making of *Angelcynn*.[68] However, it is important to bear in mind that the words 'scolam Anglorum' appear in the report of a late tenth-century archbishop of Canterbury, which survives in a slightly later English manuscript, rather than in a strictly Roman source. In other words, we do not have evidence indicating that in the late tenth century the Romans would have defined the English quarter in the city as *schola Anglorum*. In fact, a 955 bull of Pope Agapetus II refers to this area as the location of a water mill on the River Tiber by using the traditional label *schola Saxonum*.[69] The impression is that although in Rome too the English came progressively to be called *Angli*, rather than *Saxones*, which previously had been the most commonly used term, the area in the city with which they were associated continued to be referred to through labels which retained the 'Saxon' element. This is what emerges from a bull of Leo IX for the canons residing at the monastery of St Martin at the Vatican, dated 1053. The bull casts light on several different aspects of the status of the *scholae peregrinorum* in the mid-eleventh century and, while dealing with the English *schola*'s right to bury those who got ill and died

---

65 The church of San Pancrazio, like the *schola Saxonum/Anglorum*, stood on the west side of the River Tiber and was the last one to be visited by Sigeric after a long clockwise tour around Rome. On the following morning ('mane'), he went to the Pantheon, the church which would have been closest, among those he visited, to his base at the *schola*. See Ortenberg, 'Archbishop's Sigeric Journey to Rome', p. 199, and below, the section on intramural churches.

66 Ermini Pani, 'Per un organico funzionamento della corte papale', pp. 286–91.

67 Santangeli Valenzani, 'Hosting Foreigners in Early Medieval Rome', p. 79; Ermini Pani, 'Per un organico funzionamento della corte papale', pp. 283–84.

68 Wormald, '*Engla Lond*'; Foot, 'The Making of *Angelcynn*'; Brooks, 'English Identity from Bede to the Millennium'. See also Keynes, 'Alfred the Great and the Kingdom of the Anglo-Saxons'.

69 Jaffé 2816; Moore, *The Saxon Pilgrims to Rome*, p. 96, n. 1: 'etiam confirmamus vobis aquimolum molentem unum in integrum in fluvium Tyberis justa Schola Saxonum positum'.

there, it uses the words 'Anglos venientes de Anglia qui, si in scola Saxie infirmantur et ibi moriuntur, ibi sepelliantur'.[70]

In England, by contrast, it would have probably made less sense to keep referring to the site in this way, as is confirmed by a passage of the eleventh-century *Life* of St Kenelm referring to a dove's miraculous delivery to the altar of St Peter's of a letter inscribed with golden letters in English. The pope, who was celebrating Mass, looked at the strange sheet written with 'ignotis uerbis ac litteris' and asked the people of various nations who came flocking to St Peter's whether anyone could understand the text. There were, of course, English people among them and these are said to have been 'either staying at the *Anglica scola* in Rome [...], or just recently arrived from England'.[71] The *Life* places this event in the early ninth century, but the words used to refer to the English quarter in Rome reflects what its likely author, Goscelin of St-Bertin, would have called the institution in the second half of the eleventh century rather than early ninth-century usage. It is also interesting that the text should refer to the *scola* as functioning both as a colony of permanent residents and as a hostel for English visitors, thus confirming continuity with what we know for the earlier period.[72] Goscelin is not known to have ever been in Rome but, as we have seen, his patron, Bishop Herman of Ramsbury and Sherborne, was there in 1050 and may have been the source of this information about the existence and functions of the *Anglica scola*. Whether translation and interpretation were also included among such functions, as the *Life* would seem to suggest, is impossible to determine, but as linguistic difficulties were already experienced by Boniface in his meetings with Pope Gregory II in 722, one should certainly account for the possibility that those who resided permanently at the English *scola* may have acted as interpreters for prominent visitors.[73]

Burial, an aspect of the *schola Saxonum*'s functions already touched upon, is a further area in which continuity between the earlier and later periods can be identified. As mentioned above, Leo IX's bull of 1053 says explicitly that the English residents or visitors who died while at the *schola* could be buried within its limits.[74] As Wilfrid J. Moore noted, this seems to have already been the case in the second

---

70 Jaffé 3260; Schiaparelli, 'Le carte antiche dell'archivio capitolare di San Pietro', no. 16, p. 469. On the substantial authenticity of this privilege see Stocchi, 'San Michele dei Frisoni', pp. 17–20, and di Carpegna Falconieri, 'Roma e Leone IX', pp. 333–34. Cf. Johrendt, 'Die Anfänge des Kapitels von St Peter im Vatikan?'. The word *Saxia* used in this document has survived to this day in the Italian name of the hospital and church of Santo Spirito in Sassia, which can be found on the site of the early medieval *schola Saxonum*. It would seem, in other words, that the name of the *schola*, which originally referred to the ethnicity of those who resided there, crystallized as a place-name, preserving the root of its original designation.

71 *Three Eleventh-Century Anglo-Latin Lives*, ed. and trans. by Love, pp. 64–67.

72 Ermini Pani, 'Per un organico funzionamento della corte papale', pp. 284–86.

73 On Boniface and Gregory II see Wright, *A Sociophilological Study of Late Latin*, pp. 95–109.

74 This is an exception that the English appear to have negotiated with the church of S. Salvatore, where all pilgrims and strangers who died in Rome and its vicinity were supposed to be buried. See Birch, *Pilgrimage to Rome in the Middle Ages*, p. 146, and, more recently, Stocchi, 'San Michele dei Frisoni', pp. 17–18.

half of the ninth century, when Burgred of Mercia fled to Rome, died there and was buried 'in Schola Saxonum in ecclesia Sanctae Mariae', as attested by Asser's *Life of Alfred*.[75] However, the information that the bull of Leo IX provides about the *scholae peregrinorum* in the mid-eleventh century also indicates that by this time they had lost some of the autonomy that they had probably enjoyed earlier on.[76] Among other things, it establishes the pope's involvement ('consilio nostro') in the ordination of the *archipresbiter* of the 'ecclesia Sancte Dei genitricis virginis Marie que vocatur scola Saxonum', while the ordination of the other priests and *scholenses* was left in the hands of the canons of the Vatican Basilica residing in the monastery of St Martin, which seems to have exercised some sort of jurisdiction over the four *scholae peregrinorum* since the time of Leo IV (790–855).[77] By the mid-eleventh century, the church of St Mary was therefore served by a number of clerics headed by an archpriest; we do not know how large this group was, but it included further priests as well as *scholenses*, a word which in this context would seem to indicate clerics in lower orders. The provision of burial in the cemetery of the *schola* for English people who happened to die there would seem to have been one of their major responsibilities.[78]

Extramural Churches

Going back to Sigeric's tour, it would seem that on his first full day of sightseeing, his main focus was on the extramural churches, which he visited following a clockwise route.[79] This first day's pronounced interest in the extramural sites can perhaps be related to surviving mid-seventh-century itineraries of Rome, which were especially focused on the burial places of the early martyrs.[80] The clockwise direction of Sigeric's tour is also present in one such itinerary, the so-called *Notitia ecclesiarum urbis Romae*,

---

75 Moore, *The Saxon Pilgrims to Rome*, p. 111. Incidentally, it is interesting to note that Asser's Latin text (*Asser's Life of King Alfred*, ed. by Stevenson, c. 46, p. 35) seems likely to echo traditional Roman usage, whereas the *Anglo-Saxon Chronicle*, on which Asser's account is based, describes the same event *s.a.* 874 through the words 'on sancta Marian cyrican on Angelcynnes scole': *Two of the Saxon Chronicles Parallel*, ed. by Plummer, pp. 24–25. On Asser's thinking of Alfred's subjects and their language as 'Saxon', see Brooks, 'English Identity from Bede to the Millennium', p. 47.

76 Santangeli Valenzani, 'Hosting Foreigners in Early Medieval Rome', p. 85.

77 'in hac tamen ecclesia ordinatio archipresbyteri consilio nostro fiat; aliorum vero presbyterorum, atque scholensium per vos fiat absque omni venalitate'. Schiaparelli, 'Le carte antiche dell'archivio capitolare di San Pietro', no. 16, p. 470. For the partially extant text of a bull of Leo IV of 854 granting various properties to the monastery of St Martin including the 'ecclesia Sanctae Dei genitricis virginis Marie que vocatur scola Saxonum', see Jaffé 1990 and Schiaparelli, 'Le carte antiche dell'archivio capitolare di San Pietro', no. 2, p. 433. Schiaparelli believed the phrase used to describe the church of St Mary in the later bull was lifted directly from the document of Leo IV. The earlier text also refers to the 'ecclesia Sancti Salvatoris nostri ad sepeliendos omnes peregrinos'; see Birch, *Pilgrimage to Rome in the Middle Ages*, p. 144. For a recent analysis of Leo IV's bull tentatively confirming its substantial authenticity, see Stocchi, 'San Michele dei Frisoni', pp. 13–17.

78 Stocchi, San Michele dei Frisoni', p. 10.

79 Ortenberg, 'Archbishop Sigeric's Journey', pp. 208–21, with a useful map at p. 209.

80 Thacker, 'Rome: The Pilgrims' City', p. 119.

which mentions all the extramural churches visited by the archbishop, with the exception of S. Anastasio.[81] This does appear, however, in another seventh-century itinerary known as *De locis sanctis martyrum quae sunt foris civitatis Romae*, as well as in the somewhat later one which William of Malmesbury included in his *Gesta regum Anglorum*.[82] This last itinerary, of English provenance, is especially interesting because it is the only one to share two features with Sigeric's list, namely, the clockwise direction of his first day's tour and the inclusion of all the extramural churches visited by the archbishop.[83] This is not to suggest that Sigeric would have used the Malmesbury itinerary or any of the other earlier ones while in Rome; in fact, he would not have found them particularly useful, given the amount of information they provide on the catacombs and cemeteries which were the highlights of the pilgrims' city in the seventh century, but which by Sigeric's time had long ceased to attract visitors. It can be maintained, however, that the archbishop's choices and organization of his tour may preserve traces of the earlier pilgrims' experience as reflected in the surviving itineraries, especially that of Malmesbury. For some of the extramural churches which Sigeric visited, Alan Thacker has presented further evidence confirming that they were clearly also known to earlier Anglo-Saxons, as is the case, for instance, with the major basilicas of S. Lorenzo and S. Paolo fuori le mura.[84] Although the others, S. Valentino, S. Agnese, S. Sebastiano and S. Pancrazio, cannot be directly linked to any known earlier Anglo-Saxon pilgrim, their fame as opulent suburban basilicas, as well as the fact that they all appear in the Malmesbury itinerary, make it very likely that they had also attracted the English pilgrims who preceded Sigeric on the way to Rome.

Intramural Churches

On his first full day, however, Sigeric did not see just extramural churches. He started off with a visit 'ad sanctum Laurentium in craticula' (S. Lorenzo in Lucina), the first of the three Roman churches dedicated to St Laurence which the archbishop would visit.[85] From there he moved north beyond the walls to S. Valentino and proceeded clockwise to visit various suburban churches until he reached S. Paolo on the Via Ostiense. Then, he went back north into the city and up the Aventine to the churches of S. Sabina and S. Bonifacio, before going down on the other side of the hill 'ad sanctam Mariam scolam grecam' (the predecessor of S. Maria in Cosmedin), crossing the Tiber to reach S. Cecilia, S. Crisogono and S. Maria in Trastevere. He

---

81 *Codice topografico*, ed. by Valentini and Zucchetti, II (1942), pp. 72–99. For a discussion of S. Anastasio as the possible site of the monastery where Theodore of Tarsus lived while in Rome, see Ferrari, *Early Roman Monasteries*, pp. 33–48.

82 *Codice topografico*, ed. by Valentini and Zucchetti, II (1942), pp. 106–31, 141–53.

83 For the suggestion that the Malmesbury itinerary may have found its way to England in the late 680s through Aldhelm, another famous early English pilgrim to Rome, see Lapidge, 'The Career of Aldhelm', p. 57.

84 Thacker, 'Rome: The Pilgrims' City', pp. 128–29.

85 Ortenberg, 'Archbishop's Sigeric Journey to Rome', pp. 212–25. On the importance of the cult of St Laurence for the earlier English pilgrims see Thacker, 'Rome: The Pilgrims' City', p. 129.

then proceeded further west to S. Pancrazio before finally going back home. On the following day he went straight into the city 'ad sanctam Mariam rotundam' (i.e., the Pantheon) and to SS. Apostoli. From there he headed south-east to reach the Lateran, visit the Basilica of S. Giovanni and have lunch with the pope. Only in the afternoon could he resume his tour by going first to the nearby S. Croce in Gerusalemme, then S. Maria Maggiore, S. Pietro in Vincoli and the church now known as S. Lorenzo in Panisperna ('ubi corpus eius assatus fuit').

Most of these intramural churches are listed in an unfinished catalogue, headed 'ISTAE VERO ECCLESIAE INTVS ROMAE HABENTVR', which is appended to the seventh-century *De locis sanctis* itinerary in all three manuscripts in which they have both been preserved.[86] Moreover, nearly all of them also appear in another itinerary surviving in a ninth- or tenth-century manuscript kept in the monastery of Einsiedeln (Switzerland).[87] Composed towards the end of the eighth century, the Einsiedeln itinerary guided visitors through the main roads which crossed the city. The churches which Sigeric visited within the city can therefore also be interpreted in terms of continuity with past pilgrims' routes; however, unlike the Einsiedeln itinerary, which aimed at describing all the main features of the route, identifying sights to the pilgrim's left and right, Sigeric's diary names just churches, the only targets of his tour, even though he would obviously have seen much else when going from one religious site to the next. Moreover, his religious and devotional interests emerge clearly from the fact that, unlike the Einsiedeln text, his diary never fails to name the churches' dedicatees. For instance, while the earlier itinerary simply refers to *Rotunda*, Sigeric has *sancta Maria rotunda*, and, similarly, where that says *ecclesia Graecorum*, Sigeric has *sancta Maria scola greca*.[88]

It is important to bear in mind that, as Veronica Ortenberg has noted, Sigeric's itinerary is the result of selection, given the wide number of churches which were extant in late tenth-century Rome.[89] His preferred route may have been determined by various factors, including plans made before leaving England, based on his knowledge of the sites previous pilgrims to Rome, such as the former archbishops of Canterbury, had visited. Such intentions may have obviously been modified when he reached the city because of the advice received at the English *schola* or from other people he may have met during his sojourn. Visits by Sigeric to intramural churches which point towards continuity with previous English experiences of Rome include S. Maria Maggiore, S. Pietro in Vincoli and S. Maria in Trastevere.[90] Marian churches in general appear

---

86 *Codice topografico*, ed. by Valentini and Zucchetti, II (1942), pp. 118–31.

87 *Codice topografico*, ed. by Valentini and Zucchetti, II (1942), pp. 155–207. The only exceptions are the churches on the Aventine which are not explicitly named in the Einsiedeln itinerary, though it does refer to the Aventine. The church of S. Bonifacio is mentioned in the list of intramural churches appended to the *De locis sanctis*.

88 Cf. *Codice topografico*, ed. by Valentini and Zucchetti, II (1942), pp. 171, 181, and Ortenberg, 'Archbishop's Sigeric Journey to Rome', p. 199.

89 Ortenberg, 'Archbishop's Sigeric Journey to Rome', p. 201.

90 Thacker, 'Rome: The Pilgrims' City', p. 129. For S. Maria Maggiore see also Colgrave, 'Pilgrimages to Rome', p. 165, and Lapidge, 'The Career of Aldhelm', pp. 54–62.

to have impressed both Benedict Biscop and Wilfrid, and the various sites associated with St Laurence which Sigeric visited can also be interpreted in the light of earlier Anglo-Saxon tradition of Laurentian devotion.[91] Perhaps more surprising is Sigeric's choice to ascend the Aventine to visit the churches of S. Sabina and S. Bonifacio, as these cannot be associated with any known earlier English visitors, although it ought to be noted that the latter church is mentioned in both the catalogue appended to the *De locis sanctis* and the Malmesbury itinerary.

Conclusions

In many respects the evidence for the presence of the English in Rome in the tenth and eleventh centuries attests to significant continuities with the earlier period. Anglo-Saxon pilgrims were still flocking to Rome to reach the thresholds of the Apostles and many of the cult sites that constituted the main attractions in the earlier period were also visited later on. Leading ecclesiastics also continued to go to Rome when the papacy's involvement was required to solve delicate issues of episcopal authority. At the same time, however, pilgrimage, piety, and politics developed in new ways. Some of the changes were the result of developments in Rome itself. The powerful attraction of the catacombs to pilgrims, including English ones, who left a noticeable amount of graffiti on their walls, was weakened considerably when the popes of the second half of the eighth century encouraged the translation of saints' relics from the suburban cemeteries to the city's intramural churches, though the major extramural basilicas continued to attract later visitors such as Sigeric. Moreover, the acquisition of Roman relics, which was one of the major aims of early Anglo-Saxon visitors such as Biscop and Wilfrid, no longer featured among the main goals of the later English pilgrims.[92] It must be borne in mind that by this time the movement of relics in Rome was not as active as it had been in previous centuries, and that efforts to acquire relics were normally more typical of regions where ecclesiastical organization was still nascent, which was no longer the case in late Anglo-Saxon England.[93]

The transcription of the *tituli* or inscriptions which could be found at several major Roman Christian sites also occupied a number of learned English visitors, such as Aldhelm, in the earlier period, but active English interest in Roman *syllogae* does not seem to have continued later on.[94] One wonders, however, whether the detailed text on the succession of tenth-century popes which Sigeric most likely brought back from

---

91 Thacker, 'Loca sanctorum', p. 39; Cubitt, 'Universal and Local Saints', p. 444.
92 Exceptions include Archbishop Plegmund of Canterbury who, by the time of Gervase of Canterbury (d. c. 1210), was believed to have returned from Rome in 908 with relics of St Blaise. Ælfstan, abbot of St Augustine's, Canterbury also brought back relics from Rome in 1022, which he gave to his monastery. See Ortenberg, The English Church, p. 161.
93 Smith, 'Care of Relics in Early Medieval Rome', pp. 183, 187; Smith, 'Old Saints, New Cults', pp. 320–21; Costambeys, 'Alcuin, Rome and Charlemagne's Imperial Coronation', pp. 261–64.
94 Cf. Sims-Williams, 'Milred of Worcester's Collection'; Orchard, The Poetic Art of Aldhelm, pp. 203–12; Lapidge, 'The Career of Aldhelm', pp. 52–62; Thacker, 'Rome: The Pilgrims' City', pp. 100, 103, 125, 127.

Rome, and which is now preserved with his diary in Cotton Tiberius B V, fol. 23ᵛ, could be a parallel to the earlier interest in *syllogae*. Of course, there are limits to the extent to which one can compare such collections with a specific event like Sigeric's putative copying of the information on tenth-century papal succession.[95] It can be noted, however, that the copying of inscriptions and the written collection of local knowledge were both activities that learned visitors could perform while in Rome, either through access to monumental inscriptions or manuscripts or encounters with informed sources. In both cases, they attest to literacy as the means through which such visitors could bring back with them valued information about Christian Rome.

As we have seen, continuity can also be observed in the area of ecclesiastical politics. However, here too novel elements have been identified. The journeys of the archbishops-elect to collect the pallium probably represent the most remarkable innovation of the later period, though the enthusiasm with which the practice appears to have been embraced at Canterbury can be contrasted with the irregularity with which such trips seem to have been undertaken by contemporary incumbents at the northern archiepiscopal see of York. More importantly, the so-called letter of protest to the papacy regarding the very practice of the journey to Rome to collect the pallium, probably drafted by Archbishop Wulfstan of York, reveals criticisms absent from earlier English sources dealing with Rome. The letter's tone becomes particularly harsh in its final section, which deals with the payments seemingly expected by the popes in exchange for the pallium; similar complaints are reiterated, though in milder terms, in Cnut's letter of 1027. Ultimately, a telling contrast comes to light: on one side, some of the most significant novelties among the reasons which took the English to Rome in the tenth and eleventh centuries emerged from a specifically English context, as is the case both with the trip to fetch the pallium and the role assigned to the pope in determining the penance for serious sinners; on the other side, late Anglo-Saxon sources indicate that the English attitude towards the papacy could also be far from deferential. At the very end of our period, especially in the time of Leo IX and Nicholas II, further new elements in the relations with the English were introduced by the papacy; these would affect their experiences in the city in various ways. As we have seen, the initially disastrous results of the mission of 1061 offer an illuminating example of the ways in which the reforming popes could use the grant of the archiepiscopal pallium as a means to ensure proper canonical observance in episcopal elections.[96] Moreover, the bull of Leo IX of 1053 indicates direct papal control of the institution which represented the most tangible sign of the presence of the English in Rome, that is, the *schola Saxonum*. Many of the latter's principal functions, such as hospitality and burial, were still being performed, but against a background of more active papal involvement.

---

95 On Sigeric's and other catalogues of tenth-century popes see above n. 29. For an example of a tenth-century author combining information gathered from various texts with that provided by inscriptions such as the papal tombs' epitaphs which he had seen in Rome, see Duchesne's discussion of Flodoard of Reims's poem *De triumphis Christi apud Italiam* in *LP*, II, pp. ix–xi. On Flodoard's sources see also Roberts, *Flodoard of Rheims and the Writing of History in the Tenth Century*, pp. 145–87.

96 Schoenig, 'Withholding the Pallium'.

Abbreviations

S P. H. Sawyer, *Anglo-Saxon Charters: An Annotated List and Bibliography*, Royal Historical Society Guides and Handbooks, 5 (London: Royal Historical Society, 1968) (cited by charter number) (available in an electronic and updated form at https://esawyer.lib.cam.ac.uk/)

Jaffé Philipp Jaffé, *Regesta pontificum Romanorum ab condita ecclesia ad annum post Christum natum MCXCVIII*, 2nd edn, 2 vols (Leipzig: Veit, 1885–1888; repr. Graz: Akademische Druck- u. Verlagsanstalt, 1956)

LP *Le 'Liber Pontificalis': texte, introduction et commentaire*, ed. by Louis Duchesne, 2nd edn, 3 vols (Paris: Boccard, 1955–1957)

Works Cited

Manuscripts and Archival Sources

Cambridge, Corpus Christi College, MS 44
London, British Library, MS Cotton Tiberius B V

Primary Sources

Alfred the Great: Asser's Life of Alfred and Other Contemporary Sources, trans. with an introduction and notes by Simon Keynes and Michael Lapidge (Harmondsworth: Penguin, 1983)

The Anglo-Saxon Chronicle: A Collaborative Edition, vol. v: MS C, ed. by Katherine O'Brien O'Keeffe (Cambridge: Brewer, 2001)

The Anglo-Saxon Chronicle: A Collaborative Edition, vol. vi: MS D, ed. by G. P. Cubbin (Cambridge: Brewer, 1996)

The Anglo-Saxon Chronicle: A Collaborative Edition, vol. vii: MS E, ed. by Susan Irvine (Cambridge: Brewer, 2004)

The Anglo-Saxon Chronicle: A Collaborative Edition, vol. viii: MS F, ed. by Peter S. Baker (Cambridge: Brewer, 2000)

Anglo-Saxon Wills, ed. and trans. by Dorothy Whitelock (Cambridge: Cambridge University Press, 1930)

Les Annales de Flodoard, ed. by Philippe Lauer, Collection de textes pour servir à l'étude et à l'enseignement de l'histoire, 39 (Paris: Alphonse Picard, 1905)

Asser's Life of King Alfred, together with the Annals of St Neots, erroneously ascribed to Asser, ed. by William Henry Stevenson (Oxford: Clarendon Press, 1959)

Bede, *Historia ecclesiastica gentis Anglorum*, ed. and trans. by Bertam Colgrave and R. A. B. Mynors (Oxford: Clarendon Press, 1969)

Charters of St Augustine's Abbey, Canterbury and Minster-in-Thanet, ed. by S. E. Kelly, Anglo-Saxon Charters, 4 (Oxford: Oxford University Press, 1995)

Charters of Selsey, ed. by S. E. Kelly, Anglo-Saxon Charters, 6 (Oxford: Oxford University Press, 1998)

The Chronicle of Æthelweard, ed. by Alistair Campbell (London: Nelson, 1962)

Codice topografico della città di Roma, ed. by Roberto Valentini and Giuseppe Zucchetti, Fonti per la storia d'Italia, 81, 88, 90, 91, 4 vols (Rome: R. Istituto Storico Italiano per il medio evo, 1940–1953)

Eadmer, *Historia novorum in Anglia*, ed. by Martin Rule, Rolls Series 81 (London: Longman, 1884; repr. Cambridge: Cambridge University Press, 2012)

English Historical Documents, i: *c. 500–1042*, ed. by Dorothy Whitelock, 2nd edn (London: Eyre Methuen, 1979)

Flodoard of Reims, *De triumphis Christi apud Italiam*, in *Patrologiae cursus completus: series latina*, ed. by Jacque-Paul Migne, 221 vols (Paris: Migne, 1844–1864), 135 (1853), cols 491–886

Die Gesetze der Angelsachsen, ed. by Felix Liebermann, 3 vols (Halle: Max Niemeyer, 1903–1916)

Goscelin, *Historia translationis S. Augustini* in *Patrologiae cursus completus: series latina*, ed. by Jacque-Paul Migne, 221 vols (Paris: Migne, 1844–1864), 155 (1854), cols 13–46

Liber Eliensis, ed. by Ernest O. Blake, Camden Series, third ser., 92 (London: Royal Historical Society, 1962)

The Life of King Edward Who Rests at Westminster, ed. and trans. by Frank Barlow, 2nd edn (Oxford: Clarendon Press, 1992)

The Lives of the Ninth-Century Popes (Liber Pontificalis): The Ancient Biographies of the Popes from AD 817–91, trans. by Raymond Davis, Translated Texts for Historians, 20 (Liverpool: Liverpool University Press, 1995)

Memorials of St Dunstan, Archbishop of Canterbury, ed. by William Stubbs, Rolls Series, 63 (London: Longman, 1874, repr. Wiesbaden: Kraus, 1965)

Three Eleventh-Century Anglo-Latin Lives: Vita S. Birini, Vita et miracula S. Kenelmi, and Vita S. Rumwoldi, ed. and trans. by Rosalind Love, Oxford Medieval Texts (Oxford: Clarendon Press, 1996)

Two of the Saxon Chronicles Parallel (787–1001 A.D.), ed. by Charles Plummer (Oxford: Clarendon Press, 1889)

Secondary Studies

Aronstam, Robin Ann, 'Penitential Pilgrimages to Rome in the Early Middle Ages', *Archivum Historiae Pontificiae*, 13 (1975), 65–83

Barlow, Frank, *The English Church 1000–1066: A History of the Later Anglo-Saxon Church*, 2nd edn (London: Longman, 1979)

Birch, Debra J., *Pilgrimage to Rome in the Middle Ages*, Studies in the History of Medieval Religion, 13 (Woodbridge: Boydell, 1998)

Bolton, Timothy, *The Empire of Cnut the Great: Conquest and the Consolidation of Power in Northern Europe in the Early Eleventh Century*, The Northern World, 40 (Leiden: Brill, 2009)

Brooks, Nicholas, *The Early History of the Church of Canterbury: Christ Church from 597 to 1066* (London: Leicester University Press, 1984)

————, 'Canterbury, Rome and the Construction of English Identity', in *Early Medieval Rome and the Christian West: Essays in Honour of Donald A. Bullough*, ed. by Julia M. H. Smith, The Medieval Mediterranean, 28 (Leiden: Brill, 2000), pp. 221–46

————, 'Canterbury and Rome: The Limits and Myth of *Romanitas*', in *Roma fra Oriente e Occidente*, Settimane di studio del Centro italiano di studi sull'alto medioevo, 49, 2 vols (Spoleto: Centro italiano di studi sull'alto medioevo, 2002), II, 797–829

————, 'English Identity from Bede to the Millennium', *The Haskins Society Journal*, 14 (2003), 33–51

Bullough, Donald A., *Alcuin: Achievement and Reputation*, Education and Society in the Middle Ages and Renaissance, 16 (Leiden: Brill, 2004)

di Carpegna Falconieri, Tommaso, 'Roma e Leone IX', in *La reliquia del sangue di Cristo: Mantova, l'Italia e l'Europa al tempo di Leone IX*, ed. by Glauco Maria Cantarella and Arturo Calzona (Verona: Scripta, 2012), pp. 325–39

Colgrave, Bertram, 'Pilgrimages to Rome in the Seventh and Eighth Centuries', in *Studies in Language, Literature, and Culture of the Middle Ages and Later*, ed. by E. Bagby Atwood and Archibald A. Hill (Austin: University of Texas at Austin, 1969), pp. 156–72

Conner, Patrick W., *Anglo-Saxon Exeter: A Tenth-Century Cultural History*, Studies in Anglo-Saxon History, 4 (Woodbridge: Boydell, 1993)

Costambeys, Marios, 'Alcuin, Rome and Charlemagne's Imperial Coronation', in *England and Rome in the Early Middle Ages: Pilgrimage, Art and Politics*, ed. by Francesca Tinti, Studies in the Early Middle Ages, 40 (Turnhout: Brepols, 2014), pp. 255–89

Cubitt, Catherine, 'Universal and Local Saints', in *Local Saints and Local Churches in the Early Medieval West*, ed. by Alan Thacker and Richard Sharpe (Oxford: Oxford University Press, 2002), pp. 423–53

————, 'The Politics of Remorse: Penance and Royal Piety in the Reign of Æthelred the Unready', *Historical Research*, 85 (2012), 179–92

————, 'Individual and Collective Sinning in Tenth- and Eleventh-Century England', in *Religion und Politik im Mittelalter: Deutschland und England im Vergleich*, ed. by Ludger Körntgen and Dominik Wassenhoven (Berlin: De Gruyter, 2013), pp. 51–70

Dockray-Miller, Mary, *The Books and the Life of Judith of Flanders* (Farnham: Ashgate, 2015)

Dumville, David N., 'The Catalogue Texts', in *An Eleventh-Century Anglo-Saxon Illustrated Miscellany: British Library Cotton Tiberius B.V Part 1, together with Leaves from British Library Cotton Nero D.II*, ed. by P. McGurk and others, Early English Manuscripts in Facsimile, 21 (Copenhagen: Rosenkilde and Bagger, 1983), pp. 55–58

Ermini Pani, Letizia, 'Per un organico funzionamento della corte papale: le *scholae peregrinorum*', in *Le corti nell'alto medioevo*, Settimane di studio del Centro italiano di studi sull'alto medioevo, 62, 2 vols (Spoleto: Centro italiano di studi sull'alto medioevo, 2015), I, 281–317

Ferrari, Guy, *Early Roman Monasteries: Notes for the History of the Monasteries and Convents at Rome from the V through the X Century*, Studi di antichità cristiana, 23 (Vatican City: Pontificio Istituto di archeologia cristiana, 1957)

Foot, Sarah, 'The Making of *Angelcynn*: English Identity before the Norman Conquest', *Transactions of the Royal Historical Society*, sixth ser., 6 (1996), 25–49

————, *Veiled Women, I: The Disappearance of Nuns from Anglo-Saxon England*, Studies in Early Medieval Britain and Ireland (Aldershot: Ashgate, 2000)

Gem, Richard, 'Gabatae Saxiscae: Saxon Bowls in the Churches of Rome in the Eighth and
    Ninth Centuries', in Early Medieval Art and Archaeology in the Northern World: Studies
    in Honour of James Graham-Campbell, ed. by Andrew Reynolds and Leslie Webster
    (Leiden: Brill, 2013), pp. 87–110

Halpin, Patricia A., 'Anglo-Saxon Women and Pilgrimage', Anglo-Norman Studies, 19 (1997),
    97–122

Howe, Nicholas, 'Rome: Capital of Anglo-Saxon England', Journal of Medieval and Early
    Modern Studies, 34 (2004), 147–72

Izzi, Luisa, 'Anglo-Saxons Underground: Early Medieval graffiti in the Catacombs of
    Rome', in England and Rome in the Early Middle Ages: Pilgrimage, Art and Politics, ed. by
    Francesca Tinti, Studies in the Early Middle Ages, 40 (Turnhout: Brepols, 2014),
    pp. 141–77

Johrendt, Jochen, 'Die Anfänge des Kapitels von St Peter im Vatikan? Zu den Urkunden
    Leos IX. für die Basilikalklöster der Peterskirche (1053)', Deutsches Archiv für
    Erforschung des Mittelalters, 65 (2009), 83–110

Keynes, Simon, 'Anglo-Saxon Entries in the "Liber Vitae" of Brescia', in Alfred the Wise:
    Studies in Honour of Janet Bately on the Occasion of her Sixty-Fifth Birthday, ed. by
    Jane Roberts, Janet L. Nelson, and Malcolm R. Godden (Cambridge: Brewer, 1997),
    pp. 99–119

——, 'Alfred the Great and the Kingdom of the Anglo-Saxons', in A Companion to Alfred
    the Great, ed. by Nicole Guenther Discenza and Paul E. Szarmach, Brill's Companions
    to the Christian Tradition, 58 (Leiden: Brill, 2015), pp. 13–46

Lapidge, Michael, 'The Career of Aldhelm', Anglo-Saxon England, 36 (2007), 15–69

Levison, Wilhelm, England and the Continent in the Eighth Century: The Ford Lectures
    Delivered in the University of Oxford in the Hilary Term, 1943 (Oxford: Clarendon Press,
    1946)

Matthews, Stephen, The Road to Rome: Travel and Travellers between England and Italy
    in the Anglo-Saxon Centuries, BAR International Series 1680 (Oxford: Archaeopress,
    2007)

Moore, Wilfrid J., The Saxon Pilgrims to Rome and the Schola Saxonum (Fribourg: Society
    of St Paul, 1937)

Naismith, Rory, 'Peter's Pence and Before', in England and Rome in the Early Middle Ages:
    Pilgrimage, Art and Politics, ed. by Francesca Tinti, Studies in the Early Middle Ages, 40
    (Turnhout: Brepols, 2014), pp. 217–53

Naismith, Rory, and Francesca Tinti, The Forum Hoard of Anglo-Saxon Coins. Il ripostiglio
    dell'Atrium Vestae nel Foro Romano, Bollettino di numismatica 55–56 (Rome: Istituto
    Poligrafico e Zecca dello Stato, 2016)

Naismith, Rory, and Francesca Tinti, 'The Origins of Peter's Pence', The English Historical
    Review, 134 (2019), 521–52

Noble, Thomas F. X, 'The Rise and Fall of the Archbishopric of Lichfield', in England and
    Rome in the Early Middle Ages: Pilgrimage, Art and Politics, ed. by Francesca Tinti,
    Studies in the Early Middle Ages, 40 (Turnhout: Brepols, 2014), pp. 291–305

Ó Carragáin, Éamonn, and Alan Thacker, 'Wilfrid in Rome', in Wilfrid: Abbot, Bishop and
    Saint. Papers from the 1300th Anniversary Conference, ed. by N. H. Higham (Donnington:
    Shaun Tyas, 2013), pp. 212–30

Old St Peter's, Rome, ed. by Rosamond McKitterick, John Osborne, Carol M. Richardson, and Joanna Story, British School at Rome Studies (Cambridge: Cambridge University Press, 2014)

Orchard, Andy, *The Poetic Art of Aldhelm,* Cambridge Studies in Anglo-Saxon England, 8 (Cambridge: Cambridge University Press, 1994)

Ortenberg, Veronica, 'Archbishop Sigeric's Journey to Rome in 990', *Anglo-Saxon England,* 19 (1990), 197–246

——, *The English Church and the Continent in the Tenth and Eleventh Centuries: Cultural, Spiritual and Artistic Exchanges* (Oxford: Clarendon Press, 1992)

Pesci, Benedetto, 'L'itinerario romano di Sigerico arcivescovo di Canterbury e la lista dei papi da lui portata in Inghilterra (anno 990)', *Rivista di archeologia cristiana,* 13 (1936), 43–60

Piazzoni, Ambrogio M., 'Biografie dei papi del secolo X nella continuazione del *Liber Pontificalis*', *Mittellateinisches Jahrbuch,* 24–25 (1989–1990), 369–82

Roberts, Edward, *Flodoard of Rheims and the Writing of History in the Tenth Century* (Cambridge: Cambridge University Press, 2019)

Santangeli Valenzani, Riccardo, 'Hosting Foreigners in Early Medieval Rome: From *xenodochia* to *scholae peregrinorum*', in *England and Rome in the Early Middle Ages: Pilgrimage, Art and Politics,* ed. by Francesca Tinti, Studies in the Early Middle Ages, 40 (Turnhout: Brepols, 2014), pp. 69–88

Schiaparelli, Luigi, 'Le carte antiche dell'archivio capitolare di San Pietro in Vaticano', *Archivio della Società romana di storia patria,* 24 (1901), 393–496

Schoenig, Steven A., 'Withholding the Pallium as a Tool of the Reform', in *Proceedings of the Thirteenth International Congress of Medieval Canon Law: Esztergom, 3–8 August 2008,* ed. by Peter Erdö and Szabolcs Anzelm Szuromi, Monumenta iuris canonici, ser. C, Subsidia, 14 (Vatican City: Biblioteca Apostolica Vaticana, 2010), pp. 577–88

——, *Bonds of Wool: The Pallium and Papal Power in the Middle Ages* (Washington, DC: Catholic University of America Press, 2016)

Sims-Williams, Patrick, 'Milred of Worcester's Collection of Latin Epigrams and its Continental Counterparts', *Anglo-Saxon England,* 10 (1981), 21–38

Smith, Julia M. H., 'Old Saints, New Cults: Roman Relics in Carolingian Francia', in *Early Medieval Rome and the Christian West: Essays in Honour of Donald A. Bullough,* ed. by Julia M. H. Smith, The Medieval Mediterranean, 28 (Leiden: Brill, 2000), pp. 317–39

——, 'Care of Relics in Early Medieval Rome', in *Rome and Religion in the Medieval Worlds: Studies in Honor of Thomas F. X. Noble,* ed. by Valerie L. Garver and Owen M. Phelan (Farnham: Ashgate, 2014), pp. 179–205

Stancliffe, Clare, 'Kings Who Opted out', in *Ideal and Reality in Frankish and Anglo-Saxon Society: Essays Presented to J. M. Wallace-Hadrill,* ed. by Patrick Wormald, Donald Bullough, and Roger Collins (Oxford: Blackwell, 1983), pp. 154–76

Stocchi, Mirko, 'San Michele dei Frisoni nelle fonti medioevali dell'archivio capitolare di San Pietro in Vaticano (854–1350)', in Tiemen Brouwer, Mirko Stocchi and Luigi Marsili, *La chiesa dei Santi Michele e Magno in Borgo S. Spirito e l'Arciconfraternita del SS.mo Sacramento nella Basilica Vaticana: Storia e documenti* (Vatican City: Capitolo Vaticano, 2010), pp. 7–34

Story, Joanna, 'Aldhelm and Old St Peter's, Rome', *Anglo-Saxon England*, 39 (2010), 7–20

Stroll, Mary, *Popes and Antipopes: The Politics of Eleventh Century Church Reform* (Leiden: Brill, 2012)

Thacker, Alan, 'In Search of Saints: The English Church and the Cult of Roman Apostles and Martyrs in the Seventh and Eighth Centuries', in *Early Medieval Rome and the Christian West: Essays in Honour of Donald A. Bullough*, ed. by Julia M. H. Smith, The Medieval Mediterranean, 28 (Leiden: Brill, 2000), pp. 247–77

——, '*Loca sanctorum*: The Significance of Place in the Study of the Saints', in *Local Saints and Local Churches in the Early Medieval West*, ed. by Alan Thacker and Richard Sharpe (Oxford: Oxford University Press, 2002), pp. 1–44

——, 'Rome: The Pilgrims' City in the Seventh Century', in *England and Rome in the Early Middle Ages: Pilgrimage, Art and Politics*, ed. by Francesca Tinti, Studies in the Early Middle Ages, 40 (Turnhout: Brepols, 2014), pp. 89–139

Tinti, Francesca, 'England and the Papacy in the Tenth Century', in *England and the Continent in the Tenth Century: Studies in Honour of Wilhelm Levison (1876–1947)*, ed. by David Rollason, Conrad Leyser, and Hannah Williams, Studies in the Early Middle Ages, 37 (Turnhout: Brepols, 2010), pp. 163–84

——, 'Introduction: Anglo-Saxon England and Rome', in *England and Rome in the Early Middle Ages: Pilgrimage, Art and Politics*, ed. by Francesca Tinti, Studies in the Early Middle Ages, 40 (Turnhout: Brepols, 2014), pp. 1–15

——, 'The Archiepiscopal Pallium in Late Anglo-Saxon England', in *England and Rome in the Early Middle Ages: Pilgrimage, Art and Politics*, ed. by Francesca Tinti, Studies in the Early Middle Ages, 40 (Turnhout: Brepols, 2014), pp. 307–42

——, 'The Preservation, Transmission and Use of Papal Letters in Anglo-Saxon England', in *Fruits of Learning: The Transfer of Encyclopaedic Knowledge in the Early Middle Ages*, ed. by Rolf H. Bremmer Jr. and Kees Dekker (Leuven: Peeters, 2016), pp. 93–114

——, 'The Pallium Privilege of Pope Nicholas II for Archbishop Ealdred of York', *Journal of Ecclesiastical History*, 70 (2019), 708–30

Treharne, Elaine, *Living through Conquest: The Politics of Early English, 1020–1220* (Oxford: Oxford University Press, 2012)

——, 'The Performance of Piety: Cnut, Rome and England', in *England and Rome in the Early Middle Ages: Pilgrimage, Art and Politics*, ed. by Francesca Tinti, Studies in the Early Middle Ages, 40 (Turnhout: Brepols, 2014), pp. 343–64

Wood, Ian, 'The Continental Journeys of Wilfrid and Biscop', in *Wilfrid: Abbot, Bishop and Saint, Papers from the 1300th Anniversary Conference*, ed. by Nicholas H. Higham (Donnington: Shaun Tyas, 2013), pp. 200–11

Wormald, Patrick, '*Engla Lond*: The Making of an Allegiance', *Journal of Historical Sociology*, 7.1 (1994), 1–24

Wright, Roger, *A Sociophilological Study of Late Latin* (Turnhout: Brepols, 2002)

ÉAMONN Ó CARRAGÁIN

A Renaissance Synthesis of Ancient Christian Themes: Architecture, Altarpieces, and Imagined Spaces in San Giovanni Crisostomo, Venice, 1495–1520

One of the fascinations of Venice, a city I have had the privilege of exploring more than once with Alan Thacker and other friends, is the ways in which its Renaissance churches provide fresh syntheses of early Christian and medieval ideas.[1] Those churches that have not been despoiled fascinate in another way: individual works of art often relate, not only to each other, but to the church for which they were designed. The present paper explores these two ideas in San Giovanni Crisostomo, some ten minutes' walk from the Rialto. This church was renovated by Mauro Codussi (1440–1504) and his workshop;[2] three major artists (with their workshops) provided the first three of its new altarpieces: Pietro Lombardo (1435–1515), Sebastiano Luciani later known as Sebastiano del Piombo (c. 1485–1547),[3] and finally the aged Giovanni Bellini (1430–1516).[4] The individual altarpieces have been much studied; but there has been little discussion of how each relates to the others and to the design of the church.

---

1 I am grateful to the late Jennifer O'Reilly, with whom I discussed the first versions of this paper; to Emily Goetsch and Christos Kakalis, who invited me to present an early version at their 'Mountains' conference (Edinburgh, 2014); and to Terence O'Reilly, Daragh O'Connell and Eoghan Ó Carragáin, with whom I discussed later drafts. I am particularly grateful to Don Cesare Maddalena, the present Parish Priest of San Giovanni Crisostomo, for his courteous permission to examine and photograph in the interior of the church. As good photographs of all three altarpieces are easily available on the web, my illustrations are chosen to illustrate the relations between the altarpieces and other features of the church. Full-resolution versions of each figure can be viewed at https://doi.org/10.5281/zenodo.2561359, 'Images to accompany "A Renaissance Synthesis of Ancient Christian Themes"'.
2 Olivato and Puppi, *Mauro Codussi*, pp. 215–18; Jestaz, *Monuments vénitiens*, pp. 211–45.
3 Strinati and Lindemann, *Sebastiano del Piombo*, pp. 106–09.
4 Poldi and Villa, *Bellini a Venezia*, pp. 232–57.

Éamonn Ó Carragáin • is professor emeritus of Old and Middle English at University College Cork.

Cities, Saints, and Communities in Early Medieval Europe, ed. by Scott DeGregorio and Paul Kershaw, SEM 46 (Turnhout: Brepols, 2020), pp. 373-396
BREPOLS PUBLISHERS
DOI 10.1484/M.SEM-EB.5.119636

The Bernabò Chapel: Mauro Codussi, Pietro Lombardo, and their Workshops

In 1475, the medieval church of San Giovanni Crisostomo was damaged by fire.[5] It was not totally destroyed: the campanile still stood, and appears in the bird's eye view of Venice by Jacopo de' Barbari, published in 1500; the church remained in continuous use.[6] Ludovico (vernacular, Alvise) Talenti was appointed *piovano* (parish priest) in 1480: he would remain in this position until his death in 1516. He set about collecting money, persuading the Senate to obtain from Rome an indulgence of ten years for people who contributed to the restoration. The letter to Rome of January 1489, requesting the indulgence, was no doubt largely drafted by Talenti: it does not even mention the fire, but instead details the age and poor condition of the church.[7] The renovation of the church, in which Talenti was closely involved, got going from 1495.[8] Talenti provided the pulpit between the sacristy door and the Bernabò chapel at his own expense, and it is inscribed with his name and the date (1501) (Fig. 3).[9]

There was a lively debate in early sixteenth century Venice about how one should best serve society: in the active life (such as that of an administrator, soldier or parish priest) or in the contemplative life (that of a scholar, monk, or hermit)?[10] These preoccupations are progressively explored in the three altarpieces commissioned during Talenti's lifetime. In December 1508, Venice was threatened by the League of Cambrai, a powerful coalition which included France, the Habsburg Empire, the Papacy, Mantua, and Ferrara.[11] Venice suffered a severe defeat at the battle of Agnadello (14 May 1509); the war would not end until 1517. The war had been waged for some four years when the third altarpiece (that by Bellini, for the Diletti chapel) was painted. It is of interest, therefore, that the search for wisdom, implicit in all three altarpieces, is given verbal expression in the third.

San Giovanni Crisostomo was among Mauro Codussi's last projects.[12] His design, a Greek cross within a square and with three apses, around a central dome, was a variant, not only on his earlier designs for churches, but also (appropriately, for a church dedicated to St John Chrysostom) on aspects of early byzantine architecture.[13]

---

5   Olivato and Puppi, *Mauro Codussi*, p. 215.
6   Olivato and Puppi, *Mauro Codussi*, p. 214.
7   Jestaz, *Monuments vénitiens*, pp. 211–12.
8   Olivato and Puppi, *Mauro Codussi*, p. 215; on Talenti's involvement, Jestaz, *Monuments vénitiens*, pp. 212 and 217.
9   Jestaz, *Monuments vénitiens*, p. 212.
10 Pinchi, *À quels saints se vouer?*, pp. 45–46.
11 Hale, *Titian: His Life*, pp. 81–86.
12 Other late projects included the church of Santa Maria Formosa (1492–1504), the clock tower in St Mark's square (1494–1504) and Palazzo Loredan Vendramin Calergi (1502–1504): Olivato and Puppi, *Mauro Codussi*, pp. 206–25.
13 Jestaz, *Monuments vénitiens*, pp. 229–31; Boccato, *Chiese di Venezia*, p. 171.

Figure 2. The Madonna Greca, legacy of Giacomo de'Bernabò, d. 1438; below, altarpiece by Tullio Lombardo, inserted 1506. Photo by the author.

Figure 3. The Bernabò Chapel and altarpiece; Pulpit donated by Ludovico Talenti.
Photo by the author.

The Bernabò family, rich local merchants, commissioned Pietro Lombardo to rebuild their chapel (1499–1500), dedicated to the Virgin Mary.[14] Money for the rebuilding came via the testament of Giacomo de' Bernabò (dated 11 July 1438, shortly before his death that same year).[15] The chapel stands out in the general austerity of the church. It is the only chapel completely clad in marble, and designed as a chantry: marble benches to right and left of the altar provide seats for up to three persons aside to chant the office or assist at Mass. On either side of the altar, there is a tall window in the external (north) wall: each window overlooks, and provides excellent light for, the nearest bench. The bright marble cladding of the sides of the chapel reflects some of this light back, onto the altar and its altarpiece. Marble cladding encloses the inner and outer sides of each bench: chanting in the chapel would be heard throughout the church, but not all people in the church could easily see the chanters. To construct a chapel as a chantry was to encourage thoughts of liturgical celebration and cosmic harmony: ideas also symbolized by the four sculpted musician-angels in the Bernabò altarpiece.

A standing Madonna *orans* (with her lower arms raised in prayer) is set high in the wall under the chapel's vault, above the altarpiece and within a rectangular frame of blue marble (Figure 2).[16] The Madonna probably dates from the fourteenth

14   Jestaz, *Monuments vénitiens*, pp. 233–35.
15   Jestaz, *Monuments vénitiens*, p. 232.
16   Zanin, *Chiesa S. Giovanni Grisostomo*, unnumbered Plate [23]. On the orant Madonna, I rely on Annalisa Bristot, 'Note a margine'; Davis, *Byzantine Relief Icons*, Appendix I, pp. 24–26.

century: it is clear from Giacomo de' Bernabò's testament (1438) that he had long prized it, in his own home, as an object of devotion.[17] It differs stylistically from all Venetian examples: Giacomo had probably acquired it years before, on one of his journeys to the Levant as a silk merchant.[18] In 1499 it was fittingly described as a 'madonna greca'.[19] Soon after 1438, it had been set high in the wall of the chapel, above a wooden altarpiece. As part of the refurbishment that wooden altarpiece was removed to store, and eventually given to another church, Santa Maria Maggiore. The Lombardo workshop carefully remodelled the orant Madonna: they removed gilding mentioned in Giacomo's will, retouched some details of the Madonna, and covered the background of the panel in dark slate so as to make the Madonna stand out clearly, seeming to float within its frame, against the new bright marble cladding of the altar wall.[20]

By January 1500, Giacomo's Madonna had been carefully remodelled and restored to its position in the north wall. The other work on the chapel was completed by April 1501; but it was only much later, in October 1506, that the Lombardo workshop inserted the new marble altarpiece on which Pietro's son Tullio Lombardo (c. 1455–1532), had been working since 1501.[21] Tullio designed his altarpiece so as to provide a visual prologue or introduction to the Bernabò family heirloom, the orant Madonna: as we shall see, his new altarpiece was designed to complement the Madonna, visually and theologically. Tullio used two closely-fitting slabs of Carrara marble, an upper and a lower. He sculpted a fictive room, with a coffered vault and a receding colonnade which, as it were, extends the actual Bernabò chapel towards the north. Christ stands at centre foreground, between two fictive ionic columns which support a beam topped by a triangular pediment. On the basis of the accounts for the chapel, which refer to a throne, Bertrand Jestaz has recently argued that this structure is a throne, from which Christ has risen up, to stand before it.[22] The triangular pediment above Christ's head (which has a smaller triangle of porphyry at its centre) points upwards, towards the other members of the Holy Trinity who hover under the fictive barrel vault, just above Christ. A bust portrait of God the Father (with a triangular 'trinitarian' halo) looks benignly downward towards his son, the Virgin Mary, and the gathered apostles. The bust portrait of the Father is flanked by six cherubim. Four full-length angel-musicians, and below them another four cherubim, flank the dove of the Holy Spirit and the rays which stream down

17 Jestaz, *Monuments vénitiens*, pp. 234 and 238.

18 Davis, *Byzantine Relief Icons*, pp. 24–25.

19 Jestaz, *Monuments vénitiens*, p. 242, par. 34, accounts for 20 December 1499: 'per chonzar una Madona greca'.

20 Jestaz, *Monuments vénitiens*, p. 234: Jestaz is highly critical of the account given in Davis, 'La cappella Bernabò'.

21 Tullio had acquired the two plaques of marble on 7 December 1500: Jestaz, *Monuments vénitiens*, p. 238 and par. 99 on p. 245.

22 Jestaz, *Monuments vénitiens*, p. 238, and par. 100 on p. 245; earlier, Markham Schulz, *The Sculpture of Tullio Lombardo*, p. 84, suggested that the structure represents the closed door of the room in which Christ appears in John 20. 19.

towards Christ, Mary, and the apostles. Christ has just placed a crown on the head of the young Virgin Mary. She kneels before him, her arms clasped before her body in a gesture of acceptance: 'be it done to me according to thy word'.[23]

Christ appears as in his thirties, the age of his public ministry or of his post-Resurrection appearances. The long-haired girl who kneels before him seems half his age, perhaps fifteen to eighteen. To understand this reversal of biological facts, a good place to start is the letter *Cogitis me*, composed about AD 835 by the Carolingian writer Paschasius Radbertus (*c*. 799–865).[24] Paschasius wished to encourage the aristocratic nuns Theodrada and Emma to celebrate the feast of the Assumption of Mary into Heaven, without being distracted by unreliable apocryphal narratives such as the *Transitus Mariae*.[25] He is sceptical about apocryphal stories that Mary's body was assumed into heaven, and makes it clear that this was not the point of the feast.[26] The nuns should concentrate instead on the liturgical chants, based on scripture, for the feast. Some of these antiphons and responsories went back to the time of Ambrose (*c*. 340–397); but the repertoire had greatly increased in Paschasius' own lifetime.[27] Many of these antiphons and responsories adapted erotic texts from the Song of Songs.[28] Paschasius drew on these liturgical *libretti* to argue that it was the intensity of her love for Christ, her longing to be in his presence, that drew Mary towards heaven; and that the Assumption fulfilled her role in the Incarnation, when she became Theotokos (God-bearer). Paschasius therefore devotes much of his letter to the Incarnation; he is the first theologian to use the Assumption antiphons to provide a rationale for the feast.[29]

Where, and when, is Tullio's scene set? Paschasius says that after the Resurrection Mary lived with the apostles in the Cenacle, and instructed them informally about the Incarnation and its implications.[30] The Cenacle (dining room, upper room) in Jerusalem was where both the Last Supper and Pentecost took place: it would have been particularly appropriate to represent the Cenacle just over the altar of the Bernabò chapel.[31] None of the twelve apostles in Tullio's sculpture has been identified

---

23 'Fiat mihi secundum verbum tuum', Luke 1. 38.

24 References to *Cogitis me* are to the paragraphs in Ripberger's two editions, this numbering is also followed in Dezzuto's edition. Page references to these editions refer to Introductions, notes or appendices.

25 The various *Transitus Mariae* narratives are discussed in Clayton, *The Apocryphal Gospels of Mary*.

26 *Cogitis me*, §§ 7–9.

27 *Cogitis me*, §§ 21–23, §§ 38–45, and §§ 57–59; Ripberger, *Der Pseudo-Hieronymus Brief IX*, pp. 36–43; Matter, *The Voice of My Beloved*, pp. 151–77.

28 There is a concordance between the antiphons quoted in *Cogitis me* and those in the Antiphonary of Compiègne in Ripberger, *Der Pseudo-Hieronymus Brief IX*, pp. 146–50; for some critical comments on Ripberger's identifications of the antiphons, see Dezzuto, p. xxxix, note 103.

29 Matter, *The Voice of My Beloved*, p. 152.

30 The narrative of Acts 1. 13–14 is expanded in *Cogitis me*, §§ 15–16.

31 See Cross and Livingstone, *The Oxford Dictionary of the Christian Church*, p. 315, under 'Cenaculum'. Another link between altarpiece and altar is the fact that the first Good Friday, commemorated in each Mass, was, like the Annunciation, believed to have occurred on 25 March: see Ó Carragáin, *Ritual and the Rood*, pp. 83–95.

as Judas; therefore it seems that the scene is set after Mathias was chosen to replace him, just before Pentecost.[32] This would mean that Tullio's sculpture represents a post-Resurrection appearance of Christ.[33] His pose, calm and authoritative, and his affectionate gesture towards the young kneeling woman, suggests that Christ here formally confirms what Mary has told the apostles informally about the Incarnation. To drive home the importance of the Incarnation, Christ grants the apostles (and the onlookers) an object-lesson: a vision of his mother as a young woman 'gracilis et delicata',[34] as she was at the very moment (some thirty-four years before[35]) when she had consented to became mother of God. The scene is stunningly original: it expresses the mystery of the Incarnation no longer by the mediating image of the angel Gabriel. The omission of Gabriel at the moment of Annunciation is intended to startle the apostles (and the onlookers) into awareness that, in willing the Incarnation, the Trinity itself acted in its fullness:

> And Mary said to the angel: How shall this be done, because I know not man? And the angel answering, said to her: the Holy Spirit shall come upon thee, and the power of the Most High shall overshadow thee and therefore also, the Holy One which shall be born of thee shall be called the Son of God.[36]

Tullio's Christ, to confirm the mystery, telescopes time. His right hand rests affectionately on the young woman's crowned head, to show that from the very moment she agreed to become God-bearer she was already potentially Queen of Heaven. Christ's gesture prophesies that the mutual love between Mary and the Trinity will lead to her final glory.

We can now understand the ways in which Tullio's altarpiece was designed to provide a visual and theological context for Giacomo de' Bernabò's 'Madonna greca'. The mission of the Apostles would be to proclaim to the ends of the earth the startling mystery of the Incarnation: without the Incarnation, they had no message to bring. To enlighten the Apostles, Christ, Son of God combines (in a Pentecostal setting) a vision of the past (Annunciation) with a prophetic gesture (Crowning). He shows how, some thirty-four years before, it was her consent to the proposed action of the Trinity that made his Incarnation possible; through his gesture of crowning Mary, Christ prophesies that Mary's original act of obedient faith ('fiat mihi') will finally lead, after her death, to her becoming Queen of Heaven.

Tullio's fusion of Annunciation and Crowning in this altarpiece had an authoritative Venetian precedent in the Doge's Palace. In the Sala del Consiglio, Guariento di Arpo (1300–1370) had already (1365–1366) flanked his great fresco, in which Christ

---

32 Acts 1. 23–26.

33 See, for example, I Corinthians 15. 7: 'after that he was seen by James: then by all the apostles'; see Markham Schulz, *The Sculpture of Tullio Lombardo*, p. 84.

34 *Cogitis me*, § 46.

35 On medieval calculations of Christ's age, see Ó Carragáin, *Ritual and the Rood*, pp. 83–84.

36 Luke 1. 34–35. A Venetian audience would have been sensitive to any reference to the Annunciation: because tradition held that the city was founded on the Feast of the Annunciation, 25 March AD 421, Annunciation scenes are ubiquitous in the city: Sinding-Larsen, *Christ in the Council Hall*, pp. 49–55.

crowns Mary Queen of Heaven (in the presence of the apostles and angels), with images of Gabriel and Mary at the Annunciation.[37] In Dante's *Paradiso*, St Bernard had called Mary 'daughter of your son' (figlia del tuo figlio).[38] The inscription to Guariento's fresco provides a creative variant of this famous Dantesque conceit: it calls her 'daughter of the Trinity'. Like Dante, and like *Cogitis me*, the inscription sees love as the central motive for the action of the Trinity:

> L'Amor che mosse già l'eterno Padre
> Per figlia hauer de sua deità trina
> Chostei che fu del suo figliuol poi madre
> Del'universo qui la fa Regina.

>> The love which once moved the Eternal Father
>> To have a daughter out of his triple divinity
>> (She who then became mother of his little Son)
>> Here makes her the Queen of the universe.[39]

Of European cities, Venice was the place where an educated parish priest (like Ludovico Talenti), who knew not only his Dante and also the local variant of the Dantesque paradox in the Sala del Consiglio, might have worked out with Tullio, during the years (1501–1506) in which Tullio worked on the altarpiece, how the Annunciation (celebrated on 25 March, and understood to be the date on which Venice was founded) might be fused with 'Santa Maria Gloriosa', the Queen of Heaven (that feast was celebrated on 15 August). Just above the altarpiece, the attitude of prayer of Giacomo di' Bernabò's Madonna represents her role in the present life of this church and its congregation: she prays for humankind to the Trinity, whose love had, for the sake of humankind, made her God-bearer. This role was given classic expression in the traditional hymn for Terce of the Little Office of the Blessed Virgin:

> Maria, mater gratiae,
> Dulcis parens clementiae,
> Tu nos ab hoste protege
> Et mortis hora suscipe.

>> Mary, mother of grace,
>> Sweet parent of mercy,
>> Protect us from the enemy
>> And at the hour of our death receive us.[40]

---

37 Sinding-Larsen, *Christ in the Council Hall*, pp. 45–56 and Plates XXXIX and XL. The juxtaposition of Annunciation and Crowning is also central to Filippino Lippi's altarpiece (1488) in the Carafa chapel of Santa Maria sopra Minerva, Rome: see Nelson, 'La cappella Carafa', pp. 40 and 44.

38 Dante, *Paradiso*, 33:1–3, p. 907.

39 Sinding-Larsen, *Christ in the Council Hall*, p. 45, note 3, who states that Guariento's inscription was traditionally attributed to Dante himself. I am grateful to Dr Daragh O'Connell for help with this matter.

40 *The Little Office of the Blessed Virgin Mary*, p. 120; see Cross and Livingstone, *The Oxford Dictionary of the Christian Church*, p. 992, under 'Little Office of Our Lady (Officium Parvum Beatae Mariae Virginis)'.

Placed above Tullio's altarpiece as though soaring through the heavens towards the firmament symbolized by Codussi's 'byzantine' dome, the orant 'Madonna greca' is already 'Sancta Maria Gloriosa' the glorified Mary of the Assumption.[41] Those art historians who interpret Tullio's altarpiece in isolation from the iconography of the chapel as a whole tend to interpret its young kneeling Virgin reductively, as a static and conventional allegory: for example, as an image of 'Ecclesia'.[42] We should instead see the chapel's two images of Mary as forming a dynamic sequence. Giacomo Bernabò's 'Madonna Greca' presents Mary's powerful role as intercessor and protector. Tullio Lombardo's altarpiece, just over the altar where Christ's body would be made present at each Mass, fuses the beginning of Mary's story (the Annunciation) with its ending (the Crowning). Her 'fiat' ('let it be done') made her the preeminent model for human responses to God in Christ: the outstanding Christian exemplar of human wisdom.[43]

Several of the apostles are startled to see Christ crown the young Virgin (their various reactions provide models for how onlookers might react to Tullio's highly unusual iconography). Christ and the Virgin are flanked by two rows of six apostles. The figures of the front row are identifiable. To the left of Christ, just behind the Virgin, the astonishment of St Peter at what Christ has just done is shared by St Andrew (immediately to the left, identified by his attribute, a cross). On the left of the front row, St Mark is identified by his gospel book. To the right of Christ, however, John the Evangelist looks calmly towards the middle distance, as though he is already contemplating the sign that will appear in heaven: 'the woman clothed with the sun, and with the moon under her feet, and upon her head a crown of twelve stars'.[44] John's youth associates him with the youthful Virgin, and recalls that he was 'the disciple whom Jesus loved',[45] to whom Christ on the cross entrusted Mary.[46] Paschasius stresses that John is a model for his monastic audience: 'the virgin to whom the Virgin was entrusted by Christ'.[47] St James the Greater, identifiable by his family likeness (and similar haircut) to Christ his cousin, turns to discuss the scene with St Matthew, who stands, holding his gospel, on the right of the front row.

In this altarpiece the apostles take second place. They will soon be teachers, here they are taught: the good news of the Incarnation is more important than its messengers. How to attain wisdom, of which Mary was the outstanding human exemplar, will be progressively explored in the other two altarpieces commissioned in the lifetime of Ludovico Talenti. Christ will appear once more, as the baby borne by

41 The name of the Venetian church 'Santa Maria Gloriosa dei Frari', refers to its dedication to the Assumption: Boccato, *Chiese di Venezia*, p. 77.
42 Markham Schulz. *The Sculpture of Tullio Lombardo*, pp. 83–84.
43 From the seventh century, scriptural passages in which Wisdom speaks of herself (such as Proverbs chapter 8, or Ecclesiastes (Sirach) chapter 24) were read at Mass on feasts of the Virgin: Calduch–Benages, 'Sapienza', especially pp. 1065–72. On the feast of the Assumption, Ecclesiastes (Sirach) 24 was often read. On the importance, in late medieval Italian art, of Mary as intercessor, see Sinding–Larsen, *Christ in the Council Hall*, pp. 46–55.
44 St John's Apocalypse (Revelation) 12. 1 (Douai–Rheims version).
45 John 13. 23, 19. 26, 20. 2, 21. 7, 21. 20.
46 John 19. 26–27.
47 *Cogitis me*, § 10: 'cui uirgini a Christo uirgo commisa est'; see also § 14.

St Christopher (in Bellini's painting for the Diletti chapel). Otherwise, the pursuit of divine wisdom will usually involve a search (by contemplation, study or martyrdom) for something hidden.

The Central Altarpiece: Sebastiano Luciani and Domenico Codussi

When Mauro Codussi died in 1504, the Bernabò chapel was already finished, apart from its new altarpiece; it is likely that the domed roof of the church was also in place.[48] Domenico Codussi, Mauro's son, took over as proto or foreman, to complete the church, its furnishings, and its two ornamental portals. The brown and yellow floor tiling was perhaps laid under Domenico's direction: in an age which did not yet cover the floors of churches with pews, marble floors were an important feature of church design. To flank the altarpiece over the main altar, Domenico erected two matching ionic pillars (they recall the pair of ionic pillars which, in Tullio's imagined room, flank Christ). Sebastiano Luciani, from whom the main altarpiece was commissioned, would make striking use of the floor, of the framing pillars, and of the main altar over which his painting was placed. The altarpiece may have been painted by 1508 or 1509.[49]

In the foreground of the painting, tiled paving corresponds to the tiles of the actual church (Figs 5 and 6). Counting from the bottom of the painting, there are six rows of white painted tiles, and seven of brown (as we shall see, sixes and sevens recur throughout the painting). In the actual church, two steps mark off the body of the nave from the area around the altar; in the painting two steps of similar height, leading to a much shallower third step, mark off a raised area immediately in front of the painted building (Fig. 5). St John Chrysostom (patron saint of the church) sits on this raised area, together with another aged male saint. To concentrate on his writing, Chrysostom has laid aside his episcopal mitre and staff, placing them conveniently behind him at the base of the building's prominent corner-pillar. Its entrance side, directly behind Chrysostom, is in shadow, but we can make out that it consists of a row of pillars: two large corner pillars and four (or perhaps five?) intermediate pillars. The dark shadow towards the right of the façade makes it difficult to be certain of the number of pillars: this lack of clarity increases our sense of enigma and mystery. The massive and brightly-lit base of the nearest corner-pillar in the painting echoes Codussi's actual ionic pillar, which provides a frame for the left side of the painting (Fig. 6). The viewer's eye moves naturally from the real pillar to the painted one: the imaginary sight-lines thus created converge towards the hill, topped by a little hill-town, on the horizon. References to aspects of the actual church (tiling, steps, pillar-frame) encourage us to see this church as leading into, and extended by, the painted space and landscape. In the painting, as in the actual church, we face east.

---

48   Olivato and Puppi, *Mauro Codussi*, p. 217.
49   See Strinati and Lindemann, *Sebastiano del Piombo*, p. 108; Grave, *Giovanni Bellini*, p. 248.

Figure 4. View of the Bernabò Chapel. Photo by the author.

Figure 5. High altar, and Sebastiano Luciani's altarpiece. Note its framing pillars, and the steps leading to the altar area: these are echoed by the pillar, and the steps, in the painting. Photo by the author.

The dawning sun, still hidden, is reflected from the salmon-coloured clouds on either side of the distant hill-village. Fictive light also shines from the nave of the actual church, onto the 'west' wall of the painted building on the left of the painting, onto its nearest corner-pillar, and onto the faces of each of the seven human figures in the foreground. The upper half of the painting is divided into blocks of light (the 'west' side wall of the painted building), dark (its pillared entrance wall) and again light (the distant hill and its village) (Fig. 6).

Three female saints advance in the left foreground (Sebastiano has portrayed his favourite model in three different poses).[50] St Mary Magdalen, the central figure of the group, is the only figure in the painting to challenge us with her direct gaze. Light from the nave illuminates her left foot, ample green dress, red bodice and blue silk blouse: relatively few details can be seen of the clothing of her two companions. We know the Magdalen by her attribute, the gold-coloured jar in her right hand. This is the 'spikenard, of great price' which she poured on Christ's feet and dried off with her hair; when Judas objected to such extravagance, Christ defended her:

> Let her alone, that she may keep it against the day of my burial. For the poor you have always with you: but me you have not always'.[51]

---

50   Luchs, *Tullio Lombardo and Ideal Portrait Sculpture*, p. 75.
51   John 12. 7–8, where the woman is Mary of Bethany; see Ó Carragáin, *Ritual and the Rood*, p. 134.

The female saint to the right of the group carries, before her closed, unseeing eyes, a small glass filled with liquid. She may be St Lucy (from the fourteenth century, visual representations represented her as having her eyes put out during her martyrdom); or perhaps St Caecilia (also associated with blindness).[52] Sebastiano apparently added the lady on the left (the third portrait of his favourite model) as an afterthought. It is possible that she represents St Catherine of Alexandria.[53] This group of three female saints visually recalls a famous mosaic in San Marco (at the keystone of the vault between the 'Ascension' and 'Pentecost' domes).[54] That mosaic represents the three women who, in St Mark's gospel, sought out the body of Christ in the tomb at dawn on Easter Sunday morning ('Mary Magdalen, and Mary the mother of James, and Salome brought spices, that they might go and anoint Jesus')[55] They find the stone rolled back; a young man (an angel) tells them 'he is not here' (in the mosaic he points at the empty shroud in the tomb). He instructs them to tell Peter and the other disciples to go to Galilee, where they will see him. From the time of St Gregory the Great, references in the gospels to 'the woman who was a sinner', and to various women named Mary, were combined to construct the figure of St Mary Magdalen as the type of faithless Israel who, through repentance and love for Jesus, became the 'teacher of the teachers', bringing the news of Christ's resurrection to Peter and the Apostles.[56] It is interesting that Sebastiano's three women advance from the left of the painting, that is, from the north side of the actual church where the Bernabò chapel (dedicated to Mary) stands. In Luke's gospel, the angel Gabriel and Elizabeth (mother of John the Baptist), both, affirm that the Virgin Mary is 'blessed among women'.[57] St Gregory the Great had constructed his 'biography' of the Magdalen to provide a clear contrast between her fruitful repentance and the sinless Virgin Mary, in whom human wisdom had reached perfection.[58] The Gregorian contrast between the Virgin and the Magdalen is reflected in the progression between the Marian imagery of the Bernabò chapel and Sebastiano's altarpiece for the main altar of the church.

Sebastiano's three women advance towards an area (at the foreground of the painting) directly above the main altar of the actual church. The Mass was seen

---

52 Caraffa and others, eds, *Bibliotheca Sanctorum*, VIII, cols 252–54, under 'Lucia di Siracusa'; Connolly, *Mourning into Joy*, pp. 23–59.

53 For discussion, see Strinati and Lindemann, *Sebastiano del Piombo*, pp. 106–09. It is perhaps the kind of afterthought a parish priest, aware that larger issues demanded that there should be three women in the group, might suggest.

54 Demus, *The Mosaics of San Marco in Venice*, vol. I, Part 1, pp. 204–05 and figs 28–29; vol. I, Part 2, Plate 331; Demus and others, *San Marco: Patriarchal Basilica in Venice*, I, p. 115 (illustration) and p. 125 (discussion); II, p. 67 (iconography and inscription).

55 Mark 16. 1–7. Only Mark names these three women.

56 See Ward, *Harlots of the Desert*, p. 15; Ó Carragáin, *Ritual and the Rood*, pp. 128–37.

57 Luke 1. 28; 1:42.

58 From the seventh century, Luke 10. 38–42, the story of Martha and Mary of Bethany, often came to be read on the feast of the Assumption (15 August): when this happened, the liturgy applied the last verse of the lection, 'Mary has chosen the better part, which will not be taken away from her' (Luke 10. 42) to the Virgin Mary herself, on the day of her death and entry into heaven: Ó Carragáin, *Ritual and the Rood*, p. 102.

as the memorial of Christ's Passion and death; altars of churches were commonly interpreted as symbolizing Christ, and in particular his dead body, wounded by the spear.[59] The three women in Sebastiano's painting and the three women in the San Marco mosaic have in common the figure of Mary Magdalen. They have something else in common: both groups of women are engaged in a search for Christ. Here, the Magdalen seeks him in love, to anoint his body. St Lucy, even in her blindness, seeks and finds him in martyrdom. If the lady on the left can be identified with St Catherine, she sought him in the intellectual debate (with the learned men of Alexandria) which led to her martyrdom.[60]

At the centre of the painting, against the massive corner-pillar, sits the patron of the church, Saint John Chrisostom. He holds a large clasped book open above his lap, and with his left hand holds open its first quires, so that we can see some of what he has written on the verso of the opening (Greek letters can be deciphered). With a pen held in his right hand, John writes on the recto of the next folio. Thus, his whole right arm can be seen, and is central to the painting: of the 'great many relics' which this church claimed to possess, St John's arm was the outstanding one.[61]

To the right of John Chrysostom, there is a second group of three, this time of male saints. As Mary Magdalen was the central figure of the group of female saints to the left, so John the Baptist is the central figure of the trio of male saints towards the right. Each group of three saints forms a triangle. John the Baptist is the only male saint to stand in the foreground, on the same level as the three women. He leans forward eagerly towards Chrysostom and his book, as though about to deliver an urgent message: indeed, the writing Chrysostom could be taking dictation from the young man. The Baptist grasps with his right hand not only his slender staff, but also the top of a scroll which winds itself downwards around the staff. The inscription on the scroll indicates the likely theme of the message the young man proclaims: the words '[ECCE] AGNUS DE[I]'[62] are visible. The initial word '[ECCE]', is concealed on the scroll, but is clearly implied by John's gesture. Near the scroll, the index finger of his left hand points downwards, not at the scroll, but out of the painting, towards the high altar of the actual church. From the late seventh century, Christ was addressed as Lamb of God in the 'Agnus Dei' chant, sung in each Mass, just before communion.[63] The Baptist's pointing finger provides, in addition, an answer to the implied question of the Magdalen and her companions ('where is Christ's body?'). The figures of the Magdalen and the Baptist, the protagonists in the foreground of the painting, together provide a dramatic inner frame to the painting. The question implied by her questioning

59 Martimort, 'Liturgical signs', vol. I, pp. 207–08.
60 Jacobus de Voragine, Legenda Aurea, pp. 791–92.
61 Jestaz, Monuments vénitiens, p. 211, quoting the request (29 January 1489) for an indulgence, a document in which Ludovico Talenti probably had a large part: 'cujus sacratissimum brachium et alie complures reliquie in ea reperiuntur et maxima devotione custodiuntur' (whose most holy arm, and very many more relics are to be found [in that church] and are kept with the greatest devotion).
62 'Behold the Lamb of God': John 1. 29 and 36.
63 The origins of the chant are discussed in Ó Carragáin, Ritual and the Rood, pp. 160–64.

gaze, and the answer implied by his pointing finger, are central to the painting's discourse.

If the Bernabò Madonna, and altarpiece, together presented the trajectory of a single life (that of the Virgin Mary), this painting provides a wide-ranging epitome of scriptural history. Youth and age are juxtaposed and balanced. Of the four male figures, the military saint on the extreme right (George or Theodore?) is in his mature prime (say, thirty to forty years of age?). He wears armour, which gleams in the 'interior' light source, and he holds a spear which disappears upwards at the top right of the painting. The Baptist is younger: say, about twenty years of age. He is the only one who seems about to speak: all the other figures listen intently to what he is about to say, except for the Magdalen who looks challengingly at us, as though to interrogate us. But there is a particularly intimate relationship (of speaking and rapt listening) between the Baptist and the aged saint who sits on the dais together with Chrysostom. He is not identified by an attribute. Who is he? Of the various scholarly suggestions, the most attractive is St John the Evangelist: no longer young (as he appeared in the front row of the Bernabò altarpiece) but now the aged seer who would die on Patmos: the author, not only of John's gospel, but of his Apocalypse.[64] John the Evangelist not only wrote of the eschatological future (including the 'woman clothed with the sun'); he, alone among the evangelists, saw Christ as the Word who 'was in the beginning with God. All things came into being through him, and without him not one thing came into being'.[65] The Evangelist's comprehensive vision of history complemented that associated with the Baptist. The latter was understood to be the last prophet of the Old Testament, and to sum up what the earlier prophets had to say of Christ: 'to the prophets who went before, it was given to announce beforehand the things that were to come to pass concerning Christ; but to this man it was given to point him out with his finger'.[66] Between them, Evangelist and Baptist were seen to testify to the full course of scriptural history.

There is an eschatological dimension to the little hill-village on the eastern horizon. The cross at the top of the Baptist's staff is placed to the right of the head of the aged Evangelist, and just to the left of the hill-village. Its placing may hint at the Crucifixion, which took place outside the walls of Jerusalem.[67] While the hill-town on the horizon represents neither the actual city of Jerusalem nor the heavenly Jerusalem, it perhaps provides a hint of the former and a tiny foretaste of the latter. As for the dawn breaking at the horizon, it is of interest to note that one

---

64 Strinati and Lindemann, *Sebastiano del Piombo*, p. 106. The legendary acts of St John the Evangelist at Ephesus and on Patmos are set forth in the mosaics of the north transept of San Marco: Demus, *The Mosaics of San Marco in Venice*, Vol. I, Part 1, pp. 84–93; Vol. I, Part 2, Pl 2, 31–34, 88–102; Demus and others, *San Marco: Patriarchal Basilica in Venice*, I, pp. 113–14 and plates; II, pp. 69–83 (iconography and inscriptions).

65 John 1. 3.

66 'prophetis praecedentibus praenuntiare de Christo futura concessum est; huic autem digito ostendere': Augustine, *In Ioannis Evangelium*, IV, 1, ed. Willems, p. 31. Augustine, reasonably, assumes that the repeated 'Ecce' ('behold') of John 1. 29, 36 implies the action of pointing.

67 Hebrews 13. 12–14.

of the Assumption antiphons addressed Mary as 'quasi aurora consurgens' (like the dawn rising aloft).[68]

What is the significance of the painted building to the left of the painting? The façade of pillars, and the closeness of St John Chrysostom to the prominent corner-pillar, suggests an answer:

> Wisdom hath built herself a house: she hath hewn out her seven pillars
> She hath slain her victims, mingled her wine, and set forth her table.
> She hath sent her maids to invite to the tower, and to the walls of the city:
> Whoever is a little one, let him come to me. And to the unwise she said:
> Come, eat my bread, and drink the wine which I have mingled for you.
> Forsake childishness, and live, and walk by the ways of prudence. [...]
> The fear of the Lord is the beginning of wisdom: and the knowledge of the
> holy is prudence.[69]

The seven saints in the painting are gathered *al fresco* at wisdom's feast, where they are fed by reading, contemplation, listening, and awareness of the real presence of Christ. The proximity of the main altar, to which the Baptist points, suggests that this 'feast' has a Eucharistic dimension.[70] If we imagine the façade as comprising six pillars (two corner pillars, four intermediate pillars) the symbolism is particularly powerful. Chrysostom would then figure not merely as the central saint of the seven, but also as the seventh pillar. Paul said that the apostles Peter, James and John were seen as 'pillars' of the Jerusalem church; he instructed Timothy to learn how 'to conduct oneself in God's house, which is the assembly of the living God, the pillar and base of the truth'.[71] The images of Sebastiano's altarpiece raise questions relevant to this Venetian church, its *piovano*, and its congregation.[72] From the twelfth century, Wisdom's house was identified with the womb of the Virgin Mary, in which Wisdom, the Word of God, had dwelt, and from which he was born.[73] The powerful Marian references in this painting develop the symbolic discourse begun in the sculptures of the Bernabò chapel.

---

68 Canticle 6. 9 Canticle 6. 9; ; *Cogitis me* § 42; see Ripberger, ed., *Der Pseudo-Hieronymus Brief IX*, p. 149: 'Quae est ista, quae ascendit sicut aurora consurgens ...'; the way in which this antiphon adapts the Song of Songs is discussed by Matter, *The Voice of My Beloved*, p. 154.

69 Proverbs 9. 1–6, 10. For another visual reference (1482) to the seven pillars of Wisdom's house (Botticelli's *Rebellion of the sons of Korah* in the Sistine Chapel), see Ó Carragáin 'Ut Poesis Pictura', pp. 501–05.

70 From early Christian times, Wisdom's feast in Proverbs chapter 9 was seen to have a Eucharistic dimension: Oden and Wright, *Ancient Christian Commentary on Scripture, Old Testament*, vol. IX, pp. 71–77.

71 Galatians 2. 9; I Timothy 3. 15; cf. Revelation 3. 12. If the façade comprises seven pillars (two corner pillars and five intermediate pillars) the symbolism is even plainer, but perhaps less rich. In that case, the seven pillars of wisdom are balanced by the seven Christian saints; in either case, Chrysostom is central.

72 For this wider relevance of the 'building' imagery, see I Peter 2. 5: 'Be you also as living stones built up, a spiritual house, a holy priesthood, to offer up spiritual sacrifices, acceptable to God by Jesus Christ'.

73 Caldach-Benages, 'Sapienza', p. 1067: see especially Bernard of Clairvaux, 'De domo divinae sapientiae'.

Giovanni Bellini and the Diletti Chapel

The concern with wisdom is finally put into words in the Diletti chapel (directly opposite the Bernabò chapel), the third and last altarpiece completed in the lifetime of Ludovico Talenti (Figs 7 and 8). The merchant Giorgio Diletti made his will in 1494 and died in 1505; his widow provided money for the chapel in 1509.[74] In his will Diletti specified that his altarpiece should represent the figures of St Jerome, St Christopher and St Louis of Toulouse (St Louis, the patron saint of the *piovano* Ludovico [Alvise] Talenti).[75]

Bellini took account both of the Bernabò chapel and of Sebastiano's altarpiece for the main altar. Like Sebastiano's, this painting has two sources of imaginary light, an inner and an outer (Figs 7 and 8). The painting itself is divided into inner and outer areas, marked off by a waist-high marble chancel and by a broad arch (Fig. 8).[76] Visually, the arch echoes both the actual vault of the Bernabò chapel, and Tullio's sculpted fictive barrel vault within it, both vaults directly across the church. In the mountainous and rocky landscape 'outside', ramparts are visible, recalling Wisdom's invitation (quoted above): 'She hath sent her maids to invite to the tower, and to the walls of the city: / Whoever is a little one, let him come to me'.[77] St Jerome meditates on a large folio placed on the trunk of a crooked and almost-bare tree; his eyes are closed in contemplation.[78] Two other large books lie on the rocks near his legs. On the left of the scene, just under the crooked tree and its book, dawn breaks, as in the 'aurora consurgens' of Sebastiano's altarpiece. Both altarpieces therefore agree on where, in this church, the east end lies. The arch is inscribed with a psalm verse in Greek capital letters. Translated, it reads:

> The Lord hath looked down from heaven on the children of men,
> To see if there be any that understand and seek God.[79]

The short psalm from which this verse is taken paints a corrupt and strife-ridden society. It begins, 'The fool hath said in his heart, there is no God. They are corrupt, and are become abominable in their ways; there is none that doth good, no, not one'. The next verse is that on the broad arch; then the jeremiad is repeated: '[t]hey have all gone astray, they have become unprofitable together: there is none that doth good, no, not one' (Psalms 14. 3). The psalm concludes with a prayer: 'Who shall give out of Sion the salvation of Israel? When the Lord shall have turned away the captivity of his people, Jacob shall rejoice and Israel be glad' (Psalms 14. 7). As scholars have

---

74 Olivato and Puppi, *Mauro Codussi*, p. 218; Jestaz, *Monuments vénitiens*, p. 219: before the widow Diletti provided her husband's bequest, the chapel had been dedicated to the Holy Cross.

75 Jestaz, *Monuments vénitiens*, p. 219, gives the text of the will, with French translation.

76 For discussion of the fictive 'inner' and 'outer' in this painting, see Grave, *Giovanni Bellini*, pp. 248–49.

77 Proverbs 9. 4.

78 Poldi and Villa, *Bellini a Venezia*, pp. 233 and 245. The bare tree recalls St Luke's Passion narrative, where Christ says: 'for if in the green wood they do these things, what shall be done in the dry?' (Luke 23. 31). The original dedication of the chapel, to the Holy Cross, may be relevant to this feature.

79 Psalm 14. 2; Septuagint and Vulgate, 13. 2. Poldi and Villa, *Bellini a Venezia*, p. 237.

Figure 6. Nave of San Giovanni Crisostomo, showing steps and tiled floor, both echoed in the altarpiece. Photo by the author.

Figure 7. Diletti Chapel (viewed from the Bernabò Chapel), showing the light from the side windows. Photo by the author.

Figure 8. Diletti Chapel, showing St Christopher and St Louis of Toulouse standing inside the painted chancel, and looking across the nave towards the Bernabò Chapel. Photo by the author.

seen, the psalm was appropriate to the defeats and disturbance of the war against the League of Cambrai, which had by now lasted over four years.[80]

The 'inner' scene in the painting is illuminated (as in Sebastiano's altarpiece) by imaginary light from the interior of the church. Here, however, the interior light is greatly strengthened by imaginary light from the right-hand (western) side-window of the chapel.[81] Firm contrasts of light and shadow define the pillars of the painted arch, and the two saints who stand beside the pillars on this side of the marble chancel (Fig. 8). The chancel (to which Bellini has fixed his signature, dated 1513) shows the inner scene to be part of this very church. A gleaming pilaster, at its centre, is decorated with grotesque ornament. Part of the ornament is a bearded head,[82] which echoes two similar grotesque heads at the top of an external pilaster, just to the east of the nearest (south) door of the actual church. In Bellini's painting, St Christopher, bearing the Christ-child, is about to set off towards this very door:

80   Poldi and Villa, *Bellini a Venezia*, p. 237.
81   Jestaz, *Monuments vénitiens*, p. 219, suggests that the chapel was extended towards the south, and that the two side windows were inserted, in the period 1511–13, to provide good light for Bellini's altarpiece. We might therefore have here a good example of architect and painter working together.
82   Good illustrations in Poldi and Villa, *Bellini a Venezia*, p. 248, and Grave, *Giovanni Bellini*, p. 247.

he stands, not in a river, but in this Diletti chapel (Fig. 8).[83] St Louis carries another large folio, bound in red. The title 'De civitate dei' has been added later to the binding (perhaps at the suggestion of the parish priest?).[84] This added title identifies the book as St Augustine's classic treatise which sees the heavenly Jerusalem as the goal towards which the Christian Church travels through history. St Louis is in full and elaborate canonical dress (unlike the two theologian–bishops painted in the church, St John Chrysostom and St Jerome). Bishops were understood to be successors of the apostles. This bishop looks out, with a calm and level gaze, not only straight at us, the onlookers, but also across the nave to the apostles, his forebears, in the Bernabò altarpiece. We have seen that in the Bernabò chapel (to paraphrase Psalm 14. 2, quoted in the Diletti chapel) God the Father looks down from heaven: not only on his own son (who brought salvation to the world) but also on Mary, the virginal 'daughter of Sion' *par excellence*, whose perfect response to the Trinity has led to her becoming queen of heaven. In Bellini's altarpiece, St Christopher also looks across the church at the Bernabò chapel. His strikingly intense and visionary gaze is fixed, not on the apostles, but higher: towards the orant 'Madonna greca' who soars above Tullio's altarpiece. After all, St Christopher, like Mary herself, was a bearer of Christ.[85]

Saint Jerome, the contemplating scholar–hermit, searching for wisdom in the breaking dawn ('aurora consurgens') would have been understood to provide authority for the unusual Marian imagery of the Bernabò chapel, opposite. Throughout the Middle Ages, Jerome was thought to be the author of the letter *Cogitis me*. This mistaken attribution ensured that the letter would become a major authority: clerics who wanted to understand the Feast of the Assumption went primarily to *Cogitis me*.[86] We need not suppose that the large folio which Jerome reads is a text of his letters: rather, it is more likely to be his Vulgate translation of the Bible, the source of the many scriptural allusions, and antiphons, in *Cogitis me*.

To conclude: three masterpieces were commissioned for the church of San Giovanni Crisostomo when Ludovico Talenti was its parish priest. They have hitherto been studied separately, and without much reference to their functions within the church for which they were made. However, they are better understood as a progressive series, designed to complement each other, and to expand the liturgical space of the church. Each of the altarpieces leads the viewer's gaze from the actual church towards visionary perspectives and landscapes. The altarpieces progressively explore what, in a Christian context, wisdom and understanding might involve. They present the Virgin Mary, in her cooperation with the divine challenge of the Incarnation which

---

83 Contrast Bellini's polyptych of St Vincent Ferrer in Santi Giovanni e Paolo, where the saint crosses a river: Boccato, *Chiese di Venezia*, p. 227; Poldi and Villa, *Bellini a Venezia*, p. 30; Caraffa and others, *Bibliotheca Sanctorum*, IV, cols 349–64, under 'Cristoforo di Licia'.

84 Poldi and Villa, *Bellini a Venezia*, pp. 237–38, 244.

85 For the implications of the term 'bearing Christ' in early Christian commentary, see Ó Carragáin, *Ritual and the Rood*, pp. 137–41.

86 Jerome's authorship was first disproven by Erasmus (d. 1536); Paschasius Radbertus was identified as the author in 1880: Ripberger, ed., *Der Pseudo-Hieronymus Brief IX*, pp. 7–14; Dezzuto, ed., *La lettera di Girolamo*, p. xxxvii, note 98.

led to her crowning, as the primary example of human wisdom. The church and its early altarpieces exemplify a central concern of renaissance humanism: the need to return, with greater understanding, to the classics of early Christian and medieval theology, such as the works of John Chrysostom, Augustine and Jerome (or, as we now know the author of *Cogitis me* to be, Paschasius Radbertus). It is likely that the guiding intelligence behind this dynamic synthesis of early Christian theology was the learned *piovano*, Ludovico Talenti. It is reasonable to think that it was under his guidance that the artists made the church of San Giovanni Crisostomo a place of contemplation and a *lieu de mémoire*.

Works Cited

Primary Sources

Augustine of Hippo, *In Ioannis Evangelium Tractatus CXXIV*, ed. by Radbod Willems, Corpus Christianorum Series Latina, 36, second edition (Turnhout: Brepols, 1990)

Bernard of Clairvaux, 'De domo divinae sapientiae', *Sermones de diversis, Sermo LII*, in *Patrologiae cursus completus: series latina*, ed. by Jacques-Paul Migne, 221 vols (Paris: Migne, 1844–1864), 183, cols 674–76

Dante, *Paradiso: Dante Alighieri Commedia*, con il commento de Anna Maria Chiavacci Leonardi, volume terzo, *Paradiso* (Milan: Mondadori, 1994)

Jacobus de Voragine, *Legenda Aurea*, ed. by Johann Georg Theodor Graesse, *Jacobi a Voragine Legenda Aurea: vulgo Historia Lombardica dicta* (Osnabrück: Otto Zeller, 1969 reprint)

Jestaz, Bertrand, *Monuments vénitiens à la lumière des documents de la première renaissance* (Venice: Istituto Veneto di Scienze, 2017)

The Little Office of the Blessed Virgin Mary fully explained and annotated (London: Burns, Oates and Washbourne, 1914; reprinted 1954)

Paschasius Radbertus, *Cogitis me*, ed. by Carlo Dezzuto, *La lettera di Girolamo: un saggio di spiritualità monacale* (Milan: Glossa, 2009)

——, *Cogitis me*, ed. by Albert Ripberger, *Der Pseudo–Hieronymus Brief IX "Cogitis me": ein erster Marianischer Traktat des Mittelalters von Paschasius Radbert*, Spicilegium Friburgense, 9 (Freiburg Schweiz: Universitätsverlag, 1962)

——, *Cogitis me*, ed. by Albert Ripberger, in *Paschasii Radberti de Partu Virginis, cura et studio E. Ann Matter; De Assumptione Sanctae Mariae Virginis, cura et studio Alberti Ripberger*, Corpus Christianorum Continuatio Mediaevalis, 56C (Turnhout: Brepols, 1985)

Secondary Studies

Boccato, Alessandra, *Chiese di Venezia* (Venice: Arsenale, 2010)

Bristot, Annalisa 'Note a margine di restauri lombardeschi', in *Tullio Lombardo scultore e architetto nella Venezia del Rinascimennto*, ed. by Michele Ceriana (Atti del convegno di studi, Venezia, Fondazione Cini, 4–6 aprile 2006). (Venice: Fondazione Giorgio Cini, 2007), pp. 440–66 and colour plates

Calduch-Benages, Nuria, 'Sapienza', in *Mariologia*, ed by Stefano De Fiores, Valeria Ferrari Schiefer, and Salvatore M. Perrella (Milan: Edizioni San Paolo, 2009), pp. 1059–71

Caraffa, Filippo, and others, (eds), *Bibliotheca Sanctorum: Enciclopedia dei Santi*, 15 vols, fourth edition (Rome: Città Nuova editrice, 1998)

Ceriana, Michele, *Tullio Lombardo scultore e architetto nella Venezia del Rinascimennto* (Atti del convegno di studi, Venezia, Fondazione Cini, 4–6 aprile 2006). (Venice: Fondazione Giorgio Cini, 2007)

Clayton, Mary, *The Apocryphal Gospels of Mary in Anglo-Saxon England* (Cambridge: Cambridge University Press, 1998)

Connolly, Thomas, *Mourning into Joy: Music, Raphael, and Saint Cecilia* (New Haven: Yale University Press, 1994)

Cross, F. L., and E. A. Livingstone, *The Oxford Dictionary of the Christian Church*, third edition revised (Oxford: Oxford University Press, 2005)

Davis, Charles, *Byzantine Relief Icons in Venice and along the Adriatic Coast: Orants and Other Images of the Mother of God*. University of Heidelberg, Art–Dok series, on line: https://archiv.ub.uni–heidelberg.de/artdok/270/1/Davis_2006.pdf. Consulted 27 December 2018

———, 'La cappella Bernabò in San Giovanni Crisostomo: storia e immagine', in *Tullio Lombardo scultore e architetto nella Venezia del Rinascimennto*, ed. by Michele Ceriana (Atti del convegno di studi, Venezia, Fondazione Cini, 4–6 aprile 2006). (Venice: Fondazione Giorgio Cini, 2007), pp. 217–78

Demus, Otto, *The Mosaics of San Marco in Venice*, 2 vols in four (Chicago: University of Chicago Press, 1984)

Demus, Otto, and others, *San Marco: Patriarchal Basilica in Venice*, 2 vols (I, *The Mosaics, the History, the Lighting*; II, *The Mosaics, the Inscriptions, the Pala d'Oro*). (Milan: Fabbri, 1990–1991)

Grave, Johannes, *Giovanni Bellini: The Art of Contemplation* (Munich: Prestel, 2018)

Hale, Sheila, *Titian: His Life* (London: Harper, 2012)

Luchs, Alison, *Tullio Lombardo and Ideal Portrait Sculpture in Renaissance Venice, 1400–1530* (Cambridge: Cambridge University Press, 1995)

Markham Schulz, Anne, *The Sculpture of Tullio Lombardo* (Turnhout: Brepols, 2014)

Matter, E. Ann, *The Voice of My Beloved: The Song of Songs in Western Medieval Christianity* (Philadelphia: University of Pennsylvania Press, 1990)

Martimort, Aimé Georges, 'Liturgical Signs', in *The Church at Prayer*, ed. by Irénée Henri Dalmais and others, 4 vols (London: Geoffrey Chapman, 1987), I, pp. 173–226

Nelson, Jonathan K. 'La cappella Carafa: un nuovo linguaggio figurativo per la Roma del Rinascimento' in *Filippino Lippi e Sandro Botticelli nella Firenze del'400*, ed. by Alessandro Cecchi (Exhibition catalogue, Rome, Scuderie del Quirinale, 5 October 2011–15 January 2012) (Rome: 24 ore cultura), pp. 40–49

Ó Carragáin, Éamonn '*Ut poesis pictura*: The Transformation of the Roman Landscape in Botticelli's *Punishment of Korah*', in *New Offerings, Ancient Treasures: Studies in Medieval Art for George Henderson*, ed. by Paul Binski and William Noel (Stroud: Sutton, 2001), pp. 492–518

———, *Ritual and the Rood: Liturgical Images and the Old English Poems of the 'Dream of the Rood' Tradition* (London: British Library, 2005)

Olivato, Loredana, and Lionello Puppi, *Mauro Codussi* (Milan: Electa, 2007)

Oden, J. Robert, and J. Robert Wright, eds, *Ancient Christian Commentary on Scripture, Old Testament, IX, Proverbs, Ecclesiastes, Song of Solomon* (Dower's Grove: Intervarsity Press, 2005)

Pinchi, Dominique, *À quels saints se vouer? Regards sur la peinture vénitienne de la Renaissance* (Paris: La tour verte, 2014)

Poldi, Gianluca, and Giovanni C. F. Villa, *Bellini a Venezia* (published in relation to the exhibition at Rome, Scuderie del Quirinale, 29 September 2008–11 January 2009) (Rome: Silvana, 2008)

Sinding-Larsen, Staale, *Christ in the Council Hall: Studies in the Religious Iconography of the Venetian Republic* (Rome: Bretschneider, 1974)

Strinati, Claudio, and Bernd Wolfgang Lindemann, eds, *Sebastiano del Piombo 1485–1547* (Exhibition catalogue: Rome, Palazzo di Venezia, 8 February – 18 May 2008; Berlin, Gemäldegalerie, 28 June–28 September 2008) (Milan: Federico Motta, 2008)

Ward, Benedicta, *Harlots of the Desert: A Study of Repentance in Early Monastic Sources* (London: Mowbray, 1987)

Zanin, Giovanni, *Chiesa S. Giovanni Grisostomo e Santuario Madonna delle Grazie in Venezia* (Venice: Dolo, 1978)

Index

Studies in the Early Middle Ages

All volumes in this series are evaluated by an Editorial Board, strictly on academic grounds, based on reports prepared by referees who have been commissioned by virtue of their specialism in the appropriate field. The Board ensures that the screening is done independently and without conflicts of interest. The definitive texts supplied by authors are also subject to review by the Board before being approved for publication. Further, the volumes are copyedited to conform to the publisher's stylebook and to the best international academic standards in the field.

Titles in Series

The Old English Homily: Precedent, Practice, and Appropriation, ed. by Aaron J. Kleist (2007)

James T. Palmer, *Anglo-Saxons in a Frankish World, 690–900* (2009)

Challenging the Boundaries of Medieval History: The Legacy of Timothy Reuter, ed. by Patricia Skinner (2009)

Peter Verbist, *Duelling with the Past: Medieval Authors and the Problem of the Christian Era, c. 990–1135* (2010)

Reading the Anglo-Saxon Chronicle: Language, Literature, History, ed. by Alice Jorgensen (2010)

England and the Continent in the Tenth Century: Studies in Honour of Wilhelm Levison (1876–1947), ed. by David Rollason, Conrad Leyser, and Hannah Williams (2010)

Early Medieval Northumbria: Kingdoms and Communities, AD 450–1100, ed. by David Petts and Sam Turner (2011)

Conceptualizing Multilingualism in Medieval England, c. 800–c. 1250, ed. by Elizabeth M. Tyler (2011)

Neglected Barbarians, ed. by Florin Curta (2011)

The Genesis of Books: Studies in the Scribal Culture of Medieval England in Honour of A. N Doane, ed. by Matthew T. Hussey and John D. Niles (2012)

Giselle de Nie, *Poetics of Wonder: Testimonies of the New Christian Miracles in the Late Antique Latin World* (2012)

Lilla Kopár, *Gods and Settlers: The Iconography of Norse Mythology in Anglo-Scandinavian Sculpture* (2012)

R. W. Burgess and Michael Kulikowski, *Mosaics of Time: The Latin Chronicle Traditions from the First Century BC to the Sixth Century AD, vol. I: A Historical Introduction to the Chronicle Genre from its Origins to the High Middle Ages* (2013)

Sacred Sites and Holy Places: Exploring the Sacralization of Landscape through Space and Time, ed. by Sæbjørg Walaker Nordeide and Stefan Brink (2013)

Christine Maddern, *Raising the Dead: Early Medieval Name Stones in Northumbria* (2013)

Landscapes of Defence in Early Medieval Europe, ed. by John Baker, Stuart Brookes, and Andrew Reynolds (2013)

Sara M. Pons-Sanz, *The Lexical Effects of Anglo-Scandinavian Linguistic Contact on Old English* (2013)

Society and Culture in Medieval Rouen, 911–1300, ed. by Leonie V. Hicks and Elma Brenner (2013)

Shane McLeod, *The Beginning of Scandinavian Settlement in England: The Viking 'Great Army' and Early Settlers, c. 865–900* (2014)

England and Rome in the Early Middle Ages: Pilgrimage, Art, and Politics, ed. by Francesca Tinti (2014)

Luigi Andrea Berto, *In Search of the First Venetians: Prosopography of Early Medieval Venice* (2014)

Clare Pilsworth, *Healthcare in Early Medieval Northern Italy: More to Life than Leeches* (2014)

Textus Roffensis: Law, Language, and Libraries in Early Medieval England, ed. by Bruce O'Brien and Barbara Bombi (2015)

Churches and Social Power in Early Medieval Europe: Integrating Archaeological and Historical Approaches, ed. by José C. Sánchez-Pardo and Michael G. Shapland (2015)